I was Jerry Lewis' Bodyguard for 10 Minutes!

...and other celebrity encounters

Irv Korman

Loconeal Publishing
Amherst

I was Jerry Lewis' Bodyguard for 10 Minutes!

...and other celebrity encounters

Loconeal books may be ordered through booksellers or by contacting:
www.loconeal.com
216-772-8380

Loconeal Publishing can bring authors to your live event. Contact Loconeal Publishing at 216-772-8380.

Published by Loconeal Publishing, LLC
Printed in the United States of America

First Loconeal Publishing edition: November, 2011

Visit our website: www.loconeal.com

ISBN 978-0-9825653-4-6 (Paperback)

Dedication

This book is dedicated to the *Pauline Eisler* I met in the winter of 1967: Wherever you are today, thank you for the care, faith, support, loyalty, devotion, love, and encouragement that started me on a journey of creativity that eventually lead to the publication of this book.

Acknowledgments

Very few things are accomplished alone.

An analogy of this book can be likened to an iceberg: what you see on the surface of the water is only about 10 % of the entire iceberg. My book is what you see in front of you but many people helped me along the way to get it into your hands. For their help I am very grateful. Among them were:

Larry Alltop, Dave "Radar" Andrews, David Auburn, Charlie Aukerman, Larry Aylward, Barbara "Bunny" Balance, James O. Barnes, Linda Bennett, Anne Bentzel, Micki Brook, Carolyn Bosworth, Katherine Bowman, Judy Casey, Kate Clark, Carol Masky-Callahan, J. Albert Callahan, Robert and Suanne Crowley, Emily Deal, Mary DeHaven, Marie Duffy-Dusini, Patti Eddy, Jeanne Emser, Al Fitzpatrick, Laurie Filicky, David Fulford, Jennifer Gaglione, Ed George, David Giffels, Christine Gregor, Prescott Griffith, Jeff Haller, Pat and Jerry Hanley, April Helms, Phil Hoffman, Bonnie Keiper, John Kenley, Francine Korman, Fred Kraus, Mary Maxson, Ellie Meindl, Carolyn Narotsky, June Nolls, Bill O'Connor, Paige Palmer, Roland Paolucci, Peggy Parmelee, Larry Penecost, Ron Riegler, Les Roberts, Melanie Korman Roddy, Julie Korman Ross, Sue Round, Heidi Rotbart, Jack Schantz, Mike Senuta, Scott Shriner, David W. Slaght, Howard K. Slaughter, "Red" Staneck, Michael Stein, Gail Tankersley, Marge Tannehill, Marge Thomas, Joanne Tortoriello, Jane Turzillo, Frank Wallick, Julie Washington, Betty and Earl Webb, Betty Wilson.

Two people are worthy of mention and very special recognition:

David Ritchey, my friend, for always looking out for my best interests, and David Mull, my "Write Brother," who sits across from me every Thursday morning, working on his books.

If it wasn't for David Mull this book would never have been written or completed. When anything had to be done electronically, David knew what to do and how to do it. I will always be grateful for his assistance, patience, and encouragement.

Table of Contents

Chapters are in chronological order of the celebrity's death, Chapters 1-21.

Celebrities still with us as of October, 2011:

PREFACE

Many separate yet related events led me to meeting famous people and writing about my experiences with them. These separate events were quite varied and require some explanation.

The first event occurred when I entered grade school as well as summer day camp talent shows, usually pantomiming (lip-synching) Jerry Lewis 45-RPM records (oddly enough that's how he got his start in show business) in front of children my own age and maybe a few adults. Consequently, I can still recite the lyrics of Jerry Lewis' *Never Smile at a Crocodile* at the drop of a hat.

As a teenager I was not much of an athlete or a "jock." Those guys got the adulation, the girls, and peer recognition. I figured I could get some form of that adulation, peer recognition, and, hopefully, girls by performing on a stage instead of on an athletic field, thus doing something the popular male athletes *could not* do. The feeling of performing onstage, in front of an audience, with everyone staring at me, gave me a "rush" that was hard to explain. My friends feared being in front of a large crowd. I did not have that fear. I could do something they could not do!

As I entered my teenage years I continued pantomiming records for junior high school talent shows, usually as part of the school carnival. I had graduated from lip-synching Jerry Lewis comedy records to Jerry Lee Lewis rock and roll records.

About the same time my uncle, George Korman, then president of the Akron Jewish Center Theatre Guild in Akron, Ohio, encouraged me to try out for a minor role, that of a shoeshine boy (with one spoken line) in one of their upcoming productions: the comedy play, *Make A Million*, in 1960. I got the part. It was a step up from pantomiming records at school and summer camp talent shows. I was now working with and performing in front of adults while still getting that "rush" and recognition. In fact most adults dreaded being on stage in front of a crowd. I was now doing something that even some adults feared!

In the fall of 1960, I began acting in plays in high school. My first experience was a memorable one. The all-school play was the only opportunity for a sophomore to be in a play production with junior and senior upperclassmen at John R. Buchtel High School. The only other play productions at the school were the junior class play and the senior class play. I was one of only two sophomores in the all school production of the classic comedy, *Arsenic and Old Lace*. The other sophomore was a tall blonde and lanky fellow classmate with a deep, strong speaking voice and a crew cut. His name was John Lithgow. His father, Arthur, was the director of Shakespearean plays at nearby Stan Hywet Hall and Gardens. Stan Hywet (old English for "stone quarry") was the residence of F.A. Seiberling, founder of Goodyear Tire and Rubber Company. The Tudor mansion and its grounds were and still are a popular tourist attraction. During the summer months John's father, Arthur Lithgow, directed the Shakespearean plays on the mansion's back terrace staging the popular and quite elaborate productions.

About this same time my father, Ben Korman, suggested I try out for an upcoming play at a nearby neighborhood community theatre. My father, a mailman, walked by Weathervane Community Playhouse on his way to work at Maple Valley Branch Post Office, located in West Akron. One evening, not knowing the play being cast was a musical, I ventured into Weathervane Community Playhouse to audition for a role in an upcoming production of *Down in the Valley*. I panicked when I learned the play was a musical. Even though I come from a musical family (my mother was a dancer, father a big band musician, and sister a singer) I felt (and was told on many occasions) I was tone-deaf and could not carry a tune. When I informed the play's director, Bob Belfance, that I made a mistake by showing up and should not try out for the musical play, he implored, "Everybody can sing," and coaxed me to try something simple like the lyrics to "Mary Had a Little Lamb." After singing a few bars he immediately agreed, "You're right. You can't sing." Leaving the theater, I thought my budding acting career was over.

A few months later I received a telephone call from Weathervane director Belfance to play a minor role, that of Wint Selby, in their upcoming non-musical production of Eugene O'Neil's *Ah, Wilderness!* I even secured special permission from my high school principal to grow a moustache for the role in order to make me look older. I was the only one in the entire high school with permission to grow a moustache! Talk about attention among my teenage high school peers! Thus began a relationship with Weathervane Community Playhouse that still exists today.

While still acting in plays in high school and at Weathervane Community Playhouse, I was taking elocution lessons from an amazing little woman: Billie Lahrmer. Every Saturday morning I would take the bus to her studio apartment in downtown Akron for my lesson. She was also the play director at another local community theatre, Coach House Theatre. One day she invited me to act in one of her productions, the courtroom drama, *Inherit the Wind*, loosely based on the 1920's Monkey/Scopes Trial that pitted the Bible's version of Creation against Darwin's Theory of Evolution. I played several minor roles, including a hot dog vendor and a courtroom reporter. I began appearing in other Coach House Theatre productions as well. Billie Lahrmer was famous in the area for many years nurturing the careers of such actors as actors Mark Stevens ("Objective Burma" with Errol Flynn, 1945, plus television's "Martin Kane, Private Eye"), David McLean (star of the television western "Tate") and Jesse White (the lonely Maytag Repairman). I'll never forget the little dynamo that was Billie Lahrmer. She was under five-feet tall and always wore slacks. She had jet black hair and would always emphasize a point by saying, "Now, goddamn it, you can do it!" I can still recall her lining me up against her apartment wall and imploring me to recite the five vowels while putting her small fist into my stomach and diaphragm. As I recited each vowel I had to make my stomach muscles move her fist outward, away from my diaphragm. To this day I have no problem with volume or being heard when I perform onstage. I took great pride and satisfaction in that, especially when I did three months of summer stock at Priscilla Beach Theatre in Cape Cod, Massachusetts in 1968. One young male actor, quite enamored with himself, had frequent throat problems because, for all his self-importance, he was never taught to project from his diaphragm. I quietly relished his pompous hoarseness. He went on to act professionally on Broadway, television, and in motion pictures.

Also during my high school years, I began writing creatively. At the urging of my English teacher, Mrs. Emily Deal, I wrote a story expressing my emotions and thoughts upon entering the empty auditorium of a theater after a play performance, long after the audience had left. I described how I felt after the performance, looking at the discarded ticket stubs scattered about the auditorium floor. Mrs. Deal liked the story so much she sent it to the Akron Public Schools' administration building, where it was put on display with written works by other students.

After high school graduation (having performed in the junior class play as well as the senior class play), in June of 1963, I entered The University of Akron. As an undergraduate (from 1963 to 1967) I appeared in numerous university theatre productions. While taking a freshman English course, the instructor, Mrs. Mary DeHaven, was kind enough to look at some of my written short stories and gave me valuable suggestions and encouragement. It was at this time I also began writing poetry.

After earning a Liberal Arts Degree at the University of Akron, I was employed as a speech pathologist for the Akron Public Schools. I returned to The University of Akron in 1970 to begin work on a Masters Degree in Theatre, receiving the degree in 1973. My thesis was an original children's musical, *The Adventures of Aaron Aardvark*, which was performed onstage at The University of Akron in July of 1972. I wrote the book and lyrics while the music was provided by my good friend, the very musically talented and gifted Bill Forsch.

One required course for my Masters Degree in Theatre was Drama Criticism. The class involved attending about four plays and writing a critical review of each performance. I enjoyed the experience so much that I reviewed 10 plays! My advisor, Howard K. Slaughter, remarked, "If you check a dictionary once in a while, you may have something here." I kept the encouraging comment in mind.

While teaching school one day in the fall of 1973, I received a telephone call from my wife who was at home taking care of our infant daughter. My wife asked me if I wanted to act in a play with Mickey Rooney.

I told her I was having a rather challenging day at school and that her prank was not particularly funny at the moment. She told me it wasn't a joke. One of the public relations girls I knew at Carousel Dinner Theatre in Ravenna, Ohio, Barbara "Bunny" Balance, called to ask if I was interested in appearing in an upcoming production of the comedy play, *See How They Run*, starring Mickey Rooney. Would I!

The next day after school I followed Bunny's directions to Carousel Dinner Theatre in Ravenna. I met the director, David Fulford, as we walked into the auditorium. The theater was a former grocery store that had been recently remodeled into a theater-in-the-round configuration with several levels of tables and chairs for dining, then watching a play.

The Carousel Dinner Theatre format featured a star actor or actress in a play (usually a comedy) for about a month-long run. This format was not new to Fulford, who also owned Canal Fulton Summer Theatre in nearby North Canton, Ohio. It was a summer stock venue in which a star appeared in a play for one week. Fulford thought this format could work on a year round basis, thus opening Carousel Dinner Theatre in April of 1973.

Fulford had me read several lines from the script of *See How They Run*. The small role was of a British policeman: a "bobby," named Sgt. Towers who comes in toward the end of the play to, more or less, straighten things out amid the chaotic climax of the comic confusion. I read the lines with what I thought was a credible cockney "British accent." Fulford said the role was mine if I wanted it. Are you kidding? So for four weeks, with an eventual extension of two more, I appeared in a play with Mickey Rooney! It was my first real close encounter with a celebrity.

With the growing responsibility of fatherhood and being the sole provider for my wife Francine, daughter Julie and eventually my second daughter, Melanie, I looked for part-time evening employment to supplement my income. It seemed my acting days were over. Acting in community theatre productions is strictly voluntary.

One day in 1975, I was reading an article in the Akron daily newspaper about the local, Northeastern Ohio Ronald McDonald, the fast food clown. The article told about the local gentleman's background. McDonalds ruthlessly guarded the identity and everything else relating to their trademark clown. After reading the article I thought to myself, "What skills does he possess that I don't have? I can act, I have a master's degree in theatre, and I am not afraid of performing in front of people." I also knew a little magic. Two friends of mine, Marv Cohen, a dentist, and Jeff Spector, a podiatrist, had signed up for a magic class at The University of Akron's Community College. It was a non-credit course in the fundamentals of magic, using coins, cards, and other household items. The doctors thought if they learned magic that some of their younger patients would not be as frightened of them; if the children were entertained with some sleight-of-hand wizardry, it might calm their fears. Being an elementary school teacher, I figured I could use the magic tricks and illusions to reward my students for good behavior, so I joined my two friends in enrolling in the magic class. So, now I could act *and* do magic. I decided to write the McDonald's Corporation at their national headquarters in Oak Brook, Illinois, and ask what the qualifications were for being a local Ronald McDonald. I soon received an answer to my letter. My inquiry letter had been forwarded to the Ohio office of McDonalds in Columbus, Ohio. Timing is everything. I was informed that the Canton, Ohio area (about 30 miles south of Akron) was presently in the market for a Ronald McDonald. I interviewed at a local Canton advertising agency and got the position. Needless to say, the experience was memorable. I portrayed the hamburger trademark character from 1975 to 1989 in countless parades, grand openings, magic shows, Muscular Dystrophy Telethons, and other personal appearances. The periodic Ronald McDonald conventions at the corporate headquarters for their most recognizable advertising symbol were most enjoyable and enlightening. In the beginning my Ronald McDonald appearances were few and seasonal, mostly during the spring and summer months.

How do I keep "on my toes" during the off-season? I decided to create my own clown character, the exact opposite of the happy, white -faced, trademark Ronald McDonald. Thus, in July of 1978 "Marlowe the Magic Clown" was born. He was (and still is) a traditional sad-faced tramp clown. "Marlowe" is entirely my own creation. Though I learned a lot being Ronald McDonald for 14 years, the 33 years as "Marlowe the Magic Clown" have been most gratifying and rewarding personally. In a reversal of situations I, as Ronald or Marlowe, was the celebrity. This gave me the perspective of being the famous person sought after at appearances. The shoe, as they say, was on the other foot! In another ironic twist, my being Ronald and Marlowe got *me* to meet celebrities. As Ronald McDonald I met many local Northeastern Ohio celebrities such as athletes and elected officials. One memorable experience was in 1986, when I appeared in the National Football League's Hall of Fame Parade and got to meet inductee and former Green Bay Packer great, Paul Hornug, before the parade. As "Marlowe" I have met animal activist Jim Fowler, Bob McGrath of TV's "Sesame Street," and Bob Keeshan, TV's "Captain Kangaroo."

In March 1978, my next-door neighbor introduced me to a friend who owned the local franchise of a weekly publication called "TV Facts." The magazine contained the local area's TV listings for the week. It appeared on the checkout counters of area supermarkets. The publication was free to customers and earned its income by selling advertising space to local merchants. At the time, the Akron daily newspaper theatre critic did not review the plays at Carousel Dinner Theatre because he looked down on the venue as not "real theatre." When I met my neighbor's friend I mentioned to her the fact that the Akron daily paper did not review Carousel Dinner Theatre plays, yet the same reporter would interview and do a story about the star appearing in the same Carousel production. Her immediate response was, "Why don't *you* review the plays?" She then immediately informed me that she could not, of course, pay me for the play reviews.

Remembering my connection with Carousel Dinner Theatre from *See How They Run*, starring Mickey Rooney, in 1973, I called the public relations director, Ellie Meindl, to ask her if I could review the current production at Carousel for "TV Facts" magazine. Ellie said she would set aside two "press tickets" for me to see the production *You Know I Can't Hear You When the Water's Running*, starring comedian Shelly Berman. She also informed me of the opening night press party where we (the press and other media) could meet the cast and the star immediately following the performance.

Thus began my foray into reviewing plays and the beginning of meeting famous entertainers on a semi-regular basis. The thought of interviewing the star of each Carousel Dinner Theatre star did not enter my mind until about one year later in 1979, at the behest of Carousel's public relations director, Ellie Meindl, when she set up an interview with actor Richard Egan. He was starring in the comedy play *Hanky Panky* at Carousel Dinner Theatre. Though the interview was not my idea, something amazing happened during the process of interviewing Richard Egan: I felt that same "rush" sensation I had when I performed onstage. Since the interview process was a positive one for me, I made it a point to try to interview other stars appearing at Carousel Dinner Theatre, and review the play as well. My first encounters with the famous at Carousel Dinner Theatre included Pat O'Brien, Morey Amsterdam, Dorothy Lamour, Pat Paulsen, and Dodie Goodman, among others. I did the same at David Fulford's summer venue, Canal Fulton Summer Theatre, where I met and interviewed Robert Alda, Nanette Fabray, and Noel Harrison, and had my second encounter with Dorothy Lamour.

The Carousel Dinner Theatre experience led to seeing other performers there. Occasionally, on Monday evenings (when traditionally there is no play production), one-night concerts were scheduled, showcasing the talents of such entertainers as Eddy Fisher, Patti Paige, The Lettermen, Donald O'Connor, Katherine Grayson, The Amazing Kreskin, Rosemary Clooney, Pat Boone, Jim Nabors, and Ricky Nelson.

To further pursue entertainment stories; in 1980 I noticed the upcoming appearance of former teen idol and singer Frankie Avalon in the Sultan's Cabaret, a Las Vegas-style nightclub showroom located in Akron's Tangier Restaurant. Now writing for an area weekly newspaper, The Village Views, I called Tangier public relations director Marge Thomas and explained I was interested in writing a story on Frankie Avalon. I had no intention of meeting or interviewing him. I just wanted to do a story prior to his appearance. Thomas told me the best way to find out about Avalon would be to see him perform. She asked me how many "press tickets" I wanted for his opening night performance and private press party reception immediately afterward. Thus began interviews and reviews of such entertainers at Tangier Restaurant as Milton Berle, Dottie West, Buddy Rich, Woody Herman, Harry Blackstone, Jr., Phyllis Diller, Crystal Gayle, the Hager Twins, Bo Diddley, Ray Charles, Joan Rivers, Frank Gorshin and Sam Kinison.

In subsequent years I wrote for other area publications: The West Side Leader (weekly), The Medina County Gazette (daily), as well as "Focus" (monthly). The Medina Gazette (now The Gazette) enabled me to review plays and concerts at Playhouse Square in downtown Cleveland, as well as the Cleveland Playhouse. Playhouse Square consists of several renovated movie theaters, including the Allen, the Ohio, the State, and the Palace, located in the heart of downtown Cleveland, Ohio. Speaking of Cleveland, I also wrote several stories for The Cleveland Plain Dealer (daily) weekend entertainment magazine, "Friday!"

Since 1978, I have written countless play reviews and interviewed numerous famous entertainers. I had the stories piled on a shelf in my basement office, separated by year, but never knew how many times a famous person had appeared in the area nor how many times I saw them perform or met them. I also did not know the number of times I reviewed different productions of the same play, such as *Fiddler on the Roof, South Pacific, Hello, Dolly!* or *The Sound of Music.*

In the summer of 2002, I began the arduous task of going through all my written stories, by year, and cataloging each article, by publication. The end result was several full spiral notebooks of information.

At the same time I realized I had a filing cabinet full of information on famous performers that I had compiled since 1978, when I began writing the original stories. Going through the files I discovered that eighteen famous people I had written about since 1978 were no longer living. I pulled the files of the deceased and put them in a separate file drawer. Many of the files contained show and play programs, newspaper articles, authorized biographies and autographed publicity photographs.

While I was visiting my oldest daughter and her husband in Florida in the summer of 2002, Milton Berle passed away. I recalled meeting him at Tangier Restaurant in Akron many years before. But when? What were the circumstances? What could I recall of the encounter? Occasionally I sat on my daughter and son-in-law's porch and wrote in a spiral notepad what I remembered about many of the famous people I had met. I concentrated on recalling the exact circumstances, anecdotes, quotes and other bits and pieces of information that came to mind when I thought of a particular entertainer I had met and spent some time with.

Why not write about my encounters with the famous, especially the ones now deceased, no matter how long or short the experience? I often told people stories of meeting famous entertainers and showing a personalized autographed picture or a photo of us together.

People are continually amazed I did not have to travel to Hollywood or New York City to meet them! It was all done right here within a 30-mile radius of Akron, Ohio!

to Lou:
All good
wishes!

Jerry Lewis
'95

Foreword

I was Jerry Lewis' Bodyguard for 10 Minutes!

On the night of April 24, 1990, I was Jerry Lewis' bodyguard for ten minutes!

It happened during a reception following opening night of a five-day, ten-show appearance by entertainment legend, Jerry Lewis at Carousel Dinner Theatre in Akron, Ohio.

Publicity for Lewis' appearance advertised patrons could meet the star opening night. After Jerry Lewis' first show everyone proceeded upstairs to Prescott's Lounge for the reception. As soon as my wife and I entered the lounge I looked around and sensed something quite different than the usual, traditional Northeastern Ohio press corps scene. At the time I was writing play reviews and celebrity interviews for a local daily newspaper and was to review Jerry Lewis' performance to be published the next day.

I became concerned when I did not see familiar media people. Instead I witnessed a strange array of apparent ardent, die-hard Jerry Lewis fans. Some carried old Jerry Lewis 45 rpm record albums while others clutched aging Muscular Dystrophy posters. My suspicions were confirmed when Carousel Dinner Theatre public relations director Betty Wilson confided in me of her concern. She had recently been informed a Jerry Lewis "stalker" was in attendance. What to do?

Meanwhile, people were milling around waiting for Jerry Lewis to make his appearance. Before long I was approached by Dennis Kancler, son of Carousel Dinner Theatre's director of sales and marketing, Virginia Kancler. Dennis' daytime job was police chief of nearby Brecksville, Ohio. He was quite massive in stature, especially when compared to my five foot, nine-inch, 185 pound frame. Dennis told me Carousel Dinner Theatre was also concerned about Jerry Lewis' safety in light of the strange assembly of people now impatient to meet their idol.

What Dennis confided in me almost knocked me over. He told me that he and I, of all people, were going to protect Lewis. I couldn't believe what he just said. He and I were to stand on either side of the

Lewis' podium and face the crowd. Dennis would be on one side of Lewis and me on the other. We were to face the audience, taking a menacing stance, with legs apart and arms folded across our chest, to imply we were hired bodyguards. Right! I was numb with my assignment but did as he asked. I told my wife to stand apart from the crowd just in case...

Dennis and I assumed our "menacing stance," me with both knees continually knocking together with fear and anticipation. After a few minutes, amid cheers and applause, Jerry Lewis entered Prescott's Lounge and approached the podium with Dennis on one side and nervous, sweating me on the other. We both faced the crowd with serious, stern grins on our faces.

Lewis thanked those in attendance for coming to see him. After a few remarks one fan asked, out loud, to autograph something for him. "No," said Lewis. "Because if I sign that one thing for you, then everyone will expect me to sign whatever they have and we'd be here till three o'clock in the morning and I just can't do that." Jerry then bid the assembled farewell, turned around and left the room.

That was it. Dennis Kancler and Betty Wilson thanked me for participating in the charade. I asked Betty if I could have the 8" x 10" publicity photo of Jerry Lewis from my press packet autographed at his convenience. Betty said Lewis would autograph several photos before he left Carousel Dinner Theatre and one of them would be mine.

The next week, during the press party at the next Carousel Dinner Theatre event, I approached Betty Wilson about my promised autographed Jerry Lewis photo. She informed me Lewis did not leave any as he promised. My rule-of-thumb was that any non-autographed photo was worthless to me so I let the matter go.

A few years later I learned Jerry Lewis was appearing on Broadway in a revival of the musical comedy, *Damn Yankees,* as the Devil. "How appropriate," I thought. I bought a copy of a Sunday New York Times and found the ad for *Damn Yankees* in the entertainment section. It had Jerry Lewis' picture in it. The next day I called the main library in downtown Akron and got the address of the Marquis Theatre at Broadway and 46th Street in New York City.

I wrote Lewis a letter about attending his opening night performance at Carousel Dinner Theatre, in Akron, Ohio, in April of

1990. I informed him I was one of the two "bodyguards" (the smaller one) who stood on either side of him at the opening night press party. I told him of my admiration of him and his talents. I included the unsigned 8" x 10" publicity photo and a self-addressed stamped envelope. I asked him if he would be kind enough to sign the photo, put it in the self-addressed envelope and mail it back to me. Frankly, I expected no response based on what I had heard about Lewis and his notoriously negative reputation.

A few weeks later I went my mailbox to find a self-addressed stamped 8" x 10" envelope! It was postmarked from Las Vegas, Nevada. I opened it to find the Jerry Lewis photo personalized and autographed. He wrote: "Irv, All good wishes. Jerry Lewis '95' "

Imagine!

So, I can truthfully claim I was Jerry Lewis' bodyguard for ten minutes. How do you suppose the aforementioned event will look on my next job application's resume?

To Fred Bless
god Bless
you
Pat
O'Brien

Chapter 1
Pat O'Brien

"They're (nuns) some of our best audiences."

He was the quintessential Irish-American priest and cop: always soft-spoken, yet a strong character with equally powerful convictions. He was part of Hollywood's "Irish Mafia" at Warner Brothers' motion picture studio in the 1930s and 1940s that included other Irish-type actors like James Gleason, Allen Jenkins, Rhys Williams, Edward S. Brophy, James Flavin, Allan Hale, Edgar Kennedy, Tom Kennedy, Frank McHugh, Thomas Mitchell, and Arthur Shields (as well as Shield's brother Barry Fitzgerald).

William Joseph Patrick O'Brien was born on November 11, 1899, in Milwaukee, Wisconsin, where he eventually attended Marquette University. A law major, he made a name for himself both in the classroom and on the football field. During World War I, he and his boyhood friend, Spencer Tracy, enlisted in the U.S. Navy and trained at Great Lakes Naval Training Station. Following the end of World War I and his discharge from the Navy, O'Brien enrolled, along with pal Tracy, at the American Academy of Dramatic Art in New York. Upon graduation, he started his professional acting career in stock companies, road shows, and finally on Broadway. In 1928, the struggling young actor reported for rehearsal in Chicago for the play *Broadway*. It was there that he met a beautiful and talented member of the cast named Eloise Taylor. They were married January 21, 1931. They would be married for over 50 years and have four children, three of them adopted.

Also in 1931, then movie mogul Howard Hughes sent for O'Brien to come to Hollywood from Broadway to play the role of Hildy Johnson in Hughes' motion picture based on the stage hit, *The Front Page*. Over his long acting career O'Brien starred in 114 motion pictures, nine with friend and fellow Irish-American, James Cagney. Unlike Cagney, who was constantly at odds with Warner

Brothers Studio over choice of scripts and salary increases, O'Brien was a team player who accepted his assignments, generally without protest.

Who can forget Pat O'Brien in *Knute Rockne, All American* (1940) as the famous Notre Dame football coach urging his players to win the big game for "the Gipper", played by a young Ronald Reagan? For the rest of his life O'Brien willingly repeated his famous locker-room pep-talk at countless dinners and various public functions.

Other memorable O'Brien motion picture portrayals included Father Duffy in *The Fighting 69th (*1940), Father Dunne in *Fighting Father Dunne* (1948), Frank Cavanaugh in *The Iron Major* (1943), Colonel Patty Ryan in *Bombardier* (1943) and Capt. Oren Hayes in 1969's television movie *The Over-the-Hill Gang*. Ironically, one of O'Brien's last motion pictures was also friend Cagney's: *Ragtime* in 1981.

While appearing in motion pictures O'Brien also performed in dozens of plays and on television. In 1960 he starred in his own television comedy courtroom series *Harrigan and Son* with Roger Perry (husband of comedienne Joanne Worley).

Towards the end of O'Brien's career, he and wife Eloise spent many years touring in stage plays together. Among them were *Hot Line to Heaven, Paris Is Out, Me and Thee, Absence of a Cello, Holiday for Lovers, Love and Kisses, Time Out for Ginger, Dear Ruth, Never Too Late, Our Town, Father of the Bride* and *Second Time Around.*

Pat O'Brien's own book on the story of his life, *The Wind At My Back,* was published in 1964 and received both critics' and the public's accolades. O'Brien has two stars on the famed Hollywood Walk of Fame: one for his work in motion pictures and one for his work in television.

From June 10 to June 29, 1980, Pat O'Brien and his wife Eloise starred in *Second Time Around* at Carousel Dinner Theatre, a theater-in-the-round then located in Ravenna, Ohio. The comedy is the story of two smitten senior citizens (Pat and Eloise O'Brien) who decide to live together rather than marry, much to the dismay of their respective and respectable families

At the play's opening "press night" performance it was my good fortune to be seated on the ground floor, stage-side, very close to the play's onstage action. I was reviewing the play for a local weekly newspaper, *The Village Views*. O'Brien was 80 years old at the time of *Second Time Around*. During the play's blackouts for scene changes the lights remained out longer than usual. Being stage-side I could see the reason: a stagehand was helping O'Brien (with cane) walk onstage. When O'Brien was seated, the stagehand quickly grabbed the actor's cane and ran offstage. The stage lights then came up to begin the next scene with O'Brien seated.

At the play's conclusion, after the well-deserved curtain call, O'Brien ambled out from backstage to talk to the audience. It was customary, at Carousel Dinner Theatre, for the featured performer of the current production to give a short speech after the cast curtain call. The audience waited in anticipation because they all knew some classic Irish stories would, no doubt, be in the offing.

Midway through a few of O'Brien's stories I spied a nun seated at an upper level patron table. Instead of paying attention to O'Brien's next story (complete with genuine Irish accent), I decided to watch the nun's reaction to the upcoming joke's punch line. After O'Brien delivered the tale's punch line I spied the nun laughing as the entire audience also roared with laughter. I then directed my attention back at O'Brien stage-side listening for the next story. I froze when I realized O'Brien was staring directly at me! I also realized I was the only one in the entire theater audience who did not laugh at the last story's punch line.

"Didn't you think it was funny?" Pat O'Brien asked me out loud in front of the entire audience. Embarrassed, I nervously smiled, broke out in a cold sweat, and nodded "yes" that I thought the story was, indeed, funny.

After each of the next several stories O'Brien would stare directly at me for my visual approval of his last joke's punch line.

When the stories finally ended and O'Brien's curtain speech was over, the audience filed out of the theater. As was the usual press night custom, all the press and media people waited behind to spend time with Pat and Eloise O'Brien and the rest of the cast as well. Patiently waiting in line, I wondered what Pat O'Brien would say to me. As my turn came, I presented him with one of his publicity pictures and asked him to autograph it. He obliged. Feeling very guilty, I confessed to O'Brien that the reason I did not laugh at his one story's punch line was because I was anticipating the reaction of a nun in the audience. O'Brien smiled. His deep blue eyes glistened as he said, "They're some of our best audiences." He then graciously posed for a photograph with me.

I felt a warm glow deep inside me as I left the theater. It wasn't until I got home that I read the salutation Pat O'Brien inscribed on the publicity picture. Above his signature he wrote: "To Irv, God Bless You."

Pat O'Brien passed away on October 15, 1983, in Santa Monica, California.

The body, face, and gait of the Pat O'Brien I saw that June night in 1980, three years before his death, were, indeed, aged. But the voice I heard and the gleam in his two, crystal-clear, blue eyes had the same brilliance I had observed in the same Pat O'Brien in his prime as Knute Rockne, numerous Irish-American parish priests and countless cops in his 114 motion pictures.

To Irv—
Best of
luck

Robert
Alda

Chapter 2
Robert Alda

"I prefer appearing in front of live audiences because you get your instant reaction. The most compensating in the long run is film because they last for years."

The telephone rang early one Saturday afternoon in September of 1979. It was the first time someone famous had actually called me at home. "Hello, Irv. This is Robert Alda calling from Canal Fulton Dinner Playhouse in North Canton," said a deep baritone voice at the other end of the line.

The reason for the personal call became quite apparent later. Canal Fulton Dinner Playhouse was, at the time, owned by David Fulford, who also owned Carousel Dinner Theatre in Ravenna, Ohio. Canal Fulton Dinner Playhouse was a summer stock (summer-only) theater with the same format of featuring a name actor or actress per show as did the Carousel Dinner Theatre. But the summer format was usually for a one-week run instead of the three-week to one-month run at Carousel.

Robert Alda (father of TV's *M*A*S*H** Alan Alda) was starring at Canal Fulton Dinner Playhouse with his younger son (and Alan's stepbrother), Antony. Alan and Antony had the same father but different mothers. Robert and Antony were performing in a comedy play, *Later, Leonardo,* written by George Tibbles (also the composer of "The Woody Woodpecker Song") at Canal Fulton Dinner Playhouse from September 4 through September 30, 1979.

Alda had obtained my name and phone number from Ellie Meindl, the director of publicity for both Carousel Dinner Theatre and Canal Fulton Dinner Playhouse. The reason for the personal phone call was Alda's unhappiness with the publicity, or rather the lack of it, being put forth to advertise *Later, Leonardo.* During our phone conversation Alda confessed he could not believe with a large shopping mall just down the road from Canal Fulton Dinner

Playhouse that there was not even a kiosk set up in the mall's main entrance to sell tickets or even some sandwich board-type billboards strategically located throughout the mall to advertise the production.

Our phone conversation ended by making an appointment for me to interview Robert Alda at his apartment at the Imperial House Hotel located across from Belden Village Mall in North Canton, Ohio, on Wednesday, September 12, 1979, at 4:30 PM.

The day of the interview did not get off to a very good start. My one-year old Volkswagen convertible broke down about half way between Akron (where I live) and North Canton, Ohio, on Route 77. Luckily I was near an exit ramp. I found a telephone at the nearest gas station, as this was before cell phones, and called the local branch of the American Automobile Association to have my car towed. In a short period of time a tow truck arrived, and my car was towed to the nearby garage. After I explained my plight to the mechanic, I borrowed his telephone to call Alda at his apartment to tell him of my dilemma. Alda assured me everything was still planned for the interview and not to worry, which was very reassuring to me. The car's problem was merely a broken fan belt. The mechanic quickly replaced it, and I was on my way to Alda's apartment.

Nearly one hour after our appointment was originally scheduled to begin, I found myself knocking on the door of Robert Alda's rented apartment. The handsome mature-looking man who opened the apartment door was tall, thin, and tanned, with a full head of silver-white hair very neatly combed and styled. He wore a dark blue silk shirt with tiny white polka dots and black trousers. I introduced myself. Upon entering the apartment I took out my notepad and plugged my portable tape recorder into a nearby wall outlet. Then we both sat down on a couch in the apartment's living room area. I nervously looked at my list of pre-written questions as we both settled in.

Robert Alda fondly recalled his beginnings in show business. Alphonso Giuseppe Giovanni Roberto D'Abruzzo was born on February 26, 1914, in New York City. A graduate of New York City's prestigious Stuyvesant High School, he was a student of architecture at New York University when the Depression hit. Alda entered amateur night contests at local theaters as a singer and dancer. One night he won the first prize of $30. Considering that architects working for the WPA (Works Progress Administration) at the time were earning only $24.75 per week, Alda decided to continue his singing career. He entered the last vestiges of vaudeville with his song -and-dance act, and also sang in nightclubs. The owner of one club was so impressed by Alda's talent that he became his manager. Alda was then booked onto the Catskill Mountains circuit of summer resorts.

In 1943, after a return engagement to New York City nightclubs, Alda received offers for screen tests from MGM, Paramount, and Warner Brothers motion picture studios. He opted for the Warner Brothers offer because the screen test would be conducted in Hollywood, California.

Thirteen months later, in 1945, Alda starred in the Warner Brothers' motion picture *Rhapsody in Blue*, about the life of famous American composer George Gershwin. It would become, and remain, Alda's most famous vehicle.

Since his beginning in show business Alda had done radio, TV and movies. He originated the role of Sky Masterson in Broadway's *Guys and Dolls,* for which he won a Tony Award. He also starred on Broadway in *What Makes Sammy Run?*

Alda's movie career was not as promising, appearing in such films as *Tarzan and the Slave Girl* in 1950 and *Won Ton Ton, the Dog That Saved Hollywood* in 1976.

Alda appeared on such early "live" television shows as *Robert Montgomery Presents* and *Lux Video Theatre* in 1950. He performed equally well in comedies and dramas. While living in Italy in the 1950s, '60s, and '70s, he did several Italian motion pictures before returning to the United States.

Back in the states Alda made guest appearances in such weekly hit television series as *Quincy, The Love Boat, The Incredible Hulk, Laverne and Shirley, Rockford Files, Wonder Woman, Fantasy Island, Kojak, Police Story, Mission Impossible, Rhoda,* and *Here's Lucy.* He also appeared in the daytime drama, *Love of Life,* as Jason Ferris.

During my conversation with Robert Alda I asked which he preferred: live plays or motion pictures. He smiled. "I prefer appearing in front of live audiences because you get your instant reaction", he said. "You get immediate reaction. When doing the show here (*Later, Leonardo* at Canal Fulton Dinner Playhouse) I get to do the after piece for 10 minutes, depending on audience reaction, and I get a chance to feel out the good jokes I do. It gives me the 'stand-up' or nightclub 'feel' for which I've done many all over the world." Then Alda added, "The most compensating in the long run is films because they last for years and years and years. It's been 35 years since the Gershwin picture and people still talk about it because they see it every once in a while on television or a rerun in a movie theater. That was my first movie. It's nice to have something that lasts that long that's still talked about and thought about so well."

I could not let the opportunity pass without asking Alda to compare his two sons, Alan and Antony.

"Alan was fooling around with writing since he was nine years old," Alda recalled. "He'd write a local paper on a mimeograph machine of two or three pages of the happenings in the canyon. We lived in a canyon in California. He'd write it and distribute it door-to-door. Then when he got to high school he actually wrote his first play. It was a musical comedy that made $3,000 for the high school. He thought: 'Wow! This is it! Let's go off into show business.' I told him, 'Hold it. Times are changing. Things are getting rougher. I'd like you have a little more on the ball. How about going to college? Let's make a deal: you go to college and I'll see that you get into summer stock. I'll help you with anything I can.' That worked out. He graduated Fordham University. He majored in English Literature. I think it helped him a great deal in his writing."

Then Alda's thoughts and comments turned toward his younger son. "Antony showed signs at 9 ½ years old when he made his first TV pilot. Alda talked about how rough it is for children to work on television and in movies while also being tutored so many hours a day on the set. "When this started happening to Antony," recalled Alda, "I said 'What the heck. I'm going to Europe and work on a picture or two. We'll go there and do his high school in Europe.' All during high school Antony was in plays. After high school Antony did some English-speaking theatre in Rome and some on his own. He eventually came back here (to the United States) and we had the college problem: was it college or musical college? So he went to musical college: Julliard for a couple of years, which gave him a good base for music. Today (1979) he plays five instruments, he composes, writes words and music. He's almost an engineer. He has practically a recording studio in his home and records his own stuff and overdubs everything. Everything on the soundtrack is his from beginning to end. He's waiting for the day he can put out his first album when this 'Disco Fever' is gone."

Returning to the present (1979), I asked Alda about his current wife (Flora Martino). A former Italian actress, she was in the next room doing her exercises. Alda and his wife had just published a book called *99 Ways to Cook Pasta*. "She did about eight or nine movies in Italy," said Alda. "We wound up with Antony. Alan's mother was another woman (Joan Browne whom he divorced) and she died. This is meditation hour for my wife," Alda informed me in a softer tone of voice. "She's into 'Self-Realization Fellowship.' It's a Far Eastern Philosophy. Not just yoga in the exercises but the complete yoga: the lessons and the teachings and the Eastern philosophy with heavy meditation. There is an aura about her; about all those people. It's magnificent. They're constantly smiling."

The Akron-Canton area's entertainment publicity (or lack of it) greatly bothered Robert Alda, especially how live stage plays were typically reviewed in the Northeastern Ohio publications. Alda said that the local Canton, Ohio, daily newspaper reviewed *Later, Leonardo* but that the nearby Cleveland, Ohio (about 60 miles north), and Akron, Ohio (about 30 miles north), daily papers did not. "People here (in Canton, Ohio) will buy both the Cleveland and Akron newspapers," he said matter-of-factly. Alda was particularly irritated that the Akron, Ohio, daily newspaper play reviewer who had interviewed him for a story but refused to review *Later, Leonardo* because the writer had an aversion to dinner theater, claiming it was not "real theatre." The writer further believed, considering himself a traditional theatergoer, he would be shortchanged "artistically" by attending a dinner theatre production. This greatly annoyed Alda. "When I go into dinner theatre," asserted Alda, "I give 100% and I believe my cast has to do the same. We don't do any 'asides' to the audience or jokes or out of character things until the curtain comes down. Then we might 'kibitz' around and talk to the audience. As a matter of fact, I have another session with the cast for 15 minutes to a half an hour to meet the audience to talk to them there and shake hands or sign autographs. But while the show is on for two or two and a half hours, we try to give as good a show as we can give them anywhere. For dinner theaters to survive today, audiences are too sophisticated to be cheated on food or the production. You have to give them maximum performance in both areas because you cannot duplicate a show and dinner for the price they give it to you for. Therefore, if you have any kind of attraction or live performances or good plays and you can combine the two, it's worth that extra five- to ten-mile drive in the country to see the thing."

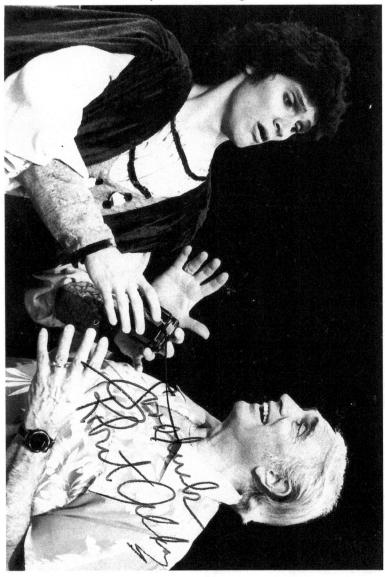

I glanced at my watch and realized it was time for Robert Alda to get ready for his performance in *Later, Leonardo*. I unplugged my tape recorder and thanked Alda for his time and candor. Before I left, he graciously honored my request by autographing an 8" x 10" publicity picture and we had a photograph taken of us together.

Not too long after my interview story was published, I learned Alda actually pulled his production of *Later, Leonardo* from Canal Fulton Dinner Playhouse before the end of its scheduled run because of his continual annoyance at the lack of publicity efforts.

I also learned of another incident at the end of one of the performances of *Later, Leonardo*. At the conclusion of each performance Alda would give an after-curtain speech depending on the audience response to that evening's production. It was after one evening's favorable performance that he decided to entertain a few questions from the theater audience. One spectator asked Alda how his son Alan was. Robert Alda smiled and said to the patron, "Why don't you ask him yourself?" Then quite suddenly, Alan Alda himself strolled out from backstage to the complete and utter surprise of the astonished audience! Alan had been in the area visiting his daughter at Kenyon College and decided to take in a performance of his father and half-brother's appearance in *Later, Leonardo*.

After pulling *Later, Leonardo* from Canal Fulton Dinner Playhouse, Robert Alda returned to work in television. Having already appeared in one *M*A*S*H** episode in 1972 as Dr. Borelli with his son Alan, Alda returned in another episode in 1980, which also included son Antony. Alda even returned as Dr. Stuart Whyland on *Days of Our Lives* in 1981. He also appeared on television in episodes of *The Facts of Life*, *The Dukes of Hazard*, and *Matt Houston*.

Robert Alda passed away on May 3, 1986, in Los Angeles, California, from the effects of a stroke.

I recently found Alan Alda's New York City address online, and wrote a letter informing him that I had an audio tape recording of his father from that September 1979, Canal Fulton Dinner Playhouse interview. I wrote I would be glad to mail him a copy of the audio taped interview. I also asked for an autographed 8" x 10" photograph. Several days later I received a large envelope in the mail that contained only an autographed 8" x 10" photograph of Alan Alda.

The envelope did not contain a note or letter indicating whether or not he desired a copy of the taped interview of his father.

In case you are wondering how Alphonso Giuseppe Giovanni Roberto D'Abruzzo became "Robert Alda," he took his name "Robert" for his first name and the first two letters of his first name, Alphonso (AL) and combined it with the first two letters of his last name, D'Abruzzo (DA) for his last name of "Alda."

Alas, today neither Canal Fulton Dinner Playhouse nor the Imperial House Hotel is in existence. Luckily for me, neither is

"Disco Fever!" Yet, thanks to a tape-recorded interview and a personalized, autographed photo of Robert Alda, plus the photograph of the two of us together, I have three treasured possessions from one special encounter that began with my very first celebrity phone call at home.

Buddy Rich
"DRUMMIN' UP DELIGHT"

Featuring
STEVE MARCUS
TENOR SAX
BARRY KIENER
PIANO

SUNDAY, JANUARY 12, 1986
8:30 p.m. in the Tangier Cabaret

Chapter 3
Bernard "Buddy" Rich

"I never think about a (drum) solo until I'm four bars into it."

Mention the term "big band drummer" and the first name that comes to mind has to be either Gene Krupa or Buddy Rich. Encounters with drummer extraordinaire Buddy Rich and, eventually, clarinetist Woody Herman were two experiences I had because of my father.

My father, Ben Korman, was a local big band musician for over 65 years. By his teens he was already accomplished on the saxophone, clarinet and violin. After graduating West High School in Akron, Ohio, in 1928, instead of attending college he decided to go on the road with a musical revue, touring the Deep South at the beginning of the Depression. Until the day he died, at age 91, my father hated fried chicken because it was mostly what the band was fed on the road during that long tour. Returning to Akron from his travels, he married my mother, Bertha Wolfand, in 1936, and settled down. All during his daytime job years he continued to earn extra income by playing in numerous local dance bands at night and on weekends.

Legendary drummer Buddy Rich and his big band orchestra were scheduled for a one-concert performance on January 12, 1986, at 8:30 PM locally in the Sultan's Cabaret at The Tangier. One of Akron's top restaurants, The Tangier periodically featured (and still does today) top-notch entertainment in its nightclub room, the Sultan's Cabaret. The room is set up like a small Las Vegas lounge with high-backed upholstered booths and tables for patrons, plus a stage for performing. The Tangier's lobby walls are lined with countless autographed pictures of famous entertainers who have appeared there over the years.

I contacted the cabaret manager, Larry Alltop, and explained to him that my father and I were coming to see the Buddy Rich concert.

Alltop had already supplied me with an official Buddy Rich biography and copies of newspaper articles from his publicity packet for a story I was writing about the concert for a local weekly newspaper. I explained to Alltop that my father was a big band musician and asked if my father could meet Rich the evening of the concert.

Bernard Rich was born September 30, 1917, in New York City. Eighteen months after his birth he was already standing on the stage with his parents in their vaudeville act. At four years of age he was on Broadway; at six he was known as "Baby Traps" and worked as a single act managed by his parents. He led a band at fifteen and was making $1,000 a week, a salary that reportedly was topped only by child movie star Jackie Coogan at the time.

Rich's jazz career began at age twenty-one with clarinetist Joe Marsala in 1938. Rich then turned up in the bands of Bunny Berigan, Artie Shaw, Tommy Dorsey, and Benny Carter. In 1946 Rich formed his own band just as the "Big Band Era" was ending. His ex-roommate, Frank Sinatra, had so much faith in Rich's ability that he decided to back the new band. Rich, more and more, wanted to play jazz. Unfortunately, not enough people felt the same way, and after about two years as a bandleader, Rich decided to accept an offer to join the touring "Jazz at the Philharmonic" troupe in the late 1940s.

Between tours Rich was a permanent fixture on New York City's 52nd Street where he was one of the spearheads of a new form of music called "Bebop," later shortened to "Bop." It was at this time Rich worked and recorded with such legendary musicians as Charlie "Bird" Parker (saxophone), Dizzy Gillespie (trumpet), Thelonius Monk (piano), Al Haig (piano) , Buddy de Franco (clarinet), Errol Garner (piano), Dexter Gordon (tenor saxophone), George Duvuvier (bass) , and J.J. Johnson (trombone).

Thereafter followed a period during which Rich could be heard alternately with the bands of Harry James and Tommy Dorsey until 1959 when he suffered his first heart attack. In 1961, despite poor health, Rich was still the driving force behind the swinging bands.

In April 1966, Rich formed a big band with Gene Quill (saxophone) and Pepper Adams (saxophone). In subsequent bands Rich featured the talents of Don Menza (saxophone and arranger), Art Pepper (saxophone), Al Porcino (trumpet), Joe Romano (saxophone),

Pat LaBarbera (saxophone), Bruce Paulson (trombone), Bobby Shew (trumpet), Chuck Findlay (trumpet), Joe DeBartolo (bass), Barry Kiener (piano), Alan Kaplan (trombone), Lin Biviano (trumpet), Dave Stahl (trumpet), and Steve Marcus (saxophone).

In the summer of 1967, Rich's career received a tremendous boost when his band was selected by Jackie Gleason as a regular on his summer replacement television series, along with singer Buddy Greco and comedian George Carlin. In the fall of that same year Rich went on a concert tour with Frank Sinatra. He continued his big band format except for a brief period in 1974 when he formed a small group that included Sal Nestico (tenor saxophone), Sonny Fortune (saxophone), Joe Romano (saxophone), Jack Wilkins (guitar), Kenny Baron (piano), and John Bunch (piano). But Rich still missed the power of the big band sound and assembled a new band. That same band format is what Buddy Rich brought to the Tangier Restaurant Sultan's Cabaret at The Tangier January 12,1986, for a one-performance concert that featured Steve Marcus on tenor saxophone and Barry Kiener on piano.

As I sat at a stage-side table with my father to watch the concert, I was amazed at how many young men were in Buddy Rich's orchestra. The band filled Tangier's Cabaret stage with Rich on a raised platform, upstage center where he could be clearly seen. Under his very own spot light, drummer Buddy Rich would squint and continuously smile, displaying a mouthful of large white teeth. After each musical number Rich called out a number. I later learned it was the page number in the band's massive music book that contained the next musical number. Apparently there was no set pre-planned repertoire. After each musical number Rich decided, on the spur-of-the-moment, which tune he wanted the band to play next and merely shouted out its page number.

After several musical numbers, many featuring Buddy Rich on drums, the bandleader announced that there would be an intermission. Much like Rich's repertoire that evening, the break was apparently unplanned, as the facial expressions on several of the band members attested.

The band members put down their instruments and followed Rich offstage. A few minutes later Larry Alltop, the Cabaret manager, approached our table and told my father and me to quickly follow him into an unused restaurant banquet room across the carpeted hall. The three of us entered the room where the band members were relaxing, some sitting in chairs. In one corner was Buddy Rich, changing his clothes, getting out of his dark suit and tie and putting on a freshly starched white shirt and a light blue, v-neck sweater. While he was putting on his shirt, I caught a quick glimpse of him from his waist up. His torso appeared scarred from one massive or several lesser operations.

Today, as I look back on meeting Buddy Rich that night in 1986, I recall that he seemed a bit "out of it" or somewhat disoriented as to where he was or what was going on at the moment. Alltop introduced Rich to my father and me. My father, a man of few outward emotions or words, seemed impressed at meeting the legendary big band drummer. Within a few minutes the introductions and conversations were over, but not before I asked Rich to autograph two publicity photos: one for my father and one for me. There was also a little bit of time for a few photographs with Rich since I had brought my camera along.

We quickly left the room and returned to our table where we anxiously awaited the rest of the concert. As the band resumed their performance, I recalled some publicity articles I had read prior to the Buddy Rich concert. It seemed Rich never ceased to amaze his audience as a performer. Reported to be outwardly "cocky" and often insulting, Rich was also reported to be charming and thoughtful. He was famous for respecting talent while abhorring phonies no matter their so-called expertise.

Because of his frequent appearances on Johnny Carson's *Tonight Show*, Rich often gave the impression of being his own biggest fan. Often referred to as "The World's Greatest Drummer," Rich never seemed to discourage the label. In his own defense Rich was quoted as saying, "That's a lot of bull! When I say that, I say it with my tongue all the way back in my cheek. Who's the greatest at anything? Babe Ruth? Muhammad Ali? At one time we all go down."

When asked how he prepared for a drum solo, Rich once said, "I don't. I never think about a solo until I'm four bars into it. I have no preconceived ideas. It depends upon how I feel at that moment what direction the solo takes." While on the topic of music, Rich was once asked about what makes a great band. "Fifteen excellent musicians, obviously," he replied matter-of-factly.

If you thought Buddy Rich's music was merely a nostalgia act, he would be the first to tell you about reaching out to young people. "A ten-year old came backstage," recalled Rich, "and said, 'Mr. Rich, you are utterly awesome!' I loved it!"

Buddy Rich received much deserved recognition throughout his musical career. The Downbeat Magazine Hall of Fame Award, the Modern Drummer Magazine Hall of Fame Award, and the Jazz Unlimited Immortals of Jazz Award are just a few of his numerous honors.

About one year after my father and I experienced Buddy Rich and his concert at The Tangier, I read of Rich's death on April 2, 1987. He died of heart failure following surgery for a malignant brain tumor.

Rich had a quadruple heart bypass in 1983 after a massive heart attack and was advised to retire. He completely ignored the doctors and went on to play at levels he had never reached before. According to Rich's daughter, Cathy, six weeks after the bypass Rich was opening at Ronnie Scott's club in London. Rich's daughter thought that if her father had listened to his doctors and stayed at home, he might start thinking he would never play again. So he got up and left for New York City to rehearse his band. From all accounts Rich played greater than ever. He may have been a little stiff but he never looked back.

The most astonishing thing I read about Buddy Rich was that he never took a drum lesson! As a youngster he sang and danced as well as played the drums. In his early teens he became more interested in drumming and began to listen to the best drummers of his time, such as Chick Webb, Davey Tough, Sid Catlett and Gene Krupa (who actually introduced Buddy Rich to his wife). Later Rich would actually duel Krupa in numerous "battle of the drums" as part of the Jazz at the Philharmonic tours around the world.

In fact, it was Krupa who paid Buddy Rich the ultimate compliment when he said Rich was "...the greatest drummer ever to draw breath."

Chapter 4
Richard Egan

"It's the part that makes the performer. If he doesn't have the right tools to work with, he's not going to be remembered too long."

I was shivering on the afternoon of February 4, 1979, for two reasons: cold and fear. I had never interviewed anyone before. This was to be my 14th published story, most of which were play reviews for a local weekly magazine called *TV Facts*. The closest I had ever been to a famous person was in 1973, when I appeared with Mickey Rooney in *See How They Run* at Carousel Dinner Theatre for six memorable weeks.

Actor Richard Egan was appearing at the same Carousel Dinner Theatre, then located in Ravenna, Ohio, in the comedy *Hanky Panky* that played January 30 through February 25, 1979. The comedy was advertised as "the story of Phil Stockdale (Egan), a recently divorced man who comes between two 'lukewarm' lovers. Egan as a middle-aged Lothario is in search of a new life and new loves. Stockdale's ex-wife provided the 'frosting' on the cake in the play's supposed sophisticated vehicle of razor-sharp wit and repartee."

Ellie Meindl, Carousel's publicity director, had arranged an interview with Egan. I thought her telephone call concerned reviewing the opening night performance of *Hanky Panky*. I had no intention of interviewing actor Egan. Then when Ellie called and asked if I wanted to interview him, I recalled that "rush" I felt when in the company of Mickey Rooney and when acting on stage with him in *See How They Run* in 1973. So I figured, "why not?" and told Ellie to go ahead with arranging the interview.

Days before the interview I prepared questions in advance and wrote them down on a small note pad. Because I wanted to pay as much attention as I could to Egan, I decided to take my portable tape recorder along. That way I could play the taped interview back for accurate and precise quotes to include in the finished article. Also, I wouldn't have to stop Egan in mid-sentence to write something down, thus hindering his train of thought. The only time I would have to stop Egan was to get the correct spelling of a particular name and/or place.

I met Ellie at Carousel Dinner Theatre in Ravenna and we drove several blocks to Egan's rented apartment. As I got out of the car and followed Ellie up to Egan's apartment, I could hear my heart pounding more and more loudly. I had never interviewed anyone famous before! I was getting that "rush."

The door opened. Ellie and I greeted Richard Egan who cordially invited us in. I pulled out my pen and notepad as Egan served us coffee. I noticed the television was on. Egan had been watching a boxing match. He was wearing a short sleeved, multi-colored striped golf shirt and dark trousers. Egan was a large man at six feet two inches in height. He also looked as if he hadn't shaved that morning. As I plugged in my tape recorder, Egan sat down in a big easy chair. His deep, resonant, rugged, masculine voice truly matched his large, powerful demeanor.

I began the interview by asking some biographical questions. The beefy, handsome movie star of the 1950s was born on July 29, 1921, in San Francisco, California. Following his stint in the Army during World War II, Egan attended The University of San Francisco for undergraduate work in theatre history and dramatic literature. He studied at Stanford University for graduate work. He attended and taught at Northwestern University as well. It was while studying at Stanford that he did a screen test for Metro Goldwyn Mayer Studios. He decided to stay in Hollywood when he got his first movie bid.

Egan admitted at the beginning of the interview that he had really begun acting very early in life in grammar school, then high school and college. "Since I had an aptitude for it I decided to go for it as a career," Egan recalled. "I decided to go through academic theatre in order to do it because I thought I could learn much faster and be more immersed in it. Someone saw me in a play and I got a bid to do a screen test."

Egan's brawny physique and rugged manner came to the forefront in the early 1950s in such motion pictures as *The Damned Don't Cry, Bright Victory, Hollywood Story, The Golden Horde, Cripple Creek, One Minute To Zero*, with Robert Mitchum,

Blackbeard the Pirate, The Glory Brigade, Demetrius and the Gladiators, 300 Spartans, Underwater, with Jane Russell, *Untamed,* with Tyrone Power, Seven *Cities of Gold, The View From Pompey's Head, Slaughter On Tenth Avenue,* and *Love Me Tender* with Elvis Presley.

"Certainly Presley will always stand out in my mind," Egan said when asked about Elvis. "*Love Me Tender* was his first movie. He was a wonderful boy. I like him very much. He's very modest, unassuming, and very impressive. He wanted to learn and he did learn. I always thought he wasn't given what he should've been given in the way of material and scripts. I think they got the money, but the movies weren't much. I don't think you can guide a career like that with simply what you can get out of it financially. I think you have to be a little more choosey about the scripts or you'll hurt that talent badly. Some of them survive but Elvis had a low point in his career. In fact, I think in his last picture he had a non-singing role in a picture called *Charro*. It was a western. Can you imagine him in a picture and not singing? How many gold records does he have, and him in a picture with a non-singing role? That shows bad guidance. I don't care how much money you've got: it shows bad guidance! It was only his tremendous talent that allowed him to go back to nightclub performing and making records and maintain the top level of stardom he should've had in motion pictures."

After *Love Me Tender* (1956), Richard Egan appeared in *The Revolt of Mamie Stover* (also in 1956) with Jane Russell, *These Thousand Hills* (1959) with Don Murray and Lee Remick, *Summer Place* (also in 1959) with Dorothy McGuire, *Pollyanna* (1960) with Jane Wyman and Karl Malden, *Esther and the King* (also in 1960) with Joan Collins, *300 Spartans* (1962) with Ralph Richardson and Diane Baker, *Chubasco* (1968) with Susan Strasberg, Ann Sothern and Preston Foster, and *The Destructors* (also in 1968) with Michael Ansara.

Egan sat back in his easy chair, sipping his coffee and casually spoke of his friends and acquaintances. I asked if any were in the motion picture business. "Yes. I have a friend: Robert Mitchum," Egan said matter-of-factly. "Actors who play leads usually don't associate with each other. It's the nature of the business. You travel so much you seldom run into anyone more than once or twice a year. I did three pictures with Bob Mitchum. I have another friend in Jane Russell. Lee Marvin is also a friend of mine as is Ernest Borgnine. I have a close friend in Rory Calhoun. I did two pictures with Rory. As far as the ones who've passed on (as of 1979) I was struck with Tyrone Power. I also worked with Susan Hayward. She was a striking person. So was Joan Crawford. I admired Barbara Stanwyck and Lana Turner. I can't say they are close friends of mine, but we're friends. If we see each other there's no animosity or anything."

Egan's one foray into network television came from 1962 to 1963. Egan starred in a one-hour modern western called *Empire* on NBC. The next season the series was cut to one-half hour and retitled, *Redigo.*

"*Empire* was like making a movie: the same pace," recalled Egan. "Maybe you worked longer hours than in motion pictures but when you went into a half-hour (format) you even doubled that because they tried to do two episodes a week: two and a half days an episode. It's backbreaking and it's very wrong. But that's what they try to do. It was from 6:00 AM in the morning until there was no sunshine. We were shooting outside. There was no break between this episode and that episode. If you finish this episode at 1:00 PM, you started the next one at 1:30 PM. The next director came in and said, 'Okay, we want you over here and start going.' I thought it was silly but that's what they wanted.

"They were late beginning. They wanted to be four or five episodes ahead of airtime. At least at that time (early 1960s) they did. They'd like to be ten if they could. That would give them time to polish it a little more. The difference essentially is 'speed.' Speed doesn't necessarily mean economy. And it certainly doesn't mean 'artistry.' The show was cut from one hour to a half hour. It wasn't done deliberately. NBC decided then they didn't want to pick up *Empire* for the next year. They tried to sell the hour but could only sell a half hour. So they came back and said, 'How about going to a half hour? We can sell that.' NBC decided not to pick up the second year of *Empire*. ABC bought 32 outright. NBC wouldn't let us go over there. They just held on to their option until September and that killed it. That hurt me badly because I owned a third of it. That was Screen Gems. It was part of Columbia Pictures. But that wasn't Screen Gems' fault. It was the network's decision. One of the heads

of the network said, 'Oh, well. That's business.' Charming person,"
said Egan sarcastically. "I'd like to meet him someday."

Egan relished the good old days of motion picture film making
while disdaining the ways of today. "There isn't any unity like they
used to have," noted Egan. "No matter what they said about Louis B.
Mayer or Harry Cohn, who was much maligned, he had a great talent.
They were great cutters (motion picture editors) like Darryl Zanuck.
He could put together a picture. They knew what would sell. Louis B.
Mayer had a sense of 'rightness.' So did Jack Warner. Even Howard
Hughes did. If Hughes were more interested in pictures it would be
better for all of us. But then he became involved with the Government
and outer space and the things he really liked and enjoyed.

"It's the part that makes the performer. The performer adds a
great deal to the part or the tools to work. If he doesn't have the right
tools to work with he's not going to be remembered too long. There
are a couple of guys who've come up and vanished in the last five or
ten years that looked like they'd get somewhere but there was nothing
to follow up with. The heads of studios used to guide people. They'd
say, 'Okay, let's get another picture like that.' (Clarke) Gable became
great because they repeated all his strong parts. He was strong in that
they gave him different roles. John Wayne lasted years being
'typecast.' Gable was the same, as was (Gary) Cooper and Jimmy
Cagney."

Egan fondly recalled the directors who brought their own
personal life experiences into their craft like Raoul Walsh, John Ford,
and William Wellman. "These men had enormous experiences in
life," said Egan. "Walsh was everything before he became a director."
Having done some research before the interview I added to the
conversation: "William Wellman was a member of Lafayette
Escadrille in World War I." The outfit was a group of United States
pilots who flew for France several years before the United States
entered the conflict against Germany.

"(Raoul) Walsh worked his way across the country as a hand on
a ranch," added Egan. "He used to have to pull the teeth of horses and
of the men! He had a patch over his one eye most of his life from a
jackrabbit that went through his car windshield and the glass went
into his eye. He met Pancho Villa. He was on a train a mile long and
he went with him to meet (Emilio) Zapata in Mexico City. He wrote

about it in his autobiography, *Each Man in His Time*."

Egan did not have anything positive to say about the films of the day (the late 1970s). "Have you seen some of the pictures they put on? Frightening," Egan said disgustedly, "Frightening! I guarantee if I'd seen these pictures I'd never have gone into motion pictures in the beginning. If they had things like *Looking for Mr. Goodbar* and that stuff. Ilk! There would be no appeal."

But all was not lost. I asked Richard Egan if he had seen any pictures lately that he did like. "Yes," he said. "I liked *Rocky*. I liked *The Longest Yard*. That one was funny. The language was raw but it seemed to be in keeping with the nature of the vehicle itself. They just didn't throw that in. It was the way they talked. I like a lot more than I dislike."

My interview then turned toward Richard Egan's family and his wife Patricia. How did he and his wife meet? All three of us (Egan, Ellie, and I) burst out laughing when Egan confessed, "She picked me up in a bar."

Then Egan's attention turned toward his children. "They all like to eat. That's for damn sure! My oldest likes to write. Her name's Tricia (age 19). She's at Loyola Marymount. She's a good writer. She's talked about giving acting a fling," Egan revealed. My second is Kathleen (age 14). She thinks there's a place in this entertainment world for her as a model or whatever. We'll have long talk about that before she makes her move. My third is a marvelous athlete. She's extraordinary. Colleen, age 12. She can outrun anybody. She's an excellent basketball player as well as volleyball and baseball. She plays on a boys' baseball team. I think she's so extraordinary that I better do something about her. I think she can make it on the Olympic Team. That's how good she is. She can outrun boys her own age and outrun them by three or four yards. That's an enormous talent. She's so well coordinated in dancing and ice-skating and yet she's very feminine. My son, Richard, Jr. (age 9), of course, is a lot like me: sort of a baby bear. He's a rough one. Then there's my youngest, Maureen (age 5). We call her 'Puff'. She's yet to indicate which facet of the world she's going to conquer first. I'm sure she'll go right into college."

Was there a show business career for any of his children? Egan was serious in his response. "I'd steer them all away from entertainment until they learn to control this new freedom of language and nudity of excess until it comes under control and they stop acting like children and act more like adults, like Zefferelli. He knows how to act and handle a thing like that," Egan said with passion. "These B-Picture 'cats': they can take a script or a reel off their library of stag movies and just rewrite them and put it in lascivious actions and say, 'Well, what do we call this one?'"

When asked about plans for the immediate future, Egan was not sure. "I'll stay with this play (*Hanky Panky*). I'll look for a new play. I have a friend who owns some theaters and he read a play he liked and is going to bring it over here before I leave. He has good taste and he knows what I like. I might be doing that. There's another fellow I know who took over a picture I did, called *Mission To Glory*, who says he has a script for me to do. I haven't read it yet. It's a movie. I don't even know the name of it."

As our time together came to an end I asked Richard Egan if there was anything he wanted me to add to my interview article that I didn't cover in our interview. "No," he said politely.

My first star interview was over. I realized my initial fears had been unfounded. Thanks to actor Richard Egan's relaxed, easygoing manner I was completely at ease during the interview process. The "rush" this experience gave me also gave me some confidence that I felt I needed at the time.

Egan continued to appear on television after the run of *Hanky Panky*. He appeared in such series as *Police Story, The Streets of San Francisco*, and *Capitol*.

Richard Egan died on July 20, 1987 of prostate cancer at age 65 in Los Angeles, California. He is buried in Holy Cross Cemetery in Culver City California.

I often wonder how Egan's children have turned out. Did some go into show business or excel in athletics? Which facet of the world did Egan's youngest, Maureen or "Puff", eventually conquer? Did Egan's wife, Patricia, remarry? Is she alive today?

The coldness of that frigid February day in 1979 was tempered with the warm kindness extended to me by actor Richard Egan, my first celebrity interview.

Chapter 5
Woody Herman

"Woody Herman was heralded not so much for his talent as a clarinetist . . . but for his talent in selecting exceptional groups of sidemen . . . and by combining clever arrangements with skill, style and discipline. He also held importance as an organizer, having the rare ability to assemble and sustain bands notable for the quality of their musicians that consisted of brilliant improvisers."

. . . Film maker Ken Burns

The second "big band" experience I had with my father was at the behest of legendary big band clarinetist Woody Herman.

In the spring of 1986, the annual, age-old question once again popped into my mind: What can I get my dad for Father's Day? Scanning the local daily newspaper I saw an advertisement of an upcoming entertainment event at Tangier Restaurant the Sultan's Cabaret at The Tangier. Big band clarinetist Woody Herman and his band, The Thundering Herd, were scheduled for two matinee performances on June 9 and 10.

Like Herman, my father had played the clarinet for more than fifty years, mostly in numerous area "big bands." I decided that taking my dad to see Woody Herman and His Thundering Herd would, indeed, be a very special Father's Day gift.

I contacted Tangier Restaurant's Cabaret manager, Larry Alltop, and asked him to reserve two seats for my father and me for one of the matinee performances. I also informed Alltop that I would be joining my father a bit later during the performance since I would still be teaching school at show time. The matinee would begin at 3:30 PM after a 2:00 PM buffet brunch. Senior citizens largely attended the matinees. Tangier Restaurant owner, Ed George, usually had special entertainment to accommodate older "bus tour" and senior citizen groups.

Woody Herman

Thomas Cassidy, Inc.
Artist Management
423 Marauood Drive • Woodstock, Illinois 60098
815-338-9075

    Woodrow Charles Herman was born on May 16, 1913, in Milwaukee, Wisconsin. He started playing the saxophone at age 11. Within four years he was already a professional musician. In Chicago he gained experience with such bands as Tom Gerun and Harry Sosnik. He also toured with Gus Arnheim. The year 1934 was pivotal for clarinetist Herman. It was the year he joined the Isham Jones Orchestra. In 1936, when the Jones orchestra disbanded, Herman decided to take a risk and formed his own band from the members who chose to stay. He used the Jones's band sidemen as the nucleus for his own orchestra. It was the recordings of this particular band that Herman made during this period that emphasized vocals. But the band was also becoming known for its instrumentals. In 1939 Herman recorded his first hit and the band's theme song of "At the Woodchoppers' Ball." Later the band was renamed, The First Herd. Famous musician Duke Ellington influenced Herman's band during this period. The band went through a number of changes of personnel, such as the inclusion in 1943 of Chubby Jackson (double bass) and in 1944 of Neal Hefti (trumpet and arranger), Ralph Burns (piano and arranger), Flip Phillips (tenor saxophone), and Bill Harris (trombone). By the mid 1940s, under the name Herman's Herd, the band was internationally famous for the force and originality of its music and was considered the most exciting big band in jazz.

Some music writers agreed with Herman's term of "herd" for his orchestra because of the boisterous, energetic side of the band's work. This description did not necessarily catch the beautiful, reflective side of the band's output, especially in the hands of such arrangers as Ralph Burns when featuring star soloists Stan Getz (tenor saxophone), Zoot Sims (tenor saxophone), Serge Chaloff (baritone saxophone), Gene Ammons (tenor saxophone), and Al Cohn (tenor saxophone).

It was also during this time period that Herman's famous "Four Brothers" lineup of three tenors and one baritone saxophone became legendary. Besides "At the Woodchopper's Ball," Herman's high energy hit tune "Apple Honey" became a big band favorite. Composer Igor Stravinsky was so impressed by the "Herman sound" that he composed "Ebony Concerto" especially for the band in 1945.

Unfortunately, Herman's First Herd broke up in 1946 because of family troubles, just at the height of the band's success. It was the only one of his bands to make real money. Herman formed the Second Herd in 1947. This band was not as extroverted as the original Herd but still had some popular numbers such as "The Goof and I." Soon after, the "Four Brothers" trademark sound came to an end.

After the demise of the Second Herd, Herman started his Third Herd, which was a little more conservative than the first two "herds." This band lasted from 1950-1956. He started the Thundering Herd, also referred to as the Anglo-American Herd, in 1959. The Swinging Herd was formed in 1962. It featured such soloists as Bill Chase (trumpet), Phil Wilson (trombone), and Sal Nistico (tenor saxophone).

In the late 1960s Herman took up the soprano saxophone and included young jazz-rock players in his subsequent bands.

Woody Herman toured with his band throughout the 1970s and 1980s. He held residency in a club in New Orleans. Thereafter, he worked principally on the West Coast before taking up another residency in the St. Regis Hotel in New York City in 1985. In 1986 he celebrated his 50th year as a bandleader.

In retrospect, Woody Herman was heralded not so much for his talent as a clarinetist, but rather for in his talent in selecting exceptional groups of sidemen, and by combining clever arrangements with skill, style, and discipline, turning his various "herds" into a series of great ensembles. He also held importance as an organizer. He had the rare ability to assemble and sustain bands notable for the quality of their musicians that consisted of brilliant improvisers.

It was about 4:15 P.M. when I arrived at the Tangier Restaurant Sultan's Cabaret that June afternoon in 1986. I had arranged for my father to attend the matinee performance without me, meeting him after work. The matinee performance of Woody Herman and his band began at 3:00 P.M. The stage area was brightly lit. I looked for my father who was supposed to be seated somewhere in the crowd, listening to the concert. When I arrived at the assigned table, he was not there. I quietly retreated to the round bar area near the nightclub's entrance door. I sat on one of the tall barstools, ordered a cocktail, and began listening to the concert already in progress.

There, onstage, was the Woody Herman playing his legendary clarinet with his orchestra; his current Thundering Herd. The audience was seated tableside, listening to the nostalgic melodies emanating from the stage. Head swaying, toe tapping and rhythmic body movements were quite evident in the older crowd. Too bad there was no space for a dance floor available by the stage. No doubt a significant number of those in attendance had actually danced to Woody Herman and one of his Herds years ago and would like to recreate the memory once again.

Herman played numerous songs with his band and spoke to the audience, often telling jokes between musical numbers. It was about one year before his death and Herman looked frail and gaunt. But when he played his clarinet, accompanied by his band, he seemed much younger.

Just as the matinee concert ended, I saw the nightclub manager, Larry Alltop, and asked him where my father was. He told me that since he knew my father was a big band clarinet player and this was my Father's Day present, Alltop saw to it that my father had a seat closer to the stage bandstand. I thanked Alltop for his kindness. He then asked me if I would like to meet Woody Herman. Pulling a camera from my sport coat pocket, I said I would like to take a photo of my father with Woody Herman. After the concert Alltop escorted us up to the bandstand. Several people were already talking to Woody Herman, no doubt about when and where they saw him with his band in the past.

Alltop introduced Herman to my father. The bandleader was very cordial and accommodating. While the two veteran clarinet players talked to each other about what make of clarinet each favored I snapped a picture of them together. My father and I left the Sultan's Cabaret after thanking Alltop for all he had arranged for us. My father seemed pleased. I thought the occasion was a better Father's Day present than a tie. Several weeks later I presented my father with an 8" x 10" photograph of him with Woody Herman and put it in a frame. My father hung it on his wall next to the 8" x 10" photograph I took of him with drummer Buddy Rich the year before.

In the late 1980s the Internal Revenue Service continually hounded Woody Herman, because his manager had not paid taxes from his sidemen's salaries during the 1960s.

About one month before Woody Herman died; I saw his photo in the local daily newspaper. The article that accompanied the photo told of Herman's financial plight and how much his friends were helping him out. He was pictured sitting in a wheelchair sporting a beard. I had seen the same sort of photograph of Henry Fonda just after he had won an Oscar as Best Actor for his role in *On Golden Pond* in 1981. Fonda was too frail with a heart condition to accept the award in person. Shortly thereafter Fonda died. Similarly, Woody Herman died about one month later on October 29, 1987, of cardiac arrest. Simply put: a broken heart.

Buddy Rich and Woody Herman are both gone. Even though I was too young at that time to have experienced the original Big Band Era, thanks to Buddy Rich and Woody Herman, I was able to relive the era with my father: him for the "umpteenth" time and me for the first.

DOTTIE WEST

L/A

Management:
KRAGEN & COMPANY
1112 N. Sherbourne Drive
Los Angeles, California 90069
(213) 659-7914

Chapter 6
Dottie West

"You can knock me down, but better have a big rock to keep me there. This, too, shall pass."

All I knew about Dottie West before her concert one September night in 1980 was that she was a female country western singer. To me, the term "female country western singer" conveyed the picture of a thick-accented Southern girl in a gingham dress with countless rows of fringe, wearing a cowboy hat atop a large bouffant hairdo, singing songs about how painful love is, accompanied by a "twangy" steel guitar with maybe some yodeling thrown in. I was raised in a house filled with recordings of classical symphonies, big band music, and opera. My own personal preference back then was rock 'n' roll. Then I recalled that West had recently recorded some duets with singer Kenny Rogers who had recently crossed over from country to pop music. Maybe Dottie West wasn't so "hillbilly" after all.

Kenny Rogers would not only play a part in West's life but, indirectly, in her death as well.

Armed with my image of a female country western singer, yet with an open mind, I ventured into Tangier Restaurant's Sultan's Cabaret to review her performance for a local weekly newspaper.

West's one-hour set on the Sultan's Cabaret stage would feature thirteen songs, an Elvis Presley medley, and one encore. West's backup band consisted of three guitars, percussion, electronic keyboard, piano, and two female backup singers. The band members' backgrounds were, indeed, diverse. Three of the musicians were from Texas and one from Arkansas, while the pianist hailed from Maryland and the electronic keyboardist was from Boston.

Then there was the actual, personal appearance of Dottie West herself: she was not dressed in fringed gingham sporting a big bouffant hairdo, even though she did wear a hat. The hat was for a very good reason which she revealed to the audience later. West had long flowing red hair with Farah Fawcett-style layered tresses. That evening she had dressed in one of her famous Bob Mackie designer dresses! Hardly "hillbilly."

West knew that the Tangier audience had come to see her. She could have easily taken up the entire one-hour performance by herself. But she didn't. Dottie West was a gracious entertainer. Occasionally, when a musical bridge surfaced during some of her vocal numbers, West turned away from the audience and faced the band. With her back to the audience, West cleverly drew the spectators' attention away from her and directly on the band musicians performing the bridge music. West occasionally stood between her two back up singers, Nanette and Becky, so the spotlights would shine on them simultaneously.

Another country western myth was dispelled that autumn evening when I realized that Dottie West had no thick country accent or southern drawl. Like Dolly Parton, West had been born in Tennessee. She drew upon the similarities of their birth during verbal patter between musical numbers. "I wore a hat," she informed the Tangier audience, "so you wouldn't confuse me with Dolly Parton. I know she's bigger than me," West went on, "She's five foot ten inches . . . laying down!"

Another aspect of West's relaxed demeanor surfaced during her performance. Many of her fans had brought cameras and continually snapped pictures during the concert. West never mentioned being annoyed by the constant clicking of camera shutters or the popping of flashbulbs.

Some of West's repertoire included songs by Pete Seeger, Hank Williams, and Kenny Rogers. One of the concert's most popular songs was "Raised on Country Sunshine." If the title doesn't sound familiar, it was the song she sang in the late 1970s and early 1980s for Coca Cola television commercials. Dottie West could, indeed, sing of heartache and disappointment if she chose to. Her rags-to-riches story was eventually made into a television movie.

Much like Loretta Lynn and Dolly Parton, Dottie West came from a very large family and extreme poverty. Born Dorothy Marie Marsh on October 11, 1932, in Smithville, Tennessee, about 70 miles outside of Nashville, West was the oldest of 10 children. The family literally lived in a shack in the woods. West's father, Hollis Marsh, was an alcoholic who abused the entire Marsh household. He had an extremely violent temper that he constantly took out on the family. Hollis regularly molested his oldest daughter, Dottie. This horror continued until one day at school when Dottie broke down and cried, telling her principal what she had been going through at home for years. The principal immediately called the local sheriff. Hollis was arrested and charged with rape, incest, and violating the age of consent law. He was sentenced to 40 years in prison where he eventually died.

Dottie's mother, Pelina, a very good cook, eventually opened two restaurants. For the first time in years things began to look up for the Marsh family. They moved out of their old shack in the woods into a decent apartment. At seventeen years of age Dottie was presented with her very first birthday cake.

Young Dottie Marsh knew that music would become an important part of her life. She set out to major in music at Tennessee Tech located near her home. While at Tennessee Tech she met Bill West, who would eventually become her first husband. They played the local party and club circuits on a regular basis. Their first two children, Kerry and Morris, were born during this period.

Northeastern Ohio, Cleveland in particular, played an important part in the next phase of Dottie West's life. After graduating from Tennessee Tech, Dottie, Bill and the children moved to Cleveland, Ohio, where Bill obtained a job as an electrical engineer. Both performed on a local television show, *Landmark Jamboree*, which originated from Cleveland. While the Wests lived in Cleveland, daughter Shelly West was born. She would later become a country singer in her own right.

One day, while driving back to Cleveland from Nashville, Dottie and Bill passed Starday Records. Other record labels had recently turned them down. Dottie West was feeling particularly confident that day when she walked into the Starday Record studio and said, "I am a singer and I want to record a record." One week later, at the cost of $5ll, she recorded "Angel on Paper." The song was played all over the Nashville radio airwaves and eventually led to Grand Ole Opry manager Ott Devine inviting West to appear on the Grand Ole Opry stage. It was there that West met lifelong friend, Patsy Cline, who gave her some advice: "If you can't do it with feeling, don't."

Dottie West was on her way. She and singer Jim Reeves teamed up and recorded some duets. She wrote, "Is This Me?" for Reeves which became a hit. They teamed up to record "Love Is No Excuse" and toured together. She also recorded another duet, "Slowly," with Jimmy Dean.

In 1964, West was brought to RCA records by legendary guitarist Chet Atkins where they began working together. She recorded "Here Comes My Baby Back Again" which climbed to number 1. It was later recorded by Perry Como and Wayne Newton. West eventually won a Grammy Award for the song. She immediately began touring with such country luminaries as Minnie Pearl and Charlie Rich.

The next several years produced such hit songs as "Paper Mansions," "Would You Hold It Against Me?" and "Last Time I Saw Him." In 1969, West teamed up with Don Gibson and recorded "Rings of Gold."

In 1974, Bill and Dottie West's marriage ended in divorce. It was the same year West recorded "Country Sunshine" for a Coca-Cola television commercial. The song won her a Clio Award (the Academy Award of commercials). Two years later she signed with United Artists/Liberty records. It was also the year she married Byron Metcalf, the drummer in her band.

In 1978 Dottie West met Kenny Rogers quite by accident during a recording session. Rogers apparently had the wrong recording time scheduled. Since he was already in the studio, he casually sang along with West during her recording of "Every Time Two Fools Collide." The teaming of Rogers and West seemed such a good idea that they recorded a complete record album of duets. The new duo proved so popular, they began touring together and recorded the album, *Classics*, the following year. Rogers and West went on to win "Vocal Duo of the Year" in 1978 and 1979, challenging Conway Twitty and Loretta Lynn as country music's hottest new duo.

For West it was a far cry from the forest shack of Tennessee to the sold-out crowds at county fairs and superdomes, and traveling 300 days a year. West was acquiring entertainment "smarts." She began touring overseas, establishing an international following, especially in England. The British Country Music Association named her Country Music Artist of the Year in 1972 and again in 1973.

From 1977 to 1983, Dottie West never missed the Country Top

40. Her *Special Delivery* album went to number 78 on Billboard's top 200 hottest selling albums for 1980, followed by her *Wild West* album released later the same year.

It was during this high point in her life and career that Dottie West appeared in Akron, Ohio, in the Sultan's Cabaret at Tangier Restaurant in September of 1980. By this time she had been nominated for 16 Grammy Awards and had recorded 33 albums. Before arriving for her Tangier concert appearance, West had spent 3 ½ days in her tour bus traveling to Akron from her previous engagement in Fresno, California.

Halfway through her Akron performance, Dottie West thought her audience deserved something "country," so she sang Hank Williams's "Lonesome Road." Her evening's 13-song set was highlighted by her single hit tunes plus duets with recorded tracks of Kenny Rogers's voice. West ended her performance with a medley of Elvis Presley songs including "Dixieland." Her one encore was Anne Murray's "You Needed Me."

As was the custom those days, Tangier owner Ed George held a press reception in a small private banquet room so that the featured performer could meet the local media. Back then the Tangier headliner usually had a five- or six-day appearance.

The press people filed into the private banquet room to sample the buffet and anticipate the appearance of Dottie West. When West finally entered, she was most gracious, cordial, and accommodating, continually sporting a warm, friendly smile. I patiently waited as the press reception wore on. I eventually approached West as she casually sat at a small round table in the middle of the small banquet room. After introductions and some friendly conversation, she kindly honored my request by signing an 8" x 10" publicity picture while a photo was taken of us casually conversing.

After West's six day appearance in Akron, she was on her way again, appearing in her $100,000 dollar Bob Mackie dresses and having the best time of her life. She was reportedly earning $2 million annually. West was also known for helping newcomers break into the country music business, especially Larry Gatlin and Steve Wariner.

During this time Dottie West moved into her dream house. The mansion was located on 40 acres just outside of Nashville, Tennessee. It contained 30 rooms, an elevator, bowling alley, and a nursery for her granddaughter, Tess-Marie. West also continued to turn out such hit songs as "A Lesson in Leavin'," "You Pick Me Up and Put Me Down," "Come See Me and Come Lonely," "All I Ever Need Is You," "Together Again," "Leavin's For Unbelievers," and "Are You Happy Baby?"

One year later, in 1981, life began to change for Dottie West. Her second marriage to Byron Metcalf was over because of his infidelity. Not only was West's personal life a mess, but her finances as well.

In 1985, West took a break from recording and accepted the role of the Madam in a touring company's play production of *The Best Little Whorehouse in Texas*. She also made guest appearances on television's *The Dukes of Hazzard, The Love Boat, Austin City Limits*, and *Lifestyles of the Rich and Famous*. She also appeared in the motion picture *Aurora Encounter*. West began touring again, even to the Middle East and Europe. She hosted her own TV Christmas special, sold out Carnegie Hall and performed at the White House (as First Lady Barbara Bush's favorite singer). She also performed extremely well in Las Vegas and Lake Tahoe. It was during this period West married her third husband, Allen Carter Winters, 20 years her junior. The age difference concerned her friends, as did West's drinking habits. Her continued consumption of alcohol resulted in late show and concert appearances.

By 1986, West's concert appearances and recording dates became sparse, but she continued to appear on television's popular Nashville Network, singing at the Grand Ole Opry, and doing some voice-overs for a popular cartoon series, *The Raccoons*.

By August 1990, Dottie West was financially broke. She owed almost $2 million to various agencies, plus interest. The IRS claimed she owed them almost $1.3 million. A West Coast management firm sued her for $130,000, and her manager was suing her for $110,000. Even her third husband, Byron Metcalf, sued her for $7,500. West was so busy paying attention to her career that she was not keeping up with her finances. At this point the IRS seized all of Dottie West's assets including her mansion, Corvette, and even her many music awards. All were eventually auctioned off to satisfy the IRS and other creditors.

West quietly moved into an apartment complex in Nashville after sleeping in an abandoned car. She told a newspaper reporter, "You can knock me down but you better have a big rock to keep me there! This, too, shall pass."

West decided to return to her singing career. She was making plans to record a comeback album with friends Tammy Wynette and Tanya Tucker. She also began writing her autobiography.

On August 30, 1991, West was running late for an 8:30 P.M. Grand Ole Opry appearance. Her car, the one her friend Kenny Rogers had given her, was not working properly. West's neighbor, 81 year-old George Thackston, tried to help by driving West to the Grand Ole Opry appearance. To make up for lost time, Thackston drove too fast. The car was going about 55 mph on the 25 mph Opryland exit ramp when he lost control of the car. The car became airborne before hitting an embankment.

Thackston suffered leg, back and hip injuries. West was in critical condition. Both were conscious when admitted to a hospital. Just before West's surgery, Kenny Rogers rushed to her side. Rogers promised West that they would record another song together. West's liver was severely injured and her spleen was ruptured. She spent five days in intensive care and was given nearly 35 units of blood. During surgery, Dottie West died on the operating table on September 4th at 9:43 A.M., at the age of 58. She was laid to rest beside her mother.

My lasting memory of Dottie West has never faded, especially when I look at the photo of the two of us casually talking to each other after her opening night performance at Tangier Restaurant that September evening in 1980. Although I've looked at that photo as well as her autographed publicity picture for years, I just recently discovered that in the lower right-hand corner of the publicity picture is the name and address of a West Coast management agency. Could it possibly be the same agency that sued her in 1990 for $130,000? I have often thought of finding out, but what good would pursing the matter accomplish? I would rather recall that early fall evening when I met a female country music legend, and a preconception was completely dispelled when I became a musical convert.

SAM KINISON

Chapter 7
Sam Kinison

"We put a video camera in a smart bomb that will kill once. But thanks to the video camera we can relive the moment time and time again."

At the time of his premature death, comedian Sam Kinison was truly Leader of the 'Banned'. "Sex, drugs, and rock 'n' roll" only partially described the comic whose routines were peppered with high, ear-piercing screams. Further defining Kinison was "volume," "enthusiasm," and for his language; "controversial." Kinison seemed to have picked up the mantle of Lenny Bruce and George Carlin in his choice of contemporary topics and most notably, his language. Even today, years after his death, video clips of his routines on television are heavily censored with "bleeps." Ironic for a comedian whose beginnings were extremely religious. He was not only the son of a preacher; he actually preached himself, extolling the virtues of the religious life and the Holy Bible.

The "shock comic" had two evening performances scheduled in the Sultan's Cabaret at Tangier Restaurant in Akron, Ohio, on Sunday (of all days!), October 27, 1991. It was six months before his untimely death in an automobile accident near Laughlin, Nevada, only a few days after his marriage to Malika Souiri.

Sam Kinison was born in Yakima, Washington, on December 8, 1953, the son of a traveling Pentecostal preacher. For a period of time the entire Kinison family lived in a church in Peoria, Illinois. Sam and his brothers eventually became preachers and traveled the Bible Belt. Regions in the South where fundamentalist beliefs prevail and Christian clergyman are especially influential. Eventually Sam decided preaching was not for him. After seven years of preaching young Kinison began to frequent comedy clubs to explore his thoughts further and express his ideas.

The 1980s showcased Kinison's explosion onto the comedy

scene. His loud and rude routines were perfect for HBO television cable specials. Comedian Rodney Dangerfield befriended him and even included Kinison in his 1986 movie, *Back to School*. Besides appearing in three Dangerfield specials, Kinison appeared on television with guest appearances on *Saturday Night Live, In Living Color, The Tonight Show, The Arsenio Hall Show, The Joan Rivers Show*, and *The David Letterman Show*.

Kinison's religious upbringing eventually became lost in a hazy fog of sex, drugs, and rock 'n' roll. Speaking of rock 'n' roll, Kinison was an accomplished guitarist who earned the respect of such 1980s rock groups as Motley Crue, Guns n' Roses, and Ozzy Osbourne. Kinison appeared on stage with Aerosmith, Billy Idol, and White Snake. He even joined Bon Jovi at a Giant Stadium concert performing to a crowd of over 80,000 people.

Kinison had three multi-platinum comedy albums on Warner Bros. Records, which rivaled the sales of Bill Cosby and Robin Williams at the time of his Akron, Ohio appearance in October of 1991.

Sam Kinison's 7:30 P.M. Tangier performance began at 7:55 P.M., opening with comic C. D. (Carl) LeBove. Surprisingly, LeBove had a far fouler mouth than and more risqué comedy routine than Kinison! LeBove concluded his "blue" comedy routine at 8:15 P.M. Suddenly, Sam Kinison bounded on stage, wearing a black, double-breasted suit (in desperate need of pressing), black silk shirt opened at the collar, and red, high top tennis shoes. His long, shaggy, sandy-colored hair freely hung beneath a long and flowing black and white cloth bandana. At first glance, Kinison's stature and demeanor resembled a young, hippie-looking Mickey Rooney.

Sam Kinison's almost one-hour performance was a relentless verbal attack on the days' current events. Nothing escaped the "equal-opportunity-offender," who was billed as "the most controversial comic in America."

Pacing back and forth on the Tangier stage, Kinison humorously poked fun at the Jeffrey Dahmer murder case, Jimmy Swaggart and his "spiritual death wish," James Jones, Richard Simmons, the gay community, recently appointed Supreme Court Justice, Clarence Thomas, Pee Wee Herman, children's shows in general, especially Captain Kangaroo, while questioning Mr. Rogers' sexual preference, the current situation in Russia, and most notably, Operation Desert Storm (this was, after all, 1991).

While venting about Desert Storm, Kinison continually poked fun at the Kurds. He referred to them as "two million idiots." He emphasized they were "the largest concentration of idiots in one place. Usually a village has one or two idiots but not the Kurds!" Also on the topic of Desert Storm, Kinison described the United States' use of the "smart bomb": "We put a video camera in a smart bomb that will kill a person once. But thanks to the video camera we can relive the moment time and time again." Scud missiles also occupied some of the comic's acerbic remarks. "The Iraqis buy a scud missile at K-Mart at a midnight sale and launch them from their car trunk," Kinison observed, "then turn on CNN to see where it landed!"

Kinison touched only lightly on the then-current political scene, referring to Massachusetts senator Ted Kennedy as the "Shemp" (from The Three Stooges) of the Kennedys.

Kinison called Russia a "screwed-up country." The United States' response to Russia's economic plight did not escape the comic's acid tongue when he observed, "The U.S. shows how we help Russia by giving them a McDonald's restaurant when the average Russian can't afford a loaf of bread. We should have a pawnshop to trade jewels for McDonald's food!"

The audience seemed younger than the usual Tangier Restaurant nightclub crowd, reflecting the comic's "Generation X" fan base. Instead of the more expensive exotic alcohol cocktails, the youthful crowd seemed to favor beer, guzzling it directly from the bottle.

Kinison did not pass up the opportunity to plug his upcoming television show *Charlie Hoover* with Tim Matheson on the Fox Network and a more recent guest appearance on another television show, *In Living Color.*

Some of Sam Kinison's comic tirade will not be reprinted due to subject matter and, most of all, language. One of Kinison's observations was a favorite of the young crowd. One of his biggest audience laughs came after he referred to a particular variation on an oral sex act as "like a snowflake" because "no two are exactly alike."

After almost one hour, the rapid-fire staccato, ear-piercing, often "blue" rhetoric of Sam Kinison was over. Rousing and thunderous applause followed "the leader of the banned" off the Tangier stage.

Within six months comic Sam Kinison was dead, killed in an automobile accident in the Nevada desert.

It is a testament to Sam Kinison's uniqueness that no other comic has picked up his mantle. Today's comics merely spew filthy language without the clever, thought-provoking insight into current affairs and controversial subjects that so trademarked the routines of Sam Kinison.

Chapter 8
Robert Reed

"This (television) pilot of 'The Brady Bunch' will never sell to any of the networks."

Certain actors are associated with specific roles. When you think of the Broadway musical *The Music Man*, you automatically think of Robert Preston as traveling salesman Harold Hill. Mention *The King and I* and you immediately think of Yul Brynner as the King of Siam. *The Sound of Music* conjures up Julie Andrews as Maria von Trapp. Television's family comedy *The Brady Bunch* will eventually make you think of Robert Reed as Mike Brady, patriarch of the Brady family.

Stories of Reed's discontent on *The Brady Bunch* set are legendary. He frequently walked off the Brady soundstage after arguments with creator/producer Sherwood Schwartz. Reed would later confess in an interview that the role of Mike Brady embarrassed him.

On a whim, actor Robert Reed decided to make the pilot episode of the television family comedy *The Brady Bunch*, thinking it would never sell to any of the networks. As television history has taught us he was very wrong.

One of the most popular television situation comedy series of all time, *The Brady Bunch*, about a widower with three sons who marries a widow with three daughters and their nutty housekeeper Alice, co-starred actress Florence Henderson. *The Brady Bunch* aired for five seasons, beginning in 1969, and is still in worldwide syndication today. Post-*Brady Bunch* TV specials, in 1977 and 1988, followed the show's original five-year run that ended in 1974. Two Brady TV movies, *The Brady Girls Get Married* (1981) and *A Very Brady Christmas* (1988) were also made. Two *Brady Bunch* motion pictures with entirely new casts were also released.

What the general public does not know about Robert Reed is that he was a classically trained stage actor in London.

Reed's local connection was his appearance at Carousel Dinner Theatre as Clarence Day in *Life with Father* in 1990, from May 8 to June 17. Historically, *Life with Father* was significant for Carousel Dinner Theatre for two reasons: it was one of the last Carousel productions featuring a famous actor or actress (the format that made the theater the success it continues to be today) and it was the last non

-musical play production at the Akron dinner theater. Since *Life with Father*, starring Robert Reed, Carousel Dinner Theatre has done only musical plays with a professional cast. The performers are mostly recruited and rehearsed in New York City, with some local actors and/or dancers included in some of the productions.

Born Robert Rietz in Highland Park, Illinois, on October 19, 1932, Reed attended Northwestern University and trained as a stage actor. Transferring to The Royal Academy of Dramatic Arts, in London, England, Reed trained with fellow actors Brian Bedford, Peter O'Toole and Albert Finney.

Returning to the United States, Reed joined the award-winning off-Broadway troupe The Shakespearewrights. In 1956 he became a resident member of Chicago's Studebaker Theatre where he appeared with actor E.G. Marshall (whom he would later co-star with on television in *The Defenders*), and starred opposite Geraldine Page in Eugene Leontovitch's production of *A Month in the Country*.

Reed also starred in the original company of Richard Rodgers' *Avanti!* He acted in the Broadway comedy *Barefoot in the Park*, plus two successful national tours of *The Owl and the Pussycat* and *California Suite*. Until his Carousel Dinner Theatre appearance in *Life with Father* in 1990, Reed had been last seen on Broadway in productions of *Deathtrap* and *Doubles*.

Arriving on the West Coast, Reed began landing numerous acting roles on television. The turning point in his career came during a guest appearance as a young attorney on the popular family TV series, *Father Knows Best,* starring Robert Young. The role led to his first series, *The Defenders,* with E.G. Marshall, then followed, *The Brady Bunch*. But that was by no means the end of Reed's acting career, especially on television. Reed was a regular in a serious role, that of Lt. Adam Tobias on *Mannix* starring Mike Connors as private investigator Joe Mannix.

Reed was nominated for television's Emmy Award several times: in 1969 as a husband and father who undergoes a transsexual operation in *Medical Center—The Third Sex*; in 1976 as the decadent millionaire Teddy Baylan in the mini-series *Rich Man, Poor Man*; and in 1977 as Dr. William Reynolds in the mini-series *ROOTS*.

In Carousel Dinner Theatre's production of *Life with Father* in 1990, Reed would again portray the head of a family, that of a crusty, rambunctious father of four redheaded sons and a wife who knows the secret to handling her husband and the family. Adapted from author Clarence Day's work by playwrights Howard Lindsey and Russell Crouse, *Life with Father*, chronicles Day's saga of his own family during the turn-of-the-century in Manhattan. The play treads familiar ground in such similar plays as *I Remember Mama, Ah, Wilderness*, and especially *Cheaper by the Dozen*.

Carousel's production of *Life with Father* was a three-act, two intermission play, with a three-hour running time, and was generally well received by local theater patrons and newspaper critics.

Carousel Dinner Theatre used the usual Tuesday through Thursday "preview" format before the official Friday evening opening night gala. The preview performances gave the cast a chance to get the feel of the dinner theater stage, lights, and sound system while enabling the public to see the three preview performances for a reduced admission fee.

The official opening night of Carousel Dinner Theatre's production *Life with Father*, starring Robert Reed, was held on Friday, May 11, 1990. Food service began at 6:30 P.M. The play started at 8:30 P.M., following a master of ceremonies singing a few songs from upcoming productions, acknowledging birthdays and anniversaries of audience members and displaying examples of Carousel Dinner Theatre's famous after-dinner desserts.

After the three-hour opening night performance, the audience was cordially invited to Carousel's upstairs banquet room called "Prescott's", in honor of then-Carousel Dinner Theatre owner, Prescott Griffith, who traditionally greeted audience members as they entered.

Press night patrons were treated to champagne, a light buffet, and desserts. Members of the local press, wearing special nametags that came with their press packet, were permitted free drinks at the bar. The tags also alerted cast members to which patrons were local press and other media for introduction purposes.

Several minutes into the press party the cast of *Life with Father* casually strolled into Prescott's. Theatre patrons and the press were free to mingle and meet the cast. Naturally, most of the patrons wanted to meet "Mike Brady," Robert Reed. He was attired in white casual slacks, turquoise pullover shirt, white cloth jacket and a matching white cloth Ivy-League cap. Reed's hair was dyed red for his role. He had grown a moustache that was also dyed red. The 6-foot-3-inch actor looked tall, skinny and gaunt. He milled about Prescott's Lounge, quite accommodatingly, holding a mixed drink in his right hand with a paper napkin under it. While I casually spoke to Reed, the local daily newspaper critic Bill O'Connor approached, and we shook hands in front of Reed. At that precise moment a photo of the friendly social occasion was taken. Upon request Reed signed a publicity photo from the production as I posed for a picture with him.

Almost two years to the week of his appearance in *Life with Father* at Carousel Dinner Theatre in Akron, 59 year-old actor Robert Reed died after a six-week battle with intestinal cancer in Pasadena, California, on May 12, 1992. The cause was later revealed to be AIDS -related. Reed left behind a wife, daughter, and mother.

As with most of my encounters with famous people, all the "hype" and controversies that may surround the person were not noticeable to me at the time. A famous person, like Robert Reed, tends to be down-to-earth, very accommodating, and appreciative of the fact that the public still holds him in high esteem. Such was the case with Robert Reed.

Unlike actors or actresses who are type-cast as one memorable character that continually sticks in the public's mind, (like George Reeves as *Superman* and Clayton Moore as *The Lone Ranger*) Robert Reed got to perform as other, non-Mike Brady characters and make a living long after his *Brady Bunch* years.

Chapter 9
George "Spanky" McFarland

"I didn't know what was going on around me because my world was the studio, the school, and that camera, and those lights. That was my world. That was my childhood. That's what I grew up with."

Meeting a celebrity once is quite a thrill. But when it happens twice, wow!

Such was the case with George "Spanky" McFarland of *Our Gang* and *The Little Rascals* fame, first on April 4, 1987, and again on May 12, 1990, both times at the Akron Civic Theatre in downtown Akron, Ohio.

The Akron Civic Theatre was originally a Loews Theater on Main Street in downtown Akron. The building was completed as a vaudeville house in 1929, just before the beginning of the Depression. With the advent of talking motion pictures the theater was quickly converted to a "sound" movie house, and the Loews Theater was a prominent fixture on Akron's Main Street until the early 1960s. Suburban mall movie theaters and twin cinemas in shopping plazas doomed downtown movie theaters, as well as businesses in general, all over the country, largely due to the lure of free parking close to the business venue. The Loews Theater became run down, reflecting the overall tone of downtown Akron and downtown America in general. By 1964 the Loews Theater was the lone survivor of 10 movie houses that had once thrived in downtown Akron. The Loews Theater was to be sold and torn down to make way for a parking lot, but in December of 1964, the Junior Chamber of Commerce took the option to buy the building and land for $65,000. In 1965, a nonprofit organization was formed called The Community Hall Foundation. The foundation purchased the old Loews, renamed it the Akron Civic Theatre, and began slowly repairing the building to required building codes. Film festivals dominated the theater's calendar. The theater was also rented out for dance recitals and high school graduations.

During Halloween season the Akron Civic Theatre was converted to a haunted house. Another asset to the historic structure was that numerous entertainers preferred historic buildings such as the Akron Civic Theatre instead of newer performing arts halls. One such entertainer was Bob Dylan.

Under the stewardship of general manager Patti Eddy, the Akron Civic Theatre played host to such festivities and venues as The Three Stooges Film Festival (which featured the world's largest pie fight at the time), a Marx Brothers Film Festival, a *Rocky and Bullwinkle* Film Festival, an International Animation Film Festival, plus the showing of such classic films as *Casablanca, The Maltese Falcon, They Died With Their Boots On,* Jeanette MacDonald and Nelson Eddy movies as well as many classic MGM musicals and the re-release of a 70-millimeter edition of the 1939 classic *Gone With the Wind.* Every fall the dedicated group that maintained the massive Akron Civic Theatre Wurlitzer organ, The Organ Guild, featured a classic silent film to raise funds to keep the organ in working order. The Akron Civic Theatre was the perfect setting to see such celluloid luminaries as Lon Chaney in *Phantom of the Opera* (1925) and Douglas Fairbanks in *Thief of Baghdad* (1924).

It was into this atmosphere that George "Spanky" McFarland was first scheduled on Friday, April 4, 1987. The publicity boasted "An Evening with Spanky," featuring a lecture by McFarland that would highlight his 13-year film career and film clips from some of the 95 *Little Rascal/Our Gang* comedies featuring Spanky. The evening program was scheduled to begin at 8:00 P.M. The price of admission was $7.00 in advance and $8.50 at the door.

I had arranged with Patti Eddy to interview McFarland one hour before his appearance on the Akron Civic Theatre stage in a retrospect of *The Little Rascals/Our Gang* short subject films. He was to speak to the audience about his life with Hal Roach, creator of Our Gang, and tell some tales and anecdotes of the "gang" members, both past and present. But something quite unusual happened late in the afternoon of April 4, 1987: a spring blizzard! Patti Eddy telephoned to inform me that McFarland's flight into Cleveland Hopkins Airport was delayed because of the snowstorm. Undaunted, I drove to the Akron Civic Theatre in the snowstorm, repeatedly asking myself, "What am I doing?"

Since it was now impossible to interview and tape record McFarland personally, I decided to audiotape record his appearance so that I could do a story for the weekly newspaper I was currently writing for. As 8:00 P.M came and went, the patiently loyal Akron Civic Theatre audience waited in anticipation for McFarland's arrival while Patti Eddy sent someone in a four-wheel drive vehicle to Cleveland Hopkins Airport in Cleveland (about 30 miles north) to pick up McFarland. In the meantime, what to do? General Manager Eddy quickly sent a member of her staff to a nearby neighborhood movie house, the Highland Theater, for something, anything, to show on the Akron Civic Theatre movie screen. Meantime, Eddy announced to the Akron Civic Theatre audience that McFarland's plane was being delayed in Chicago because of the snowstorm and that until his arrival, the classic movie serial *Mysterious Dr. Satan* (Republic Pictures, 1940) would be shown. Between each episode, Eddy would announce "Spanky Sightings" from areas between Cleveland Hopkins Airport and the Akron Civic Theatre. Eddy later confessed to me that she did not know what hamlets were actually located between the airport and downtown Akron so she made them up. After several episodes of *Mysterious Dr. Satan*, Eddy scoured the Akron Civic Theatre for cartoons to show.

Finally, at 10:00 P.M Eddy announced, "Spanky has been sighted on Main Street!" Shortly thereafter she announced, "Spanky has been sighted in the Akron Civic Theatre lobby!" The crowd went wild. Two hours late, George "Spanky" McFarland casually walked onto the Akron Civic Theatre stage to a standing ovation. Eddy later told me McFarland quickly changed his clothes upon arrival and requested a glass of wine while the projectionist readied a reel of Spanky's films.

George "Spanky" McFarland may have actually been 58 years old at the time of his first Akron appearance in 1987, but that short-of-stature, portly man with the trademark baby face still looked like the movie screen's little Spanky. Spanky McFarland promised the audience it would not be cheated on time. He intended to stay as long as it took to tell about his adventures as a member of Hal Roach's *Our Gang*.

"A lot of the stuff we'll be dealing with tonight has to do with a very special time in my life, and for that matter a special time in your life. Otherwise you all wouldn't be here. If I get choked up just bear with me and we'll get through it," McFarland said with a slight Texas drawl. "We'll have some fun tonight. It's not a sad show."

It would later be revealed that only two patrons out of the entire Akron Civic Theatre audience actually requested a refund due to the show's weather-related two-hour delay.

"This is gonna be a night of reminiscing," McFarland confessed. "I got some film that'll knock your socks off. If you came here thinking the little fat man was going to perform, you're wrong." With a mischievous gleam in his eye, McFarland confessed, "I don't perform anymore. If you don't believe that just ask my wife!"

With that short introduction McFarland began his two-hour appearance on the Akron Civic Theatre stage by filling us in on his humble beginnings. "I was born in Dallas, Texas, [on Oct. 2] in 1928," McFarland began. "When I was in my 'late three's' I was doing modeling for baby clothes for some department stores in Dallas. My aunt, my mother's sister, was a fashion artist for Neiman-Marcus Department Stores, so I did some modeling for them. I also did a film commercial for the Wonder Bread Company in Dallas. It was shown in local movie houses. I'd love to see that film today, but I've been unable to find it. As a result of that film, I had some publicity in the local newspapers. My aunt sent a copy of the film commercial to Hal Roach (Motion Picture) Studios in Hollywood, California."

McFarland went on to explain how Roach (still alive at age 95 in 1987) was then making short, two-reel comedies starring such funnymen as Stan Laurel and Oliver Hardy, Harold Lloyd, Snub Pollard, and Charlie Chase. He already had a few child actors on his lot for these comedies. According to legend, one day in 1922, Roach was looking out his office window at a lumberyard across the street from the studio. McFarland explained Roach became fascinated by watching how a gang of five or six kids decided who got what size stick of wood. He watched for about 15 minutes and observed that the smallest kid got the biggest stick. Roach was amazed at how much he was entertained for 15 minutes before the gang of kids walked away. This observation gave him an idea. He scoured his studio for a "gang" of his own. He already had a few children under contract, including an African-American boy, Ernie "Sunshine Sammy" Morrison who had been in some of his Snub Pollard and Harold Lloyd comedies. Roach also had Jackie Condon and a cute little girl named Peggy Cartwright under contract. Harold Lloyd's leading lady, Mildred David, had a tough-looking younger brother, Jackie. Allen "Farina" Hoskins reportedly followed Ernie "Sunshine Sammy" Morrison to the studio one day, so he stayed. Still photographer Gene Kornman volunteered his blonde daughter, Mary, for the gang and also recommended to Roach a friend's freckled-faced son, Mickey Daniels. A chubby kid, Joe Cobb, would join later. Add some neighborhood pets, and Roach's *Our Gang* was complete!

Historically, Hal Roach's *Our Gang* would always have a fat kid, an African-American kid, etc. As each "gang" member grew, he/she would be replaced. Roach conducted an ongoing search for spontaneous kids, not child actors, as replacements.

McFarland emphasized to the Akron Civic Theatre audience in 1987 that Hal Roach did not hire actors, he hired kids. "He hired them for the way they walked, the way they talked, the way they looked, something unusual," explained McFarland. "They maybe became actors later but that's not what he hired them for originally." In early 1925 Roach began making *Our Gang* comedies as a series and hired six or seven other kids. These were the silent shorts that featured Dorothy DeBorba, Norman "Chubby" Chaney, and Bobby "Wheezer" Hutchins.

Such was the atmosphere at the Hal Roach Studios in Hollywood, California, in 1931, when Roach saw the film commercial Spanky's aunt had sent him. Roach liked what he saw immediately and contacted McFarland's parents to come out to Hollywood so that Spanky could be given a proper screen test.

McFarland's actual screen test became the *Our Gang* short, "Spanky." McFarland recalled some of the actual filming of the comedy short. It featured Spanky going after a bug with a hammer. "The hammer was rubber," he recalled, "and the bug was not real. It was on a string manipulated by prop man Don Sandstrom. I remember director Bob McGowan from behind the camera hollering, 'Hit it, Spanky. Hit it!' I was very frustrated and told him, 'If Don will hold the damn thing still, I will'!"

Roach liked what he saw in Spanky. "I was a talker," recalled McFarland at the time of his screen test. "I couldn't read yet, but I had a good memory and could recite stories and nursery rhymes. I was very gregarious and up front which Roach liked. As I said before: he hired kids not actors." To illustrate this point, McFarland told the audience that in 1933 Shirley Temple had an audition to be in *Our Gang*. "She was turned down because she was too cute," said McFarland. "She was too polished. She was in acting school and drama school. She did not fit the mold for *Our Gang*.

The McFarland family moved to Hollywood from Texas and rented a little house in Culver City. "I worked for Roach for 13 years and did 95 comedies," said McFarland. "My first contract was from

1931-1936 for $50 per week. Men were supporting families on $10 to $15 per week then (during the Depression). I was paid per week whether I worked or not. My last contract was from 1939-1944 for $1,750 per week. Kids who did feature films made the real money, such as Jackie Coogan, Jane Withers, Mickey Rooney and Shirley Temple."

This principle also affected Hal Roach on a much larger scale. The most money to be made in the motion picture business was in feature films, not two-reel comedy shorts. Roach saw the market for short comedies drying up. Comedies were going from two-reel to feature full-length motion pictures. Comedy shorts were being replaced by double bills (two full-length motion pictures). Even cartoons (cheaper to make) were becoming very popular. Because MGM already had distributed *Our Gang* comedies, in order to raise money for his first feature-length film, Roach sold the rights to Our Gang, Laurel and Hardy, and Charlie Chase to MGM in 1938. McFarland told the Akron Civic Theatre audience an interesting tidbit of unknown historical motion picture news about Laurel and Hardy. "At one time Laurel and Hardy split up due to a contract dispute Stan Laurel had with Hal Roach," said McFarland. "Roach proposed a series with Oliver Hardy and me as his son. But before it got any further Stan Laurel came back."

McFarland confessed the MGM *Our Gang* scripts were not very good. They all had moral lessons. Some were nothing more than World War II propaganda films. MGM stopped making *Our Gang* comedies in 1944. By then some of the gang members changed. "Porky was the first to leave," said McFarland, "then Alfalfa, then me. They hired a kid named Mickey Gubitosi (now Robert Blake) and then Billy "Froggy" Laughlin (also McLaughlin)." In retrospect McFarland told the Akron Civic Theater audience he was in the gang the longest, 13 years (1931-1944). Billie "Buckwheat" Thomas was second with 10 years (1934-1944).

Spanky McFarland let us in on what it was like to work at Hal Roach Studios as a member of *Our Gang*. "We worked at the studio five days per week for eight to nine hours a day," he recalled. "We got to the studio at 8:30 A.M. I may have gotten to the studio school by 9:00 A.M. but then I may have been needed on the set at 9:15 A.M. I had to get three hours of school in, Monday through Friday.

Education came in dribs and drabs, pieces and bits, here and there, once in a while, now and again. We had one hour for lunch. That left about five hours a day to shoot films. Sometimes our education came in 10 or 15-minute sections. That's how I got my elementary education. I got a good one because there were no more than five or six in the class at one time." McFarland fondly recalled his studio teacher, Mrs. Fern Carter.

There are several stories as to how George McFarland got the name "Spanky." One version has the name merely coming from a suggestion by a reporter. Another tale has the name originating from one of Hal Roach's gag writers. Still another story has the name stemming from the precocious little McFarland being pulled aside by his mother and being reprimanded, "Mommy (is going to) spankee." In hindsight, I never made a mental note to ask how he actually got the nickname, "Spanky."

Spanky McFarland was not exclusively relegated to *Our Gang* comedies at Hal Roach Studios. "I made 14 full length films between 1931 and 1944 when Roach loaned me out to other studios when I was not needed in a (Our Gang) short," recalled McFarland. "I worked with Edward G. Robinson, Joan Bennett, Fred MacMurray, Henry Fonda, and Sylvia Sydney (at other studios). We got our Hal Roach Studio contract salary and Roach kept any difference in pay the other studios would pay for my services." This despite McFarland's informing his audience that "you couldn't work for another studio as long as you were under contract to one particular studio. The studio paid you per week if you worked or not. That was a whale of a deal during the Depression!"

One of the feature-length movies McFarland was in, on a loan-out basis, was very significant in the history of motion pictures. On loan to another studio, McFarland appeared with Henry Fonda in the remake of a 1915 movie titled, *Trail of the Lonesome Pine* in 1936. The feature film is the classic story of feuding families and the changes that occur when a railroad is built on their land. Why was the film significant in the annals of motion picture history? *Trail of the Lonesome Pine* was the first outdoor film filmed entirely in Technicolor. That fact may not seem so significant on the surface, but if the film had not worked out in Technicolor, *Gone with the Wind* would have certainly been filmed in black and white three years later.

Would *Gone with the Wind* have been the great success it was, and still is, if it had been filmed in black and white?

McFarland explained who replaced whom in *Our Gang* as they grew. "When Stymie (Matthew Beard), who replaced Allen 'Farina' Hoskins, started getting too big Roach replaced him with Billie "Buckwheat" Thomas. I replaced Joe Cobb as the fat kid. Cobb had replaced Norman 'Chubby' Chaney." Then McFarland revealed that his replacement was to be Eugene "Porky" Lee from Ft. Worth, Texas, who began in *Our Gang* comedies at age two and appeared in 42 "Gang" comedies over four years. "They hired him in 1934 to take my place," recalled McFarland. "They thought I was gonna grow up like everyone else. But I fooled them! Porky literally grew himself out of a job. My replacement outgrew his part! In 1939 Porky was taller than Buckwheat, Alfalfa or Darla. Everyone was taller than me!"

Spanky McFarland looked back on his 13 years (and 95 comedies) as a member of *Our Gang* and flatly stated, in a matter-of-fact way: "Growing up in the comedies was unique. I was five or six before I realized kids weren't performers. I began at three. I don't remember beginning at three. Every Monday through Friday I would go to the (Hal Roach) studio and stand in front of a camera for eight hours a day. Then I'd go home. I grew up with this. I went to the studio school three hours per day Monday through Friday whether we worked or not. On the days we weren't working, we still had to go into the studio for school, and then go home at noon." McFarland referred to the experience as a *closed situation*. "I didn't know what was going on around me because my world was the studio, and school, and that camera, and those lights. That was my world. That was my childhood. That's what I grew up with. Some people say I didn't have a childhood, but that *WAS* my childhood. I didn't know the difference until later. Then it was too late and it didn't make a difference." McFarland considers 1934-1938 as the "heyday" of *Our Gang's* golden era. It was when half of the 217 *Our Gang* comedies were made.

Incidentally, according to McFarland, each comedy took about three to four months to make.

Before going on with his life after he left *Our Gang*, McFarland took one more look back, at Hal Roach. "Hal Roach was a businessman first, last, and always," informed McFarland. "He was good to work for. He kept out of the way of the people doing the creative work. He hired people to do a job and then stepped aside to let them do their job." McFarland believed that Hal Roach was far ahead of his time by having an African-American child as an integral part of the *Our Gang* cast. "Hal Roach was not making a statement by having a black kid in the *Gang*. The only statement he was interested in was a bank statement," said McFarland. "He was a bona-fide man. None of the black kids ever said they felt put upon or were in any way put in uncomfortable social situations. They never felt put upon in stereotypical situations either. It was just part of the script."

McFarland then returned to his life in 1944, when MGM stopped production of the *Our Gang* comedies. "I was 16 years old," recalled McFarland. "Fortunately for me I stayed small. If you started shaving or your underarms began to smell, your career was over! I was lucky."

The McFarland family moved from Hollywood back to Lancaster, Texas, in 1944, where Spanky finished his schooling. "I was 16 years old," said McFarland. "We went from the lap of luxury into the pits of poverty in one easy lesson. We had to chop wood to keep the house warm. I thought it was fun because I never had to do it before. I have not only seen the good side of life, but I've seen the tough side of it also. I think it made me a better man out of me and gave me a little more idea of what the world was about, especially just after World War II. All my life has not been roses. Trust me. We had some hard times but it all works out. The 'American Dream' is there if you are willing to work toward it."

When he was in high school back in Texas, McFarland's class elected him class president. This made the former child star wonder out loud to the Akron Civic Theatre audience, "Did they elect me because they thought I'd do a good job or because I was Spanky McFarland?"

After high school McFarland did odd jobs. He did not go to college. Instead, he joined the Air Force. "It (Air Force) provided income for my family because my dad was too ill to work. I could send money home so my family could survive," confessed McFarland. "After eight months I decided to leave the Air Force. The war was over and my father was able to work again." McFarland tried to figure out just how to get out of the Air Force. "I went to the post library and got a book on *101 Discharges*. I found one in fifteen minutes! I decided I was a hardship case. I figured I helped the war effort because they signed a peace treaty three weeks after I left the Air Force!"

McFarland married his high school sweetheart, but the marriage did not last. "I call that my 'practice round,'" said McFarland. "I did a lot of odd jobs," recalled the former child actor after leaving the Air Force. "In the 1950s I couldn't get back into pictures because directors couldn't see me other than 'Spanky.' I couldn't get work even as an extra. So I put that part of my life behind me."

McFarland got into sales for consumer products. "I represented Swiss Colony Wine," he said. "Then I was with Philco-Ford as national sales training manager in Philadelphia for four years. I was with the company for a total of 11 years altogether. When Ford sold the company, I went to work for Magic Chef Kitchen Appliances in Tennessee. I left them two years ago (1985) to retire. My second wife and I have been married 32 years. I have a boy 37, another boy 32, and a 26-year-old daughter. I have a 2-year-old granddaughter."

McFarland also did some promotional work for the Justin Boot Company since he lived in Fort Worth, Texas. "I also do some promotional work for Republic Pictures," he said. "They are restoring the original silent *Our Gang* comedies. They release a couple every year." McFarland appeared locally a few times after his 1990 appearance at video store grand openings to promote the restored *Our Gang* comedies.

As of that 1987 Akron Civic Theatre appearance Spanky McFarland was 58 years old, age 60 as of the 1990 appearance.

"I do these shows now. I'm not wealthy but I'm comfortable," confessed the former child actor. With those closing remarks on his life, McFarland began to show slides of some of the favorite *Our Gang* members.

Before getting into each *Our Gang* member's personal history, McFarland cleared up the *Our Gang* and *Little Rascals* dual titles. "In 1949, television was buying up all kinds of films because they didn't have enough live talent for 24 hour-a-day programming," said McFarland. "Hal Roach owned his package of *Our Gang*. He sold them to MGM in 1938. But the comedies he made from 1925 to 1938 (pre-MGM) that are on TV today were retitled, *The Little Rascals*.

When Roach sold his package of *Our Gang* comedies to television he had to come with a different name to differentiate his batch from MGM's after 1938. Roach recalled calling the kids "little rascals" several times and chose that trademark name.

Spanky McFarland never got any "residuals" later in life for his work in Hal Roach's or MGM's *Our Gang*. The residuals agreement began in 1948. Simply put "residuals" meant you got paid again for something you did before. "I made good money back then (1931-1944)," confessed McFarland during his 1990 Akron Civic Theatre appearance. "I have no regrets about my career. I enjoyed what I did back then as far as my memory goes. It helped me in my sales career. It helped me to be at ease in any social situation and enabled me to be quick on my feet and think quickly when I answered (questions). I did not go to college. That *WAS* my college education! I do get 'residuals' in the form of nice folks like yourself who remember *Our Gang* and who remember me and the kids that I worked with." McFarland was clearly getting sentimental and it showed as the portly former child star said, "I can feel the love coming from the audience and I hope I can return it to you because without you, the fans, there would not have been *Our Gang* comedies. Your love and interest is the only 'residual' I need."

From Spanky McFarland's two Akron Civic Theatre appearances (1987 and 1990) the following information appears. Some of the facts may differ from one McFarland appearance to the other and, in some instances, may not be entirely accurate. The book, *Our Gang, The Life and Times of the Little Rascals* by Leonard Maltin and Richard W. Bann (Crown Publishers, 1977), to date, is the definitive reference for more accurate *Our Gang* and *Little Rascals* information.

Matthew "STYMIE" Beard

"Stymie" was born Matthew Beard in Los Angeles, California, on January 1, 1925. He was the sole support for 13 brothers and sisters. His father was a non-denominational preacher in Los Angeles. Stymie was in *Our Gang* from 1929 to 1934, appearing in 36 of the short comedies. He had to leave the "gang" when he got too tall. Another African-American, Billie "Buckwheat" Thomas, would replace him. When Stymie left the "gang" and grew older, he got in with the wrong crowd. He got into trouble and into drugs. He did finish high school but could not find a job. He got into heroin and crime. He was caught and convicted, spending eight years in federal prison. Synanon House helped Stymie get his life back in order. He worked for Synanon driving their bus until the day he died. After beating his drug habit Stymie got work in television on such shows as *Maude, Good Times*, and even got to work with Red Foxx on *Sanford and Son*. He also worked on some documentaries on the Public Broadcasting System (PBS) and motion picture films like *The Buddy Holly Story*. He still looked the same even when he was older.

Stymie showed up for Spanky McFarland's annual celebrity golf tournament in Indiana a few times. "He didn't golf but would wear his derby and sign autographs," recalled McFarland fondly. In 1981, after returning from one of Spanky McFarland's golf tournaments Stymie suffered a stroke in his apartment. "That did not kill him," said McFarland, "but the fall and banging his head on a piece of furniture did. McFarland divulged that Matthew Beard actually had a fine singing voice. The character name "Stymie" is actually credited to *Our Gang* director Bob McGowan. "Stymie was always on the set and into everything," recalled McFarland, "prompting director McGowan to remark, 'Get that kid outta here. He 'stymies' me all the time.'" Historically, Matthew Beard was going to be called "Hercules" before he "stymied" director McGowan.

William "BUCKWHEAT" Thomas

William Thomas was born in Los Angeles, California, in 1931. Buckwheat's character was modeled after African-American *Our Gang* member Allen Clayton "Farina" Hoskins. Before William Thomas became Buckwheat, his part, believe it or not, was played by a girl, actually two girls. In one short, Buckwheat was played by Stymie's (Matthew Beard) sister, Carlena, and in three other shorts by Willie Mae Taylor. It was the only time an *Our Gang* member had the same name but was played by different children. William Thomas as Buckwheat joined *Our Gang* in 1934 to replace Stymie and eventually left show business entirely in 1944 when MGM stopped making *Our Gang* comedy shorts. He worked for more than 20 years as a film technician for the Technicolor Corporation, retiring in 1977. Thomas was a "ham radio operator" and talked to people all over the world. Thomas held the second longest tenure in the *Our Gang* shorts: 10 years, appearing in 93 of the *Our Gang* comedies. Spanky McFarland was in *Our Gang* the longest with 13 years, appearing in 95 *Our Gang* comedies. "He (Buckwheat) was very shy about not talking right," recalled McFarland. "He 'stumbled' over his words. But as he got older his speech improved, thanks in part, to studio teacher, Mrs. Fern Carter." Thomas died in 1980 of a massive heart attack shortly after an *Our Gang* reunion. Thomas was married and had one son. In a conversation with Thomas' son, an attorney in Los Angeles, McFarland was told there was no history of heart problems in the family.

Carl "ALFALFA" Switzer

Carl "Alfalfa" Switzer was born in Paris, Illinois, on August 8, 1927. He and his younger brother, Harold, sang in many places around their town. McFarland repeatedly told both the 1987 and 1990 Akron Civic Theatre audiences that Carl was not disciplined at all by his parents. Carl's parents thought their two sons were talented enough to be in *Our Gang* comedies. So, in 1935 they sold their Illinois farm and actually drove to Hollywood. They arrived with $31 in their pocket. At the time the Hal Roach Studios had a commissary cafeteria called the *Our Gang Café*, where the public as well as studio employees could eat lunch. Carl's parents dressed both sons in cowboy outfits and headed for the *Our Gang Café*. They put their two sons on one of the café tables one afternoon during lunch. Harold played the mandolin while Carl sang, *She'll Be Comin' Around the Mountain When She Comes*. Some *Our Gang* directors just happened to be eating lunch at the *Our Gang Café* when they caught the impromptu performance. They never heard the song sung quite that way before (off key with a high-pitched, squeaky voice) and thought it was funny.

The fact that Hal Roach was actually in New York City at the time did not matter. One of the directors called Roach and told him about the Switzer brothers. Roach instructed the director to put the family up in a nearby hotel until he returned from New York a few days later. The rest is history.

As Spanky McFarland said, Carl was not very disciplined. McFarland sighted several incidents to illustrate his point. "He'd put some gang members up to a prank," McFarland said, "and disappear when they were caught. One day he stuck bubble gum in one of the motion picture cameras' gear mechanism. He was also never around when he was needed on the set. He was a born troublemaker." McFarland sighted one of Carl's most disgusting pranks. "We heard loud popping noises on the set one day," recalled McFarland. "The stage floor lights began popping loudly because Carl was urinating on them! We had to stop shooting for an entire day and open the soundstage doors to bring in large fans to air the place out."

McFarland thought Carl's lack of discipline resulted from the fact that his parents were not educated and did not know right from wrong. "He (Carl/Alfalfa) was not stupid," said McFarland, "but he was wild."

Over a six-year period, Carl "Alfalfa" Switzer appeared in 61 *Our Gang* short comedies. His brother Harold was also in several *Our Gang* shorts, nicknamed "Slim" and "Deadpan." Being a farm boy from Illinois, the name "Alfalfa" suited Carl. The name had been used by Will Rogers for one of his country characters in a silent movie series he did for Hal Roach. Carl "Alfalfa" Switzer was a very popular *Our Gang* character with his waxed (actually Vaseline) cowlick of hair, bug-eyed double take facial expression, bulging crossed eyes, and squeaky, off-key singing voice. Incidentally, his trademark cowlick hair caused some delays in filming. The cowlick of hair would unceremoniously begin to droop under the hot studio stage lights. Then a stagehand would rush over to "Alfalfa" and wrap a towel full of ice around the hair until it got stiff enough again to resume filming.

By 1941, Alfalfa had grown too tall to be an *Our Gang* member. He stayed in motion pictures but did not make enough money to support himself. He had to supplement his income by bartending and leading hunting parties up into the hills that surrounded Hollywood to hunt bear. Carl formed a business partnership with another man to lead hunting parties up into the hills. They bought expensive hunting dogs (about $2,500 each according to McFarland). One day in 1959, Carl's partner led a hunting party up into the hills. One of the expensive hunting dogs wandered away. When he returned, he advertised a reward of $50 for the return of the hunting dog. A few weeks later Carl led a party into the hills to hunt bear when the missing dog wandered into the camp. Carl brought the dog back to his partner's house and demanded the $50 reward. The man told Carl that the dog was joint property and if *HE* returned one of Carl's lost dogs he wouldn't want a reward. "An ugly argument ensued," McFarland recounted, "at which point Carl drew a knife. Feeling threatened, the partner drew a gun and asked Carl to leave the property. When Carl went toward his partner with the knife, he was shot and killed. The case was later ruled justifiable homicide at a coroner's inquest. Carl "Alfalfa" Switzer was only 31 years old."

Ironically, the incident surrounding Carl's death did not get much press. The death of one of the most popular *Our Gang* members coincided with the death of legendary motion picture director Cecil B. DeMille. DeMille garnered all the newspaper headlines and media attention. Another twist of fate had Carl "Alfalfa" Switzer in one of his last motion picture appearances in *The Defiant Ones* in 1958 as a dog handler!

McFarland also related an act of revenge on Alfalfa's father by some *Our Gang* members. According to McFarland, "It was popular in the 1930s to give people a 'hot foot.' Alf's dad would always be on the *Our Gang* set, sitting in a director's chair, continually reading a newspaper. You'd slip the wood end of a match in the sole of someone's shoe. You light the match, retreat and watch the man jump when he got the 'hot foot.' I thought we'd do it to Mr. Switzer. We put it in his shoe. Nothing happened. We did it again. It burned up one side of his shoe and lit the (news) paper. He jumped up, pulled his pant leg up and put out the fire." It was at that moment the pranksters realized Mr. Switzer had a wooden leg and could not feel the fire!

"DARLA" Hood

Darla Hood (actual first name Dorla) was born in Oklahoma (Enid, Oklahoma, according to McFarland and Leedey, Oklahoma, according to Maltin and Bann's book) on November 4, 1931. Her first *Our Gang* appearance was in *Our Gang Follies of 1936*. She was a member of *Our Gang* for six years (1936-1942) appearing in 50 comedies. Darla was always the apple of Alfalfa's eye. Usually Darla left Alfalfa for someone else and another gang member would figure out a way to get them back together. Originally Darla's mother named her daughter "Dorla" but someone at the Roach Studios accidentally misspelled it. Darla took singing and dancing lessons growing up in

Oklahoma. Her voice teacher took her on a trip to New York City. One night the bandleader at the Edison Hotel invited her up to the bandstand to sing and conduct the orchestra. The crowd loved the performance. It just so happened, that Roach casting director Joe Rivkin was in the audience at the time. He immediately arranged for a screen test for Darla in New York. Hal Roach saw the test and signed Darla Hood to a seven-year contract beginning at $75 per week.

While an *Our Gang* regular, Darla appeared in other Hal Roach motion pictures including *Neighborhood House* with Charley Chase and *The Bohemian Girl* with Stan Laurel and Oliver Hardy. After leaving *Our Gang*, Darla, a marvelous singer, did voice-overs. She was the original voice of the mermaid in the Chicken of the Sea Tuna television commercials, the voice of Tiny Tears dolls, and was the voice of one of the Campbell Soup Kids. Some experts said she had a three-octave voice range, while others claim it was four octaves. Darla was married twice and had two daughters. Her second husband had a record company and eventually became a paraplegic. Spanky McFarland was surprised to see five-foot-one-inch tall Darla on television's *The Mike Douglas Show* one day in the early 1970s. McFarland would eventually appear with her on the show late in 1973. They had not seen each other in 35 years.

In 1987, McFarland told his Akron Civic Theatre audience Darla Hood died in 1979 of inadvertently taking an overdose of sleeping pills. McFarland told his 1990 audience Darla died of a heart attack shortly after another joint television appearance on *The Mike Douglas Show*. Since Maltin and Bann's book was published two years before Darla died, there is no information there about the cause of her death. The International Motion Picture Database website has Darla Hood dying under rather mysterious circumstances in 1979, at a North Hollywood hospital of acute hepatitis following a minor surgery operation. Darla was 47 years old. She is interred at the Hollywood Memorial Cemetery (now called Hollywood Forever) in Hollywood, California. According to McFarland, he did not have a crush on Darla. He thought Alfalfa really might have. "No 'Hanky Panky' with Spanky," McFarland said about Darla.

Eugene "PORKY" Lee

Eugene "Porky" Lee was born in Ft. Worth, Texas, in 1933. He joined *Our Gang* in 1935, at age two and appeared in 42 shorts in four years. As mentioned before, Porky was the "fat kid" who was to replace Spanky but outgrew his part. Eugene's mother sent a photograph of her son to Hal Roach because she thought he looked a little like Spanky. Roach, struck by the resemblance, arranged a screen test. Porky first appeared in *Our Gang's* "Little Sinner" as Spanky's brother. Who can forget the classic conversations between Porky and Buckwheat punctuated by Porky's classic refrain of, "Oh, tay!"? By 1940, Porky was physically larger than Spanky. After his *Our Gang* tenure, Eugene "Porky" Lee left show business entirely.

During both of his Akron appearances Spanky McFarland offered little information on Porky. He all but disappeared, never wanting to attend any of the *Our Gang* reunions. Eugene Lee became a college teacher of Political Science and has been reported to have taught in colleges in Minnesota, Colorado, and Texas. One of the last slides Spanky McFarland showed at his 1990, Akron Civic Theater appearance was a picture of the last Our Gang reunion to date (1985 or 1986). Standing in the back row of the photograph was a six-foot, five-inch, 275 pound man with very dark hair and an equally dark beard: it was Porky!

"Pete" the Dog

There were actually two Petes! "The original had a ring around his right eye," explained McFarland. "It was natural in color but not dark enough to photograph, so they enhanced it. He was a good dog but got wild in crowd scenes. He'd get excited and would start nipping at people in the heels. We used a double for the crowd scenes." The problem was the "crowd scene Pete" had a circle around the left eye! "Sometimes, if you look close," instructed McFarland, "you can see both dogs in the same short." Then McFarland startled his audience by revealing Pete the Dog was a pit bull! "The American Kennel Club did not recognize the pit bull as a breed until the mid-1930s," said McFarland. "In order to get the breed established in this country they called the breed Staffordshire Terrier. Pete the Dog was the first Staffordshire Terrier to be recognized by the AKC in the United States!"

Spanky McFarland also offered little tidbits of information on lesser-known *Our Gang* members. Billy "Froggy" Laughlin was in 29 of the *Our Gang* shorts in two years at MGM. According to McFarland, Froggy's trademark deep voice was really his. It was not dubbed. "He couldn't do the deep voice for more than a few minutes at one time," said McFarland, "or he'd swallow his tongue. The veins used to stick out in his neck when he did the voice." Unfortunately, Laughlin died in 1953, when a car hit him while he was on a motorcycle.

Scotty Beckett was the cute kid with the big turtleneck sweater and baseball cap turned sideways. He was born in 1929, and was in 15 *Our Gang* comedy shorts in two years. He did other movies after he left the gang. The last ten years of his life were not very good, according to McFarland, punctuated by divorce, violence, drugs, and numerous arrests. In May of 1968, Beckett was found in the bathroom of a bar in New York City severely beaten. "He died two days later," said McFarland. "Pills and a note were found but no conclusion was made by the coroner as to the exact cause of death. He was 38 years old."

Bobby "Wheezer" Hutchins was born in 1925. He made 58 *Our Gang* comedies in six years. Not much is known about him after he left the gang. He was killed in a training exercise during World War II.

As of his 1990 appearance Spanky McFarland said there were no more *Our Gang* reunions planned for the near future. Besides himself, McFarland informed his audience that Tommy "Butch" Bond, Sidney "Woim" Kibrick, Robert "Mickey" (Gubitosi) Blake, Jackie Cooper were still alive. He did not mention that Darwood "Waldo" Kaye and Dickie Moore were also still alive.

McFarland fondly spoke of attending a special ceremony in 1985 in Hollywood, when Hal Roach received an Honorary Oscar Award. "There was a dinner that night," recalled McFarland. "I sat at a table with Roach, his two daughters, me and my wife, Dickie Moore and his wife, Jane Powell. I met Michael Jackson at the award dinner." McFarland then went on to relate how Jackson wanted to meet him. "I admired him," confessed McFarland, "because he made it all by himself by not using drugs, dirty words, etc. We were fans of each other." Michael Jackson was currently on a concert tour and would be appearing in Texas near McFarland's home. McFarland invited him to his house to rest during the tour. Jackson even invited McFarland to see the show. After the performance they ate dinner and returned to McFarland's home. "He shows up in three vans with security, a chef, and a doctor," said McFarland. "We went through my scrapbook and had a great two-and-a-half days together. Michael loves the *The Little Rascals.*"

What was the secret of *Our Gang* lasting so long? When asked by an audience member during the question-and-answer period at the Akron Civic Theatre, McFarland replied, "Besides being damn good entertainment it's funny and you don't have to work at it. We don't have a moral each time and we don't have to hit you over the head with it. We're not unzippin' our pants and Darla's dress isn't blowing open every 30 minutes. It's just plain good entertainment. It's nostalgia. Kids today wish to heck they could've lived back then."

Another audience member asked McFarland why they don't make movies like *The Little Rascals* anymore. McFarland's answer was simple: "We did it right the first time. The times were different. The gang reflected what kids did back then to entertain themselves. We were primarily from low-income families. We were left on our own to make our own entertainment. That's the way kids did back then in those days. That's what Hal Roach tried to capture. That's why you can't recapture that moment again."

Of the 95 *Our Gang* shorts he made over his 11 years Spanky McFarland's favorite comedy was 1933's "The Kid from Borneo." It was the short that had the gang mistaking Bumbo, a sideshow jungle wild man, for Spanky's itinerant Uncle George. The gang calls the wild man "Uncle George," who is continually hungry and keeps saying, "Yum-Yum! Eat 'em up! Eat 'em up!" Bumbo is merely hungry and wants food, but the gang thinks he is a cannibal and wants to eat them.

Spanky McFarland ended each of his appearances by notifying his audience he would be in the theater lobby following his performance. He emphatically stressed he would not sign any unauthorized *Our Gang* or *The Little Rascals* photos or items. "I won't sign any duplicate photos; only originals," McFarland said. "They are not copyrighted." He further explained that some photographs (especially some 8" x 10"'s) had been duplicated without authority of license and this was the only way of protesting this copyright infringement.

"There are a lot of rip-off items and pirated things out there that I have nothing to do with," McFarland said.

I made my way to the lobby with the rest of the Akron Civic Theatre crowd and patiently waited in line to meet and greet Spanky McFarland. Luckily, I had the Maltin and Bann book with me. McFarland was most cordial as he personalized the book and posed for a photograph with me. Several days later Pattie Eddy of the Akron Civic Theatre sent me a personalized autographed, 8" x 10" picture of Spanky McFarland.

George "Spanky" McFarland died of a heart attack in Grapevine, Texas, on June 30, 1993. Though 64 years old, McFarland was still recognizable as the chubby little rascal of *Our Gang* and *The Little Rascals* fame.

To Sue—
Good Luck &
God Bless You
Dorothy
Lamour

Chapter 10
Dorothy Lamour

"I only recently visited the South Seas due to the fact all my South Seas pictures were shot on the back lot of the studio!"

As stated at the beginning of the previous chapter, one personal encounter with a celebrity, like child actor George "Spanky" McFarland, produced quite a "rush." But twice is even more of an indescribable "rush." In that regard, I was lucky enough to experience movie actress Dorothy Lamour on two separate occasions as well.

Movie actress Dorothy Lamour is forever etched into our minds as a long, dark-haired beauty, eternally clad in a South Seas cloth sarong and/or cavorting with Bob Hope and Bing Crosby in their numerous and highly successful "Road" motion pictures.

The true facts are that Lamour actually wore a sarong in only six of her career total of 59 motion pictures and appeared in all seven Hope and Crosby "Road" pictures.

I had the good fortune of spending some time with Ms. Lamour in April of 1979, and again three years later in July of 1982.

In April of 1979, actress Dorothy Lamour was starring for three weeks in Neil Simon's comedy play *Barefoot in the Park,* in the role of Mrs. Banks, at Carousel Dinner Theatre, then located in Ravenna, Ohio. Three years later, in July of 1982, at Carousel Dinner Theatre's summer venue, Canal Fulton Dinner Playhouse, Lamour appeared for one week in a retrospect of her film career, showing film clips and adding commentary about her numerous co-stars and leading men.

The public may not be aware that Dorothy Lamour began as a singer, not an actress.

She was born Mary Leta Dorothy Slaton in New Orleans, Louisiana, on December 10, 1914. Of French, Scotch-Irish and Spanish extraction, in 1931 the already stunning beauty was named "Miss New Orleans", clad in a blue linen dress that cost her $2.98.

Shortly thereafter, Lamour began working at odd jobs, finally settling on becoming a secretary. Friends convinced the beautiful

Lamour to become a singer instead of a secretary. Lamour and her mother moved to Chicago, Illinois, where Lamour landed a job as an elevator operator in a large department store. After hard work, knocking on doors, and countless auditions, Lamour was discovered by bandleader Herbie Kay who recommended the songstress to Rudy Valee. With Valee's orchestra, Lamour played all the major nightclubs, including New York's Waldorf-Astoria. Lamour also performed with legendary pianist Eddie Duchin. From band singer to solo-vocalist at Sherman Billingsly's Stork Club to an NBC radio contract for her own program, *The Dreamer of Songs,* Dorothy Lamour's career was on its way. Even after her movie career was established, Lamour returned to radio where she starred and co-starred in several radio series including *Front and Center, The Sealtest Variety Theater,* and *The Chase and Sanborn Hour.* She worked with such radio luminaries as Don Ameche, Edgar Bergen and Charlie McCarthy, Nelson Eddy, W.C. Fields, Lionel Barrymore, Dean Martin and Jerry Lewis, as well as Ronald Reagan, George Murphy, Bob Hope and Bing Crosby.

Lamour began her movie career as a non-credited chorus girl in *Footlight Parade* in 1933. In 1935 Dorothy Lamour married her discoverer, bandleader Herbie Kay. The marriage lasted four years. In 1936 Lamour was among the 250 actresses who auditioned for the upcoming Paramount motion picture, entitled *Jungle Princess*, which starred Ray Milland and Akim Tamiroff. "I guess the one reason I got the part (of Ulah)," recalled Lamour at a 1982 Canal Fulton Dinner Playhouse press party, "was because I had long black hair down to my waist." Her next major movie role was in 1937's *The Hurricane* (as Marama), directed by John Ford, and starring Jon Hall. The supporting cast included Mary Astor, C. Aubrey Smith, Raymond Massey, Thomas Mitchell and John Carradine. Lamour's memories of the epic picture were quite clear some 35 years later (at the 1982 Canal Fulton press conference). "I remember endless hours in a huge studio water tank on a sound stage being buffeted by several wind machines," she recalled. "All my (jungle) pictures were done on the back lot, you see. Only the second unit went out on location for the outdoor shots." Then Lamour confessed, "I only recently visited the South Seas due to the fact all my South Seas pictures were shot on the back lot of the studio!"

Lamour stole the movie audience's attention in *The Hurricane* with her wrap-around sarong and long, waist-length black hair. She became an instant movie star as Marama, the child of nature. She went on to portray similar characters in *Her Jungle Love* in 1938 (as Tura), *Typhoon* in 1940 (as Dea) and *Beyond the Blue Horizon* in 1942 (as Tama).

In 1940, Lamour starred in her first Bob Hope and Bing Crosby "Road" picture as Mima in *Road to Singapore.* For you movie buffs, the other "Road" pictures included *Road to Zanzibar* (1941) as Donna Latour, *Road to Morocco* (1941) as Princess Shalmar, *Road to Utopia* (1946) as Sal Van Hoyden, *Road to Rio* (1947) as Lucia Maria de Andrade, *Road to Bali* (1952) as Princess Lala, and *Road to Hong Kong* (1962) as herself. Lamour frequently remarked, "I was the happiest and highest-paid straight woman in the business."

Dorothy Lamour was not limited to comedic glamour roles during her motion picture career. Among her more serious film roles were Mabel "Lucky" DuBarry with Tyrone Power in *Johnny Apollo* (1940) and Albany Yates with Henry Fonda in *Chad Hanna* (also in 1940).

When the 1950s heralded a slowdown in her movie career, Lamour turned to nightclubs and the stage. She toured successfully in *Hello, Dolly!* for David Merrick in 1967. The one-year tour covered almost 29,000 miles and 91 cities. The tour made Merrick about $7 million dollars. "Right from the beginning the show should have been called *Hello, Dollars!"* Lamour once remarked.

Lamour also performed on television. She guest performed on such series as *Murder, She Wrote, The Love Boat, Marcus Welby, M.D., Burke's Law,* and *Remington Steele.*

During her later performance years, Lamour did the dinner theater circuit acting in *Anything Goes, Fallen Angel,* and Neil Simon's comedy, *Barefoot in the Park.* It was during Lamour's appearance in *Barefoot in the Park* in 1979, at Carousel Dinner Theatre (then located in Ravenna, Ohio), that I met Ms. Lamour for the first time. As stated in a previous chapter, Carousel Dinner Theater had a press night party for the local media after the first Thursday night performance, when the general public exited the theater and the press stayed behind to mingle with the cast and most notably the star: Dorothy Lamour.

It was Thursday evening, April 5, 1979, that I first met actress Dorothy Lamour after her performance in the comedy *Barefoot in the Park* as Ethel Banks, mother of newlywed daughter, Corie. Corie and new husband, lawyer Paul, had just moved into a cramped, fifth-floor apartment in New York City. In typical Neil Simon comedic fashion, the audience witnesses the trials and tribulations of the newlyweds in the cramped NYC apartment when mother, Mrs. Banks (Ms. Lamour), decides to pay a visit.

After the Thursday evening performance, as the general public exited the theater, I watched patiently as the stage set was cleared and a light buffet was rolled out onstage for the pending press party reception. This was early on in my entertainment writing career. I had not met many celebrities in person. I had interviewed my very first celebrity, actor Richard Egan, only two months before. I was just beginning to realize the "rush" I felt meeting a famous person was identical to the "rush" I felt onstage as a performer in front of a live audience.

My first impression of actress Dorothy Lamour turned out to be a false one. Ms. Lamour walked out to the center of the stage and sat directly behind a table previously set up especially for her. As she sat down, she remained motionless for several minutes as a hairdresser meticulously and gingerly rearranged some of her long, dark tresses. I immediately thought, "Oh, boy, a pampered, arrogant starlet who will not be very approachable." I was totally wrong!

Ms. Lamour was polite and very accommodating. Scott Griffith, owner of Carousel Dinner Theatre at the time, said that Lamour knew she came from the studio star system and she realized the system did not exist any longer. Her appearance in *Barefoot in the Park* at Carousel Dinner Theatre that April of 1979, was only a few months after her second husband, William Ross Howard, had passed away. Lamour had just come out of a long retirement. I truly feel Ms. Lamour was very grateful that the public still remembered her and was appreciative of the local media attention.

I patiently waited my turn to greet Ms Lamour. She smiled as I requested that she autograph an 8" x 10" publicity photograph for me. She also let me pose with her for a photograph of us together. Carousel owner Griffith later told me that Lamour had brought a Scottish terrier puppy with her. It was a recent gift from one of her two sons. Griffith recalled how everyone at the theater helped in training the pup. "We even bought it a toy fire hydrant," Griffith joyfully recalled.

Before the next time I saw Ms. Lamour again, she had penned her autobiography, *My Side of the Road*, published by Prentice-Hall in 1980. The second time I met Dorothy Lamour was three years after her Carousel Dinner Theatre appearance at Canal Fulton Dinner Playhouse near Canton, Ohio, also owned by Scott Griffith. This time Lamour was appearing for one week in a retrospective of her film career. Her show included film clips and photos of her co-stars and leading men, and comments and stories about them. She even sang some of the songs from her motion pictures. She was, after all, originally a band vocalist!

Owner Griffith decided to throw a lavish press party the week of her appearance at Canal Fulton Dinner Playhouse. The purpose for the publicity stunt was to present Lamour with the world's largest floral carnation lei, to be given by the Akron Floral Association just before her scheduled press conference and party. As the party progressed, the press and media people sipped pina coladas and talked among themselves and with Ms. Lamour. At one point Lamour sat down at a table, prepared to answer questions from the assembled media. As cameras clicked, Lamour fielded questions.

As with some local media events, one or two local media types seemed to monopolize the situation by asking redundant questions. They provided a further annoyance by purposely laughing at anything and everything Lamour said. Lamour answered all questions frankly and candidly as she sat clad in a tan pants suit with several gold necklaces around about her neck. She also wore a yellowish-gold shawl draped about her shoulders. Later, she proudly revealed that she had made the shawl herself.

While she sipped white wine and puffed on a Vantage cigarette, Dorothy Lamour seemed quite comfortable in her "element." Before being widowed some three years before, she was married for 35 years to husband William Ross Howard, an Air Force officer she had met during World War II. They had two sons: Ridgeley, born in 1946, and Tom, born in 1949.

Dorothy Lamour was proud of her work during World War II, selling more than $300 million worth of war bonds. It was her idea for the 10% payroll savings plan.

The press conference continued amid more pina coladas, redundant questions, and photo opportunities. Ms. Lamour revealed that her home was decorated in "contemporary everything." She confessed to staying up late some nights to watch *Colombo* reruns on television. She also liked to watch TV game shows, particularly *Tic Tac Dough*. She was particularly thrilled to personally meet the Air Force captain who won the most money in the history of the program. Ms. Lamour also liked daytime dramas, especially *General Hospital* and *One Life to Live*. She liked *One Life to Live* because one of her co-stars from *Barefoot in the Park* (from her 1979 Carousel Dinner Theatre appearance) appeared in it.

Lamour was also impressed with the local area's stately homes and how well-kept they were. When asked whether she preferred performing in plays or motion pictures, she wisely replied, "I like anything I am doing at the time."

During the entire press conference I merely sat toward the back of the area and silently took notes. Suddenly, Dorothy Lamour stopped and looked directly at me! "Don't you have any questions to ask me, young man?" she asked me point-blank! I was startled and immediately replied, "No, ma'am." Lamour smiled and declared to the assembled media, "You gotta watch out for those quiet ones." What a lasting memory!

When I learned on September 22, 1996 of Dorothy Lamour's death of undisclosed causes (one source indicated diverticulitis) I called Carousel Dinner Theatre (now located in Akron) and spoke to owner Scott Griffith about what he remembered about Lamour's two appearances for him. "I was getting off Route 77 (near the Canal Fulton Dinner Playhouse) when I saw a familiar car off the side of the road," he recalled. "An attractive woman had raised her dress just high enough to show the lower part of her leg in an effort to flag someone down to help her with a flat tire. It was Dorothy Lamour!"

Besides Lamour singling me out at her Canal Fulton Dinner Playhouse press conference, I recalled that the week before her Canal Fulton appearance the weather had been rainy and dismal. When Dorothy Lamour arrived in the area, the weather became sunny and warm. I like to believe that Dorothy Lamour brought her South Seas weather along that July in 1982.

Chapter 11
Morey Amsterdam

"If anyone can make a living at what they like to do, they got it made!"

Who can forget the character of Buddy Sorrell, the funny little comedy writer on *The Dick Van Dyke Show* with the shiny black hair and perennial speech impediment (lateral lisp)?

It was October, 1979, my first year of interviewing famous people for the weekly *TV Facts Magazine*. Morey Amsterdam would be only my third celebrity interview, after Richard Egan and Robert Alda.

Morey Amsterdam was appearing at Carousel Dinner Theatre in Ravenna, Ohio, but not in the usual Carousel comedy play format. Amsterdam and other comics like Phyllis Diller appeared at Carousel with locally popular Carousel Dinner Theater emcee, singer Mark Thomsen. Thomsen, who had a regional following and fan base, would sing a medley of songs for the first half of the evening's entertainment. After intermission, Diller or Amsterdam would do their comedy routine for the second half of the show.

Amsterdam was appearing at Carousel Dinner Theatre from October 16 - 21, with singer Thomsen. Ellie Meindl, the public relations director at Carousel, had arranged for me to interview Amsterdam, late in the afternoon, on Wednesday, October 17, 1979. I followed Ellie to the apartment Carousel rented for him during the run of his appearance. Assuming that Ellie would remain with me during the entire interview, I had brought along my camera for Ellie to snap a photograph of Amsterdam with me. It never happened. After our introductions Ellie left to return to her duties at the dinner theater.

My first impression of Morey Amsterdam in person was of his stature. He was not very tall. People look much larger on the movie screen as well as the television picture tube. Amsterdam looked very healthy. He was extremely tan, well groomed with his trademark, shiny jet-black hair. He was wearing dark trousers, laundered shirt open at the collar, and a sport coat.

While setting up my battery-powered tape recorder, Amsterdam and I discussed the merits of different name-brand recorders. I had just "graduated" from an electronic tape recorder to a battery-operated one for better portability and easier access to whom I was interviewing. I was previously embarrassed and uneasy about snooping around a celebrity's apartment looking for an electric wall outlet. Then there was the matter of where to place the microphone and how long the microphone cord could actually reach. My battery-operated tape recorder had the microphone built into the unit, thus placing the recorder closer to the celebrity and ultimately resulting in a clearer tape recording of the interview.

Being a Wednesday, Amsterdam had already appeared in a matinee performance at Carousel and would return later to do an evening show. I told him I would be brief since I figured he might want to rest.

"What rest?" he said. "I walk out there and talk to people!"

I marveled at the man who had gained immortality on television in *The Dick Van Dyke Show*. But there was more to Morey Amsterdam than his portrayal of the wily comedy writer Buddy Sorrell on a popular weekly television program. Before getting into the success of *The Dick Van Dyke Show,* I inquired into Amsterdam's beginnings in show business. As of 1979, he had been in "the business" 53 years.

Amsterdam was born in Chicago, Illinois, on December 14, 1908. His father was a concert violinist with the Chicago Symphony and later the San Francisco Symphony. "My father wanted me to be a musician," revealed Amsterdam, "and my mother wanted me to study law." But show business began flowing in Morey Amsterdam's veins at an early age. By age ten, Amsterdam was a boy soprano on radio in the Chicago area, and also an accomplished cellist.

Amsterdam's first appearance on a vaudeville stage occurred because an illness of an unknown comic and the behest of Amsterdam's brother. Morey's older brother was already appearing in vaudeville as a piano player who had also become the "straight man" for a comedian.

"When the comic got sick," recalled Amsterdam, "my brother

decided to recruit me."

The young comedian began getting bookings in local clubs around the Chicago area. When Amsterdam was 16 years old, he was already performing in a Chicago speakeasy owned by an "Al Brown," better known as Al Capone. One night young Amsterdam was caught in the middle of a shootout and immediately decided to seek safer bookings elsewhere.

Amsterdam moved west to California where he became a writer and gag man for such comedy legends as Fanny Brice, Jimmy Durante, Will Rogers, Jack Benny, and Red Skelton.

By the 1930s and 1940s, Amsterdam was on three different daily radio shows, which prompted famous radio personality Fred Allen to joke, "The only thing I can turn on without getting (Morey) Amsterdam is the faucet!"

Amsterdam would become known as the "Human Joke Machine" because he could instantly tell a joke about any subject upon request. The most unique aspect about the comedy of Morey Amsterdam was that he wrote all his own material. "Most funnymen began (their careers) by stealing bits from other comedians," said Amsterdam, "until they eventually established their own style, at which time they hired their own writers."

From vaudeville to radio, Amsterdam gained immortality on television as comic writer Buddy Sorrell on *The Dick Van Dyke Show.* But Amsterdam had had other forays into television before his 1961 debut on *The Dick Van Dyke Show.* In 1950, Amsterdam hosted *Broadway Open House.* The format was something never before seen or heard on the new medium of television: the talk show. *Broadway Open House* was the granddaddy of NBC's *The Tonight Show* that starred Jack Paar, and then eventually, Johnny Carson and Jay Leno.

Amsterdam's appearance on *The Dick Van Dyke Show* was not planned. In fact it originally had an entirely different cast and title.

"The original show pilot was a Carl Reiner creation called *Head of the Family,*" according to Amsterdam. "It starred Carl Reiner in the Dick Van Dyke role. The cast was also completely different." Amsterdam credits Reiner's genius for the turn of events in the show's metamorphosis. "Reiner, along with producers Sheldon Leonard and Danny Thomas, looked at the pilot episode and concluded it just wasn't right," according to Amsterdam. "Carl Reiner was perceptive enough to see he wasn't right for the part. Looking for another actor, he spotted Dick Van Dyke in the Broadway production of *Bye, Bye Birdie* and offered him the part. The entire TV comedy show was recast with Mary Tyler Moore, Richard Deacon, and former child actress Rose Marie."

For television trivia buffs, Mary Tyler Moore had previously been seen as the little pixie in the Hotpoint appliance television commercials in the early 1950s. Later, her legs and sultry, breathy voice were all that was revealed in her portrayal as Sam, David Jansen's telephone answering service operator on television's popular detective series, *Richard Diamond, Private Eye.*

The cast of *The Dick Van Dyke Show* lacked one more character. A combination actor-writer was needed. Rose Marie suggested her good friend Morey Amsterdam, who had written for her since she was 12 years old. Rose Marie was also godmother to Amsterdam's daughter.

"Reiner calls me," said Amsterdam, "as I was digging out of a blizzard in Yonkers, New York. That afternoon I flew out (to California) to do the pilot of the show."

Amsterdam credits two things to the success of *The Dick Van Dyke Show* from 1961-1966. "First off, all the stories were believable," said Amsterdam. "They could happen to anyone. The true-life situations were ones the audience could relate to. Second was the blending of the right people in front of the camera with people behind the camera. There was no 'temperament.' Everyone was pushing for each other. It was a perfect relationship of good writing with good performing."

Amsterdam chuckled at some of the benefits resulting from the success of *The Dick Van Dyke Show.* "The show appears today (1979) in 38 countries," said Amsterdam. "I've seen myself talk in seven different languages!"

Before, during, and even after Amsterdam's stint on *The Dick Van Dyke Show*, the comedian performed in motion pictures and guest -starred on other television series. On television, Amsterdam appeared on episodes of *The Love Boat, Alice, Adam 12, The Partridge Family, Love, American Style, Have Gun, Will Travel, The Hollywood Squares,* and *Caroline in the City.*

Motion picture appearances included Amsterdam as Michael

"Fanny" Fandango in *Machine Gun Kelly* (1958), Walter Sage in *Murder, Inc.* (1960), Cappy in *Beach Party* (1963) and again as Cappy in *Muscle Beach Party* (1964), Charlie Blake in Disney's *The Horse in the Gray Flannel Suit* (1968), and as the custard pie star in *Won Ton Ton, the Dog Who Saved Hollywood* (1976). His voice was also featured in two animated films: *Mr. Magoo's Christmas Carol* and *Gay Purr-ee*, both in 1962.

Back in his rented apartment, in Ravenna, Ohio, between performances at Carousel Dinner Theatre, in October of 1979, Morey Amsterdam spoke fondly of his family: his wife, Kay, of 38 years, and his two children. His son, age 35, was a writer-director-producer and his daughter, age 27, a psychologist.

After his Carousel Dinner Theatre appearance was over, Amsterdam would be off to a one-week engagement in Florida. Then it was on to Amsterdam's home in Beverly Hills, California, to play golf and rest for the remainder of 1979.

Morey Amsterdam seemed to exemplify his personal philosophy on life: "If anyone can make a living at what they like to do, they got it made."

Amsterdam spoke of his amazement during a recent appearance in Florida. "I played an apartment complex called Century Village," he recalled. "Thirty-five hundred families! I played ten nights in an auditorium to a different audience each night!"

Amsterdam also liked to appear occasionally on tour with former strip tease artist Ann Corio in *This Was Burlesque.*

One of Amsterdam's hobbies was the history of words. He educated me on the origin of three words (of his choice) based on his understanding of their origin: "You know where the word *kike* comes from?" he asked. "It comes from a Jewish dance in the Old Country, (called) the *kikel*. Jews who were good at it were called *kikes*."

To further educate me, Amsterdam asked me if I knew the origin of the term, "WOP." Showing my ignorance, I answered in the negative. "When Italians came over to this country and had no proper documentation," said Amsterdam, "the immigration authorities stamped them, '<u>W</u>ith <u>O</u>ut <u>P</u>apers.'"

Amsterdam saved the best for last. "You know where the term *fuck* came from? In England, authorities didn't know what to book prostitutes for, so they decided on '<u>F</u>or <u>U</u>nlawful <u>C</u>arnal

Knowledge.'"

Speaking of England, Amsterdam said he made many television appearances in England and Australia. "Television in England is wonderful," said Amsterdam, "but the programming is lousy. You have two hours of two priests just sitting talking to each other. It's ridiculous."

During the interview I was trying to think of a way to ask Amsterdam about his trademark speech impediment, a lateral lisp. As a public school speech pathologist at the time, I was curious as to Amsterdam's feelings on the subject. I realized I had wasted my time when he revealed: "I went to speech class when I was a kid. I had a lisp. I still have it. I'm so well-known now there's nothing I can do about it," he admitted. "Kids three and four years old come up to me on the street and say, 'Uncle Buddy! Uncle Buddy!'"

Just before my interview with Morey Amsterdam concluded, he excused himself to make a phone call to a comedy group appearing in Cleveland who had asked him to view a video tape of one of their recent performances. My most lasting memory of comedian and actor Morey Amsterdam is not the autographed photo I eventually obtained, but, rather, the image of the famous comedian taking the time between appearances at a dinner theater, to view the video tape of a struggling comedy group and offer them his own personal professional advice, free of charge.

I had a similar experience years later when I had the privilege of visiting blues guitarist B. B. King between sets at Akron's Tangier Restaurant. There, the musical legend was sweating after his first performance, sitting in a corner of his dressing room, listening to an audiotape of another Blues guitarist. To me that's a prime example of "Class" in the first degree.

Comedian Morey Amsterdam passed away of a heart attack at age 86, in Los Angeles, California, on October 27, 1996.

Chapter 12
Pat Paulsen

"What if I win this time?" (on being perennial Presidential candidate)

The old saying "the third time's the charm" was *not* the case concerning the third and final encounter I had with comedian Pat Paulsen, whose distinguishing trademarks were constantly running for President of the United States, a puny physique, a monotone voice, and most notably, a continual deadpan face. The first two encounters with the comedian were more pleasant and fruitful.

My first encounter with Paulsen occurred while he was appearing at Carousel Dinner Theatre (then located in Ravenna, Ohio) from September 4-30 in 1973, in the Woody Allen comedy play, *Play It Again, Sam*. Traditionally, while one show was being performed at Carousel in the evening, the next upcoming production was being prepared and rehearsed during the day.

As stated in the Foreword, I had the opportunity of appearing in *See How They Run* at Carousel Dinner Theatre, starring Mickey Rooney, from October 2nd to November 4th of 1973. *See How They Run* was the show rehearsing in the day while Paulsen was starring in *Play It Again, Sam* during the evening.

Born and raised in California, Paulsen, with his continual deadpan face (akin to silent screen star Buster Keaton's), skinny physique, and understated, low-key comic demeanor, burst upon the comedy entertainment horizon during the folk club craze of the 1960s, first as a comic guitarist in such places as "The Ice House" in Pasadena, "The Troubadour" in Los Angeles, and "The Gaslight" in New York. It was while appearing at San Francisco's "The Purple Onion" that he was discovered by the Smothers Brothers. They immediately put him on their weekly variety television show in 1967, as the television station manager with a weekly editorial commentary. Subsequent appearances on popular singer Glen Campbell's and guitarist Mason Williams's television shows kept Paulsen's comic façade on television for several more years.

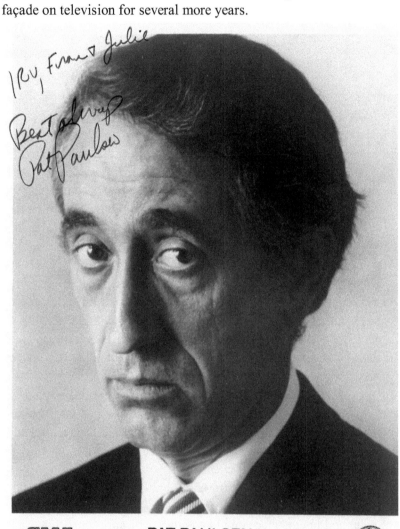

Irv, From Julie
Best always
Pat Paulsen

PAT PAULSEN

    Paulsen's trademark low-key approach to any subject was unique and subtle, much like Don Knotts's deputy sheriff Barney Fife character from TV's *The Andy Griffith Show*. Paulsen's popularity eventually led him to run for President of the United States, beginning in the1968 election campaign, under the banner of the STAG (Straight Talking American Government) Party. Subsequent presidential bids were under other party banners such as the All Night Party.

During an afternoon rehearsal for *See How They Run* at Carousel Dinner Theatre in September, 1973, another local actor and I were sitting at a stageside table eating our brown-bag lunches when a very plain-looking, inconspicuous man, with his deadpan face, wandered into the theater. He meandered over to our table and struck up a conversation.

"You guys in the next show?" he nonchalantly asked. He was holding a handful of letters, having just been to the box office to pick up his daily mail. "I'm in the show that's here now, *Play It Again Sam,*" he said. "My name is Pat Paulsen." We shook hands. "Nice meeting you guys. Good luck." Paulsen turned around and went out the back door, got into his rented car and drove off.

At Carousel Dinner Theatre, it was customary on the last night of the current show for its star to introduce the next play's star and their cast. Such was the case on Sunday night, September 30, 1973, when the cast of *See How They Run* was invited to dine and watch the last performance of Pat Paulsen starring in *Play It Again, Sam.*

After his final night performance, Paulsen came onstage for an after-curtain speech and introduced the next show's star, Mickey Rooney, to the crowd with the rest of the upcoming cast of *See How They Run.* I didn't see Pat Paulsen again until 13 years later, in 1986.

One day I picked up the local daily newspaper to see an ad for Pat Paulsen appearing at the nearby (now defunct) "Akron-Canton Comedy Club" in Canton, Ohio. At the time I was writing for *The Medina Gazette*, a daily newspaper. I asked the newspaper's entertainment editor if I could do a story on Paulsen and, perhaps, even review his nightclub comedy act. When the okay was given, I made arrangements with club manager, Jeff Haller, to review a performance of Paulsen and perhaps meet him after the show. I recounted to the club manager my meeting the comic 13 years before at Carousel Dinner Theatre when we both were appearing in separate play productions. Haller told me that two press tickets would be waiting for me at the box office for the upcoming 11:30 PM show.

My friend, Sam, and I arrived at the Akron-Canton Comedy Club by 11:30 P.M. Just before midnight the two comics preceding Paulsen had completed their *schtick*. The comic immediately preceding Paulsen was unusually annoying. With evidently nothing better to do, he strolled up to the stageside table that my friend and I occupied and asked what we "two guys" were doing together at the club. I was beginning to sense a very *negative* and *suggestive* drift to his line of "comedy." The comic startled me by suddenly asking me my name. Concentrating on jotting some notes down on the notepad resting on my lap under the small round table, I was momentarily stunned, not realizing that he was talking directly to me. The comic then began making fun of me for not knowing my name, not to mention being at a small, intimate table with another male. Get the *drift*?

When the comic again asked me what I was doing at the club with my "male friend," I quickly discovered the "Power of the Press." I immediately exposed the reporter's notepad from beneath the table. With a pen in one hand and a notepad in the other I smiled and loudly proclaimed to all within earshot, "I am reviewing *your* act for a daily newspaper." That was enough. The comic immediately put both hands up in the air, like he was surrendering to me, backed away from my table, and went on to another part of the audience to ply his "craft."

Pat Paulsen came out onstage with two "bodyguards" who were wearing sunglasses to look as if they were part of the Secret Service. Paulsen immediately launched into his campaign rhetoric for the 1988 Presidential Campaign. This current Presidential campaign's slogan was "The Future Lies Ahead."

Though not declaring allegiance to any political party, Paulsen immediately differentiated between Republicans and Democrats. "A Democrat takes a woman to dinner and a movie," said Paulsen, "then takes her home to bed. A Republican takes a woman to dinner and a movie, then the chauffer takes her home to bed."

Candidate Paulsen's platforms were very timely (1986). On the topic of senior citizens, candidate Paulsen said, "We have an abundance of old people and a shortage of gas. What we need is a way to convert old people *into* gas!"

Paulsen also had a platform for Women's Liberation. "A woman should not be discriminated against just because of the shape of her skin," he stated. Birth control was also on the Paulsen Presidential platform. Speaking from personal experience, Paulsen confessed "the coil" was too expensive for his wife to use. "I gave my wife a Slinky instead," Paulsen said. "Boy, you should see how she walks down those steps!" He also explained how his wife joined a health spa and lost 20 pounds in one day . . . "when an exercise machine tore her leg off."

M ANAGEMENT
T ALENT
A SSOCIATES
1745 Camino Palmero Ste. 304
Los Angeles, CA 90046

RON MASON

PAT PAULSEN

WILLIAM MORRIS AGENCY, INC

Paulsen then dismissed his "bodyguards" and went into a non-presidential, stand-up comedy routine. At one point in his routine Paulsen told his audience that he had been a Marine. "I could take apart a rifle in 11 seconds blindfolded," he proudly declared. "So if we were ever attacked, I can blindfold myself and take apart my gun in 11 seconds!"

Paulsen produced a guitar and performed several folksong parodies of the day. Then several impressions were in order. Among the most memorable was Richard Nixon as captain of the *Titanic*.

Paulsen was an excellent mime. His fluid slow motions rivaled pantomime legends Marcel Marceau and even Red Skelton. Particularly funny and amusing was his rendition of a tennis match in played slow motion.

After about 45 minutes Paulsen thanked his audience and left the small Akron-Canton Comedy Club stage. A few minutes later I found Paulsen backstage in the club manager's office. He was sitting on a couch in the corner, relaxing with a cigarette in one hand and a bottle of Molson Ale in the other. I related to the comic our first meeting 13 years before at Carousel Dinner Theatre in Ravenna when he was in, *Play it Again Sam.* He smiled and remembered the production fondly, confessing it was a bit hard to do the play since it was a popular Woody Allen vehicle. His concern was that he would be compared with Woody Allen and not judged on his own merits.

The comic and I talked for some time about the last 13 years. Paulsen seemed quite serious about the 1988 Presidential Campaign. He reflected for a moment. More deadpan than ever, when he looked me straight in the eye and said, "Gosh, what if I win this time?"

After the second Pat Paulsen meeting at Akron-Canton Comedy Club meeting, in 1986, I had received periodic mailings from Paulsen's daughter, Terri (his public relations manager), about his upcoming Presidential campaign and his recent acquisition of the small town of Asti, California. I wondered why Paulsen purchased an entire town. Actually this was *serious* business for the comic. He was, believe it or not, in the wine business.

Pat Paulsen Vineyards were located in Asti, California, with Pat Paulsen as its mayor. The business venture was noteworthy enough to garner space in Akron's daily newspaper, touting Paulsen's award-winning wines. In 1970, Paulsen and his wife were looking to invest in some land in Northern California, then move up their daughter and two sons from Southern California. They found and bought a 600-acre ranch near Cloverdale, California, located in northern Sonoma County. Paulsen was familiar with the area having grown up there. After considering the area he decided to plant grapes. After all, Sonoma County was famous the world over as California's "wine country."

Beginning in 1979, Paulsen hired a full-time winemaker and began planting grapes: 35 acres to sauvignon blanc, chardonnay and cabernet sauvignon. Pat Paulsen Vineyards 1983 Cabernet Sauvignon was voted the best of 140 cabernets in a much coveted competition in Reno, Nevada. Also worthy of note were Pat Paulsen Vineyards Dry Muscat Canelli 1985, Refrigerator White 1985, and Paulsen Vineyards Sauvignon Blanc Select 1984. Paulsen's goal in 1986 was for his winery to produce 25,000 cases of wine in the following year or so.

The Paulsen public relations machine kept churning out periodic press releases about Asti, California. With Paulsen as mayor, how could there *not* be fodder for comic press releases? On July 3, 1986, Paulsen declared himself mayor of Asti, California, and had an inaugural celebration dubbed "Hands Across My Asti," riding into town in a rusted out 1927 Ford, complete with "Secret Service" escort.

My third and last conversation with Pat Paulsen, via telephone on December 28, 1987, had been pre-arranged with Paulsen's daughter, Terri. I was to call Paulsen at a hotel in Denver, Colorado, where he was currently appearing. Terri gave me the phone number of the Denver hotel and the extension number. It was a Monday evening. I waited until halftime of ABC-TV's *Monday Night Football* to call Paulsen just in case he was also watching the game.

After introducing myself (reminding him of our two previous meetings) and commencing with the interview, I instantly felt uncomfortable when Paulsen stated, "You can do it now. Let's get it over with." To make me feel more uncomfortable he said, "You can say you talked to Pat Paulsen and he didn't say anything."

I began the task of asking Paulsen questions tailored to a presidential candidate, big mistake. I asked about Social Security, defense spending, etc. "That's getting into my act for you to put on paper. You don't wanna do that," he said. Then he matter-of-factly stated, "I give short answers to all presidential questions."

Undaunted, I pursued my intent by asking about Paulsen, the presidential candidate's platform on Social Security. "Social Security should remain like it is. Okay? What else?" he seemed to say rather hurriedly. The knot in my stomach was tightening. "What about defense spending?" I asked. "We shouldn't spend so much money. Good, huh? These are my position papers," he replied.

"What about crime?" I inquired. "We shouldn't have crime," was his terse answer. Then he explained, "All the candidates go into a long harangue about it but mine are short. I've got an answer for everything." About the current events in (1987) Iran, Paulsen said, "We should clear that situation up." Then, toying with me he asked, "Not getting much help are you?" I contained my frustration. I refused to lower myself to his level and did not reply to his question.

I continued with the phone interview. About raising campaign funds Paulsen confessed, "I have about $400. I take a sack. We intend to send mimeograph copies to all who contributed to let them know where the money goes, like amaretto and coffee at the O'Hare airport coffee shop."

When asked about keeping his presidential image clean, Paulsen admitted, "I don't have one. I intend to keep it that way." On the subject of pollution, Paulsen continued his theme of short, terse answers when he flatly stated, "We shouldn't have pollution."

On the subject of foreign aid, Paulsen actually said more than just a few terse words. After thinking a moment about the subject, candidate Paulsen replied, "I don't think we need any. Maybe we do. Then we can return to the real pleasure of hating *them*. We gave *them* aid and they hated us for that. They got real strong and then they have to send us aid and we can get back to hating *them*."

Paulsen declared, "I'm presenting a new vision. That's it: a new vision. I don't know what the hell it means but I'm presenting it."

What was Pat Paulsen's campaign slogan for *this* try at the White House? "Pat Paulsen for President. He's Got To Sleep Some Place."

"Just remember," warned candidate Paulsen, "I intend to lead America into the past. That way we'll get to see our mistakes before we make them."

Japanese whaling concerned Presidential candidate Paulsen enough to comment, "I'm against Japanese whaling. I can't stand Yoko Ono. I'm tired of her *wailing*."

I thought if I changed the subject, perhaps Paulsen would soften his terse tone. I began by asking about his town of Asti, California. "I'm having trouble with the 'Asti-Nistas.' There's a revolt going on there and I'm not there to handle it," Paulsen said, tongue-in-cheek. "I left my son, Justin 'Baby Doc' Paulsen in charge."

Justifying his current mood, Paulsen admitted, "Sorry I couldn't be more explicit. It's so much easier talking to guys like you if I just say: 'Pollution: I'm against it.' It works."

Then Paulsen apparently concluded the phone interview, putting me off with, "I'm sure your story will be something. 'I talked to Pat Paulsen and he didn't say anything.' Sounds basically what it should be."

And so it was. As I mentioned before, a story never materialized from that winter evening's audio-taped telephone interview. It seemed that the weather was not the only thing chilling the air (and telephone wires) that cold December evening. I had paid for the long distance phone call out of my own pocket and was also out the money I would *not* get for *not* writing the story.

I could have written a story about Pat Paulsen's negative attitude that night and how he treated me, but that wasn't (and still isn't) my style. After some soul-searching, I decided that there was basically nothing to write about concerning his upcoming northeastern Ohio appearance and filed the tape and notes away until 1997 when I learned of Pat Paulsen's death.

Pat Paulsen died at age 69 on April 24, 1997, of terminal brain and colon cancer while undergoing experimental treatment in Tijuana, Mexico. I immediately thought of how actor Steve McQueen had died in very much the same way. I was writing for the daily newspaper, *The Gazette* (formally *The Medina County Gazette)* at the time. I secured permission from the paper's entertainment editor to write a story about my encounters with the late comic. In the published story I related our first two meetings, at Carousel Dinner Theatre in 1973 and at The Akron-Canton Comedy Club in 1986. The frustrating phone interview of December 28, 1987, was never mentioned.

In looking back at our three encounters I can't help thinking of the frustrating phone interview and recalling how wrong Pat Paulsen was when he said that I had talked to him and he didn't say anything. The taped interview was, after all, useful in concluding this chapter when I could finally use its content to reflect on my third and final encounter with the perennial, deadpan-faced presidential candidate.

Since his death I always wondered what had happened to his beloved winery and town of Asti, California. After some research I discovered that Paulsen had lost his winery and vineyard during his divorce from his wife, June, which ultimately led to an IRS seizure of the property in 1990. It was purchased several years later by Kristine and Chris Williams, who renamed it Wattle Creek Winery.

When I periodically think about Pat Paulsen, I mostly recall his presidential campaigns. With politics the way it is today, I now realize how justified comic Pat Paulsen was in being very concerned, almost scared, that night in 1986, after his performance at The Akron-Canton Comedy Club, when he worried about his then-current Presidential bid. I can vividly see him staring at the floor, with a lit cigarette in one hand and a cold beer in the other lamenting, "Gosh. What if I win this time?"

Chapter 13
Harry Blackstone, Jr.

"I will never do a trick I have not mastered completely, especially if it involves danger. When I go onstage to perform I don't want any surprises. I learned that lesson in Detroit when I sawed a reporter in half. The man is now working in Detroit AND Chicago!"

Harry Blackstone Jr. was a reluctant magician. He bore his father's famous name, yet he did not want to follow in his father's profession. Through his early years Blackstone Jr. tried his best to avoid his father's fame and avocation. At age 34, he succumbed to his father's profession, improved upon it, and the entertainment world is better for it. I am thankful for having had the opportunity to spend time with him on two separate occasions, one at an afternoon brunch and another, watching him perform onstage at the Tangier Restaurant.

The reluctant magician was born June 30, 1934, in Colon, Michigan, the son of the famous magician, Harry Blackstone Sr., who ranked very close to Harry Houdini in popularity in his day. When Blackstone Jr. was six months old, he began appearing and disappearing from his famous father's illusions. By age four he was already performing feats of "mental telepathy" for visitors to the Blackstone home in Michigan. By age seven he was traveling with his famous father's illusion show, learning the elements of magic under the watchful eyes of his father and uncle. All the famous Blackstone Sr. illusions were eventually mastered by the younger Blackstone, including the dancing handkerchief, the vanishing birdcage, the floating light bulb and the buzz saw.

After a stint in the U.S. Army, Blackstone Jr. attended college for a while at Swarthmore. He then earned a degree in drama from The University of Southern California and a Master of Fine Arts degree in theatre arts from The University of Texas. While working on his degree at The University of Texas, he worked as a disc jockey for a local radio station owned by then-United States Senator Lyndon B.

Johnson. Blackstone Jr. migrated to Hollywood, California, where he eventually managed three West Coast companies of the rock musical play *Hair*. He also became an associate producer for the Smothers Brothers television show.

HARRY BLACKSTONE

It was the Smothers Brothers who finally persuaded Blackstone Jr. to become a fulltime magician and were instrumental in getting him to perform in nightclubs and, eventually, on television. Besides being an associate producer for the Smothers Brothers television show, Blackstone Jr. became involved with Tommy Smothers in the production of a motion picture titled *Get to Know Your Rabbit.* The movie bombed and was quickly removed from distribution. In the movie Tommy Smothers portrays a tap-dancing magician. Smothers enjoyed the part so much in the movie that he decided to include the character in his Las Vegas routine. Smothers needed a real magician. Blackstone Jr. volunteered.

Blackstone Jr.'s part of the show involved making Tommy Smothers disappear and reappear from a box, along with the 28 members of the entire orchestra, the 13 Edwin Hawkins Singers, the Everly Brothers and Leslie Uggams, as well as Dick Smothers and his bass fiddle. Blackstone Jr.'s performance was so well received that Tommy Smothers offered to help him raise $50,000 to start a magic act of his very own.

"Men and women who had worked for my father started sending me all sorts of material and tricks my father had used or plans for illusions he had made but never completed," recalled Blackstone Jr. "With the assistance of my friends and colleagues, we started recreating many of the famous tricks and illusions used by my father and incorporating them into a nightclub act." In 1969, three years after his famous father passed away, Blackstone Jr. opened in Lake Tahoe at Harrah's as a solo act.

Though Blackstone Sr. never had the opportunity to see his son perform professionally, he did witness a performance in 1959 at The University of Texas. As part of his master's thesis in theatre arts, titled "The Development of the Levitation from the Deus Ex Machina to the Present," Harry Jr. demonstrated 10 variations on how objects floated. Unknown to him, one of his professors invited Blackstone Sr. to the session. "I had no idea he was there," recalled Blackstone Jr. "Then, after I had finished and was accepting some scattered applause, I heard someone whistling from the back of the room, one I had heard hundreds of times. And when I heard it that day, well, it was as though somebody had pressed a cube of ice into the middle of my back. Somehow I managed to maintain my stage presence and introduced him to the group." Blackstone Jr. related what happened next. "Not only did my father get a three-minute standing ovation, he also came on stage and did 15 minutes of material. Later I was told my performance was okay but that my supporting act was really great!"

By 1976, Blackstone had dropped the "Jr." from his name and was hosting a British TV show for the British Broadcasting Corporation (BBC) called *The Magic Show* in England and performed for Queen Elizabeth II's Silver Jubilee. Also in 1976, Blackstone was named America's Official Bicentennial Magician. In 1977, Blackstone had his own syndicated television show in the U.S. called *MAGIC! MAGIC! MAGIC!* From 1978 to 1979, Blackstone produced the largest traveling illusion show since his father's and appeared in *Blackstone on Tour* for Home Box Office in 1979. *The Blackstone Magic Show* tour from 1979-1980, set box office records in 16 of 151 cities in a 30-week, $3 million tour. In 1980, *Blackstone!* opened on Broadway and became the largest and longest running illusion and magic show in the history of New York Theater.

Blackstone's performances always contained some of his father's famous routines as well as many creations of his own. He had two Golden Rules. The first axiom was: "I will never do a trick I have not mastered completely, especially if it involves danger." The second axiom was: "When I go on stage to perform I don't want any surprises. I learned that lesson in Detroit when I sawed a reporter in half." Blackstone then smiled. "The man is now working in Detroit *and* Chicago!"

Tangier Restaurant, in Akron, Ohio, had the good fortune to sponsor a Blackstone appearance on its Sultan's Cabaret nightclub stage several times in the 1980s and 1990s. I wrote two stories before Blackstone's two appearances at Tangier, both in 1981: one in February and another in October.

I had the good fortune to attend Blackstone's February 11, 1981, evening performance at Tangier Restaurant. The 65-minute, 10-illusion show was, indeed, very entertaining. The performance featured his trademark floating light bulb, sawing a woman in half, and disappearing bird cage illusions. The disappearing birdcage was the magician's first illusion. Blackstone casually strolled onstage, in black tuxedo and black flowing cape, carrying a small, square wooden-bar birdcage with a bird in it, directly in front of him. Without warning, the cage mysteriously vanished into thin air. Blackstone then committed one of the cardinal sins of performing magic: he repeated the illusion. Magicians are taught not to repeat an illusion ever, for fear the audience may figure out how it was done. Blackstone was so enamored with the audience's positive reaction to the disappearing birdcage illusion, however, that he amazed the audience making the birdcage vanish once again.

Blackstone had a very deep, resonant voice that could host any radio or television show or pitch any commercial product. Another of his assets was his "patter" or verbal presentation. He could make one illusion last longer than usual because of his relaxed, easy-going performance style. Tangier scheduled a Sunday matinee performance especially tailored for children. Blackstone liked children's audiences so much that he would usually pay a visit to Akron Children's Medical Center when he was "appearing" in town.

The second time I saw Blackstone was at a local hotel restaurant that featured a Sunday brunch. My immediate family had decided to attend the brunch one Sunday morning in July of 1984. After the family had gone through the buffet line and sat down at a table, I glanced across the room and recognized Harry Blackstone. He was sitting at a table with his wife, Gay.

As mentioned in the Foreword to this book, for 14 years I portrayed Ronald McDonald locally. Every two years or so McDonalds Corporation would hold a Ronald McDonald Convention at its corporate headquarters in Oak Brook, Illinois. This gathering of Ronald McDonald portrayers from all over the country, and world, would be about a five-day convention to educate their "Ronalds" on the latest available skits and the new, upcoming McDonald promotions. The last evening of the convention would feature a renowned performer after the evening's festivities and banquet. The 1984 convention featured Blackstone. But, alas, due to obligations, I could not attend the convention but had heard, from some of my other "Ronald" buddies that Blackstone gave a great show that last evening of the 1984 convention.

I walked over to where Blackstone and his wife were seated and asked, "Excuse me. Are you Blackstone?" He answered yes. Then I said, "I heard you were fantastic last week at the Ronald McDonald Convention at Oak Brook." Blackstone looked up and stared at me in disbelief. Knowledge of the Ronald McDonald program and even its occasional conventions was as much a secret as some of our government's defense department files! I then confessed that I was a local Ronald McDonald and, regretfully, had missed the convention. Blackstone seemed to be more in awe that I was a Ronald McDonald than I was at meeting Blackstone the Magician! He then introduced me to his wife, Gay. I told him I had seen him perform before at Tangier Restaurant and knew that he was in town to appear at Tangier again.

I told Blackstone that I was at the hotel brunch with my family. I pointed to our table across the room and where my father was seated. I then told the magician that my father was a big band musician who played in the orchestra pits of the local vaudeville houses in downtown Akron during the 1920s and the Depression. I related a story to Blackstone that my father had related to me about playing in the orchestra pit when Blackstone Sr. appeared at a downtown Akron vaudeville house many, many years ago.

I thanked Blackstone for letting me speak to him and his wife and went back to our table. A few minutes later, Blackstone approached our table and spoke to my father. "Hello. My name is Blackstone and I understand you played in the orchestra pit when my father appeared in Akron." The two men conversed for a while. Blackstone asked my father what he remembered from the appearances, especially what illusions Blackstone Sr. had performed.

After the conversation I asked Blackstone if he would mind posing for a photograph with me since I happened to have my camera to photograph the family gathering at the hotel brunch. Blackstone posed with me for a picture. I knew the famous magician had older children by his first marriage and some younger children with wife, Gay. I asked Blackstone for the names of his younger children so that I could write them a letter on Ronald McDonald stationery if he didn't mind. He seemed most pleased. He gave me the names of his children and I wrote them down. He then told me to let him know which performance I would like to attend at Tangier and how many complimentary tickets I would need for that performance. I was surprised and told him of my appreciation of the gesture. As I stated before, he seemed to be just as thrilled I was a Ronald McDonald as I was he was the famous Blackstone the Magician. My family and I eventually attended a performance of Blackstone at Tangier at which time I presented him with the Ronald McDonald letters for his children.

I eventually framed the photo of me with Blackstone along with a personalized 8" x 10" autographed publicity photo of the famous magician.

In 1993, a very mysterious thing happened. I had hung the Blackstone photos on a wall in my basement office. They were placed along with other signed celebrity autographed photos. Blackstone's photos hung directly in the center of a particular wall. One day in 1993, I was looking at the photos on the wall when I noticed that the autographed Blackstone photo did not seem right. Upon closer examination I noticed what looked like water damage in the frame containing the autographed photo but none on the photo of us standing next to each other. No other pictures on the wall had water damage. When I opened the damaged frame, I discovered that some moisture and dampness had fused part of the autographed Blackstone publicity photo to the glass. When I tried to take the picture out of the frame, part of it stuck to the glass. It was a mess. I called Tangier Restaurant and spoke to Marge Thomas, the restaurant's director of publicity. I told her what had happened. She gave me a few addresses for Blackstone and told me which one would be the one I should send a letter to request another autographed photo. I wrote Blackstone a letter telling him who I was and informed him of what happened to the autographed photo. Within a few weeks I had a new autographed photo to replace the damaged one!

As one can imagine I was very sad when I learned of Blackstone's premature death, at age 62, on May 14, 1997, of pancreatic cancer. I read all the tributes and personal remembrances in local publications as well as the professional magazines of the International Brotherhood of Magicians and the Society of American Magicians. All testimonies referred to Blackstone's dedication to his profession, his friendliness, and his sense of humor.

One excerpt quoted the eulogy at Blackstone's funeral in California. The funeral was held at the First Congregational Church in Redlands, California, on May 18, 1997. The eulogy by Rich Block told a story of Blackstone's humor. In Chicago, Blackstone was set to 'vanish' a live elephant and its trainer. Just as screens were placed all around the pair and Blackstone was about to utter his magic words to make the elephant and trainer disappear, the audience heard the trainer call out the animal's name quite loudly: "Luella, NO!" Evidently it was too late. When the screens dropped, the elephant and trainer had, indeed, disappeared, almost! The elephant had left something "natural" behind. Not missing a beat, Blackstone walked down to the edge of the stage and told the audience, "In the event some of you believed we were not using a real elephant..."

Another testimony from the eulogy concerned Blackstone's raw courage in the face of his illness. He actually arose out of his hospital bed to go to Atlantic City, New Jersey, to fulfill his obligations to the people who came every Christmas to see his show. As Blackstone was rehearsing his trademark floating light bulb illusion, he was mounting the steps to the stage when pain and fatigue suddenly overcame him, causing him to topple backwards down the steps. Gay, Blackstone's wife, caught his head as he lay on the ground with shards of broken light bulb glass all around him. As Gay ran for the medics, a bystander took off his coat and put it under the fallen magician's head. The man asked Blackstone, "Are you comfortable?" The magician looked the man straight in the eye, and again, without missing a beat, replied, "I make a living."

When Blackstone died, some said it was the end of an era. The Blackstone legend will stay in the public eye thanks to his wife Gay and other members of the Blackstone family, who advise both corporations and the entertainment world on special effects and other projects. The Blackstone Foundation was recently established to promote theater, magic and education throughout the world. In the works are three books to be published by Blackstone's wife, Gay, daughter Bellamie and Charles Reynolds.

The legacy of Harry Blackstone will live not only on through motion pictures, video tape, and books, but also in the mind of one local entertainment writer who had the good fortune to experience Blackstone the Magician twice, once on a professional level and another on a more personal, memorable level.

Dear Korman
my thanks
dear friend

Red Skelton

Chapter 14
Richard "Red" Skelton

"That's what's so nice about show business: I haven't met a stranger in 50 years."

Whenever I am asked who my favorite is of all the famous people I have met, without any hesitation, I always answer: "Red Skelton."

How could a press conference in the lobby of the Palace Theater in downtown Cleveland, Ohio, one April morning in 1992 make such a lasting impression? The answer is quite easy. Red Skelton had such a genuine and honest demeanor about him that you immediately and unconditionally liked him. He *truly* enjoyed what he did. It was very obvious that he loved performing. Moreover, he loved people. Skelton habitually laughed and giggled uncontrollably in anticipation of uttering the punch line. His laugh and manner were so infectious that you could not help but laugh along with him before he was even close to the punch line. For a person who spread so much joy and happiness, Richard "Red" Skelton's personal life seemed to reflect the opposite.

Meeting Red Skelton was quite accidental. I had just completed an entertainment article for *The Medina Gazette*. The entertainment editor was not around but a bright red piece of paper in the middle of his desk caught my eye. It was an invitation to a press conference for Red Skelton to be held in the lobby of the Palace Theatre located in downtown Cleveland. The conference was scheduled for Thursday morning, April 9, 1992, at 10:00 AM, before his evening appearance. The invitation featured a caricature drawing of Red Skelton holding a cigar, the logo of his CBS television show.

The following day I called the entertainment editor at the newspaper to ask if he planned to attend the press conference. He was not attending but informed me that the newspaper photographer was going. The photographer had taken a photograph of Skelton some years before in Minnesota and wanted Skelton to autograph an enlargement of it.

The morning of May 9th, I met the photographer in the newspaper parking lot to drive to the Palace Theatre. As we arrived in downtown Cleveland, I spied a long limousine pulling up in front of the theater. After the photographer had parked the car, we approached the front of theater. I noticed a man slowly getting out of the long limo. The brim of his hat was pulled down over his face. He walked with a noticeable limp, carrying a cane along with a camera bag, and a small, hand-held video camera. Several people walking by the theater stopped and approached the man. The man was Red Skelton! He stood by the limo door and patiently spoke to the people who had gathered around him. He was cordial as he made his way to the front door of the theater. While the photographer and I made our way into the Palace theater lobby, Red Skelton was still talking to the people outside.

Inside, were about 30 media people milling about the lobby. When the guest of honor entered, we immediately formed a large circle. Skelton entered the circle and personally greeted everyone. I had a black moustache at the time. When Skelton made his way around to me he pointed to my upper lip and said, "Hey, buddy, you got a loose thread there!"

Skelton eventually made it over to a red-carpeted stairway leading from the balcony of the theater. In front of the staircase a long table held about a dozen strategically placed microphones. Skelton approached the table and greeted his audience. He put his cane, camera bag and video camera down, pulled up his beltless trousers and took out a cigar which he held but never lit during his entire press conference. I had heard he chewed, but never smoked, about 30 cigars a day. I made a mental note to ask him what brand of cigar he preferred since I enjoyed a good cigar myself every now and then.

Skelton picked up his video camera and panned the lobby. He explained that at home he wrote his wife a love letter every morning. When he was on the road he videotaped his daily happenings, instead of writing love letters, so she could see what he was doing.

The first thing out of Skelton's mouth was, of course, a funny line: "I just got out of the hospital. A team of five Palm Springs doctors removed my wallet." The theater lobby immediately reverberated with laughter. The laughter would continue with regularity during the entire press conference as we all fell in love with the beloved entertainment icon.

Richard "Red" Skelton was born on July 18, 1913, in Vincennes, Indiana. His father, Joseph, a clown with the Hagenback and Wallace Circus, died of alcohol abuse a few months before Red's birth, leaving Red's mother and three older brothers in dire poverty. Red began working at age seven. At age 12 he began his show business career with *Doc Lewis' Patent Medicine Show* when it came to town. Red's audition for the talent part of the show failed but Lewis felt sorry for him and let him sell bottles of his patent medicine, a salt water and brown sugar solution. One day Red tripped up the steps as he approached the stage to sell the medicine. The audience laughed. They thought it was part of the act. Lewis then asked Red to fall off the stage every performance from then on. Thus began Red's famous physical, slapstick comedy that would eventually take a heavy toll on his body.

In the fall Red returned to school. Since he had no burning desire to learn to read or write, he played hooky whenever the local circus or carnival came to town. By age 14, Red was six feet tall but still in the fifth grade. After quitting school he took any job he could with any traveling show that pitched its tent in town. He even obtained a job on a stern-wheel showboat *Cotton Blossom,* eventually playing every part in the play *Uncle Tom's Cabin* except for the part of Little Eva. In 1928, when the showboat was in the same town as the Hagenback and Wallace Circus, Skelton was hired and became a walk-around clown.

In 1929 the stock market crashed causing the Great Depression. At the same time the intense competition from radio and talking movies resulted in circuses folding or cutting personnel. In 1931, Skelton was hired as a clown for a Walkathon, a dance marathon featuring up to 100 couples who danced for days and weeks. The last remaining couple standing could win a prize of $500 to $1,000. Skelton's job as a clown was to entertain the crowd and keep them amused between couples collapsing. Red Skelton became known as the best of the Walkathon clowns. This fact was proven when I witnessed a conversation between Skelton and an elderly gentleman at the end of the press conference in Cleveland. The elderly man approached Skelton and told him that he remembered him from a

Walkathon in 1933 in Cleveland. Skelton was very cordial to the man and even recalled the ballroom where the Walkathon took place. It was also during a Walkathon that Skelton met his first wife, Edna, whom he married in 1931. Edna would remain his closest confidant in his personal and business matters the rest of his life.

Skelton's big break came in Atlanta, Georgia, when he appeared as a clown with the *W.E. Tibbets Walkathon*. Tibbets also produced a nightly musical review called *As Thousands Hear*, spoofing a popular Broadway musical, *As Thousands Cheer*. Skelton was the show's emcee. He also did comedy routines, sang, and danced. A veteran vaudeville entertainer who was in the audience one evening introduced Skelton to theatrical agent Tom Kennedy. Skelton was on his way to stardom. Ultimately he would alternate between two vaudeville houses in Montreal and Toronto, Canada.

After one performance, Skelton went to a coffee shop for a late-night snack. Skelton intently watched as a man was clumsily dunking a doughnut in his coffee. Ever the observer of human nature, Skelton eventually came up with a comedy routine demonstrating different types of doughnut-in-coffee dunkers. This idea led to other comedy routines based on how people did things. Among the most famous was his "Guzzler's Gin" sketch.

In those days, the next logical step up from vaudeville was radio. In 1938, Red Skelton appeared as a guest on *The Fleischmann Hour*, starring Rudy Vallee. At the time ad agencies put together radio shows and sold them to networks. Skelton also began providing comedy for *The Red Foley Show*, as a country bumpkin character.

Because of his radio popularity, a motion picture screen test was arranged for Skelton at MGM in 1940 where he did his famous Guzzler's Gin routine. Traditionally, motion picture studios introduced a new star in established movie series. Red Skelton debuted in 1941 in MGM's *The People Versus Dr. Kildare*. Thinking Skelton would be another Bob Hope, MGM cast Skelton in a comedy series called *Whistling in the Dark* with Skelton portraying Wally Benton, a radio detective who becomes involved in real-life murders. Between 1941 and 1943, Skelton starred in 27 films for MGM while guest-appearing in three others. Silent screen legend Buster Keaton was working as a gagman for MGM at the time and supplied jokes for such Skelton movies as *A Southern Yankee, The Yellow Cab Man,* and

Watch the Birdie, which was a remake of Keaton's silent movie classic *The Cameraman.*

In 1941 Red Skelton was offered his own coast-to-coast radio show, *The Red Skelton Scrapbook of Satire.* Incidentally, the show's bandleader was Ozzie Nelson and the vocalist was Harriet Hillard, who later became Harriet Nelson. The radio show enabled Skelton to create trademark characters that would eventually make the transition to his television show. Skelton created San Fernando Red, a crooked politician; Clem Kadiddlehopper, a country bumpkin; Cauliflower McPugg, a punch-drunk ex-prizefighter; Sheriff Deadeye, a cowardly gunfighter; and Junior, the Mean Widdle Kid. At the behest of Red Skelton, most of his alter egos put in an appearance in the Palace Theater lobby in Cleveland during his press conference on April 9, 1992. Skelton's radio show premiered in October, 1941, and was broadcast on Tuesday nights at 7:30 p.m. (Pacific Time) on NBC, following Bob Hope's *Pepsodent Show.*

The only medium left for Red Skelton to conquer was television. In September of 1951 Skelton's television show premiered on NBC. When CBS eventually cancelled his show in 1971, Skelton had been on television for 20 years.

Red Skelton's television show always followed the same format: a monologue while dressed in a tuxedo, a musical interlude, a series of short blackout sketches, and a serious curtain speech at the end of the show followed by, "Good night and may God bless."

Skelton developed one of his most endearing characters just for television. Inspired by his friend Emmett Kelly, the famous Ringling Brothers, Barnum and Bailey Circus clown, Skelton created Freddy the Freeloader, a happy tramp clown. The character was so popular that Skelton eventually made an HBO special called *Freddy the Freeloader's Christmas Dinner.*

Red Skelton reminisced about two of his favorite television guests at the Cleveland press conference, especially their ad-libs on camera. He fondly recalled Vincent Price and John Wayne. In one Freddie the Freeloader sketch, Price played an unscrupulous art collector who discovers an original Leonardo DaVinci painting hanging in Freddie's rundown shack. Price tries to cheat Freddie out of it. Skelton explained that all spoken lines were read off cue cards just out of camera range. Price accidentally mispronounced DaVinci

(DaVin-chee) as DaVin-*Key*. Skelton recalled, "You must realize this gentleman (Price) has a vocabulary that is perfect. He never slurs a word and is as proper as can be." Then Skelton related how, without missing a beat, Price looked right into the camera lens and said, "And it was an ori-*Guh*-nal!"

Skelton also fondly spoke of a John Wayne appearance just after the popularity of his Rooster Cogburn character in *True Grit,* for which he won the Academy Award for Best Actor. In a comedy sketch for Skelton's television show, Wayne was dressed as Cogburn, complete with a patch over one eye. According to Skelton, Wayne was supposed to take a sip of coffee from a coffee cup. Someone offstage, however, had forgotten to remove a spoon from the cup. Wayne took a look at the spoon in the cup and ad-libbed, "Better take that out. Don't want this (pointing to patch on his bad eye) to happen again!"

While Skelton was recalling his favorite guests I gathered enough nerve to ask if he recalled Errol Flynn's guest appearance. Flynn had appeared on the show just before his death in 1959. "That was the last show he did," recalled Skelton. "There was that little girl with him (Beverly Aadland). She was kind of mean, you know? He kept putting vodka bottles in his (dressing) room and we'd take them out and fill them with water. Then she'd come back and put the stuff back in again. He was so crocked on the show that we worked around it to make it look like he was doing it on purpose." He went on about Flynn's heavy reliance on vodka. "Out of the clear blue sky," Skelton said, "while we were taping, he'd hand me a bottle and I'd pretend it was water but it was really vodka. People thought he was just acting like that. He died two weeks later. He was a nice gentleman." Skelton stopped and reflected momentarily then said, "He was a nice fella."

In 1971, CBS canceled Skelton's show because of demographics, believing Skelton's audience was older than the target audience of the show. Red Skelton refused to just sit around. He had other interests such as composing, writing, and most profitable of all, painting. Skelton also took to the road presenting symposiums on college campuses and making one-night appearances throughout the United States and Canada. "I do about 75 a year," Skelton said. Though he would not elaborate, Skelton mentioned, "This year I'm going into the hospital so I only booked about 50."

All Red Skelton's success and adulation came at a very high price, both personally and physically. Skelton was married three times. In 1958, while married to his second wife, his son died of leukemia at age nine, resulting in the eventual suicide of the boy's distraught mother. Also, as a result of Skelton's heavy reliance on physical comedy, his body paid a high price. When he appeared in Cleveland in April of 1992, he was walking with a cane. One of the first things Red Skelton did was to thank the media for not mentioning to the public that he wore steel braces on both legs.

Red Skelton confessed at the beginning of his press conference that he liked appearing in old, remodeled theaters. As he gazed around at the Palace Theater lobby, he noted, "These theaters to me are temples. They do as much good as church but in a different way of course. When they started cutting them up in two's (for movie theaters), it was a sacrilege."

Because it was 1992, Red Skelton did not waste the opportunity to mention the upcoming Presidential election in the fall. As his crooked political character, San Fernando Red, Skelton puffed up his chest, took a "political" pose then said, "This is gonna be a clean campaign. I'm not gonna throw mud at my opponent. He's a fine man. And his wife: a mighty fine woman, mighty fine. What he sees in that thing he's running around with I'll never know!"

Skelton also took a jab at H. Ross Perot, who was running for president against George Bush and Bill Clinton. Referring to Perot, Skelton observed, "I like that little guy. He dropped out because of a speech impediment: no one could understand what he was saying! I shouldn't make fun of anyone because of their speech. I have a speech impediment of my own: I stop every once in a while to breathe!"

Cleveland was a special place for Red Skelton. As he looked around the Palace Theater lobby again, he recalled his many appearances in Cleveland. "I was in Cleveland a long time ago on 155th street," he said. "I played a walkathon. I was master of ceremonies. I was also here with the Hagenback and Wallace Circus. I also played at the Hippodrome Theater. I played there in vaudeville. Then I played here at the Palace. I delivered a baby here (in Cleveland). I did. It was at a walkathon (dance marathon). One of the little nurses was pregnant. I didn't know what I was doing, but I put newspapers down on the bed and I delivered this little baby here in Cleveland."

Skelton even recalled appearing in vaudeville in nearby Akron, Ohio. "I played at the Palace Theatre there. (He even recalled the two unique entrances to the theater: one down on Main Street and the other a block up on High Street.) Then I played in burlesque there at an opera house. As a matter of fact I got the show closed," Skelton recalled. "I did a joke. I'll show you how humor has changed. Burlesque in those days was a little bit different. We did a satire on a few things. The first act was Cleopatra and the second act was the Gay Nineties. We were doing a song in Gay Nineties outfits and were singing this song. I kneel in front of this girl and say, 'Would you like to take a walk?' She lifts her skirt to her ankles and says, 'I think it's going to rain.' I said, 'What?' She says, 'I think it's going to rain.' I said (looking at her ankles and up her skirt) 'I'd like to see it *clear up*.'" That remark closed the show. A judge fined each cast member $25. According to Skelton, "There were 35 people in the show. They hated me because they didn't have that kind of money and because I got the show closed for this lousy joke I did."

Red Skelton was very frugal when he prepared for a one-night performance. "I come into town early and go to K-Mart to pick up my props. Going to K-Mart is cheaper than paying freight on my props," he explained. "I go in and get a chair, mop, broom, and stool and I always buy white socks. They're cheaper than sending them to the laundry. It costs 75 cents to send them to the hotel laundry. I wear them once and then throw them away. You can get the others for 30 cents a pair. So you save money in the long run." Skelton has ulterior motives for frequenting Kmart. "People will come up and say things to you and things come to you and you find your humor that way. That way you know basically what's going on in town. I mention politics and they say, 'Yeah, do a joke on so-and-so.' I'll go over there this morning and talk with people."

When home in California, Skelton was a creature of habit. He explained his morning routine with a few humorous detours, of course. "My day starts at 5:30 in the morning. After I shower and shave the first thing I do is write a love letter to Mrs. Skelton. Then I do a pencil sketch to illustrate something in the letter. Then I write five musical selections. I have 18,000 copyrighted musical selections that I've done very little with. My marches are played. You've probably marched to some of my music in school. I've written 64 symphonies. The London Philharmonic has recorded four of them and they're going do six more in October. I write an outline for a short story every day and on Sunday I take the best of seven stories and write a complete story. That way I have 365 ideas a year to work from and 52 short stories. I publish 20 of them a year from a mail order business. I have an unusual thing with my list of people: I have over 750,000 people that we have addresses to. I print 15,000 (book copies) only. The brochure is sent out. They send for the book and they send the $15.00 for the book. If they read it and don't like it, they send it back and return all but $2.00. If they do like it, they send it back. I autograph it personally and mail it back to them." Skelton then shrugged his shoulders and smiled confessing, "So it's a racket, really!" To further tickle our funny bones, he said, "I do inventions. I just finished an invention that's coming out. It's a dartboard with an automatic return!" Skelton smiled and laughed just before the punch line.

Red Skelton is also well known for his clown paintings. He's painted Freddie the Freeloader in various poses for many years. He did several per year and lithographed a few thousand of each for sale. "I have 36 galleries across the country and 21 in Canada," Skelton informed the assembled media. "I made more off my artwork than I ever did being in show business." Skelton then told us how he hoped the press would help in fulfilling a dream. "When I was a boy I wanted to be a painter. I was sitting in an elevator back in Washington, Indiana, with my grandmother. My mother couldn't take me home and she (my grandmother) ran the elevator in a building in Indianapolis. I was seated on this little stool sketching her running the elevator, you know? A guy got on the elevator and said, 'Hey, kid, what do you do, sell those?' I said, 'Yeah.' He said, 'Will you take a buck for that (drawing)?' I said, 'Yeah.' (Recently) I was in Muncie, Indiana, at Ball State University and the press was there from Indianapolis. I offered $50,000 if someone, still by chance, had that sketch, because I signed it. Not that it would mean anything. That guy could have thrown it away or put it in his pocket. No one has come up with it yet. I would just like to have it to see if I've improved."

Speaking of painting, Skelton was always amazed at the public.

One time an old lady heard he was an artist and asked him, "Do you think you can paint me in the nude?" Not wanting to miss an opportunity for humor, Skelton immediately replied, "I never did it before. Can I leave my socks on?" Skelton also lamented feeling sorry for another famous painter; Michelangelo: "He lays on his back for seven years painting the Sistine Chapel. The Pope comes in and says, 'That's nice but we're gonna need a second coat!'"

Several of Red Skelton's alter egos put in humorous appearances during the memorable mid-morning press conference. Having already experienced San Fernando Red, the crooked politician, commenting on the upcoming Presidential election, Skelton treated us to other favorite characters.

In the middle of one topic Skelton said, "I like Klem (Kadiddlehopper)," as he took off his hat and put a crease down the middle of it. He fluffed up both sides of his red hair with his finger tips and put the creased hat back on his head, brim up. Now as Klem he said, "Since I saw you I was in a military wedding. There were guns there, let's put it that way!" Sensing the crowd's instant laughter, Skelton, as Klem, went on. "My wife's brother says to me, 'Wanna meet my sisters? One's named Hortense and the other's named Lassie.' I said, 'Lassie's a dog.' He says, 'Wait till you see Hortense!'"

Skelton, still as Klem, was clearly on a roll. "A guy's brother-in-law is the laziest man in the world. He won't work. He saw the 1992 recession coming so he quit work in 1950! I got even with him on Halloween. I scared him to death. I went to the party dressed like a job!"

While on the subject of employment, Skelton immediately changed persona and became his trademark funny tramp clown, Freddie the Freeloader. Skelton, now as Freddie, reflected momentarily then said, "I just had a narrow escape. A fella offered me a job!"

Later, when Red Skelton took off his hat, fluffed out his hair again, put both hands under his armpits like wings, and momentarily crossed his eyes, and instantly became his two famous seagulls, Heathcliff and Gertrude. "Heathcliff and Gertrude are standing on the beach and their little friend, the sparrow comes up to them and he's limping," related Skelton. "He's got a broken wing and doesn't have a feather on him. Heathcliff says, 'What on Earth happened to you?' 'Oh,' replied the sparrow, 'I was flying over the athletic club and got into the damnedest badminton game!'"

As himself again, Red Skelton relished his countless true-life experiences as an entertainer, on and off the stage. One particular small town in Pennsylvania amused Skelton when he was picked up to be taken to the town's fair for his appearance. He related how large the limousine was that pulled up in front of his hotel. Then Skelton off-handedly remarked, "By the way, all my life I work at being recognized so they meet me at the airport yesterday and the limo has black windows!" Getting back to his Pennsylvania story, Skelton related how the limo driver explained that the limousine was not his. "Oh, it's not mine," the driver confessed. "It belongs to the local undertaker." The driver insisted Skelton stop by the local hotel to say hello to his parents. When he went into the hotel lobby, an old lady was standing there. "Oh, I'm so glad to see you," said the old lady. "First time I felt so good in a long time. I lost my husband about a month ago." Skelton thought a minute then replied, "Want me to help you find him?" The old lady replied, "You rascal!" Skelton confessed he was just trying to make her laugh. "That's all right. Forget it," she replied. "At least I know where he is at night now."

Skelton asked the limo driver how he could thank the undertakers during his performance on stage to give them some recognition and free advertising. "Just knock 'em dead," replied the driver.

After Skelton's performance at the town's fair, it was time to go to the airport. No limo. "Instead it's a hearse," said Skelton. "We put my trunks and luggage in the back. I'm just sitting there. It's early morning and I hadn't been to sleep yet, so the driver says, 'Wanna lay down in the back?'" At that precise moment in the story, Skelton, as he had done previously, stopped to make a few remarks on a related subject. "I noticed something strange here (in Cleveland)," he observed seriously, "people die in alphabetical order!" Then he made a profound statement: "If you figure you're gonna die, let your creditors be your pallbearers." Skelton then smiled one of his impish smiles and while he laughed, he continued, "If they've carried you this far..."

Meanwhile back to his small town Pennsylvania story after his performance, Skelton had been driven to the airport in a hearse instead of a limousine. "We get to the airport and everybody's looking. I get out of the hearse and a little old lady walks up to me and asks, 'Is it too late to ask for an autograph?'" Skelton again smiled and confessed, "I like stories like that." Without missing a beat he told about seeing a show in New York. "What was going on in the audience was worse than what was going on onstage. This man was laying in the aisle and not moving. An usher came over thinking he was a drunk and said, 'Hey, get up and get out of here.' The man mumbled something but didn't move. The manager then comes over to the guy still lying in the aisle and tells him to get up and get out. The man mumbles but doesn't move. Finally, a policeman is sent for. 'Get up and get out of here! By the way, where are you from?' The guy mumbles, 'From the balcony.'"

As mentioned, Red Skelton was an excellent mime. His fluid movements rivaled his friend's, world famous French mime Marcel Marceau. Skelton even had a "silent spot" on his television show to display his physical, non-verbal pantomime genius. Skelton told us a story about Marceau. "He took some of his friends to attend an opera at the Paris Opera House and got the best seats," Skelton said. "He didn't like the music so he sat there with earplugs in his ears. The incident got back to the opera cast. They were, naturally, offended. Marceau's show opened two weeks later. All the people from the opera cast sat there in the (front row of the) audience... with blindfolds on!"

The press conference was winding down. Red Skelton answered questions from the media about his HBO specials, as well as the circumstances that led up to his famous version of The Pledge of Allegiance after viewing a Vietnam War protest demonstration in Canada. He also touched on why we will never see some releases of his black-and-white television shows.

At the end of the conference everyone patiently formed a line to meet Red Skelton. A chair had been provided for him. He politely posed for photographs and signed autographs. I took a picture of the newspaper staff photographer with Skelton as Red personalized the enlargement of a photo taken years before in Minnesota.

When it was my turn to meet Skelton, I politely greeted him and handed him a page from my reporter's notebook to sign. Thinking back, I should have asked him to sign the page, "Richard 'Red' Skelton," instead of "Red Skelton." I did not pass up the opportunity to ask him what kind of cigars he preferred. "Don Tomas," he replied. The newspaper photographer took a picture of us as Skelton autographed the notebook page.

I have two framed displays of Red Skelton. One is a collage of photos I took of him doing each trademark character at the press conference in 1992, with the article I wrote about him. Also in the frame is the invitation I saw on my entertainment editor's desk that led me to attend the memorable press conference and the autographed piece of paper. The other display is an article I wrote in September of 1997, just after Skelton passed away, recalling the press conference. In the display is the photo of me with Skelton. Both displays are, appropriately, mounted on *red* background paper.

In another part of my home is a double 8" x 10" frame of an autographed photo of Red Skelton I had obtained years before. He had a one-night performance at E. J. Thomas Performing Arts Hall on the campus of The University of Akron. In advance of his appearance I had requested an 8" x 10" photo of him and mailed it to Skelton in care of E. J. Thomas Performing Arts Hall with a letter and a self-addressed envelope. The autographed photo arrived at my home, inscribed, "Irv Korman, My thanks, dear friend." It was signed, "Red Skelton." I took the photo and put it in the double frame with an 8" x 10" enlargement of the picture of me with Skelton autographing the page from my reporter's notebook.

The most memorable thing I recall about the April 1992 press conference is a quotation that came from Red Skelton. It is etched in my mind forever when I think of the lovable comedian: "That's what's nice about show business: I haven't met a stranger in 50 years."

One of my greatest regrets is not attending one of his famous one-night performances.

I have lithographs of two of Red Skelton's famous Freddie the Freeloader paintings hanging on a wall, prominently displayed in my family room at home. One is entitled, "Freddie's Birthday," with the tramp clown holding a piece of cake, and the other is entitled, "Freddie and His Kitty Cat," showing the tramp clown holding a white kitty in the palm of one hand. How I acquired the two paintings would easily make up another chapter in this book.

Richard "Red" Skelton passed away in Rancho Mirage, California, on September 17, 1997. Mr. Skelton died of pneumonia at age 84.

Chapter 15
Douglas Fairbanks, Jr.

"They destroy everything they don't use in Hollywood."

Webster's New Collegiate Dictionary defines "junior" as . . . "being younger, used chiefly do distinguish a son with the same name given as his father." Also . . . "lower in standing or rank."

To be named "junior" can be a burden. But not for Douglas Fairbanks *Jr*, especially Friday evening, December 13, 1991 at the Akron Civic Theatre in downtown Akron, Ohio. The occasion seemed so right: a movie legend in a legendary movie *palace*.

About the time of Loews Theater's construction, Douglas Fairbanks Sr. was approaching the end of his movie career: just as his son's was beginning to prosper.

Douglas Fairbanks Sr. was the famous silent screen star and dashing, swashbuckling hero of such adventurous silent films as *The Mark of Zorro* (1921), *The Three Musketeers* (1921), *Robin Hood* (1922), *The Thief of Baghdad* (1924), *The Black Pirate* (1926), and *The Gaucho* (1927).

Douglas Sr.'s movie star status began to rise in 1915 when silent film directors William Ince, D.W. Griffith, and Mack Sennett formed Triangle Film Corporation and starred Doug Sr. in its silent films. In 1920, Fairbanks Sr., along with silent screen comic star Charlie Chaplin, director D.W. Griffith, and "America's Sweetheart," actress Mary Pickford, formed United Artists Corporation. This merging of talent enabled the group to choose their scripts, make their own movies, and, most importantly, distribute their films.

In 1923, Douglas Sr. married "America's Sweetheart," movie actress Mary Pickford. The two were treated as America's royalty reigning from their famed palatial estate, *Pickfair*, in Hollywood.

Douglas Fairbanks Jr's mother was Anna Beth Sully, Doug Sr.'s first wife. Doug Jr. was born in New York City on December 9, 1909. He began his movie career in silent films in 1923, at the age of 13, in

Stephen Steps Out. Fairbanks Sr. discouraged his son from going into film acting because he strongly felt the industry would only be capitalizing on the father's name; not the son's acting ability or potential.

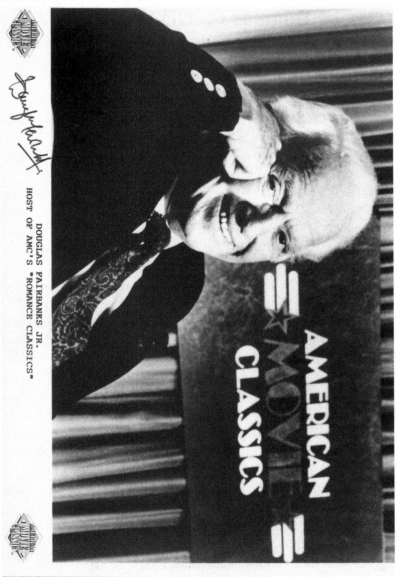

DOUGLAS FAIRBANKS JR.
HOST OF AMC'S "ROMANCE CLASSICS"

"The real reason I went to work (in films) was because my mother and I needed the money and we didn't want to make a public display of it," explained Fairbanks. "We didn't want to trouble my father with that."

On December 13, 1991 Fairbanks Jr. appeared at Akron at the Akron Civic Theatre to promote The American Movie Classics Channel inclusion into the Warner Cable choice of television program selections. Fairbanks was also scheduled to appear the following evening at the remodeled Palace Theatre in nearby Canton, Ohio (another refurbished Loews movie house) for the showing as well as personal observations and recollections concerning his appearance in the 1939 adventure classic RKO motion picture *Gunga Din*. The motion picture also starred Cary Grant. Fairbanks's appearance in Akron was for the showing and personal observations and recollections about his appearance in the 1933 RKO motion picture *Morning Glory* with a very young Broadway stage actress named Katharine Hepburn.

Fairbanks had just celebrated his 82nd birthday. He appeared moved and surprised when feted to a large birthday cake and a vocal rendition of "Happy Birthday" during a press party given by Warner Cable of Akron for the actor and the local media on the mezzanine level of the Akron Civic Theatre. The press party was scheduled just prior to his appearance before a general audience to introduce *Morning Glory,* accompanied by a few personal remarks. The Deputy Mayor of Akron attended the press party to present the distinguished actor with a proclamation from the mayor designating December 12, 1991 "Douglas Fairbanks Day" in Akron in honor of his 82nd birthday.

Fairbanks was truly a dashing figure with a tan face, accented by a pencil-thin moustache. He stood tall in a tailor-made suit accented by a fresh boutonniere in his lapel. Fairbanks freely mingled with the media during the press party. At times he sat on a richly carved antique chair that was strategically placed in front of a large Warner Cable American Movie Classics logo. He posed for photographs and signed autographs. I mentally visualized Fairbanks sitting in the antique chair, dressed in a period costume of a wealthy nobleman, surveying his kingdom and subjects as he did in many of his motion pictures. After the party I observed Fairbanks walking down the carpeted mezzanine lobby toward the Akron Civic Theatre stage. He stopped momentarily at a large table. He cautiously and patiently surveyed the dessert trays and carefully selected a few sweets, savoring them before continuing down to the auditorium.

Fairbanks had had an adventurous career in motion pictures. In 1930 Fairbanks appeared in three memorable movies: *Dawn Patrol, Outward Bound,* and *Little Caesar.* During the rest of that decade Fairbanks starred in British motion pictures *Catherine the Great* (1934), *Jump for Glory* (1937), and *The Prisoner of Zenda* (1937).

The Prisoner of Zenda, in particular, showcased Fairbanks in his very first action-packed swashbuckling portrayal that rivaled the films of his father. Father and son grew much closer in the late 1930s. There was even some speculation of a movie starring both father and son just before Fairbanks Sr. died in 1939.

Fairbanks made *The Corsican Brothers* in 1941 just before the outbreak of World War II, playing a dual role of twin brothers. Fairbanks then put his acting career on "hold" to help the Allied Cause during World War II.

During the war Fairbanks served with distinction as a lieutenant commander with the U. S. Navy. He was eventually awarded the Silver Star and the Legion of Merit with "V" for *valor* from the U. S. government for his combat service on PT boats and gunboats.

After World War II, Fairbanks returned to making films in both England and the United States. In the early 1950s the actor saw the potential of the new medium of television. He produced a series of 160 one-act plays for television, appearing in 40 of them. The program was called *Douglas Fairbanks Presents.* About the same time, another motion picture swashbuckler, Errol Flynn, also noticed the potential of television and did the very same thing in England.

Fairbanks's career and talent were not relegated to 80 motion pictures. He also appeared in dozens of live stage theatrical touring productions of *Romeo and Juliet, The Pleasure of His Company, My Fair Lady*, and *Sleuth.*

Fairbanks appeared in his last motion picture, *Ghost Story*, in 1981, co-starring Fred Astaire, Melvin Douglas, and John Houseman.

During Fairbanks's remarks to the Akron Civic Theatre audience on December 13, 1991, he reflected on *Ghost Story,* wishing the movie would have been released in its original four-hour length format, not the final two-hour drastically edited version. "The rest of it was probably destroyed. They destroy everything they don't use in Hollywood," Fairbanks said.

Fairbanks further lamented about the term *Golden Age of Hollywood.* "There never was a *Golden Age of Hollywood,*" he explained. "It was always *yesterday.* We looked over our shoulders in the 1930s and 1940s and said World War I films were the *Golden Age.*"

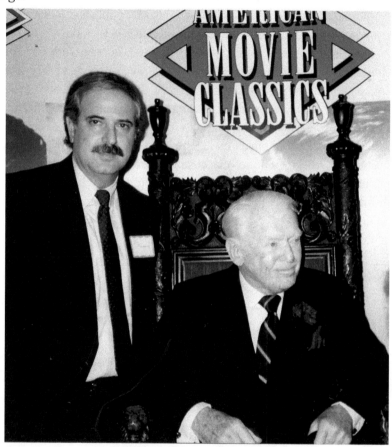

Fairbanks had humorously begun his remarks earlier after glancing out at the large audience and observing, "I feel like a mosquito at a nudist camp: I don't know where to begin!" He then apologized for having a slight limp when he walked out onstage to the podium after his introduction. "I injured my knee during the filming of a little picture called *Gunga Din* in 1939." After the audience applauded Fairbanks added, "I liked working with Betty Grable, Greta Garbo, Greer Garson, and did six films with Loretta Young."

At age 82, Douglas Fairbanks Jr. was a widower, having been

married to Mary Lee Epling from 1939 to 1988. He had three married daughters, Daphne, Victoria, and Melissa, and eight grandchildren. Fairbanks had been previously married to actress Joan Crawford from 1929 to 1933.   He married Vera Shelton in 1991 and remained married to her until his death in May of 2000.

Fairbanks's autobiography *Salad Days* was published in 1988. A second book, *A Hell of a War,* was published in 1993.

Douglas Fairbanks Jr. died on May 7, 2000, in New York City, of respiratory problems. He was 90. When I learned of his death I fondly recalled meeting him in December of 1991. I still think of his Akron appearance as a movie legend appearing in a legendary movie theater. The image of him is still very clear to me today; that of a handsome, physically fit and tanned male movie star with a pencil-thin moustache, wearing a tailor-made suit adorned with a freshly cut boutonniere and flashing a pearly-white movie star smile. This image will forever be etched in my mind as the epitome of a male movie star with *class*.

Chapter 16
Steve Allen

"Steve Allen does so many things, he's the only man I know who's listed on every one of the Yellow Pages!"

>...... Andy Williams, singer and friend of Steve Allen

The most multitalented person I ever interviewed and/or reviewed was Steve Allen. Allen appeared in Akron, Ohio, at Carousel Dinner Theatre, from August 10-13, 1988, and again from April 14-16, 1991. Not only was he prolific on radio and television, but Allen was also an actor (Broadway and motion pictures), a composer (writing over 7,400 songs and recording 49 albums) and author of over 50 books. How could he NOT be multitalented?

From reports I had received until actually interviewing Allen via telephone on April 9, 1991, I heard that he was very quiet and reserved on a one-to-one basis. This would immediately change when Allen was in a crowd or in front of a live television audience.

Stephen Valentine Patrick William Allen was born on December 26, 1921, in New York City. Both parents were vaudeville comedians. His father, Carroll Allen, died when Steve was only 18 months old. His mother, Isabelle (Belle Montrose), continued in vaudeville as a single act, moving to Chicago, where young Steve was raised by her family. Allen's childhood was very unhappy, due in part to attending 18 different public schools. He attended, but never graduated from Iowa University and Arizona University. It was in Phoenix, Arizona, that Allen met and married his first wife, Dorothy Goodman. They had three sons together (Steve Jr., born in 1944, is a doctor; Brian, born in 1947, is now in real estate; and David, born in 1949, is a songwriter). Allen divorced Goodman in 1952 and married actress Jayne Meadows in 1954.

Following a brief military career (drafted in 1943 then released due to asthma) Allen became a writer and announcer for Phoenix, Arizona, radio station KOY. In 1945, Allen with his wife and infant son (and a total savings of $1,000) moved to Los Angeles, California. In 1946 he was hired as a disc jockey for a Los Angeles radio station. After two years on the Mutual Broadcasting Company, Allen got a half-hour music and talk show on the local CBS radio outlet, KNX. He began inviting Hollywood celebrities to his show to plug their movies. Within a year the format was expanded to one hour and quickly became the most popular nighttime show in the history of Los Angeles radio, with a standing-room-only audience in the broadcast studio.

One evening Allen had arranged for movie actress Doris Day to be on his radio show, setting aside a 25-minute block of time. When Doris Day failed to show up, Allen picked up the floor microphone and ad-libbed with the total strangers in the studio audience, beginning Allen's famous ad lib, man-on-the-street, interview format (which would eventually become the basic trademark for *The Tonight Show*).

By 1950, the CBS executives decided Steve Allen was ready for the next logical step: television in New York City. For the next three years Allen guest-starred on numerous early CBS television daytime and evening programs such as *This Is Show Business,* and *What's My Line?* Allen also hosted a weekly series called *Songs for Sale.*

Though it looked like Allen was attaining success, he personally felt that he'd reached a stagnant plateau. Also, his marriage to Dorothy Goodman was failing, eventually ending in divorce in 1954.

But things steadily improved for Allen. NBC had a 90-minute block of television airtime for a program titled, *Tonight*. NBC turned this concept over to Allen who developed the nightly show into *The Tonight Show.*

Also, by this time, Allen had met actress Jayne Meadows. Meadows was born in Wu Chang, China, where her parents were Episcopalian missionaries for 14 years. By the time she met Allen, Meadows had been on every continent except Australia and could speak several languages. She would eventually star in motion pictures with Katharine Hepburn, Gregory Peck and David Niven. She also appeared on Broadway in *Another Love Story, Kiss Them for Me*, and *Spring Again.* Allen and Meadows had one son, Bill, born in 1957, who is an internet executive. Within one year Allen's personal life and television career had turned completely around. He married Jayne

Meadows and *The Tonight Show* was the most talked-about show on television. This thrust Steve Allen into the rank of television superstar.

By 1956, thanks to *The Tonight Show*, Allen had discovered Steve Lawrence and Eydie Gorme, as well as Andy Williams. Other stars that owe Allen for early appearances on *The Tonight Show* include Louis Nye, Don Knotts, Tom Poston, the Smothers Brothers, Don Adams, Bill Dana, Jim Nabors, Jackie Vernon, Lenny Bruce, Jonathan Winters, Tim Conway, Lou Rawls, Jackie Mason, and Miriam Makeba.

There seemed to be no end to Allen's talent or stamina. For a few months in 1956 Allen was doing his 90-minute weeknight *The Tonight Show,* plus a weekly Sunday night hour-long comedy show opposite *The Ed Sullivan Show,* while starring in Universal-International's motion picture, *The Benny Goodman Story.* It was also in 1956 that Allen became one of the first variety show hosts to book an up-and-coming rock 'n' roll singer named Elvis Presley. The singer had just come out with his hit song, "Hound Dog" and was being criticized for his unorthodox and controversial lower-body gyrations. Allen came up with the idea of having Elvis appear in a formal tuxedo while standing still and singing "Hound Dog" to an actual hound dog, a basset hound, also dressed in a formal tuxedo outfit.

The pace, even for Allen, was becoming too much. He decided to give up *The Tonight Show,* suggesting to NBC that either Jack Paar or Ernie Kovacs would make an excellent host replacement. At first NBC ignored Allen's suggestion and came up with a show called *America After Dark.* A few months later, after very low ratings, NBC decided Allen was right after all. *The Tonight Show* returned with Jack Paar as host.

Allen's other television efforts included *The Steve Allen Show* for NBC on Sunday nights that ran neck-and-neck with *The Ed Sullivan Show* until 1960 when the show ended. It earned Allen an Emmy Award for Best Comedy Show of 1960.

From 1961-62 Allen appeared in a weekly comedy hour series on ABC and the following year returned to NBC with his old *Tonight Show* format. After three years he then went to CBS for another three years to emcee *I've Got a Secret.*

Allen's proudest television accomplishment was *Meeting of the Minds,* which ran on PBS (Public Broadcast System) from 1977-1980. Allen, as host, moderated a panel of actors impersonating historic figures such as Galileo, Charles Darwin and Attila the Hun, who explained their various philosophies and spoke on great issues. Many of the female roles, such as Emily Dickinson and Cleopatra were played by Allen's wife, Jayne Meadows.

In his later years Allen became a critic of the increased sexual content on television, accusing tabloid talk shows of "taking television to the garbage dump."

I usually interview a celebrity over the telephone about one week prior to their area appearance. Then I also review the actual performance. With Steve Allen it was the reverse: I reviewed his performance at Carousel Dinner Theatre in 1988 and then interviewed him over the telephone just prior to his 1991 appearance at Carousel.

I reviewed Allen's matinee show on August 10, 1988, at Carousel Dinner Theatre. Since it was our 19th wedding anniversary I took my wife to the performance. Carousel's usual format with a single star was to have an opening act (usually a singer or comedian), an intermission, and then the featured performer. Not with Allen. He *was* the entire evening. While people ate dinner before the show, note cards found at each place setting were filled out by each patron, if they so chose. The completed cards were then taken to Allen backstage who would eventually read several selected cards aloud and then immediately respond to them onstage during the second act of his performance. That's how spontaneous and witty he was.

As soon as the first-act curtain rose, there was six-foot, three inch, 193-pound Steve Allen in a tuxedo seated at a piano. He informed his audience that he was staying at "the Oatmeal Hilton," which was then a Hilton Hotel, called the Quaker Square Hilton, located in downtown Akron. The facility had once been the headquarters of the Quaker Oats Company. Its visual trademark was a group of several imposing tall cement silos which stored the company's oats that would eventually be made into cereal. The developer who purchased the property constructed hotel rooms out of the massive silos. Each room was, naturally, round. The rest of the property was turned into a multi-level retail shopping complex.

Allen told his audience that his first job in show business was as an "ah-ah" man at a theater in Chicago. "My job," explained Allen, "was to stand between the men's and women's bathrooms at the theater. If a patron headed for the wrong door, I'd say, 'ah-ah.'"

Allen said he would try to be *straight* during his performance but that, "my mind sometimes goes *sideways*." This was followed by not only audience laughter but Allen laughing as well with his trademark high-pitched vibrato laugh. At times he laughed so hard that his shoulders shook up and down.

Allen's entire performance seemed relaxed and informal. One got the impression that they were in Allen's living room, spending an informal evening with him. He seemed momentarily annoyed by two large spotlights directly trained on him. He looked up at them, winced and said, "I've seen lights nowhere else except maybe at the Nuremberg Trials."

Allen mentioned that there were many songs written and sung about countless islands, all except one. He began playing a Latin, tropical melody on the piano and singing about "Three-Mile Island." He continued his obscure lyrics by singing the menu from a Mexican restaurant. It reminded me of a classic Allen routine from *The Tonight Show* where he attempted to seriously read the lyrics to the popular rock 'n' roll tune, "Be-Bop-A-Lu-La."

Allen would periodically stop during his performance and drink a glass of orange juice. "I need to wet my whistle," he said. "I can't sing with a *dry* whistle!"

After a short intermission, at which time he remained at his piano backstage eating dinner and going over the note cards from the audience, Allen once again appeared in his tuxedo at the piano. "You know," he observed, "flying is the best way of getting anywhere late."

Allen then began reading from the audience note cards. One card praised Allen of having a clean act. "Damn right," he replied. Another card commented on Allen's infectious laugh. "I'd better have that infection taken care of," he said.

One card asked Allen if he'd ever visited the fjords. "Yes," replied Allen. "As a matter of fact we visited Betty and Gerald 'Fjord' quite recently!"

Allen confessed that the music of the 1920s, '30s and '40s was his favorite. He liked the music of Jerome Kern, Irving Berlin, George Gershwin and Cole Porter. Allen played so effortlessly on the piano that the instrument seemed to be a natural extension of his body.

Allen next sang a song about mouth-to-mouth resuscitation, followed by another song made up of love song titles to the melody of "Honeysuckle Rose."

Toward the end of his performance, Allen sang two of his more notable musical compositions, "South Rampart Street Parade" and "Gravy Waltz." Responding to my wife's note card he honored the occasion of our wedding anniversary by playing one of my wife's favorite tunes, the theme from the movie *Picnic*, which he wrote. You may not be aware of the fact he also wrote the theme song for the popular television sitcom, *Mary Hartman, Mary Hartman*.

Steve Allen concluded the show by playing his theme song, "This Could Be the Start of Something Big," which was a hit recording for one of Allen's discoveries; Steve Lawrence and Eydie Gorme.

Though I did not get to meet Allen personally that night, I was later presented with a personalized, autographed 8" x 10" publicity photograph, inscribed: "To Irv-Best Wishes." It was signed "Steve Allen."

Another aspect about Steve Allen that I learned about from his 1988 Carousel Dinner Theatre appearance was that he traveled alone, employing no agent, road manager, or publicity agent. I eventually learned from Larry Pentecost, the man who chauffeured Allen around town during his two Akron appearances, that Allen always carried a pocket tape recorder with him to record his many spontaneous ideas so that he would not forget them.

Almost three years later, on April 6, 1991, I had the opportunity to interview Steve Allen via telephone before his upcoming appearance, again, at Carousel Dinner Theatre from April 14 to 16.

I prefaced the interview by thanking Allen for playing the theme from the movie *Picnic,* during his 1988 concert, in honor of my 19th wedding anniversary since I did not get the opportunity to thank him in person after his performance.

I began the telephone interview by asking Allen if there was anything he had not done yet that he would like to try. "No," was his immediate reply, "the world has let me do everything I ever imagined that might be amusing to experiment with. I have no complaints." Allen explained that he had the same enjoyment factor whether working in television, movies, writing, or other creative endeavors. "I have no favorite artistic pursuit," he admitted. As of the 1991 telephone interview Allen had been in his "artistic pursuits" for 45 years.

I asked Allen what was in his near future. "More comedy shows, symphony concerts, and my 35th book," he said. "The book was originally titled 'The Mystery of the Bible' but was changed to 'Steve Allen on the Bible, Religion, and Morality.'"

I was curious as to how Steve Allen learned about performing at Carousel Dinner Theatre in Akron, Ohio. "They must have written me," he said. As an after-thought he added, "Everyone in show business is available anywhere. You can have Michael Jackson or Bob Hope at your daughter's 'coming out party.' It's just a matter of money. I'm not joking. For a million bucks I assure you Michael Jackson would show up."

Recalling how much fun and publicity wife Jayne Meadows' shopping sprees had received during Allen's 1988 Akron appearance I asked if she was coming to Akron this trip. "No," replied Allen, "she has commitments in Florida, New York City, and Washington."

I always wanted to ask Steven Allen about his talk show format that so revolutionized late night television. "I will take bows for some other things I have accomplished (but) I really feel uncomfortable for creating that (talk show)." He further explained. "There is not much to a talk show. Millions of years ago cavemen sat on a stump one evening and one caveman remarked he caught a fish that day. Another one asks if that is a bear skin he is wearing. 'Yes, I killed it about three weeks ago.' Literally, there is a talk show!" Allen would later expound on the topic. "Inventing the talk program was, frankly, rather like inventing, oh, the paper towel. The result is useful, a source of enormous profits, and the world is somewhat better off for it. But it's hardly to be compared to doing a successful weekly prime-time comedy series, painting an unforgettable picture, composing a beautiful musical score or discovering a cure for a crippling disease."

I strongly felt Steve Allen's second passion (television being his first) was writing, due to having authored 35 books as of 1991. Allen's latest book, "Dumbth," had just come out in paperback. The book concerned the current situation in education in America. His interest had nothing to do with the fact that he traveled a lot as a child and attended many schools. "Whatever I'm interested in is something I will write about," was Allen's explanation.

I asked Allen about getting people in America to read more. "Convince people when they are young and impressionable," was his answer. "It's too late to begin with someone who is 47 years old. If you can get them when they are seven and read to them, give them books for Christmas, etc. Television is so much easier: your brain is on hold and your eyes are affixed to it." Allen himself was a voracious reader. He did not understand people who thought nothing of spending a lot of money for a bottle of liquor that is consumed in a few days while balking at paying the same amount of money on a book that would last a lifetime. Allen was also appalled at the fact that our nation, with the highest literacy rate in the world, had such a deplorable reading record.

With Allen always working on several projects at once I asked him how he relaxed. "I was born relaxed," he replied. "I am not a 'hyper-type.' My brain never stops nor should it. The one part of your body that doesn't sleep is your brain. I'm perfectly willing to work seven days a week. I always enjoy it. I'll stay at home Saturday or Sunday but I'm always working, painting, writing music, or editing a manuscript. It's all fun for me so I feel no pressure from it." At the time of Allen's 1991 Akron appearance he had eight books in the works, six plays or musicals in various stages of preparation, motion picture properties, and plans to release another record album.

I asked Allen what he thought of television of the day (1991). "TV always was lousy as it is today." He liked *The Golden Girls, Cheers* and *The Cosby Show.* *"The Roseanne Barr Show* is funny," he said, "if you can get over certain problems having to do with taste, but the funniness is certainly there. The new show based on a movie where a baby talks, is funny. Classics like *Taxi* and *Barney Miller* are good sitcoms. *All in the Family* improved comedies. 1950s sitcoms like *Leave It to Beaver* were stupid; for nine year-olds. Yes, *I Love Lucy* and Gleason were great. But name 14 more!"

While on the subject of current television trends I asked Allen what he thought of cable television. "They haven't improved anything," he said. "They merely have watered things down." After a few seconds Allen then said, "But I am grateful to The Comedy Channel because my old NBC comedy series from the 1950s is on every morning and night."

Having an entertainment legend on the other end of the telephone, I asked Allen what advice he had for up-and-coming comics. His response was quick and short. "See Red Skelton," was his reply.

Allen said he still socially met with his famous "Man On the Street" cast from his old *Tonight Show,* including Dayton Allen (whose famous retort was, "Why not?"), Gabe Dell (who often spoofed Dracula), Tom Poston (whose persona was always forgetting his name), Louie Nye ("Hi, ho, Steverino!"), Don Knotts (Question:

"Are you nervous?" Knotts' answer: NOOO!"), Bill Dana (Jose Jimenez), and Pat Harrington.

Allen concluded the telephone interview by confessing he liked to answer questions from audience note cards in the second half of his performances. "No two shows are alike," he said matter-of-factly.

Steve Allen garnered many honors in his lifetime, including induction into The TV Academy's Hall of Fame in 1986. He was honored in the 1985 edition of *The Guinness Book of Records* as the most prolific composer of modern times, yet he considered himself a musical illiterate because he did not read music!

One of Steve Allen's greatest personal accomplishments was beating colon cancer in 1986, which later went into remission.

Prescott Griffith, owner of Carousel Dinner Theatre during Allen's two Akron appearances, fondly recalled Allen mentioning Carousel Dinner Theatre on television on *The Larry King Show*, describing Carousel "looking like a Las Vegas show room." Griffith also recalled Jayne Meadows' publicity during her memorable shopping sprees during Allen's 1988 appearance. "We enjoyed him," said Griffith. "He kept sending us a copy of a musical version of *A Christmas Carol* he was working on for us to think about doing. I also got a Christmas card from him every year until about five years before his death." Griffith also recalled Allen carrying a portable tape recorder around to record his ideas on.

At the time of his death, Allen had written 52 books, composed 7,400 songs and recorded 49 record albums.

Allen considered himself a self-styled advocate of "radical middle-of-the-roadism," speaking out on political matters such as capital punishment, nuclear policy and freedom of expression.

Allen's death, on Monday, October 30, 2000, was officially ruled "a coronary event due to road accident." He and wife Jayne Meadows were driving to son, Bill Allen's house in Encino, California, for dinner when they were involved in a minor car accident that thrust Allen into the car's steering wheel, unknowingly bruising his heart. "He was a little tired after dinner," son Bill recalled. "He went to relax, peacefully, and never reawakened." Allen was 78 years old.

The life and talent of Steve Allen can best be summed up by his friend, singer Andy Williams: "Steve does so many things, he's the only man I know who's listed on every one of the Yellow Pages."

Chapter 17
Milton Berle

"I don't steal other people's jokes. I find them before they're lost."

"A *comic* says funny things; a *comedian* says things funny."

He did it all during his 93 years: the model for Buster Brown shoes, appearing in silent films (with Charlie Chaplin in "Tillie's Punctured Romance" and with Pearl White in "The Perils of Pauline"), vaudeville, radio, television, and motion pictures. He was known as "Uncle Millie," "Mr. Tuesday Night," "The Thief of Bad Gags," and "Mr. Television." He was overbearing, smoked big cigars, and often appeared on his weekly television show in drag. One of his famous tag lines was, "I'll kil-wul; I swear I'll kil-wul you."

On a local, more personal level, Berle remembered performing in Akron several times in his vaudeville career, recalling appearances at the Colonial theater in the 1920s. He also remembered babysitting a little boy backstage for a vaudeville comedienne named Belle Montrose. The little boy's name was Steve Allen. I had the good fortune of meeting Milton Berle after his March 1980 appearance in the Sultan's Cabaret at Tangier Restaurant.

When one looks back on Berle's life it seems he didn't quite find his niche in the entertainment world until the advent of television. He seemed to do well in vaudeville, movies, radio and theatre. That was before he earned such accolades as "Mr. Television" and "Mr. Tuesday Night."

Born in New York City as Mendel Berlinger on July 12, 1908, to Moses and Sarah Berlinger, Berle was one of five children (Phil, born in 1901; Francis, born in 1904; Jack, born in 1905; and Rosalind, born in 1913). Berle's strong-willed mother, Sarah, saw to it her son, Milton, was educated at New York's Professional Children's School when he began performing at age five. His first stage appearance was in "Floradora" in Atlantic City. In his autobiography, *Milton Berle*, published by Dell Publishing in 1974, Berle's impersonation of Charlie Chaplin led to his appearance in a silent motion-picture serial being filmed in nearby New Jersey, called *The Perils of Pauline* in 1914. As a result of Berle's "pushy" mother, Sarah, little Milton eventually was taken to Hollywood, California, to appear in such silent films as *Tillie's Punctured Romance* with Marie Dressler and Charlie Chaplin, directed by Mack Sennett (1915), *Rebecca of Sunnybrook Farm* with Mary Pickford (1917), and *The Mark of Zorro* with Douglas Fairbanks, Sr. (1920).

A foray into vaudeville soon followed with Berle studying Eddie Cantor, Al Jolson, and other entertainers of the day (he was already emulating others). The 1930s showcased Berle as a working comedian in vaudeville houses and even on Broadway in such revues as "The Ziegfeld Follies" and "The Earl Carroll Vanities." In the late 1930s and early 1940s Berle was featured on radio and tried to break into Hollywood movies once again. His early motion picture parts were of usually brash and pushy funnymen. He scored in the motion picture, *Broadway Faces of 1937*, followed by roles in such films as *Tall, Dark, and Handsome* (1941), *Whispering Ghosts* (1942) and *Margin for Error* (1943).

Vaudeville, radio, and Broadway kept Berle working steadily but not attaining "headliner" or "star" status. That all changed in 1948. Although Berle was earlier involved in a 1929 experiment with a new invention called "scanning-wheel television" in Chicago, it was the *new* medium of television that changed his career and the entertainment world forever.

Milton Berle was a middle-aged vaudeville and nightclub comic in 1948 when he was asked by the National Broadcasting Corporation (NBC) to create a variety show for the new medium of television. At the time the United States had a population of 150 million with only 150,000 television sets.

Looking back on his early entrance into television, Berle said, "When I started out with the Texaco series in 1948, television was brand new, and I knew as much about it as anyone else. I was in charge of everything because I wanted to be," he recalled. "We didn't have any (television) experts in 1948." *Texaco Star Theater* ran eight years, beaming entertainment into the home 34 weeks per year, *live*. Back then NBC gave Berle a weekly budget of $15,000 per show. In today's dollars that amount could easily exceed over a half-million dollars!

The original NBC concept was a weekly, live variety show with a different host each week. The opening telecast on June 8, 1948, had Berle as the program's first host. The following weeks featured Henny Youngman, Jack Carter, and Harry Richmond as guest hosts. It wasn't until September that NBC invited Berle back. The sponsors decided on a permanent host and settled on Berle.

In 1948 not everyone had a television set in their home. It was not uncommon for half the neighborhood to gather in someone's living room on Tuesday night to watch Berle's *Texaco Star Theater*. It was also not uncommon for people to gather outside on the sidewalk in front of an appliance store to watch Uncle Miltie through a plate glass window. Neighborhood bars had a new draw to entice customers into their establishments by mounting a television console behind the bar. Patrons could watch television while socializing and imbibing their favorite alcoholic beverage. Many media experts credit Berle with being a major factor in households purchasing their very first television set. Decades later Berle would reflect on this phenomenon and joke, "I helped sell television sets. When I was on, my aunt sold her set, my uncle sold his!"

For eight years the *Texaco Star Theater*, with Berle as host, featured brash and raucous comedy skits, guest stars, and lavish production numbers. The hour began with Berle entering onstage in an outrageous costume, often in drag (which he frequently did in vaudeville) after being introduced by a singing quartet in Texaco service uniforms.

Some early television trivia buffs may recall Berle's cast of regulars. Comic actress Ruth Gilbert portrayed Berle's secretary, Max, who had a terminal crush on the host. She would always remind Berle that the love she had for him was "bigger than both of us." Also in Berle's cast of characters was pitchman Sid Stone who, in derby hat, would roll up his sleeves, look the television viewer in the eye and say, "Tell you what I'm gonna do." Ventriloquist Jimmy Nelson and his alter ego, Danny O'Day, were also permanent cast members, usually dressed in Texaco gas station uniforms. Arnold Stang would be on hand wearing thick glasses and bowtie, continually putting Berle in his place by mocking, "Chip. Chip. Big Man. Big Man!" Whenever Berle would holler "make up!" a midget in smock and beret would immediately run onstage and pelt the host with an enormous powder puff leaving Berle reeling off balance, covered in white powder, almost knocking him over.

The historical impact of Berle on Tuesday night television was staggering for its time. On Tuesday nights restaurants almost emptied, stores had to close early while theater and movie attendance plummeted. It is reported Berle had a staggering 80% of the television audience (recent televised Academy Award shows garnered only

25%) on Tuesday nights all to himself and his *Texaco Star Theater.* The show was the top rated television program in 1950 and 1951. It was in the top ten rated shows through 1954.

Berle was not the only one on television Tuesday nights. Bishop Fulton J. Sheen's *Life Is Worth Living* began broadcasting in 1953. "Uncle Miltie" often acknowledged the competition between him and Sheen by referring to him as "Uncle Fultie." Berle would also remark, "We both work for the same boss: Sky Chief." Sheen reportedly enjoyed the ribbing. Berle would also remark about the competition, "He (Fulton) stayed on longer than I did because, let's face it, he had better writers: Mark, Luke..."

NBC would eventually award Berle a 30-year contract. Upon hearing the news Groucho Marx reportedly stated, "30 years with NBC? That's not a contract that's a sentence!" Speaking of Groucho, Berle once confessed, "You know, Groucho, I've stolen some of my best jokes from you." Marx, without missing a beat, replied, "Then you weren't listening."

With changing demographics and a new television generation emerging, *Texaco Star Theater* went off the air in 1956. Berle returned to television to launch new series in 1958 and 1966, but they fell flat. Undaunted, Berle discovered he was in demand as a guest star on talk-shows, television series and even movies. A few of his more memorable performances on television included "Louie the Lilac," one of Batman's villains on the popular 1960's series, as well as guest shots on *Roseanne, The Nanny, Murder, She Wrote, Burke's Law, Matlock, Fresh Prince of Bel-Air, The Love Boat, Different Strokes,* and on the game show, *Hollywood Squares.*

Berle received rave reviews for his serious portrayal as one of seven blind passengers stranded in the desert in the made-for-television movie, *Seven in Darkness* in 1969. Motion picture parts included him as himself in Woody Allen's *Broadway Danny Rose* (1984), a female patient in Jerry Lewis' *Cracking Up* (1983), used-car salesman Mad Man Mooney in *The Muppet Movie* (1979), a blind man in *Won Ton Ton, the Dog Who Saved Hollywood* (1976), Luther Burton in *Who's Minding the Mint?* (1967), and J. Russell Finch in *It's a Mad Mad Mad Mad World* (1963). Berle appeared in the 1965 cult classic motion picture, *The Loved One*, as Mr. Kenton. Billed as "the movie to offend everyone," *The Loved One* took a satirical poke at the "business" of the funeral business.

In 1980, Milton Berle was scheduled to appear in the Sultan's Cabaret in Akron's Tangier Restaurant, February 26th through March 2nd for two shows nightly. Ticket prices back then ranged from $10.00 to $15.00 with the usual two-drink minimum.

Opening night at the Tangier Restaurant usually featured a small press party for invited guests and the press after the show in one of

the restaurant's many banquet rooms.

At age 72, Milton Berle had not slowed down one bit. It was 8:30 PM. After his introduction to the opening night crowd, followed by thunderous applause, Berle turned to the band onstage behind him and said, "This is a good audience." Berle's one-hour-and-fifteen-minute set had begun.

Opening remarks lovingly ridiculed restaurant owner Ed George, the city of Akron, and his accommodations in the nearby downtown Cascade Holiday Inn. Berle would periodically look at someone in the audience seated close to the stage and ask, "Are you gonna listen or laugh?" or "Are you awake?" Berle even laughed at some of his own punch lines. Polish jokes, ridiculing current television commercials and women who were intimidating were the topics of most of Berle's comic jabs.

Berle was a crafty spinner of funny yarns. He wisely protected himself by prefacing most of his jokes by saying, "Danny Thomas told me this story...," "Frank Sinatra told me this one...," "Buddy Hackett told me this joke...," or "Johnny Carson told me this one..."

Berle held a trumpet for about 20 minutes but never played it. The band behind him played "Muskrat Ramble" and "When the Saints Come Marching In." Berle did sing, quite tenderly as a matter of fact, to "May To December." He remarked about some silver strands in his hair. He said they reminded him of his dear mother, Sarah, who passed away in May of 1954. If you view old kinescope recordings of the *Texaco Star Theater*, you can occasionally spy Sarah in the audience. But you can also hear her outlandish laugh that often made the rest of the audience giggle.

"It's nice to see you face to face," Berle told the Tangier audience. "You are very entertaining." Recalling the precision timing of live television, Berle confessed, "It's nice *not* to have to watch a clock all the time." Berle, at age 72, did not seem to sweat. He looked completely dry and relaxed on the Sultan's Cabaret stage. "I like to make people laugh," he confessed to his audience. Reacting to the thunderous applause and warm audience responses to his jokes, Berle said, "Give me an audience like you for the rest of my life." The Tangier audience also learned that Berle had a stock of heckler retorts in case of an emergency. Luckily, he did not have to employ any of them during his initial performance. He also said he had a file at home of six-and-a-half million jokes. It made me wonder if they were divided into two sections: his and ones he "borrowed" from others. I later recalled his quote from a 1986 interview when the subject of his "borrowing" surfaced. "I don't steal other people's jokes," he said. "I find them before they're lost."

Berle also observed, "Audiences are the same as vaudeville audiences, but older. Older jokes are still funny today."

Immediately after Berle's one-hour-and-fifteen-minute performance, invited guests made their way to the nearby reserved party room for the Berle reception. Guests and the press mingled as all waited for the guest of honor. Owner Ed George strolled in and sampled some of the buffet food. Nibbling on a delicacy he was heard to remark, "This is better than the stuff in the restaurant."

Milton Berle bounded into the reception room and began table hopping. As I followed his moves from table to table I heard some of his comments to patron questions. "My advice to new comics is to keep your eyes and ears open," he advised. "Know what to do and not to do. Do community theater. Get out in front of an audience. Do comedy and improv stores."

Berle also equated a comic to being a boxer: "Train and shadow box by and with yourself. But the true test is in the ring (onstage) with your opponent (audience)."

One of Berle's more enduring observations about being a professional comedian was: "to be a comic you need to be born with a funny bone." I also learned that after his Tangier appearance Berle was going back to California to begin rehearsal in the role of Nathan Detroit for the Civic Light Opera's upcoming production of "Guys and Dolls" at the Dorothy Chandler Pavilion. Berle said the part of Nathan Detroit was originally written for him.

Having a printed program for him to sign and a camera in my pocket I thought I would approach Berle to sign the program and pose for a photograph. As I scanned the room I suddenly realized he was gone! I approached Marge Thomas, the public relations person for Tangier Restaurant, and inquired where he was. "Oh, he just left," she said. We immediately bounded into the hallway and saw Berle down the hall. We called for him to stop. As he turned around I politely introduced myself, told him I did a story about him for a local newspaper and presented him with a copy. I then asked him if he would kindly autograph my printed program and pose for a quick photograph with me. With a large cigar in his left hand he obliged on both accounts, turned around and preceded back down the hallway. Much later, after the photograph was developed I looked at the cigar in Berle's left hand and noticed the cigar band. I wish I had a strong enough magnifying glass to determine what brand he smoked. I recalled asking Red Skelton what brand he "chewed" and found out it was Don Tomas.

After his 1980 appearance at Tangier Restaurant in Akron, Ohio, Berle continued to guest star on television programs and game shows. He continued his college seminars on humor. He also appeared on talk shows and in motion pictures.

Berle returned to Northeastern Ohio, four years later, in 1984, to appear at Carousel Dinner Theatre (then located in Ravenna) with Bernie Wayne from November 6-11.

In a 1996 interview with Larry King, Berle confessed he lives to laugh and laughs to live. When King asked him about retirement, at age 88, he retorted, "Retire to what?" Berle was now adding nursing homes to his list of places to visit.

Berle also recalled to Larry King about a $600 cigar humidor he had purchased and presented President John F. Kennedy. Berle then confessed he did not want to pay the asking price $595,000 it eventually sold for at a recent auction.

On a more humorous topic, King asked Berle about his 51-year-old wife. "We almost make love every night of the week," he boasted. "We *almost* made love Monday, we *almost* made love Tuesday . . ."

On the same subject Berle told King, "We made love for one hour and three minutes. That's the night they turned the clocks back!"

Two years later, now at age 90, Berle was once again interviewed by King and was asked about television censorship. It was immediately evident that age had not affected his mental capacities. Berle immediately retorted, "I was just in Las Vegas and saw Hoover *Darn*. (Recently) when I was in New Jersey we came in on a *heck*-a-copter."

Berle disagreed with King about the observation, "A comedian says funny things; a comic says things funny." Berle strongly felt the opposite: "A *comic* says funny things; a *comedian* says things funny."

Berle began to suffer health problems in the early 1990's. In

December, 1991, he suffered a mild stroke at his home in California. In April of 2001, he was diagnosed with a slow-growing cancerous tumor in his colon. Doctors said he did not need surgery at the time and the cancer would take 10 to 12 years to affect him. He passed away at his home on March 27, 2002, as a result of the advancing cancer.

I like to think "Mr. Television" is still "knockin' 'em dead" on that big entertainment stage in the sky competing against other greats such as Jackie Gleason, Eddie Cantor, and Jack Benny while, unknown to them, still stealing their best material (including Groucho's).

In retrospect, I often wonder what happened to Berle's collection of over 6 million jokes. Where are the joke collections of Bob Hope, Jackie Gleason, George Burns, plus other standup comics? Hopefully they are in a university library or in a museum collection for the public to refer to and historians to consult. The vaults better have first -rate locks to prevent the ghost of Milton Berle from stealing them to outdo his contemporaries on the big comedy stage in the sky.

Chapter 18
"Captain Kangaroo" Bob Keeshan

"We are the only nation dumb enough to use television as a selling tool. Here in America we believe in free commercial speech and exploitation of anybody, including children and the future."

"Mr. Korman, could you come to the office? Captain Kangaroo is on the phone!"

That was my first introduction to Bob Keeshan, at the behest of my secretary, Helen Lawrence, at Findley Elementary School, on the morning of May 7, 1987.

At the time I was a speech/language pathologist for the Akron (Ohio) Board of Education. To supplement my income (as a husband and a father of two young daughters) I was writing for *The West Side Leader*, a weekly newspaper, on a freelance basis. I reviewed local community theater productions and interviewed celebrities appearing in the area.

I was well into a morning speech therapy session with several students when the Captain Kangaroo message came over the room's public address system. I dismissed my students and went to the school office across the hall.

I thought something was wrong, because I had previously arranged with the advertising agency handling Bob Keeshan's Akron appearance to interview him over the telephone later that afternoon. I was to telephone *him* and conduct the phone interview before his upcoming appearance the next week at the Quaker Square Hilton Hotel, sponsored by Children's Hospital Medical Center of Akron, to speak on the topic, "Children's (Hospital) and the Captain-Partners in Advocacy." I left my school telephone number with the agency in the event they had to contact me about any schedule change. Signals got crossed and Keeshan thought he was to call *me*.

I apologized to Keeshan on the phone, explaining I was to call *him* for a telephone interview. I asked him if I could call him back during my lunch from home to conduct an interview. He insisted on calling *me* and asked for my home telephone number and when to call.

I ended my conversation with Keeshan, smiled at my confused secretary, and resumed my morning group speech therapy sessions. I drove home during lunch and readied my tape recorder while jotting down a few questions to ask. I was anxious to ask him what it was like to be the first "Clarabell the Clown" on "The Howdy Doody" television show. Was it his own creation? Why was Clarabell an auguste, instead of a whiteface or tramp clown? At precisely the agreed time the telephone rang and I began my interview with Bob Keeshan a.k.a. Captain Kangaroo.

By May, 1987, when the phone interview took place, Keeshan, as his creation, Captain Kangaroo, had already appeared on CBS (Columbia Broadcasting System) television for 30 years (1955-1985). This was his second year (of eventually six) on non-commercial PBS (Public Broadcasting System). His low-key approach to his children's television show had won him countless awards, including six Emmys and three Peabody Awards.

Robert James Keeshan was born June 27, 1927, on Long Island, in Lynbrook, New York, the son of immigrant parents. He was one of four children (two brothers and one sister). His mother died when he was 15 years old. While attending high school, Keeshan got a job as a page (a low-level "go-fer") at NBC (National Broadcasting Company). After high school he continued working as a page at NBC for popular radio personality Bob Smith, who had an adult radio program as well as a popular morning children's show.

Keeshan's career was put on hold during World War II when he enlisted in the Marines in 1945. At war's end he returned to NBC, still working for Bob Smith during the day, while attending Fordham University at night, to become a lawyer.

In 1947, NBC wanted Bob Smith to transfer his popular children's radio show to the new medium of television. Smith took his page, Keeshan, with him. The new television show, "Puppet Playhouse," was an instant hit. It was quickly expanded and renamed after the lead puppet character, to become "The Howdy Doody Show." On the show, Keeshan was relegated to menial tasks, such as handing out prizes to children and keeping them quiet when they were not supposed to be heard.

One of the show's producers, while viewing the program one day, was rather appalled that Keeshan appeared on the show as a "normal" person, when the program's setting was that of a circus. Shortly thereafter, Keeshan became an auguste-type clown named "Clarabell Hornblower." Clarabell did not speak but communicated by honking his "yes" or "no" horn mounted on either side of a box strapped to his waist on the front of his costume. Inside the box was a bottle of seltzer water, usually meant for Bob Smith (now named "Buffalo Bob") that followed a slapstick chase around the circus set.

But all was not "rosy" for Keeshan. Bob Smith (a former big band singer) was musically-inclined and wanted the musical theme to be part of the children's show's format. But Keeshan could not sing nor play an instrument. Also, some parents began complaining to NBC that Clarabell's seltzer antics and slapstick chases were getting their children too excited before dinnertime. Clarabell was the apparent culprit. The solution? NBC fired Keeshan in 1950. Actor Gil Lamb was hired to replace Keeshan as Clarabell the Clown. Lamb was theatrically trained in dance and mime. It did not take very long for the young audience to realize a more-gentle and shy Clarabell the Clown had suddenly become taller, thinner and uncharacteristically very polite. Ratings immediately plummeted. The solution? NBC quickly rehired Keeshan as Clarabell and resumed his seltzer-spraying, slapstick, Buffalo Bob-chasing ways.

In 1952, Keeshan's tenure as Clarabell the Clown on "The Howdy Doody Show" came to an end. Keeshan and several other characters on the show were putting in long hours on the television show five days a week. More time was demanded of them for additional promotions and numerous personal appearances. Keeshan considered his pay ($600 per week) not commensurate with his additional responsibilities. He and three other performers from the show decided to get an agent. NBC's solution? Keeshan was immediately fired.

In August of 1953, Keeshan was back on television as Corny the Clown on a new children's television show called "Time for Fun." In addition to the new show, Keeshan began work on another children's television show called "Tinker's Workshop," with Keeshan playing a grandfatherly-type character named Tinker. The character would eventually evolve into Captain Kangaroo.

The very first question I asked Keeshan, in my telephone interview, was how it felt to be the first Clarabell the Clown on "The Howdy Doody Show." His reply took me by surprise when he nonchalantly stated, "Oh, well, I hardly remember that. That goes way back. It's difficult to remember what it was except that it was a role and I certainly was young at the time. I was 19 when I started. It was just a different formula and a different age. It would not be considered appropriate today." My heart sank, so much for the anticipated inside story of Clarabell the Clown.

I then asked Keeshan about his upcoming child advocacy appearance in conjunction with Akron Children's Medical Center of Akron. "It will be relative to children's issues that will be 'Keeshan' (not Captain Kangaroo) and it will be directed to adults," was his reply. "My remarks," he continued, "will entitle all phases of nurturing children. It offends me (that he would even have to explain the importance of child advocacy) making the case, telling people why child advocacy is so important in this day and this age (1987) and in this world of change, and why it is appropriate for the hospital (Akron Children's Medical Center of Akron) to be designated advocate, if you will, to serve as a catalyst working with other agencies already established and helping to establish new services devoted to helping young people and families."

Keeshan was well aware of the problems of latch-key children and after school daycare. "This is not only an isolated problem or a problem for parents or a problem for working parents, but is, in fact, a community-wide problem," he explained. "When we fail to give proper care, we fail to nurture the children properly and a very large extent of those children turn out to need a remedial program of some kind, including programs that eventually lead to prison and all of that is a vastly more expensive approach than would be getting in place a much more modest expenditure of public funds and developing those children as healthy taxpaying adults, sharing the burden along with us." I was used to the voice at the other end of the telephone speaking very slow and deliberate on television to young children. Now he was speaking as an adult on very lofty and mature subjects and timely topics.

"Different children have different needs," Keeshan went on. "What we are really saying is that there are many needs that children have and many conditions that children do not flourish. For example, you know we talk about the popular thing, now-a-days, is substance abuse. I think it's fine and wonderful that (First Lady) Nancy (Reagan) says let's just say 'no.' But, you know, you're just treating the symptom, not the disease. I'm not talking against that. That's fine," Keeshan said, "but, you know, the chances are pretty good that a kid is not going to be just taught to say 'no' when you haven't talked to the kid through a lifetime. And that's one of the reasons he or she has turned to drugs or alcohol at this particular point. You're not going to solve this by calling an ad agency and getting them to develop a bumper sticker. That's the typical approach to problem solving. What we really have to do is do it the hard way: pay attention to kids and pay attention to programs that support kids and the American family. That takes a little more time and that takes more effort and commitment and it does take some money. But more than anything it's the commitment to the family that what is really going to solve substance abuse in the end. The kids will be saying 'no' quite naturally. You won't have to teach them."

Keeshan went on to further differentiate between the types of abuse children suffer (emotional, physical, and sexual). "Emotional abuse may have the most long-lasting effects on children. Of course when we start talking about abuse we are talking about education, prevention, and if those fail, we're talking about identification, intervention and counseling, all of which are tremendous community problems and if we fail to do it, not just because we feel sorry for abused children and neglected children, we feel sorry for ourselves as taxpayers. Because, if we fail to do it we're going to be paying for the breakfast, lunch, and dinner for a lot of people in the institutions of this country. We, as taxpayers across the nation, pay for 2 million meals a day, and those people represent the mistakes of the past, and that is an expensive way out. We could have been a lot better reaching them earlier on. We have a nation that's made children their principal underclass. Isn't that wonderful? Isn't that great? America that brags about being the land of plenty, the land of promise, yet studies indicate over 80% of the inmates of penal institutions admit to having been abused as children and that has played a considerable role in their past crimes. We have 14 million children below the poverty line," emphasized Keeshan. I told him those statistics reminded me of an interview the previous week I had with comedienne Phyllis Diller. I told Keeshan that Diller was born and raised in Lima, Ohio, where a state mental institution is located. Diller informed me (and I informed Keeshan) that 90% of that state hospital's inmates were abused as children. "If only we had programs in place to aid these children," Keeshan replied, "we probably wouldn't have caught all of them, but maybe, if we caught half of them, put aside cost that we'd be saving now, the economic expense we'd be saving now, think of the social value of that. Half of those people now being productive human beings. That would be wonderful. That's really what we have to do with all of those programs."

I asked Keeshan about his low key, soft-spoken, approach on his "Captain Kangaroo" television show. "(Today) we've moved from low-key to excitement. Prior to low-key we had a lot of formulas that were developed for motion pictures and radio; more dramatic formats and so on and the low-key approach really took advantage of the television medium and its intimacy," he explained. "I've always felt it was appropriate for this age group. They needed that kind of gentle stimulation, a kind of modeling behavior and the friendship that is implicit in it. It's worked well and it continues to work well and there are certainly others doing it, like Mr. Rogers."

Keeshan liked his Captain Kangaroo program better on non-commercial PBS. He had definite opinions on commercial television. "Of course we don't use the medium very well because in the commercial sector it's now devoted to selling. It's a selling tool. Then, again, it's the American way: let the marketplace be the determining factor. To heck with kids and the family and the future and the effect of television on them and leave that to do-gooders and teachers and a few others. We are the only nation dumb enough to use television as a selling tool. England, France, Germany, Japan, and the Soviet Union know the value of television and nurturing children as well," he said. "They prohibit its use for the exploitation of children. But, here in America we believe in free commercial speech and exploitation of anybody, including children and the future."

Keeshan was not at all surprised when CBS cancelled "Captain Kangaroo" in 1985, after 30 years. "There was nothing abrupt about it," he recalled. "It had been going on for a decade. When they deregulated broadcasting it was inevitable. There was no shock about it." On his non-commercial PBS format of "Captain Kangaroo," Keeshan is executive producer. "I'm in charge of everything," he said. "I'll take the blame." He went on further: "We are delighted (with PBS). Unfortunately when we started 32 years ago there was no public television as we know it today. There were only about a half-dozen stations across the country. So we had to go with the commercial network. It worked out fairly well but we are much more comfortable in the public television setting. I think it's much more appropriate to the Captain and think it's more appropriate for his audience."

Getting back to his upcoming Akron appearance, Keeshan said that he spoke on the topic of child advocacy once or twice a week. "It's always exciting to be able to reach out and to join in a partnership with other people, in this case Children's Hospital Medical Center and to tell people of the community how important their participation in children's programs are, that without their advocacy, whether they have anything to do with children or not, children are not going to be well served, and if children are not going to be well served, all of us are in jeopardy in the future because every one of us pays the price if we don't do a good job."

I looked at my watch and saw my lunchtime was about over. I had to get to my next elementary school for afternoon speech therapy sessions. I thanked Keeshan for the opportunity to interview him and told him I was looking forward to meeting him the following week at his lecture.

On the evening of Wednesday, May 13, 1987, at 7:30 PM, Bob Keeshan began his lecture, "Children's and the Captain—Partners in Advocacy," in the Grand Ballroom of the Quaker Square Hilton Hotel in downtown Akron, Ohio. The room was filled to capacity. I noticed a large number of parents who had brought their children along with them.

Keeshan began his lecture by telling his audience, point blank, he was *not* appearing as Captain Kangaroo *but* as Bob Keeshan, child advocate. I immediately heard a soft, barely-audible disturbance in the audience, especially coming from those with children. I sensed the parents wanted their children to meet Captain Kangaroo after the lecture or even, more important: meet the man who *they* watched on television when they were their children's age, themselves. Throughout the lecture Keeshan reiterated he was appearing as private citizen, Bob Keeshan, not Captain Kangaroo. If that was the case, then, in retrospect, perhaps the title of his advertised lecture should have deleted the term "the Captain." But then, perhaps, attendance would have been much smaller.

This oversight manifested itself, after his lecture, when Keeshan repeatedly refused to sign autographs, especially as "Captain Kangaroo." The adults with children were visibly displeased. I patiently waited in line and eventually introduced myself to Keeshan.

A few days later I received a personalized autographed publicity photograph of Keeshan as Captain Kangaroo.

Nine years later (in 1996) I had the opportunity, once again, to meet Bob Keeshan, but under totally different circumstances.

In the spring of 1996, my oldest daughter, Julie, was majoring in Communications at The University of Akron. As a requirement her senior year, she had to intern for one semester at a local business to create and implement publicity for several special events. She interned at Borders Books in nearby Montrose. One of her tasks was to formulate a publicity campaign for the appearance, on Sunday, April 21, 1996, of Bob "Captain Kangaroo" Keeshan.

Keeshan was to appear, beginning at 1:30 PM, for a discussion, then autograph session of his latest children's book, "Alligator in the Basement." My daughter's publicity advertised . . . "activities for the kids, including a clown and refreshments."

Since 1978, I had performed locally as my own creation, "Marlowe the Magic Clown", clown and magician. Capitalizing on her father's talents, my daughter suggested "Marlowe" to Borders Books for the clown. It worked. My job as "Marlowe the Magic Clown" was to entertain children while they waited to meet Keeshan/ Captain Kangaroo.

I arrived at Borders Books in costume to assume my afternoon clown duties just before the public began arriving to meet Keeshan. About 1:30 PM, in through the front door of the store came Bob Keeshan. There was immediate audible recognition and excitement from his assembled fans as Keeshan walked toward the children's book area.

He was dressed in gray slacks, burgundy turtleneck sweater, and navy-blue blazer. He saw me as "Marlowe the Magic Clown" as he walked by. He stopped momentarily. He gave me a sort of smile and a look that told me he was acknowledging my presence as a clown and that he also knew, quite well, what it was like to be in greasepaint and costume. I never forgot his positive facial recognition and smile as stopped on his way to meet and greet his fans.

I noticed he had aged a great deal since our previous meeting nine years before.

As the afternoon wore on, my daughter escorted me to where Keeshan was standing during a lull in his appearance activities. She then introduced me. I told Keeshan who I was from his 1987 Akron Children's Medical Center appearance. He smiled as he recalled the event.

I purchased a copy of "Alligator in the Basement" and had Keeshan personalize it for me. He wrote: "To Irv, Captain Kangaroo." A day or so later my daughter presented me with a publicity poster of "Alligator in the Basement," also personalized by Captain Kangaroo.

I reflected on the two totally different circumstances concerning Bob Keeshan. In 1987 he appeared in Akron as Bob Keeshan, all but disavowing his persona as Captain Kangaroo while simultaneously disappointing many parents and children. Nine years later, in order to publicize his children's book, he gladly acknowledged his alter ego, Captain Kangaroo, to the extent he actually signed his book "Captain Kangaroo."

I was saddened to learn of Bob Keeshan's death, of natural causes, on January 23, 2004, in his hometown of Hartford, Vermont.

Not only do I have Bob Keeshan's 1987 tape-recorded telephone interview, plus two personalized publicity photos (one as Bob Keeshan and one as Captain Kangaroo) from his 1987 Akron appearance, to remember him, but I also have a more personal memento: a photo my daughter Julie snapped of Keeshan with me as "Marlowe the Magic Clown" from his 1996 Borders Books appearance. I like to think it is a photo of two performers frozen in time one Sunday afternoon in April of 1996: one man dressed as a clown and one man, in gray slacks, burgundy sweater, and navy blazer; an eternally gentle clown-at-heart.

A few years ago, Helen Lawrence, my secretary at Findley Elementary School, who had informed me, "Captain Kangaroo is on the phone" retired. At her retirement banquet when people were asked to come up to the microphone to recall a particular event concerning Helen, I fondly told the little-known episode we both had with Captain Kangaroo that April morning in 1987. Everyone laughed at the story as I fondly recalled Bob Keeshan all over again.

MARY TRAVERS

ROGERS & COWAN, INC.

PUBLIC RELATIONS

Chapter 19
Mary Travers
Folksinger/Political Activist

"My politics? I've never heard of a Republican folksinger."

"You want to know how I got involved in Soviet Jewry? Am I Jewish? No. But I didn't have to be black to get involved with the Civil Rights movement either."

"Tyranny functions best in silence."

"Those of us who live in a Democracy have a responsibility to be the voice for those whose voices are stilled."

"How tall am I? I'm five feet, ten inches; six feet in good heels."

"I'd like to sing 'My Beloved.' I've never recorded it but the K.G.B. has."

"America has to stop asking for charisma rather than leadership."

"A great deal of politics is show business."

"Democracy must function by law and must function in the light."

"I'd now like to sing some songs because it's easier than speaking."

Mary Ellin Travers was born on November 7, 1936, in Louisville, Kentucky. She moved with her mother and father to New York City. There her mother took her to folk music concerts and other cultural events. In her teens she was singing with various folk groups in and around Greenwich Village. She was a member of a group, *The Song Swappers*, and was quite involved in the folk-singing scene in and around Greenwich Village. She appeared twice at Carnegie Hall with Pete Seeger and also sang in a Broadway review starring comedian and political satirist Mort Saul.

In the 1950s Travers met an electric guitarist, originally from Maryland, who moved to New York City from Michigan. His name was Noel Stookey. He played rock 'n' roll music while trying his hand at stand-up comedy. He had been trying his stand-up comedy routines at a club called The Gaslight, across the street from Travers' third floor walk-up apartment. The two began performing together, as *Stookey and Travers*, when folk impresario Albert Grossman introduced them to a native New Yorker, who had studied psychology at Cornell University. His name was Peter Yarrow.

"I had just gotten out of a lousy marriage," Mary recalled, "and had a small child and a funky day job in a bar."

The trio rehearsed for a few months in Travers' apartment, then made their debut at The Bitter End coffee house in 1961. Shortly before their debut Noel changed his name to "Paul." Thus began the trio of *Peter, Paul, and Mary*. Within one year (1962) they signed a contract with Warner Brothers Records. Their first album, "Peter, Paul, and Mary," ended up seven weeks at No. 1, ten months in the Top Ten, and the Top 20 for two years. The album contained the hit, "If I Had a Hammer." Their first single, "Lemon Tree," soon followed.

The early 1960s was a fertile time for the folksong. Historically, in the years prior to the '60s, folksingers such as Woody Guthrie, The Weavers, and Pete Seeger had used the folksong for sociopolitical commentary. This movement had been forced underground due to the Anti-Communist "witch-hunts" of Senator Joseph McCarthy in the 1950s. Between the Cold War, the Civil Rights Movement, and later, the Vietnam War, folksingers and folk singing groups became spokespersons for these and other social movements through their songs.

Actually, Peter, Paul, and Mary were continuing the folk music genre of the Kingston Trio from the 1950s. "If I Had A Hammer" was written a decade earlier by Pete Seeger and Lee Hays of The Weavers. The trio also gave boosts to the careers of Bob Dylan ("Blowin' In the Wind," "Don't Think Twice, It's All Right"), Lauro Nyro, Phil Ochs, Tom Paxton and Gordon Lightfoot ("For Lovin' Me") as well as John Denver by recording their songs.

The 1960s were alive with folk singing groups such as The New Christy Minstrels, The Brothers Four, The Limelighters, The Chad Mitchell Trio, The Rooftop Singers, among others. Even England got into the mode with the folk sounds of Chad Stuart and Jeremy Clyde and Peter and Gordon.

Together as well as individually, Peter Yarrow, (Noel) Paul Stookey, and Mary Travers championed many political and social causes of the time.

One of Mary Travers' causes manifested itself locally when she appeared in Akron, Ohio, Thursday evening, December 11, 1986, at the Akron Jewish Center, for the cause and plight of Soviet Jewry.

At the time (1986) countless Soviet Jews, called *Refusniks*, risked everything to make known to the Soviet government their intention to try and migrate to Israel. To do this the Soviet Jews risked their jobs, income, social status, and even their lives to reach their ancestral homeland in Israel. They *refused* to buckle under to the relentless Soviet social and governmental pressure. This *Refusnik* movement called attention to the Soviet Union on an international level, which the Soviet government did not want. Many prominent Americans, Mary Travers included, visited the Soviet Union and met with the *Refusniks* to give them whatever support they could. This was during the era after the Civil Rights movement and the Vietnam War.

Mary Travers scheduled a press conference at the Akron Jewish Center prior to her public appearance on behalf of Soviet Jewry.

I prepared questions in the hope of asking Travers a few at the anticipated news conference located in the small auditorium in the Akron Jewish Center. I arrived early in order to get a good seat, down front and center. I had a battery-powered tape recorder to record the news conference for accurate quotes. I was writing for a local weekly publication, *The West Side Leader*. As time went by the only other media person in attendance was the editor of *The Akron Jewish News,* a monthly publication of the Akron (Ohio) Jewish community. So, there we were; just the three of us: "Irving, Tobie, and Mary."

In walked Travers and immediately surveyed the scene. Without skipping a beat she looked down at me in the two-person audience and told me to come up onstage. She spotted my tape recorder, grabbed the microphone and told me to turn it on. She seemed completely in control of the impromptu situation.

Travers began speaking directly into the microphone, not being concerned in the least about only two media people being present. She immediately began her press conference.

"You'd probably ask, 'Miss Travers, may I call you Mary?' And I would have said, 'Of course.'"

"You'd ask, 'How did you get involved in Soviet Jewry? Are you Jewish?' I am not Jewish but then I didn't have to be black to be in the Civil Rights movement."

"How did I get involved in Soviet Jewry? In 1983, I was invited to be part of a delegation that was going to El Salvador to study the impact of foreign policy on El Salvador's Human Rights abuses. The group consisted of a lot of former (United States) government officials: the former assistant secretary of state under the Carter administration, former director of VISTA (the Domestic Peace Corp.), and two congressmen of the Foreign Relations Committee. Several academics and church people were also in attendance. As many of us previously discovered, the (El Salvador) military was directly responsible for the majority of the Human Rights abuses in the country. They managed political assassinations of over 50,000 civilians in four years. The U.S. was indirectly responsible for not putting controls on our aid (to El Salvador). It reminded me, in a sense, of the Soviet Union, with organized tyranny."

"When I came back from my first trip to El Salvador I was really upset and angry. I wrote an article about the trip. I asked a friend of mine, who happens to be a rabbi, to edit it for me. He edited the piece and then said, 'Well, Mary, now that you witnessed the terror of the Right, how about experiencing the terror of the Left?' And so that's how I left for the Soviet Union to visit with 'Refusnik' Jews and Hebrew teachers. It was a meaningful trip. Because it was such a small group we didn't have tourist supervision."

At this point in the press conference I informed Travers the weekly newspaper I was writing for had a circulation of about 25,000 homes. I then asked her, "What if someone was reading this article and wanted to do something about Soviet Jewry, what could they do?"

"Well, there are a lot of things you can do," she said. "It has been my experience that tyranny functions best in silence. The moment you see press restrictions in a country you know that there is a reign of Totalitarianism occurring, like the censoring of the press in South Africa and the Republic of South Korea. It is not so healthy, when we invade a country, that we don't allow any reporters along either. It is a bad sign. It means somebody wants to do something they don't want anybody to know about and, as anyone knows, when anybody does something that they don't want anybody to know about, it's because they are doing something wrong. So, the first thing you have to do is raise these issues with the press, again and again, and with elected officials. You have to make sure human rights abuses are a top priority for your own government. In the case of South Africa you have to make the nation know their behavior is unacceptable. That's why people march, why they talk about it. It is to raise the country's awareness that there is terror and injustice to humanity in South Africa. The same is true for the Soviet Union."

Mary Travers lit the first of her three Marlboro Light cigarettes that she consumed during the half-hour press conference, and began to expound about the Soviet Union.

"The Soviet Union is not quite as vulnerable to this kind of pressure as, say El Salvador, who is dependent on the United States. But it is not impervious either. The Soviet Union has a historical world image which it would like to change," Travers said between puffs on her first cigarette. "It's been considered a barbaric, underdeveloped country, living in the 20th century perhaps militarily, but certainly not in the 20th century culturally or industrially. It is viewed as a barbaric country of the East. It has been viewed that way since the czars started and is still viewed that way. They would like to be perceived as a major Western world power. We even refer to our problems with the Soviets as 'East-West' dialogue. They don't consider themselves in the East. They never even did in the czarist times. The royal court spoke French and thought of themselves as being European, not as being in the East. However, we see their desire, especially now (1986), to be viewed as a Western nation."

"Three years ago Gorbachev visited Europe, with what was for the Soviet Union a new invention: a 'First Lady'. This was pure confection, something they invented."

I remarked to Travers it was also the first time the Soviet leader was younger than the U.S. President (Reagan).

"It was the beginning of the younger politicians who did NOT go through the (Communist) Revolution, but who were born during World War II, that were starting to enter higher office. That could be good. It certainly can't get much worse. The Soviets are in trouble.

They have an economy that doesn't work."

I asked Travers, "How can we, as Americans, get more Jews out of the Soviet Union?" She replied, "Take up a writing campaign. You can write Soviet Jews. They may not get your letters or you may not get their responses. But that is not the point. The point is that the Soviets don't like it when you put a light on one of their subjects." She went on, "Also get to know the issue. I think it is important to read a little bit. Americans are always being accused of being the most ill-informed on foreign affairs. There are two excellent books by David Shipler, correspondent for *The New York Times,* on Russia. He's written two books. One has just come out called, *The Arab and the Jew.* It will really explain the Middle East Crisis to you if you don't understand it. He's a very fine measured writer. He's not a propagandist. He's a very level-headed journalist who was stationed in the Soviet Union for some time and in Jerusalem. I met him in Jerusalem."

Travers said she does about 20 "Soviet Jewry" concerts a year.

"This last summer I was going to do a concert in South Africa but was denied a visa. It must have been something I said. So I went back to El Salvador and also Nicaragua for the first time." Besides El Salvador, Nicaragua, South Africa, and the Soviet Union, Travers also speaks out against (South) Korea, which she feels is a very fascinating non-democratic country which has no collective bargaining. It doesn't have free elections. It has total censorship of the press. "Democracy must function by law and must function in the light. There is an upside and a downside to Democracy." Travers went on to explain. "The downside is that you don't always get things done quickly when you rule by committee. But when things get done by consensus you do get them done. I think we lose moral 'high ground' when we tell our allies not to do something."

It was quite clear during the press conference Mary Travers did not think much of then-President Ronald Reagan or his administration's policies, especially on foreign affairs.

"The President (Reagan) has done great injury to the United States," Travers began. "Not because he knew something or because he didn't know. That's not really the question. The question is something went wrong in his Cabinet that was absolutely wrong, probably illegal. He cannot say, 'I did not know.' What's he going to tell us, he (Reagan) was taking a nap? He may have been! The fact of the matter is America has to stop asking for charisma rather than leadership. I'm sure Churchill was not the most charming man all the time but he was a leader. I think we should begin to decide what is dividing us. The question is, what are we looking for? If it's charisma it does not always happen that we get competent leadership and charisma. There is no substitute for character. It depends what charisma does. If a leader inspires people it can be the placebo that works. A great deal of politics is show business, which is probably why this particular President (Reagan) functions so well."

"People who love America, and I count myself as one of them, want America to be, in deed, what she is in myth. I don't want a large separation between the deed and the myth. I feel Americans must, especially in light of embracing this concept of anti-totalitarianism, that we have to really be against totalitarianism wherever it may be. And, certainly, insist that basic human rights be observed. Insist of our allies and attempt to make human rights the bargaining chip with our adversaries. It should be a vested interest for both countries. One should not have to bargain with one's allies. It should be a vested interest for both countries."

It had been about a half-hour since the press conference began. Travers looked at her wrist watch, put out her last (third) cigarette, and said she had to prepare for her concert. About another half-hour later, in the Jewish Center's multi-purpose room, the program began.

At the program's inception several elected officials were introduced. After a moment of silence a letter was read to the assembled from Ohio Governor Richard Celeste. The letter was about a Soviet *Refusnik* family he had "adopted." It concerned the family of Benjamin Bogomony. At the end of the letter reading, Benjamin Bogomony stood up and was introduced to a standing ovation. He had made it out of Russia, to Israel, and to the United States. After a few remarks by Bogomony, Mary Travers was introduced. She told, in more detail, of her trip to the Soviet Union.

Travers remarked, "where but in a Democracy can three generations (Mary, her mother, and her daughter) be arrested on the steps of the South African embassy in Washington?" She gave a brief statement concerning her political leanings. "There has never been a Republican folksinger," she remarked. "I'd now like to sing some songs," she said, "because it's easier than speaking."

She began by singing, "My Beloved" in Hebrew. "I never recorded it," she said, "but the KGB did!" She was referring to the time she sang it to *Refusniks* in the Soviet Union and knew the room she was in at the time was being bugged.

When she sang, "Where Have All the Flowers Gone?" she encouraged the audience to sing along. She then sang, "I Am Your Child." It was a song to her parents but she dedicated to her own children. When singing "Carry On" Travers dedicated it to all the "sweet survivors."

As she continued to sing about half-a-dozen songs, Travers swung and swayed just as she did when singing with Paul Stookey and Peter Yarrow. Her long, straight blonde hair moved with her body, her face framed by her trademark blonde bangs.

She saved her favorite song for last. "This song is like a tool because it fits in so many places." The she began "Blowing in the Wind." The concert lasted about an hour-and-a-half. As the applause intensified at the end of Travers' last song, I recalled another song that I thought described her: "Proud Mary."

Since the concert by Mary Travers at the Akron Jewish Center in December of 1986, *Peter, Paul, and Mary* have focused on such issues as gun violence against children, the rights and organizing efforts of strawberry pickers in California, homelessness and world hunger. "We've always been involved with issues that deal with the fundamental rights of people, whether that means the right to political freedom or the right to breathe air that's clean," Travers pointed out.

Peter, Paul, and Mary have lasted over four generations, won five Grammy Awards, and produced thirteen Top 40 hits, of which six climbed into the Top 10, as well as earning eight gold and five platinum albums.

One cannot talk about Mary Travers' accomplishments without including Paul Stookey and Peter Yarrow. Their success in the 1960's music scene included such hits as "Blowin' In the Wind", "If I Had a Hammer", "Leaving On a Jet Plane", "Where Have All the Flowers Gone?", "500 Miles", and "Puff, the Magic Dragon".

During the 1970s the trio gave themselves seven years to pursue individual interests. Mary Travers continued her support of various causes and recorded four solo albums. She performed with symphonies, hosted a syndicated radio show, lectured at colleges on "Society and Its Effect on Music," and wrote newspaper editorials and commentary. She also produced, wrote, and starred in the British Broadcasting Corporation's (BBC) series "Rhymes and Reasons," which dealt with societal mores and changes in recent times.

The trio reunited in the 1980s while still pursuing their individual social agendas. The produced and appeared in several Public Broadcasting Corporation (PBS) specials including their *25th Anniversary Concert* and *A Holiday Celebration.*

In 1992, *Peter, Paul and Mary* resigned with Warner Brothers Records. In 1996 they did a TV special and album, *Life Lines*. This enabled *Peter, Paul, and Mary* to perform with such mentors and friends as onetime Weavers Ronnie Gilbert and Fred Hellerman, plus Richie Havens, Tom Paxton, Odetta, Dave Van Ronk, John Sebastian, Buddy Mondlock and Susan Werner.

In 2004, Mary Travers was diagnosed with leukemia. She was

given a 40% chance of survival. She was eventually given a bone marrow/stem cell transplant. The last performance of *Peter, Paul, Mary* and was on May 20, 2009, in New Brunswick, New Jersey.

Mary Travers passed away from complications of chemotherapy on September 16, 2009. She was 72 years old.

Mary's private life had been kept *very* private. She had been married three times. Her last marriage was to Ethan Robbins (in 1991), a retired restaurateur. She is also survived by two daughters, Erika (age 50) and Alicia (age 43) and by her mother, who was head of public relations at Danbury Hospital, where Mary passed away. Travers also has a sister, Ann Gordon, as well as two granddaughters, Wylie and Virginia.

Mary Travers will always be associated with the folk singing trio of *Peter, Paul and Mary*. She will also be remembered for her social causes.

"Folk music has sort of a bubbling-under quality," she once remarked. "The stream runs through the cultural consciousness, and whether or not it's on the radio is not the issue. Folk music is always there."

Through recordings, both audio and visual, "Proud Mary keeps on churning" and "Proud Mary keeps on burning" … in our soul.

Chapter 20
Eddie Fisher, Crooner/Survivor

"For those who don't remember me, I'm Carrie Fisher's father. That's better than (being known as) MISTER Elizabeth Taylor!"

"Today I sing for pleasure. My real job is a marriage counselor."

"Just point me to a microphone and I automatically sing."

     . . . Eddie Fisher

"I only hope you will be as happy as I might have been on several occasions!"

     . . . Toast given by George Jessel at Fisher/Reynolds wedding

Mention the name, "Eddie Fisher" and the response will reveal your age. Your response may be one of the following:

"The crooner?"

"Wasn't he married to Debbie Reynolds?"

"Wasn't he married to Elizabeth Taylor?"

"Isn't he Princess Leia's (from *Star Wars*) father?"

"Carrie Fisher's dad?"

"Joley Fisher's (television show *Ellen*) dad?"

"Eddie who?"

I reviewed singer Eddie Fisher at Carousel Dinner Theatre, in Ravenna, Ohio, in May of 1987. Eight years later I interviewed him, via telephone, in April of 1995, prior to an appearance at Landerhaven (an entertainment complex) in Mayfield Heights, Ohio, a suburb near Cleveland. Both instances revealed many sides of a complex personality.

Edwin Jack Fisher was born in Philadelphia, Pennsylvania, on August 10, 1928. He was the fourth of seven children of Russian-born Jewish immigrants Kate (nee Winokura) and Joseph Fisher. His father's surname was Tisch or Fisch, but was anglicized to Fisher upon entry into the United States. Eddie was always called "Sonny

Boy" by his family, a nickname derived from the song of the same name from Al Jolson's motion picture, *The Singing Fool* (1928).

EDDIE FISHER

At an early age, Fisher displayed talent as a vocalist and began singing in amateur contests, which he usually won. He made his debut on radio on *Arthur Godfrey's Talent Scouts*, a very popular radio show. The show was so popular that it later moved to the new electronic medium of television.

Due to his local singing success in the Philadelphia area, Fisher quit high school in the middle of his senior year at South Philadelphia High School. By 1946, he was crooning with Buddy Morrow's and Charlie Ventura's orchestras. 1949 was his breakout year. He was singing at Grossinger's Resort in the Borscht Belt (of the Catskill Mountains of New York State) when he was discovered by popular entertainer Eddie Cantor. After appearing on Cantor's radio show, Fisher became a hit, gaining him a national audience. He eventually signed with RCA Victor records. His first few singles for RCA included "Thinking of You" and "Turn Back the Hands of Time." Both spent time near the top of the charts.

In 1951, Fisher was drafted into the U.S. Army. He had basic training in Texas and served one year in Korea. President Harry S. Truman referred to Fisher as "my favorite PFC." While in Korea, Fisher entertained the troops. From 1952 to 1953 he was the official vocalist for The United States Army Band.

After his military discharge, Fisher hit the nightclub circuit as a crooner, appearing in the top night clubs across the country. The early 1950s were very kind to tenor Eddie Fisher. He sold millions of records with 32 hit songs including "Any Time," "Oh! My Pa-pa," "Wish You Were Here," "Lady of Spain," and "Count Your Blessings."

In 1952, Fisher scored with "Any Time," "Tell Me Why," and "Wish You Were Here." In 1953 his hit records included "I'm Walking Behind You," and "Oh! My Pa-pa."

Fisher's recordings led to two televisions shows. *Coke Time* was a daily, fifteen-minute show on NBC from 1953 to 1957. The show proved to be so popular that Coke offered Fisher one million dollars to be their national spokesperson. Such a deal was unheard-of at this time, but helped push the crooner into being one of the most popular singers by 1954. *The Eddie Fisher Show*, also on NBC, aired from 1957 to 1959.

A pre-Rock-and-Roll-era singer, Fisher's tenor singing voice made him a teen idol and one of the most popular singers of the 1950s. He scored seventeen songs in the Top 10 on the music charts between 1950 and 1956 and thirty-five in the Top 40.

His first three much-publicized marriages were to Debbie Reynolds (from 1955 to 1959), Elizabeth Taylor (from 1959-1964) and Connie Stevens (from 1967 to 1969). His marriage to Reynolds produced daughter Carrie and son Todd. His marriage to Stevens produced two daughters, Tricia and Joley. He also was married to Terry Richard (from1975 to 1976) and Betty Lin (from 1993 until her death of lung cancer in 2001).

Fisher chronicled his life twice, once in 1981, with *Eddie, My Life, My Loves,* and a more controversial autobiography in 1991 entitled, *Been There, Done That.* The second autobiography upset both Reynolds and Taylor. Daughter Carrie Fisher even threatened to change her last name from "Fisher" to "Reynolds."

Fisher's marriage to Elizabeth Taylor, and her affair and eventual marriage to Richard Burton seemed to drain the crooner. He would later confess that he gave up his singing career catering to Taylor. His bookings dried up and his finances dwindled. He got hooked on gambling and drugs. He tried a comeback in 1983 but his old fans were turned off by his private-turned-public life, scandals, and addictions.

It was between his comeback try in 1983, and the publishing of his second autobiography, *Been There, Done That* in 1991, that I had a chance to review Fisher in concert at Carousel Dinner Theatre in Ravenna, Ohio, in May of 1987. He was on a double-bill with singer Patti Paige from May 19-24. Paige was popular in the early 1950's, as was Fisher, singing such hit tunes as "In Old Cape Cod," "Tennessee Waltz," "Allegheny Moon," and "How Much Is That Doggie In the Window?" At the time "Tennessee Waltz" was the biggest selling single record ever recorded by a female vocalist.

Fisher performed first that May evening in 1987. Before the concert I met the public relations director of Carousel Dinner Theatre, Micki Brook, in the theater lobby. I had a copy of Fisher's first autobiography (*Eddie, My Life, My Loves*) in hand hoping to meet Fisher after the performance, have him sign an 8" x 10" publicity photo and his book, and pose for a photograph with him. Neither event happened. When Brook saw the autobiography in my hand she said, "Whatever you do, don't let him see that book." I asked why and was informed he and the book publisher were not on the best of terms. It had something to do with wanting some parts of the book left in that the publisher edited out. That may have eventually prompted Fisher to write the second autobiography in 1991 (*Been There, Done That*). I recently looked at both autobiographies and noticed each one was published by a different book company.

Eddie Fisher's one-hour concert (from about 8:15 to 9:15 PM) included eight songs plus a nine-song Al Jolson medley. His conductor/accompanist was Peter Thompson. Though Paige and Fisher had different conductor/accompanists, the orchestra remained the same for both performers.

Fisher put the audience at ease immediately, after a vocal medley, by saying, "For those of you who don't remember me, I'm Carrie Fisher's father." After the laughter died down he then said, "That's better than (being known as) Mr. Elizabeth Taylor!" He stood upright in a simple black tuxedo, white shirt, and black bow tie. He wore no jewelry. As his one-hour set progressed he seemed unaccustomed to Carousel Dinner Theatre's "theater-in-the-round" stage set up. He seemed to be used to a proscenium or thrust stage, not a three-quarter or totally "in-the-round" setting. Some of the patrons only saw Fisher's profile or back of his head during the performance. He did not move around a lot. It also seemed apparent the band was not 100%. Perhaps the conductor/accompanist Peter Thompson should have warmed up the orchestra a bit more before Fisher's concert. Carousel's sound system was not co-operating either. It seemed to be in need of constant attention and monitoring.

The same orchestra was in fine tune after intermission when Patti Paige was under the direction of conductor/accompanist Rocky Cole for the second half of the concert. Perhaps the fact Cole had been with Paige for 35 years had something to do with Paige's more polished performance.

During Fisher's one-hour concert he peppered his audience with comments from his show business friends. "I asked George Burns how his sex life was. He told me, 'Like shooting pool with a rope.'" He also confessed, "Today I sing for pleasure. My real job is a marriage counselor!"

Fisher ended his appearance with the Irish axiom: "May the Lord take a liking to you, but not too soon."

One week later I returned to Carousel Dinner Theatre to review their next production, "My One and Only" on press night. After the performance I saw the theater's owner, Prescott Griffith, and asked him about Eddie Fisher the week before, especially his sub-par performance. Griffith looked at the floor and shook his head. "You won't believe this," he said. He then told me a most interesting story about Eddie Fisher.

Griffith told me that after Fisher's less-than-stellar opening night, Griffith placed a long-distance telephone call to Fisher's manager and reported to him about the disappointing opening night performance. Griffith then said to me, "You're not going to believe what Fisher's manager told me to do." The manager told Griffith to promise Eddie Fisher an ice-cream cone after the concert! That's right: an ice-cream cone! He told Griffith to stand offstage to reassure Fisher he would, indeed, be treated to an ice-cream cone after his performance.

Griffith followed the manager's advice and approached Fisher before the next night's performance. Fisher was excited. During his one-hour performance Fisher gave it his "all." After each song he raced offstage up to Griffith and would ask, "Are you sure we're going to get an ice-cream cone after the show?" Each time Fisher asked, Griffith reassured the crooner of the after-concert reward. At evening's end, sure enough, Fisher got his promised ice-cream cone. After that, Fisher's remaining performances were much better, according to Griffith.

I never got to meet Fisher after the opening night performance. I did not get to meet Patti Paige either. I eventually met Ms. Paige two years later at Tangier Restaurant in Akron, Ohio, after a solo concert.

Eight years later, in 1995, I noticed an ad in a local paper for an upcoming Eddie Fisher concert in a nearby suburb of Cleveland, Ohio. It was for a two-day appearance (Sunday, April 23rd and Monday, April 24th) with Fisher, featuring The Ray Stone Orchestra. I was writing for a daily newspaper at the time and proposed to my entertainment editor doing a telephone interview a week prior to Fisher's appearance. I got the okay and was eventually given Fisher's telephone number. When I called the number I spoke to a woman who I eventually figured out was Fisher's current wife, Betty Lin. Fisher was not available at the time but we worked out another day and time for a telephone interview.

A few days later I called the telephone number again and, again, spoke to Betty Lin who eventually put Fisher on the phone, thus beginning another "interesting" Eddie Fisher experience.

I began the telephone interview by telling him I wanted to ask him some questions about appearing in concert at Landerhaven on Sunday, April 23rd and Monday, April 24th.

"I am?" was his reply. "What is Landerhaven? What is that?" he asked. "It's not a theater is it?" I told him it was a very upscale party center that could, very easily accommodate a concert. "Well," he replied, "I worked all kinds of places. I'm going to be there. I was told I was going to be around some place near Cleveland."

I told Fisher he would be accompanied by The Ray Stone Orchestra. "I don't know who that is," he said, "but it's an orchestra and I have a musical director. Just point me to a microphone and I automatically sing!"

I informed him I had seen him in 1987 at Carousel Dinner Theatre in Ravenna, Ohio, in concert with Patti Paige. "Oh, yeah," he replied, "I've done a lot of stuff with Patti Paige for a long time for many years."

I then related a story to Fisher about my grandmother. In Yiddish a grandmother is called a *bubbe*. I told Fisher that my *bubbe* used to like to listen to him sing, especially when she watched his television show, *Coke Time*. Fisher laughed. "I haven't heard that word (*bubbe*) used in a long time. Jerry Seinfeld called his (grandmother) 'Nana.' I guess that's for the American public. They don't know what a *bubbe* is. They know what a 'Nana' is."

Then, out of nowhere Fisher began telling a story. "I used to tell a joke onstage," he recalled. "I had a young musical director, a piano player. I'd say, 'How old are you?' He'd say, 'Thirty-three.' I'd say, 'Thirty-three. Do you know how much fun I had at your age?' He'd say, 'I heard.' I'd say, 'What do you mean, you heard?' He said, 'Well, somebody told me.' I said, 'Who told you?' He said, 'My grandmother told me!' That would get a laugh."

Without skipping a beat, Fisher related another story. "Then there was (comedian) Joey Lewis," he said. "He would do a line with me. He'd take the microphone away from me and ask, 'Can I say a few words?' I'd say, 'Sure, go ahead.' He'd say, 'You know, Eddie, a lot of comedians around are saying things and remarks. Don't worry. You're a wonderful singer and don't pay any attention what they say. Whatever happened between you and Elizabeth Arden is your business.' Then I would say to him, 'You got the wrong Elizabeth.' And he'd say back, 'And so did you!' That would bring the house down."

Before Fisher began to relate another story I quickly asked, "What has happened since your 1981 autobiography?"

"I'm smack in the middle of another autobiography," he confessed. "As a matter of fact the writer is right on the other side of the apartment. You took me away from my writer. It's one of the toughest things to do. Trust me. I've already written an autobiography. I just made a deal with St. Martin's Press and I'm really going to do a spectacular thing. It's going to be really good."

I asked Fisher if he had a title yet. "No," he replied. "How about: 'I Burned My Candle at Both Ends and In the Middle Too'? I'm just playing around." The second autobiography would eventually be titled, *Been There, Done That* and published in 1999.

I then asked Fisher if he still did many nightclub appearances. "No," he replied, "as a matter of fact my Betty, my beloved Betty, made this commitment (the upcoming Landerhaven concert). I think I have one other. I've cancelled going to Israel to do two concerts. I've cancelled New York. I've cancelled Las Vegas. I'm going to start recording in a few weeks and it's going to be shocking and I really want to wait until then. I am coming to whatever you say I'm coming to (again, the upcoming Landerhaven concert). I made that commitment. The Israel thing is flexible. I can go there and work with the Israeli Philharmonic or whatever sometime with my new songs and stuff, you know."

I asked Fisher to elaborate on his upcoming album. "I can't talk about it," he said. "I don't want to . . . I can't. I promised the producer I wouldn't."

I told Fisher my two daughters watch *The Ellen Show,* referring to his daughter Jolie (by Connie Stevens). I asked Fisher if he would do a "cameo role" on the show with his daughter. "I see her all the time and she hasn't asked me," he replied. "I don't think it's gonna happen. It doesn't fit the format, or whatever. Speaking of Jolie, May 1st she's taking over Brooke Shields' role in 'Grease' on Broadway. It just happened. I don't think anyone knows about it yet." I asked Fisher if I could print that information in my article. "Oh, sure. Her name will be above the title: Jolie Fisher in 'Grease' on Broadway."

I was curious as to what Eddie Fisher did in his spare time, when not performing or writing another autobiography, so I asked him. "I work now and then," he revealed. "You, know, I don't work all the time. I work out with weights. I walk. I go to museums. I go to the opera. I go to the symphony. I'm a big reader of books. Non-fiction. My wife (Betty) and I are not very social but we have friends here and there and we are living a good, wonderful life."

I noticed Fisher's telephone area code was California and asked him about it. "We live in the heart of San Francisco," Fisher said, "where Tony Bennett left it!"

"He's a good painter," I said. "I know," replied Fisher. "He painted me. He's a wonderful guy and I'm thrilled about his success. He played up here a couple of times. We hung out here and in New York and Los Angeles. He's a sweetheart. I've known him for 40 years."

"So you decided to settle in San Francisco," I said. "I've been here six years," he said. "I put in 20 years in L.A., 10 years ('79-'89) in New York and '45-'56 in New York, and sixteen years in Philadelphia."

I did not know Fisher came from a family of seven children. "Yeah," Fisher reflected, "There are three of us left. My mother passed away a couple of years ago. She was 90. I'm going for her genes. I don't think I have her genes. I think I have my father's. I hope to live to be 73 like he did. I have a 75 year-old brother in good health. I try to take care of myself. I eat well and I exercise. I take care of my wife and myself."

I knew my interview was coming to a close when Fisher changed the subject and said,

"Come and see me or I'll call your *bubbe*." Jokingly I asked, "Can I come backstage and see you?" "If you don't come back, don't come," was Fisher's reply. "You're a Jew. You gotta come. You'll be my guest. You're a *lanzman* (a fellow-countryman). I love Jews. If you're not there I'm not going on." After a moment Fisher said to me, "You're a funny, straight-forward guy." I replied, "Than you, sir." He said, "Don't call me 'sir.' Call me what my mother used to call me: 'Honey.' No wait, Jolson used to call me that."

I quickly interjected, "Your mother, I think, called you 'Sonny Boy'."

"Yep," replied Fisher. So ended my telephone interview with Eddie Fisher.

For some reason I cannot recall, I never made it up to Landerhaven to Eddie Fisher's concert.

A few years ago I was channel-surfing with my remote and saw Eddie Fisher being interviewed on a television show by his daughter Carrie. Outwardly he looked good with (dyed) dark hair. Having been a speech pathologist for 30 years, I could tell by the way he spoke that he may have had too-large caps on his teeth or ill-fitting false teeth.

Then the news came that Eddie Fisher passed away on September 22, 2010. He had died at his home in Berkeley, California, of complications from hip surgery. He had broken his hip on September 9th at his home. He was 82 years old. He had reached the age halfway between the ages of death of his mother (90) and his father (73).

He never did record the record album he spoke of during the 1995 telephone interview. His last album, *After All*, was released in 1984. Fisher tried to stop the album from being released (under the Bainbridge label) but to no avail. It was produced by William J. O'Malley and arranged by Angelo DiPippo. DiPippo had worked with Fisher for countless hours to better his vocals but it became useless.

Fisher garnered several entertainment accolades in his lifetime. He received Emmy Award nominations for Best Male Singer in both 1955 and 1956.

In 1958 Fisher was awarded a Golden Globe Award for Best TV Show, *Coke Time*.

Eddie Fisher has two stars on the Hollywood Walk of Fame: one for Recording (at 6241 Hollywood Boulevard) and one for Television (at 1724 Vine Street).

In recalling the life of crooner Eddie Fisher, his highly publicized marriages, additions to gambling and drugs, his try at a comeback, I came across a quote. It was a toast given by George Jessel at the Eddie Fisher-Debbie Reynolds wedding and, I think, sums up Fisher's life: "I only hope you will be as happy as I might have been on several occasions!"

Chapter 21
Bob Feller, Baseball Legend/Patriot

"Did you want me to autograph something?"
    . . . Bob Feller to author

"I've been in public life almost all of my whole life. So I'm not going to hide this."
    . . . upon revelation of leukemia at age 91.

"As far as I'm concerned I'm no hero. Heroes didn't come back to this country. They're (still) in Europe, in the bottom of the Pacific or on the islands of the Pacific. Survivors return home. If anyone thinks I'm a hero, I'm not."
    . . . response to being called a World War II hero.

"I just reared back and let them go!"
    . . . description of how to throw his famous fastball.

Who would have thought attending a local community theatre play production would lead to meeting a childhood hero?

Friday, April 25, 2001, at Weathervane Community Playhouse in Akron, Ohio, was the opening night of the play, "Mr. Rickey Calls a Meeting", by playwright Ed Schmidt. The play concerns a meeting at the Roosevelt Hotel in New York City in April of 1947, held by Branch Rickey, then general manager of the Brooklyn Dodgers of the National League professional baseball team. Rickey plans to give Negro League Baseball player Jackie Robinson a chance to play for the Dodgers. Before a press conference announcing Robinson as the first African-American in professional baseball's National League, Rickey solicits the support of several prominent African-American celebrities. He invites heavyweight boxing champion Joe Lewis, dance legend Bill "Bojangles" Robinson, and actor, and recently banned Communist, Paul Robeson to his hotel suite to discuss his strategy for the upcoming press conference. The play concerns the dynamics of this historic event. As one can imagine, with so many strong personalities, the play is full of drama. (Incidentally, the first African-American to play baseball for the American League was Larry Doby of the Cleveland Indians).

Opening night of "Mr. Rickey Calls a Meeting," at Weathervane Community Playhouse, was to include an after-performance talk-back session onstage that included the play's cast plus Wilmer Fields, President of the Negro League Baseball Players Association, and Baseball Hall of Fame and Cleveland Indians pitching legend Bob

Feller.

Growing up in the late 1940s and early 1950s in Northeastern Ohio, I recall listening to the voice of Cleveland Indians radio announcer Jimmy Dudley exhorting diehard baseball fans to the talents of such immortal Cleveland Indians as Jim Hegan, Bobby Avila, Vic Wertz, Early Wynn Jr., Al Rosen, Mike (the Bear) Garcia, Bob Lemon, Luke Easter, Larry Doby, and, of course, pitcher Bob Feller.

What was the likelihood of meeting such idols aside from hanging around Municipal Stadium in downtown Cleveland before or after a baseball game?

About a month before the opening night performance of "Mr. Rickey Calls a Meeting," a friend of mine, Frank Wallick, went to Winter Haven, Florida, to watch the Cleveland Indians in spring training. Frank told me that Bob Feller often sat at an umbrella table outside the practice field and signed autographs for fans. Frank was kind enough to secure a black-and-white, 8" x 10", personally autographed photo of Bob Feller for me. I promptly framed the photo and put it on my wall with other autographed photos at home. I thought to myself that a photograph of me with Feller would certainly look nice framed right next to the autographed photo of him. But what was the likelihood of that happening?

I was scheduled to review "Mr. Rickey Calls a Meeting" for a local weekly newspaper on opening night. Upon arrival at the theater, I learned a pre-show reception was in progress upstairs for Bob Feller and Wilmer Fields. I hurriedly ran upstairs to the reception room, only to find it mostly empty. The reception had concluded. As I turned around to leave I saw an open elevator door at the end of the hallway. A few people from the reception were entering the elevator. One of the people inside the elevator turned around, saw me and said, "There's room for one more!" As I stepped into the elevator I looked up right into the face of Bob Feller! I eventually said, "I guess I'm too late to ask for an autograph. I don't want to bother you right now before the play so I'll wait to see if you are available after the show for one." Feller and I got off the elevator and into a line to enter the theater to see the play. While in line I mentioned to Feller I vividly remember listening to radio announcer Jimmy Dudley in the late 1940s and early 1950s and the Cleveland Indians line-up. Feller lamented the fact that Jimmy Dudley recently passed away at a nursing home in Arizona. I thought to myself that even if I didn't get an autograph or have my picture taken with Feller, I would always have the memory of this intimate conversation. I eventually went to my reserved seat in the theater as Feller went to his.

I watched the play, "Mr. Rickey Calls a Meeting," and jotted down notes for my newspaper review. As advertised, after the play the cast came out onstage, followed by Wilmer Fields and Bob Feller. The group discussion concerned Jackie Robinson, whether the historic meeting in the play actually took place, plus personal reminiscences by both Fields and Feller. Following the discussion onstage everyone exited into the theater lobby, where I spotted a crowd assembled around Feller. I decided to wait at the end of the long line until the crowd thinned out before approaching Feller for an autograph and asking him to pose for a photo with me.

Before he began signing autographs Feller spotted me out of the corner of his eye and said to the crowd, "Before I do anything, I want to do something." He looked directly at me and said, "Didn't you want me to autograph something?"

Imagine my surprise when I realized he was speaking to me! I was both speechless and flattered. Since I already had the autographed photo (thanks to my fiend Frank's recent visit to Florida), I had Feller autograph a piece of paper I tore out of my reporter's notebook for my grandnephew, Andrew, a true sports participant as well as fan. Then Feller graciously consented to a photo with me before going back to signing autographs for the general crowd. While initially waiting in line I had purchased a baseball conveniently for sale at the playhouse boutique. Feller kindly consented to sign the ball also.

My Bob Feller shrine was now complete with the black-and-white, 8" x 10" autographed photo, a photograph of Feller and me, and an autographed baseball. The display sits next to an autographed baseball and two autographed trading cards of my other Cleveland Indians idol: former third baseman, No. 7, Al Rosen, all of which I bought on eBay.

Bob Feller's kindness continued after that Friday evening of April 25, 2001. My oldest daughter's first husband was an ardent Cleveland Indians fan. Since Bob Feller gave me his business card the night I met him at Weathervane Community Playhouse, I thought an autographed photo of Feller would be an appropriate birthday present for him. I wrote to Feller explaining my son-in-law's devotion to the Cleveland Indians and asked if he would be kind enough to send him an autographed photo. A few months later my daughter informed me her husband had just received a *color*, autographed photo of Bob Feller! Feller later wrote me a letter apologizing for taking so long in sending the photo to my son-in-law since he had just returned from wintering in Florida.

Whenever I look at the display of Bob Feller on the wall in my home, I think of how I acquired the personalized autographed, black-and-white 8" x 10" photo, the picture of Feller and me, and the autographed baseball from one of my childhood idols who is, truly, a gentleman, and who acts and deserves the title of "idol" and earns it every day of his life.

In August of 2010, it was revealed in a local newspaper that Feller was being treated for a form of leukemia that frequently occurs in older men. Feller was three months shy of his 92nd birthday. A series of blood transfusions and chemotherapy followed but did not slow "Rapid Robert" down. "I've been in public life almost all of my whole life," he said. "So I'm not going to hide this." While undergoing chemotherapy he fainted and eventually had a pacemaker implanted. Up until then Feller regularly attended Cleveland Indians home games, sitting in his seat in the Progressive Field press box. He would also trek to Indians spring training camp in Winter Haven, Florida (and, more recently, Goodyear, Arizona), sit under an umbrella table and sign autographs for fans. He would also participate in the Indians' yearly fantasy camp, pitching and striking out men 50 years his junior!

Within a few months of Feller being diagnosed with leukemia, he was moved into hospice care. He passed away December 15, 2010, at the age of 92. He was survived by his wife, Anne, and three sons, Steve, Martin, and Bruce.

Bob Feller was the longest tenured living Baseball Hall of Famer. "Bullet Bob" came off his father's farm in Van Meter, Iowa, and made his major league pitching debut at age 17 on August 23, 1936. He was the youngest player to ever pitch in a major league game. In that game Feller struck out 15 St. Louis Browns players, just two shy of the league record, and won the game 4-1.

Feller was born November 13, 1918. He was seventeen when he caught the eye of Cleveland Indians scout Cy Slapnicka at an amateur game in Dayton, Ohio. He signed Feller for one dollar and an autographed baseball. Feller never pitched in the minor leagues. He went straight to the Cleveland Indians!

Feller's fastball was known as the "Van Meter Heater." Before radar guns were invented it was estimated he could throw the baseball at 104 miles per hour. It was calculated in 1940 by Major League Baseball in a test involving a man on a Harley-Davidson motorcycle traveling at a high speed and two bulls-eye targets on a closed street in Chicago's Lincoln Park. There is newsreel film footage of the event.

Over his career Feller helped win 266 games and strike out 2,581 hitters in his 18-year career. He had a lifetime ERA (Earned Run Average) of 3.25. He was the first major league pitcher to win 20 games before he was 21. He led the American League in victories six times. He is still the Cleveland Indians shutout leader (46), innings pitched (3,827), walks (1,764), complete games (279), wins and strikeouts.

Feller won a World Series title with Cleveland in 1948. He retired from baseball in 1954, having made eight All-Star teams. He was enshrined in the Baseball Hall of Fame in Cooperstown, New York, in 1962, the very first year of his eligibility. His jersey, No. 19, was retired by the Cleveland Indians in 1957. When the Cleveland Indians opened their new baseball stadium in downtown Cleveland in 1994, Feller was immortalized outside the main gate entrance with a statue posed in the middle of his famous "windmill" windup, rearing back to fire another pitch.

Feller's statistics could have been far more staggering had his career not been interrupted by World War II. He volunteered to join the Navy the day after Pearl Harbor in December of 1941, the first major league player to do so. Feller missed three full seasons from 1942 to 1944, during which time he earned five campaign ribbons and eight battle stars for his service to his country. He spent time in Iceland and on the U.S.S. Alabama, where he helped take supplies to Russia, eventually going to the Japanese front, where he saw action in numerous battles. Originally Feller had hoped to join the Air Force, but was rejected due to a hearing loss, suffered by driving a tractor on his father's farm in Van Meter, Iowa.

In the three years before Feller enlisted he won 76 games and posted a 2.88 ERA with 767 strikeouts in 960 innings. He never regretted leaving baseball to serve his country. "I'm no hero," he said. "Heroes don't come back. Survivors return home. If anyone thinks I'm a hero, I'm not."

Feller threw three no-hitters, including one on Opening Day in 1940. He shares the record for the most one-hitters in major league history with 12. He set a modern record that has since been broken, by striking out 18 Detroit Tigers in one game in 1938.

Bob Feller, a man of few words, said of his pitching prowess: "I just reared back and let them go."

After retiring from baseball, Feller worked in the insurance business. One of his sons, an architect, constructed a Bob Feller Museum for his father in his hometown of Van Meter, Iowa, where it is a tourist attraction.

Recently heroes of our century, such as Charles Lindbergh and Jacques Cousteau have had "skeletons in their closet" revealed. Both men had extra-marital affairs and children out of wedlock. I do not expect any such story to ever be revealed about Bob Feller. Plain and simple he regarded himself as we did: a baseball player and a patriot. To his legions fans, he was much, much more. To me he was a modern-day hero, sports legend, and a World War II hero who has never let me down, as a child or an adult.

Chapter 22
Tony Bennett

"Tony Bennett is the best singer in the business; the best exponent of song. He excites me whenever I watch him. He moves me. He's the singer who gets across what the composer has in mind and probably a little more."
                    . . . Frank Sinatra

"(Tony Bennett) . . . is the best singer I've ever heard."
                    . . . Bing Crosby

When writing about a celebrity there may be many resources available. Among them may be: the celebrity's public relations agency official printed biography, telephone interview, personal interview, even writing a review of the celebrity in concert. In the case of singing legend Tony Bennett, all of the above were utilized concerning my two encounters with him.

Before reviewing Bennett's opening night performance at Carousel Dinner Theatre in Akron, Ohio, in the summer of 1989, I received his printed biography in the mail at the behest of then-Carousel public relations director Betty Wilson. I wrote a pre-concert article for *The Medina Gazette*, a daily newspaper, based on the information from the printed biography. Later, I wrote another article, a review of Bennett's actual performance on July 8, 1989. After the concert performance I was able to meet him in person immediately after the show backstage. I was amazed at his appearance: perfectly dry; not a bead of sweat visible on his five-foot, seven-and-half inch frame, still looking fresh and dapper in his black tuxedo! He was cordial enough to let my wife take a photograph of us together.

The second time I encountered Bennett was a little over a year later, again, before a Carousel Dinner Theatre concert that began a week-long appearance in November of 1990. This time I was able to conduct a telephone interview with Bennett two weeks before he came to Akron. At that time he was appearing in Palm Beach, Florida, at the Indian River Plantation Hotel. The phone interview was scheduled for October 18, 1990, in the late afternoon when I was sure to be at home after a day of teaching school.

PHOTO CREDIT: ANNIE LEIBOVITZ

In 1989, Tony Bennett was 63 years old. He was in the ninth month of his "Spirit of Family Tour," promoting his latest Columbia Records recording of *Astoria: Portrait of the Artist*. It was his 91st record for Columbia Records. The album was Bennett's most personal to date because each song was personally hand-picked by the singer.

Born in Astoria, a working-middle class section of Queens, New York, the son of a grocer father and seamstress mother, Bennett explained, "I chose the songs on this album to recall the very special moments that so often touched my heart. I was a kid in pursuit of that often-elusive 'American Dream' with a desire to make it in the big city. That goes to show you how a little faith in oneself can go." The album was produced by eldest son Danny and mixed by youngest son Daegal. One of the songs on the album is titled after one of his two daughters, *Antonia*. Other songs in the album feature Bennett singing old standards as well as a few new songs. The album cover was unique in that there were two photographs of Tony Bennett, both in front of his apartment house in Astoria, New York. One is of him taken in 1942 at age fifteen and the other, very recent (1989). He recorded the album in Astoria the previous June, at the same studio where singer Bing Crosby was taping his current hit NBC sitcom television show.

Both of Bennett's Akron concerts at Carousel Dinner Theatre were intimate affairs in that Bennett was accompanied by The Ralph Sharon Trio, consisting of Ralph Sharon on piano, Paul Langosch on bass and Joe LaBarbera on drums. No big band accompaniment seemed necessary, yet some of Bennett's trademark songs would have benefited from such a musical arrangement, at least for part of the concert. Both concerts had no opening act or intermission. Each concert lasted about an hour-and-a-half, containing 25-28 songs. The Ralph Sharon Trio is featured on the *Astoria* album, although some songs are accompanied by a full orchestra, conducted by Jorge Calandrelli.

Both Carousel Dinner Theatre concerts featured familiar Bennett hit tunes (*Rags to Riches, Because of You, Boulevard of Broken Dreams, From This Moment On, Rags to Riches, Fly Me to the Moon, Who Can I Turn To?, Just In Time, If I Ruled the World, The Good Life,* and, of course, *I Left My Heart In San Francisco*) plus songs by such tunesmiths as Cole Porter, Jule Styne, Irving Berlin, Duke Ellington, and George Gershwin.

Bennett, born Anthony Dominick Benedetto, on August 3, 1926, was a graduate of Manhattan's High School of Industrial Arts where he took up art and music. He dropped out at age 16 to support his family. His mother was a seamstress. His father, a grocer, had passed away when Bennett was only nine years old. After World War II (he was drafted on his eighteenth birthday in 1944), having served in the U.S. Army in Europe, Bennett began a singing career, enrolling in the

Bel Canto singing discipline at the American Theatre Wing on the GI Bill. He continued singing while waiting tables in countless New York restaurants. Things looked pretty grim until he was put into an all-Black revue by entertainer Pearl Bailey, in 1949, at a Greenwich Village nightclub.

One night comedian Bob Hope spotted Bennett (singing under the name of Joe Bari) and immediately liked what he heard. Hope befriended the young singer by first changing his name to "Tony Bennett," then taking him under his wing. In 1950, Bennett came in second, on Arthur Godfrey's *Talent Scouts* program, to a young female singer named Rosemary Clooney. Thanks to Bob Hope's exposure, Bennett was singing at the Paramount Theatre. His first hit recording of *Boulevard of Broken Dreams* launched Bennett's singing career under the guidance of Mitch Miller at Columbia Records. *Because of You, Cold, Cold Heart* (a Hank Williams song), *Rags to Riches*, and *Stranger In Paradise* soon followed. The relationship between Bennett and Miller at Columbia lasted until 1971. After 88 record albums, Columbia and Bennett eventually parted company.

For the next 15 years Tony Bennett did not record for any record label. He continued singing in upscale night clubs and doing concerts around the world, purposely avoiding larger venues such as Las Vegas.

It was during this time, the early 1960s, that Bennett recorded his trademark, *I Left My Heart in San Francisco.*

The story of how Bennett came to record it is worthy of mention. In the late 1950s, in New York City, tunesmiths peddled their songs to singers and musicians. One duo, George Cory and Douglass Cross, were always hanging around singers and accompanists to promote their songs. Several times the composers would see Bennett's pianist/ accompanist Ralph Sharon and give him several of their songs. One day they bumped into Sharon and handed him some songs. Sharon took them and promised he'd look them over. He promptly deposited them in his dresser drawer and forgot about them. In mid-1961, Bennett, accompanied by Ralph Sharon and his trio, was set to go on a concert tour to Hot Springs, Arkansas, and then to the Fairmont Hotel in San Francisco, California. While Sharon was packing for the trip, he rummaged through his dresser drawer for some shirts and came upon the songs Cory and Cross had given him two years earlier.

On top of the pile was a song titled, *I Left My Heart in San Francisco*. Since the tour would end up in San Francisco, Sharon packed the song with his shirts. One night on the first leg of their tour in Arkansas, Sharon and Bennett retired to the bar of the Vapors Restaurant after one of their concerts. Sharon took out *I Left My Heart in San Francisco* and began playing it for Bennett on the bar's piano. Bennett thought it was a great song. What added to his judgment was the comment, "If you guys record that song, I'll buy the first copy," from the bartender!

Bennett sang the song for the first time on opening night at the Fairmont Hotel in San Francisco. It was an immediate smash with the crowd. As luck would have it, local representatives from Columbia Records just happened to be at Bennett's rehearsal the previous afternoon and liked it also. After the tour Bennett recorded the song on January 23, 1962, in one take, with another song, *Once Upon A Time,* from a Ray Bolger Broadway show called *All American.* The next day Sharon called Cory and Cross and told them he had recorded one of their songs. *Once Upon A Time* was released as a single with *I Left My Heart in San Francisco* as the B-side. So sure that *Once Upon A Time* was a hit, Bennett began plugging it during his concerts. The Columbia Records reps called Bennett and said the public was reacting more positively to the B-side of the record, *I Left My Heart in San Francisco*, so he immediately began plugging it instead. Bennett, in his autobiography, further adds to the phenomenon of the song as being a "grass roots" effort in that the song came from nowhere, it was written by two unknowns and it wasn't from a Broadway show or movie. Also, Columbia Records didn't have to spend millions of dollars to promote it. The public responded to it because it was a great song, not because a record company executive was telling them what to like. *I Left My Heart in San Francisco* sold thousands of copies a week for the next four years, became a gold record and garnered Bennett his first Grammy Award. Though it never reached number one, the song stayed on the charts for twenty-five months! When people ask Bennett if he ever gets tired of singing his trademark song he responds, "Do you ever get tired of making love?"

The 1970s and 1980s were rough years for Tony Bennett, personally as well as professionally. His first marriage to artist

Patricia Beech, whom he married in 1952, was in shambles. He and Beech separated in 1965, and then divorced in 1971, due mostly to the pressures of too much traveling and not being home. Bennett also had developed a cocaine habit that later nearly killed him in 1979. In desperation he then turned to Daegal and Danny, his two sons by Patricia Beech. Daegal became the recording master and Danny became his father's manager. The result was a rebirth for Tony Bennett. It was also during this time Bennett met, and in December of 1971 (shortly after his divorce), married aspiring actress Sandra Grant, with whom he had two daughters, Joanna and Antonia. Since he was no longer under contract to Columbia Records he was now free to record whatever he wanted. No more edicts from Columbia to sing popular ballads and "upscale tunes" of their choosing, and Mitch Miller's. Bennett had also left Ralph Sharon and his trio.

Thanks to his sons, Bennett recorded albums (under the *Improv* label) of songs by composers Rodgers and Hart and did an album with jazz pianist Bill Evans. Bennett's sons kept their father's name and persona in the public eye by having him appear as a guest artist on countless television variety shows and talk show formats for such television personalities as Johnny Carson, Merv Griffin, Mike Douglas, etc.

But Bennett's second marriage was failing. He and second wife Sandra soon separated, although they did not finally divorce until 1984. The end of the 1970s not only took a toll on Bennett's health, due to his drug habit, but he was also living way beyond his means. The Internal Revenue Service was trying to seize his Los Angeles home. Thanks to Daegal and Danny, Bennett's life got back on track. The boys got their father to move back to New York City from California, got him booked into colleges and small night clubs. Bennett also reunited with Ralph Sharon and his trio.

By early 1986, Bennett was once again recording with Columbia Records and has been producing successful albums there with his two sons ever since. Danny discovered that a new generation was beginning to listen to Bennett. He was immediately booked on such upscale shows as *Late Night with David Letterman, Late Night with Conan O'Brien,* and *MTV Unplugged.* The *Unplugged* soundtrack album went platinum! Bennett even had a part on *The Simpsons.* Also, thanks to son Danny, Bennett began doing a series of benefit concerts organized by alternative rock radio stations around the country. As planned, a whole new generation was rediscovering Tony Bennett.

The second time I saw Tony Bennett, I did not want to write another pre-concert article from another printed biography sent to me by his public relations agency. I arranged to interview Bennett over the telephone two weeks before his 1990 Carousel Dinner Theatre concert. As stated previously, he was appearing at a club in Florida. I arranged with his public relations agency to call Bennett at his convenience, anytime, anywhere. A date and time were arranged with his agency. I was to call *him*.

It did not start out that simple, though. As I drove my car up my driveway after teaching school on the afternoon of the scheduled telephone interview, my oldest daughter, Julie, ran up to the car. She said someone claiming to be Tony Bennett had just called me on the telephone. My daughter, thinking the call was a prank, said, "Oh, yeah. Sure," and did not believe the caller. Needless to say I was a bit upset. I ran into the house and found the Florida telephone number the agency had given me and immediately called the number. The voice on the phone said Bennett was speaking to someone else at the moment. I explained what had happened: that *I* was supposed to call him. I was told to call back a few minutes later to speak with Mr. Bennett. This gave me enough time to set up my telephone microphone adapter and my tape recorder while locating my notes containing questions to ask Bennett that I had previously jotted down. A few minutes later I finally got Bennett on the telephone. I apologized for the miscommunication. He did not seem to mind and we got on with the telephone interview.

I asked Bennett to explain his longevity in the music business. He said he once asked his friend, Frank Sinatra, the same question. Bennett said Sinatra paralleled his career with the garment business: "If you use good material the product will stand the test of time."

I then asked Bennett about his stamina. "How do you manage to stay in shape and do over 200 concerts a year?" "I play a lot of tennis," he replied, "eat good food, and take very good care of myself." Accompanist Ralph Sharon added that Bennett practices scales for twenty minutes, three times a day, every day.

Was an autobiography in the future? "I don't want to do a *tell-all* thing," replied Bennett. "I'd like to do just stories about relationships with other artists. I am working on it. It will come out sooner or later." About eight years later, in 1998, Bennett's autobiography *The Good Life* was published.

While Bennett was appearing in Akron he was chauffeured around town by Larry Penecost. Larry told me one evening Bennett wanted to go to a good Italian restaurant in the area for some authentic, *al dente* Italian food. Penecost knew of an-upscale Italian restaurant and contacted the owner about providing a quiet, out-of-the-way table for Bennett. As he was dropped off at the restaurant door, Bennett insisted Larry accompany him inside and dine with him. Larry was flattered by Bennett's generous offer.

During Bennett's first Akron appearance he was given a room at a downtown Akron hotel. Prescott Griffith, owner of Carousel Dinner Theatre at the time, liked to sequester his famous guests at different hotels around town, in order to be fair and not favor one particular area hotel over another. When Penecost picked up Bennett to be driven to Carousel Dinner Theatre for a rehearsal, Bennett nonchalantly asked Penecost, "Do you think the hotel could get someone to sweep the dead flies off the window sill in my room?" While Bennett rehearsed at Carousel Dinner Theatre, Penecost informed Carousel owner Griffith of Bennett's question. Griffith immediately telephoned another local hotel and asked the hotel manager if he could immediately accommodate Tony Bennett. "No problem," was the reply. Bennett's belongings were removed from the downtown hotel and transported to the other hotel. After the rehearsal Bennett was driven to his new hotel location. As the limo drove up to the front door, the manager greeted the singer. While Bennett was personally escorted to his room by the manager, a recording of Tony Bennett songs was heard over the hotel lobby speaker system. Bennett later said he enjoyed his stay at that particular hotel because it had a picturesque balcony that overlooked a wooded area and a small waterfall. Bennett enjoyed the view because he is, besides a legendary vocalist, a renowned painter and artist.

Art and music were both a constant tug-of-war with Tony Bennett. He originally aspired to become a commercial artist, as his father wanted. "I had this teacher, Mr. Sonberg, who kept telling me I should be a singer," recalls Bennett. "He steered me into music class and he had me sing on all the assembly days, and he got all my art teachers mad at him." After World War II, Bennett tried to make a living as a singer. "I came into the business at a tough time," he said. "By the time the war was over, it was uneconomical for big bands to stay together. So I had to play the little lounges rather than the big dates with the big bands I had grown up listening to. So it was pretty rough, but somehow I just kept pursuing."

There were several influences on Tony Bennett's vocal and musical career. "Louis Armstrong, Sarah Vaughn, Billy Eckstine were in my head at the beginning, and Bing Crosby and Sinatra. And Mel Torme—he made some beautiful records with Artie Shaw. And the Mel-Tones," said Bennett. "They were all very impressive to me...as was Billy Holiday." Advice by singer Joe Williams has always stayed with Bennett. Williams gave the young Bennett this to ponder: "It's not that you want to sing, it's that you have to sing." Another piece of advice came long ago from voice teacher Mimi Spier: "Never imitate a singer. Imitate musicians, players."

On his way to singing stardom Bennett never let go of his art talent. Still, today, he keeps his two worlds of talent separate. There is singing legend Tony Bennett and there is world renowned painter Antonio Benedetto.

Bennett's art passion goes way back to Astoria, Queens, when he drew chalk drawings on the sidewalk outside his apartment at age five. Today, at age 82, Bennett still finds time to paint every day, sketching the view from the windows of his New York City hotel suite or out in the country to which he travels. He has received many accolades for his paintings. The United Nations commissioned his artwork on two separate occasions including their 50th Anniversary. An original watercolor, *Peace*, created for a first-day cover for the United Nations 1987 Flag Stamp Series, is on permanent display in the lobby of the UN headquarters in Manhattan; an honor rarely accorded an individual artist. One of his paintings is also on permanent display at the Butler Institute of American Art in Youngstown, Ohio. His original oil painting, *Boy on Sailboat, Sydney Bay*, is part of the permanent collection at the prestigious National Arts Club in Gramercy Park in Manhattan. Bennett was also commissioned to be the official artist of the 2001 Kentucky Derby, and created two original watercolors for the historic racing event called *Kickin' Up Dirt 1* and *Kickin' Up Dirt 2*.

Among the many owners of original Bennedetto artworks are Carol Burnett, Whoopie Goldberg, the late Frank Sinatra, Donald Trump, Oprah Winfrey, Mickey Rooney, Katie Couric, and the late Cary Grant.

Several of Bennett's paintings have been published as museum-quality, limited-edition, fine-art lithographs. With the publication of a beautifully-bound book of his paintings, *TONY BENNETT: WHAT MY HEART HAS SEEN*, by Rizzoli International in 1996, a lifelong dream has been realized.

There is one accolade Bennett will never forget. "One day I picked up Cary Grant at his house to go to the Hollywood Bowl where I was appearing," he recalls. "When we got there I couldn't believe the horde of photographers and reporters that were waiting for him. He never had given interviews before or appeared on talk shows; but for the first time in his life he agreed to be interviewed live, on camera. Then he told everyone that he thought I was a fine painter. That was about eight months before he died, and it was a great gift from him to me."

Bennett keeps both his performing and painting worlds separate, yet they are intertwined. Bennett thinks it's in his heritage. "Italians have it in their genes to excel in music and art," he believes. "When it comes to the creative eye, the creative feeling, the soul of things, they feel free to express their creativity."

"What I love about my life is being able to combine business with pleasure. I never get burned out. First, I'll be in front of a large audience entertaining; then I go back and paint quietly and have a chance to learn what to do with myself and how to discipline my life better," admits Bennett, thus proving both entertaining and painting *can* co-exist together.

Painting and singing work well together for Bennett. He spends about forty weeks a year singing all over the world, but his painting never suffers because of this; wherever he is, one-third of his waking hours is spent at the easel.

Bennett has garnered his share of music awards, including several Grammys, Emmys, a Golden Laurel award, and even a Cable ACE award.

Since his comeback, Bennett has also prospered financially, with assets worth between $15 to 20 million, with no intention of retiring. He continues to paint and sing, doing 100-200 shows a year. To show his vocal prowess and powerful voice projection, Bennett makes a point, during his concert appearance, to sing *Fly Me to the Moon*, without microphone amplification!

One show, *Tony Bennett's Wonderful World: Live from San Francisco*, was made into a PBS special. He also created and starred in the first of A&E Network's *Live by Request* series, for which he won an Emmy Award. Bennett has also had cameo appearances as himself in such motion pictures as *The Scout, Analyze This, and Bruce Almighty.*

Among the more prominent achievements for Tony Bennett is the simple fact that he has sold over 50 million records!

Bennett has continued to garner many artistic awards. He was given a star on the Hollywood Walk of Fame (at 1560 Vine Street). He was inducted into the Big Band and Jazz Hall of Fame in 1997, and was awarded the Grammy Lifetime Achievement Award in 2001. It was also the year Bennett and Susan Crow, a former New York City schoolteacher (born in 1960, whom he married in a civil ceremony on June 21, 2007) founded Exploring the Arts, a charitable organization dedicated to creating, promoting, and supporting arts education. At the same time they founded (and named after Bennett's friend) the Frank Sinatra School of Arts in Queens, a public high school dedicated to teaching the Performing Arts.

The following year, in 2002, he received a lifetime achievement award from the American Society of Composers, Authors and Publishers (ASCAP), and *Q* magazine named him in the list of the "50 Bands To See Before You Die." It was also in 2002 that Bennett joined Michael Jackson, Chris Tucker, and former President Bill Clinton in a fundraiser for the Democratic National Committee at New York's Apollo Theater. No wonder he's been dubbed, "Tony Benefit."

In 2004, Bennett shared the Grammy Award for best traditional pop vocal album, for *A Wonderful World* with K. D. Lang. In 2005, Bennett was named as a recipient of the 2005 Kennedy Center Honors in the Performing Arts. The same year he was named a member of the National Endowment for the Arts Class of 2006 Jazz

Masters. In 2006 (at age 80), Bennett won a Traditional Pop Vocal Album Grammy Award for his *The Art of Romance* album. Also that year Bennett won multiple Emmy Awards for his television special *Tony Bennett: An American Classic* for NBC. The year of awards continued with the Billboard Century Award and guest-mentoring on season 6 of *American Idol,* performing during its finale. This was also the year Bennett was inducted into the Long Island Music Hall of Fame. The year 2006 concluded with Bennett being awarded the National Endowment for the Arts Jazz Masters Award, the highest honor the United States bestows on jazz musicians. In 2008 Bennett made two appearances with singer Billy Joel at the final concerts given at Shea Stadium. He also released the album *A Swingin' Christmas* with the Count Basie Big Band, for which he made a number of promotional appearances at holiday time.

"I have a lot of fun," admits 83 year-old Tony Bennett today. "I enjoy life. I paint and play tennis, and I sing and study music. I also study painting on a daily basis, and I feel alive. You might say I'm in love with life."

To Bennett's quote I would unceremoniously add: *"Amen!"*

Chapter 23
Mickey Rooney

"The most talented person in films is Mickey Rooney."

. . . Cary Grant

"I don't regret anything I've ever done in life. I only wish I could've done more."

. . . Mickey Rooney

"The fact is the good Lord was good enough to let me be in a business and have a vocation that I got paid for."

. . . Mickey Rooney

"After all, actors and actresses are nothing but grown up children playing 'make-believe'."

. . . Mickey Rooney

"On your way out of the theater there is a display in the lobby of all my wedding cakes. Don't touch the last one. It's still wet!"

. . . Mickey Rooney

All the previous chapters about celebrities were relatively brief encounters, telephone interviews, personal interviews, and/or reviews in performance.

My celebrity encounter with actor Mickey Rooney was nothing like the previous ones because I actually spent one month *performing* with him! It was in the play *See How They Run* a comedy, at Carousel Dinner Theatre, in the fall of 1973. After one week of rehearsal, the show ran from October 2nd to November 4th.

As stated before in previous chapters, Carousel Dinner Theatre began as a theater-in-the-round in Ravenna, Ohio, in the spring of 1973, in a renovated A & P Supermarket. Each play production, usually a comedy, ran about four weeks and featured a television or motion picture personality. Founder-producer-director David Fulford had successfully staged a summer stock format (with a television or movie star in a production for one week) in a barn in Canal Fulton, Ohio, for years. He figured he could do a similar format year-round, extending the run for a month instead of merely one week.

The comedy *See How They Run* was scheduled between *Play It Again, Sam* (Sept. 4th to Sept. 30th), starring television comic Pat Paulsen, and *The Tender Trap* (Nov. 6th to Nov. 25th), starring movie actor Tab Hunter.

It all began one fall morning with a telephone call. At the time I was a speech/language pathologist, working for the Akron Board of Education in Akron, Ohio. This particular morning I was at King Elementary School. I decided, between speech/language therapy sessions, to go to the school office and call home to see how my wife and six-month old daughter were doing. During the brief conversation my wife suddenly asked, "You want to be in a play with Mickey Rooney?" Since I was not having the most productive day, and had not been in a play for a few years, I replied, "That's not very funny considering I'm having a bad morning."

"I'm not kidding," she replied. "You got a call from Carousel Dinner Theatre in Ravenna, Ohio, about being in a play with Mickey Rooney." My wife told me the only other information the theater needed to know was how tall I was. To me that was a funny question in light of all the publicity I had heard about Mickey Rooney not really being concerned with *his* lack of height.

Needless-to-say, when I got home that afternoon, I immediately called Carousel Dinner Theatre. I was told my name was mentioned when a small part became available, that of an English policeman, a "bobby," in the last scene of the play. Carousel Dinner Theatre often employed local talent in their productions. Their Actor's Equity contract stipulated one or two non-Equity actors/actresses could be employed each production at a non-union rate of pay.

During the phone conversation a day and time was agreed upon. A few days later I followed the directions to Ravenna, Ohio, about a half-hour drive east, to Carousel Dinner Theatre. It was located just outside of town in a small, unassuming strip plaza. The theater took up about half the plaza and was in a renovated A&P Supermarket. I entered the carpeted theater lobby. It still had the large plate glass windows that you would see in the very front of a supermarket. On the wall were photos of the cast of the current production, *Play It Again, Sam* starring television comic Pat Paulsen.

I went up to the desk in the Carousel Dinner Theatre lobby and told the person standing there that I had an appointment with founder/ director David Fulford. A few minutes later a man strolled into the lobby and introduced himself as David Fulford. As we shook hands I noticed he was very tall, well over six feet. He had light brownish, sandy-colored coarse hair and a very deep, theatrical-sounding voice. He had a very commanding presence. Mr. Fulford told me my name came up in a conversation with public relations manager, Marie Duffy and group sales manager, Barbara "Bunny" Balance. I had done summer stock theater with Barbara's younger brother, Jack, during the summer of 1968 at Priscilla Beach Theatre in White Horse Beach, Massachusetts, just outside Plymouth. Jack was Priscilla Beach Theatre's set designer. I also knew Barbara from doing local community theater in the Akron, Ohio, area.

Mr. Fulford informed me he needed an actor to portray Sgt. Towers, a British policeman, who comes in the last scene of the play, during a very chaotic situation, and tries to get to the bottom of the mess, created by Mickey Rooney's character, and finally tries to restore some kind of order. Mr. Fulford handed me a script and asked me to read a few lines. I quickly conjured up in my mind what an English "bobby" might sound like. I tried to convey a "cockney" persona. After reading several lines I expected to be told I would get a phone call in a few days about whether I got the part or not. That was not the case. He told me, point blank, "You've got the part!"

Mr. Fulford told me about rehearsals and the performance schedule. I informed him I was employed by the Akron Board of Education and my hours were Monday through Friday from about 8:00 AM to 4:00 PM. He said since my part was small that I could come in when available for rehearsals. The only problem concerned one part of the performance schedule. Tuesday through Sunday night performances were no problem. But there was a Wednesday matinee at 2:00 PM. besides the regular 8:30 PM performance that evening. That could be a big problem unless there was an understudy for me for those matinees. I told Mr. Fulford that I would ask the director of special education (my department) about getting Wednesday afternoons off, even if it was without pay. For me, Wednesdays were routinely reserved for paperwork, testing students, or working one-on -one with students who needed individual speech/language therapy sessions in addition to their weekly, two, 30-minute group sessions.

I made an appointment with my superior, the director of special education, for the Akron Board of Education, and explained my situation. She told me she would have to take the matter up with the assistant superintendent, who was in charge of such matters. I eventually was told I could have the three Wednesday afternoons off without pay. I was elated. Carousel Dinner Theatre would later call me for two comedies: *The Odd Couple* in 1975, starring Dan Dailey, and *No Hard Feelings* in 1976, starring Forrest Tucker. Both requests to my superior and the assistant superintendent to be in these productions were denied. I was told the assistant superintendent did not want this to become "a habit." The irony is that when I eventually retired from Akron Board of Education in 1997, and was very available to be in plays at Carousel Dinner Theatre (now located in Akron, Ohio), they had changed their format to musical comedies only. Since I do not sing my only association with Carousel Dinner Theatre was a one-time situation.

My routine during weekday rehearsals for *See How They Run* were that I would immediately drive to Ravenna after school and rehearse with the cast minus Mickey Rooney. We would rehearse up until just before the nightly performance of *Play It Again, Sam* that starred Pat Paulsen. The theater staff needed time to set up the buffet dinner room and reset the stage for *Play It Again, Sam*. Mickey would eventually arrive in Ravenna a day or two before the show opened so we could rehearse with him.

We went through rehearsals, David Fulford directing, with the cast members saying, "Mickey will do this here," and "this line is changed to this." Most of the cast had just done *See How They Run* with Mickey Rooney at The Alhambra Dinner Theatre in Jacksonville, Florida. Two parts were now taken by local talent: myself as Sgt. Towers and a Canton native, Gary Wilbanks, as Rev. Lionel Toop. The other three female parts and three male parts were holdovers from the Jacksonville production.

On weekends, when we rehearsed long hours, it was very enlightening to hear the stories from the rest of the supporting cast members about working in other productions with famous actors and actresses. I absorbed the stories like a sponge and immediately retold them to my wife when I got home.

Each cast member had worked on Broadway, in motion pictures, and many dinner theaters across the country with famous movie and television personalities. One story concerned an actor that was so old and senile that he had a terrible time remembering lines. It got to the point where he had to wear an electronic receiver in his ear to be fed the lines he was continually forgetting during productions.

One other cast member recalled an incident when appearing with actor Allan Jones and one of his personal habits. During a break in rehearsal Jones brought out the latest public sensation: a Polaroid SX-70 camera that had just been put on the market. As he was demonstrating it to someone, a cast member reached for what he thought was a cup of black coffee. Jones immediately said, "Stop. Don't drink that. It's my chewing tobacco juice!"

David Fulford was a hands-on director. That is, until Mickey Rooney arrived for rehearsals. Fulford wisely deferred to Mickey taking over. After all, people came to see Mickey Rooney, not a production of *See How They Run* directed by David Fulford. Mickey changed a lot of the play, tailoring it to himself, especially lines. In the play, for example, there is the part of a Russian spy. For reasons known only to him, he changed the spy's nationality to Lithuanian. His own first name in the play is Clive. He "Americanized" it to Clyde. I suspect he did this because he played the part of an American soldier in Great Britain and because the play was written by a British playwright.

In the last chaotic scene I enter, as Sgt. Towers, and ask Mickey's character, American solder, Sgt. Clyde Vinton, "And who are you?" Instead of the written line identifying himself as Sgt. Clyde Vinton, Mickey would routinely reply, "I'm Andy Hardy as a midget!" Of course the line brought instant laughter followed by thunderous applause from the audience every time.

The week-long rehearsal schedule was a bit awkward without the star, yet the spectre of Mickey Rooney was ever-present.

When thinking of Mickey Rooney, many images come to mind: silent film star, television pioneer, *Andy Hardy* movies, films with Judy Garland, and, of course, several marriages, the first to Ava Gardner. In 1973, just before his Carousel Dinner Theater appearance in *See How They Run*, Mickey was in the public eye, appearing on the popular television variety series *NBC Follies*. Years after *See How They Run* at Carousel Dinner Theatre, there would be a revival of his career in such films as *Pete's Dragon, Black Stallion* and *Bill*, plus his legendary Broadway appearance in *Sugar Babies*. But in 1973, most television and movie stars would do dinner theater, like Carousel Dinner Theatre, not as a career first choice but to earn a living. Historically, summer-stock theater gave television performers added income, since summer re-runs and residuals were not yet the norm for such personalities. Performers were actually unemployed over the summer months, while summer replacement shows took their place. Dinner theaters were, actually, year-round summer-stock venues.

Born on September 23, 1920, in Brooklyn, New York, Mickey Rooney (original name Joseph Yule, Jr.) made his vaudeville stage debut at age 15 months. It was no surprise since both parents were vaudeville performers. Shortly after Mickey was born, his parents divorced. Thinking her son had lots of untapped talent; Mickey's mother bought a used car and drove her son to Hollywood, California, to get him into silent films. She had an appointment with "Our Gang" producer Hal Roach. After an audition Mickey was offered a contract but his mother held out for more money, causing Hal Roach Studios to withdraw the offer. Undaunted, Mickey's mother heard that a popular comic strip, "Mickey McGuire", would begin filming silent short films. One problem: Mickey was blonde and McGuire had dark hair. No problem. Black shoe polish solved the dilemma and Mickey got the part. Between 1927 and 1933, Rooney performed in 50 silent Mickey McGuire comedies. According to Rooney, he did 76 shorts.

In 1934, Rooney signed a contract with MGM. Besides starring in 15 "Andy Hardy" films, Rooney was paired in memorable, uplifting films with Judy Garland. He also got rave reviews as Puck in *A Midsummer Night's Dream* (1935), as Huck in *The Adventures of Huckleberry Finn* (1939) and a jockey, with Elizabeth Taylor, in *National Velvet* (1944). From 1938 to 1940, the Theater Owners of America made Rooney their Box Office Champion. In 1939, he received a special Oscar from the Academy of Motion Picture Arts and Sciences.

Mickey Rooney let the cast of *See How They Run* in on an interesting fact about the filming of *A Midsummer Night's Dream* for Warner Brothers in 1935. There are scenes with Rooney as Puck walking and running around. Then, suddenly, all you begin to see is of him is sitting down, whether on the ground or in a tree. There is a reason for this. During filming Mickey learned that Big Bear, up in northern California, had just had a snowfall. He asked his mother to drive him up there. He was warned by Warner Brothers executives not to play football, baseball or do any high diving. It would be a breach of his contract and result in his firing. They did not say anything about sledding or going on a toboggan. Going down a steep hill he put his left leg out to slow his toboggan down. You guessed it: it broke! The sitting scenes in the movie are to hide the cast on his leg!

After filming *National Velvet* with a young Elizabeth Taylor, in 1944, Rooney was drafted into World War II. He spent two years in the Army, mostly entertaining troops. Rooney would relate his wartime experiences by telling tales of doing three-man shows with just a Jeep, very close to the front lines of combat. He spent five months in Patton's Third Army in Europe. Rooney would come out of his Army experience as a Tech Sgt. 5 and a Bronze Star. He would repeatedly state, of all his lifetime awards and accolades, his Bronze Star, in the service of his country during World War II, was his most treasured. Rooney would relate some of his war stories to the cast during intermission when we would sit with him outside his dressing room. He was assigned to entertain the troops, but did not get a huge stage and large audiences like Bob Hope and other celebrities did. He did "three-guys-and-a-jeep" tours very close to actual combat zones, and was proud to entertain the troops. Whenever he could, he would take it upon himself to visit sick and injured soldiers near the front. He related one story concerning a soldier he saw at one hospital. The soldier had just had one leg amputated and was quite depressed. Rooney spoke to him and said how lucky the soldier was. Rooney related a story about a famous British actor who had a false leg and was quite the dandy with the women. Rooney said he got all those women due to the fact the actor had an artificial leg. During these intermission sessions I also learned of Rooney's fondness for Judy Garland. I also learned what actor or actress was ill or, worse yet, terminally ill.

Rooney's career was never the same after World War II. He was too old for *Andy Hardy* films. The public's taste had changed from "hometown" and "home spun" to "worldly" and "realistic." Like other child stars, Rooney found it hard to get a break as an adult actor.

From the late 1940s and into the 1950s, Rooney made of string of not-so-successful films. He tried his hand at early television in *Hey, Mulligan*, as a young page at a television studio, in 1954. From 1942 to 1974, Rooney was married and divorced seven times, most notably to his first wife, Ava Gardner. His current wife, country-western singer Jan, has been married to Rooney since 1978. In his 89th year, Rooney, at the urging of his wife, Jan, is currently touring the country in a one-man show of his career. Rooney once confessed to me that he thought enough of his women to marry them and not just live with them.

The closing night of *Play It Again, Sam*, at Carousel Dinner Theatre, was the Sunday before *See How They Run* with Mickey Rooney would open. Traditionally, the next cast and its star attended the final performance of the production they are replacing. At the end of the performance of *Play It Again Sam*, comedian Pat Paulsen introduced the cast of *See How They Run* and its star, Mickey Rooney. That was my first glimpse of Mickey Rooney. The next day, Monday, was spent going over the play several times, since the next day would be opening night. I arrived at the theater as soon as I could after teaching all day. I was formally introduced to Rooney, who insisted everyone call him "Mickey." To this day I do not know what I was thinking when introduced to him. "How do you feel?" asked Mickey. For some unknown reason I replied, "With my hands." Mickey's immediate reply was, "Oh, one of those." So began a month-long association with Mickey Rooney.

When recalling the month-long run of *See How They Run* with Mickey Rooney, so many images and events flood my mind. Foremost was that Rooney was always moving, mentally as well as physically. You could never interrupt him but he could always interrupt you.

It was the policy of Carousel Dinner Theatre that the cast got two complimentary tickets for dinner and show. Beyond that the cast had to pay for each dinner they requested. In speaking with the waiters and waitresses who worked at the theater I discovered they could get as many free meals as they wanted. This kind of irritated me a bit.

Rooney's private dressing room was located stage left of the theatre-in-the-round main stage. Across from Rooney's dressing room was a dressing room for the next-important actors and actresses. Further down the hall was another dressing room for the lesser performers, like myself. During the early days of the performances the sewer system backed up in this room through the floor grate, causing the carpet to get wet. I got a case of athlete's foot because of it. We were eventually moved to another room, just above the Carousel Dinner Theatre kitchen. In fact you passed a table with plates of rolls and pats of butter to go up the few stairs to that dressing room. It was not unusual for cast members to casually grab a plate of rolls and butter on their way up to the dressing room. The few of us in that room did not feel slighted because the Actor's Equity representative of the cast was in our dressing room. He was the one who got our room moved when the carpet in the other dressing room got soaked.

One more item concerning food comes to mind during the run of *See How They Run*. One Wednesday, between the 2:00 PM matinee and the 8:30 PM performance, Rooney treated the entire cast to a local German restaurant and picked up the entire tab. That is when I discovered German potato salad, as well as German sauerkraut, is served warm. As I said previously, Rooney was always "on the go." Most Wednesdays the cast would return to their rooms and take a nap between the matinee and evening performances. Not Rooney. He would play 18 holes of golf before the matinee performance and another 18 before the evening performance! On rainy Wednesdays when Rooney could not golf he would be seen at the local race track.

I observed, first hand, the cost of stardom. When I entered the theater before each performance there was always a stack of mail on the theater lobby desk for Rooney. There were scripts local people wanted him to read. There were business cards with notes like, "let's play golf sometime together" or "let's do lunch" or "let's do dinner" from total strangers.

Rooney never stayed after a performance to meet the public. After a very brief "curtain speech" he would immediately run backstage to his private dressing room, change clothes, splash on lemon aftershave, and bolt out the backdoor to his leased Chevrolet and drive back to his rented apartment nearby. There was one exception to Rooney's bolting after a performance.

Matinees traditionally consisted of groups of bused-in senior citizens, mostly women. They remembered a young Mickey Rooney as Andy Hardy and in films with Judy Garland. One matinee performance concluded with the usual short curtain speech, dash to the dressing room, change of clothes, lemon aftershave, and dash out the back door. This time Rooney was unaware a bus of senior citizens was loading up next to his rented car. He ran right into the middle of the crowd. He was mobbed by the older, gray and white-haired women. He eventually got into his car and drove off. He was more careful when he opened the back door to the theater to get to his car from then on.

Rooney's after-performance speech would consist of thanking the audience for attending. He would then add: "If you enjoyed the show please tell your friends. If you did not enjoy the show still tell your friends you enjoyed the show so they can get stuck just like you did!" Then Rooney would tell the audience, "On your way out of the theater there is a display of my wedding cakes in the lobby. Don't touch the last one. It's still wet!" He would also say a few things about his wives. "Ava Gardner, my first wife, laughed at everything I did," confessed Rooney. "That probably explains why we never had children!" If he then had nothing else to say he would immediately turn to any cast member and inform the audience it was their birthday. "Let's all sing *Happy Birthday.*" By the time the audience had sung the song to the surprised cast member, Rooney was gone!

Rooney made one exception to not seeing anyone after a performance. During one intermission, a Carousel Dinner Theatre waitress came backstage and handed Rooney an old black-and-white photograph. It was of a young Rooney in his army uniform standing beside another young soldier. Mickey looked at the photo and said to the waitress, "I'll see him after the show."

During intermissions the cast would gather in the small ante-room between Rooney's dressing room and the other one across from it. Rooney would sit on a chair and talk about many things. One night during one of those intermission sessions a patron casually strolled into our midst to speak to Rooney. Mickey was quite cordial to the man until he left. Then Rooney (and rightly so) lost his temper, raised his voice, and demanded to see the stage manager. He told him, in so many words, that the intrusion *would not* happen again. As a precaution the rest of the male cast took it upon itself to post a "guard" outside Rooney's area backstage so there would be no more wanderers interrupting our intermission sessions.

Rooney's approach to his appearance in *See How They Run* had many positive aspects as I recall the play's run. One matinee in particular sticks out in my mind. Wednesday matinees were at 2:00 PM. After lunch, the play would begin. As stated before, the matinees were usually attended by busloads of senior citizens who fondly recalled the Mickey Rooney of the MGM years, starring in musical comedies with Judy Garland and, of course, the *Andy Hardy* movie series. The series, by the way, gave Lana Turner and Ava Gardner, among others, their first screen appearances.

This particular Wednesday matinee was going along quite well. There is one scene in which many characters are seated on stage in a large room of an English house. The female housekeeper, a flighty cockney maid named Ida, is most paramount to the scene. When the time came for her entrance she did not appear! Since most of the cast had just been in the production of *See How They Run* with Mickey Rooney one month earlier, the cast was relatively familiar with each other's lines and carefully pieced the scene together, the audience being none the wiser. Then, after masterfully getting by Ida's input information, Ida walks in to the scene! Then everyone on stage just stopped and stared at each other in disbelief. What to do? Mickey immediately stood up, walked over to the corner of the stage, lifted one end of an area rug, looked at the cast and said, "You guys work this out, I'm going down the basement!." He came back out from under the carpet and informed the audience that there was obviously some problem with the play. He asked the audience, "Are you all having a good time?" Of course the response was immediate applause. Mickey then explained these things happened and, nonchalantly, resumed his position on stage and the play continued as if nothing happened.

Mickey Rooney treated his cast like family. Everyone was close, especially members of the cast who performed *See How They Run* previously at a dinner theater in Florida.

One day before a rehearsal, I was smoking a pipe after eating my brownbag lunch. Mickey walked in and noticed I was smoking a pipe. He stopped to smell the tobacco. "Hey, that smells good," he said. "Why don't we go the drugstore and get more of it. I smoke a pipe too." I explained the tobacco was not from the local drugstore. I told him I ordered it from Iwan Ries, a tobacco shop out of Chicago, Illinois. He immediately walked over to the box office and picked up the telephone and asked "information" for the telephone number of the Iwan Ries Company in Chicago, Illinois. I had followed Mickey to the box office and stood next to him. He got the phone number and called the shop. He informed whoever answered the telephone on the other end that he was Mickey Rooney, appearing in Ravenna, Ohio, and that one of their loyal customers, Irv Korman, had turned him on to their tobacco. "Send me four, one-pound cans of the tobacco and four pipes." He gave them the Carousel Dinner Theatre address in Ravenna, Ohio, and then hung up the telephone. I stood there in amazement.

A few days later, as I entered the lobby of the theater to go to the dressing room, I noticed a large cardboard box on the box office counter with a stack of mail. Mickey came out, got the cardboard box, read the return address label, and instructed me to follow him back to his dressing room. I obeyed. In his dressing room he opened the box. He lined up the four, one-pound cans of tobacco on his make-up table and said, "Take two of them." I was dumbfounded and couldn't think of anything to say. He said, "Go ahead, take two of them." I thanked him and stood there stunned for the moment. He then took four pipes out of the box. He took the time to put one at a time in his mouth, posed with each one, and asked what I thought. I told him one in particular looked good. He immediately took it out of his mouth and handed it to me. "Here," he said, "it's yours. I want you to have it." He told me he enjoyed a good pipe and tobacco. I believed him! I still stood there stunned and, again, thanked him. At the end of the run of "See How They Run" Mickey gave everyone connected with the production a wristwatch. I did not receive one but did not mind. I enjoyed the pipe and tobacco and it was more personal than a Timex wristwatch to me. I eventually received a very nice letter from the Iwan Ries Co., thanking me for being a loyal customer and for getting Mickey Rooney as a customer also. The letter also invited me to the store for a tour if I was ever in Chicago. I still have that letter and intend to take them up on their offer even if 36 years have gone by so far!

Rooney, as I said before, was always in motion. He had a "trick knee" that would occasionally go out on him during a performance. He would be running back stage from one exit to enter onstage somewhere else when the knee would go out of place. He would momentarily stop, "snap" the knee back in place, and continue running to get onstage on cue. For quick changes, he had strips of Velcro sewn behind the buttons on his shirts so he would not have to take the time to unbutton then re-button the shirt. He merely pulled open the shirt, changed, and pressed down the Velcro on the next shirt he had just put on. He also had a pair of white tennis shoes painted brown to look like leather.

When not in costume, Rooney would wear loose-fitting clothes and a wool ski cap. His glasses, when not in use, would always be on his forehead or front of the wool hat. This was very consistent. The proof of this habit was verified when I looked through the personal file I had collected on Rooney over the years. Not only were the hat and glasses in the usual place on his head in a photo taken of the two of us together, but also in two photos of him from the Akron Beacon Journal newspaper, one from 1973 and another from 1986, when he appeared again in Akron.

In 1986, Rooney was in Akron, Ohio, appearing for Kenley Players at the Akron Civic Theatre, in the comedy *Go Ahead and Laff.* I thought it would be a great idea to take my now 13-year-old daughter, Julie, with me to see the play and meet Rooney afterwards, since he held her when she was six months old in 1973, at Carousel Dinner Theatre in Ravenna. By 1986, I was reviewing plays for the weekly "West Side Leader" newspaper. I knew producer John Kenley by then, and told him the story of appearing with Rooney in 1973 at Carousel Dinner Theatre and him holding my daughter. Kenley said it was okay to go down to his dressing room after the show. I arrived early before the performance and saw Rooney onstage taking care of last-minute stage business being opening night. I could not see him then and told Kenley. Mr. Kenley said he would personally meet me at the stage right door to escort me and my daughter to Rooney's dressing room immediately after the show. Knowing Rooney's habit of bolting soon after the curtain call (from previous experience in 1973), Julie and I ran down to the stage right door to catch him before he left. We waited for him and suddenly he ran into his dressing room. What happened next initially shocked me. While he was changing quickly (as usual) I told him I appeared with him at Carousel Dinner Theatre in 1973, in *See How They Run.* I told him I played Sgt. Towers. I took out a photo of us together taken then.

Rooney quickly looked at the photo and said, "I guess we've both changed a bit." He then called to the rest of the cast and said, "Hey, guys, let's go!" Now dressed, Rooney and the rest of the cast bolted out the back door.

There I stood, photo in hand, next to my daughter, who was holding a camera I was going to use to take a photo of with Rooney. I immediately looked down at my daughter and said, "I'm sorry, honey." Her response showed more maturity than I could ever imagine. "Oh, that's okay, dad," she said with a sour-like angry look on her face. Undaunted, after writing a review of the play I wrote a companion piece about being in a play with Rooney 13 years before and the hasty and disappointing attempted mini-reunion. I poignantly ended the article by saying, "As the proverb says (with a slight alteration), 'Time wounds all heels!'"

What I later realized was that each cast Rooney was in was like a close-knit family. Anyone not connected with that particular production was an "outsider." I was not a part of the current production of *Go Ahead and Laff.* Therefore, even though I had been in a previous production with him, I was now an outsider to Rooney.

There are still other more-fond memories of the autumn in 1973. Rooney autographed an 8" x 10" photo for me. Before he signed it he looked at the publicity photo, obviously taken years before, and looked at all the hair on the head of his image in the older picture. Now, obviously thinner on top, he remarked as he personalized the photo, "Just look. Back then I used to have *waves*. Now all I have is *beach.*" The only reference I heard Rooney utter in regards to his stature was when he jokingly mentioned trying to trace his family tree. "You know," he said, "I was trying to trace my roots recently and I discovered they lead to a stump!"

Rooney showed another helpful side of himself on another occasion. When you entered the theater to go to your dressing room before the show, there was a bulletin board posted backstage. On it was a sign-in sheet and copies of stories and reviews of the production. One day I signed in and noticed a new review posted. I read it and could not believe it. It was from the Kent State University student newspaper. Kent State University was located close to Ravenna where Carousel Dinner Theatre. There was an intense rivalry between Kent State University and The University of Akron, where I earned a Bachelor of Arts Degree and Master of Arts Degree a few years later. Being a graduate of The University of Akron was mentioned in the program notes. The fact I had a minor part, particularly at the end of the play, meant I would hardly expect to be mentioned in any play reviews of the production, though a few reviews did actually mention me, referring to the "local talent" angle. The review from the Kent State newspaper ended by singling me out, personally, for ruining the last and final act of the play! Imagine. I guessed the rivalry between the two universities went beyond sports activities. I was standing at the bulletin board reading and reacting to the negative review after signing in when Rooney came up to me and saw me reading the article. "What do you think?" he asked. I was actually too numb and stunned to react. Rooney immediately sensed this and asked me, "Are you having a good time doing this play?" I replied, "Yes." Rooney told me he thought I was doing a spectacular job and that one negative review should not mean anything, especially when he, the star of the production, thought I was doing just fine. That helped since none of the other of the reviews were negative, especially where my minor part was concerned. I never forgot Rooney consoling me that day.

Rooney, despite his trick knee, seemed to be in good health. He attributed his present condition to being a student of Christian Science. He once told me of all his carousing, alcohol problems, etc. But now he said, because of being Christian Science, he was okay. "I want to die healthy," he said. I also noticed he wore a copper bracelet on his wrist at all times. Every time I see Rooney on television or in a recent photograph, I always look for and find the bracelet on him.

Speaking of health and alcohol, I once asked Rooney about the actor, Errol Flynn, since I was an admirer of his action films and equally action-filled life. Rooney was a close friend of his and even a pallbearer at his funeral in October of 1959. Rooney would shake his head about Flynn. "I tried to get him to stop drinking (vodka)," he said. "It got so bad he carried a quart bottle of the stuff in his pants." Rooney related all the times men would come up to Flynn and try and pick a fight with him to prove he wasn't so tough in real life. Rooney said Flynn would always try to avoid a confrontation by saying, "Come on, mate, let's have a drink." When this tactic would not work and the man would not back down, Flynn would immediately slam the heel of one of his shoes onto the very top of the man's foot, making him reel in instant, incapacitating pain, unable to move or respond.

As the weeks flew by I anticipated, with dread, the end of the run of *See How They Run* and an unbelievable association with "show biz" and Mickey Rooney.

Two of the cast members, George Emch (originally from nearby Youngstown, Ohio) and James Galvin told me about a movie they had just completed in New York City before doing *See How They Run* with Mickey Rooney. It was a movie about a New York City policeman who goes undercover but finds out some of the policemen in his department are taking bribes. A lot of his section is corrupt. The movie starred Al Pacino. No one had heard about it yet because it was still in post-production. The motion picture was *Serpico*. Emch and Galvin told me what parts they portrayed (as un-credited extras) in the movie and when I eventually went to see it I saw them. Emch was in a high-ranking police uniform sitting on stage during Serpico's graduation ceremony as he becomes a New York City policeman. Galvin was later in the film, as a television camera operator at the hearings in which Serpico testifies at the police corruption hearings.

It was truly a grind: working all day, taking a short nap at home, driving to Ravenna to be in the play, driving home late and going to sleep. My wife was always waiting for me and asking what entertainment gossip I had heard from the cast during our intermission conversations with Rooney and the rest of the cast. I sometimes had to postpone the information until the next day when I came home from work, just before my nap.

Aside from being in a professional play production with Mickey Rooney, I had other personal rewards. Coming into the lobby one day a total stranger looked at me and then saw my photo on the "cast wall." He elbowed the woman next to him. He pointed to the photo of me on the wall, then at me, and told his wife, "Yep, that's him!"

Occasionally, when exiting the front of the theater after a show some patrons would linger, probably looking for Rooney who had long gone. Some wanted the cast to sign their programs. Others just wanted to look at us, probably to see if you actually looked like our publicity pictures on the wall!

One evening as I was about to leave a familiar face approached me. "Hi, Irv," said the woman. "Remember me?" she asked. I recognized her as Nancy Salzer, a girl I recalled from acting in plays at The University of Akron several years before, as an undergraduate. Nancy, now married, introduced me to her husband, who was in an army uniform. "It's our anniversary and my husband wanted to know what I wanted to do to celebrate. I told him I'd like to see Irv in *See How They Run* at Carousel Dinner Theatre." I was quite moved. Someone actually came to see me!

The end of the production came and went and I resumed my normal life once again. I was always on the lookout for news of Mickey Rooney or any of the cast members. One other supporting player, Jim Peck (who played the Lithuanian spy) was seen on a PBS play production as a clergyman.

The following January my wife and I were visiting friends in Canton, Ohio, so I thought I would call Gary Wilbanks, who played the clergyman, Lionel Toop, in *See How They Run*. He was the other local actor in the production. I called his telephone number and a woman answered. She said Gary was not at home. He was appearing in a play with Mickey Rooney in Florida. What! I asked if the play was *See How They Run*. She said yes. I was livid! How could this happen? They went to Florida with the production and did not ask me? How could they? I was furious for a long time. Eventually I called Gary again to vent my frustration. What he told me calmed me down and actually made sense, although it took a while for me to settle down.

Professionally speaking, when a play or motion picture is finished, the participants are actually all unemployed until they get with another production. Therefore, technically, the entire cast of *See How They Run*, Rooney included, became instantly unemployed when the show at Carousel Dinner Theatre closed on November 4th. When Rooney reassembled the cast for the Florida production, they did not include me because I was the only one who still had full time employment (speech/language pathologist for the Akron Board of Education). They figured since I was married with a six-month old daughter and fully employed that it would be hard to get away to Florida for a month-long run of *See How They Run*. Gary then made me feel somewhat better when he said Rooney told him he missed the smell of my pipe tobacco. That told me he remembered me and that somewhat consoled me a bit.

As I related before Rooney was in a "down" period in his career in 1973, at the time of *See How They Run*. After that I followed his career in the media. Aside from *The Black Stallion, Bill*, and *Pete's Dragon* movies and *Sugar Babies* on Broadway, Rooney's voice was that of Santa Claus in television's 1974 animated movie of *The Year Without a Santa Claus*. His voice had been Santa before in 1970's *Santa Claus Is Comin' to Town*. Among other appearances, he was seen in the 1994 documentary, *That's Entertainment: III*, as himself, guiding us through the back lot of MGM. In 1998 Rooney's voice was that of a pig in a *Babe* sequel, *Pig in the City*.

More recently Rooney was teamed with Dick Van Dyke as a shady custodian in 2007 in the motion picture, *Night at the Museum*.

Being in show business for most of his life (91 at the time of this book) has garnered Mickey Rooney many accolades. The Academy Awards have honored Rooney six times. In 1939 he shared the Juvenile Award with actress Deanna Durbin. In 1940 he was nominated as Best Actor in a Leading Role for *Babes in Arms*. In 1944 he was nominated as Best Actor in a Leading Role for *The Human Comedy*. In 1957 he was nominated as Best Actor in a Supporting Role for *The Bold and the Brave*. In 1980 he was nominated as Best Actor in a Supporting Role for *The Black Stallion*. In 1983 he received an Honorary Award "in recognition of his 50 years of versatility in a variety of memorable film performances."

Television, in the form of an Emmy, has rewarded Rooney four times. In 1958 he was nominated for Actor- Best Single Performance- Lead or Support for "The Comedian," a Playhouse 90 production. In 1959 he was nominated for Best Single Performance by an Actor for "Alcoa Theatre." In 1982 he won for Outstanding Lead Actor in a Limited Series or a Special for. In 1984 he was nominated for an Emmy for Outstanding Lead Actor in a Limited Series or a Special for "Bill: On His Own."

Rooney has won two Golden Globe Awards. In 1964 he won for Best TV Star-Male. In 1982 he won Best Performance by an Actor in a Mini-Series or Motion Picture Made for TV for *Bill*.

He has two stars on The Hollywood Walk of Fame. One for Motion Picture (located at 1718 Vine Street) and one for Television (located at 6541 Hollywood Blvd.).

Mickey Rooney wrote about his life, an autobiography titled *Life Is Too Short*, published by Villard Books in 1991. Rooney has been married eight times and has eleven children. Presently he is married to Jan Chamberlin. Never one to merely retire, Rooney, recently was quoted as saying, "I say, 'Don't retire-inspire.'" As recently as 2010, Rooney and his wife were touring in a two-person revue inspired by his MGM musicals, called *Let's Put on a Show!* He also completed a cameo in the upcoming new Muppet movie to be released in November of 2011. How does he stay fresh and alive? "Positive thinking," he replies. "If you say you can, you can."

Best
Wishes
Irw

Phyllis
Diller

Chapter 24
Phyllis Diller,
Comedienne/Concert Pianist/Painter

"A stand-up comic is judged by every line. Singers get applause at the end of their song no matter how bad they are."

"It's a good thing beauty is skin deep, or I'd be rotten to the core."

"Always be nice to your children because they are the ones who choose your rest home."

"Aim high, and you won't shoot your foot off."

"The shortest distance between two laughs is a punch line."
                    . . . Phyllis Diller

We were both standing next to each other in a totally empty room. We obviously read the invitation incorrectly.

"Are you with the press?" she asked.

"Yes," I replied.

"What's your name?" she inquired.

"Irving," I said.

"Irving . . . *Really*?" she asked.

She was comedienne Phyllis Diller. It was our first encounter. I had reviewed a performance of hers two years earlier at Carousel Dinner Theatre in Ravenna, Ohio, for a weekly newspaper. Ms. Diller was having a press reception at Tangier Restaurant in Akron, Ohio, with owner Ed George. The party was actually being held in a room downstairs. As we walked down together I could not help but glance at the famous blonde-haired comedienne. She, indeed, looked good in her red dress. She had continually looked good since receiving her first much-publicized face-lift years before. Diller was one of the first famous entertainers to *not* hide the fact she had undergone plastic surgery; unheard-of at the time. But one glance down at her hands revealed her true age. The press reception was just before her May 1-

6 appearance at Tangier Restaurant in the Sultan's Cabaret.

I would review, interview, and meet Ms. Diller about half a dozen times, either at Tangier or Carousel Dinner Theatre between 1985 and 1996. What was significant about Tangier Restaurant was that it was the first *and* last place I met her in person: first in 1987 at the press reception, and last, just after a matinee performance in 1996.

Mention "Phyllis Diller" and a flood of images come to mind: the trademark "guffaw" laugh, the silver lame` sack dress with matching, high-heel boots, skinny legs, blonde fright wig, and a long cigarette-holder. The first one-liner out of her mouth was usually, "I'm known as the Bo Derek of the Geritol Set!" Then the endless and effortless one-liners began to flow, punctuated by that trademark "guffaw" laugh.

But that late April afternoon during the press reception Diller was cordial and friendly, neatly attired in a red dress. The reception was scheduled from 5:00 PM to 7:00 PM for Wednesday, April 29, 1987. It was for the local press and media prior to her Tangier appearance. As Diller and I entered the correct reception room a jazz combo was playing. As soon as the honored guest was spotted the combo stopped playing and Ms. Diller was announced to the assembled. She stood at the bar by a buffet table and began an informal press conference while sipping a glass of wine.

"My doctors follow me around with knives," she lamented and went into detail about her latest operation. "They suctioned fat through my navel and injected it into my face by my lower mouth to get rid of a few wrinkles." After a pause she said, "Barbara Walters has been done-over more than me and needed it more!"

Through the rest of the question-and-answer period the press learned, at the time (1987), Ms. Diller had been married twice: for 25 years the first time and 12 years the second time.

"Got any more questions?" Diller inquired. "I have answers left over from my last show!"

Ms. Diller revealed she recently completed a motion picture with comic Jonathan Winters, called *T.I.P.S.* (*To Insure Proper Service*) in which she portrayed his mother. The script, according to Diller, was mostly ad-libbed. Diller confessed she liked the comedy work of entertainers like Winters, Shecky Greene, Joan Rivers, Bob Newhart, and Roseanne Barr.

When asked about her immediate plans after her Tangier appearance, Diller told the select crowd she was off to Ft. Bragg for Bob Hope's 84th birthday, then to New York, Washington D.C., and on to Los Angeles. "I love to travel," Diller confessed. "Talk about lost luggage," Diller said, "I look good in men's suits!"

On a more personal side Diller confessed her first facelift was in 1971. She mixed personal childhood psychological pain with her own style of humor. "I got tired of playing witch roles. With me it was Halloween every day! I never liked my old face. Why was I born wrong-side-out? I always wanted to be pretty. I played in comic roles in high school. It was a defense. I was so ugly as a baby my mother put my bonnet on backwards!" After another sip of wine, Diller said, "I have quite a cross to bear . . . It's in my car!"

Ms. Diller confessed to having recently read books about Carol Burnett and Joan Rivers. "Such sad childhoods," she observed. It would be another eighteen years until she would pen her own revealing autobiography (*Like a Lampshade in a Whorehouse* in 2005).

"You have to have a good attitude toward yourself," Diller advised. "If you can't accept *yourself* you can't get things done."

Diller said she presently lived in the Brentwood suburb of Los Angeles. She said she grew up in Lima, Ohio, as Phyllis Driver. She even entertained at Lima State Hospital, mentioning an amazing statistic: 90% of the criminals in the institution were abused as children.

Phyllis Ada Driver was born on July 17, 1917, to Perry Marcus and Frances Ada (Romshe) Driver in Lima, Ohio, the only child of older parents. She graduated Lima's Central High School, and then studied three years at the Sherwood Music Conservatory in Chicago. Not many people know what an accomplished classical concert pianist Diller is. She even considered it as a career. From Chicago she transferred back to Ohio's Bluffton College, where, among other activities, she wrote humorous articles for the college newspaper. It was at Bluffton College she met her future husband, Sherwood (later to become "Fang" in her trademark comedy nightclub act).

At age 22, Diller married Sherwood Anderson Diller in 1939 (they divorced in 1965). Before she knew it she was mother of six children (one died in infancy in 1945 at the age of two weeks). Peter was born in 1940 (died of cancer in 1998), Sally was born in 1944, Suzanne born in 1946, Stephanie in 1948 (died of a stroke in 2002), Perry in 1950.

During World War II, the Diller family moved to Michigan, where Sherwood found work at the Willow Run Bomber Plant. Diller found work as an advertising copywriter. She began writing one-line jokes about household situations and garnered encouragement from other housewives in the same situation. After the war the family moved to California for more lucrative job opportunities for

Sherwood. While living in San Francisco, Phyllis became a secretary at a San Francisco television station. After trying out her nightclub act on a few local television stations, in 1955, at age 37, she made her comedy debut at the famed Purple Onion nightclub. Her two-week engagement lasted 1 ½ years! Her nightclub performance eventually landed her on television shows with Jack Paar, Jack Benny, and Red Skelton. She was even a contestant on Groucho Marx' *You Bet Your Life* television show.

One of Diller's closest professional relationships was with Bob Hope. She appeared in three motion pictures with him (*Boy, Did I Get the Wrong Number* in 1966, *Eight On the Lam* in 1967, and *The Private Navy of Sgt. O'Farrell*, in 1968). She went on Hope's 1967 USO Viet Nam tour (plus two others) and appeared on 23 of his television specials.

While appearing in the comedy motion picture, *Did You Hear the One about the Traveling Saleslady?* in 1965, Diller met singer Warde Donovan, who appeared with her in the movie. They married but divorced ten years later. Two tries at her own television show, *The Phyllis Diller Show,* both failed in 1966 and 1967. But she continued to be popular as a guest on other television shows such as *Laugh-In*, Dean Martin's *Celebrity Roasts*, *The Hollywood Squares*, and *The Gong Show*. On a more personal television note, Diller was featured on Ralph Edwards' *This Is Your Life* in 1971.

Obviously Phyllis Diller loves television. "It's not my fault if the tubes blow out when I laugh," she once observed. Ms. Diller also recorded many successful comedy albums. Of course her "bread-and-butter" eventually became her trademark popular nightclub comedy act.

At the time of the Tangier reception (1987), Phyllis Diller was approaching her 70th birthday. She told the press party she had five children between the ages of 37 and 46. One of her grandchildren (the oldest) would be starting college. "Just think," she then observed, "if I married Mel Tillis, I'd be *Phyllis Tillis!*"

Diller then talked about impersonator Jim Bailey. Bailey gained fame by impersonating female entertainers like Judy Garland, Peggy Lee, Barbra Streisand, and Phyllis Diller. Diller said Bailey memorized a comedy album of hers and repeated it word-for-word in his nightclub act. It was done so well that meticulous Bailey even inserted Diller's sniffles in his act: you see, Ms. Diller had a cold when the album was recorded live at one of her nightclub performances!

Diller told the Tangier press crowd that her first national exposure was at the behest of Groucho Marx, as a contestant, on his television quiz show in the early 1950's.

At that moment in the press reception, Ms. Diller let us all watch her latest creative endeavor: a video tape of "How to Have a Money-Making Garage Sale." The humorous, 20-minute video was classic Diller. Her topics, in the video, included what sells and what doesn't, how to display merchandise, how to price it, how to advertise, when to hold the garage sale, how to deal with shoplifters, what to do with leftovers, how to establish inventory control, and how to deal with the "morning after" the garage sale. "When in doubt, put it out!" was Diller's motto for the video. Then she advised: "Buy it (the video tape) then sell it in *your* garage sale!"

Following the video, Tangier owner Ed George took charge and told those present at the reception about the upcoming attractions in Sultan's Cabaret, his Las Vegas-style nightclub lounge. George told the crowd it was the restaurant's 35th anniversary. He told of the establishment's 6 million-dollar-a-year business in giving a reason for people to go out: good food, free parking in a covered parking deck, and new entertainment. "We have 4,000 busloads a year for our matinees alone," George proudly stated.

As I left the reception and walked to my car I recalled the very first time I saw and reviewed Phyllis Diller on stage, almost two years earlier at Carousel Dinner Theatre in Ravenna, Ohio, in November of 1985. The printed Carousel program noted that it was Ms. Diller's sixth appearance at the dinner theater since it opened in 1974. That fact alone was a testament to Diller's popularity, particularly in the northeastern Ohio area.

The evening's festivities began with a buffet dinner, a Carousel trademark at the time. At about 8:00 PM singer Larry Stuart (singer Enzo Stuarti's son) came out to begin the first part of the evening's entertainment. For almost a half hour, Stuart sang several songs, including a medley of Bobby Darin tunes.

After about a half-hour intermission, the house lights dimmed and the announcer said, "Here she is: The Bo Derek of the Geritol Set: Phyllis Diller!" And out she came, resembling a female version of the Tin Man from *The Wizard of Oz*. Her dress looked like it was made of aluminum foil with high-heel boots to match. The boots supported a pair of very skinny legs. The teased blonde fright wig and trademark cigarette holder completed the visual-trademark Phyllis Diller the audience came to see. What followed was about an hour's worth of her favorite targets and one-liners to go with them.

Diller told the Northeastern Ohio crowd about the recent floods near her home in southern California. "It was so bad that a flasher opened his raincoat and caught a trout!" The punch line was immediately punctuated by one of her trademark "guffaws." After the audience laughter died down she looked at her outfit and remarked, "I look like I was raped by the Bird of Paradise."

Then the assault began on one of her most favorite targets: her husband, "Fang" and his cheapness. She told the Carousel crowd about the night she got her engagement ring from Fang. "He said it was a square-cut diamond," Diller said then confessed: "It was a Chicklet!"

"The other night I told Fang I wanted to eat out," she said "We ate in the garage!" A barrage of bad cooking jokes ensued punctuated by, "The kids bought me a stove that flushes."

More acerbic attacks were reserved for Diller's mother-in-law and her huge stature. "At Halloween we don't have a jack-o-lantern," she noted. "We put her head in the window with a match in her mouth." About the upcoming Yuletide season Diller remarked, "I didn't get my mother-in-law a Christmas present this year. She didn't use last year's present: a cemetery plot."

Then Ms. Diller went back to the types of restaurants Fang took her to. "At this one place I asked for Russian dressing and got a photograph of Gorbachev (the current prime minister of the Soviet Union) putting his pants on." How bad was a recent trip to a Mexican restaurant with Fang? "The food was so hot that before you ate you put (a roll of) toilet paper in the freezer." Any specials at the place? "The catch of the day was *hepatitis*!" How about the service? "I asked the waiter to heat up my coffee. He threw a (lit) cigarette in it."

What is a comedy routine without period (1985) political jokes? Ronald Reagan was President at the time. Ms. Diller noted his age, "His last birthday cake looked like a prairie fire." Diller then observed, "To him a second term was like a double feature." We were informed by Ms. Diller why Reagan wore a hearing aid. "It's because the Democrats told him to 'stick it in his ear'."

Speaking of Democrats, former President Jimmy Carter did not escape Diller's observations. "He's from Plains, Georgia," Diller told the crowd. The town is so small that "the fire department is an eight-year-old bed-wetter."

Diller then made a few semi-comedic recollections about her career as a mother, having all five of her children within nine years. "I had so many kids it was standing room only in the playpen," she recalled. "It was so wet there was always a rainbow over the playpen."

Then back to her mother-in-law and her large body. "She puts on make-up with a roller," she recounted. "In a 'hula hoop' she looks like Saturn." Recalling her mother-in-law's trip downtown one day Diller recalled, "She blew her nose and the construction crew broke for lunch." About the woman's size Diller lamented, "She's so big they use her once a month to clean the Holland Tunnel! She's so big that she was born on the eighth, ninth, and tenth of June! One day a VW Beetle hit her. They still haven't found it. She has a chafing problem: her legs caught fire running after a bus." Then Diller added two more insults about the lady concerning her pets. "She left us a Persian rug: she sat on the cat! Then she stepped on the dog's tail. We now call him 'Beaver.'"

Ms. Diller pulls no punches about housework and her house cleaning habits; or rather, lack of them. "I keep a flea collar on both ankles. My Roach Motel is booked for the next two months."

"I love my LA lifestyle," confessed Diller. "I was invited to a *pot* party so I brought a tuna casserole." Then there is driving in LA, especially getting her driver's license. "I got two tickets on the written test. I even have a phone in my car: I hit a telephone booth."

As her set wound down, Diller returned to Fang and her mother, with more punch lines. Even her dog was not spared. "My mother was once asked if anyone in the family suffered from insanity. 'No,' mother replied, 'we enjoyed it.'" Diller once told Fang she was going to improve their sex life with an *aphrodisiac*. Fang said, "No black women in this house!" Then there is Diller's German Shepherd dog. "I say 'attack'," says Diller, "and it *has* one!"

As her comedy set ended, I realized what a trailblazer Phyllis Diller was. She began her career at age 37, after having five children. Female nightclub comedians were a rarity in 1985. I tried to think of female comediennes of the day. I could only think of a handful, like Totie Fields, Pat Carroll, Joanne Worley, Joan Rivers, Lily Tomlin, and Roseanne Barr.

Four years later was the second time I reviewed Ms. Diller's comedy performance. It was on a perfect night for her: Halloween! It was October 31, 1989, again at Carousel Dinner Theatre, but this time at their new location in Akron, Ohio, near the Akron-Fulton airport, in the former Breakaway Nightclub. Instead of the trademark Carousel buffet, as in their old home (a renovated A&P super market converted into a theater-in-the-round) in Ravenna, the new, much larger, Carousel (now a more traditional three-quarter-front thrust stage configuration) featured menus and table-side service by waiters and waitresses.

Diller's opening act was, again, a singer, but this time it was Carousel resident vocalist, Mark Thomsen. He opened for Ms Diller with about a half-.hour medley of tunes. After the usual half-hour intermission, Carousel had contestants vying for prizes in a "Phyllis Diller Look-a-like Contest." After all, it was Halloween! Prizes were awarded, and then the Carousel house lights dimmed. Diller was introduced the same way; as the "Bo Derek of the Geritol Set." Would her topics and punch lines be the same as four years ago? Would there be new topics and new material?

Reflecting on the holiday and the contest preceding her entrance, Diller said, "Every night is Halloween for me!" Then noting the contest she said, "I entered a Phyllis Diller look-a-like contest…and lost!"

Diller looked into the audience and inquired, "Is Shirley MacLaine in the audience tonight? She could be any one of you."

Without missing a beat, Ms, Diller began a verbal assault on one of her usual favorite targets: husband, Fang. "Fang couldn't make the trip (to Akron). He had an accident: he was doing pushups in the nude and didn't see the mousetrap!" The verbal assault continued. "The happiest day of my life will be when I open the refrigerator and see Fang's picture on the milk carton. You know, he's so dumb he went up to the thermostat. It said '70.' 'My goodness,' he said, 'I lost 50 pounds!'" Then the audience learned of Fang's recent fishing trip. "Fang went ice fishing," Diller said, "and he caught 50 pounds of ice."

Next Diller began observations on another favorite topic: her appearance. "The best contraceptive for old people is nudity. It works for me. You've heard of 'the total woman.' You're looking at a fraction! Did you know Geritol pays me five-hundred dollars a month to say I *didn't* use it?"

More Fang insults followed that I remembered from Diller's 1985 appearance. But some new material was also present. After all, we had another president: George Bush. "Remember when he recently said Pearl Harbor was bombed on September 7th? He was *bombed* on December 7th!" Diller even had an observation about Japanese businesses recently buying up California real estate: "The Japanese bought Forest Lawn (cemetery) and changed the name to

Jap in the Box."

Verbal assaults and observations were made about Zsa Zsa Gabor, Liz Taylor, Dolly Parton ("Poor thing. She's a hunch-front!"), the Reagans ("Someone asked Nancy Reagan if she understood 'the poor.' 'Yes,' she said, 'only if they speak slowly.'"), George and Barbara Bush, Jimmy Carter, Gary Hart, Jimmy Swaggart, Oral Roberts, and Tammy Fae Bakker. "Tammy looks like an Exxon oil spill. One of her eyelashes fell off and broke her foot. You know what P.T.L. stands for? 'Part Thy Legs.'"

Another favorite target of Diller's is her California lifestyle. "I went to the doctor and he told me to take off my clothes. Then *he* put them on!" Other California observations included: "I went to the store the other day and said, 'I'd like to see something in a bra.' The clerk took one look at me and said, 'I'll bet you would.'" Driving in Los Angeles: "I'm sure glad I have group insurance: I hit a group!" Diller's dog, once again, garnered some attention. "My German Shepherd bites his nails, barks with a lisp, and has bumps on his head from chasing parked cars." About a recent costume party that Diller attended in LA, she observed, "I went topless: my upper plate fell out!"

What would a Phyllis Diller appearance be without some cracks about her mother-in-law? "Our wedding was a civil ceremony. Fang's mother didn't come." Her size is a constant topic for ridicule: "She's so fat she has a racing stripe on her fork." Diller's brother-in-law wasn't even spared. "He used to sell airplane horns. He was killed by a falling star: an actress fell on him."

Then there's Diller's "fast" sister. "She's been in more hotels than a Gideon Bible. Joan Collins called *her* a slut! Her bedroom has a revolving door on it."

Even though the topics were the same, most of the jokes were newer and different than her performance four years earlier. When a comic returns to the same location, the same punch lines are okay if the audience is totally different. But if a large portion of the audience is repeat business, it would be smart if most of the material is new and fresh even if the subjects remain the same. Phyllis Diller knows her craft and delivers mostly new material on the same familiar topics. Besides her appearance, her topics, too, are part of her famous stage performances. She knows her territory and it is obvious. Her timing is perfect. She knows not to step on audience laughter. Her pacing shows, with just the right amount of time between her laughs (or guffaws) and the audience's immediate responsive laughter.

Having seen Diller on stage in her "Bo Derek of the Geritol Set" persona twice and observing her offstage self at the Tangier reception party, what would Diller be like during a telephone interview? The question was answered on Wednesday, April 24, 1996, prior to her appearance at Tangier Restaurant, once again for three days, May 3, 4, and 5. Each date included a matinee as well as an evening performance.

Ms. Diller was speaking from her Brentwood home in Los Angeles, California. According to Diller the house is a large, English-style home. "The place used to be haunted but the ghosts haven't been seen back since the night I tried on all my wigs!"

Even though Diller currently lives in California, she is still very proud of her Lima, Ohio, roots. "Hugh Downs and Helen O'Connell came from Lima. I went to Bluffton College with him (Downs)." I asked Ms. Diller if Jonathan Winters came from Lima. "No, he came from Springfield, Ohio, from a very wealthy family. His parents owned a bank. Paul Lynde was from (nearby) Washington Courthouse. Dodie Goodman is from Ohio, as is Cliff Arquette." Arquette first gained national attention by appearing as Charlie Weaver on *The Jack Paar Show* reading his humorous "Letters from Mama." He later gained fame on TV's *The Hollywood Squares*. Other celebrities from Ohio, Diller noted, were Danny Thomas and Jamie Farr (Klinger on TV's *M.A.S.H.*) from Toledo, Dean Martin from Steubenville, and Tim Conway and Bob Hope from the Cleveland area. "Seven Presidents were born in Ohio," added Diller.

Speaking of Ohio, Diller told me of her upcoming three-day appearance at Tangier Restaurant. "Each date has a matinee," she said. "I love coming back to Ohio. It's my home state."

I asked where she'd been recently. "I was in Canada, Dallas, and Tennessee. All three in six days," she said, "Two days in each town. In Tennessee I opened Dolly Parton's 'Dollywood.' You know, I have enough *frequent flier miles* to go to the moon!"

I asked if she had any new hobbies or pursuits in her spare time. "I'm painting now," she replied. "It was an accident. With me everything is an accident, you know. People used to call up and they say, 'we need a piece of art for charity,' and I'd sit down and do something. They started selling for five thousand (dollars) and I thought, 'wait a minute. Wait a minute! *I* should be painting!'" Diller couldn't pass up an opportunity to add a comment about her onstage appearance. "I paint a little like Picasso: I look very much like a lot of Picasso's!" I asked her what form her medium was and what she painted. "I specialize in faces, impressionist things. I really can't give a name to it. Sometimes I paint trees, houses, and churches. I use acrylics, sometimes watercolors and pen-and-ink." She then told me, "Red Skelton makes a million (dollars) a year on his paintings. He's a natural-born artist. Henry Fonda used to do wonderful art so I thought, 'Well, I'll do that!'"

I reminded Ms. Diller that one of the first times I caught her nightclub act was on Halloween. "Well, you know," she replied, "that's my night!"

I asked Diller if she still played concert events as a classical pianist. "No," she said, "I plan to do just one this year. I do not do that anymore because I don't practice. I don't have time because I'm too busy. I love being on the go all the time."

Speaking of being "on the go", I asked Diller where she would be appearing immediately after her three-day appearance in Ohio. "I go to Joliette, Illinois, then Wabash, Indiana, with Roger Williams, and then I go to Las Vegas for a Mother's Day show." She then, once again, repeated, "I love to travel!"

I asked Diller if she still writes most of her own material. "Yep!" she replied.

She spoke fondly of her friend, Bob Hope. "His joke file is larger than mine. Everything about him is bigger than me!" I recalled to Diller what he said about her on a Christmas tour of Vietnam: "If Diller had been cooking for the Viet Cong, the war would have been over much sooner!" "You know," Diller said, "he'll be 93 this year (1996)? He loves to make jokes about me and I love for him to do it."

I read in Diller's printed biography that she owns several classic automobiles: a 1967 custom-made Checker wagon, an Excalibur, a 1927 red Mercedes Phaeton, a 1959 Silver Cloud Rolls Royce, and a 1971 SL Mercedes sedan. The reason I mention this fact is that Diller brought up the subject of a recent gas crises and how expensive gasoline was in California in 1996: $3.00 a gallon while it was $1.23

at the time in Ohio. "You double your car's value by filling up with gas," Diller joked. "Your Chevron card maxes out before your Visa (card)!" Then Diller jokingly confided in me how expensive gasoline in California really was: "Elizabeth Taylor just announced a brand of gas named after her!"

I knew the telephone interview was over when Ms. Diller said, "Well, Irv, looking forward to seeing you."

Phyllis Diller had been a lot like she was the first time I met her in person in 1987: cordial, pleasant, yet did not pass up the opportunity to let the stage "Phyllis Diller" occasionally appear to plug a joke or make a comic observation about her trademark outrageous onstage persona.

My oldest daughter, Julie, and I did catch a matinee of Diller's at Tangier the following week that May in 1996. I felt embarrassed for her, because the matinee performance we attended in the Sultan's Cabaret seemed sparsely attended. Nonetheless Diller gave it her usual first-rate, trademark performance. I like to think the audience, sparse in numbers, was "quality, not quantity." After the show we went back to the dressing room. Diller had taken off her onstage outfit and looked like I had seen her years before at the press reception. Ms. Diller noted that her dresser for her performances in Akron was one of her daughters. She cordially signed and personalized the 8" x 10" black-and-white publicity photograph I handed her. She also posed for a photograph with me. Seeing Ms. Diller again was a most pleasant and personally rewarding experience: like no time had passed since our meeting for the first time some nine years before.

Phyllis Diller continued her famous nightclub act across North America as well as across the world. She appeared in serious roles on television in *Boston Legal* and *Seventh Heaven.* Her first movie role was a cameo role, that of larger-than-life nightclub hostess Texas Guinan in 1961 with Warren Beatty in Elia Kazan's *Splendor in the Grass.* She also appeared in many live stage productions such as *Wonderful Town, Happy Birthday, Everybody Loves Opal, Nunsense,* and for three months as the lead on Broadway in *Hello, Dolly!*

Awards and much-deserved accolades have not eluded Phyllis Diller. Among the more notable ones: 1992 American Comedy Awards, USA: recipient of the Lifetime Achievement Award in

Comedy; 1996 winner of a Golden Apple Award for Most Cooperative Actress; the 1967 Laurel Awards gave her a Golden Laurel for Female New Face; 2004 San Diego Film Festival's Governor's Award; and a star on the Hollywood Walk of Fame in 1993 (located at 7003 Hollywood Blvd). She was awarded honorary degrees from Bluffton College and Kent State University in her home state of Ohio.

PHYLLIS DILLER

Probably Phyllis Diller's most unusual award was being the recent recipient of the American Academy of Cosmetic Surgery for "the tremendous breakthrough in acceptance of our field, recognizing the fact she was the first person to have the courage to proclaim her surgery and show her results publicly."

Diller's talents as a classic concert pianist resulted in over 100 appearances with symphonies throughout the U.S. and Canada, where she billed herself as "Dame Illya Dillya." One of her best reviews was for her interpretation of Beethoven's Concerto #1 as well as various works of Bach.

Within six years of seeing Phyllis Diller in 1996, she announced her retirement, in 2002. At age 84, Diller's health was failing. She suffered a heart attack in 1999 and had a pacemaker implanted. She lives in her Brentwood mansion with her classic cars and prizes a custom-made harpsichord. She has become known as quite a fabulous cook. She also has a large collection of Waterford Crystal that took 50 years to compile. In 1996 a ten-year affair ended with lawyer Robert Hastings when he passed away. She penned her autobiography, *Like a Lampshade in a Whorehouse* in 2005. Also in 2005, Diller underwent diagnostic tests in the hospital after injuring her head and neck in a fall at her Brentwood home. On a happier note, also in 2005 (October to be exact), Ms. Diller's voice was on an episode of television's *The Family Guy*. The episode, for trivia buffs, was "Padre de Familia" (episode six, season six).

One fact of interest concerns her trademark sack dresses. They were actually designed by Gloria Johnson of Omaha, Nebraska, who Diller jokingly referred to as "Omar of Omaha," since tent dresses were popular in the 1960s and 1970s. Another Diller trademark is worthy of note: her cigarette holder. It is merely a prop since Ms. Diller is a life-long non-smoker.

Alas, comedienne Phyllis Diller is now retired. Carousel Dinner Theater is no longer in existence. Tangier Restaurant, however, still has entertainment in the Sultan's Cabaret.

Even though Diller may not be active, she lives on in my memory and, even, actions.

A retired co-worker friend of mine retired and eventually became quite ill. I wrote Phyllis Diller and requested an autographed photograph of her be sent to my ailing friend to cheer her up. Without hesitation it was.

In 1997, a local middle school asked if I would address an advanced English class about writing stories for newspapers. I put together a packet for each student. Thinking about Phyllis Diller, I included in the packet a list of questions I asked her for the 1996 telephone interview, a copy of her agency's biography, a publicity 8" x 10" photograph, Tangier Restaurant's publicity about the May 1996 appearance, a copy of my first draft of the story resulting from the telephone interview, a copy of the galley-proof I typed into the newspaper's computer, and finally, the printed final copy of the story. Therefore, the students saw the transition of the story from its inception to the final, printed product. The highlight of the presentation was to play the actual recorded telephone interview so the students could her Diller's trademark "guffaw" laugh and how she commented seriously, then comically on the topics discussed that I had written down before the interview. This proved to be a most-rewarding experience for me as well as the English class.

I may have not spent the longest time with Phyllis Diller as I did with some other celebrities I was lucky enough to meet, but it is Ms. Diller that I met and wrote about the most. In concluding my recollections of celebrities with this chapter, I can truly say that in the case of comedienne Phyllis Diller, I did indeed save the best for last!

Another legacy from Ms. Diller is one of her unforgettable punch lines. I cannot find its source in my notes, her printed biographies, or other written publicity about her. Every time I feel depressed or "down", though, I will immediately recall what I think is one of her funniest lines: "I was lying on a nude beach in southern California one afternoon, when a group of Hell's Angels (the notorious motorcycle gang) came up to me and gang-dressed me!"

Photo courtesy of David Mull.

Irv Korman is a writer, theatre critic, actor, clown and magician. He was also a senior lecturer for thirteen years in the School of Communication at The University of Akron.

A native of Akron, Ohio (where he has lived for over sixty years), Irv has received four Communicator Awards and one Chanticleer Award for his talents as a writer, theater critic, and actor. When he isn't teaching public speaking, working on his books, or strutting the stages of local community theaters, Irv can be found portraying one of his alter egos-Marlowe the Magic Clown (hobo clown/magician), or Mildew the Mundane (magician).

Irv received both his Bachelor of Arts degree in Speech Pathology and his Master's Degree in Theater at The University of Akron. He and his wife of 42 years, Francine, reside in Fairlawn, Ohio. He has two married daughters, Julie and Melanie.

VISIT THE LOCONEAL BLOG AT

www.loconeal.com

Breaking News
Forthcoming Releases
Links to Author Sites
Loconeal Events

BASIC ELECTRICITY

Prepared by

BUREAU OF NAVAL PERSONNEL

DOVER PUBLICATIONS, INC.
NEW YORK · NEW YORK

Published in the United Kingdom by
Constable and Company Limited, 10 Orange
Street, London W. C. 2.

This new Dover edition, first published
in 1962, is an unabridged and unaltered republication of the work first published by the
United States Government Printing Office in
1960. *Basic Electricity* was prepared by the
Bureau of Naval Personnel, Department of
the Navy, as Navy Training Course NAVPERS
10086-A.

The United States Government Printing
Office edition has been slightly reduced photo-
graphically in order to make the book fit into
a more convenient format.

Library of Congress Catalog Card Number: 62-4907

Manufactured in the United States of America

Dover Publications, Inc.
180 Varick Street
New York 14, N. Y.

PREFACE

Basic Electricity is written primarily to provide coverage of the electrical knowledge factors required of men of the U. S. Navy and Naval Reserve who desire to advance in certain ratings. The RE-QUIREMENTS FOR ADVANCEMENT for each rating specify the exact electrical knowledge factors required in each case. Some ratings require a much broader and more thorough coverage of electricity than others. For this reason, *Basic Electricity* is written to provide either the broad or the more limited knowledge of electrical fundamentals, depending on which chapters of the text are studied. To provide this type of coverage, the text is written in two main parts—Part 1 and Part 2.

Part 1 provides the more limited coverage of electrical theory. Starting with the fundamental electrical nature of matter, it goes on to cover such subjects as the production of a voltage by various methods, the characteristics of simple electric circuits, magnetism, and the solving of problems in simple direct-current circuits. It also contains an introduction to fundamental alternating-current electricity, and a discussion of the effects of capacitance and inductance in electric circuits. The final chapter in Part 1 covers the basic indicating instruments commonly used to measure electrical voltage, current flow, resistance, and power. (NOTE: When you are going to study only the material in Part 1, you should also read chapters 20 and 21 in Part 2.) Chapter 20 covers electrical drawings and technical manuals, and chapter 21 is on safety.

Part 2 is written for the student who is held responsible for more difficult knowledge factors than those covered in Part 1. It also serves to provide material for the student who is interested in studying more difficult subject matter not actually required of him. In Part 2, the general theories of electricity studied in Part 1 are applied to electrical machines, such as generators, motors, transformers, and magnetic amplifiers. Also, more complicated instruments, synchros, and servomechanisms are discussed. The final chapters of the text cover electrical blueprints and wiring diagrams, and safety.

As one of the Navy Training Courses, this book was prepared by the U. S. Navy Training Publications Center for the Bureau of Naval Personnel.

CONTENTS

SKIP→ (handwritten, pointing to item 6)

CONTENTS (Continued)

CONTENTS (Continued)

CONTENTS (Continued)

BASIC ELECTRICITY

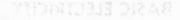

PART 1

CHAPTER 1

FUNDAMENTAL CONCEPTS OF ELECTRICITY

What is Electricity?

The word "electric" is actually a Greek-derived word meaning AMBER. Amber is a translucent (semitransparent) yellowish mineral, which, in the natural form, is composed of fossilized resin. The ancient Greeks used the words "electric force" in referring to the mysterious forces of attraction and repulsion exhibited by amber when it was rubbed with a cloth. They did not understand the fundamental nature of this force. They could not answer the seemingly simple question, "What is electricity?". This question is still unanswered. Though you might define electricity as "that force which moves electrons," this would be the same as defining an engine as "that force which moves an automobile." You would have described the effect, not the force.

We presently know little more than the ancient Greeks knew about the fundamental nature of electricity, but tremendous strides have been made in harnessing and using it. Elaborate theories concerning the nature and behavior of electricity have been advanced, and have gained wide acceptance because of their apparent truth and demonstrated workability.

From time to time various scientists have found that electricity seems to behave in a constant and predictable manner in given situations, or when subjected to given conditions. These scientists, such as Faraday, Ohm, Lenz, and Kirchhoff, to name only a few, observed and described the predictable characteristics of electricity and electric current in the form of certain rules. These rules are often referred to as "laws." Thus, though electricity itself has never been clearly defined, its predictable nature and easily used form of energy has made it one of the most widely used power sources in modern time. By learning the rules, or laws, applying to the behavior of electricity, and by learning the methods of producing, controlling, and using it, you will have "learned" electricity without ever having determined its fundamental identity.

THE MOLECULE

One of the oldest, and probably the most generally accepted, theories concerning electric current flow is that it is comprised of moving electrons. This is the ELECTRON THEORY. Electrons are extremely tiny parts, or particles, of matter. To study the electron, you must therefore study the structural nature of matter itself. (Anything having mass and inertia, and which occupies any amount of space, is composed of matter.) To study the fundamental structure or composition of any type of matter, it must be reduced to its fundamental fractions. Assume the drop of water in figure 1-1 (A) was halved again and again. By continuing the process long enough, you would eventually obtain the smallest particle of water possible—the molecule. All molecules are composed of atoms.

A molecule of water (H_2O) is composed of one atom of oxygen and two atoms of hydrogen, as represented in figure 1-1 (B). If the molecule of water were further subdivided, there would remain only unrelated atoms of oxygen and hydrogen, and the water would no longer exist as such. This example illustrates the following fact—the molecule is the smallest particle to which a substance can be reduced and still be called by the same name. This applies to all substances—liquids, solids, and gases.

When whole molecules are combined or separated from one another, the change is generally referred to as a PHYSICAL change. In a CHEMICAL change the molecules of the

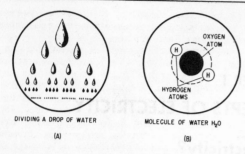

(A) DIVIDING A DROP OF WATER

(B) MOLECULE OF WATER H₂O

Figure 1-1.—Matter is made up of molecules.

substance are altered such that new molecules result. Most chemical changes involve positive and negative ions and thus are electrical in nature. All matter is said to be essentially electrical in nature.

THE ATOM

In the study of chemistry it soon becomes apparent that the molecule is far from being the ultimate particle into which matter may be subdivided. The salt molecule may be decomposed into radically different substances—sodium and chlorine. These particles that make up molecules can be isolated and studied separately. They are called ATOMS.

The atom is the smallest particle that makes up that type of material called an ELEMENT. The element retains its characteristics when subdivided into atoms. More than 100 elements have been identified. They can be arranged into a table of increasing weight, and can be grouped into families of material having similar properties. This arrangement is called the PERIODIC TABLE OF THE ELEMENTS.

The idea that all matter is composed of atoms dates back more than 2,000 years to the Greeks. Many centuries passed before the study of matter proved that the basic idea of atomic structure was correct. Physicists have explored the interior of the atom and discovered many subdivisions in it. The core of the atom is called the NUCLEUS. Most of the mass of the atom is concentrated in the nucleus. It is comparable to the sun in the solar system, around which the planets revolve. The nucleus contains PROTONS (positively charged particles) and NEUTRONS which are electrically neutral.

Most of the weight of the atom is in the protons and neutrons of the nucleus. Whirling

around the nucleus are one or more smaller particles of negative electric charge. THESE ARE THE ELECTRONS. Normally there is one proton for each electron in the entire atom so that the net positive charge of the nucleus is balanced by the net negative charge of the electrons whirling around the nucleus. THUS THE ATOM IS ELECTRICALLY NEUTRAL.

The electrons do not fall into the nucleus even though they are attracted strongly to it. Their motion prevents it, as the planets are prevented from falling into the sun because of their centrifugal force of revolution.

The number of protons, which is usually the same as the number of electrons, determines the kind of element in question. Figure 1-2 shows a simplified picture of several atoms of different materials based on the conception of planetary electrons describing orbits about the nucleus. For example, hydrogen has a nucleus consisting of 1 proton, around which rotates 1 electron. The helium atom has a nucleus containing 2 protons and 2 neutrons with 2 electrons encircling the nucleus. Near the other extreme of the list of elements is curium (not shown in the figure), an element discovered in the 1940's, which has 96 protons and 96 electrons in each atom.

The *Periodic Table of the Elements* is an orderly arrangement of the elements in ascending atomic number (number of planetary electrons) and also in atomic weight (number of protons and neutrons in the nucleus). The various kinds of atoms have distinct masses or

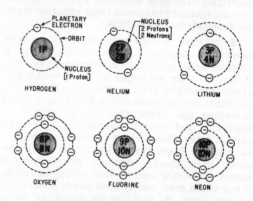

Figure 1-2.—Atomic structure of elements.

2

weights with respect to each other. The element most closely approaching unity (meaning 1) is hydrogen whose atomic weight is 1.008 as compared with oxygen whose atomic weight is 16. Helium has an atomic weight of approximately 4, lithium 7, fluorine 19, and neon 20, as shown in figure 1-2.

Figure 1-3 is a pictorial summation of the discussion that has just been presented. Visible matter, at the left of the figure, is broken down first to one of its basic molecules, then to one of the molecule's atoms. The atom is then further reduced to its subatomic particles—the protons, neutrons, and electrons. Subatomic particles are electric in nature. That is, they are the particles of matter most affected by an electric force. Whereas the whole molecule or a whole atom is electrically neutral, most subatomic particles are not neutral (with the exception of the neutron). Protons are inherently positive, and electrons are inherently negative. It is these inherent characteristics which make subatomic particles sensitive to electric force.

When an electric force is applied to a conducting medium, such as copper wire, electrons in the outer orbits of the copper atoms are forced out of orbit and impelled along the wire. The direction of electron movement is determined by the direction of the impelling force. The protons do not move, mainly because they are extremely heavy. The proton of the lightest element, hydrogen, is approximately 1,850 times as heavy as an electron. Thus, it is the relatively light electron that is most readily moved by electricity.

When an orbital electron is removed from an atom it is called a FREE ELECTRON. Some of the electrons of certain metallic atoms are so loosely bound to the nucleus that they are comparatively free to move from atom to atom.

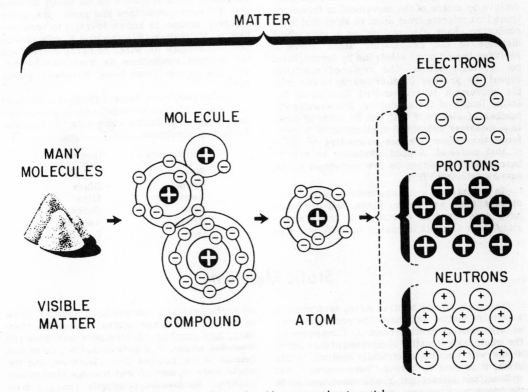

Figure 1-3.—Breakdown of visible matter to electric particles.

3

Thus, a very small force or amount of energy will cause such electrons to be removed from the atom and become free electrons. It is these free electrons that constitute the flow of an electric current in electrical conductors.

If the internal energy of an atom is raised above its normal state, the atom is said to be EXCITED. Excitation may be produced by causing the atoms to collide with particles that are impelled by an electric force. In this way, energy is transferred from the electric source to the atom. The excess energy absorbed by an atom may become sufficient to cause loosely bound outer electrons to leave the atom against the force that acts to hold them within. An atom that has thus lost or gained one or more electrons is said to be IONIZED. If the atom loses electrons it becomes positively charged and is referred to as a POSITIVE ION. Conversely, if the atom gains electrons, it becomes negatively charged and is referred to as a NEGATIVE ION. Actually then, an ion is a small particle of matter having a positive or negative charge.

Conductors and Insulators

Substances that permit the free motion of a large number of electrons are called CONDUCTORS. Copper wire is considered a good conductor because it has many free electrons. Electrical energy is transferred through conductors by means of the movement of free electrons that migrate from atom to atom inside the conductor. Each electron moves a very short distance to the neighboring atom where it replaces one or more electrons by forcing them out of their orbits. The replaced electrons repeat the process in other nearby atoms until the movement is transmitted throughout the entire length of the conductor. The greater the number of electrons that can be made to move in a material under the application of a given force the better are the conductive qualities of that material. A good conductor is said to have a low opposition or low resistance to the current (electron) flow.

In contrast to good conductors, some substances such as rubber, glass, and dry wood have very few free electrons. In these materials large amounts of energy must be expended in order to break the electrons loose from the influence of the nucleus. Substances containing very few free electrons are called POOR CONDUCTORS, NONCONDUCTORS, or INSULATORS. Actually, there is no sharp dividing line between conductors and insulators, since electron motion is known to exist to some extent in all matter. Electricians simply use the best conductors as wires to carry current and the poorest conductors as insulators to prevent the current from being diverted from the wires.

Listed below are some of the best conductors and best insulators arranged in accordance with their respective abilities to conduct or to resist the flow of electrons.

Conductors	Insulators
Silver	Dry air
Copper	Glass
Aluminum	Mica
Zinc	Rubber
Brass	Asbestos
Iron	Bakelite

Static Electricity

In a natural, or neutral state, each atom in a body of matter will have the proper number of electrons in orbit around it. Consequently, the whole body of matter comprised of the neutral atoms will also be electrically neutral. In this state, it is said to have a "zero charge," and will neither attract nor repel other matter in its vicinity. Electrons will neither leave nor enter the neutrally charged body should it come in contact with other neutral bodies. If, however, any number of electrons are removed from the atoms of a body of matter, there will remain more protons than electrons, and the whole body of matter will become electrically positive. Should the positively charged body come in contact with another body having a normal charge, or having a negative (too many electrons) charge, an electric current will flow between them. Electrons will leave the more negative body and enter the positive body. This electron flow will continue until both bodies have equal charges.

When two bodies of matter have unequal charges, and are near one another, an electric force is exerted between them because of their unequal charges. However, since they are not in contact, their charges cannot equalize. The existence of such an electric force, where current cannot flow, is referred to as static electricity. "Static" means "not moving." This is also referred to as an ELECTROSTATIC FORCE.

One of the easiest ways to create a static charge is by the friction method. With the friction method, two pieces of matter are rubbed together and electrons are "wiped off" one onto the other. If materials that are good conductors are used, it is quite difficult to obtain a detectable charge on either. The reason for this is that equalizing currents will flow easily in and between the conducting materials. These currents equalize the charges almost as fast as they are created. A static charge is easier to obtain by rubbing a hard nonconducting material against a soft, or fluffy, nonconductor. Electrons are rubbed off one material and onto the other material. This is illustrated in figure 1-4.

When the hard rubber rod is rubbed in the fur, the rod accumulates electrons. Since both fur and rubber are poor conductors, little equalizing current can flow, and an electrostatic charge is built up. When the charge is great enough, equalizing currents will flow in spite of the material's poor conductivity. These currents will cause visible sparks, if viewed in darkness, and will produce a crackling sound.

CHARGED BODIES

One of the fundamental laws of electricity is that LIKE CHARGES REPEL EACH OTHER and UNLIKE CHARGES ATTRACT EACH OTHER. A positive charge and negative charge, being unlike, tend to move toward each other. In the atom the negative electrons are drawn toward the positive protons in the nucleus. This attractive force is balanced by the electron's centrifugal force caused by its rotation about the nucleus. As a result, the electrons remain in orbit and are not drawn into the nucleus. Electrons repel each other because of their like negative charges, and protons repel each other because of their like positive charges.

The law of charged bodies may be demonstrated by a simple experiment. Two pith (paper pulp) balls are suspended near one another by threads, as shown in figure 1-5.

If the hard rubber rod is rubbed to give it a negative charge, and then held against the right-hand ball in part (A), the rod will impart a negative charge to the ball. The right-hand ball will be charged negative with respect to the left-hand ball. When released, the two balls will be drawn together, as shown in figure 1-5 (A). They will touch and remain in contact until the left-hand ball acquires a portion of the negative charge of the right-hand ball, at which time they will swing apart as shown in figure 1-5 (C). If positive charges are placed on both balls (fig. 1-5 (B)), the balls will also be repelled from each other.

COULOMB'S LAW OF CHARGES

The amount of attracting or repelling force which acts between two electrically charged bodies in free space depends on two things—(1) their charges, and (2) the distance between them. The relationship of charge and distance to electrostatic force was first discovered and written by a French scientist named Charles A. Coulomb. Coulomb's Law states that CHARGED BODIES ATTRACT OR REPEL EACH OTHER WITH A FORCE THAT IS DIRECTLY PROPORTIONAL TO THE PRODUCT OF THEIR CHARGES, AND IS INVERSELY PROPORTIONAL TO THE SQUARE OF THE DISTANCE BETWEEN THEM.

ELECTRIC FIELDS

The space between and around charged bodies in which their influence is felt is called an ELECTRIC FIELD OF FORCE. The electric field is always terminated on material objects and extends between positive and negative charges. It can exist in air, glass, paper, or a vacuum. ELECTROSTATIC FIELDS and DIELECTRIC FIELDS are other names used to refer to this region of force.

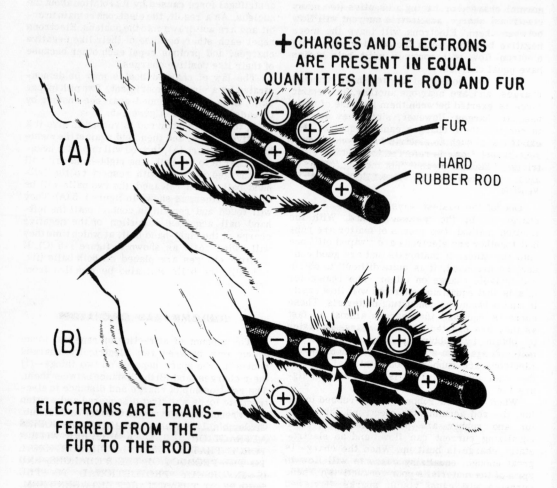

+ CHARGES AND ELECTRONS ARE PRESENT IN EQUAL QUANTITIES IN THE ROD AND FUR

FUR

HARD RUBBER ROD

(A)

(B)

ELECTRONS ARE TRANS-FERRED FROM THE FUR TO THE ROD

Figure 1-4.—Producing static electricity by friction.

Fields of force spread out in the space surrounding their point of origin and, in general, DIMINISH IN PROPORTION TO THE SQUARE OF THE DISTANCE FROM THEIR SOURCE.

The field about a charged body is generally represented by lines which are referred to as ELECTROSTATIC LINES OF FORCE. These lines are imaginary and are used merely to represent the direction and strength of the field. To avoid confusion, the lines of force exerted by a positive charge are always shown leaving the charge, and for a negative charge they are shown as entering. Figure 1-6 illustrates the use of lines to represent the field about charged bodies.

Figure 1-6 (A) represents the repulsion of like-charged bodies and their associated fields. Part (B) represents the attraction between unlike-charged bodies and their associated fields.

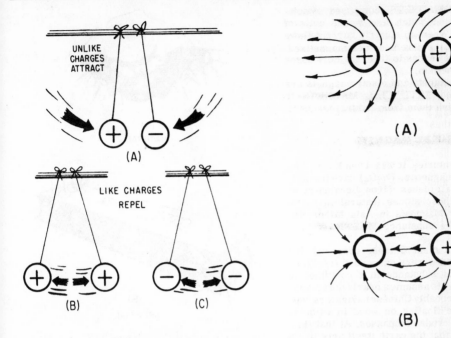

UNLIKE CHARGES ATTRACT

(A)

LIKE CHARGES REPEL

(B)   (C)

Figure 1-5.—Reaction between charged bodies.

(A)

(B)

Figure 1-6.—Electrostatic lines of force.

Magnetism

A substance is said to be a magnet if it has the property of magnetism—that is, if it has the power to attract such substances as iron, steel, nickel, or cobalt, which are known as MAGNETIC MATERIALS. A steel knitting needle, magnetized by a method to be described later, exhibits two points of maximum attraction (one at each end) and no attraction at its center. The points of maximum attraction are called MAGNETIC POLES. All magnets have at least two poles. If the needle is suspended by its middle so that it rotates freely in a horizontal plane about its center, the needle comes to rest in an approximately north-south line of direction. The same pole will always point to the north, and the other will always point toward the south. The magnetic pole that points northward is called the NORTH POLE, and the other the SOUTH POLE.

A MAGNETIC FIELD exists around a simple bar magnet. The field consists of imaginary lines along which a MAGNETIC FORCE acts. These lines emanate from the north pole of the magnet, and enter the south pole, returning to the north pole through the magnet itself, thus forming closed loops.

A MAGNETIC CIRCUIT is a complete path through which magnetic lines of force may be established under the influence of a magnetizing force. Most magnetic circuits are composed largely of magnetic materials in order to contain the magnetic flux. These circuits are similar to the ELECTRIC CIRCUIT, which is a complete path through which current is caused to flow under the influence of an electromotive force.

Magnets may be conveniently divided into three groups.

1. NATURAL MAGNETS, found in the natural state in the form of a mineral called magnetite.

2. PERMANENT MAGNETS, bars of hardened steel (or some form of alloy such as alnico) that have been permanently magnetized.

7

3. ELECTROMAGNETS, composed of soft-iron cores around which are wound coils of insulated wire. When an electric current flows through the coil, the core becomes magnetized. When the current ceases to flow, the core loses most of its magnetism.

Permanent magnets and electromagnets are sometimes called ARTIFICIAL MAGNETS to further distinguish them from natural magnets.

NATURAL MAGNETS

For many centuries it has been known that certain stones (magnetite, Fe_3O_4) have the ability to attract small pieces of iron. Because many of the best of these stones (natural magnets) were found near Magnesia in Asia Minor, the Greeks called the substance MAGNETITE, or MAGNETIC.

Before this, ancient Chinese observed that when similar stones were suspended freely, or floated on a light substance in a container of water, they tended to assume a nearly north-and-south position. Probably Chinese navigators used bits of magnetite floating on wood in a liquid-filled vessel as crude compasses. At that time it was not known that the earth itself acts like a magnet, and these stones were regarded with considerable superstitious awe. Because bits of this substance were used as compasses they were called LOADSTONES (or lodestones), which means "leading stones."

Natural magnets are also found in the United States, Norway, and Sweden. A natural magnet, demonstrating the attractive force at the poles, is shown in figure 1-7 (A).

ARTIFICIAL MAGNETS

Natural magnets no longer have any practical value because more powerful and more conveniently shaped permanent magnets can be produced artificially. Commercial magnets are made from special steels and alloys—for example, alnico, made principally of aluminum, nickel, and cobalt. The name is derived from the first two letters of the three principal elements of which it is composed. An artificial magnet is shown in figure 1-7 (B).

An iron, steel, or alloy bar can be magnetized by inserting the bar into a coil of insulated wire and passing a heavy direct current through the coil, as shown in figure 1-8 (A). This aspect

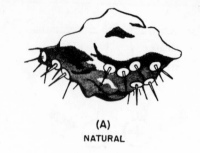

(A)
NATURAL

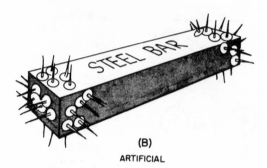

(B)
ARTIFICIAL

Figure 1-7.–(A) Natural magnet; (B) artificial magnet.

of magnetism is treated later in the chapter. The same bar may also be magnetized if it is stroked with a bar magnet, as shown in figure 1-8 (B). It will then have the same magnetic property that the magnet used to induce the magnetism has—namely, there will be two poles of attraction, one at either end. This process produces a permanent magnet by INDUCTION—that is, the magnetism is induced in the bar by the influence of the stroking magnet.

Artificial magnets may be classified as "permanent" or "temporary" depending on their ability to retain their magnetic strength after the magnetizing force has been removed. Hardened steel and certain alloys are relatively difficult to magnetize and are said to have a LOW PERMEABILITY because the magnetic lines of force do not easily permeate, or distribute themselves readily through the steel. Once magnetized, however, these materials retain a large part of their magnetic strength and are called PERMANENT MAGNETS. Permanent magnets are used extensively in electric instruments, meters, telephone receivers, permanent-magnet loudspeakers, and magnetos. Conversely, substances

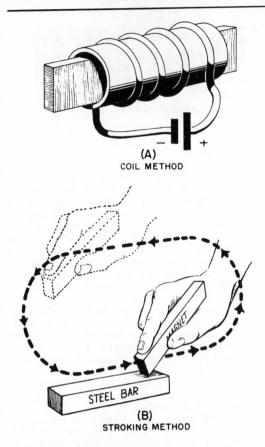

(A)
COIL METHOD

(B)
STROKING METHOD

Figure 1-8.—Methods of producing artificial magnets.

that are relatively easy to magnetize—such as soft iron and annealed silicon steel—are said to have a HIGH PERMEABILITY. Such substances retain only a small part of their magnetism after the magnetizing force is removed and are called TEMPORARY MAGNETS. Silicon steel and similar materials are used in transformers where the magnetism is constantly changing and in generators and motors where the strengths of the fields can be readily changed.

The magnetism that remains in a temporary magnet after the magnetizing force is removed is called RESIDUAL MAGNETISM. The fact that temporary magnets retain even a small amount of magnetism is an important factor in the buildup of voltage in self-excited d-c generators.

NATURE OF MAGNETISM

Weber's theory of the nature of magnetism is based on the assumption that each of the molecules of a magnet is itself a tiny magnet. The molecular magnets that compose an unmagnetized bar of iron or steel are arranged at random, as shown by the simplified diagram of figure 1-9 (A). With this arrangement, the magnetism of each of the molecules is neutralized by that of adjacent molecules, and no external magnetic effect is produced. When a magnetizing force is applied to an unmagnetized iron or steel bar, the molecules become alined so that the north poles point one way and the south poles point the other way, as shown in figure 1-9 (B).

If a bar magnet is broken into several parts, as in figure 1-10, each part constitutes a magnet. The north and south poles of these small magnets are in the same respective directions as those of the original magnet. If each of these parts is again broken, the resulting parts are likewise magnets, and the magnetic orientation is the same. If this breaking process could be continued, smaller and smaller pieces would retain their magnetism until each part was reduced to a molecule. It is therefore logical to assume that each of these molecules is a magnet.

A further justification for this assumption results from the fact that when a bar magnet is held out of alinement with the earth's field and is repeatedly jarred, heated, or exposed to a powerful alternating field, the molecular alinement is disarranged and the magnet becomes demagnetized. For example, electric measuring instruments become inaccurate if their permanent magnets lose some of their magnetism because of severe jarring or exposure to opposing magnetic fields.

A theory of magnetism that is perhaps more adequate than the MOLECULAR theory is the DOMAIN theory. Much simplified, this theory may be stated as follows:

In magnetic substances the "atomic" magnets, produced by the movement of the planetary electrons around the nucleus, have a strong tendency to line up together in groups of from 10^{14} to 10^{15} atoms. This occurs without the influence of any external magnetic field. These groups of atoms having their poles orientated in the same direction are called DOMAINS. Therefore, throughout each domain an intense magnetic field is produced. These

UNMAGNETIZED STEEL
(A)

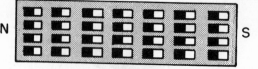

MAGNETIZED STEEL
(B)

Figure 1-9.—Molecular theory of magnetism.

fields are normally in a miscellaneous arrangement so that no external field is apparent when the substance as a whole is unmagnetized. Each tiny domain (10^6 of them may be contained in 1 cubic millimeter) is always magnetized to saturation, and the addition of an external magnetic field does not increase the inherent magnetism of the individual domains.

However, if an external field that is gradually increased in strength is applied to the magnetic substance the domains will line up one by one (or perhaps several at a time) with the external field.

MAGNETIC FIELDS AND LINES OF FORCE

If a bar magnet is dipped into iron filings, many of the filings are attracted to the ends of the magnet, but none are attracted to the center of the magnet. As mentioned previously, the ends of the magnet where the attractive force is the greatest are called the POLES of the magnet. By using a compass, the line of direction of the magnetic force at various points near the magnet may be observed. The compass needle itself is a magnet. The north end of the compass needle always points toward the south pole, S, as shown in figure 1-11 (A), and thus the sense of direction (with respect to the polarity of the bar magnet) is also indicated. At the center, the compass needle points in a direction that is parallel to the bar magnet.

When the compass is placed successively at several points in the vicinity of the bar magnet the compass needle alines itself with the field at each position. The direction of the field is indicated by the arrows and represents the direction in which the north pole of the compass needle will point when the compass is placed in this field. Such a line along which a compass needle alines itself is called a MAGNETIC LINE

OF FORCE. As mentioned previously, the magnetic lines of force are assumed to emanate from the north pole of a magnet, pass through the surrounding space, and enter the south pole. The lines of force then pass from the south pole to the north pole inside the magnet to form a closed loop. Each line of force forms an independent closed loop and does not merge with or cross other lines of force. The lines of force between the poles of a horseshoe magnet are shown in figure 1-11 (B).

The space surrounding a magnet, in which the magnetic force acts, is called a MAGNETIC FIELD. Michael Faraday was the first scientist to visualize the magnet field as being in a state of stress and consisting of uniformly distributed lines of force. The entire quantity of magnetic lines surrounding a magnet is called MAGNETIC FLUX. Flux in a magnetic circuit corresponds to current in an electric circuit.

The number of lines of force per unit area is called FLUX DENSITY and is measured in lines per square inch or lines per square centimeter. Flux density is expressed by the equation

$$B = \frac{\Phi}{A},$$

where B is the flux density, Φ (Greek phi) is the total number of lines of flux, and A is the cross-sectional area of the magnetic circuit. If A is in square centimeters, B is in lines per square centimeter, or GAUSS. The terms FLUX and FLOW of magnetism are frequently used in textbooks. However, magnetism itself is not thought to be a stream of particles in motion, but is simply a field of force exerted in space.

A visual representation of the magnetic field around a magnet can be obtained by placing a plate of glass over a magnet and sprinkling iron filings onto the glass. The filings arrange themselves in definite paths between the poles.

10

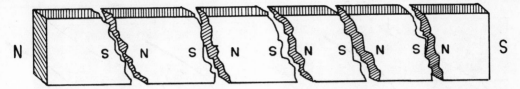

Figure 1-10.—Magnetic poles of a broken magnet.

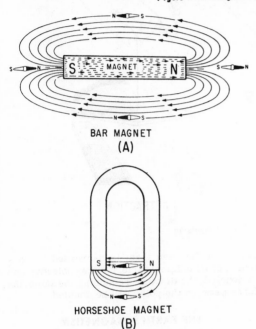

BAR MAGNET
(A)

HORSESHOE MAGNET
(B)

Figure 1-11.—Magnetic lines of force.

This arrangement of the filings shows the pattern of the magnetic field around the magnet, as in figure 1-12.

The magnetic field surrounding a symmetrically shaped magnet has the following properties:

1. The field is symmetrical unless disturbed by another magnetic substance.

2. The lines of force have direction and are represented as emanating from the north pole and entering the south pole.

LAWS OF ATTRACTION AND REPULSION

If a magnetized needle is suspended near a bar magnet, as in figure 1-13, it will be seen

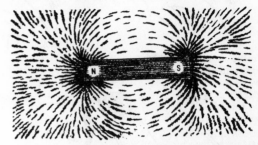

Figure 1-12.—Magnetic field pattern around a magnet.

that a north pole repels a north pole and a south pole repels a south pole. Opposite poles, however, will attract each other. Thus, the first two laws of magnetic attraction and repulsion are:

1. LIKE magnetic poles REPEL each other.

2. UNLIKE magnetic poles ATTRACT each other.

The flux patterns between adjacent UNLIKE poles of bar magnets, as indicated by lines, are shown in figure 1-14 (A). Similar patterns for adjacent LIKE poles are shown in figure 1-14 (B). The lines do not cross at any point and they act as if they repel each other.

Figure 1-15 shows the flux pattern (indicated by lines) around two bar magnets placed close together and parallel with each other. Figure 1-15 (A) shows the flux pattern when opposite poles are adjacent; and figure 1-15 (B) shows the flux pattern when like poles are adjacent.

The THIRD LAW of magnetic attraction and repulsion states in effect that the force of attraction or repulsion existing between two magnetic poles decreases rapidly as the poles are separated from each other. Actually, the force of attraction or repulsion varies directly as the product of the separate pole strengths and inversely as the square of the distance separating the magnetic poles, provided the poles are small enough to be considered as points. For example, if the distance between two north poles is increased from 2 feet to 4 feet, the force of

11

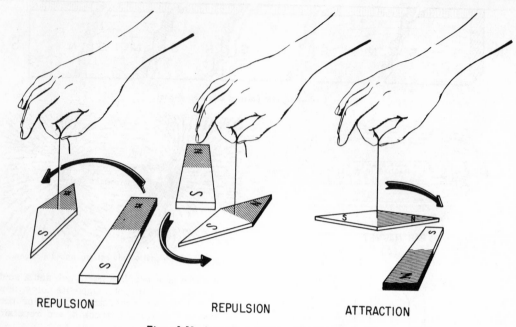

REPULSION   REPULSION   ATTRACTION

Figure 1-13.—Laws of attraction and repulsion.

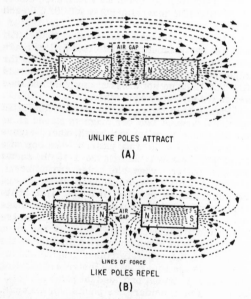

UNLIKE POLES ATTRACT

(A)

LINES OF FORCE

LIKE POLES REPEL

(B)

Figure 1-14.—Lines of force between unlike and like poles.

repulsion between them is decreased to one-fourth of its original value. If either pole strength is doubled, the distance remaining the same, the force between the poles will be doubled.

THE EARTH'S MAGNETISM

As has been stated, the earth is a huge magnet; and surrounding the earth is the magnetic field produced by the earth's magnetism. The magnetic polarities of the earth are as indicated in figure 1-16. The geographic poles are also shown at each end of the axis of rotation of the earth. The magnetic axis does not coincide with the geographic axis, and therefore the magnetic and geographic poles are not at the same place on the surface of the earth.

The early users of the compass regarded the end of the compass needle that points in a northerly direction as being a north pole. The other end was regarded as a south pole. On some maps the magnetic pole of the earth towards which the north pole of the compass pointed was designated a north magnetic pole. This magnetic pole was obviously called a north pole because of its proximity to the north geographic pole.

12

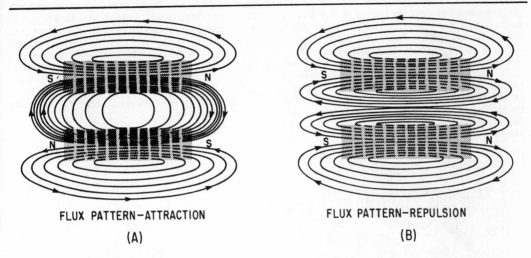

FLUX PATTERN—ATTRACTION

(A)

FLUX PATTERN—REPULSION

(B)

Figure 1-15.—Flux patterns of adjacent parallel bar magnets.

When it was learned that the earth is a magnet and that opposite poles attract, it was necessary to call the magnetic pole located in the northern hemisphere a SOUTH MAGNETIC POLE and the magnetic pole located in the southern hemisphere a NORTH MAGNETIC POLE. The matter of naming the poles was arbitrary. Obviously, the polarity of the compass needle that points toward the north must be opposite to the polarity of the earth's magnetic pole located there.

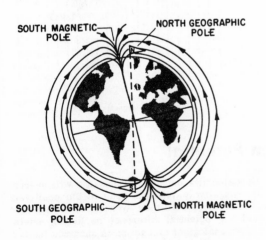

Figure 1-16.—Earth's magnetic poles.

As has been stated, magnetic lines of force are assumed to emanate from the north pole of a magnet and to enter the south pole as closed loops. Because the earth is a magnet, lines of force emanate from its north magnetic pole and enter the south magnetic pole as closed loops. The compass needle alines itself in such a way that the earth's lines of force enter at its south pole and leave at its north pole. Because the north pole of the needle is defined as the end that points in a northerly direction it follows that the magnetic pole in the vicinity of the north geographic pole is in reality a south magnetic pole, and vice versa.

Because the magnetic poles and the geographic poles do not coincide, a compass will not (except at certain positions on the earth) point in a true (geographic) north-south direction—that is, it will not point in a line of direction that passes through the north and south geographic poles, but in a line of direction that makes an angle with it. This angle is called the angle of VARIATION OR DECLINATION.

MAGNETIC SHIELDING

There is not a known INSULATOR for magnetic flux. If a nonmagnetic material is placed in a magnetic field, there is no appreciable change in flux—that is, the flux penetrates the nonmagnetic material. For example, a glass plate placed between the poles of a horseshoe magnet will have no appreciable effect on the field although glass itself is a good insulator in an electric circuit. If a magnetic material (for example, soft iron) is placed in a magnetic field, the flux may be redirected to take advantage of the greater permeability of the magnetic material as shown in figure 1-17. Permeability is the quality of a substance which determines the ease with which it can be magnetized.

The discussion of magnetism up to this point has been mainly intended to clarify terms and meanings, such as "polarity," "fields," "lines of force," and so forth. Only one fundamental relationship between magnetism and electricity is discussed in this chapter. This relationship pertains to magnetism as used to generate a voltage and it is discussed under the headings that follows.

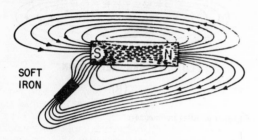

SOFT IRON

Figure 1-17.—Effects of a magnetic substance in a magnetic field.

The sensitive mechanism of electric instruments and meters can be influenced by stray magnetic fields which will cause errors in their readings. Because instrument mechanisms cannot be insulated against magnetic flux, it is necessary to employ some means of directing the flux around the instrument. This is accomplished by placing a soft-iron case, called a MAGNETIC SCREEN OR SHIELD, about the instrument. Because the flux is established more readily through the iron (even though the path is longer) than through the air inside the case, the instrument is effectively shielded, as shown by the watch and soft-iron shield in figure 1-18.

The study of electricity and magnetism, and how they affect each other, is given more thorough coverage in later chapters of this course.

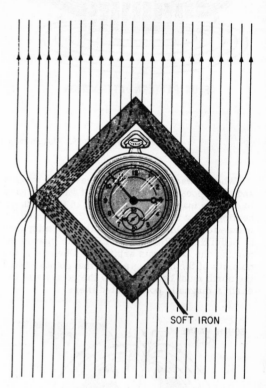

SOFT IRON

Figure 1-18.—Magnetic shield.

Difference in Potential

The force that causes free electrons to move in a conductor as an electric current is called (1) an electromotive force (e.m.f.), (2) a voltage, or (3) a difference in potential. When a difference in potential exists between two charged bodies that are connected by a conductor, electrons will

flow along the conductor. This flow will be from the negatively charged body to the positively charged body until the two charges are equalized and the potential difference no longer exists.

An analogy of this action is shown in the two water tanks connected by a pipe and valve in figure 1-19. At first the valve is closed and all the water is in tank A. Thus, the water pressure across the valve is at maximum. When the valve is opened, the water flows through the pipe from A to B until the water level becomes the same in both tanks. The water then stops flowing in the pipe, because there is no longer a difference in water pressure between the two tanks.

Current flow through an electric circuit is directly proportional to the difference in potential across the circuit, just as the flow of water through the pipe in figure 1-19 is directly proportional to the difference in water level in the two tanks.

A fundamental law of current electricity is that the CURRENT IS DIRECTLY PROPORTIONAL TO THE APPLIED VOLTAGE.

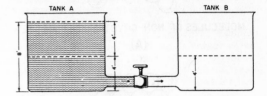

Figure 1-19.—Water analogy of electric difference in potential.

Primary Methods of Producing a Voltage

Presently, there are six commonly used methods of producing a voltage. Some of these methods are much more widely used than others. The methods of utilizing each source will be discussed, and their most common applications will be included. The following is a list of the six most common methods of producing a voltage.

1. FRICTION.—Voltage produced by rubbing two materials together.

2. PRESSURE (Piezoelectricity). — Voltage produced by squeezing crystals of certain substances.

3. HEAT (Thermoelectricity).—Voltage produced by heating the joint (junction) where two unlike metals are joined.

4. LIGHT (Photoelectricity).—Voltage produced by light striking photosensitive (light sensitive) substances.

5. CHEMICAL ACTION.—Voltage produced by chemical reaction in a battery cell.

6. MAGNETISM.—Voltage produced in a conductor when the conductor moves through a magnetic field, or a magnetic field moves through the conductor in such a manner as to cut the magnetic lines of force of the field.

VOLTAGE PRODUCED BY FRICTION

This is the least used of the six methods of producing voltages. Its main application is in Van de Graf generators, used by some laboratories to produce high voltages. As a rule, friction electricity (often referred to as static electricity) is a nuisance. For instance, a flying aircraft accumulates electric charges from the friction between its skin and the passing air.

These charges often interfere with radio communication, and under some circumstances can even cause physical damage to the aircraft. You have probably received unpleasant shocks from friction electricity upon sliding across dry seat covers or walking across dry carpets, and then coming in contact with some other object.

VOLTAGE PRODUCED BY PRESSURE

This action is referred to as piezoelectricity. It is produced by compressing or decompressing crystals of certain substances. To study this form of electricity, you must first understand the meaning of the word "crystal." In a crystal, the molecules are arranged in an orderly and uniform manner. A substance in its crystallized state and in its noncrystallized state is shown in figure 1-20.

For the sake of simplicity, assume that the molecules of this particular substance are spherical (ball-shaped). In the noncrystallized state, in part (A), note that the molecules are arranged irregularly. In the crystallized state, part (B), the molecules are arranged in a regular and uniform manner. This illustrates the major physical difference between crystal and noncrystal forms of matter. Natural crystalline matter is rare; an example of matter that is crystalline in its natural form is diamond, which is crystalline carbon. Most crystals are manufactured.

Crystals of certain substances, such as Rochelle salt or quartz, exhibit peculiar electrical characteristics. These characteristics,

15

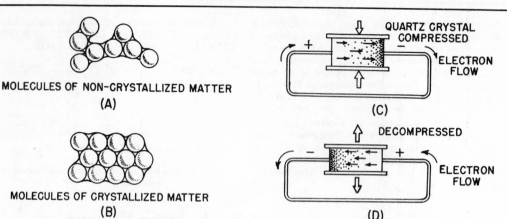

Figure 1-20.—(A) Noncrystallized structure, (B) crystallized structure, (C) compression of a crystal, (D) decompression of a crystal.

or effects, are referred to as "piezoelectric." For instance, when a crystal of quartz is compressed, as in figure 1-20 (C), electrons tend to move through the crystal as shown. This tendency creates an electric difference of potential between the two opposite faces of the crystal. (The fundamental reasons for this action are not known. However, the action is predictable, and therefore useful.) If an external wire is connected while the pressure and e.m.f. are present, electrons will flow. If the pressure is held constant, the electron flow will continue until the charges are equalized. When the force is removed, the crystal is decompressed, and immediately causes an electric force in the opposite direction, as shown in part (D). Thus, the crystal is able to convert mechanical force, either pressure or tension, to electrical force.

The power capacity of a crystal is extremely small. However, they are useful because of their extreme sensitivity to changes of mechanical force or changes in temperature. Due to other characteristics not mentioned here, crystals are most widely used in radio communication equipment. The more complicated study of crystals, as they are used for practical applications, is left for those courses that pertain to the special ratings concerned with them.

VOLTAGE PRODUCED BY HEAT

When a length of metal, such as copper, is heated at one end, electrons tend to move away from the hot end toward the cooler end. This is true of most metals. However, in some metals, such as iron, the opposite takes place and electrons tend to move TOWARD the hot end. These characteristics are illustrated in figure 1-21. The negative charges (electrons) are moving through the copper away from the heat and through the iron toward the heat. They cross from the iron to the copper at the hot junction, and from the copper through the current meter to the iron at the cold junction. This device is generally referred to as a thermocouple.

Thermocouples have somewhat greater power capacities than crystals, but their capacity is still very small if compared to some other sources. The thermoelectric voltage in a thermocouple depends mainly on the difference in temperature between the hot and cold junctions. Consequently, they are widely used to measure temperature, and as heat-sensing devices in automatic temperature control equipment. Thermocouples generally can be subjected to much greater temperatures than ordinary thermometers, such as the mercury or alcohol types.

VOLTAGE PRODUCED BY LIGHT

When light strikes the surface of a substance, it may dislodge electrons from their orbits around the surface atoms of the substance. This occurs because light has energy, the same as any moving force.

Some substances, mostly metallic ones, are far more sensitive to light than others. That is, more electrons will be dislodged and emitted

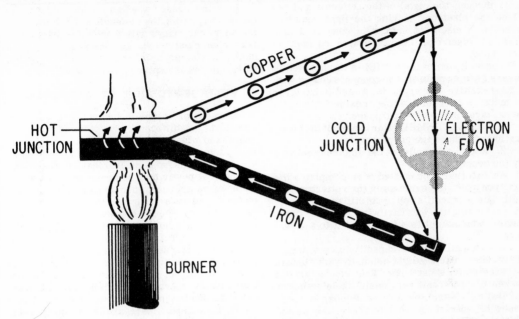

Figure 1-21.—Voltage produced by heat.

from the surface of a highly sensitive metal, with a given amount of light, than will be emitted from a less sensitive substance. Upon losing electrons, the photosensitive (light sensitive) metal becomes positively charged, and an electric force is created. Voltage produced in this manner is referred to as "a photoelectric voltage."

The photosensitive materials most commonly used to produce a photoelectric voltage are various compounds of silver oxide or copper oxide. A complete device which operates on the photoelectric principle is referred to as a "photoelectric cell." There are many sizes and types of photoelectric cells in use, each of which serves the special purpose for which it was designed. Nearly all, however, have some of the basic features of the photoelectric cells shown in figure 1-22.

The cell shown in part (A) has a curved light-sensitive surface focused on the central anode. When light from the direction shown strikes the sensitive surface, it emits electrons toward the anode. The more intense the light, the greater is the number of electrons emitted. When a wire is connected between the filament and the back, or dark side, the accumulated electrons will flow to the dark side. These electrons will eventually

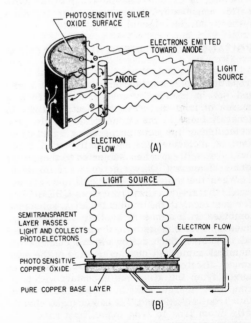

Figure 1-22.—Voltage produced by light.

pass through the metal of the reflector and re-place the electrons leaving the light-sensitive surface. Thus, light energy is converted to a flow of electrons, and a usable current is developed.

The cell shown in part (B) is constructed in layers. A base plate of pure copper is coated with light-sensitive copper oxide. An additional layer of metal is put over the copper oxide. This additional layer serves two purposes:

1. It is EXTREMELY thin to permit the pene-tration of light to the copper oxide.

2. It also accumulates the electrons emitted by the copper oxide.

An externally connected wire completes the electron path, the same as in the reflector type cell. The photocell's voltage is utilized as needed by connecting the external wires to some other device, which amplifies (enlarges) it to a usable level.

A photocell's power capacity is very small. However, it reacts to light-intensity variations in an extremely short time. This characteristic makes the photocell very useful in detecting or accurately controlling a great number of proc-esses or operations. For instance, the photo-electric cell, or some form of the photoelectric principle, is used in television cameras, auto-matic manufacturing process controls, door openers, burglar alarms, and so forth.

VOLTAGE PRODUCED BY CHEMICAL ACTION

Up to this point, it has been shown that elec-trons may be removed from their parent atoms and set in motion by energy derived from a source of friction, pressure, heat, or light. In general, these forms of energy do not alter the molecules of the substances being acted upon. That is, molecules are not usually added, taken away, or split-up when subjected to these four forms of energy. Only electrons are involved.

When the molecules of a substance are al-tered, the action is referred to as CHEMICAL. For instance, if the molecules of a substance combines with atoms of another substance, or gives up atoms of its own, the action is chemi-cal in nature. Such action always changes the chemical name and characteristics of the sub-stance affected. For instance, when atoms of oxygen from the air come in contact with bare iron, they merge with the molecules of iron. This iron is "oxidized." It has changed chemi-cally from iron to iron oxide, or "rust." Its molecules have been altered by chemical action.

In some cases, when atoms are added to or taken away from the molecules of a substance, the chemical change will cause the substance to take on an electric charge. The process of pro-ducing a voltage by chemical action is used in batteries and is explained in chapter 2.

VOLTAGE PRODUCED BY MAGNETISM

Magnets or magnetic devices are used for thousands of different jobs. One of the most useful and widely employed applications of mag-nets is in the production of vast quantities of electric power from mechanical sources. The mechanical power may be provided by a number of different sources, such as gasoline or diesel engines, and water or steam turbines. However, the final conversion of these source energies to electricity is done by generators employing the principle of electromagnetic induction. These generators, of many types and sizes, are dis-cussed in later chapters of this course. The important subject to be discussed here is the fundamental operating principle of ALL such electromagnetic-induction generators.

To begin with, there are three fundamental conditions which must exist before a voltage can be produced by magnetism. You should learn them well, because they will be encountered again and again.
They are:

1. There must be a CONDUCTOR, in which the voltage will be produced.

2. There must be a MAGNETIC FIELD in the conductor's vicinity.

3. There must be relative motion between the field and the conductor. The conductor must be moved so as to cut across the magnetic lines of force, or the field must be moved so that the lines of force are cut by the conductor.

In accordance with these conditions, when a conductor or conductors MOVE ACROSS a mag-netic field so as to cut the lines of force, elec-trons WITHIN THE CONDUCTOR are impelled in one direction or another. Thus, an electric force, or voltage, is created.

In figure 1-23, note the presence of the three conditions needed for creating an induced voltage:

1. A magnetic field exists between the poles of the C-shaped magnet.

2. There is a conductor (copper wire).

3. There is relative motion. The wire is moved back and forth ACROSS the magnetic field.

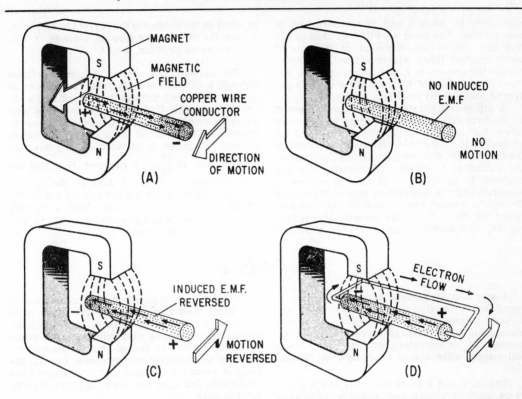

Figure 1-23.—Voltage produced by magnetism.

In part (A) the conductor is moving TOWARD you. This occurs because of the magnetically induced electromotive force (e.m.f.) acting on the electrons in the copper. The right-hand end becomes negative, and the left-hand end positive. In part (B) the conductor is stopped. This eliminates motion, one of the three required conditions, and there is no longer an induced e.m.f. Consequently, there is no longer any difference in potential between the two ends of the wire. In part (C) the conductor is moving AWAY from you. An induced e.m.f. is again created. However, note carefully that the RE-VERSAL OF MOTION has caused a REVERSAL OF DIRECTION in the induced e.m.f.

If a path for electron flow is provided between the ends of the conductor, electrons will leave the negative end and flow to the positive end. This condition is shown in part (D). Electron flow will continue as long as the e.m.f. exists. In studying figure 1-23, it should be noted that the induced e.m.f. could also have been created by holding the conductor stationary and moving the magnetic field back and forth.

In later chapters of this course, under the heading "Generators," you will study the more complex aspects of power generation by use of mechanical motion and magnetism.

Electric Current

The drift or flow of electrons through a conductor is called ELECTRIC CURRENT. In order to determine the amount (number) of electrons flowing in a given conductor, it is

19

necessary to adopt a unit of measurement of current flow. The term AMPERE is used to define the unit of measurement of the rate at which current flows (electron flow). The symbol for the ampere is I. One ampere may be defined as the flow of 6.28×10^{18} electrons per second past a fixed point in a conductor.

A unit quantity of electricity is moved through an electric circuit when one ampere of current flows for one second of time. This unit is equivalent to 6.28×10^{18} electrons, and is called the COULOMB. The coulomb is to electricity as the gallon is to water. The symbol for the coulomb is Q. The rate of flow of current in amperes and the quantity of electricity moved through a circuit are related by the common factor of time. Thus, the quantity of electric charge, in coulombs, moved through a circuit is equal to the product of the current in amperes, I, and the duration of flow in seconds, t. Expressed as an equation, $Q = It$.

For example, if a current of 2 amperes flows through a circuit for 10 seconds the quantity of electricity moved through the circuit is 2 x 10, or 20 coulombs. Conversely, current flow may be expressed in terms of coulombs and time in seconds. Thus, if 20 coulombs are moved through a circuit in 10 seconds, the average current flow is $\frac{20}{10}$, or 2 amperes. Note that the current flow in amperes implies the rate of flow of coulombs per second without indicating either coulombs or seconds. Thus a current flow of 2 amperes is equivalent to a rate of flow of 2 coulombs per second.

Resistance

Every material offers some resistance, or opposition, to the flow of electric current through it. Good conductors, such as copper, silver, and aluminum, offer very little resistance. Poor conductors, or insulators, such as glass, wood, and paper, offer a high resistance to current flow.

The size and type of material of the wires in an electric circuit are chosen so as to keep the electrical resistance as low as possible. In this way, current can flow easily through the conductors, just as water flows through the pipe between the tanks in figure 1-19. If the water pressure remains constant the flow of water in the pipe will depend on how far the valve is opened. The smaller the opening, the greater the opposition to the flow, and the smaller will be the rate of flow in gallons per second.

In the electric circuit, the larger the diameter of the wires, the lower will be their electrical resistance (opposition) to the flow of current through them. In the water analogy, pipe friction opposes the flow of water between the tanks. This friction is similar to electrical resistance. The resistance of the pipe to the flow of water through it depends upon (1) the length of the pipe, (2) the diameter of the pipe, and (3) the nature of the inside walls (rough or smooth). Similarly, the electrical resistance of the conductors depends upon (1) the length of the wires, (2) the diameter of the wires, and (3) the material of the wires (copper, aluminum, etc.).

Temperature also affects the resistance of electrical conductors to some extent. In most conductors (copper, aluminum, iron, etc.) the resistance increases with temperature. Carbon is an exception. In carbon the resistance decreases as temperature increases. Certain alloys of metals (manganin and constantan) have resistance that does not change appreciably with temperature.

The relative resistance of several conductors of the same length and cross section is given in the following list with silver as a standard of 1 and the remaining metals arranged in an order of ascending resistance:

Silver.	1.0
Copper.	1.08
Gold.	1.4
Aluminum.	1.8
Platinum.	7.0
Lead	13.5

The resistance in an electrical circuit is expressed by the symbol R. Manufactured circuit parts containing definite amounts of resistance are called RESISTORS. Resistance (R) is measured in OHMS. One ohm is the resistance of a circuit element, or circuit, that permits a steady current of 1 ampere (1 coulomb per second) to flow when a steady e.m.f. of 1 volt is applied to the circuit.

QUIZ

1. Soft iron is most suitable for use in a
   a. permanent magnet
   b. natural magnet
   c. temporary magnet
   d. magneto

2. Static electricity is most often produced by
   a. pressure
   b. magnetism
   c. heat
   d. friction

3. A fundamental law of electricity is that the current in a circuit is
   a. inversely proportional to the voltage
   b. equal to the voltage
   c. directly proportional to the resistance
   d. directly proportional to the voltage

4. A substance is classed as a magnet if it has
   a. the ability to conduct lines of force
   b. the property of high permeability
   c. the property of magnetism
   d. a high percentage of iron in its composition

5. If a compass is placed at the center of a bar magnet, the compass needle
   a. points to the geographic south pole
   b. points to the geographic north pole
   c. alines itself parallel to the bar
   d. alines itself perpendicular to the bar

6. When electricity is produced by heat in an iron-and-copper thermocouple,
   a. electrons move from north to south
   b. electrons move from the hot junction, through the copper, across the cold junction to the iron, and then to the hot junction
   c. electrons move from the hot junction, through the iron, across the cold junction to the copper, and then return through the copper to the hot junction
   d. none of the above is true

7. The four factors affecting the resistance of a wire are its
   a. length, material, diameter, and temperature
   b. size, length, material, and insulation
   c. length, size, relative resistance, and material
   d. size, insulation, relative resistance, and material

8. Electricity in a battery is produced by
   a. chemical action
   b. chemical reaction
   c. a chemical acting upon metallic plates
   d. all of the above

9. Resistance is always measured in
   a. coulombs
   b. henrys
   c. ohms
   d. megohms

10. The magnetic pole that points northward on a compass
    a. is called the north pole
    b. is actually a south magnetic pole
    c. points to the north magnetic pole of the earth
    d. indicates the direction of the north geographic pole

11. Of the six methods of producing a voltage, which is the least used?
    a. Chemical action
    b. Heat
    c. Friction
    d. Pressure

12. As the temperature of carbon is increased, its resistance will
    a. increase
    b. decrease
    c. remain constant
    d. double

13. Around a magnet, the external lines of force
    a. leave the magnet from the north pole and enter the south pole
    b. often cross one another
    c. leave the magnet from the south pole and enter the north pole
    d. may be broken by a piece of iron shielding

14. When a voltage is applied to a conductor, free electrons
    a. are forced into the nucleus of their atom
    b. are impelled along the conductor
    c. unite with protons
    d. cease their movement

15. When the molecules of a substance are altered, the action is referred to as
    a. thermal
    b. photoelectric
    c. electrical
    d. chemical

16. When matter is separated into individual atoms, it
    a. has undergone a physical change only
    b. has been reduced to its basic chemicals
    c. retains its original characteristics
    d. has been reduced to its basic elements

17. Most permanent magnets and all electromagnets are
    a. classed as natural magnets
    b. manufactured in various shapes from lodestone
    c. classed as artificial magnets
    d. manufactured in various shapes from magnetite

18. When a conductor moves across a magnetic field
    a. a voltage is induced in the conductor
    b. a current is induced in the conductor
    c. both current and voltage are induced in the conductor
    d. all of the above occurs

19. The nucleus of an atom contains
    a. electrons and neutrons
    b. protons and neutrons
    c. protons and electons
    d. protons, electrons, and neutrons
20. An alnico artificial magnet is composed of
    a. magnetite, steel, and nickle
    b. cobalt, nickle, and varnish
    c. aluminum, copper, and cobalt
    d. aluminum, nickle, and cobalt
21. A material that acts as an insulator for magnetic flux is
    a. glass
    b. aluminum
    c. soft iron
    d. unknown today
22. The force acting through the distance between two dissimilarly-charged bodies
    a. is a chemical force
    b. is referred to as a magnetic field
    c. constitutes a flow of ions
    d. is referred to as an electrostatic field

23. An atom that has lost or gained electrons
    a. is negatively charged
    b. has a positive charge
    c. is said to be ionized
    d. becomes electrically neutral

24. Which of the following is considered to be the best conductor?
    a. Zinc
    b. Copper
    c. Aluminum
    d. Silver

25. As the temperature increases, the resistance of most conductors also increases.
    A conductor that is an exception to this is
    a. aluminum
    b. carbon
    c. copper
    d. brass

CHAPTER 2

BATTERIES

Storage batteries are widely used as sources of d-c voltage in automobiles, boats, aircraft, ships, telephone systems, and in portable lighting equipment. In most cases, they are used as standby power supplies.

In others, batteries are the only source of power.

A battery consists of a number of CELLS assembled in a common container and connected to each other.

Common Battery Terms

THE CELL

A cell is a device that transforms chemical energy into electrical energy. The simplest cell, known as either a galvanic or voltaic cell, is shown in figure 2-1. It consists of a piece of carbon (C) and a piece of zinc (Zn) suspended in a jar that contains a solution of water (H_2O) and sulfuric acid (H_2SO_4).

The cell is the fundamental unit of the battery. A simple cell consists of two strips, or electrodes, placed in a container that also holds the electrolyte. The electrolyte in a battery may be in the form of either a liquid or a paste.

ELECTRODES

The electrodes are the conductors by which the current leaves or returns to the electrolyte. In the simple cell, they are carbon and zinc strips that are placed in the electrolyte; while in the dry cell (fig. 2-2), they are the carbon rod in the center and the zinc container in which the cell is assembled.

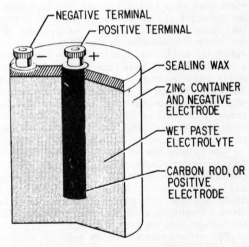

Figure 2-2.—Dry cell, cross-sectional view.

ELECTROLYTE

The electrolyte is the solution that acts upon the electrodes which are placed in it. The

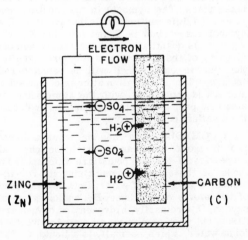

Figure 2-1.—Simple voltaic cell.

electrolyte may be a salt, an acid, or an alkaline solution. In the simple galvanic cell and in the automobile storage battery, the electrolyte is in a liquid form; while in the dry cell, the electrolyte is a paste.

PRIMARY CELL

A primary cell is one in which the chemical action eats away one of the electrodes, usually the negative. When this happens, the electrode must be replaced or the cell must be thrown away. In the galvanic type cell the zinc electrode and the liquid solution are usually replaced when this happens. In the case of the dry cell, it is usually cheaper to buy a new cell. The simple voltaic cell is a primary cell.

SECONDARY CELL

A secondary cell is one in which the electrodes and the electrolyte are altered by the chemical action that takes place when the cell delivers current. These cells may be restored to their original condition by forcing an electric current through them in the opposite direction to that of discharge. The automobile storage battery is a common example of the secondary cell.

THE BATTERY

The battery consists of two or more cells placed in a common box or container. The cells are connected to each other in series, in parallel, or in some combination of series and parallel, depending upon the amount of voltage and current required of the battery. For example, a 45-volt B battery used for radio work may consist of 30 cells of 1-1/2 volts each, connected in series. The 12-volt battery used in the automobile of today consists of 6 cells of 2 volts each, connected in series.

Battery Chemistry

ACTION ON DISCHARGE

If a conductor is connected externally to the electrodes of a cell, electrons will flow under the influence of a difference in potential across the electrodes from the zinc (negative) through the external conductor to the carbon (positive) returning within the solution to the zinc. After a short period of time, the zinc will begin to waste away because of the "burning" action of the acid. If zinc is surrounded by oxygen, it will burn(become oxidized) as a fuel. In this respect, the cell is like a chemical furnace in which energy released by the zinc is transformed into electrical energy rather than heat energy.

The voltage across the electrodes depends upon the materials comprising them and the composition of the solution. The difference of potential between carbon and zinc electrodes in a dilute solution of sulfuric acid and water is about 1.5 volts. In most practical primary cells the voltage does not exceed 2 volts.

The current that a primary cell may deliver depends upon the resistance of the entire cuurcuit, including that of the cell itself. The internal resistance of the primary cell depends upon the size of the electrodes, the distance between them in the solution, and the resistance of the solution. The larger the electrodes and the closer together

they are in solution (without touching), the lower will be the internal resistance of the primary cell and the more current it will be capable of supplying to a load.

When current flows through a cell, the zinc will gradually be dissolved in solution and the acid will be neutralized. A chemical equation is sometimes used to show the chemical action that takes place. The symbols in the equation represent the different materials that are used. The symbol for carbon is C and for zinc Zn. The equation is quantitative and equates the number of parts of the materials used before and after the zinc is oxidized. It will be remembered from chapter 1 that all matter is composed of atoms and molecules, with the atom being the smallest part of an element and the molecule the smallest part of a compound.

A COMPOUND is a chemical combination of two or more elements in which the physical properties of the compound are different from those of the elements comprising it. For instance, a molecule of water, H_2O, is composed of two atoms of hydrogen, H_2, and one atom of oxygen, O. Ordinarily, hydrogen and oxygen are gases, but when combined, as stated above, they form water, which normally is a liquid. On the other hand, sulfuric acid, H_2SO_4, and water,

24

H_2O form a MIXTURE (not a compound), because the identity of both liquids is preserved when they are in solution together.

When a current flows through a primary cell having carbon and zinc electrodes and a dilute solution of sulfuric acid and water, the chemical reaction that takes place can be expressed as:

$$Zn + H_2SO_4 + H_2O \xrightarrow{discharge} ZnSO_4 + H_2O + H_2\uparrow.$$

The expression indicates that as current flows, a molecule of zinc combines with a molecule of sulfuric acid to form a molecule of zinc sulfate ($ZnSO_4$) and a molecule of hydrogen (H_2). The zinc sulfate dissolves in solution and the hydrogen appears as gas bubbles around the carbon electrode. As current continues to flow, the zinc is gradually consumed and the solution changes to zinc sulfate and water. The carbon electrode does not enter into the chemical changes taking place but simply provides a return path for the current.

In the process of oxidizing the zinc, the solution breaks up into positive and negative ions that move in opposite directions through the solution (fig. 2-1). The positive ions are hydrogen ions that appear around the carbon electrode (positive terminal). They are attracted to it by the free electrons from the zinc that are returning to the cell by way of the external load and the positive carbon terminal. The negative ions are SO_4 ions that appear around the zinc electrode. Positive zinc ions enter the solution around the zinc electrode and combine with the negative SO_4 ions to form zinc sulfate, $ZnSO_4$, a grayish-white substance that dissolves in water. At the same time that the positive and negative ions are moving in opposite directions in the solution, electrons are moving through the external circuit from the negative zinc terminal, through the load, and back to the positive carbon terminal. When the zinc is used up, the voltage of the cell is reduced to zero. There is no appreciable difference in potential between zinc sulfate and carbon in a solution of zinc sulfate and water.

POLARIZATION

The chemical action that takes place in the cell (fig. 2-1) while the current is flowing causes hydrogen bubbles to form on the surface of the positive carbon electrode in great numbers until the entire surface is surrounded. This action is called POLARIZATION. Some of these bubbles rise to the surface of the solution and escape into the air. However, many of the bubbles remain until there is no room for any more to be formed.

The hydrogen tends to set up an electromotive force in the opposite direction to that of the cell, thus increasing the effective internal resistance, reducing the output current, and lowering the terminal voltage.

A cell that is heavily polarized has no useful output. There are several ways to prevent polarization from occurring or to overcome it after it has occurred. The very simplest method might be to remove the carbon electrode and wipe off the hydrogen bubbles. When the electrode is replaced in the electrolyte, the e.m.f. and current are again normal. This method is not practicable because polarization occurs rapidly and continuously in the simple voltaic cell. A commercial form of voltaic cell, known as the DRY CELL, employs a substance rich in oxygen as a part of the positive carbon electrode, which will combine chemically with the hydrogen to form water, H_2O. One of the best depolarizing agents used is manganese dioxide (MnO_2), which supplies enough free oxygen to combine with all of the hydrogen so that the cell is practically free from polarization.

The chemical action that occurs may be expressed as

$$2MnO_2 + H_2 \longrightarrow Mn_2O_3 + H_2O.$$

The manganese dioxide combines with the hydrogen to form water and a lower oxide of manganese. Thus the counter e.m.f. of polarization does not exist in the cell, and the terminal voltage and output current are maintained normal.

LOCAL ACTION

When the external circuit is opened, the current will cease to flow, and theoretically all chemical action within the cell will stop. However, commercial zinc contains many impurities, such as iron, carbon, lead, and arsenic. These impurities form many small cells within the zinc electrode in which current flows between the zinc and its impurities. Thus the zinc is oxidized even though the cell itself is an open circuit. This wasting away of the zinc on open circuit is called LOCAL ACTION. For example, a small local cell exists on a zinc plate containing impurities of iron, as shown in figure 2-3. Electrons flow between the zinc and iron and the solution around the impurity becomes ionized. The negative SO_4 ions combine with the positive

Zn ions to form $ZnSO_4$. Thus the acid is depleted in solution and the zinc consumed.

Local action may be prevented by using pure zinc (which is not practical), by coating the zinc with mercury, or by adding a small percentage of mercury to the zinc during the manufacturing process. The treatment of the zinc with mercury is called AMALGAMATING the zinc. Since mercury is 13.6 times as heavy as an equal volume of water, small particles of impurities having a lower relative weight than that of mercury will rise (float) to the surface of the mercury. The removal of these impurities from the zinc prevents local action. The mercury is not readily acted upon by the acid, and even when the cell is delivering current to a load, the mercury continues to act on the impurities in the zinc, causing them to leave the surface of the zinc electrode and float to the surface of the mercury. This process greatly increases the life of the primary cell.

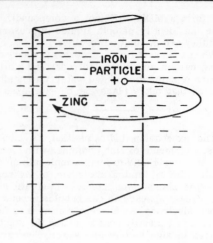

Figure 2-3.—Local action on zinc electrode.

Types of Batteries

THE DRY (PRIMARY) CELL

The dry cell is so called because its electrolyte is not in a liquid state. Actually, the electrolyte is a moist paste. If it should become dry, it would no longer be able to transform chemical energy to electrical energy. The name DRY CELL, therefore, is not strictly correct in a technical sense.

Construction of the Dry Cell

The construction of a common type of dry cell is shown in figure 2-4. The internal parts of the cell are located in a cylindrical zinc container. This zinc container serves as the cell's negative electrode. The container is lined with a nonconducting material, such as blotting paper, to insulate the zinc from the paste. A carbon electrode is located in the center, and it serves as the positive terminal of the cell. The paste is a mixture of several substances. Its composition may vary, depending on its manufacturer. Generally, however, the paste will contain some combination of the following substances: ammonium chloride (sal ammoniac), powdered coke, ground carbon, manganese dioxide, zinc chloride, graphite, and water.

This paste, which is packed in the space between the carbon and the blotting paper, also serves to hold the carbon electrode rigid in the center of the cell. When packing the paste in the cell, a small expansion space is left at the top. The cell is then sealed with asphalt-saturated cardboard.

Binding posts are attached to the electrodes so that wires may be conveniently connected to the cell.

Since the zinc container is one of the electrodes, it must be protected with some insulating material. Therefore, it is common practice for the manufacturer to enclose the cells in cardboard containers.

Chemical Action of the Dry Cell

The dry cell (fig. 2-4) is fundamentally the same as the simple voltaic cell (wet cell) described earlier, as far as its internal chemical action is concerned. The action of the water and the ammonium chloride in the paste, together with the zinc and carbon electrodes, produces the voltage of the cell. The manganese dioxide is added to reduce the polarization when line current flows, and the zinc chloride reduces local action when the cell is idle. The blotting paper serves two purposes, one being to keep the paste from making actual contact with the zinc container and the other being to permit the electrolyte to filter through to the zinc slowly. The cell is sealed at the top to keep air from entering and drying the electrolyte. Care should be taken to prevent breaking this seal.

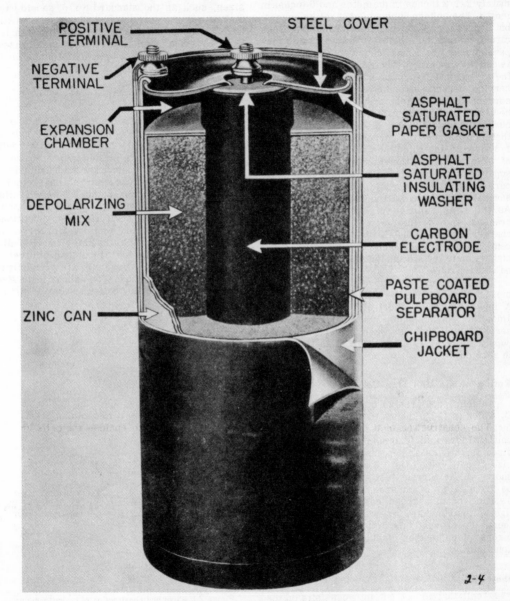

Figure 2-4.—Cutaway view of the general-purpose dry cell.

27

Rating of the Standard Size Cell

One of the most popular sizes in general use is the standard, or No. 6, dry cell. It is approximately 2-1/2 inches in diameter and 6 inches in length. The voltage is about 1-1/2 volts when new but decreases as the cell ages. When the open-circuit voltage falls below 0.75 to 1.2 volts (depending upon the circuit requirements), the cell is usually discarded. The amount of current that the cell can deliver, and still give satisfactory service, depends upon the length of time that the current flows. For instance, if a No. 6 cell is to be used in a portable radio, it is likely to supply current constantly for several hours. Under these conditions, the current should not exceed 1/8 ampere, the rated constant-current capacity of a No. 6 cell. If the same cell is required to supply current only occasionally, for only short periods of time, it could supply currents of several amperes without undue injury to the cell. As the time duration of each discharge decreases, and the interval of time between discharges increases the allowable amount of current available for each discharge becomes higher, up to the amount that the cell will deliver on short circuit.

The short-circuit current test is another means of evaluating the condition of a dry cell. A new cell, when short circuited through an ammeter, should supply not less than 25 amperes. A cell that has been in service should supply at least 10 amperes if it is to remain in service.

Rating of the Unit Size Cell

Another popular size of dry cell is the size D, which is 1-3/8 inches in diameter and 2-3/4 inches in length. This cell is also known as the unit cell. Its most common use is in standard-sized flashlights and in test instruments. The size D cell voltage is 1.5 volts when new. The short-circuit current test of a new cell should be from 5 to 6 amperes. The corrosion and swelling of discharged cells may ruin flashlights, instruments, or whatever device uses them. To prevent this action, some manufacturers place a steel jacket around the zinc container.

Shelf Life

A cell that is not put into use (sits on the shelf) will gradually deteriorate because of slow internal chemical actions (local action) and changes in moisture content. However, this deterioration is usually very slow if cells are properly stored. High-grade cells of the larger sizes, such as the standard No. 6, should have a shelf life of a year or more. Smaller size cells have a proportionately shorter shelf life, ranging down to a few months for the very small sizes. If unused cells are stored in a cool place, their shelf life will be greatly increased.

Mercury Cells

A fairly recent addition to the types of batteries used in the Navy is the mercury cell. It is known also as the "Ruben" or "RM" cell. Presently, its uses are limited mainly to precision measuring instruments and guided missiles. The mercury cell's most desirable characteristics are (1) a high power-output-to-weight ratio, (2) an almost flat discharge-voltage curve, and (3) a relatively long shelf life under conditions of high temperature and humidity. Mercury cells presently in use, such as the RM-1R and RM-4R, are very small compared to most lead-acid cells. However, larger mercury cells are presently in the developmental stage. The approximate size of two typical mercury cells is shown in figure 2-5 (A).

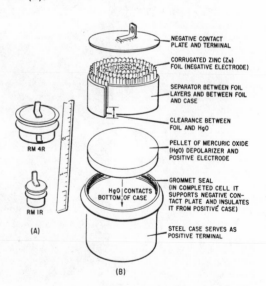

Figure 2-5.—Size and construction of typical mercury (RM) cells.

Mercury cells, as compared to lead-acid cells, are also quite different in their internal construction, as shown by the exploded view in figure 2-5 (B). The negative electrode is corrugated zinc foil, spirally co-wrapped with an inert separator. The zinc is coated with pure mercury (amalgamated) to prevent local action during shelf storage. In the completed cell, the top contact plate connects to the spiralled edge of the zinc foil. The bottom of the separator rests against the mercuric oxide pellet; and the pellet is, in turn, pressed tightly against the bottom of the steel case. There is space in the foil corrugations and in the clearance between the foil and HgO pellet. This space is filled with electrolyte. The electrolyte is an alkaline solution of potassium hydroxide, zincate, and water. The cell is sealed, since there is no gassing during discharge. Mercury cells cannot be recharged.

The overall chemical action by which the mercury cell produces electricity is given by the following chemical formula:

$$Zn + H_2O + HgO \longrightarrow ZnO + H_2O + Hg.$$

This action, the same as in other type cells, is a process of oxidation. The alkaline electrolyte is in contact with the zinc electrode. The zinc oxidizes (Zn changes to ZnO), thus taking atoms of oxygen from water molecules in the electrolyte. This leaves positive hydrogen ions, which move toward the mercuric oxide pellet, causing polarization. These hydrogen ions take oxygen from the mercuric oxide (thus changing HgO to Hg). Where one molecule of water is destroyed at the negative electrode, one molecule is produced at the positive electrode, maintaining the net amount of water constant. By absorbing oxygen, the zinc electrode accumulates excess electrons, making it negative. By giving up oxygen, the mercuric oxide electrode loses electrons, making it positive. In the discharged state, the negative electrode is zinc oxide, and the positive electrode is ordinary mercury.

Reserve Cell

A reserve cell is one in which the elements are kept dry until the time of use at which time the electrolyte is admitted and the cell starts producing current. The rigorous requirements of the proximity fuse led to the development of this type of cell. In the proximity fuse the battery consists of 63 annular (or ring-shaped) zinc and carbon electrodes. A glass container is mounted in the center of the electrodes. The shock of the acceleration produced by firing the shell breaks the glass container and forces the electrolyte between the electrodes, thus activating the cell.

The shelf life of primary reserve batteries is extremely long even under adverse tropic or arctic conditions. This life is attained by incorporating the depolarizer in the liquid electrolyte so that the elements of the cell are subject to no chemical action until the time of use.

Combining Cells

In many cases, a battery-powered device may require more electrical energy than one cell can provide. The device may require either a higher voltage or more current, and in some cases both. Under such conditions it is necessary to combine, or interconnect, enough cells to meet the higher requirements. Cells connected in series provide a higher voltage, while cells connected in parallel provide a higher current capacity. To provide adequate power when both voltage and current requirements are greater than one cell's capacity, a combination series-parallel network of cells must be interconnected.

SERIES-CONNECTED CELLS

Assume you must connect enough No. 6 dry cells to supply power to a load requiring 6 volts. At this potential, the load will draw 1/8 ampere. Since a single No. 6 cell supplies a potential of only 1.5 volts, more than one cell is obviously needed. To obtain the higher potential, the cells are connected in series as shown in figure 2-6 (A).

In a series hookup, the negative electrode of the first cell is connected to the positive electrode of the second cell, the negative electrode of the second to the positive of the third, and so on. The positive electrode of the first cell and negative electrode of the last cell then serve as the power takeoff terminals of the battery. In this way, the potential is boosted 1.5 volts by each cell in the series line. There are four cells, so the output terminal voltage is 1.5 x 4 = 6 volts. When connected to the load, 1/8 ampere flows through the load and each cell of the battery. This is within the capacity of each No. 6 cell. Therefore, only four series-connected No. 6 cells are needed to supply this particular load.

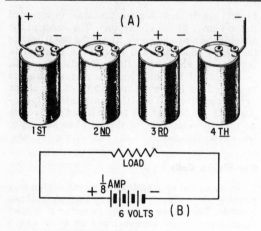

Figure 2-6.–(A) Pictorial view of series-connected cells; (B) schematic of series connection.

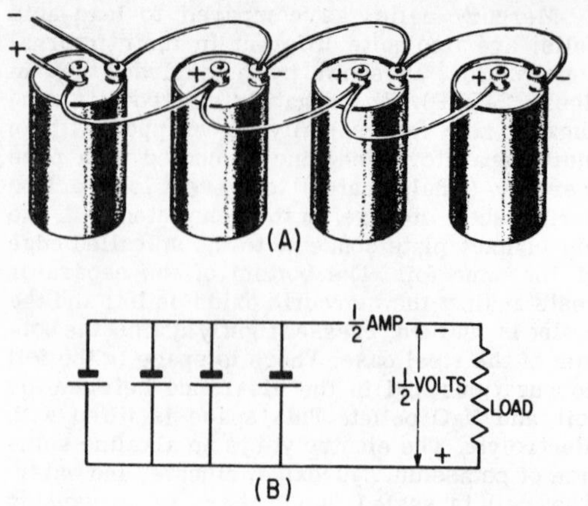

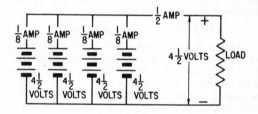

Figure 2-7.–(A) Pictorial view of parallel-connected cells; (B) schematic of parallel connections.

PARALLEL-CONNECTED CELLS

In this case, assume an electrical load requires only 1.5 volts, but will draw 1/2 ampere of current. (Assume that a No. 6 cell will supply only 1/8 ampere.) To meet this requirement, the No. 6 cells are connected in parallel, as shown in figure 2-7 (A). In a parallel connection, all positive cell electrodes are connected to one line, and all negative electrodes are connected to the other. No more than one cell is connected between the lines at any one point, so the potential between the lines is the same as that of one cell, or 1.5 volts. However, each cell may contribute its maximum allowable current of 1/8 ampere to the line. There are four cells, so the total line current is 1/8 x 4 = 1/2 ampere. Hence, four No. 6 cells in parallel have enough capacity to supply a load requiring 1/2 ampere at 1.5 volts.

SERIES-PARALLEL CONNECTED CELLS

Figure 2-8 depicts a battery network supplying power to a load requiring both a voltage and current greater than one cell can provide. To provide the required 4-1/2 volts, groups of three 1.5-volt cells are connected in series. To provide the required 1/2 ampere of current, four series groups are connected in parallel, each supplying 1/8 ampere of current.

Figure 2-8.–Series-parallel connected cells.

SECONDARY (WET) CELLS

Secondary cells function on the same basic chemical principles as primary cells. They differ mainly in that they may be recharged, whereas the primary cell is not rechargeable. Some of the materials of a primary cell are consumed in the process of changing chemical energy to electrical energy. In the secondary cell, the materials are merely transferred from one electrode to the other as the cell discharges. Discharged secondary cells may be restored (charged) to their original state by forcing an electric current from some other source through the cell in the opposite direction to that of discharge.

The storage battery consists of a number of secondary cells connected in series. Properly speaking, this battery does not store electrical energy, but is a source of chemical energy which produces electrical energy. There are three

30

types of storage cells--the lead-acid type, which has an e.m.f. of 2.2 volts per cell; the nickel-iron-alkali type; and the nickel-cadmium-alkaline type. The latter two have an e.m.f. of 1.2 volts per cell. Of these three types, the lead-acid type is the most widely used, and will be described first.

Lead-Acid Batteries

In its charged condition, the active materials in the lead-acid battery are lead peroxide (used as the positive plate) and sponge lead (used as the negative plate). The electrolyte is a mixture of sulfuric acid and water. The strength (acidity) of the electrolyte is measured in terms of its specific gravity. Specific gravity is the ratio of the weight of a given volume of electrolyte to an equal volume of pure water. Concentrated sulfuric acid has a specific gravity of about 1.830; pure water has a specific gravity of 1.000. The acid and water are mixed in a proportion to give the specific gravity desired. For example, an electrolyte with a specific gravity of 1.210 requires roughly one part of concentrated acid to four parts of water.

In a fully charged battery the positive plates are pure lead peroxide and the negative plates are pure lead. Also, in a fully charged battery, all the acid is in the electrolyte so that the specific gravity is at its maximum value. The active materials of both the positive and negative plates are porous, and have absorptive qualities similar to a sponge.

The pores are therefore filled with the battery solution (electrolyte) in which they are immersed. As the battery discharges, the acid in contact with the plates separates from the electrolyte. It forms a chemical combination with the plate's active material, changing it to lead sulfate. Thus, as the discharge continues, lead sulfate forms on the plates, and more acid is taken from the electrolyte. The electrolyte's water content becomes progressively higher; that is, the ratio of water to acid increases. As a result, the specific gravity of the electrolyte will gradually decrease during discharge.

When the battery is being charged, the reverse takes place. The acid held in the sulfated plate material is driven back into the electrolyte; further charging cannot raise its specific gravity any higher. When fully charged, the material of the positive plates is again pure lead peroxide and that of the negative plates is pure lead.

Electrical energy is derived from a cell when the plates react with the electrolyte. As a molecule of sulfuric acid separates, part of it combines with the negative sponge lead plates. Thus, it makes the sponge lead plates negative, and at the same time forms lead sulfate. The remainder of the sulfuric acid molecule, lacking electrons, has thus become a positive ion. The positive ions migrate through the electrolyte to the opposite (lead peroxide) plates, and takes electrons from them. This action neutralizes the positive ions, forming ordinary water. It also makes the lead peroxide plates positive, by taking electrons from them. Again, lead sulfate is formed in the process.

The action just described is represented in more detail by the following chemical equation

$$Pb + PbO_2 + 2H_2SO_4 \xrightleftharpoons{discharging} 2PbSO_4 + 2H_2O.$$

The left side of the expression represents the cell in the charged condition, and the right side represents the cell in the discharged condition.

In the charged condition the positive plate contains lead peroxide, PbO_2; the negative plate is composed of sponge lead, Pb; and the solution contains sulfuric acid, H_2SO_4. In the discharged condition both plates contain lead sulfate, $PbSO_4$, and the solution contains water, H_2O. As the discharge progresses, the acid content of the electrolyte becomes less and less because it is used in forming lead sulfate, and the specific gravity of the electrolyte decreases. A point is reached where so much of the active material has been converted into lead sulfate that the cell can no longer produce sufficient current to be of practical value. At this point the cell is said to be discharged (fig. 2-9 (C)). Since the amount of sulfuric acid combining with the plates at any time during discharge is in direct proportion to the ampere-hours (product of current in amperes and time in hours) of discharge, the specific gravity of the electrolyte is a guide in determining the state of discharge of the lead-acid cell.

If the discharged cell is properly connected to a direct-current charging source the voltage of which is slightly higher than that of the cell, current will flow through the cell, in the opposite direction to that of discharge, and the cell is said to be charging (fig. 2-9 (D)). The effect of the current will be to change the lead sulfate on both the positive and negative plates back to its original active form of lead peroxide and sponge lead, respectively. At the same time, the sulfate is restored to the electrolyte with the result that the specific gravity of the electrolyte increases. When all the sulfate has been restored to the electrolyte, the specific gravity will be maximum. The cell is then fully charged and is ready to be discharged again.

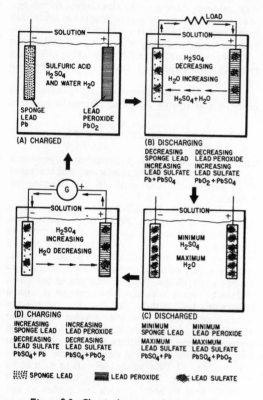

(A) CHARGED

(B) DISCHARGING
DECREASING   DECREASING
SPONGE LEAD   LEAD PEROXIDE
INCREASING   INCREASING
LEAD SULFATE LEAD SULFATE
$Pb + PbSO_4$ $PbO_2 + PbSO_4$

(D) CHARGING
INCREASING   INCREASING
SPONGE LEAD   LEAD PEROXIDE
DECREASING   DECREASING
LEAD SULFATE LEAD SULFATE
$PbSO_4 + Pb$ $PbSO_4 + PbO_2$

(C) DISCHARGED
MINIMUM   MINIMUM
SPONGE LEAD   LEAD PEROXIDE
MAXIMUM   MAXIMUM
LEAD SULFATE LEAD SULFATE
$PbSO_4 + Pb$ $PbSO_4 + PbO_2$

SPONGE LEAD   LEAD PEROXIDE   LEAD SULFATE

Figure 2-9.—Chemical action in lead-acid cell.

It should always be remembered that the addition of sulfuric acid to a discharged lead-acid cell does not recharge the cell. Adding acid only increases the specific gravity of the electrolyte and does not convert the lead sulfate on the plates back into active material (sponge lead and lead peroxide), and consequently does not bring the cell back to a charged condition. A charging current must be passed through the cell to do this.

As a cell charge nears completion, hydrogen gas, H_2, is liberated at the negative plate and

oxygen gas, O_2, is liberated at the positive plate. This action occurs because the charging current is greater than the amount that is necessary to reduce the small remaining amount of lead sulfate on the plates. Thus, the excess current ionizes the water in the electrolyte. This action is necessary to assure full charge to the cell.

PASTED PLATES

Lead-acid storage batteries use a variety of plates ranging from the spun-lead (Plante) type to the lighter pasted construction. The Plante-type plates require repeated charging and discharging to develop the active material to the proper depth. The process is slow and expensive. In 1881 Camille Faure in France made a radical improvement in the construction of storage batteries by developing a pasted plate that was manufactured with much less expense.

The pasted plate is most commonly used in portable lead-acid batteries today. The plates are formed by applying special lead-oxide pastes to a grid made of lead-antimony alloy. The grid holds in place the active material with which the spaces in the grid are filled and distributes the current evenly to all parts of the plate.

When the paste is dry, the plates are given a forming charge. They are formed by immersing them in electrolyte and passing current through them in the proper direction to change the paste to lead peroxide for the positive plates and to sponge lead for the negative plates. This type of plate takes less time to manufacture and is relatively light in weight compared to the Plante spun-lead plates, which have a more rugged and durable construction.

IRONCLAD PLATE

The ironclad plate is used extensively in submarine batteries because it has a long life. The positive ironclad plate (fig. 2-10 (A)) is quite different from the pasted plate. It consists of several slotted hard-rubber tubes filled with active material that is similar to the material used in the pasted plate. Extending through the center of each tube is a core of lead antimony, which is firmly anchored in the paste by means of radial fins that are equally spaced along the core. The core, which is lead-burned to the top and bottom of the frame, serves primarily as a conductor for the electric current and strengthens the plate. Lead-antimony cores form the

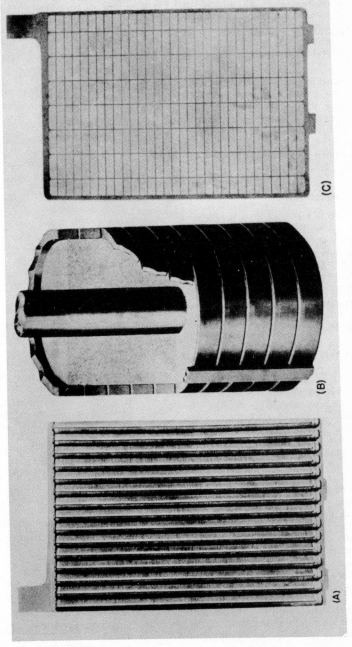

Figure 2-10.—Ironclad plate construction.

grids that comprise the conducting network between the hard-rubber tubes of the positive plate.

The hard-rubber tubes contain narrow horizontal slots to permit the passage of electrolyte through them so that it may come into contact with the active material inside the tubes (fig. 2-10 (B)).

The slotted tubes prevent the washing away, or shedding, of the active material. Each tube has two full-length ribs--one on each side--which keep the separators (spacers) from covering the slots and preventing the electrolyte from circulating freely. The ironclad negative plates are essentially the same as the negative pasted plates (fig. 2-10 (C)).

GOULD PLATE

The Gould Plate is a pasted plate that differs very little from the ordinary positive and negative pasted plates. A glass-wool mat directly over the positive plate holds the active material in place. Rubber or wood separators are used as in other batteries. The glass-wool mat prevents shedding amd makes the Gould battery almost as durable as the ironclad battery. Hence the Gould battery is used extensively in both submarines and surface vessels.

LEAD-ACID CELL ELEMENT

The plates are formed into positive and negative groups. When these groups are assembled, they become a cell element (fig. 2-11). The number of negative plates is always one more than the number of positive plates so that both sides of each positive plate are acted upon chemically. The active material on the positive plates expands and contracts as the battery is charged and discharged. The expansion and contraction must be kept the same on both sides of the plates to prevent buckling.

Separators of wood, rubber, or glass are placed between the positive and negative plates to act as insulators (fig. 2-11). These separators are grooved vertically on one side and are smooth on the other. The grooved side is placed next to the positive plate to permit free circulation of the electrolyte around the active material.

An assembled lead-acid cell with the positive and negative terminals projecting through the cell cover is shown in figure 2-12. A hole fitted with a filler cap is provided in each cell cover

to permit filling and testing. The filler cap has a vent hole to allow the gas that forms in the cell during charge to escape.

The ordinary 6-volt portable storage battery consists of 3 cells assembled in a molded hard-rubber (monobloc) case. Metal cannot be used

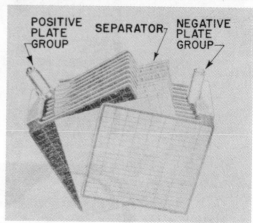

**CELL ELEMENT
PARTLY ASSEMBLED**

Figure 2-11.–Partly assembled cell element.

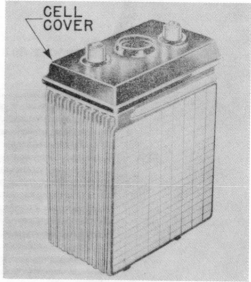

ASSEMBLED CELL

Figure 2-12.–Assembled lead-acid cell.

34

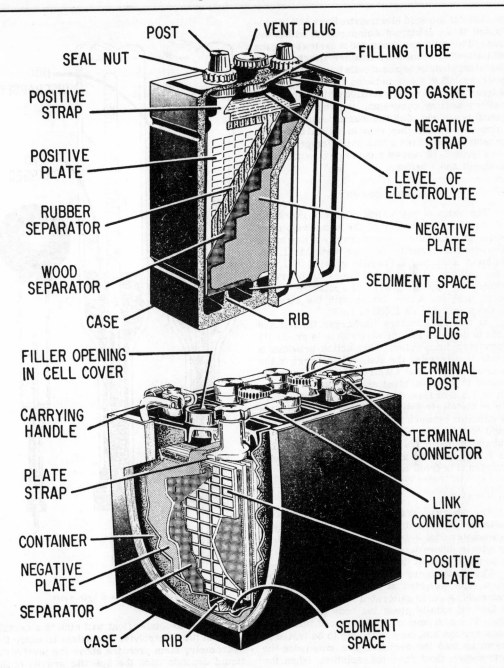

POST

VENT PLUG

SEAL NUT

FILLING TUBE

POSITIVE STRAP

POST GASKET

POSITIVE PLATE

NEGATIVE STRAP

RUBBER SEPARATOR

LEVEL OF ELECTROLYTE

WOOD SEPARATOR

NEGATIVE PLATE

CASE

SEDIMENT SPACE

RIB

FILLING OPENING IN CELL COVER

FILLER PLUG

CARRYING HANDLE

TERMINAL POST

PLATE STRAP

TERMINAL CONNECTOR

CONTAINER

LINK CONNECTOR

NEGATIVE PLATE

POSITIVE PLATE

SEPARATOR

CASE

RIB

SEDIMENT SPACE

Figure 2-13.—Lead-acid cell and battery.

35

because of the acid electrolyte. Each cell is contained in an acidproof compartment within the case. The cells are connected in series by means of lead-alloy connectors that are attached to the terminal posts of adjacent cells by a lead-burning process. The space between the case and the edges of the cell covers is filled with an acidproof battery-sealing compound, or pitch. This compound is a blend of bituminous materials that are processed so that they remain solid at high temperatures and do not crack at low temperatures.

Figure 2-13 shows a cutaway view of a lead-acid cell and a battery.

SPECIFIC GRAVITY

The ratio of the weight of a certain volume of liquid to the weight of the same volume of water is called the specific gravity of the liquid. The specific gravity of pure water is 1.000. Sulfuric acid has a specific gravity of 1.830; thus sulfuric acid is 1.830 times as heavy as water. The specific gravity of a mixture of sulfuric acid and water varies with the strength of the solution from 1.000 to 1.830.

As a storage battery discharges, the sulfuric acid is depleted and the electrolyte is gradually converted into water. This action provides a guide in determing the state of discharge of the lead-acid cell. The electrolyte that is usually placed in a lead-acid battery has a specific gravity of 1.350 or less. Generally, the specific gravity of the electrolyte in Navy portable batteries is adjusted between 1.210 and 1.220. On the other hand the specific gravity of the electrolyte in submarine batteries when charged is from 1.250 to 1.265, while in aircraft batteries when fully charged it is from 1.285 to 1.300.

Hydrometer

The specific gravity of the electrolyte is measured with a hydrometer. In the syringe-type hydrometer (fig. 2-14), part of the battery electrolyte is drawn up into a glass tube by means of a rubber bulb at the top.

The hydrometer float consists of a hollow glass tube weighted at one end and sealed at both ends. A scale calibrated in specific gravity is laid off axially along the body (stem) of the tube. The hydrometer float is placed inside the glass syringe and the electrolyte to be tested is drawn up into the syringe, thus immersing the hydrometer float into the solution. When the syringe is held approximately in a vertical posi-

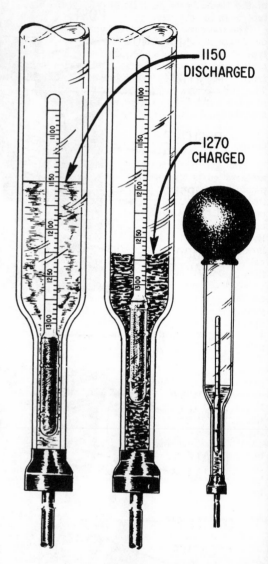

1150
DISCHARGED

1270
CHARGED

Figure 2-14.–Type-B hydrometer.

tion, the hydrometer float will sink to a certain level in the electrolyte. The extent to which the hydrometer stem protudes above the level of the liquid depends upon the specific gravity of the solution. The reading on the stem at the surface

36

of the liquid is tne specific gravity of the electrolyte in the syringe.

The Navy uses two types of hydrometer bulbs, or floats, each having a different scale. The type-A hydrometer is used with submarine batteries and has two different floats with scales from 1.060 to 1.240 and from 1.120 to 1.300. The type-B hydrometer is used with portable storage batteries and aircraft batteries. It has a scale from 1.100 to 1.300.

Corrections

The specific gravity of the electrolyte is affected by its temperature. The electrolyte expands and becomes less dense when heated and its specific gravity reading is lowered. On the other hand, the electrolyte contracts and becomes denser when cooled and its specific gravity reading is raised. In both cases the electrolyte may be from the same fully charged storage cell. Thus, the effect of temperature is to distort the readings.

All Navy standard storage batteries use 80°F. as the normal temperature to which specific gravity readings are corrected. To correct the specific gravity reading of a storage battery, add 1 point to the reading for each 3° F. above 80° and subtract 1 point for each 3° F. below 80°. The electrolyte in a cell should be at the normal level when the reading is taken. If the level is below normal, there will not be enough fluid drawn into the tube to cause the float to rise. If the level is above normal, there is too much water, the electrolyte is weakened, and the reading is too low. A hydrometer reading is inaccurate if taken immediately after water is added because the water tends to remain at the top of the cell. When water is added, the battery should be charged for at least an hour to mix the electrolyte before a hydrometer reading is taken.

Adjusting Specific Gravity

Only authorized personnel on a repair ship or at a shore station should add acid to a battery. Acid with a specific gravity above 1.350 is never added to a battery. If the specific gravity of a cell is more than it should be, it can be reduced to within limits by removing some of the electrolyte and adding distilled water. The battery is charged for 1 hour to mix the solution, and then hydrometer readings are taken. The adjustment is continued until the desired true readings are obtained.

MIXING ELECTROLYTES

The electrolyte of a fully charged battery usually contains about 38 percent sulfuric acid by weight, or about 27 percent by volume. In preparing the electrolyte distilled water and sulfuric acid that meets Navy specifications are used. New batteries may be delivered with containers of concentrated sulfuric acid of 1.830 specific gravity or electrolyte of 1.400 specific gravity, both of which must be diluted with distilled water to make electrolyte of the proper specific gravity. The container used for diluting the acid should be made of glass, earthenware, rubber, or lead.

When mixing electrolyte, ALWAYS POUR ACID INTO WATER—never pour water into acid. Pour the acid slowly and cautiously to prevent excessive heating and splashing. Stir the solution continuously with a nonmetallic rod to mix the heavier acid with the lighter water and to keep the acid from sinking to the bottom. When concentrated acid is diluted, the solution becomes very hot.

TREATMENT OF ACID BURNS

If acid or electrolyte from a lead-acid battery comes into contact with the skin, the affected area should be washed as soon as possible with large quantities of fresh water, after which a salve such as vaseline, boric acid, or zinc ointment should be applied. If none of these salves are available, clean lubricating oil will suffice. When washing, large amounts of water should be used, since a small amount of water might do more harm than good in spreading the acid burn.

Acid spilled on clothing may be neutralized with dilute ammonia or a solution of baking soda and water.

CAPACITY

The capacity of a battery is measured in ampere-hours. As mentioned before, the ampere-hour capacity is equal to the product of the current in amperes and the time in hours during which the battery is supplying this current. The ampere-hour capacity varies inversely with the discharge current. The size of a cell is determined generally by its ampere-hour capacity. The capacity of a cell depends upon many factors, the most important of which are (1) the area of the plates in contact with the electrolyte; (2) the quantity and specific gravity of the electrolyte; (3) the type of separators; (4) the general condition of the battery (degree of sulfating, plates buckled, separators warped, sediment in bottom of cells, and so forth); and (5) the final limiting voltage.

RATING

Navy storage batteries are rated according to their rate of discharge and ampere-hour capacity. All batteries, except Naval aircraft and those used for radio and sound systems, are rated according to a 10-hour rate of discharge—that is, if a fully charged battery is completely discharged during a 10-hour period, it is discharged at the 10-hour rate. Thus if a battery can deliver 40 amperes continuously for 10 hours, the battery has a rating of 40 x 10, or 400 ampere-hours. Thus the 10-hour rating is equal to the average current that a battery is capable of supplying without interruption for an interval of 10 hours. (NOTE: Aircraft batteries are rated according to a 2-hour rate of discharge.)

All Navy standard batteries deliver 100 percent of their available capacity if discharged in 10 hours or more, but they will deliver less than their available capacity if discharged at a faster rate. The faster they discharge, the less ampere-hour capacity they have.

The low-voltage limit, as specified by the manufacturer, is the limit beyond which very little useful energy can be obtained from a battery. For example, at the conclusion of a 10-hour discharge test on a Navy portable battery, the closed-circuit voltmeter reading is about 1.75 volts per cell and the specific gravity of the electrolyte is about 1.060. At the end of a charge, its closed-circuit voltmeter reading, while the battery is being charged at the finishing rate, is between 2.4 and 2.6 volts per cell. The specific gravity of the electrolyte corrected to 80° F. is between 1.210 and 1.220. In climates of 40° F. and below, authority may be granted to increase the specific gravity to 1.280. Other batteries, of higher normal specific gravity, may also be increased.

TEST DISCHARGE

The test discharge is the best method of determining the capacity of a battery. Most battery switchboards are provided with the necessary equipment for giving test discharges. If proper equipment is not available, a tender,

repair ship, or shore station may make the test. To determine the battery capacity, a battery is normally given a test discharge once every 6 months. Test discharges are also given whenever any cell of a battery after charge cannot be brought within 10 points of full charge, or when one or more cells is found to have less than normal voltage after an equalizing charge.

A test discharge must always be preceded by an equalizing charge. Immediately after the equalizing charge, the battery is discharged at its 10-hour rate until either (1) the total battery voltage drops to a value equal to 1.75 times the number of cells in series, or (2) the voltage of any individual cell drops to 1.65 volts, whichever occurs first. The rate of discharge should be kept constant throughout the test discharge. Because Navy standard batteries are rated at the 10-hour capacity, the discharge rate for a 175 ampere-hour battery is 175/10, or 17.5 amperes. If the temperature of the electrolyte at the beginning of the charge is not exactly 80° F., the time duration of the discharge must be corrected for the actual temperature of the battery.

A battery of 100-percent capacity discharges at its 10-hour rate for 10 hours before reaching its low-voltage limit. If the battery or one of its cells reaches the low-voltage limit before the 10-hour period has elapsed, the discharge is discontinued immediately and the percentage of capacity is determined from the equation:

$$C = \frac{H_a}{H_t} \times 100, \qquad (2-1)$$

where C is the percentage of ampere-hour capacity available, H_a the total hours of discharge, and H_t the total hours for 100-percent capacity. The date for each test discharge should be recorded on the storage battery record sheet.

For example, a 150-ampere-hour 6-volt battery delivers an average current of 15 amperes for 10 hours. At the end of this period the battery voltage is 5.25 volts. On a later test the same battery delivers an average current of 15 amperes for only 7 hours. The discharge was stopped at the end of this time because the voltage of the middle cell was found to be only 1.65 volts. The percentage of capacity of the battery is now $\frac{7}{10} \times 100$, or 70 percent. Thus, the ampere-hour capacity of this battery is reduced to 0.7 x 150 = 105 ampere hours.

STATE OF CHARGE

After a battery is discharged completely from full charge at the 10-hour rate, the specific gravity has dropped about 150 points to about 1.060. The number of points that the specific gravity drops per ampere-hour can be determined for each type of battery. For each ampere-hour taken out of a battery a definite amount of acid is removed from the electrolyte and combined with the plates.

For example, if a battery is discharged from full charge to the low-voltage limit at the 10-hour rate and if 100 ampere-hours are obtained with a specific gravity drop of 150 points, there is a drop of $\frac{150}{100}$, or 1.5 points per ampere-hour delivered. If the reduction in specific gravity per ampere-hour is known, the drop in specific gravity for this battery may be predicted for any number of ampere-hours delivered to a load. For example, if 70 ampere-hours are delivered by the battery at the 10-hour rate or any other rate or collection of rates, the drop in specific gravity is 70 x 1.5, or 105 points.

Conversely, if the drop in specific gravity per ampere-hour and the total drop in specific gravity are known, the ampere-hours delivered by a battery may be determined. For example, if the specific gravity of the previously considered battery is 1.210 when the battery is fully charged and 1.150 when it is partly discharged, the drop in specific gravity is 1,210 - 1,150, or 60 points, and the number of ampere-hours taken out of the battery is $\frac{60}{1.5}$, or 40 ampere-hours. Thus, the number of ampere-hours expended in any battery discharge can be determined from the following three items: (1) The specific gravity when the battery is fully charged; (2) the specific gravity after the battery has been discharged; and (3) the reduction in specific gravity per ampere-hour.

Voltage alone is not a reliable indication of the state of charge of a battery except when the voltage is near the low-voltage limit on discharge. During discharge the voltage falls. The higher the rate of discharge the lower will be the terminal voltage. Open-circuit voltage is of little value because the variation between full charge and complete discharge is so small— only about 0.1 volt per cell. However, abnormally low voltage does indicate injurious sulfation or some other serious deterioration of the plates.

TYPES OF CHARGES

The following types of charges may be given to a storage battery, depending upon the condition of the battery: (1) Initial charge, (2) normal charge, (3) equalizing charge, (4) floating charge, and (5) emergency charge.

Initial Charge

When a new battery is shipped dry, the plates are in an uncharged condition. After the electrolyte has been added, it is necessary to convert the plates into the charged condition. This is accomplished by giving the battery a long low-rate INITIAL CHARGE. The charge is given in accordance with the manufacturer's instructions, which are shipped with each battery. If the manufacturer's instructions are not available, reference should be made to the detailed instruction in current bureau directives.

Normal Charge

A normal charge is a routine charge that is given in accordance with the nameplate data during the ordinary cycle of operation to restore the battery to its charged condition. The following steps should be observed:

1. Determine the starting and finishing rate from the nameplate data.

2. Add water, as necessary, to each cell.

3. Connect the battery to the charging panel and make sure the connections are clean and tight.

4. Turn on the charging circuit and set the current through the battery at the value given as the starting rate.

5. Check the temperature and specific gravity of pilot cells hourly.

6. When the battery begins to gas freely, reduce the charging current to the finishing rate.

A normal charge is complete when the specific gravity of the pilot cell, corrected for temperature, is within 5 points (0.005) of the specific gravity obtained on the previous equalizing charge.

Equalizing Charge

An equalizing charge is an extended normal charge at the finishing rate. It is given periodically to insure that all the sulfate is driven from the plates and that all the cells are restored to a maximum specific gravity. The equalizing charge is continued until the specific gravity of

39

all cells, corrected for temperature, shows no change for a 4-hour period. Readings of all cells are taken every half hour.

Floating Charge

A battery may be maintained at full charge by connecting it across a charging source that has a voltage maintained within the limits of from 2.13 to 2.17 volts per cell of the battery. In a floating charge the charging rate is determined by the battery voltage rather than by a definite current value. The voltage is maintained between 2.13 and 2.17 volts per cell with an average as close to 2.15 volts as possible.

Emergency Charge

An emergency charge is used when a battery must be recharged in the shortest possible time. The charge starts at a much higher rate than is normally used for charging. It is seldom used because spare batteries are provided for all battery-operated equipment and this type charge may be harmful to the battery.

CHARGING RATE

The charging rate of every Navy storage battery is given on the battery nameplate. If the available charging equipment does not have the desired charging rates, the nearest available rates should be used. However, the rate should never be so high that violent gassing occurs. NEVER ALLOW THE TEMPERATURE OF THE ELECTROLYTE IN ANY CELL TO RISE ABOVE 125° F.

CHARGING TIME

The charge must be continued until the battery is fully charged. Frequent readings of specific gravity should be taken during the charge. These readings should be corrected to 80°F. and compared with the reading taken before the battery was placed on charge. If the rise in specific gravity in points per ampere-hour is known, the approximate time in hours required to complete the charge is

$$\frac{\text{rise in specific gravity in points to complete charge}}{\text{rise in specific gravity in points per ampere-hour} \quad x \quad \text{charging rate in amperes}}$$

GASSING

When a battery is being charged, a portion of the energy is dissipated in the electrolysis of the water in the electrolyte. Thus, hydrogen is released at the negative plates and oxygen at the positive plates. These gases bubble up through the electrolyte and collect in the air space at the top of the cell. If violent gassing occurs when the battery is first placed on charge, the charging rate is too high. If the rate is not too high, steady gassing, which develops as the charging proceeds, indicates that the battery is nearing a fully charged condition. A mixture of hydrogen and air can be dangerously explosive. No smoking, electric sparks, or open flames should be permitted near charging batteries.

Nickel-Cadmium Cell

The nickel-cadmium cell is an alkaline storage cell. It is used in aircraft and in the Nike and Corporal guided missiles, and may be installed aboard ship in the foreseeable future. The construction and general arrangement of the cell are similar to that of the lead-acid cell. The negative plate assembly is a cadmium-oxide compound; the positive plate assembly is a nickel-oxide compound; and the electrolyte is a 30 percent solution of potassium hydroxide (KOH). Separators between the positive and negative groups prevent internal short circuits. The cell components are assembled in a single plastic jar. The battery case is of fabricated steel. A 6-volt battery contains 5 series-connected cells. When fully charged, the cell voltage ranges from 1.39 to 1.45 volts.

The nickel-cadmium battery used in some naval aircraft is interchangeable with the present aviation type lead-acid batteries. The nickel-cadmium and lead-acid batteries have capacities that are comparable at normal discharge rates, but at high discharge rates nickel-cadmium batteries have a higher capacity. The lead-acid aircraft battery is comprised of 12 cells with a nominal cell voltage of 2 volts, while the nickel-cadmium battery contains 20 cells with a nominal voltage of 1.4 volts per cell.

CHARGING

The effect of the charging current is to change the active material of the negative plate (cadmium-oxide) to metallic cadmium (CdO to Cd). The active material of the positive plate (nickel-oxide) is changed to a higher state of oxidation (NiO to Ni_2O_3). As long as the charging current continues, this action occurs until both materials are completely converted. Toward the end of the charging process and during overcharge, the cell will gas due to the electrolysis of the water in the electrolyte. This action liberates 4 atoms of hydrogen gas ($2H_2$) at the negative plate for every 2 atoms of oxygen gas (O_2) liberated at the positive plate. The amount of gas liberated depends on the charging rate.

The electrolyte does not enter into any chemical reaction with the positive or negative plates. It acts simply as a conductor of current between the plates, and its specific gravity does not vary appreciably with the amount of charge. The effect of the reactions during charge is a transfer of oxygen from the negative to the positive plates. In this respect the nickel-cadmium storage battery is similar to the lead-acid storage battery. Unlike the lead-acid storage battery the specific gravity of the electrolyte remains constant, except at the end of a charge or on overcharge, when it increases because of the electrolysis of the water. The proper specific gravity can be obtained by adding distilled water.

Nickel-cadmium batteries can be charged by the (1) constant voltage, (2) constant current, and (3) stepped constant-current methods. The most efficient performance is obtained when the charging rate is such that 140 percent of the rated ampere-hour capacity of the cell is delivered to the cell within a 3-hour interval.

DISCHARGING

When the cell is connected to an external circuit containing a resistance, the chemical action which occurs is the reverse to that of the charging process. The negative plate gradually regains oxygen (Cd to CdO), and the positive plate gradually loses oxygen (Ni_2O_3 to NiO); that is, the action during discharge effects a transfer of oxygen from the positive to the negative plates. There is no gassing on discharge due to the interchange of oxygen. The discharge process is the conversion of the chemical energy of the plates into electrical energy. The rate at which this conversion occurs is determined by the external resistance, or load, to which the battery is connected. The internal resistance of the cell is extremely low because of the cell construction.

The nickel-cadmium battery is smaller and weighs less than the comparable lead-acid battery. There is little or no local action, and the positive plates do not shed, or flake off, as do the positive plates in the lead-acid cell. The battery life is from 10 to 15 years with constant capacity over the entire period, and satisfactory operation can be obtained over a temperature range from -65° F. to 165° F.

Silver-Zinc Batteries

Silver-zinc batteries are presently used in guided missiles. These batteries are made up of cells that are classed as "reserve cells." As stated previously, a reserve cell is one which is maintained in the dry state until power is needed. At this time, the cell is activated by adding the electrolyte solution. Once the solution has been added, the battery requires no further charging. However, once activated, the silver-zinc battery must be used immediately because it has an extremely short shelf life. This battery is also quite expensive, due to its silver content.

The physical construction of these batteries is such that they are able to withstand high accelerations and to operate effectively in spite of the shock, vibration, and extreme temperature variations present in missile flight. Other advantages also tend to offset the cost and shelf-life restrictions. Two of the major advantages are (1) the high power-to-weight ratio of silver-zinc batteries and (2) their high discharge rate while maintaining a nearly flat voltage. That is, they are able to expend their energy at a high rate over a short period of time, as in the brief flight of a missile.

In the charged or "ready" state, the positive electrode material is silver peroxide, Ag_2O_2. The negative electrode is zinc, Zn, and the electrolyte is mainly potassium hydroxide, KOH. In discharging, the silver peroxide changes to a lower state of oxidation, becoming silver oxide, Ag_2O. In giving up oxygen atoms, the silver peroxide also loses electrons, thus becoming positive. The zinc electrode, in oxidizing (absorbing oxygen), accumulates excess electrons, and thus becomes negative. Water in the electrolyte is destroyed at the negative electrode, and formed at the positive electrode, with the net amount of water remaining constant.

41

QUIZ

1. The dry cell battery is a
   a. secondary cell
   b. polarized cell
   c. primary cell
   d. voltaic cell

2. The electrolyte of a lead-acid wet cell is
   a. sal ammoniac
   b. manganese dioxide
   c. sulfuric acid
   d. distilled water

3. A battery which can be restored after discharge is a
   a. primary cell
   b. galvanic cell
   c. dry cell
   d. secondary cell

4. Lead-acid battery plates are held together by a
   a. glass wool mat
   b. wood separators
   c. grid work
   d. hard rubber tube

5. When mixing electrolyte, always pour
   a. water into acid
   b. acid into water
   c. both acid and water into vat simultaneously
   d. any of the above are correct

6. When charging a battery, the electrolyte should never exceed a temperature of
   a. 125° F.
   b. 113° F.
   c. 80° F.
   d. 40° F.

7. The plates of a lead-acid battery are made of
   a. lead and lead dioxide
   b. lead and lead oxide
   c. silver and peroxide
   d. lead and lead peroxide

8. A battery is receiving a normal charge. It begins to gas freely. The charging current should
   a. be increased
   b. be decreased
   c. be cut off and the battery allowed to cool
   d. remain the same

9. A hydrometer reading is 1.265 at 92° F. The corrected reading is
   a. 1.229
   b. 1.261
   c. 1.269
   d. 1.301

10. In the nickel-cadmium battery, KOH is
    a. the positive plate
    b. the negative plate
    c. the electrolyte
    d. none of the above

11. When sulfuric acid, H_2SO_4, and water, H_2O are mixed together, they form a
    a. gas
    b. compound
    c. mixture
    d. hydrogen solution

12. How many No. 6 dry cells are required to supply power to a load requiring 6 volts, if the cells are connected in series?
    a. Two
    b. Four
    c. Five
    d. Six

13. The ordinary 6-volt lead-acid storage battery consists of how many cells?
    a. Two
    b. Three
    c. Four
    d. Six

14. A fully charged aircraft battery has a specific gravity reading of
    a. 1.210 to 1.220
    b. 1.250 to 1.265
    c. 1.285 to 1.300
    d. 1.300 to 1.320

15. What is the ampere-hour rating of a storage battery that can deliver 20 amperes continuously for 10 hours?
    a. 20 ampere-hour
    b. 40 ampere-hour
    c. 200 ampere-hour
    d. 400 ampere-hour

16. The normal cell voltage of a fully charged nickel-cadmium battery is
    a. 2.0 volts
    b. 1.5 volts
    c. 1.4 volts
    d. 1.0 volts

17. The electrolyte in a mercury cell is
    a. sulfuric acid
    b. KOH
    c. potassium hydroxide, zincate, and mercury
    d. potassium hydroxide, water, and zincate

18. Concentrated sulfuric acid has a specific gravity of
    a. 1.285
    b. 1.300
    c. 1.830
    d. 2.400

19. The number of negative plates in a lead-acid cell is always
   a. one greater than the number of positive plates
   b. equal to the number of positive plates
   c. one less than the number of positive plates
   d. double the number of positive plates

20. A lead-acid battery is considered fully charged when the specific gravity readings of all cells taken at half-hour intervals show no change for
   a. four hours
   b. three hours
   c. two hours
   d. one hour

CHAPTER 3
THE SIMPLE ELECTRIC CIRCUIT

Whenever two unequal charges are connected by a conductor, a complete pathway for current flow exists. Current will flow from the negative to the positive charge. This was illustrated in chapter 1.

An electric circuit is a completed conducting pathway, consisting not only of the conductor, but including the path through the voltage source. Current flows from the positive terminal through the source, emerging at the negative terminal. As an example, a lamp connected by conductors across a dry cell forms a simple electric circuit. (Refer to fig. 3-1.)

Current flows from the (-) terminal of the battery through the lamp to the (+) battery terminal, and continues by going through the battery from the (+) to the (-) terminal. As long as this pathway is unbroken, it is a closed circuit and current will flow. However, if the path is broken at ANY point, it is an open circuit and no current flows.

Current flow in the external circuit is the movement of electrons in the direction indicated by the arrows (from the negative terminal through the lamp to the positive terminal). (See fig. 3-1 (A)). Current flow in the internal battery circuit is the simultaneous movement in opposite directions of positive hydrogen ions toward the positive terminal of the battery and negative ions toward the negative terminal.

A closed loop of wire (conductor) is not necessarily a circuit. A source of voltage must be included to make it an electric circuit. In any electric circuit where electrons move around a closed loop, current, voltage, and resistance are present. The physical pathway for current flow is actually the circuit. Its resistance controls the amount of current flow

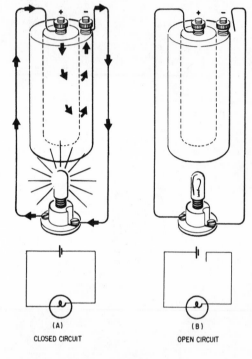

Figure 3-1.—(A) Simple electric circuit (closed); (B) simple electric circuit (open).

around the circuit. By knowing any two of the three quantities, such as voltage and current, the third (resistance) may be determined. This is done mathematically by the use of Ohm's law.

Ohm's Law

In the 19th century, a German philosopher, Georg Simon Ohm, proved by experiment the constant proportionally between electric current and voltage in the simple electric circuit and published the results of his findings in 1826. Ohm's law is fundamentally linear and therefore

44

simple. It is exact and applies to d-c circuits and devices in its basic form. In a modified form it may also be applied to a-c circuits. The unit of electrical resistance is called the OHM (designated by the Greek letter omega Ω) and finds wide application in the sources, loads, and conductors of electrical and electronics circuits.

MEANING OF OHM'S LAW

Ohm's law may be stated in words, as follows: THE INTENSITY OF THE CURRENT IN AMPERES IN ANY ELECTRIC CIRCUIT IS EQUAL TO THE DIFFERENCE IN POTENTIAL IN VOLTS ACROSS THE CIRCUIT DIVIDED BY THE RESISTANCE IN OHMS OF THE CIRCUIT.

Expressed as an equation, the law becomes

$$I = \frac{E}{R} \qquad (3\text{-}1)$$

where I is the intensity of the current in amperes, E the difference in potential in volts, and R the resistance in ohms.

If any two of these quantities are known, the third may be found by applying equation (3-1).

For example, if the voltage across the lamp in figure 3-2 is 12 volts and the effective resistance of the lamp is 2 ohms, the current through is will be $\frac{12}{2}$, or 6 amperes. If the effective resistance of the lamp remains constant

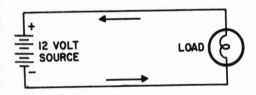

Figure 3-2.—Simple circuit.

at 2 ohms, in accordance with Ohm's law, the current will double if the voltage doubles, or halve if the voltage halves. In other words the CURRENT THROUGH THE LOAD WILL VARY DIRECTLY WITH THE VOLTAGE ACROSS THE LOAD. Thus, if the voltage across the load is reduced to zero, the current will equal $\frac{0}{2}$, or 0 amperes. If the voltage across the load is increased in steps of 1 volt starting at zero and continuing to 12 volts, the current through the

load becomes $\frac{1}{2}$ = 0.5 ampere; $\frac{2}{2}$ = 1.0 ampere; $\frac{3}{2}$ = 1.5 ampere; and so forth.

The relation between current and voltage in this example is shown in figure 3-3 as a graph in which the voltage is plotted horizontally along the X axis to the right of the origin, and the corresponding values of current are plotted vertically along the Y axis above the origin.

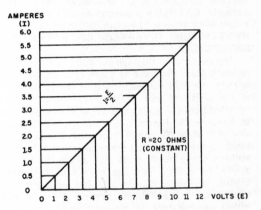

Figure 3-3.—Graph of voltage vs. current in a constant-resistance circuit.

The graph is a straight line, the equation of which is $I = \frac{E}{2}$. The constant, 2, represents the resistance in ohms of the circuit and is assumed not to change with the current in this example. This graph illustrates an important characteristic of the basic law—namely, the CURRENT VARIES DIRECTLY WITH THE APPLIED VOLTAGE IF THE RESISTANCE IS CONSTANT.

If the voltage across the load in figure 3-2 is maintained at a constant value of 12 volts, the current through the load will depend solely upon the effective resistance of the load. For example, if the resistance is 12 ohms, the current will be $\frac{12}{12}$, or 1 ampere. If the resistance is halved, the current will be doubled; if the resistance is doubled, the current will be halved. In other words, the current will vary inversely with the resistance.

If the resistance of the load is reduced in steps of 2 ohms starting at 12 ohms and continuing to 2 ohms, the current through the load

45

becomes $\frac{12}{10}$ = 1.2 amperes; $\frac{12}{8}$ = 1.5 amperes; $\frac{12}{6}$ = 2 amperes; and so forth. The relation between current and resistance in this example is expressed as a graph (fig. 3-4), whose equation is $I = \frac{12}{R}$. The numerator of the fraction represents a constant value of 12 volts in this example. As R approaches a small value the current approaches a very large value. The example illustrates a second equally important relation in Ohm's law—namely, that the CURRENT VARIES INVERSELY WITH THE RESISTANCE.

If the current through the load in figure 3-2 is maintained constant at 5 amperes, the voltage across the load will depend upon the resistance of the load and will vary directly with it. The relation between voltage and resistance is shown in the graph of figure 3-5. Values of resistance are plotted horizontally along the X axis to the right of the origin, and corresponding values of voltage are plotted vertically along the Y axis above the origin. The graph is a straight line having the equation $E = 5R$. The coefficient 5 represents the assumed current of 5 amperes which is constant in this example. Thus, a third important relation is illustrated—namely, that the VOLTAGE across a device VARIES DIRECTLY WITH THE EFFECTIVE RESISTANCE of the device provided the current through the device is maintained constant.

APPLYING OHM'S LAW

Equation (3-1) may be transposed to solve for the resistance if the current and voltage are known, or to solve for the voltage if the current and resistance are known. Thus, $R = \frac{E}{I}$ and $E = IR$. For example, if the voltage across a device is 50 volts and the current through it is 2 amperes, the resistance of the device will be $\frac{50}{2}$, or 25 ohms. Also, if the current through a wire is 3 amperes and the resistance of the wire is 0.5 ohm, the voltage drop across the wire will be 3 x 0.5, or 1.5 volts.

Equation (3-1) and its transpositions may be obtained readily with the aid of figure 3-6. The circle containing E, I, and R is divided into two parts with E above the line and IR below it. To determine the unknown quantity, first cover that quantity with a finger. The location of the

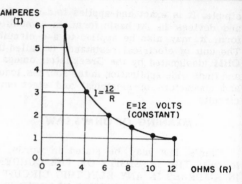

Figure 3-4.—Relation between current and resistance.

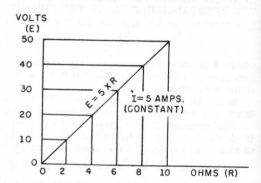

Figure 3-5.—Graph of voltage vs. resistance with constant current.

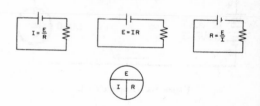

Figure 3-6.—Ohm's law in diagram form.

remaining uncovered letters in the circle will indicate the mathematical operation to be performed. For example, to find I, cover I with a finger. The uncovered letters indicate that E is to be divided by R, or $I = \frac{E}{R}$. To find E, cover E. The result indicates that I is to be multiplied by R, or $E = IR$. To find R, cover R. The result indicates that E is to be divided by I, or $R = \frac{E}{I}$.

The beginning student is cautioned not to rely wholly on the use of this diagram when transposing simple formulas but rather to use it to supplement his knowledge of the algebraic method. Algebra is a basic tool in the solution of electrical problems and the importance of knowing how to use it should not be under-emphasized or bypassed after the student has learned a shortcut method such as the one indicated in this figure.

Electric Power and Energy

POWER

Power, whether electrical or mechanical, pertains to the rate at which work is being done. Work is done whenever a force causes motion. If a mechanical force is used to lift or move a weight, work is done. However, force exerted WITHOUT causing motion, such as the force of a compressed spring acting between two fixed objects, does not constitute work.

Previously, you found that voltage is electrical force, and that voltage forces current to flow in a closed circuit. However, when voltage exists between two points, but current cannot flow, no work is done. This is similar to the spring under tension that produced no motion. When voltage causes electrons to move, work is done. The instantaneous RATE at which this work is done is called the electric power rate, and its measure is the watt.

A total amount of work may be done in different lengths of time. For example, a given number of electrons may be moved from one point to another in one second or in one hour, depending on the RATE at which they are moved. In both cases, total work done is the same. However, when the work is done in a short time, the wattage, or INSTANTANEOUS POWER RATE is greater than when the same amount of work is done over a longer period of time.

As stated, the basic unit of power is the WATT, and it is equal to the voltage across a circuit multiplied by current through the circuit. This represents the rate at any given instant at which work is being done in moving electrons through the circuit. The sympol P indicates electrical power. Thus, the basic power formula is $P = E \times I$. E is the voltage across and I is the current through the resistor or circuit whose power is being measured. The amount of power will change when either voltage or current, or both voltage and current change. This relation is shown with the graph and simple circuit in figure 3-7.

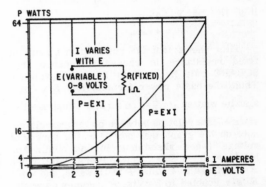

Figure 3-7.—Graph of power related to changing voltage and current.

The resistance is 1 ohm, and does not change. Voltage E is increased in steps of 1 volt from 0 to 8. By applying Ohm's law, the current I is determined for each step of voltage. For instance, when E is 4 volts, the current I is

$$I = \frac{E}{R} \qquad (3-1)$$
$$I = \frac{4}{1}$$

$$I = 4 \text{ amperes.}$$

Power P, in watts, is determined by applying the basic power formula $P = E \times I$. When E is 1 volt, I is 1 ampere, so P is

$$P = E \times I$$
$$P = 1 \times 1$$
$$P = 1 \text{ watt}$$

However, when E is 2 volts, and I is 2 amperes, P becomes:

$$P = E \times I$$
$$P = 2 \times 2$$
$$P = 4 \text{ watts}$$

47

It is important to note that when voltage E was doubled from 1 volt to 2 volts, power P doubled TWICE from 1 watt to 4 watts. This occurred because the doubling of voltage caused a doubling of current, therefore power was doubled twice. This is shown as follows:

$$P = E \times I$$
$$P = E \times 2 \times I \times 2$$
$$P = (1 \times 2) \times (1 \times 2)$$
$$P = 2 \times 2$$
$$P = 4 \text{ watts.}$$

This shows that the power in a circuit of fixed resistance is caused to change at a SQUARE rate by changes in applied voltage. Thus, the basic power formula $P = E \times I$ may also be written $P = \dfrac{E^2}{R}$. To further illustrate the square-rate relation between power and voltage, note on the graph that power is the square of voltage (when resistance is one ohm). For instance, when E is 2 volts, P is 4 watts. When E is doubled to 4 volts, P is 16 watts, and when E is redoubled to 8 volts, P becomes 64 watts. When resistance is any value other than one ohm, power will not be the exact square of voltage in QUANTITY but it will still vary at a SQUARE RATE. That is, regardless of the value of resistance, so long as it is fixed, WHEN VOLTAGE DOUBLES, POWER DOUBLES TWICE. Also, WHEN THE VOLTAGE IS HALVED, POWER IS HALVED TWICE.

Another important relation may be seen by studying figure 3-7. Thus far power has been calculated with voltage and current ($P = E \times I$), and with voltage and resistance ($P = \dfrac{E^2}{R}$). Referring to figure 3-7, note that power also varies as the square of current just as it does with voltage. Thus, another formula for power, with current and resistance as its factors, is $P = I^2 R$. Note that resistance R is a divisor in one formula ($P = \dfrac{E^2}{R}$), but is a multiplier in the other ($P = I^2 R$). This is true because of substitutions in the original formula $P = E \times I$. That is, the Ohm's law equivalent of I is $\dfrac{E}{R}$. If this equivalent is substituted for I in the power formula $P = E \times I$, the results are as follows:

$$P = E \times I \qquad (3\text{-}2)$$
$$P = E \times \frac{E}{R}$$

$$P = \frac{E^2}{R} \qquad (3\text{-}3)$$

In addition, the Ohm's law equivalent of E is $I \times R$. If this equivalent is substituted for E, the power formula becomes

$$P = E \times I$$
$$P = (I \times R) \times I$$
$$P = I^2 R \qquad (3\text{-}4)$$

In the foregoing discussion, and in figure 3-7, it was shown how variations of the voltage impressed across a fixed resistance caused variations in the circuit current and power. The following discussion refers to figure 3-8. In this circuit, the voltage E is fixed at 10 volts, and the resistance R is the variable factor. (The arrow through the resistance means it is variable).

When the resistance R is set at 1 ohm, the current I is 10 amperes, and the power is

$$P = I^2 R \qquad (3\text{-}4)$$
$$P = (10^2) \times R$$
$$P = 100 \times 1$$
$$P = 100 \text{ watts}$$

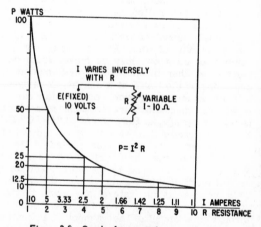

Figure 3-8.—Graph of power related to changing resistance and current.

When the resistance is DOUBLED to 2 ohms, this same calculation will show that power is HALVED to 50 watts, as the graph shows. Subsequent redoubling of the resistance to 4 and then to 8 ohms causes the power to be

48

halved each time to 25 and 12-1/2 watts, respectively. Conversely, you should note the relation when starting with resistance at 10 ohms, with 10 watts of power. If resistance is HALVED to 5 ohms, power is DOUBLED to 20 watts.

In figures 3-7 and 3-8, current and power were caused to vary as a function of voltage, in one case, and of resistance in the other. In figure 3-9, however, current is held constant. This is done by raising or lowering voltage and resistance equally and directly with each other. The resulting variations in power are LINEAR with those changes. That is, power is changed step-for-step with voltage. The changing resistance maintains a constant current despite changes of voltage. At any point on the graph, voltage divided by resistance is 1 ampere. Had the current been allowed to vary, power would have changed at a curved, or SQUARE rate, instead of linearly as on the graph.

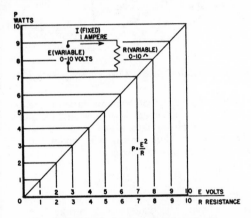

Figure 3-9.—Graph of power related to changing voltage and resistance.

Up to this point, four of the most important basic electrical quantities have been discussed. These are E, I, R, and P. It is of fundamental importance that you thoroughly understand the interrelation of these quantities. You should understand how any one of these quantities either controls or is controlled by the others in an electrical circuit. These relations are further explained in the treatment that follows. You should compare each statement carefully with its associated formula. Check each formula for correctness by applying it to the graphs in

figures 3-7, 3-8, or 3-9. (The appropriate figure number is indicated after each of the following statements)

1. Power, as related to E and I: $P = EI$ (fig. 3-7).

   This formula states that P is the product of E multiplied by I, regardless of their individual values. If either E or I varies, P varies proportionally. If both E and I vary, P varies at a SQUARE rate.

2. Power, as related to I and R: $P = I^2R$ (fig. 3-8).

   This formula states that if R is held constant, and I is varied, P varies as the square of I, because I appears as a squared quantity (I^2) in the formula. Also, if I is held constant and R is varied, P varies directly and proportionally to R, because R is a MULTIPLIER in the formula.

3. Power, as related to E and R: $P = \dfrac{E^2}{R}$ (fig. 3-9).

   This formula states that if R is held constant, as E is varied, P varies as the square of E, because E appears as a squared quantity (E^2) in the formula. Also, if E is held constant and R is varied, P varies inversely but proportionally to R, because R is a DIVISOR in the formula.

In the preceding paragraph, P was expressed in terms of alternate pairs of the other three basic quantities E, I, and R. In practice, you should be able to express any one of the three basic quantities, as well as P, in terms of any two of the others. Figure 3-10 is a summary of twelve basic formulas you should know. The four quantities E, I, R, and P are at the center of the figure. Adjacent to each quantity are three segments. Note that in each segment, the basic quantity is expressed in terms of two other basic quantities, and no two segments are alike.

RATING OF ELECTRICAL DEVICES BY POWER

Electrical lamps, soldering irons, and motors are examples of electrical devices that are rated in watts. The wattage rating of a device indicates the rate at which the device converts electrical energy into another form of energy, such as light, heat, or motion.

For example, a 100-watt lamp will produce a brighter light than a 75-watt lamp, because it converts more electrical energy into light

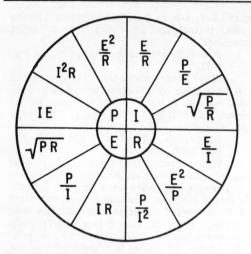

Figure 3-10.—Summary of basic formulas.

Electric soldering irons are of various wattage ratings, with the high-wattage irons changing more electrical energy to heat than those of low-wattage ratings.

If the normal wattage rating is exceeded, the equipment or device will overheat and probably be damaged. For example, if a lamp is rated 100 watts at 110 volts and is connected to a source of 220 volts, the current through the lamp will double. This will cause the lamp to use four times the wattage for which it is rated, and it will burn out quickly.

POWER CAPACITY OF ELECTRICAL DEVICES

Rather than indicate a device's ability to do work, its wattage rating may indicate the device's operating limits. These power limits generally are given as the maximum or minimum safe voltages and currents to which a device may be subjected. However, in cases where a device is not limited to any specific operating voltage, its limits are given directly in watts.

Resistors

A resistor is an example of such a device. It may be used in circuits with widely different voltages, depending on the desired current. However, the resistor has a maximum current

limitation for each voltage applied to it. The product of the resistor's voltage and current at any time must not exceed a certain wattage.

Thus, resistors are rated in watts, in addition to their ohmic resistance. Resistors of the same resistance value are available in different wattage values. Carbon resistors, for example, are commonly made in wattage ratings of 1/3, 1/2, 1, and 2 watts. The larger the physical size of a carbon resistor, the higher its wattage rating, since a larger amount of material will absorb and give up heat more easily.

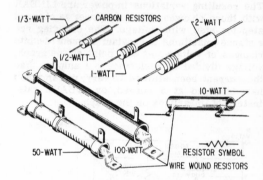

Figure 3-11.—Resistors of different wattage ratings.

When resistors of wattage ratings greater than 2 watts are needed, wire-wound resistors are used. Such resistors are made in ranges between 5 and 200 watts, with special types being used for power in excess of 200 watts.

Fuses

When current passes through a resistor, electric energy is transformed into heat, which raises the temperature of the resistor. If the temperature becomes too high, the resistor may be damaged. The metal wire in a wound resistor may melt, opening the circuit and interrupting current flow. This effect is used to an advantage in fuses.

Fuses are actually metal resistors with very low resistance values. They are designed to "blow out" and thus open a circuit when current exceeds the fuse's rated value.

When the power consumed by the fuse raises the temperature of its metal too high, the metal melts, or "blows." In service, fuses are generally connected as shown in figure 3-12.

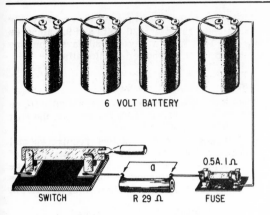

6 VOLT BATTERY

SWITCH   R 29 Ω   FUSE

0.5A. I Ω

Figure 3-12.—Simple fused circuit.

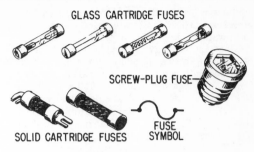

GLASS CARTRIDGE FUSES

SCREW-PLUG FUSE

SOLID CARTRIDGE FUSES   FUSE SYMBOL

Figure 3-13.—Typical fuse types.

Note that all current flowing through the load resistance of 29 ohms must also flow through the half-ampere fuse. Under normal conditions, the total resistance would be 29 + 1 = 30 ohms. If the switch were closed, the current I would be

$$I = \frac{E}{R}$$

$$I = \frac{6}{30}$$

$$I = 0.2 \text{ ampere}$$

This would be less than the rated current of the fuse, and it would not open. However, if the short conductor (a, fig. 3-12) were connected, the load resistance would be bypassed, or "shorted out." Only the fuse resistance of one ohm would remain in the circuit. Current would then be

$$I = \frac{E}{R}$$

$$I = \frac{6}{1}$$

$$I = 6 \text{ amperes}$$

Six amperes of current will cause the half-ampere fuse to open very quickly, because its wattage rating is greatly exceeded.

There are a great number of different types and sizes of fuses presently in use. Figure 3-13 shows three of the most common types.

ENERGY

Energy is defined as the ability to do work. Energy is expended when work is done, because it takes energy to maintain a force when that force acts through a distance (works). The total energy expended to do a certain amount of work is equal to the working force multiplied by the distance through which the force moved to do the work. This is the mechanical definition.

In electricity, total energy expended is equal to the rate at which work is done, multiplied by the length of time the rate is measured. Essentially, energy W is equal to power P times time t.

An equation for energy is derived by multiplying both sides of equation (3-2) by the common factor of time, t, and equating the expression to the energy, W, as

$$W = Pt$$

$$W = EIt. \qquad (3-5)$$

Similarly, both sides of equations (3-3) and (3-4) may be multiplied by the time factor, t, and equated to the energy, W, as

$$W = \frac{E^2}{R} t, \qquad (3-6)$$

and

$$W = I^2Rt. \qquad (3-7)$$

In the energy equations (3-5), (3-6), and (3-7), E is in volts and I in amperes. If t is expressed in hours, W will be in watt-hours.

If t is expressed in seconds, W will be in watt-seconds or joules (1 joule is equal to 1 watt-second). Since $Q = It$ (where Q is in coulombs, I in amperes, and t in seconds), it is possible to substitute Q for It in equation (3-5) with the resulting expression for energy. Thus

$$W = QE \qquad (3-8)$$

where W is the energy in joules or watt-seconds, Q is the quantity in coulombs, and E is in volts. (As explained in chapter 1, Q is the symbol for coulombs. This is the measure of a QUANTITY of electrons. The Q is to electricity as the gallon is to water.)

Electrical energy is bought and sold in units of kilowatt-hours $(3,600 \times 10^3$ joules), and is totalized in large central generating stations in terms of megawatt-hours $(3,600 \times 10^6$ joules). For example, if the average demand over a 10-hour period is 70 megawatts, the total energy delivered is 70 x 10, or 700 megawatt-hours. This amount of energy is equivalent to 700 x 1,000 = 700,000 kilowatt-hours, or 700 x 3,600 x 10^6 = 2,520,000 x 10^6 joules. The most practical unit to use depends in part upon the magnitude of the quantity of energy involved, and in this example the megawatt-hour is appropriate.

Problems

Ohm's law for power calculations may be applied to a great many everyday problems wherever electricity is at work.

Consider one of the most common examples —that of the incandescent electric light. Incandescent lamps for use in constant-potential circuits in homes and factories are rated in volts and watts. How much current do they take? How much resistance do they possess? If high powered, they may draw several amperes; if low in wattage rating, they may take only a small fraction of an ampere. Specifically the current rating of a 100-watt 120-volt lamp is easily found by transposing equation (3-2) and solving for the current. Thus

$$I = \frac{P}{E} = \frac{100}{120} = 0.833 \text{ ampere.}$$

The resistance of this lamp during normal operation may be found by substituting the calculated value of current and the rated voltage in equation (3-1) and transposing for R—

$$R = \frac{120}{0.833} = 144 \text{ ohms.}$$

Thus, a 100-watt 120-volt lamp draws a current of 0.833 ampere and has a hot resistance of 144 ohms. How much does it cost to use this lamp 4 hours each evening for 30 days at 3.2 cents per kilowatt-hour? Surprising little, as seen by the calculation:

$$\text{Total kilowatt-hours} = Pt = \frac{100 \times 4 \times 30}{1,000} = 12,$$

$$\text{Total cost} = 3.2 \times 12 = 38.4 \text{ cents.}$$

Consider the cost to operate a window air conditioner rated at 120 volts and 9.4 amperes in use 10 hours a day for 30 days. Applying equation (3-2), the power in kilowatts is

$$P = \frac{EI}{1,000} = \frac{120 \times 9.4}{1,000} = 1.128 \text{ kw.}$$

The total kilowatt-hours are 1.128 x 30 x 10, or 338.4 kw.-hr. At 3.2 cents per kw.-hr. the cost is $0.032 x 338.4, or $10.83.

Household electric stoves require special circuits as may be seen from the magnitude of the current drawn by a 7.5-kw. 220-v. range with all burners turned on full. The current is found by transposing equation (3-2) as follows:

$$I = \frac{P}{E} = \frac{7,500}{220} = 34 \text{ amperes.}$$

Since most household branch circuits are not permitted to carry more than 20 amperes, the possibility of a 34-ampere load requires special circuits for the range. It is also important to note that the availability of the 220-volt service (rather than 110-volt service) permits the use of smaller conductors since current varies inversely with voltage for a given power rating. Thus a 7.5-kw. range rated at 110 volts would draw a maximum of $\frac{220}{110}$ x 34, or 68 amperes.

To further illustrate the inverse ratio between current and voltage for a given power rating, consider the current drawn by a 100-watt incandescent lamp having a voltage rating of 6 volts. Transposing equation (3-2) the current is

$$I = \frac{P}{E} = 16.6 \text{ amperes.}$$

This value of current is $\frac{120}{6}$, or 20 times the value required by a 120-volt lamp of the same wattage rating.

It is important to operate incandescent lamps within their voltage rating, since any appreciable over-voltage even for a short period reduces the life of the lamp a relatively large amount. For example, an increase in the voltage on a 25-watt 110-volt lamp from 110 volts to 140 volts will increase the current proportionately from $\frac{25}{110}$ = 0.228 amperes to $\frac{140}{110}$ x 0.228 = 0.290 ampere. Since the power absorbed varies as the square of the applied voltage, increasing the applied voltage from 110 to 140 volts will increase the power to $\frac{(140)^2}{110}$, or 1.62 times the rated power. In a short time the lamp filament will burn out.

As another example illustrating the relation between the basic units, consider the current drawn by a 1,000-watt 120-volt electric flatiron. From equation (3-2) the current is found to be

$$I = \frac{P}{E} = \frac{1,000}{120} = 8.33 \text{ amperes.}$$

The hot resistance of this flatiron's heating element may be found by substituting the known values of current and voltage in equation (3-1) and solving for R. Thus

$$R = \frac{E}{I} = \frac{120}{8.33} = 14.4 \text{ ohms.}$$

The resistance of 14.4 ohms represents the operating resistance of the iron when it is carrying rated current. The resistance may also be calculated directly from equation (3-3) by substituting the values of voltage and power and transposing for R as follows:

$$R = \frac{E^2}{P} = \frac{(120)^2}{1,000} = 14.4 \text{ ohms.}$$

The appropriate equation depends upon what is given and what is to be found.

For example, find the total energy in watt-hours delivered by a 12-volt storage battery supplying an average current of 10 amperes for a 10-hour period. Applying equation (3-5),

$$W = EIt = 12 \times 10 \times 10 = 1,200 \text{ watt-hours.}$$

The product of amperes, hours, and volts is equal to watt-hours; and in this example, the battery is capable of furnishing electrical energy equivalent to 1,200 watt-hours, or 1.2 kilowatt-hours.

Another transposition of equation (3-3) may be used to solve the following problem: Find the voltage across, and the current through, a 100-ohm 500-watt resistor when it is carrying its rated load. Solving equation (3-3) for voltage in terms of the given values of power and resistance,

$$E = \sqrt{PR} = \sqrt{500 \times 100} = 224 \text{ volts.}$$

Thus, a 500-watt 100-ohm load will have a voltage of 224 volts across it. The current through the load may be found by transposing equation (3-4) and substituting the given values as follows:

$$I = \sqrt{\frac{P}{R}} = \sqrt{\frac{500}{100}} = 2.24 \text{ amperes.}$$

The power absorbed by the load may be checked by substituting the calculated value of current and the given value of resistance in equation (3-4), and solving as follows:

$$P = I^2R = (2.24)^2 \times 100 = 500 \text{ watts.}$$

The resistance of the load may be checked by transposing equation (3-1), substituting the calculated values of voltage and current, and solving for R as follows:

$$R = \frac{E}{I} = \frac{224}{2.24} = 100 \text{ ohms.}$$

You are urged to develop the habit of checking your work by using two or more equations to arrive at the same result. Two avenues of approach are more desirable than one since they tend to avoid mistakes that are frequently repeated in the single-approach method.

Current and voltage are important considerations in the operation of electric motors. Consider the power supplied to a large motor when it is drawing 125 amperes from a 600-volt d-c circuit. Applying equation (3-2),

$$P = EI = 600 \times 125 = 75,000 \text{ watts.}$$

This amount of power may be expressed in equivalent horsepower (746 watts = 1 horsepower) as $\frac{75,000}{746}$, or 100.2 horsepower. If the requirements of the load are such that the horsepower remains constant, then the input current will vary inversely with the applied voltage. Suppose, for example, that the voltage falls from 600 volts to 450 volts. The current required to maintain constant input power will be

$$I = \frac{P}{E} = \frac{75,000}{450} = 166 \text{ amperes.}$$

This current represents an increase of 41 amperes, or 32.8 percent, and probably will cause overheating of the motor. The condition is peculiar to electric motors and rotating machinery in general and represents a situation in which the effective load resistance varies as the square of the applied voltage ($R = \frac{E^2}{P}$).

The effective resistance offered by the motor to the flow of current when the voltage is 600 volts is

$$R = \frac{E}{I} = \frac{600}{125} = 4.8 \text{ ohms,}$$

and when the voltage falls to 450 volts, it is decreased to $\frac{450}{166}$, or 2.7 ohms. A check on the effective resistance at 600 volts may be obtained by transposing equation (3-3) and substituting the values of E and P as follows:

$$R = \frac{E^2}{P} = \frac{(600)^2}{75,000} = 4.8 \text{ ohms.}$$

A similar check on the effective resistance at 450 volts is

$$R = \frac{E^2}{P} = \frac{(450)^2}{75,000} = 2.7 \text{ ohms.}$$

The tendency of motors to increase their input current when the supply voltage decreases does not apply to electrical loads such as resistors, heating units, electric lights, and so forth. Therefore the action described in the preceding example should not be assumed to apply indiscriminately without regard to the characteristics of the particular load being considered.

Applying the simple three-letter equations of this chapter to the solution of elementary problems in electricity is not difficult. However, the ease of solution may be misleading to the student with an inquiring mind. Your attempt to prove your answers with practical equivalent circuits may reveal more than one variable in the elementary circuit.

For example, you find that Ohm's law states that the current through an electric circuit is directly proportional to the applied voltage, yet when the voltage is increased (for example, on an incandescent lamp), the current increase is not in direct proportion to the voltage increase. The discrepancy is explained by the tendency of tungsten to increase its resistance with temperature. Thus an increase in filament voltage causes an increase in filament current and temperature. The increase in filament temperature causes an increase in filament resistance. Two variables now affect the circuit current instead of one. These variables are voltage and resistance instead of voltage alone.

For example, the current at 110 volts and 120 ohms is

$$I = \frac{E}{R} = \frac{110}{120} = 0.917 \text{ ampere.}$$

The current at 132 volts and 130 ohms is

$$I = \frac{132}{130} = 1.015 \text{ amperes.}$$

The increase in voltage is 132 - 110, or 22 volts, and the percent increase is $\frac{22 \times 100}{110}$, or 20 percent. The increase in resistance is 130 - 120, or 10 ohms, and the percent increase is $\frac{10 \times 100}{120}$, or 8.33 percent. The increase in current is 1.015 - 0.917, or 0.098 ampere, and the percent increase is $\frac{0.098 \times 100}{0.917}$, or 10.7 percent. Thus an increase in voltage of 20 percent is accompanied by an increase in current of only 10.7 percent. If the voltage had been the only variable the current would have followed it exactly—that is, an increase in voltage of 20 percent would have resulted in an increase in current of 20 percent. Instead, the current increased only 10.7 percent because the resistance increased 8.3 percent.

The equations themselves do not reveal the behavior of circuits. They do indicate, however, the numerical relation between the volt, ampere, ohm, and watt, and to that extent they contribute basic knowledge to the learner.

QUIZ

1. In which direction does current flow in an electrical circuit?

    a. - to + externally, + to - internally
    b. + to - externally, + to - internally
    c. - to + externally, - to + internally
    d. + to - externally, - to + internally

2. Given the formula: $P = E^2/R$, solve for E.

    a. $E = \sqrt{ER}$
    b. $E = \sqrt{PR}$
    c. $E = IR$
    d. $E = \sqrt{P/R}$

3. Resistance in the power formula equals
   a. $R = \sqrt{I/P}$
   b. $R = E/I$
   c. $R = \sqrt{P \times I}$
   d. $R = E^2/P$

4. One joule is equal to
   a. 1 watt second
   b. 10 watt seconds
   c. 1 watt minute
   d. 10 watt minutes

5. A lamp has a source voltage of 110 v. and a current of 0.9 amps. What is the resistance of the lamp?
   a. 12.22 Ω
   b. 122.2 Ω
   c. 0.008 Ω
   d. 0.08 Ω

6. In accordance with Ohm's law, the relationship between current and voltage in a simple circuit is that the
   a. current varies inversely with the resistance if the voltage is held constant
   b. voltage varies as the square of the applied e.m.f.
   c. current varies directly with the applied voltage if the resistance is held constant
   d. voltage varies inversely as the current if the resistance is held constant

7. The current needed to operate a soldering iron which has a rating of 600 watts at 110 volts is
   a. 0.182 a.
   b. 5.455 a.
   c. 18.200 a.
   d. 66.000 a.

8. In electrical circuits, the time rate of doing work is expressed in
   a. volts
   b. amperes
   c. watts
   d. ohms

9. If the resistance is held constant, what is the relationship between power and voltage in a simple circuit?
   a. Resistance must be varied to show a true relationship
   b. Power will vary as the square of the applied voltage
   c. Voltage will vary inversely proportional to power
   d. Power will vary directly with voltage

10. How many watts are there in 1 horsepower?
    a. 500
    b. 640
    c. 746
    d. 1,000

11. What formula is used to find watt-hours?
    a. E x T
    b. E x I x T
    c. E x I x $\angle\theta$
    d. E x I^2

12. What is the resistance of the circuit shown below?
    a. 4.8 Ω
    b. 12.0 Ω
    c. 48 Ω
    d. 120 Ω

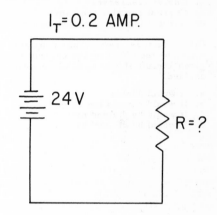

13. In the figure below, solve for I_T
    a. 0.5 a.
    b. 1 a.
    c. 13 a.
    d. 169 a.

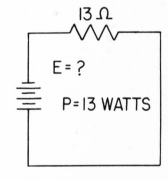

14. A simple circuit consists of one power source,
    a. and one power consuming device
    b. one power consuming device, and connecting wiring
    c. protective device, and control device
    d. one power consuming device, and protective device

15. The device used in circuits to prevent damage from overloads is called a
    a. fuse
    b. switch
    c. resistor
    d. connector

16. What happens in a series circuit when the voltage remains constant and the resistance increases?

    a. Current increases
    b. Current decreases
    c. Current remains the same
    d. Current increases by the square

17. Other factors remaining constant, what would be the effect on the current flow in a given circuit if the applied potential were doubled?

    a. It would double
    b. It would remain the same
    c. It would be divided by two
    d. It would be divided by four

18. Which of the following procedures can be used to calculate the resistance of a load?
    a. Multiply the voltage across the load by the square of the current through the load
    b. Divide the current through the load by the voltage across the load
    c. Multiply the voltage across the load by the current through the load
    d. Divide the voltage across the load by the current through the load

19. A cockpit light operates from a 24-volt d-c supply and uses 72 watts of power. The current flowing through the bulb is
    a. 0.33 amps
    b. 3 amps
    c. 600 amps
    d. 1,728 amps

20. If the resistance is held constant, what happens to power if the current is doubled?
    a. Power is doubled
    b. Power is multiplied by 4
    c. Power is halved
    d. Power is divided by 4

CHAPTER 4

DIRECT-CURRENT SERIES AND PARALLEL CIRCUITS

An electric circuit is a complete path through which electrons can flow from the negative terminal of the voltage source; through the connecting wires, or conductors; through the load, or loads; and back to the positive terminal of the voltage source. A circuit is thus made up of a voltage source, the necessary connecting conductors, and the effective load.

If the circuit is arranged so that the electrons have only ONE possible path, the circuit is called a SERIES CIRCUIT. If there are two or more paths supplied by a common voltage source, the circuit is called a PARALLEL CIRCUIT.

In any type of work that utilizes the effects of electron flow a knowledge of series and parallel circuits is desirable. None of the effects accompanying electron flow—for example, heating, lighting, or magnetic effects—would be possible without the use of electric circuits; and many electrical devices can be utilized more effectively if the operator has a knowledge of how they work. The purpose of this chapter is to give in simplified form conventional methods of calculating resistance in basic series and parallel circuits and to show how problems involving current, voltage, and power may be solved by the use of basic formulas. The next chapter is similar, except that more complex circuits are treated. In both chapters Ohm's Law or Kirchhoff's Laws are used as required to solve for various unknown values of current, voltage, or resistance.

Series Circuits

KIRCHHOFF'S VOLTAGE LAW
APPLIED TO SERIES CIRCUITS

All conductors have resistance, and therefore a circuit made up of nothing but conductors would have some resistance, however small it might be. In circuits containing long conductors through which an appreciable amount of current is drawn the resistance of the conductors becomes important. However, for the purposes of this chapter the resistance of the connecting wires is neglected, and only the resistance of each resistor element (which may be any device that has resistance) is considered.

Kirchhoff's Law of Voltages states that the algebraic sum of all the voltages in any complete electric circuit is equal to zero. In other words, the sum of all positive voltages MUST BE equal to the sum of all negative voltages. For any voltage rise there must be an equal voltage drop somewhere in the circuit. The voltage rise (potential source) is usually regarded as the power supply, such as a battery.

The voltage drop is usually regarded as the load, such as a resistor. The voltage drop may be distributed across a number of resistive elements, such as a string of lamps or several resistors. However, according to Kirchhoff's Law, the sum of their individual voltage drops MUST ALWAYS equal the voltage rise supplied by the power source.

The statement of Kirchhoff's Law can be translated into a truthful equation, from which many unknown circuit factors may be determined. (Refer to fig. 4-1.) Note that the source voltage E_S is equal to the sum of the three load voltages E_1, E_2, and E_3. In a formula, this would be written

$$E_s = E_1 + E_2 + E_3.$$

This formula may also be transposed to demonstrate that the algebraic sum of all the voltages is zero, as follows:

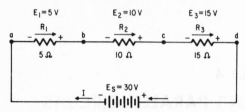

Figure 4-1.—Series circuit for demonstrating Kirchhoff's Voltage Law.

In order to solve problems applicable to figure 4-1, and others similar to it, the following procedure is suggested.

1. Note the polarity of the source e.m.f. (E_s) and indicate the electron flow around the circuit. Electron flow is out from the negative terminal of the source, through the load, and back to the positive terminal of the source. In the example being considered, the arrows indicate electron flow in a clockwise direction around the circuit.

2. To apply Kirchhoff's Law it is necessary to establish a voltage equation. The equation is developed by tracing around the circuit and noting the voltage absorbed (called voltage drop) across each part of the circuit encountered by the trace, and expressing the sum of these voltages according to the voltage law. It is important that the trace be made around a closed circuit, and that it encircle the circuit only once. Thus, a point is arbitrarily selected at which to start the trace. The trace is then made, and upon completion, the terminal point coincides with the starting point.

3. Sources of e.m.f. are preceded by a PLUS sign if in tracing through the source the first terminal encountered is positive; if the first terminal is negative, the e.m.f. is preceded by a MINUS sign.

4. Voltage drops along wires and across resistors (loads) are preceded by a minus sign if the trace is in the assumed direction of electron flow; if in the opposite direction the sign is plus.

5. If the assumed direction of electron flow is incorrect, the error will be indicated by a minus sign preceding the current, in solving for circuit current. The magnitude of the current will not be affected.

The preceding rules may be applied to the example of figure 4-1 as follows:

1. The left terminal of the battery is negative, the right terminal is positive, and electron flow is clockwise around the circuit.

2. The trace may arbitrarily be started at the positive terminal of the source and continued clockwise through the source to its negative terminal. From this point the trace is continued around the circuit to *a, b, c, d,* and back to the positive terminal, thus completing the trace once around the entire closed circuit.

3. The first term of the voltage equation is $+ E_S$.

4. The second, third, and fourth terms are respectively, $- E_1$, $- E_2$, and $- E_3$. Their algebraic sum is equated to zero as follows:

$$E_s - E_1 - E_2 - E_3 = 0.$$

Transposing the voltage equation and solving for E_S,

$$E_s = E_1 + E_2 + E_3.$$

Since $E = IR$ from Ohm's law, the voltage drop across each resistor may be expressed in terms of the current and resistance of the individual resistor as follows:

$$E_s = IR_1 + IR_2 + IR_3,$$

where R_1, R_2, and R_3 are the resistances, E_S is the source voltage, and I is the circuit current.

E_S may be expressed in terms of the circuit current and total resistance as IR_t. Substituting IR_t for E_S, the voltage equation becomes,

$$IR_t = IR_1 + IR_2 + IR_3.$$

Since there is only one path for current in the series circuit, the total current is the same in all parts of the circuit. Dividing both sides of the voltage equation by the common factor, I, an expression is derived for the total resistance of the circuit.

$$R_t = R_1 + R_2 + R_3.$$

Therefore, in series circuits THE TOTAL RESISTANCE IS THE SUM OF THE RESISTANCES OF THE INDIVIDUAL PARTS OF THE CIRCUIT.

In the example of figure 4-1, the total resistance is

$$5 + 10 + 15 = 30 \text{ ohms.}$$

The total current may be found by applying the equation

$$I_t = \frac{E_t}{R_t} = \frac{30}{30} = 1 \text{ ampere.}$$

The power absorbed by resistor R_1 is I^2R_1, or 1^2 x 5 = 5 watts. Similarly the power absorbed by R_2 is 1^2 x 10 = 10 watts, and the power absorbed by R_3 is 1^2 x 15 = 15 watts. The total power absorbed is the arithmetic sum of the power of each resistor, or 5 + 10 + 15 = 30 watts. The value is also calculated by $P_t = E_t I_t = $ 30 x 1 = 30 watts.

More than one voltage source may be used in a series circuit. If the polarities of the sources are such that they aid each other, they are simply added together, and the net result is the same as if a single source of higher voltage had been used. If the polarities of the sources are such that one or more of them tend to cancel or "buck out" the effect of the others, then the net result is the difference between the source voltages that would cause the circuit current to flow in one direction and the source voltages that cause it to flow in the opposite direction.

Actually, the current could be assumed to flow in either direction as long as the minus sign is placed before each voltage drop (when the circuit is traced in the direction of the assumed current flow) and the proper sign (the one encountered as the source is approached in the circuit) is placed before all voltage sources. As mentioned previously, if the resultant circuit current has a negative sign it merely means that the assumed direction of current flow is incorrect.

Kirchhoff's Voltage Law is readily applied in solving series circuit problems. In many cases, it is the most practical method that may be used. For example, in figure 4-2, Kirchhoff's Voltage Law is used to solve for current, I; and when this has been determined, the other unknown values may be determined by Ohm's Law or the associated power formulas.

In figure 4-2 (A), the two voltage sources are aiding each other; that is, the polarities are connected so that each source tends to make the current flow clockwise around the circuit. Starting at the left terminal of $R1$ and proceeding clockwise around the circuit, the voltage equation is,

$$- E_1 - E_2 + E_{s2} - E_3 - E_4 - E_5 - E_6 + E_{s1} = 0.$$

Expressing the voltage drops around the circuit in terms of current and resistance, and the given values of source voltage, the equation becomes,

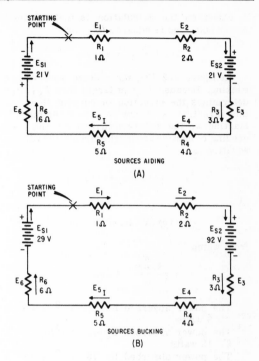

Figure 4-2.—Application of Kirchhoff's Law to series circuits.

$$- I - 2I + 21 - 3I - 4I - 5I - 6I + 21 = 0,$$
$$- 21I + 42 = 0,$$
$$42 = 21I,$$
$$I = 2 \text{ amperes.}$$

I is positive and therefore the assumed direction of current flow is correct. (In this case the direction of current flow was obvious.)

The total power absorbed by the resistors in figure 4-2 (A), is the sum of the power absorbed by each resistor.

The power in $R1$ is $I^2R_1 = 2^2$ x 1 = 4 watts.
The power in $R2$ is $I^2R_2 = 2^2$ x 2 = 8 watts.
The power in $R3$ is $I^2R_3 = 2^2$ x 3 = 12 watts.
The power in $R4$ is $I^2R_4 = 2^2$ x 4 = 16 watts.
The power in $R5$ is $I^2R_5 = 2^2$ x 5 = 20 watts.
The power in $R6$ is $I^2R_6 = 2^2$ x 6 = 24 watts.

Note that in the above calculations for power the current values in each is the same because these calculations apply to a series circuit. The total power absorbed is

$$4 + 8 + 12 + 16 + 20 + 24 = 84 \text{ watts.}$$

59

A check on the calculation is that the total power absorbed is equal to $I_t E_t$, or

$$2 \times (21 + 21) = 84 \text{ watts.}$$

In figure 4-2 (B), the voltage sources are bucking. Because E_{s2} is larger then E_{s1}, E_{s2} determines the direction of current flow, and this direction is clockwise around the circuit. Starting at the left terminal of $R1$ and proceeding clockwise around the circuit, the voltage equation is,

$$- E_1 - E_2 + E_{s2} - E_3 - E_4 - E_5 - E_6 - E_{s1} = 0,$$

or

$$- I - 2I + 92 - 3I - 4I - 5I - 6I - 29 = 0,$$

from which

$$I = \frac{92 - 29}{21} = 3 \text{ amperes.}$$

The power absorbed by $R1$ is $I^2 R_1 = 3^2 \times 1 = 9$ watts.
The power absorbed by $R2$ is $I^2 R_2 = 3^2 \times 2 = 18$ watts.
The power absorbed by $R3$ is $I^2 R_3 = 3^2 \times 3 = 27$ watts.
The power absorbed by $R4$ is $I^2 R_4 = 3^2 \times 4 = 36$ watts.
The power absorbed by $R5$ is $I^2 R_5 = 3^2 \times 5 = 45$ watts.
The power absorbed by $R6$ is $I^2 R_6 = 3^2 \times 6 = 54$ watts.
The total power is

$$9 + 18 + 27 + 36 + 45 + 54 = 189 \text{ watts.}$$

A check on the calculation is that the total power absorbed is equal to the product of the net voltage, acting in the direction of electron flow, and the current, or

$$EI = (92 - 29) \times 3 = 189 \text{ watts.}$$

TYPICAL PROBLEMS IN SERIES CIRCUITS

As seen by the preceding calculations, problems involving the determination of resistance, voltage, current, and power in a series circuit are relatively simple. It is necessary only to draw or visualize the circuit, to list the known values, and to determine by means of Ohm's Law (or Kirchhoff's adaptation of Ohm's Law) the unknown values.

In figure 4-3 (A), it is desired to find the total resistance, R_t, the current, I, and the voltage drops across $R1$, $R2$, and $R3$.

The total resistance is equal to the sum of the individual resistors. Thus,

$$R_t = R_1 + R_2 + R_3 = 5 + 10 + 25 = 40\,\Omega.$$

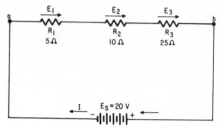

VOLTAGE AROUND SERIES CIRCUIT HAVING ONE VOLTAGE SOURCE

(A)

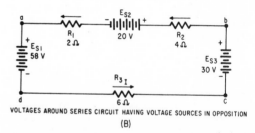

VOLTAGES AROUND SERIES CIRCUIT HAVING VOLTAGE SOURCES IN OPPOSITION

(B)

Figure 4-3.—Solving for R_t, E, and I in series circuits.

The current is

$$I = \frac{E_s}{R_t} = \frac{20}{40} = 0.5 \text{ ampere.}$$

The current is the same in all parts of the series circuit, and therefore the same current flows through $R1$, $R2$, and $R3$. The voltage drops across $R1$, $R2$, and $R3$ are indicated as

$$E_1 = I \times R_1 = 0.5 \times 5 = 2.5 \text{ volts,}$$

$$E_2 = I \times R_2 = 0.5 \times 10 = 5 \text{ volts,}$$

and

$E_3 = I \times R_3 = 0.5 \times 25 = 12.5$ volts.

According to Kirchhoff's Voltage Law, the sum of the individual voltage drops is equal to the source voltage, or

$$E_s = E_1 + E_2 + E_3 = 2.5 + 5 + 12.5 = 20 \text{ volts.}$$

The power absorbed by $R1$ is $\dfrac{E_1^2}{R_1} = \dfrac{(2.5)^2}{5} = 1.25$ watts.

The power absorbed by $R2$ is $\dfrac{E_2^2}{R_2} = \dfrac{5^2}{10} = 2.50$ watts.

The power absorbed by $R3$ is $\dfrac{E_3^2}{R_3} = \dfrac{(12.5)^2}{25} = 6.25$ watts.

The total power absorbed by the 3 resistors is 1.25 + 2.5 + 6.25, or 10 watts. This value may be checked by the equation,

$$P_t = E_t I_t = 20 \times 0.5 = 10 \text{ watts.}$$

In the example of figure 4-3 (B), the circuit trace is arbitrarily started at point a and continued in a clockwise direction completely around the circuit and back to point a. The voltage equation is written in terms of both (1) known voltages and (2) current and resistance. The equation is solved for current in terms of voltage and resistance. The three voltage sources are arranged so that E_{s1} and E_{s2} are additive and both are opposed to E_{s3}. Since the sum of E_{s1} and E_{s2} is greater than E_{s3} the electron flow is determined by E_{s1} and E_{s2} and is seen to be in a counterclockwise direction around the circuit as indicated by the arrows above the resistors.

Representing the unknown current as I, the voltage equation is,

$$2I - 20 + 4I + 30 + 6I - 58 = 0$$

$$12I - 48 = 0$$

$$I = \frac{48}{12} = 4 \text{ amperes.}$$

The voltage drop across $R1$ is $IR_1 = 4 \times 2 = 8$ volts.
The voltage drop across $R2$ is $IR_2 = 4 \times 4 = 16$ volts.
The voltage drop across $R3$ is $IR_3 = 4 \times 6 = 24$ volts.

The total voltage acting in the direction of electron flow is equal to

8 + 16 + 24, or 48 volts.

The power absorbed in $R1$ is $I^2 R_1 = 4^2 \times 2 = 32$ watts.
The power absorbed in $R2$ is $I^2 R_2 = 4^2 \times 4 = 64$ watts.
The power absorbed in $R3$ is $I^2 R_3 = 4^2 \times 6 = 96$ watts.
The total power absorbed by the three resistors is

$$32 + 64 + 96 = 192 \text{ watts.}$$

The calculation may be checked by the relation

$$P_t = E_t I = 48 \times 4 = 192 \text{ watts.}$$

The filaments of light bulbs and electron tubes are made of materials that have appreciable resistance. Most incandescent lamps have tungsten filaments. The heat produced by the current flowing through the resistance of the filament is intense enough to make the tungsten wires white hot and thus produce artificial light. Radio receivers of the common a-c/d-c variety have their filaments connected in series, as shown in figure 4-4. The tube designations are shown directly above the filament symbols, $R1$, $R2$, and so forth. The first two numerals in the designation indicate the approximate voltage that must be applied to the filament to cause rated current to flow. For example, 12 volts must be applied to the filament of the 12SA7 tube to cause the rated current of 0.15 ampere to flow.

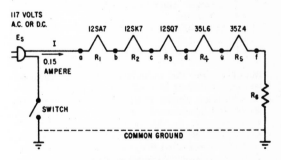

Figure 4-4.—Typical series circuit.

The first problem is to find the value of $R6$ that will cause 0.15 ampere to flow in the circuit when the applied voltage is 117 volts. By observation it is seen that the tube filaments will absorb

12 + 12 + 12 + 35 + 35 = 106 volts.

Therefore, $R6$ must absorb the difference, or

$$117 - 106 = 11 \text{ volts.}$$

The resistance of $R6$ is,

$$R6 = \frac{E_6}{I} = \frac{11}{0.15} = 73.3 \text{ ohms.}$$

The power, P_6, absorbed by $R6$ is

$$P_6 = E_6 \times I = 11 \times 0.15 = 1.65 \text{ watts.}$$

The power absorbed by the 12SA7 filament is

$$P_1 = E_1 I = 12 \times 0.15 = 1.8 \text{ watts.}$$

The power absorbed by the 12SK7 and the 12SQ7 filaments is also 1.8 watts each, since they both have equal voltages and the same value of current. The 35L6 filament absorbs an amount of power equal to 35 x 0.15 = 5.25 watts and the 35Z4 filament absorbs an equal amount of power. The total power absorbed by the entire filament circuit is equal to the sum of the power absorbed by each separate unit. Thus,

$$P_t = 1.8 + 1.8 + 1.8 + 5.25 + 5.25 + 1.65 = 17.55 \text{ watts.}$$

The total power may be checked as follows:

$$P_t = E_t I = 117 \times 0.15 = 17.55 \text{ watts.}$$

In the foregoing examples of series circuits, an important relation should be pointed out. Note that the voltage dropped across each resistor is in proportion to its resistance. This fact is important and should be thoroughly understood. It is explained as follows:

When the power switch in a series circuit is closed, current through the circuit rises very rapidly. As the current increases from zero, the total voltage drop across the load also increases until it exactly equals the source voltage, at which time the current stabilizes at a steady flow. In this natural state of balance, the voltage absorbed by each ohm of resistance will depend on two things, (1) how many source volts must be absorbed, and (2) how many ohms there are in the circuit to absorb them. The voltage that each ohm of resistance must absorb is determined by dividing the total voltage by the total number of ohms. Thereafter, when the circuit is closed, current will rise until each ohm of resistance is absorbing, or dropping, a voltage that is maximum in value, and equal to all the others. Current will stabilize when the sum of all the ohmic drops equals the source, or impressed voltage. This is Kirchhoff's Voltage Law in action. Because the voltage-per-ohm and the series current vary directly and simultaneously, they must therefore be equal. For instance, when there are 10 amperes of current through one ohm of resistance, the voltage absorbed by that one ohm is 10 volts. Thus, the division of total voltage by the total number of ohms yields TWO values, (1) the voltage absorbed per ohm, and (2) the total current.

The Ohm's Law Formula $\frac{E}{R} = I$ is most often used to express this relation. It could also be written $\frac{E}{R} = e$, where e is the volts-per-ohm value for a series circuit, because e and I are interchangeable. The voltage absorbed by any particular resistor is equal to the voltage-per-ohm value for the circuit, multiplied by the number of ohms in the particular resistor. This relation could thus be written $E = eR$. In practice, however, I is most often substituted for e, and the relation becomes $E = IR$. Hence, the commonly-used term "IR drop."

The voltages around the series circuit shown in figure 4-4 are distributed in proportion to the resistances around the circuit. Thus, the voltage between any point, for example, ground, and some other point such as a, b, or c may be determined. For example, the potential from a to ground is the full 117 volts because the entire circuit is included. From b to ground, the potential is 117 volts less the drop of 12 volts across $R1$, or 105 volts, because the circuit includes everything except $R1$. The potential between point f and ground is 11 volts because $R6$ alone is included in this part of the circuit.

In this type of circuit, when an open occurs in any of the filaments or in $R6$, the current ceases to flow. However, the input current increases if any of the points, a, b, c, and so forth, should become grounded. For example, if point f should become grounded the resistance of $R6$ is no longer in the circuit, and 117 volts is applied between points a and f instead of 106 volts. The total filament current is increased to

$$\frac{117}{106} \times 0.15 = 0.165 \text{ ampere.}$$

62

The increase in current is proportioned to the increase in voltage. Over-voltage may cause the filament to overheat because of excessive current. Thus, the entire filament circuit will be deenergized when the circuit opens at some point due to filament burnout.

Effect of Source Resistance on Voltage, Power, and Efficiency

All sources of e.m.f. have some internal resistance that acts in series with the load resistance. The source resistance is generally indicated in circuit diagrams as a separate resistor connected in series with the source. Both the voltage and power made available to the load may be increased if the resistance of the source is reduced.

The effects of source resistance, R_S, on load voltage may be illustrated by the use of figure 4-5. In figure 4-5 (A), the circuit is open, and therefore a voltmeter connected across the battery will read the open-circuit voltage. In the case of a dry cell, the open-circuit voltage is 1.5 volts. In figure 4-5 (B), the cell is short-circuited through the ammeter, and a current of 30 amperes flows from the source. In this case the voltage of the cell is developed across the internal resistance of the cell. The internal resistance of the cell is therefore,

$$R_s = \frac{E_s}{I} = \frac{1.5}{30} = 0.05 \text{ ohm.}$$

If a load, R_L, of 0.10 ohm is connected to the circuit, as shown in figure 4-5 (C), the current, I, becomes

$$I = \frac{E_s}{R_t} = \frac{1.5}{0.15} = 10 \text{ amperes.}$$

The voltage available at the load is

$$E_L = IR_L = 10 \times 0.1 = 1 \text{ volt.}$$

The voltage absorbed across the internal resistance of the cell is

$$IR_s = 10 \times 0.05 = 0.5 \text{ volt.}$$

Thus the effect of the internal resistance is to decrease the terminal voltage from 1.5 volts to 1 volt when the cell delivers 10 amperes to the load.

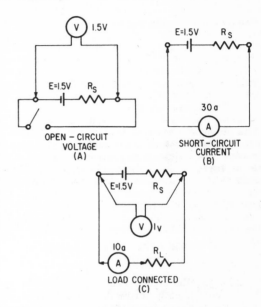

OPEN – CIRCUIT VOLTAGE (A)

SHORT – CIRCUIT CURRENT (B)

LOAD CONNECTED (C)

Figure 4-5.—Effect of source resistance on load voltage.

The effect of the source resistance on the power output of a d-c source may be shown by an analysis of the circuit in figure 4-6 (A). When the variable load-resistor, R_L, is set at the zero ohms position (equivalent to a short circuit) the current is limited only by the internal resistance, R_S, of the source. The short-circuit current, I, is determined as

$$I = \frac{E_s}{R_s} = \frac{100}{5} = 20 \text{ amperes.}$$

This is the maximum current that may be drawn from the source. The terminal voltage across the short circuit is zero and all the voltage is absorbed within the terminal resistance of the source.

If the load resistance, R_L, is increased (the internal resistance remaining the same), the current drawn from the source will decrease. Consequently, the voltage drop across the internal resistance will decrease. At the same time, the terminal voltage applied across the load will increase and will approach a maximum as the current approaches zero.

The MAXIMUM POWER TRANSFER THEOREM says in effect that maximum power is transferred from the source to the load when the resistance of the load is equal to the internal resistance of the source. This theorem is illustrated in the tabular chart and the graph of figure 4-6 (B) and (C). When the load resistance is 5 ohms, thus matching the source resistance, the maximum power of 500 watts is developed in the load.

The efficiency of power transfer (ratio of output to input power) from the source to the load increases as the load resistance is increased. The efficiency approaches 100 percent as the load resistance approaches a relatively large value compared with that of the source,

since less power is lost in the source. The efficiency of power transfer is only 50 percent at the maximum power transfer resistance of 5 ohms and approaches zero efficiency at relatively low values of load resistance compared with that of the source.

Thus the problem of high efficiency and maximum power transfer is resolved as a compromise somewhere between the low efficiency of maximum power transfer and the high efficiency of the high-resistance load. Where the amounts of power involved are large and the efficiency is important, the load resistance is made large relative to the source resistance so that the losses are kept small. In this case the efficiency will be high. Where the problem of matching a source to a load is of paramount importance, as in communications circuits, a strong signal may be more important than a high percentage of efficiency. In such cases, the efficiency of transmission will be only about 50 percent. However, the power of transmission will be the maximum of which the source is capable of supplying.

Parallel Circuits

OHM'S LAW APPLIED TO PARALLEL CIRCUITS

In the parallel circuit, each load (or branch), is connected directly across the voltage source, as shown in figure 4-7. As a result, there are as many separate paths for current flow as there are branches. When additional loads were added in the series circuit, total resistance was increased and total current decreased. In the parallel circuit, just the opposite is true. As loads are added in parallel, they simply become additional paths for current flow, and therefore the total current supplied by the source increases as they are added. If total current is increased, total resistance must have been decreased. Therefore, as branches are added in parallel, regardless of their resistances, the total resistance as seen from the voltage source DECREASES.

The voltage across all branches of a parallel circuit is the same, because all branches are connected directly to the voltage source. Consequently, the current through each branch is independent of the others, and depends only on the resistance of the particular branch, at a

given voltage. The current through each branch may thus be computed separately, simply by dividing its resistance into the source voltage. The branch currents in figure 4-7 are:

$$I_1 = \frac{E_s}{R_1} = \frac{30}{5} = 6 \text{ amperes,}$$

$$I_2 = \frac{E_s}{R_2} = \frac{30}{10} = 3 \text{ amperes,}$$

and

$$I_3 = \frac{E_s}{R_3} = \frac{30}{30} = 1 \text{ ampere.}$$

The total current, I_t, of the parallel circuit is equal to the sum of the currents through the individual branches. This, in slightly different words, is Kirchhoff's current law, which is treated later in this chapter. In this case, the total current is

$$I_t = I_1 + I_2 + I_3 = 6 + 3 + 1 = 10 \text{ amperes.}$$

In order to find the equivalent, or total resistance, R_t (for simplicity, R_t is used instead of R_{eq}), of the combination shown in figure 4-7, Ohm's law is first used to find each of the

64

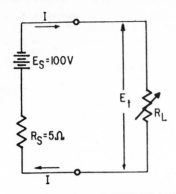

E_S= OPEN-CIRCUIT VOLTAGE OF SOURCE

R_S= INTERNAL RESISTANCE OF SOURCE

E_t= TERMINAL VOLTAGE

R_L= RESISTANCE OF LOAD

P_L= POWER USED IN LOAD

I = CURRENT FROM SOURCE

% EFF. = PERCENTAGE OF EFFICIENCY

(A)
CIRCUIT AND SYMBOL DESIGNATIONS

R_L	E_t	I	P_L	%EFF.
0	0	20	0	0
1	16.6	16.6	267.6	16.6
2	28.6	14.3	409	28.6
3	37.5	12.5	468.8	37.5
4	44.4	11.1	492.8	44.4
5	50	10	500	50
6	54.5	9.1	495.4	54.5
7	58.1	8.3	482.2	58.1
8	61.6	7.7	474.3	61.6
9	63.9	7.1	453.7	63.9
10	66	6.6	435.6	66
20	80	4	320	80
30	87	2.9	252	87
40	88	2.2	193.6	88
50	91	1.82	165	91

(B)
CHART

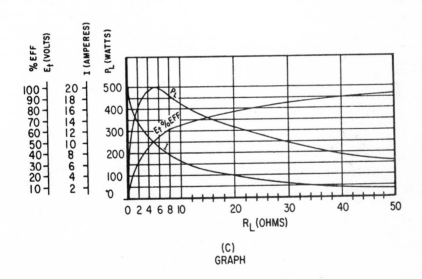

(C)
GRAPH

Figure 4-6.—Effect of source resistance on power output.

65

currents $(I_t,\ I_1,\ I_2,$ and $I_3)$. Substituting the Ohm's Law equivalent for current $(\frac{E}{R})$ in the current equation, that equation $(I_t = I_1 + I_2 + I_3)$ becomes

$$\frac{E_s}{R_t} = \frac{E_s}{R_1} + \frac{E_s}{R_2} + \frac{E_s}{R_3}$$

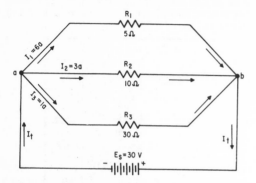

Figure 4-7.—Resistors in parallel.

This introduces the factor R_t into the equation, which is the quantity you are attempting to determine. Since E_s appears as the numerator in all four factors, it is divided out, and the equation then contains only the desired factor R_t:

$$\frac{1}{R_t} = \frac{1}{R_1} + \frac{1}{R_2} + \frac{1}{R_3},$$

$$= \frac{1}{5} + \frac{1}{10} + \frac{1}{30},$$

$$= 0.2 + 0.1 + 0.033,$$

$$\frac{1}{R_t} = 0.333,$$

$$R_t = \frac{1}{0.333},$$

$$= 3 \text{ ohms (approx.)}.$$

A useful rule to remember in computing the equivalent resistance of a d-c parallel circuit is that THE TOTAL RESISTANCE IS ALWAYS LESS THAN THE SMALLEST RESISTANCE IN ANY OF THE BRANCHES.

There are two shortcuts that may be used in solving for the equivalent resistance of a parallel circuit.

The first applies only to any number of parallel resistors all of which have THE SAME VALUE OF RESISTANCE. The equivalent resistance is determined by dividing the resistance of one resistor by the number of resistors in parallel. Thus, the equivalent resistance of five 10-ohm resistors connected in parallel is

$$R_t = \frac{10}{5} = 2 \text{ ohms.}$$

The second shortcut applies when two and only two resistors of different values are connected in parallel. The equivalent resistance is equal to their product divided by their sum. For example, if two resistors having resistances of 3 ohms and 6 ohms are connected in parallel, the equivalent resistance is

$$R_t = \frac{R_1 R_2}{R_1 + R_2} = \frac{3 \times 6}{3 + 6} = \frac{18}{9} = 2 \text{ ohms.}$$

In addition to adding the individual branch currents to obtain the total current in a parallel circuit, the total current may be found directly by dividing the applied voltage by the equivalent resistance, R_t. For example, in figure 4-7

$$I_t = \frac{E_s}{R_t} = \frac{30}{3} = 10 \text{ amperes.}$$

The quantity $\frac{1}{R}$, as used in the foregoing equations, expresses CONDUCTANCE, whose standard symbol is G. When referring to the RESISTANCE of a circuit, you visualize the degree to which it RESISTS or PREVENTS current flow. When referring to its conductance, you visualize the degree to which the circuit PERMITS or CONDUCTS current flow. It is well to be able to work from either standpoint because some problems are easier to solve using circuit conductance instead of resistance, and vice versa.

The total conductance of a circuit is the reciprocal of its total resistance (the reciprocal

66

of any quantity is that quantity dividued into one). Thus, the total conductance of a circuit is written

$$G_t = \frac{1}{R_t}$$

and

$$R_t = \frac{1}{G_t}$$

The term RELATIVE CONDUCTANCE applies to the comparison of two or more parallel branches. When two or more resistors are connected in parallel, each will conduct current in proportion to its resistance. To compare their relative conductances, each resistance is divided into the common numerator, 1. The larger a resistance the smaller its current flow, or relative conductance. The total conductance is the simple sum of all branch conductances:

$$G_t = G_1 + G_2 + G_3 + \cdots\cdots$$

or

$$\frac{1}{R_t} = \frac{1}{R_1} + \frac{1}{R_2} + \frac{1}{R_3} + \cdots\cdots$$

Since G and R are each an inversion of the other, as shown in equation (fig. 4-1), it follows that their Ohm's-Law equivalents are also inverted. That is, where R is expressed as $\frac{E}{I}$, G is expressed as $\frac{I}{E}$. Wherever R is used in Ohm's Law equations, the reciprocal of G may be used. For instance, where R is used as a multiplier in expressing E, $(E = IR)$, G would be used as a divisor, $(E = \frac{I}{G})$.

KIRCHHOFF'S CURRENT LAW APPLIED TO PARALLEL CIRCUITS

Kirchhoff's current law states that AT ANY JUNCTION OF CONDUCTORS THE ALGEBRAIC SUM OF THE CURRENTS IS ZERO. This is another way of saying that as many electrons must leave a junction as enter it. Consider junction a of figure 4-7. Assume that the current flowing toward junction a is positive and that the currents flowing away from the junction— that is, currents I_1, I_2, and I_3 —are negative. Kirchhoff's current law is then expressed mathematically as

$$+I_t - I_1 - I_2 - I_3 = 0,$$

or

$$10 - 6 - 3 - 1 = 0.$$

As in the series circuit, the total power consumed in a parallel circuit is equal to the sum of the power consumed in the individual resistors. The power P_1, consumed in $R1$ of figure 4-7 is

$$P_1 = EI_1 = 30 \times 6 = 180 \text{ watts;}$$

the power, P_2, consumed in $R2$ is

$$P_2 = EI_2 = 30 \times 3 = 90 \text{ watts;}$$

and the power P_3, consumed in $R3$ is

$$P_3 = EI_3 = 30 \times 1 = 30 \text{ watts.}$$

The total power, P_t, consumed is the sum of the power consumed in the individual branch units—that is,

$$P_t = P_1 + P_2 + P_3 = 180 + 90 + 30 = 300 \text{ watts.}$$

The total power may be checked as

$$P_t = EI_t = 30 \times 10 = 300 \text{ watts.}$$

TYPICAL PROBLEMS IN PARALLEL CIRCUITS

Problems involving the determination of resistance, voltage, current, and power in a parallel circuit are solved as simply as in a series circuit. The procedure is the same— (1) draw a circuit diagram, (2) state the values given and the values to be found, (3) state the applicable equations, and (4) substitute the given values and solve for the unknown.

For example, the parallel circuit of figure 4-8 consists of 2 branches (a and b). Branch a consists of 3 lamps in parallel. Their ratings are $L_1 = 50$ watts, $L_2 = 25$ watts, and $L_3 = 75$ watts. Branch b also has 3 lamps in parallel with ratings of $L_4 = 150$ watts, $L_5 = 200$ watts, and $L_6 = 250$ watts. The source voltage is 100 volts.

1. Find the current in each lamp.
2. Find the resistance of each lamp.
3. Find the current in branch a.

4. Find the current in branch b.
5. Find the total circuit current.
6. Find the total circuit resistance.
7. Find the total power supplied to the circuit.
8. Check 7 by a separate calculation.

1. The current in $L1$ is $I = \dfrac{P}{E} = \dfrac{50}{100} = 0.50$ ampere.

The current in $L2$ is $\dfrac{25}{100} = 0.25$ ampere.

The current in $L3$ is $\dfrac{75}{100} = 0.75$ ampere.

The current in $L4$ is $\dfrac{150}{100} = 1.50$ amperes.

The current in $L5$ is $\dfrac{200}{100} = 2.00$ amperes.

The current in $L6$ is $\dfrac{250}{100} = 2.5$ amperes.

2. The resistance of $L1$ is $R = \dfrac{E}{I} = \dfrac{100}{0.5} = 200$ ohms.

The resistance of $L2$ is $\dfrac{100}{0.25} = 400$ ohms.

The resistance of $L3$ is $\dfrac{100}{0.75} = 133$ ohms.

The resistance of $L4$ is $\dfrac{100}{1.5} = 66.7$ ohms.

The resistance of $L5$ is $\dfrac{100}{2.0} = 50$ ohms.

The resistance of $L6$ is $\dfrac{100}{2.5} = 40$ ohms.

3. The current in branch a is

$I_1 + I_2 + I_3 = 0.5 + 0.25 + 0.75 = 1.5$ amperes.

4. The current in branch b is

$I_4 + I_5 + I_6 = 1.5 + 2.0 + 2.5 = 6.0$ amperes.

5. The total circuit current is

$I_a + I_b = 1.5 + 6.0 = 7.5$ amperes.

6. The total circuit resistance is

$$R_t = \frac{E}{I_t} = \frac{100}{7.5} = 13.3 \text{ ohms.}$$

7. The total power supplied to the circuit is

50 w. + 25 w. + 75 w. + 150 w. + 200 w. + 250 w. = 750 watts.

8. The total power is also equal to

$$P_t = EI_t = 100 \times 7.5 = 750 \text{ watts.}$$

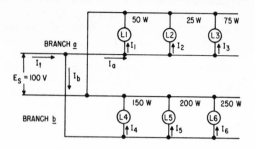

Figure 4-8.—Typical parallel circuit.

PRACTICAL APPLICATIONS OF SERIES AND PARALLEL CIRCUITS

One of the most common series circuits is the familiar string of Christmas tree lamps. When one of the lamps in the string burns out, all of the lamps go out because there is no longer a complete pathway through which the electrons can flow.

If the string is composed of 10 lamps of the same power rating and it is connected to a 120-volt source, 12 volts will be applied across each lamp. If one of the lamps burns out and the line is then shorted across the socket of the burned-out lamp, current will continue to flow through the remaining 9 lamps. However, the source voltage of 120 volts will be applied to the remaining lamps, and 13.3 volts will be developed across each lamp. The resultant increase in current flow may quickly burn out another lamp in the string.

Airport runway lamps and street lamps are other applications of series circuits. For these applications, constant-current variable-voltage sources are employed. Where long circuits like these are used, line losses are kept to a minimum by the use of high voltage and low current. When one of the lamps burns out, a device at the lamp automatically shorts out the defective lamp, thus allowing the others to continue to burn. At the variable-voltage source there is an automatic reduction in voltage when the current tends to increase so that the rise in current through the remaining lamps is checked and the circuit current remains approximately constant at the rated value.

Most power and light distribution circuits are basically parallel circuits supplied by constant-potential variable-current sources.

Ship's service distribution systems are typical parallel circuits where many branch circuits are connected in parallel across the bus bars (the massive conductors that tie to the source).

Distribution systems used in homes and factories are essentially networks of parallel circuits. The service conductors (the wires that bring the current to the home) are connected to the branch parallel circuits via a service switch and fuses. Each parallel circuit that is connected to the main circuit is likewise supplied with a fuse or circuit breaker of a lower current rating. On each individual branch circuit lamps or other loads are connected in parallel. Thus, in the home there are branch parallel circuits in parallel with other branch parallel circuits. Actually, nearly all the commonly encountered distribution electrical circuits are parallel circuits if the line resistance is disregarded.

QUIZ

1. If a circuit is constructed so as to allow the electrons to follow only one possible path, the circuit is called a/an
   a. series-parallel circuit
   b. incomplete circuit
   c. series circuit
   d. parallel circuit
2. According to Kirchhoff's Law of Voltages, the algebraic sum of all the votages in a series circuit is equal to
   a. zero
   b. source voltage
   c. total voltage drop
   d. the sum of the IR drop of the circuit
3. In a series circuit, the total current is
   a. always equal to the source voltage
   b. determined by the load only
   c. the same through all parts of the circuit
   d. equal to zero at the positive side of the source
4. The correct voltage equation for the circuit below is
   a. $E_s + E_1 + E_2 + E_3 + E_4 = 0$
   b. $E_s - E_1 - E_2 - E_3 - E_4 = 0$
   c. $E_s = - E_1 - E_2 - E_3 - E_4$
   d. $- E_s = E_1 + E_2 + E_3 + E_4$

$R_2 = 3\Omega$ $R_3 = 2\Omega$
$E_2 = ?$ $E_3 = ?$

$R_1 = 7\Omega$ $R_4 = 3\Omega$
$E_1 = ?$ $E_s = 60V$ $E_4 = ?$

5. (Refer to the circuit used with question 4.) After expressing the voltage drops around the circuit in terms of current and resistance and the given values of source voltage, the equation becomes
   a. $-60 -7I -3I -2I -3I = 0$
   b. $-60 + 7I + 3I + 2I + 3I = 0$
   c. $60 -7I -3I -2I -3I = 0$
   d. $60 + 7I + 3I + 2I + 3I = 0$

6. By the use of the correct equation, it is found that the current (I) in the circuit used with question 4 is of positive value. This indicates that the
   a. assumed direction of current flow is correct
   b. assumed direction of current flow is incorrect
   c. problem is not solvable
   d. battery polarity should be reversed
7. In what position would the variable rheostat in the circuit below be placed in order that the filaments of the tubes operate properly with a current flow of 0.15 ampere?
   a. 50 Ω position
   b. 100 Ω position
   c. 150 Ω position
   d. 200 Ω position

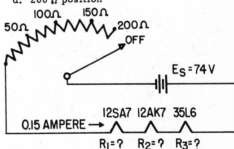

8. The power absorbed by the variable rheostat in the circuit used with question 7, when placed in its proper operating position, would be
   a. 112.50 watts
   b. 2.25 watts
   c. 337.50 watts
   d. 450.00 watts
9. In the circuit below, maximum power would be transferred from the source to the load (R_L) if R_L were set at
   a. 2 ohms
   b. 5 ohms
   c. 12 ohms
   d. 24 ohms

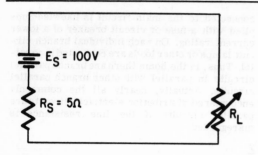

Es = 100V

Rs = 5Ω

RL

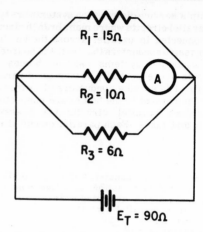

R₁ = 15Ω

R₂ = 10Ω

A

R₃ = 6Ω

ET = 90Ω

10. In the circuit below, if an additional resistor were placed in parallel to R₃ the ammeter reading would
    a. increase
    b. decrease
    c. remain the same
    d. drop to zero

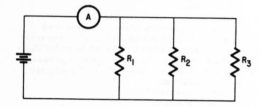

A

R₁   R₂   R₃

11. In a parallel circuit containing a 4-ohm, 5-ohm, and 6-ohm resistor, the current flow is
    a. highest through the 4-ohm resistor
    b. lowest through the 4-ohm resistor
    c. highest through the 6-ohm resistor
    d. equal through all three resistors

12. Three resistors of 2, 4, and 6 ohms, respectively, are connected in parallel. Which resistor would absorb the greatest power?
    a. The 2-ohm resistor
    b. The 4-ohm resistor
    c. The 6-ohm resistor
    d. It will be the same for all resistors

13. If three lamps are connected in parallel with a power source, connecting a fourth lamp in parallel will
    a. decrease ET
    b. decrease IT
    c. increase ET
    d. increase IT

14. What is the current flow through the ammeter in the circuit shown below?
    a. 4 amps
    b. 9 amps
    c. 15 amps
    d. 28 amps

15. In the circuit shown below, the total resistance is 24 ohms. What is the value of R₂?
    a. 16 ohms
    b. 40 ohms
    c. 60 ohms
    d. 64 ohms

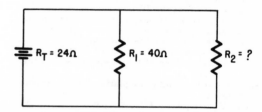

RT = 24Ω   R₁ = 40Ω   R₂ = ?

16. What is the source voltage of the circuit shown below?
    a. 40 volts
    b. 50 volts
    c. 100 volts
    d. 500 volts

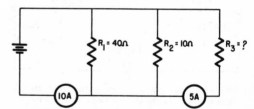

R₁ = 40Ω   R₂ = 10Ω   R₃ = ?

10A   5A

17. What is the value of R₃ in the circuit used with question 16?
    a. 8 ohms
    b. 10 ohms
    c. 20 ohms
    d. 100 ohms

8. If all 4 resistors in the circuit below are of equal ohmic resistances, what is the value of R3?
   a. 5 ohms
   b. 20 ohms
   c. 60 ohms
   d. 80 ohms

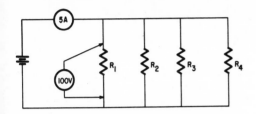

19. What is the value of the source voltage in the circuit below?
    a. 20 volts
    b. 40 volts
    c. 120 volts
    d. 160 volts

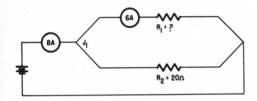

20. If lamp L2 in the circuit below should suddenly burn out, which of the below statements is correct?
    a. More current would flow through lamp L1
    b. Source voltage would decrease
    c. The filament resistance of lamp L1 would decrease
    d. Lamp L1 would still burn normal

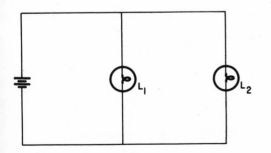

21. When referring to a circuit's conductance, you visualize the degree to which the circuit
    a. permits or conducts voltage
    b. opposes the rate of voltage changes
    c. permits or conducts current flow
    d. opposes the rate of current flow

22. The total conductance of the circuit below would be solved by which of the equations?
    a. $G_T - G_1 - G_2 - G_3 = 0$
    b. $G_T + G_1 + G_2 + G_3 = 0$
    c. $G_T = G_1 - G_2 - G_3$
    d. $G_T = G_1 + G_2 + G_3$

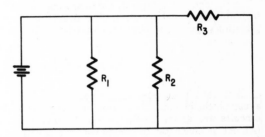

23. If the resistors in the circuit below are all rated at 250 watts, which resistor or resistors would overheat?
    a. R_1
    b. R_2
    c. R_3
    d. All

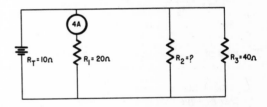

24. The total conductance of the circuit below is
    a. 0.15 G
    b. 0.20 G
    c. 0.50 G
    d. 0.75 G

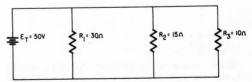

CHAPTER 5

DIRECT-CURRENT COMPOUND AND BRIDGE CIRCUITS

In the compound circuit, loads are connected in both series and parallel. For practical applications, you should become familiar with the compound circuit, since it is used more widely than any other type. You should be able to recognize and segregate the various combinations.

Series-Parallel Combinations

At least three resistors are required to form a compound circuit. Two basic series-parallel circuits are shown in figure 5-1. In figure 5-1 (A), $R1$ is connected in series with the parallel combination made up of $R2$ and $R3$.

The total resistance, R_t, of figure 5-1 (A), is determined in two steps. First, the resistance, $R_{2,3}$, of the parallel combination of $R2$ and $R3$ is determined as

$$R_{2,3} = \frac{R_2 R_3}{R_2 + R_3} = \frac{3 \times 6}{3 + 6} = \frac{18}{9} = 2 \text{ ohms.}$$

The sum of $R_{2,3}$ and R_1—that is, R_t—is

$$R_t = R_{2,3} + R_1 = 2 + 2 = 4 \text{ ohms.}$$

If the total resistance, R_t, and the source voltage, E_s, are known, the total current, I_t, may be determined by Ohm's law. Thus, in figure 5-1 (A),

$$I_t = \frac{E_s}{R_t} = \frac{20}{4} = 5 \text{ amperes.}$$

If the values of the various resistors and the current through them are known, the voltage drops across the resistors may be determined by Ohm's Law. Thus, in figure 5-1 (A),

$$E_{ab} = I_t R_1 = 5 \times 2 = 10 \text{ volts,}$$

and

$$E_{bc} = I_t R_{2,3} = 5 \times 2 = 10 \text{ volts.}$$

According to Kirchhoff's Voltage Law, the sum of the voltage drops around the closed circuit is equal to the source voltage. Thus,

$$E_{ab} + E_{bc} = E_s,$$

or

$$10 + 10 = 20 \text{ volts.}$$

If the voltage drop, E_{bc}, across $R_{2,3}$—that is, the drop between points b and c—is known, the current through the individual branches may be determined as

$$I_2 = \frac{E_{bc}}{R_2} = \frac{10}{3} = 3.333 \text{ amperes,}$$

and

$$I_3 = \frac{E_{bc}}{R_3} = \frac{10}{6} = 1.666 \text{ amperes.}$$

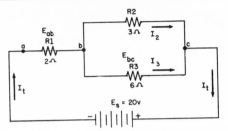

R1 IN SERIES WITH PARALLEL COMBINATION OF R2 AND R3

(A)

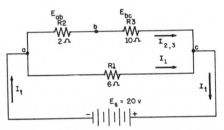

R1 IN PARALLEL WITH THE SERIES COMBINATION OF R2 & R3

(B)

Figure 5-1.—Compound circuits—series-parallel connections.

According to Kirchhoff's Current Law, the sum of the currents flowing in the individual parallel branches is equal to the total current. Thus,

$$I_2 + I_3 = I_t,$$

or

$$3.333 + 1.666 = 5 \text{ amperes (approx.).}$$

The total current flows through $R1$; and at point b it divides between the two branches in inverse proportion to the resistance of each branch. Twice as much current goes through $R2$ as through $R3$ because $R2$ has one-half the resistance of $R3$. Thus, 3.333, or two-thirds of 5, amperes flows through $R2$; and 1.666, or one-third of 5, amperes flows through $R3$.

In figure 5-1 (B), $R1$ is in parallel with the series combination of $R2$ and $R3$. The total resistance, R_t, is determined in two steps. First,

the sum of the resistance of $R2$ and $R3$—that is, $R_{2,3}$—is determined as

$$R_{2,3} = R_2 + R_3 = 2 + 10 = 12 \text{ ohms.}$$

Second, the total resistance, R_t, is the result of combining $R_{2,3}$ in parallel with $R1$, or

$$R_t = \frac{R_{2,3}R_1}{R_{2,3} + R_1} = \frac{12 \times 6}{12 + 6} = 4 \text{ ohms.}$$

If the total resistance, R_t, and the source voltage, E_S, are known, the total current, I_t may be determined by Ohm's Law. Thus, in figure 5-1 (B),

$$I_t = \frac{E_s}{R_t} = \frac{20}{4} = 5 \text{ amperes.}$$

A portion of the total current flows through the series combination of $R2$ and $R3$ and the remainder flows through $R1$. Because current varies inversely with the resistance, two-thirds of the total current flows through $R1$ and one-third flows through the series combination of $R2$ and $R3$, since R_1 is one-half of $R_2 + R_3$.

The source voltage, E_S, is applied between points a and c, and therefore the current I_1 through $R1$ is

$$I_1 = \frac{E_s}{R_1} = \frac{20}{6} = 3.333 \text{ amperes;}$$

and the current, $I_{2,3}$, through $R_{2,3}$ is

$$I_{2,3} = \frac{E_s}{R_{2,3}} = \frac{20}{12} = 1.666 \text{ amperes.}$$

73

According to Kirchhoff's Current Law the sum of the individual branch currents is equal to the total current, or

$$I_t = I_1 + I_{2,3},$$

$$5 = 3.333 + 1.667.$$

Compound circuits may be made up of a number of resistors arranged in numerous series and parallel combinations. In more complicated circuits, special theorems, rules, and formulas are used. These are based on Ohm's Law and provide faster solutions for particular applications. Series formulas are applied to the series parts of the circuit, and parallel formulas are applied to the parallel parts. For example, in figure 5-2, the total resistance, R_t, may be obtained in three logical steps.

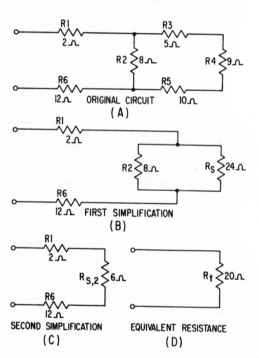

Figure 5-2.—Solving total resistance in a compound circuit.

First, $R3$, $R4$, and $R5$ in figure 5-2 (A), are in series (there is only one path for current) and may be combined in figure 5-2 (B), to give the resistance, R_S, of the three resistors. Thus,

$$R_s = R_3 + R_4 + R_5 = 5 + 9 + 10 = 24 \text{ ohms},$$

and it is now in parallel with $R2$ (because they both receive the same voltage).

The combined resistance of R_S in parallel with $R2$ is

$$R_{s,2} = \frac{R_2 R_s}{R_2 + R_s} = \frac{8 \times 24}{8 + 24} = 6 \text{ ohms},$$

as in figure 5-2 (C).

Third, the total resistance, R_t is determined by combining resistors $R1$ and $R6$ with $R_{s,2}$, as

$$R_t = R_1 + R_6 + R_{s,2} = 2 + 12 + 6 = 20 \text{ ohms}.$$

Other compound circuits may be solved in a similar manner. For example, in figure 5-3, the equivalent resistance, R_t, may be found by simplifying the circuit in successive steps beginning with the resistances, R_1 and R_2. Thus,

$$R_{1,2} = \frac{R_1 R_2}{R_1 + R_2} = \frac{3 \times 6}{3 + 6} = \frac{18}{9} = 2 \text{ ohms},$$

and it is in series with $R3$.

The resistances, $R_{1,2}$ and R_3, are added to give the resultant resistance, $R_{1,2,3}$. Thus,

$$R_{1,2,3} = R_{1,2} + R_3 = 2 + 4 = 6 \text{ ohms}.$$

$R_{1,2,3}$ is in parallel with R_4. The combined resistance, $R_{1,2,3,4}$, is determined as

$$R_{1,2,3,4} = \frac{R_{1,2,3} R_4}{R_{1,2,3} + R_4} = \frac{6 \times 12}{6 + 12} = \frac{72}{18} = 4 \text{ ohms}.$$

This equivalent resistance is in series with $R5$. Thus, the total resistance, R_t, of the circuit is

$$R_t = R_{1,2,3,4} + R_5 = 4 + 8 = 12 \text{ ohms.}$$

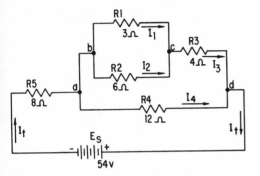

Figure 5-3.—Compound circuit for solving resistance, voltage, current, and power.

By Ohm's Law, the line current, I_t, is

$$I_t = \frac{E_s}{R_t} = \frac{54}{12} = 4.5 \text{ amperes.}$$

The line current flows through $R5$ and therefore the voltage drop, E_5, across $R5$ is

$$E_5 = I_t R_5 = 4.5 \times 8 = 36 \text{ volts.}$$

According to Kirchhoff's Voltage Law, the sum of the voltage drops around the circuit is equal to the source voltage; accordingly, the voltage between points a and d is

$$E_{ad} = E_s - E_5 = 54 - 36 = 18 \text{ volts.}$$

The current through $R4$ is

$$I_4 = \frac{E_4}{R_4} = \frac{18}{12} = 1.5 \text{ amperes.}$$

The resistance, $R_{1,2,3}$, of parallel resistors $R1$ and $R2$ in series with resistor $R3$ is 6 ohms. E_{ad} is applied across 6 ohms; therefore the current, I_3, through $R3$ is

$$I_3 = \frac{E_{ad}}{R_{1,2,3}} = \frac{18}{6} = 3 \text{ amperes.}$$

The voltage drop, E_3, across $R3$ is

$$E_3 = I_3 R_3 = 3 \times 4 = 12 \text{ volts.}$$

and the voltage across the parallel combination of $R1$ and $R2$—that is, E_{bc}—is

$$E_{bc} = I_{1,2} R_{1,2} = 3 \times 2 = 6 \text{ volts,}$$

where $I_{1,2}$ is the current through the parallel combinations of $R1$ and $R2$. By Kirchhoff's Current Law, $I_{1,2}$ is equal to I_3. The current, I_1 through $R1$ is

$$I_1 = \frac{E_{bc}}{R_1} = \frac{6}{3} = 2 \text{ amperes,}$$

and the current, I_2, through $R2$ is

$$I_2 = \frac{E_{bc}}{R_2} = \frac{6}{6} = 1 \text{ ampere.}$$

The preceding computations may be checked by the application of Kirchhoff's Voltage and Current Law to the entire circuit. Briefly, the sum of the voltage drops around the circuit is equal to the source voltage. Voltage E_5 across $R5$ is 36 volts and voltage E_{ad} across $R4$ is 18 volts—that is,

$$E_s = E_5 + E_{ad},$$

or

$$54 = 36 + 18 \text{ volts.}$$

Likewise, the voltage drop, E_{bc}, across the parallel combination of $R1$ and $R2$ plus the voltage drop, E_3, across $R3$ should be equal to the voltage across points a and d. E_{bc} is 6 volts and E_3 is 12 volts. Therefore,

$$E_{ad} = E_{bc} + E_3 = 6 + 12 = 18 \text{ volts.}$$

Kirchhoff's Current Law says in effect that the sum of the branch currents is equal to the line current, I_t. The line current is 4.5 amperes, and therefore the sum of I_4 and I_3 should be 4.5 amperes, or

$$I_t = I_4 + I_3 = 1.5 + 3 = 4.5 \text{ amperes.}$$

The power consumed in a circuit element is determined by one of the three power formulas. For example, in figure 5-3 the power, P_1, consumed in $R1$ is

$$P_1 = I_1 E_{bc} = 2 \times 6 = 12 \text{ watts;}$$

the power P_2 consumed in $R2$ is

$$P_2 = I_2 E_{bc} = 1 \times 6 = 6 \text{ watts;}$$

the power P_3 consumed in $R3$ is

$$P_3 = I_3 E_3 = 3 \times 12 = 36 \text{ watts;}$$

the power P_4 consumed in $R4$ is

$$P_4 = I_4 E_4 = 1.5 \times 18 = 27 \text{ watts;}$$

and the power P_5 consumed in $R5$ is

$$P_5 = I_5 E_5 = 4.5 \times 36 = 162 \text{ watts.}$$

The total power, P_t, consumed is

$$P_t = P_1 + P_2 + P_3 + P_4 + P_5$$

$$= 12 + 6 + 36 + 27 + 162$$

$$= 243 \text{ watts.}$$

The total power is also equal to the total current multiplied by the source voltage, or

$$P_t = I_t E_s = 4.5 \times 54 = 243 \text{ watts.}$$

Voltage Dividers

In practically all electronic devices, such as radio receivers and transmitters, certain design requirements recur again and again. For instance, a typical radio receiver may require a number of different voltages at various points in its circuitry. In addition, all the various voltages must be derived from a single primary power supply. The most common method of meeting these requirements is by the use of a VOLTAGE-DIVIDER network. A typical voltage divider consists of two or more resistors connected in series across the primary power supply. The primary voltage E_s must be as high or higher than any of the individual voltages it is to supply. As the primary voltage is dropped by successive steps through the series resistors,

any desired fraction of the original voltage may be "tapped off" to supply individual requirements. The values of the series resistors to be used is dictated by the voltage drops required.

A voltage divider circuit is shown in figure 5-4. The divider is connected across a 270-volt source and supplies three loads simultaneously—10 ma. (one MILLIAMPERE is 0.001 ampere) at 90 volts, between terminal 1 and ground; 5 ma. at 150 volts, between terminal 2 and ground; and 30 ma. at 180 volts, between terminal 3 and ground. The current in resistor A is 15 ma. The current, voltage, resistance, and power of the 4 resistors are to be determined.

Kirchhoff's law of currents applied to terminal 1 indicates that the current in resistor B is

76

equal to the sum of 15 ma. from resistor A and 10 ma. from the 90-volt load. Thus,

$$I_b = 15 + 10, \text{ or } 25 \text{ ma.}$$

Similarly,

$$I_c = 25 + 5 = 30 \text{ ma.,}$$

and

$$I_d = 30 + 30 = 60 \text{ ma.}$$

Kirchhoff's Voltage Law indicates that the voltage across resistor A is 90 volts; the voltage across B is

$$E_b = 150 - 90, \text{ or } 60 \text{ volts;}$$

the voltage across C is

$$E_c = 180 - 150, \text{ or } 30 \text{ volts;}$$

and the voltage across D is

$$E_d = 270 - 180, \text{ or } 90 \text{ volts.}$$

Before solving for the various resistances it should be recalled that in the formula, $R = \dfrac{E}{I}$, R will be in ohms if E is in volts and I is in amperes. In many electronic circuits, particularly those being considered, it is just as valid and considerably simpler to let R be in thousands of ohms (k-ohms), E in volts, and I in milliamperes. In the following formulas this convention will be followed.

Applying Ohm's law to determine the resistances—

resistance of A is $R_a = \dfrac{E_a}{I_a} = \dfrac{90}{15} = 6$ k-ohms,

resistance of B is $R_b = \dfrac{E_b}{I_b} = \dfrac{60}{25} = 2.4$ k-ohms,

resistance of C is $R_c = \dfrac{E_c}{I_c} = \dfrac{30}{30} = 1$ k-ohm,

resistance of D is $R_d = \dfrac{E_d}{I_d} = \dfrac{90}{60} = 1.5$ k-ohms.

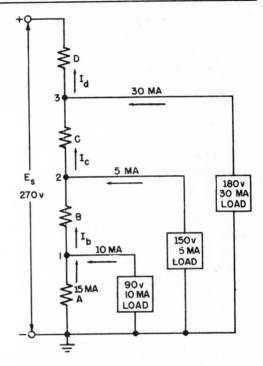

Figure 5-4.—Voltage divider, to determine R and P.

The power absorbed by

resistor A is $P_a = E_a I_a = 90 \times 0.015 = 1.35$ watts,

resistor B is $P_b = E_b I_b = 60 \times 0.025 = 1.50$ watts,

resistor C is $P_c = E_c I_c = 30 \times 0.030 = 0.90$ watts,

resistor D is $P_d = E_d I_d = 90 \times 0.060 = 5.40$ watts.

The total power absorbed by the 4 resistors is

$$1.35 + 1.50 + 0.90 + 5.40 = 9.15 \text{ watts.}$$

The power absorbed by the load connected to

terminal 1 is $P_1 = E_1 I_1 = 90 \times 0.010 = 0.90$ watt,

terminal 2 is $P_2 = E_2 I_2 = 150 \times 0.005 = 0.75$ watt,

terminal 3 is $P_3 = E_3 I_3 = 180 \times 0.030 = 5.4$ watts.

77

The total power supplied to the 3 loads is

$$0.90 + 0.75 + 5.4 = 7.05 \text{ watts.}$$

The total power supplied to the entire circuit including the voltage divider and the 3 loads is

$$9.15 + 7.05 = 16.2 \text{ watts.}$$

This value is checked as

$$P_t = E \times I_t = 270 \times 0.060 = 16.2 \text{ watts.}$$

In figure 5-5 the voltage divider resistances are given and the current in $R5$ is to be found. The load current in $R1$ is 6 ma.; the current in $R2$ is 4 ma.; and the current in $R3$ is 10 ma. The source voltage is 510 volts. Kirchhoff's Current Law may be applied at the junctions a, b, c, and d to determine expressions for the current in resistors $R4$, $R5$, $R6$, and $R7$. Accordingly, the current in $R4$ is $I + 6 + 4 + 10$, or $I + 20$; the current in $R5$ is I; the current in $R6$ is $I + 6$; the current in $R7$ is $I + 6 + 4$, or $I + 10$.

The voltage across $R4$ may be expressed in terms of the resistance in k-ohms and the current in milliamperes as $5(I + 20)$ volts. Similarly, the voltage across $R5$ is equal to $25I$; the voltage across $R6$ is $10(I + 6)$ and the voltage across $R7$ is $10(I + 10)$. Kirchhoff's law of voltages may be applied to the voltage divider to solve for the unknown current, I, by expressing the source voltage in terms of the given values of voltage, resistance, and current (both known and unknown values). The sum of the voltages across $R4$, $R5$, $R6$, and $R7$ is equal to the source voltage as follows:

$$E_4 + E_5 + E_6 + E_7 = E_s$$

$$5(I + 20) + 25I + 10(I + 6) + 10(I + 10) = 510$$

$$5I + 100 + 25I + 10I + 60 + 10I + 100 = 510$$

$$50I + 260 = 510$$

$$50I = 510 - 260$$

$$50I = 250$$

$$I = 5 \text{ ma.}$$

The current of 5 ma. through $R5$ produces a voltage drop across $R5$ of 5 x 25, or 125 volts.

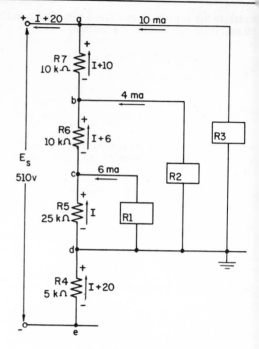

Figure 5-5.—Voltage divider, to determine E and R.

Since $R1$ is in parallel with $R5$, the voltage across load $R1$ is 125 volts. The current through $R4$ is 5 + 20, or 25 ma. and the corresponding voltage is 5 x 25, or 125 volts. Since point d is at ground potential, point c is 125 volts positive with respect to ground, whereas point e is 125 volts negative with respect to ground. The current in $R6$ is 5 + 6 or 11 ma. and the voltage drop across $R6$ is 11 x 10, or 110 volts. The current in $R7$ is 5 + 10, or 15 ma. and the voltage drop is 15 x 10 or 150 volts. The total voltage is the sum of the voltages across the divider. Thus,

$$125 + 125 + 110 + 150 = 510.$$

The power absorbed by each resistor in the voltage divider may be found by multiplying the voltage across the resistor by the current in the resistor. If the current is expressed in amperes and the e.m.f. in volts, the power will be expressed in watts. Thus the power in $R4$ is

$$P_4 = E_4 I_4 = 125 \times 0.025 = 3.125 \text{ watts.}$$

Similarly the power in $R5$ is $125 \times 0.005 = 0.625$ watts; the power in $R6$ is $110 \times 0.011 = 1.21$ watts; and in $R7$ is $150 \times 0.015 = 2.25$ watts. The total power in the divider is

$$3.125 + 0.625 + 1.21 + 2.25 = 7.21 \text{ watts.}$$

The voltage across load $R1$ is the voltage across $R5$, or 125 volts. The power in $R1$ is

$$P_1 = E_1 I_1 = 125 \times 0.006 = 0.750 \text{ watts.}$$

The voltage across load $R2$ is equal to the sum of the voltages across $R5$ and $R6$. Thus,

$$E_2 = E_5 + E_6 = 125 + 110 = 235 \text{ volts.}$$

The power in load $R2$ is

$$P_2 = E_2 I_2 = 235 \times 0.004 = 0.940 \text{ watts.}$$

The voltage across load $R3$ is equal to the sum of the voltages across $R5$, $R6$, and $R7$. Thus,

$$E_3 = E_5 + E_6 + E_7 = 125 + 110 + 150 = 385 \text{ volts.}$$

The power in load $R3$ is

$$P_3 = E_3 I_3 = 385 \times 0.010 = 3.85 \text{ watts,}$$

The total power in the three loads is

$$0.75 + 0.94 + 3.85 = 5.54 \text{ watts,}$$

and the total power supplied by the source is equal to the sum of the power absorbed by the voltage divider and the three loads, or

$$7.21 + 5.54 = 12.75 \text{ watts.}$$

The total power may be checked by

$$P_t = E_t I_t = 510 \times 0.025 = 12.75 \text{ watts.}$$

The resistances of load resistors $R1$, $R2$, and $R3$ are determined by means of Ohm's law as follows:

$$R_1 = \frac{E_1}{I_1} = \frac{125}{6} = 20.83 \text{ k-ohms,}$$

$$R_2 = \frac{E_2}{I_2} = \frac{235}{4} = 58.75 \text{ k-ohms,}$$

and

$$R_3 = \frac{E_3}{I_3} = \frac{385}{10} = 38.5 \text{ k-ohms.}$$

Attenuators

Attenuators are networks of resistors that are used to obtain the proper voltage, current, or power required by a load. They always reduce (attenuate) the source voltage to a lower value required by the load. Two of the simpler types of attenuators are the L and T types shown in figure 5-6.

If the device is adjustable, as shown, it is called an "attenuator"; if it is nonadjustable it is commonly called a "pad."

The L-type attenuator maintains constant resistance at ONE pair of terminals for any setting of the variable resistors. For example, in figure 5-6 (A), the resistance presented by the load and the attenuator to terminals ab should always be constant for any setting of ganged (grouped) resistors $R1$ and $R2$. This constant resistance must be equal to R_S in order to obtain maximum power transfer from the source to the attenuator and load.

In figure 5-6 (A), the resistance offered to the flow of current through the terminals a and b includes (1) R_S and (2) R_1 acting in series with the parallel combination of R_2 and R_L. In this circuit $R_S = R_L$, or

$$R_s = R_1 + \frac{R_2 R_L}{R_2 + R_L}$$

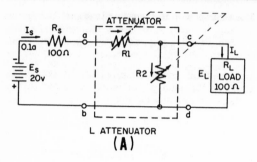

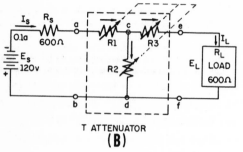

Figure 5-6.—L and T attenuators.

Thus it may be seen that R_1 and R_2 are adjusted so that

$$R_L = R_1 - \frac{R_2 R_L}{R_2 + R_L}$$

The resistance offered to the flow of current through terminals c and d includes (1) R_2 acting in parallel with the series combination of R_1 and R_S, and (2) R_L. The L attenuator operates properly only if the load is connected to terminals cd and the source to terminals ab. The load and the source are not interchangeable, because R_L is not equal to

$$\frac{R_2 (R_1 + R_s)}{R_2 + R_1 + R_s}.$$

The T-type attenuator, shown in figure 5-6 (B), maintains at BOTH pairs of terminals a constant resistance for any setting of the ganged variable resistor. As may be seen in the figure, an extra variable resistor is needed in the T-type attenuator, and the circuit is therefore more

complicated than the L-type attenuator circuit.

In the T attenuator, the resistance offered to the flow of current through terminals a and b includes (1) R_S and (2) R_1 acting in series with the parallel combination, one branch of which is R_2 and the other branch of which is R_3 acting in series with R_L. In this circuit,

$$R_s = R_1 + \frac{R_2 (R_3 + R_L)}{R_2 + R_3 + R_L}.$$

The resistance offered to the flow of current through terminals e and f includes (1) R_3 in series with the parallel combination, one branch of which is R_2 and the other branch of which is R_1 acting in series with R_S and (2) R_L. In this circuit,

$$R_L = R_3 + \frac{R_2 (R_1 + R_s)}{R_2 + R_1 + R_3}.$$

Because $R_S = R_L$ and $R_1 = R_3$, the load and the source are interchangeable without affecting the operation of the T attenuator. Thus, the resistance offered to the flow of current through terminals a and b is equal to the resistance offered to the flow of current through terminals e and f.

There are other types of attenuators that are even more complicated—for example, ladder attenuators, so called because the circuit looks like a ladder; bridge-T attenuators, in which the two resistors forming the top member of the T are paralleled, or bridged, by another resistor; and decimal attenuators, in which the resistors are arranged so that the current or voltage may be reduced in steps equal to decimal fractions of the full-load values.

It is often desirable, especially in communication circuits, to lower the voltage applied to a load in order to attenuate the signal, and yet to permit the same amount of current to be drawn from the source as was drawn before the voltage across the load was lowered. Thus the load on the source remains constant and its characteristics are not altered when the load signal is weakened. The L-type of attenuator is one of the simplest circuits that may be used to accomplish this result.

L ATTENUATOR

In the L-type attenuator shown in figure 5-6 (A), the two objectives are: (1) To vary the load voltage, and (2) to maintain constant current through the source when the load voltage is varied. The source resistance is 100 ohms, the load resistance is 100 ohms, and the source voltage is 20 volts. Before the attenuator is inserted, the current delivered to the load is

$$I_s = \frac{E_s}{R_L + R_s} = \frac{20}{100 + 100} = 0.1 \text{ ampere.}$$

The load voltage in this case is $E_L = I_S R_L$ = 0.1 x 100 = 10 volts. The voltage lost in the source is 20 - 10 = 10 volts, which is the equivalent of 0.1 ampere flowing through the source resistance of 100 ohms.

To reduce the voltage across R_L, (fig. 5-6 (A)) to 5 volts and maintain the source current at 0.1 ampere, $R1$ and $R2$ are inserted. The current, I_L, through R_L is

$$I_L = \frac{E_L}{R_L} = \frac{5}{100} = 0.05 \text{ ampere.}$$

The current through $R1$ is 0.1 ampere, since it is in series with the source, and the voltage drop across $R1$ is the difference between the source voltage and the sum of the voltage drops in the source and across the load, or 20 - (10 + 5) = 5 volts. The resistance of $R1$ is $\frac{5}{0.1}$ = 50 ohms.

The current through $R2$ is the difference between the source current of 0.1 ampere and the load current of 0.05 ampere, or 0.05 ampere. The voltage across $R2$ is 5 volts because it is in parallel with the load. The resistance of $R2$ is $\frac{5}{0.05}$ = 100 ohms.

Thus, by inserting 50 ohms in series with the source and 100 ohms in shunt(parallel)with the load, the load voltage is reduced to 5 volts and the source current is maintained at 0.1 ampere. In this way the load on the source is maintained constant while the signal voltage at the load is reduced to one-half its original value.

The parallel resistance of $R2$ and R_L is 50 ohms and the total resistance of R1 in series with the parallel combination is 50 + 50, or 100 ohms. Thus, the same resistance is presented to the source after the insertion of R1 and $R2$ as before, and the load on the source remains the same.

T ATTENUATOR

In the T attenuator of figure 5-6 (B), R_S = 600 ohms, R_L = 600 ohms, and the source voltage is 120 volts. In this example, the attenuator is adjusted to reduce the load voltage to one-half its rated value. The problem is to find the necessary resistance values of $R1$, $R2$, and $R3$. Before the attenuator is inserted, the load current is equal to $\frac{120}{600 + 600}$ = 0.1 ampere and the rated load voltage, E_L is 0.1 x 600 = 60 volts. The attenuator reduces the load voltage to $\frac{1}{2}$ of 60, or 30 volts.

The load current with 30 volts applied to the load will be $\frac{30}{600}$ = 0.05 ampere. Since the total current must remain 0.1 ampere, the current through $R2$ will be 0.1 - 0.05 = 0.05 ampere.

The algebraic sum of the voltages around circuit $dcefd$ is equal to zero, and these may be expressed in terms of current, resistance, and voltage as,

$$+ 0.05R_2 - 0.05R_3 - 30 = 0,$$

and since $R_3 = R_1$,

$$0.05R_2 - 0.05R_1 = 30. \tag{5-1}$$

The algebraic sum of the voltages around circuit $bacdb$ is equal to zero. Thus,

$$120 - 0.1 \times 600 - 0.1R_1 - 0.05R_2 = 0$$

$$0.05R_2 + 0.1R_1 = 60. \tag{5-2}$$

Subtracting equation (5-1) from equation (5-2) and solving for R_1,

$$0.05R_2 + 0.1R_1 = 60$$

$$0.05R_2 - 0.05R_1 = 30$$

$$\overline{0 + 0.15R_1 = 30}$$

$$R_1 = 200 \text{ ohms} = R_3.$$

Substituting the value of R_1 in equation (5-1),

$$0.05R_2 - 0.05(200) = 30$$

$$0.05R_2 = 40$$

$$R_2 = 800 \text{ ohms.}$$

The resistance to the flow of current through terminals a and b includes (1) the 600-ohm source and (2) the attenuator resistance, R_{ab}.

$$R_{ab} = R_1 + \frac{R_2(R_3 + R_L)}{R_2 + R_3 + R_L}$$

$$= 200 + \frac{800(200 + 600)}{800 + 200 + 600}$$

$$= 200 + 400$$

$$= 600 \text{ ohms.}$$

The resistance to the flow of current through terminals e and f includes (1) the 600-ohm load and (2) attenuator resistance, R_{ef}.

$$R_{ef} = R_3 + \frac{R_3(R_1 + R_s)}{R_2 + R_1 + R_s}$$

$$= 200 + \frac{800(200 + 600)}{800 + 200 + 600}$$

$$= 200 + 400$$

$$= 600 \text{ ohms.}$$

Thus, $R_{ef} = R_{ab}$ and both the load and the source see the same resistance "looking" into the T attenuator. The source current I_s is

$$\frac{E_s}{R_s + R_{ab}} = \frac{120}{600 + 600} = 0.1 \text{ ampere.}$$

The input voltage E_{ab} to the attenuator is

$$I_s R_{ab} = 0.1 \times 600 = 60 \text{ volts.}$$

The voltage drop across R_1 is

$$I_s R_1 = 0.1 \times 200 = 20 \text{ volts.}$$

The voltage drop across R_2 is

$$I_2 R_2 = 0.05 \times 800 = 40 \text{ volts.}$$

The voltage drop across R_3 is

$$I_3 R_3 = 0.05 \times 200 = 10 \text{ volts.}$$

Thus, the voltage across the load is

$$40 - 10 = 30 \text{ volts.}$$

Bridge Circuits

THE SIMPLE RESISTANCE BRIDGE

A resistance bridge circuit in its simplest form is shown in figure 5-7. Two identical resistors, $R1$ and $R2$, are connected in parallel across a 20-volt power source. The network be-comes a bridge circuit when a cross connection, or "bridge" is placed between the two resistors. Voltage across both resistors is dropped at the same rate, because the resistors are identical. Therefore, points $a-a'$, $b-b'$, $c-c'$, and $d-d'$ are at equal potentials. If the bridge is connected between points of equal potential, as in figure 5-7 (A), no current will flow through the bridge. However, if the bridge is connected between points of unequal potential, current will flow from the more negative to the less negative end, as shown in figure 5-7 (B). In (B), current flows right-to-left from b' to d. In (C), current flows left-to-right from a to c'. Thus, it can be seen that the direction of bridge current is controlled by the relative potential of the two ends of the bridge resistor. When the bridge is across equal potentials, and no current flows, it is said to be BALANCED. When it is across unequal potentials, and current tends to flow, it is said to be UNBALANCED. The bridge may be unbalanced in either or both of two ways —(1) by connecting the bridge to unequal potentials, or (2) by using resistors of unequal values, thus causing an unbalance.

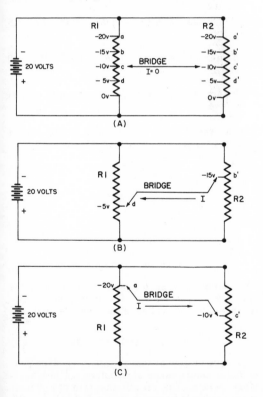

Figure 5-7.—Simple resistance bridges.

UNBALANCED RESISTANCE BRIDGE

Figure 5-8 shows an unbalanced bridge using unequal resistors. The two parallel legs are $R1$-$R4$ and $R3$-$R5$. $R2$ is the bridge. The current and voltage drop of each resistor, and the source voltage E_S, are to be determined.

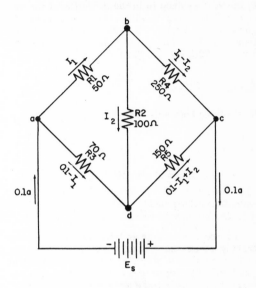

Figure 5-8.—Unbalance resistance bridge.

The current of 0.1 ampere flowing into junction a divides into two parts. The part flowing through $R1$ is indicated as I_1 and the part through $R3$ is 0.1 - I_1. Similarly, at junction b, I_1 divides, part flowing through $R2$ and the remainder through R4. The part through $R2$ is designated I_2 and the part through $R4$ is I_1 - I_2. The direction of current through $R2$ may be assumed arbitrarily.

If the solution indicates a positive value for I_2 the assumed direction is proved to be correct. The current through $R4$ is I_1 - I_2. At junction d the currents may be analyzed in a similar manner. Current I_2 through $R2$ joins current 0.1 - I_1, from $R3$; and the current through $R5$ is 0.1 - I_1 + I_2.

The unknown currents, I_1 and I_2, may be determined by establishing two voltage equations in which they both appear. These equations are solved for I_1 and I_2 in terms of the given values of current and resistance. The first voltage equation is developed by tracing clockwise around the closed circuit containing resistors $R1$, $R2$, and $R3$. The trace starts at junction a, and proceeds to b, to d, and back to a. The algebraic sum of the voltages around this circuit is zero. These voltages are expressed in terms of resistance and current. Going from a to b, the voltage drop is in the direction of the arrow and is equal to $-50I_1$; the drop across $R2$, going from b to d, is $-100I_2$; and the voltage from d to a (in the opposite direction to the arrow) is $+70(0.1 - I_1)$. Thus,

$$-50I_1 - 100I_2 + 70(0.1 - I_1) = 0.$$

Multiplying both sides by -1,

$$50I + 100I_2 - 70(0.1 - I_1) = 0,$$

and transposing and simplifying,

$$120I_1 + 100I_2 = 7. \qquad (5\text{-}3)$$

The second voltage equation is established by tracing clockwise around the circuit, which includes resistors $R4$, $R5$, and $R2$. Starting at junction b, the trace proceeds to c, to d, and returns to b. The voltage across $R4$, from b to c, is $-250(I_1 - I_2)$; the voltage across $R5$, from c to d, is $+150(0.1 - I_1 + I_2)$; and the voltage across $R2$, from d to b, is $+100I_2$. Thus,

$$-250(I_1 - I_2) + 150(0.1 - I_1 + I_2) + 100I_2 = 0$$

from which,

$$400I_1 - 500I_2 = 15. \qquad (5\text{-}4)$$

Equations (5-3) and (5-4) may be solved simultaneously by multiplying equation (5-3) by the factor 5 and then adding the equations to eliminate I_2 as follows:

$$400I_1 - 500I_2 = 15$$

$$600I_1 + 500I_2 = 35$$

$$\overline{\rule{3cm}{0.4pt}}$$

$$1{,}000I_1 = 50$$

$$I_1 = 0.05 \text{ ampere.}$$

Substituting the value of 0.05 for I_1 in equation (5-3) and solving for I_2,

$$120(0.05) + 100I_2 = 7$$

$$100I_2 = 1$$

$$I_2 = 0.01 \text{ ampere.}$$

Thus the current in $R1$ is $I_1 = 0.05$ ampere. The current in $R2$ is $I_2 = 0.01$ ampere. The current in $R3$ is $0.1 - I_1 = 0.1 - 0.05$, or 0.05 ampere. The current in $R4$ is $I_1 - I_2 = 0.05 - 0.01$, or 0.04 ampere. The current in $R5$ is $0.1 - I_1 + I_2 = 0.1 - 0.05 + 0.01 = 0.06$ ampere. The voltages E_1, E_2, E_3, E_4, and E_5 are as follows:

E_1 across $R1$ is $I_1R_1 = 0.05 \times 50 = 2.5$ volts.

E_2 across $R2$ is $I_2R_2 = 0.01 \times 100 = 1.0$ volts.

E_3 across $R3$ is $(0.1 - I_1)R_3 = 0.05 \times 70 = 3.5$ volts.

E_4 across $R4$ is $(I_1 - I_2)R_4 = 0.04 \times 250 = 10$ volts.

E_5 across $R5$ is $(0.1 - I_1 + I_2)R_5 = 0.06 \times 150 = 9.0$ volts.

The source voltage E_s is equal to the sum of voltages across $R3$ and $R5$ or $R1$ and $R4$. Thus,

$$E_s = E_1 + E_4$$

$$= 2.5 + 10 = 12.5 \text{ volts,}$$

and

$$E_s = E_3 + E_5$$

$$= 3.5 + 9 = 12.5 \text{ volts.}$$

The voltage across $R2$ is the difference in the voltages across $R3$ and $R1$. It is also the difference in the voltages across $R4$ and $R5$.

WHEATSTONE BRIDGE

A type of circuit that is widely used for precision measurements of resistance is the Wheatstone bridge. The circuit diagram of a Wheatstone bridge is shown in figure 5-9 (A). $R1$, $R2$, and $R3$ are precision variable resistors, and R_x

is the resistor whose unknown value of resistance is to be determined. After the bridge has been properly balanced, the unknown resistance may be determined by means of a simple formula. The galvanometer, G, is inserted across terminals b and d to indicate the condition of balance. When the bridge is properly balanced there is no difference in potential across terminals bd, and the galvanometer deflection, when the switch is closed, will be zero.

The operation of the bridge is explained in a few logical steps. When the switch to the battery is closed, electrons flow from the negative terminal of the battery to point a. Here the current divides, as it would in any parallel circuit, a part of it passing through $R1$ and $R2$ and the remainder passing through $R3$ and R_x. The two currents, labeled I_1 and I_2, unite at point c and return to the positive terminal of the battery. The value of I_1 depends on the sum of resistances R_1 and R_2, and the value of I_2 depends on the sum of resistances R_3 and R_x. In each case, according to Ohm's law, the current is inversely proportional to the resistance.

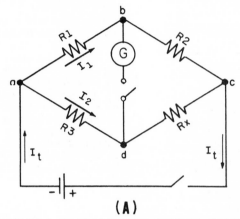

(A)

SCHEMATIC WHEATSTONE-BRIDGE CIRCUIT

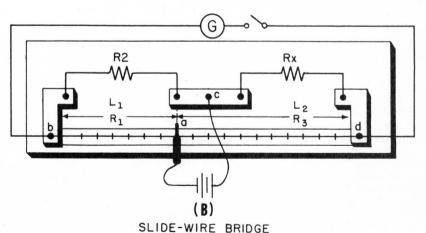

(B)

SLIDE-WIRE BRIDGE

Figure 5-9.—Wheatstone bridge circuit.

85

$R1$, $R2$, and $R3$ are adjusted so that when the galvanometer switch is closed there will be no deflection of the needle. When the galvanometer shows no deflection there is no difference of potential between points b and d. This means that the voltage drop (E_1) across $R1$, between points a and b, is the same as the voltage drop (E_3) across $R3$, between points a and d. By similar reasoning, the voltage drops across $R2$ and R_x—that is, E_2 and E_x—are also equal. Expressed algebraically,

$$E_1 = E_3,$$

or

$$I_1 R_1 = I_2 R_3,$$

and

$$E_2 = E_x,$$

or

$$I_1 R_2 = I_2 R_x.$$

Dividing the voltage drops across $R1$ and $R3$ by the respective voltage drops across $R2$ and R_x,

$$\frac{I_1 R_1}{I_1 R_2} = \frac{I_2 R_3}{I_2 R_x}.$$

Simplifying,

$$\frac{R_1}{R_2} = \frac{R_3}{R_x}.$$

Therefore,

$$R_x = \frac{R_2 R_3}{R_1}.$$

The resistance values of $R1$, $R2$, and $R3$ are readily determined from the markings on the standard resistors, or from the calibrated dials if a dial-type bridge is used.

The Wheatstone bridge may be of the slide-wire type, as shown in figure 5-9 (B). In the slide-wire circuit, the slide-wire (b to d), corresponds to R_1 and R_3 of figure 5-9 (A). The wire may be an alloy of uniform cross section; for example German silver or nichrome, having a resistance of about 100 ohms. Point a is established where the slider contacts the wire. The bridge is balanced by moving the slider along the wire.

The equation for solving for R_x in the slide-wire bridge of figure 5-9 (B), is similar to the one used for solving for R_x in figure 5-9 (A). However, in the slide-wire bridge the length L_1 corresponds to the resistance R_1, and the length L_2 corresponds to the resistance R_3. Therefore, L_1 and L_2 may be substituted for R_1 and R_3 in the equation. The resistance of L_1 and L_2 varies uniformly with slider movement because in a wire of uniform cross section the resistance varies directly with the length; therfore the ratio of the resistances equals to the corresponding ratio of the lengths. Substituting L_1 and L_2 for R_1 and R_3

$$R_x = \frac{L_2 R_2}{L_1}.$$

A meter stick is mounted underneath the slide-wire and L1 and L2 are easily read in centimeters. For example, if a balance is obtained when R2 - 150 ohms, L1 25 cm. and L2 = 75 cm., the unknown resistance is

$$R_x = \frac{75}{25} \times 150 = 450 \text{ ohms.}$$

Parallel Sources Supplying A Common Load

The circuit shown in figure 5-10 illustrates two sources of e.m.f., E_{s1} and E_{s2}, having internal resistances of 2 and 2.5 ohms respectively, connected in parallel, and supplying a 5-ohm load. Neglecting the resistance of the lead wires, it is desired to determine the current delivered by each source to the load, the load current, and the load voltage.

The problem may be solved by establishing two voltage equations in which the voltages are expressed in terms of the unknown currents I_1 and I_2, the known resistances, and the known voltages. The equations are then solved simultaneously as in previous examples, to eliminate one of the unknown currents. The other unknown current is solved by substitution.

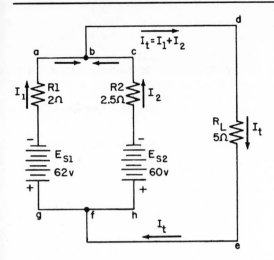

Figure 5-10.—Parallel sources supplying a common load.

The first voltage equation is established by starting at point g and tracing clockwise around circuit $gabdefg$. The total load current is equal to the sum of the source currents, $I_1 + I_2$. The first voltage equation is,

$$62 - 2I_1 - 5(I_1 + I_2) = 0,$$

from which,

$$7I_1 + 5I_2 = 62. \qquad (5-5)$$

The second voltage equation is established by starting at point h and tracing around circuit $hcbdefh$. Thus,

$$60 - 2.5I_2 - 5(I_1 + I_2) = 0,$$

from which,

$$5I_1 + 7.5I_2 = 60. \qquad (5-6)$$

I_2 is eliminated by multiplying equation (5-5) by 1.5 and subtracting equation (5-6) from the result, as follows:

$$10.5I_1 + 7.5I_2 = 93$$

$$\underline{5.0I_1 + 7.5I_2 = 60}$$

$$5.5I_1 = 33$$

$$I_1 = 6 \text{ amperes.}$$

Substituting this value in equation (5-5),

$$7 \times 6 + 5I_2 = 62,$$

from which

$$I_2 = 4 \text{ amperes.}$$

The load current is $I_1 + I_2 = 6 + 4 = 10$ amperes. Thus source E_{S1} supplies 6 amperes and source E_{S2} supplies 4 amperes.

The load voltage is equal to the voltage developed across terminals f and b and is equal to the difference in a given source voltage and the internal voltage absorbed across the corresponding source resistance.

The statement applies equally to either source since both are in parallel with the load. In terms of source E_{S1}

$$E_{fb} = E_{s1} - I_1 R_1$$

$$= 62 - 6 \times 2$$

$$= 50 \text{ volts,}$$

and in terms of source E_{S2}

$$E_{fb} = E_{s2} - I_2 R_2$$

$$= 60 - 4 \times 2.5$$

$$= 50 \text{ volts.}$$

A further check on the load voltage is to express this value in terms of the load current and the load resistance as follows:

$$E_{fb} = (I_1 + I_2) R_L$$

$$= (6 + 4)(5)$$

$$= 50 \text{ volts.}$$

87

Distribution Circuits

TWO-WIRE DISTRIBUTION CIRCUITS

Up to this point the voltage drop and the power lost in the line wires connecting the load and the source have been neglected. When the load is located at some distance from the source, the line resistance becomes an appreciable part of the total circuit resistance and the voltage and power lost in the line become significant even with moderate loads.

In figure 5-11, load M draws 7 amperes through terminals b and e, and the parallel group of lamps draws 5 amperes through terminals c and d. The current in line wires bc and de is 5 amperes. The line current in wires ab and ef is $5 + 7 = 12$ amperes.

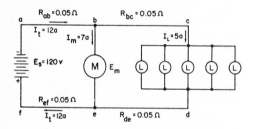

Figure 5-11.—Simple two-wire distribution circuit.

The voltage source supplies a constant potential of 120 volts between points a and f. The resistance of line wires ab and ef is $2 \times 0.05 = 0.1$ ohm. The voltage drop across line wires ab and ef is $12 \times 0.1 = 1.2$ volts. The voltage drop across line wires bc and de is $5 \times 0.1 = 0.5$ volt. The voltage across M is $120 - 1.2 = 118.8$ volts and the voltage across the five lamps is $118.8 - 0.5 = 118.3$ volts.

The power dissipated in line wires ab and ef is equal to $(12)^2 \times 0.1 = 144.4$ watts. The power absorbed by line wires bc and de is $(5)^2 \times 0.1 = 2.5$ watts. The total power absorbed by the line wires is $14.4 + 2.5 = 16.9$ watts.

The power delivered to load M is $118.8 \times 7 = 831.6$ watts, and to the 5 lamps is $118.3 \times 5 = 591.5$ watts. The total power supplied to the entire circuit is equal to $16.9 + 831.6 + 591.5 =$

1,440 watts and is equal to the product of the total applied voltage and the total current. Thus,

$$P_t = E_t I_t = 120 \times 12 = 1,440 \text{ watts.}$$

THREE-WIRE DISTRIBUTION CIRCUITS

Three-wire distribution circuits transmit power at 240 volts and utilize it at 120 volts. The direct-current 3-wire system includes a positive feeder, a negative feeder, and a neutral wire, as shown in figure 5-12 (A). The loads are connected between the negative feeder and the neutral, and between the positive feeder and the neutral. When the loads are unbalanced (unequal) the neutral wire carries a current equal to the difference in the currents in the negative and positive feeders.

In the example of figure 5-12 (A), load $L1$ draws 10 amperes, load $L2$ draws 4 amperes, and the neutral wire carries a current of $10 - 4 = 6$ amperes. The direction of flow of the current in the neutral wire is always the same as that of the smaller of the currents in the positive and negative feeders. Thus the flow is to the left in the lower (positive) wire and also in the neutral. The current in the upper (negative) wire is 10 amperes and in the lower wire is 4 amperes. The algebraic sum of the currents entering and leaving junction c is equal to zero. Thus,

$$+ 10 - 6 - 4 = 0.$$

To find load voltage, $E1$, a voltage equation is established in which $E1$ is expressed in terms of the source voltage, E_{S1}, and the IR drops in the negative feeder and neutral wire. The algebraic sum of the voltages around the circuit $fabcf$, is equal to zero. Starting at f and proceeding clockwise,

$$+ 120 - 10 \times 0.5 - E_1 - 6 \times 0.5 = 0$$

$$E_1 = 112 \text{ volts.}$$

Thus the voltage across load $L1$ is 112 volts. This voltage is less than the source voltage by an amount equal to the sum of the voltage drops in

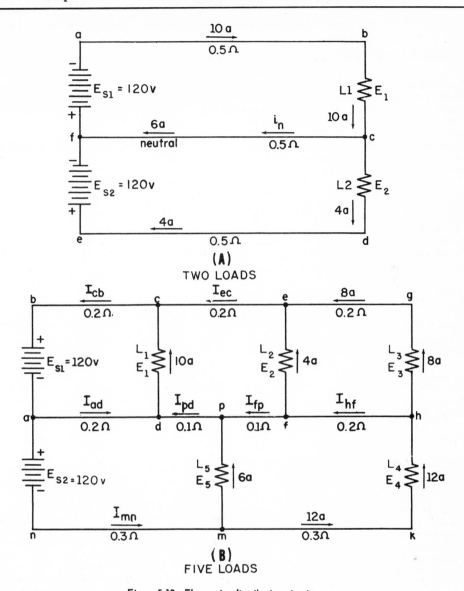

(A)
TWO LOADS

(B)
FIVE LOADS

Figure 5-12.—Three-wire distribution circuits.

the negative (5 volts) and the neutral (3 volts) wires.

To find load voltage E_2 a voltage equation is established in which E_2 is expressed in terms of the source voltage, E_{S2}, and the IR drops in the positive feeder and the neutral wire. The alge-

braic sum of the voltages around the circuit $efcde$ is zero. Starting at e and proceeding clockwise,

$$+ 120 + (6 \times 0.5) - E_2 - (4 \times 0.5) = 0$$

$$E_2 = 121 \text{ volts.}$$

89

In tracing the circuit from f to c note that the direction is against the arrow representing current flow, and therefore that the IR drop of (6 x 0.5) volts is preceded by a plus sign. The load voltage, E_2, is 121 volts, which is 1 volt higher than the source voltage, E_{S2}. The total source voltage $(E_{S1} + E_{S2})$ is 240 volts and the total load voltage $(E_1 + E_2)$ is 112 + 121 = 233 volts. This value is also equal to the difference between the total source voltage and the sum of the voltage drops in the positive and negative feeders, or 240 - (2 + 5) = 233 volts.

When the loads are balanced on the positive and negative sides of the 3-wire system, the neutral current is zero and the currents in the outside wires (positive and negative) are equal. When the loads are unbalanced the neutral wire carries the unbalanced current. The voltage on the heavily loaded side falls while the voltage on the lightly loaded side rises. The lower the resistance of the neutral wire, the less unbalance in voltage there will be for a given unbalanced load.

A more complicated 3-wire circuit is shown in figure 5-12 (B). The source voltage is 120 volts between each outside wire and the neutral, or center, wire. Load currents in the upper side of the system are indicated as 10, 4, and 8 amperes respectively for loads 1, 2, and 3. In the lower side of the system, the load currents are 12 and 6 amperes respectively for loads 4 and 5. In order to determine the various load voltages it is necessary to find the currents in each outside wire and in the neutral wire. The resistances of these wires are indicated, and therefore the voltage drops and the load voltages may be calculated after the currents are determined.

To find the currents in the various sections of the wires, it is best to start at the load farthest removed from the source. The polarities of the sources are such that electrons flow out of the negative terminal at n and return to the positive terminal at b.

Currents flowing toward a junction are assumed to be positive, and those flowing away from a junction are assumed to be negative. Applying Kirchhoff's Current Law at junction h, the neutral current, I_n (flowing from h to f) is determined as

$$12 - 8 - I_{hf} = 0$$

$$I_{hf} = 4 \text{ amperes.}$$

Applying the same rule successively to junctions f, e, p, m, d, and c, it follows that:

at junction f,

$$4 - 4 - I_{fp} = 0$$

$$I_{fp} = 0 \text{ ampere,}$$

at junction e,

$$4 + 8 - I_{ec} = 0$$

$$I_{ec} = 12 \text{ amperes,}$$

at junction p,

$$6 + 0 - I_{pd} = 0$$

$$I_{pd} = 6 \text{ amperes,}$$

at junction m,

$$+ I_{mn} - 6 - 12 = 0$$

$$I_{mn} = 18 \text{ amperes,}$$

at junction d,

$$I_{ad} + 6 - 10 = 0$$

$$I_{ad} = 4 \text{ amperes,}$$

at junction c,

$$I_{cb} + 10 + 12 = 0$$

$$I_{cb} = 22 \text{ amperes.}$$

Thus, E_{S1} supplies 22 amperes and E_{S2} supplies 18 amperes. The electron flow in all parts of the lower wire is outward from the source, and the electron flow in all parts of the upper wire is back toward the source. The current in the neutral wire is always equal to the difference in the currents in the two outside wires, and the electron flow is in the direction of the smaller of these two currents. Thus in figure 5-12 (B), the neutral current in section ad is 4 amperes, which is the difference between 18 amperes and 22 amperes; and it is in the direction of the smaller current in section nm. The neutral current in section pd is 6 amperes, which is the difference between 18 amperes and 12 amperes; and it is in the same direction as the 12 amperes in section ec. The neutral current in section fp is zero because the current in each outside wire in that section is 12 amperes. The neutral current in section *hf* is 4 amperes, which is the difference between 12 amperes and 8 amperes, and it is in the direction of the smaller outside current in section *ge*.

In order to find the voltages across the loads in figure 5-12 (B), Kirchhoff's Voltage Law is applied to the various individual circuits. Thus to find the voltage, E_1, across load L_1, the algebraic sum of the voltages around the circuit *abcda* is equated to zero, and E_1 is then readily determined. Starting at *a*,

$$- 120 + (22 \times 0.2) + E_1 + (4 \times 0.2) = 0$$

$$E_1 = 114.8 \text{ volts.}$$

To find load voltage E_2, the algebraic sum of the voltages around circuit *dcefpd* is set equal to zero. Starting at *d*,

$$- 114.8 + (12 \times 0.2) + E_2 + (0 \times 0.1) - (6 \times 0.1) = 0$$

$$E_2 = 113 \text{ volts.}$$

To find load voltage E_3, the algebraic sum of the voltages around loop *feghf* is set equal to zero. Starting at *f*,

$$- 113 + (8 \times 0.2) + E_3 - (4 \times 0.2) = 0$$

$$E_3 = 112.2 \text{ volts.}$$

To find load voltage E_4, the algebraic sum of the voltages around loop *nadpfhkmn* is set equal to zero. Loop *mpfhkm* cannot be used because it would contain two unknown voltages, E_5 and E_4. Starting at *n*,

$$- 120 - (4 \times 0.2) + (6 \times 0.1) + (0 \times 0.1) + (4 \times 0.2) + E_4$$

$$+ (12 \times 0.3) + (18 \times 0.3) = 0$$

$$E_4 = 110.4 \text{ volts.}$$

To find load voltage E_5, the algebraic sum of the voltages around loop *nadpmn* is set equal to zero. Starting at *n*,

$$- 120 - (4 \times 0.2) + (6 \times 0.1) + E_5 + (18 \times 0.3) = 0$$

$$E_5 = 114.8 \text{ volts.}$$

In each case, the equations used contain one unknown; and thus a simple solution is quickly obtained. It is necessary that the path traced include a completely closed loop and that all but one of the voltages within that loop be known. Simple transposition of the resulting equation gives the desired voltage.

QUIZ

1. The minimum number of resistors in a compound circuit is/are
   a. four
   b. three
   c. two
   d. one
2. Total resistance of the circuit shown is determined by the formula

   a. $R_1 R_2 + \dfrac{R_3 R_4}{R_4 + R_3}$

   b. $R_1 + R_2 + \dfrac{R_3 + R_4}{R_3 R_4}$

   c. $R_1 + R_2 + \dfrac{R_3 R_4}{R_3 + R_4}$

   d. $R_1 + R_2 \left(\dfrac{R_3 R_4}{R_3 + R_4} \right)$

3. In the circuit below -- what is the value of I_t?
   a. $I_t = 1.14$ amp
   b. $I_t = 0.4$ amp
   c. $I_t = 0.667$ amp
   d. $I_t = 1$ amp

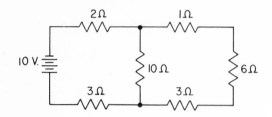

4. In the circuit in question 3, how much power is consumed by the 6-ohm resistor?
   a. 15 watts
   b. 1.5 watts
   c. 60 watts
   d. 6 watts

5. A voltage divider is used to
   a. provide different voltage values for multiple loads from a single source
   b. provide several voltage drops in parallel
   c. increase the voltage to the load at several taps
   d. provide tap points to alter power supplied

6. The total power supplied to the entire circuit by a voltage divider and 4 loads is the
   a. sum of the 4 loads
   b. voltage divider minus 4 loads
   c. voltage divider plus the 4 loads
   d. voltage divider only

7. The total voltage of a voltage divider is the
   a. input voltage minus the load's voltages
   b. the load's voltages only
   c. sum of the input and load voltage
   d. sum of the voltages across the divider

8. An attenuator is
   a. a network of resistors used to reduce power, voltage or current
   b. a network of resistors to change the input voltage
   c. also called a pad
   d. used in every power circuit

9. In an attenuator, the resistors are
   a. adjusted separately
   b. connected in parallel with the load
   c. connected in series with the load
   d. ganged

10. What two conditions may be observed in a bridge circuit?
    a. T and L network characteristics
    b. No-load and full-load bridge current
    c. Unequal potential and unequal current
    d. Balance and unbalance

11. In the circuit below—how much current flows in the 20θ resistor and what is its direction?
    a. 26 a., B to A
    b. 1 a., A to B
    c. 0.26 a., A to B
    d. 1 a., B to A

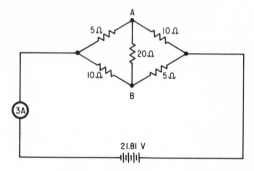

12. In a three-wire distribution system, an unbalanced situation is indicated by the
    a. potential of the positive wire being equal to the negative wire
    b. positive wire carrying more amperage than the negative wire
    c. current in the neutral wire
    d. neutral wire carrying the total current

13. In figure 5-9 (A), the galvanometer will show zero deflection when

   a. $\dfrac{R_1}{R_2} = \dfrac{R_3}{R_x}$

   b. $R_x = \dfrac{R_1 R_3}{R_2}$

   c. $\dfrac{I_1 R_1}{I_2 R_x} = \dfrac{I_2 R_3}{I_1 R_2}$

   d. $R_x = \dfrac{R_1 R_2}{R_3}$

14. In the Wheatstone bridge type circuit below, the bridge current is toward point A. The resistance of R_x is
    a. 30θ
    b. greater than 45θ
    c. 20θ
    d. less than 15θ

16. In the circuit below I line is
    a. 4.44 a.
    b. 0.444 a.
    c. 0.522 a.
    d. 5.22 a.

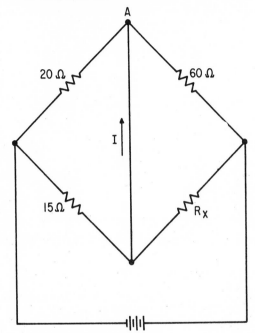

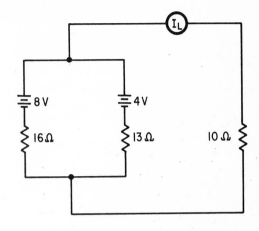

17. When checking a 3-wire distribution circuit going against the direction of current flow the IR drop is always
    a. negative
    b. positive
    c. not used
    d. always in direction of current flow

15. In the slide-wire bridge, shown in figure 5-9 (B), L_1 is equal to

    a. $L_1 = \dfrac{R_2 L_2}{R_1}$

    b. $L_1 = \dfrac{R_1 + L_2}{R_2}$

    c. $\dfrac{R_2}{R_1 L_2} = L_1$

    d. $\dfrac{R_1 L_2}{R_2} = L_1$

18. In the circuit below, the voltage drop across the 3-ohm resistor is
    a. 2.4 volts
    b. 24 volts
    c. 9.6 volts
    d. 0.96 volts

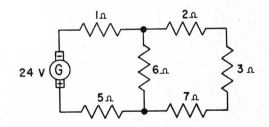

19. The resistance of the wire is taken into consideration in the 2- and 3-wire distribution systems because the
    a. source and load are very close
    b. resistance of the wire is the same throughout
    c. load and source are at a considerable distance from each other
    d. load must be decreased in order to determine accurate circuit values

20. What is Kirchhoff's second law as applied to 3-wire distribution circuits?
    a. Sum of all the voltages is zero
    b. Algebraic sum of all the voltages about a closed path is zero
    c. Alegbraic sum of all voltage is zero
    d. All IR drops in the circuit are negative

CHAPTER 6

ELECTRICAL CONDUCTORS AND WIRING TECHNIQUES

Since all electrical circuits utilize conductors of one type of another, it is essential that you know the basic physical features and electrical characteristics of the most common types of conductors.

As stated previously, any substance that permits the free motion of a large number of electrons is classed as a conductor. A conductor may be made from many different types of metals, but only the most commonly used types of materials will be discussed in this chapter.

To compare the resistance and size of one conductor with that of another, a standard or unit size of conductor must be established. A convenient unit of linear measurement, as far as the diameter of a piece of wire is concerned, is the mil (0.001 of an inch); and a convenient unit of wire length is the foot. The standard unit of size in most cases is the MIL-FOOT. That is, a wire will have unit size if it has diameter of 1 mil and a length of 1 foot. The resistance in ohms of a unit conductor of a given substance is called the specific resistance, or specific resistivity, of the substance.

Gage numbers are a further convenience in comparing the diameter of wires. The gage commonly used is the American wire gage (AWG), formerly the Brown and Sharpe (B and S) gage.

SQUARE MIL

The square mil is a convenient unit of cross-sectional area for square or rectangular conductors. A square mil is the area of a square, the sides of which are 1 mil, as shown in figure 6-1 (A). To obtain the cross-sectional area in square mils of a square conductor, square one side measured in mils. To obtain the cross-sectional area in square mils of a rectangular conductor, multiply the length of one side by that of the other, each length being expressed in mils.

For example, find the cross-sectional area of a large rectangular conductor 3/8 inch thick and 4 inches wide. The thickness may be expressed in mils as 0.375 x 1,000 = 375 mils, and the width as 4 x 1,000, or 4,000 mils. The cross-sectional area is 375 x 4,000, or 1,500,000 square mils.

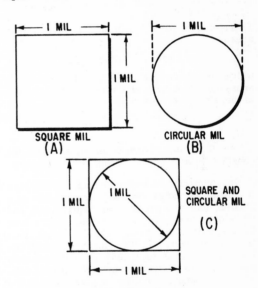

Figure 6-1.—(A) Square mil; (B) circular mil; (C) comparison of circular to square mil.

CIRCULAR MIL

The circular mil is the standard unit of wire cross-sectional area used in American and English wire tables. Because the diameters of round conductors, or wires, used to conduct electricity may be only a small fraction of an inch, it is convenient to express these diameters

95

in mils, to avoid the use of decimals. For example, the diameter of a wire is expressed as 25 mils instead of 0.025 inch. A circular mil is the area of a circle having a diameter of 1 mil, as shown in figure 6-1 (B). The area in circular mils of a round conductor is obtained by squaring the diameter measured in mils. Thus, a wire having a diameter of 25 mils has an area of 25^2 or 625 circular mils. By way of comparison, the basic formula for the area of a circle is $A = \pi R^2$ and in this example the area in square inches is

$$A = \pi R^2 = 3.14(0.0125)^2 = 0.00049 \text{ sq. in.}$$

If D is the diameter of a wire in mils, the area in square mils is

$$A = \pi \left(\frac{D}{2}\right)^2 = \frac{3.1416}{4} D^2 = 0.7854 D^2 \text{ sq. mils.}$$

Therefore, a wire 1 mil in diameter has an area of

$$A = 0.7854 \times 1^2 = 0.7854 \text{ sq. mils,}$$

which is equivalent to 1 circular mil. The cross-sectional area of a wire in circular mils is therefore determined as

$$A = \frac{0.7854 D^2}{0.7854} \quad D^2 \text{ circular mils,}$$

where D is the diameter in mils. Thus, the constant $\frac{\pi}{4}$ is eliminated from the calculation.

In comparing square and round conductors it should be noted that the circular mil is a smaller unit of area than the square mil, and therefore there are more circular mils than square mils in any given area. The comparison is shown in figure 6-1 (C). The area of a circular mil is equal to 0.7854 of a square mil. Therefore, to determine the circular-mil area when the square-mil area is given, divide the area in square mils by 0.7854. Conversely, to determine the square-mil area when the circular-mil area is given, multiply the area in circular mils by 0.7854.

For example, a No. 12 wire has a diameter of 80.81 mils. What is (1) its area in circular mils and (2) its area in square mils?
Solution:

(1) $\quad A = D^2 = 80.81^2 = 6,530 \text{ circular mils.}$

(2) $\quad A = 0.7854 \times 6,530 = 5,128.7 \text{ square mils.}$

A rectangular conductor is 1.5 inches wide and 0.25 inch thick. (1) What is its area in square mils? (2) What size of round conductor in circular mils is necessary to carry the same current as the rectangular bar?

Solution:

(1) $\quad 1.5'' \quad = 1.5 \ \times \ 1,000 \quad = 1,500 \text{ mils}$
$\quad\quad 0.25'' = 0.25 \times 1,000 \quad = 250 \text{ mils}$
$\quad\quad\quad A = 1,500 \times 250 \quad = 375,000 \text{ square mils.}$

(2) To carry the same current, the cross-sectional area of the rectangular bar and the cross-sectional area of the round conductor must be equal. There are more circular mils than square mils in this area, and therefore

$$A = \frac{375,000}{0.7854} = 477,000 \text{ circular mils.}$$

A wire in its usual form is a slender rod or filament of drawn metal. In large sizes, wire becomes difficult to handle, and its flexibility is increased by stranding. The strands are usually single wires twisted together in sufficient numbers to make up the necessary cross-sectional area of the cable. The total area in circular mils is determined by multiplying the area of one strand in circular mils by the number of strands in the cable.

CIRCULAR-MIL-FOOT

A circular-mil-foot, as shown in figure 6-2, is actually a unit of volume. It is a unit conductor 1 foot in length and having a cross-sectional area of 1 circular mil. Because it is considered a unit conductor, the circular-mil-foot is useful in making comparisons between wires that are made of different metals. For example, a basis of comparison of the RESISTIVITY (to be treated later) of various substances may be made by determining the resistance of a circular-mil-foot of each of the substances.

In working with certain substances it is sometimes more convenient to employ a different unit volume. Accordingly, unit volume may also be taken as the centimeter cube; and specific resistance becomes the resistance offered by a cube-shaped conductor 1 cm. long and 1 sq. cm. in cross-sectional area. The inch cube may also be used. The unit of volume employed is given in tables of specific resistances.

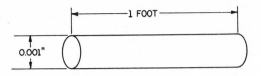

Figure 6-2.—Circular-mil-foot.

SPECIFIC RESISTANCE OR RESISTIVITY

Specific resistance, or resistivity, is the resistance in ohms offered by unit volume (the circular-mil-foot) of a substance to the flow of electric current. Resistivity is the reciprocal of conductivity. A substance that has a high resistivity will have a low conductivity, and vice versa.

Thus, the specific resistance of a substance is the resistance of a unit volume of that substance. Many tables of specific resistance are based on the resistance in ohms of a volume of the substance 1 foot long and 1 circular mil in cross-sectional area. The temperature at which the resistance measurement is made is also specified. If the kind of metal of which a conductor is made is known, the specific resistance of the metal may be obtained from a table. The specific resistances of some common substances are given in table 6-1.

The resistance of a conductor of uniform cross section varies directly as the product of the length and the specific resistance of the conductor and inversely as the cross-sectional area of the conductor. Therefore the resistance of a conductor may be calculated if the length, cross-sectional area, and specific resistance of the substance are known. Expressed as an equation, the resistance, R in ohms, of a conductor is

$$R = \rho \frac{L}{A},$$

where ρ (Greek rho) is the specific resistance in ohms per circular-mil-foot, L the length in feet (in the direction of current flow), and A the cross-sectional area in circular mils.

Table 6-1.—Specific Resistance.

Substance	Specific resistance at 20° C.	
	Centimeter cube (microhms)	Circular-mil-foot (ohms)
Silver	1.629	9.8
Copper (drawn).	1.724	10.37
Gold	2.44	14.7
Aluminum . . .	2.828	17.02
Carbon (amorphous.)	3.8 to 4.1	. . . .
Tungsten	5.51	33.2
Brass	7.0	42.1
Steel (soft) . . .	15.9	95.8
Nichrome . . .	109.0	660.0

For example, what is the resistance of 1,000 feet of copper wire having a cross-sectional area of 10,400 circular mils (No. 10 wire), the wire temperature being 20° C.?

Solution:

The specific resistance, from table 6-1, is 10.37. Substituting the known values in the preceding equation, the resistance, R, is determined as

$$R = \rho \frac{L}{A} = 10.37 \times \frac{1,000}{10,400} = 1 \text{ ohm, approximately.}$$

If R, ρ, and A are known, the length may be determined by a simple mathematical transposition. This is of value in many applications. For example, when it is desired to locate a ground in a telephone line, special test equipment is used that operates on the principle that the resistance of a line varies directly with its length. Thus, the distance between the test point and a fault can be computed accurately.

As has been mentioned in preceding chapters, conductance (G) is the reciprocal of resistance. When R is in ohms, the conductance is expressed in mhos. Where resistance is opposition to flow, conductance is the ease with which the current flows. Conductance in mhos is equivalent to the number of amperes flowing in a conductor per volt of applied e.m.f. Expressed in terms of the specific resistance, length, and cross section of a conductor,

$$G = \frac{A}{\rho L} \cdot$$

The conductance, G, varies directly as the cross-sectional area, A, and inversely as the specific resistance, ρ, and the length, L. When A is in circular mils, ρ is in ohms per circular-mil-foot, L is in feet, and G is in mhos.

The relative conductance of several substances is given in table 6-2.

Table 6-2.—Relative Conductance.

Substance	Relative conductance (Silver = 100%)
Silver	100
Copper	98
Gold	78
Aluminum	61
Tungsten	32
Zinc	30
Platinum	17
Iron.	16
Lead	15
Tin	9
Nickel	7
Mercury	1
Carbon	0.05

WIRE MEASURE

Relation Between Wire Sizes

Wires are manufactured in sizes numbered according to a table known as the American wire gage (AWG). As may be seen in table 6-3, the wire diameters become smaller as the gage numbers become larger. The largest wire size shown in the table is 0000 (read "4 naught"), and the smallest is number 40. Larger and smaller sizes are manufactured but are not commonly used by the Navy. The ratio of the diameter of one gage number to the diameter of the next higher gage number is a constant, 1.123. The cross-sectional area varies as the square of the diameter. Therefore, the ratio of the cross section of one gage number to that of the next higher gage number is the square of 1.123, or 1.261. Because the cube of 1.261 is very nearly 2, the cross-sectional area is approximately halved, or doubled, every three gage numbers. Also because 1.261 raised to the 10th power is very nearly equal to 10, the cross-sectional area is increased or decreased 10 times every 10 gage numbers.

A No. 10 wire has a diameter of approximately 102 mils, a cross-sectional area of approximately 10,400 circular mils, and a resistance of approximately 1 ohm per 1,000 feet. From these facts it is possible to estimate quickly the cross-sectional area and the resistance of any size copper wire without referring directly to a wire table.

For example, to estimate the cross-sectional area and the resistance of 1,000 feet of No. 17 wire, the following reasoning might be employed. A No. 17 wire is 3 sizes removed from a No. 20 wire and therefore has twice the cross-sectional area of a No. 20 wire. A No. 20 wire is 10 sizes removed from a No. 10 wire and therefore has one-tenth the cross section of a No. 10 wire. Therefore, the cross-sectional area of a No. 17 wire is 2 x 0.1 x 10,000 = 2,000 circular mils. Since resistance varies inversely with the cross-sectional area, the resistance of a No. 17 wire is 10 x 1 x 0.5 = 5 ohms per 1,000 feet.

A wire gage is shown in figure 6-3. It will measure wires ranging in size from number 0 to number 36. The wire whose size is to be measured is inserted in the smallest slot that will just accommodate the bare wire. The gage number corresponding to that slot indicates the wire size. The slot has parallel sides and should not be confused with the semicircular opening at the end of the slot. The opening simply permits the free movement of the wire all the way through the slot.

Stranded Wires and Cables

A WIRE is a slender rod or filament of drawn metal. The definition restricts the term to what would ordinarily be understood as "solid wire." The word "slender" is used because the length of a wire is usually large in comparison with the diameter. If a wire is covered with insulation, it is properly called an insulated wire. Although the term "wire" properly refers to the metal, it is generally understood to include the insulation.

A CONDUCTOR is a wire or combination of wires not insulated from one another, suitable for carrying an electric current.

Table 6-3.—Standard annealed solid copper wire.

(American wire gage--B & S)

| Gage number | Diameter (mils) | Cross section | | Ohms per 1,000 ft. | | Ohms per mile 25° C. (=77° F.) | Pounds per 1,000 ft. |
		Circular mils	Square inches	25° C. (=77° F.)	65° C. (=149° F.)		
0000	460.0	212,000.0	0.166	0.0500	0.0577	0.264	641.0
000	410.0	168,000.0	.132	.0630	.0727	.333	508.0
00	365.0	133,000.0	.105	.0795	.0917	.420	403.0
0	325.0	106,000.0	.0829	.100	.116	.528	319.0
1	289.0	83,700.0	.0657	.126	.146	.665	253.0
2	258.0	66,400.0	.0521	.159	.184	.839	201.0
3	229.0	52,600.0	.0413	.201	.232	1.061	159.0
4	204.0	41,700.0	.0328	.253	.292	1.335	126.0
5	182.0	33,100.0	.0260	.319	.369	1.685	100.0
6	162.0	26,300.0	.0206	.403	.465	2.13	79.5
7	144.0	20,800.0	.0164	.508	.586	2.68	63.0
8	128.0	16,500.0	.0130	.641	.739	3.38	50.0
9	114.0	13,100.0	.0103	.808	.932	4.27	39.6
10	102.0	10,400.0	.00815	1.02	1.18	5.38	31.4
11	91.0	8,230.0	.00647	1.28	1.48	6.75	24.9
12	81.0	6,530.0	.00513	1.62	1.87	8.55	19.8
13	72.0	5,180.0	.00407	2.04	2.36	10.77	15.7
14	64.0	4,110.0	.00323	2.58	2.97	13.62	12.4
15	57.0	3,260.0	.00256	3.25	3.75	17.16	9.86
16	51.0	2,580.0	.00203	4.09	4.73	21.6	7.82
17	45.0	2,050.0	.00161	5.16	5.96	27.2	6.20
18	40.0	1,620.0	.00128	6.51	7.51	34.4	4.92
19	36.0	1,290.0	.00101	8.21	9.48	43.3	3.90
20	32.0	1,020.0	.000802	10.4	11.9	54.9	3.09
21	28.5	810.0	.000636	13.1	15.1	69.1	2.45
22	25.3	642.0	.000505	16.5	19.0	87.1	1.94
23	22.6	509.0	.000400	20.8	24.0	109.8	1.54
24	20.1	404.0	.000317	26.2	30.2	138.3	1.22
25	17.9	320.0	.000252	33.0	38.1	174.1	0.970
26	15.9	254.0	.000200	41.6	48.0	220.0	0.769
27	14.2	202.0	.000158	52.5	60.6	277.0	0.610
28	12.6	160.0	.000126	66.2	76.4	350.0	0.484
29	11.3	127.0	.0000995	83.4	96.3	440.0	0.384
30	10.0	101.0	.0000789	105.0	121.0	554.0	0.304
31	8.9	79.7	.0000626	133.0	153.0	702.0	0.241
32	8.0	63.2	.0000496	167.0	193.0	882.0	0.191
33	7.1	50.1	.0000394	211.0	243.0	1,114.0	0.152
34	6.3	39.8	.0000312	266.0	307.0	1,404.0	0.120
35	5.6	31.5	.0000248	335.0	387.0	1,769.0	0.0954
36	5.0	25.0	.0000196	423.0	488.0	2,230.0	0.0757
37	4.5	19.8	.0000156	533.0	616.0	2,810.0	0.0600
38	4.0	15.7	.0000123	673.0	776.0	3,550.0	0.0476
39	3.5	12.5	.0000098	848.0	979.0	4,480.0	0.0377
40	3.1	9.9	.0000078	1,070.0	1,230.0	5,650.0	0.0299

A STRANDED CONDUCTOR is a conductor composed of a group of wires or of any combination of groups of wires. The wires in a stranded conductor are usually twisted together.

A CABLE is either a stranded conductor (single-conductor cable) or a combination of conductors insulated from one another (multiple-conductor cable). The term cable is a general one, and in practice it is usually applied only to the larger sizes of conductors. A small cable is more often called a stranded wire or cord. Cables may be bare or insulated. The

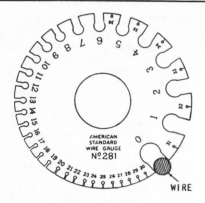

Figure 6-3.—Wire gage.

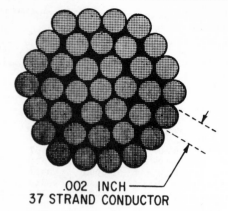

.002 INCH
37 STRAND CONDUCTOR

DIAMETER OF EACH STRAND = .002 INCH
DIAMETER OF EACH STRAND, MILS = 2 MILS
CIRCULAR MIL AREA OF
EACH STRAND = D^2 = 4 CM
TOTAL CM AREA OF
CONDUCTOR = 4 x 37 = 148 CM

Figure 6-5.—Stranded conductor.

insulated cables may be sheathed (covered) with lead, or protective armor.

Figure 6-4 shows some of the different types of wire and cables used in the Navy.

Conductors are stranded mainly to increase their flexibility. The arrangement of the wire strands in concentric-layer cables is as follows:

The first layer of strands around the center is made up of 6 conductors; the second layer is made up of 12 conductors; the third layer is made up of 18 conductors; and so on. Thus, standard cables are composed of 1, 7, 19, 37, and so forth strands.

The overall flexibility may be increased by further stranding of the individual strands.

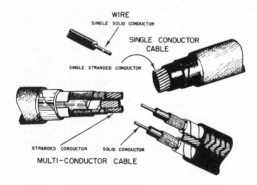

WIRE
SINGLE SOLID CONDUCTOR

SINGLE CONDUCTOR
CABLE

SINGLE STRANDED CONDUCTOR

STRANDED CONDUCTOR   SOLID CONDUCTOR
MULTI-CONDUCTOR CABLE

Figure 6-4.—Conductors.

Figure 6-5 shows a typical 37-strand cable. It also shows how the total circular-mil cross-sectional area of a stranded cable is determined.

Factors Governing the Selection of Wire Size

Several factors must be considered in selecting the size of wire to be used for transmitting and distributing electric power.

One factor is the allowable power loss (I^2R loss) in the line. This loss represents electrical energy converted into heat. The use of large conductors will reduce the resistance and therefore the I^2R loss. However, large conductors are more expensive initially than small ones; they are heavier and require more substantial supports.

A second factor is the permissible voltage drop (IR drop) in the line. If the source maintains a constant voltage at the input to the line, any variation in the load on the line will cause a variation in line current, and a consequent variation in the IR drop in the line. A wide variation in the IR drop in the line causes poor voltage regulation at the load. The obvious remedy is to reduce either I or R. A reduction in load current lowers the amount of power being transmitted, whereas a reduction in line resistance increases the size and weight of conductors required. A compromise is generally reached whereby the voltage variation at the load is within tolerable limits and the weight of line conductors is not excessive.

A third factor is the current-carrying ability of the line. When current is drawn through the line, heat is generated. The temperature of the line will rise until the heat radiated, or otherwise dissipated, is equal to the heat generated by the passage of current through the line. If the conductor is insulated, the heat generated in the conductor is not so readily removed as it would be if the conductor were not insulated. Thus, to protect the insulation from too much heat, the current through the conductor must be maintained below a certain value. Rubber insulation will begin to deteriorate at relatively low temperatures. Varnished cloth insulation retains its insulating properties at higher temperatures; and other insulation— for example, asbestos or silicon—is effective at still higher temperatures.

Electrical conductors may be installed in locations where the ambient (surrounding) temperature is relatively high; in which case the heat generated by external sources constitutes an appreciable part of the total conductor heating. Due allowance must be made for the influence of external heating on the allowable conductor current and each case has its own specific limitations. The maximum allowable operating temperature of insulated conductors is specified in tables and varies with the type of conductor insulation being used.

Tables have been prepared by the National Board of Fire Underwriters giving the safe current ratings for various sizes and types of conductors covered with various types of insulation. For example, the allowable current-carrying capacities of copper conductors at not over 30° C. (86° F.) room temperature for single conductors in free air are given in table 6-4.

COPPER VS. ALUMINUM CONDUCTORS

Although silver is the best conductor, its cost limits its use to special circuits where a substance with high conductivity is needed.

The two most generally used conductors are copper and aluminum. Each has characteristics that make its use advantageous under certain circumstances. Likewise, each has certain disadvantages.

Copper has a higher conductivity; it is more ductile (can be drawn out), has relatively high tensile strength, and can be easily soldered. It is more expensive and heavier than aluminum.

Although aluminum has only about 60 percent of the conductivity of copper, it is used extensively for high-voltage transmission lines. Its lightness makes possible long spans, and its relatively large diameter for a given conductivity reduces corona—that is, the discharge of electricity from the wire when it has a high potential. The discharge is greater when smaller diameter wire is used than when larger diameter wire is used. However, aluminum conductors are not easily soldered, and aluminum's relatively large size for a given conductance does not permit the economical use of an insulation covering.

A comparison of some of the characteristics of copper and aluminum is given in table 6-5.

TEMPERATURE COEFFICIENT OF RESISTANCE

The resistance of pure metals—such as silver, copper, and aluminum—increases as the temperature increases. However, the resistance of some alloys—such as constantan and manganin—changes very little as the temperature changes. Measuring instruments use these alloys because the resistance of the circuits must remain constant if accurate measurements are to be achieved.

In table 6-1 the resistance of a circular-mil-foot of wire (the specific resistance) is given at a specific temperature, 20° C. in this case. It is necessary to establish a standard temperature because, as has been stated, the resistance of pure metals increase with an increase in temperature; and a true basis of comparison cannot be made unless the resistances of all the substances being compared are measured at the same temperature. The amount of increase in the resistance of a 1-ohm sample of the conductor per degree rise in temperature above 0° C. is called the TEMPERATURE COEFFICIENT OF RESISTANCE. For copper, the value is approximately 0.00427 ohms. For pure metals, the temperature coefficient of resistance ranges between 0.003 and 0.006 ohms.

Thus, a copper wire having a resistance of 50 ohms at an initial temperature of 0° C. will have an increase in resistance of 50 x 0.00427, or 0.214 ohms for the entire length of wire for each degree of temperature rise above 0° C. At 20° C. the increase in resistance is approximately 20 x 0.214, or 4.28 ohms. The total resistance at 20° C. is 50 + 4.28, or 54.28 ohms.

Table 6-4.—Current-carrying capacities (in amperes) of single copper

conductors at ambient temperature of below 30° C.

Size	Rubber or thermoplastic	Thermoplastic asbestos, var-cam, or asbestos var-cam	Impregnated asbestos	Asbestos	Slow-burning or weatherproof
0000	300	385	475	510	370
000	260	330	410	430	320
00	225	285	355	370	275
0	195	245	305	325	235
1	165	210	265	280	205
2	140	180	225	240	175
3	120	155	195	210	150
4	105	135	170	180	130
6	80	100	125	135	100
8	55	70	90	100	70
10	40	55	70	75	55
12	25	40	50	55	40
14	20	30	40	45	30

Table 6-5.—Characteristics of copper and aluminum.

Characteristics	Copper	Aluminum
Tensile strength (lb/in^2).	55,000	25,000
Tensile strength for same conductivity (lb).	55,000	40,000
Weight for same conductivity (lb).	100	48
Cross section for same conductivity (C.M.).	100	160
Specific resistance (Ω/mil ft).	10.6	17

CONDUCTOR INSULATION

To be useful and safe, electric current must be forced to flow only where it is needed. It must be "channeled" from the power source to a useful load. In general, current-carrying conductors must not be allowed to come in contact with one another, their supporting hardware, or personnel working near them. To accomplish this, conductors are coated or wrapped with various materials. These materials have such a high resistance that they are, for all practical purposes, nonconductors. They are generally referred to as insulators or insulating material.

Because of the expense of insulation and its stiffening effect, together with the great variety of physical and electrical conditions under which the conductors are operated, only the necessary minimum of insulation is applied for any particular type of cable designed to do a specific job. Therefore there is a wide variety of insulated conductors available to meet the requirements of any job.

Two fundamental properties of insulation materials (for example, rubber, glass, asbestos, and plastic) are insulation resistance and dielectric strength. These are entirely different and distinct properties.

INSULATION RESISTANCE is the resistance to current leakage through and over the surface of insulation materials. Insulation resistance can be measured by means of a megger without damaging the insulation, and information so obtained serves as a useful guide in appraising the general condition of insulation. However, the data obtained in this manner may not give a true picture of the condition of the insulation. Clean-dry insulation having cracks or other faults may show a high value of insulation resistance but would not be suitable for use.

DIELECTRIC STRENGTH is the ability of the insulator to withstand potential difference and is usually expressed in terms of the voltage at which the insulation fails because of the electrostatic stress. Maximum dielectric strength values can be measured by raising the voltage of a TEST SAMPLE until the insulation breaks down.

Rubber

One of the most common types of insulation is rubber. The voltage that may be applied to a rubber-covered pair of conductors (twisted pair) is dependent on the thickness and the quality of the rubber covering. Other factors being equal, the thicker the insulation the higher may be the applied voltage. Figure 6-6 shows two types of rubber-covered wire. One is a single, solid conductor, and the other is a 2-conductor cable in which each stranded conductor is covered with rubber insulation. In each case the rubber serves the same purpose—to confine the current to its conductor.

It may be seen from the enlarged cross-sectional view that a thin coating of tin separates the copper conductor from the rubber insulation. If the thin coating of tin were not used, chemical action would take place and the rubber would become soft and gummy where it makes contact with the copper. When small,

solid, or stranded conductors are used, a winding of cotton threads is applied between the conductors and the rubber insulation.

Varnished Cambric

Heat is developed when current flows through a wire, and when a large amount of current flows, considerable heat may be developed. The heat can be dissipated if air is circulated freely around the wire. If a cover of insulation is used, the heat is not removed so readily and the temperature may reach a high value.

Rubber is a good insulator at relatively low voltage as long as the temperature remains low. Too much heat will cause even the best grade of rubber insulation to become brittle

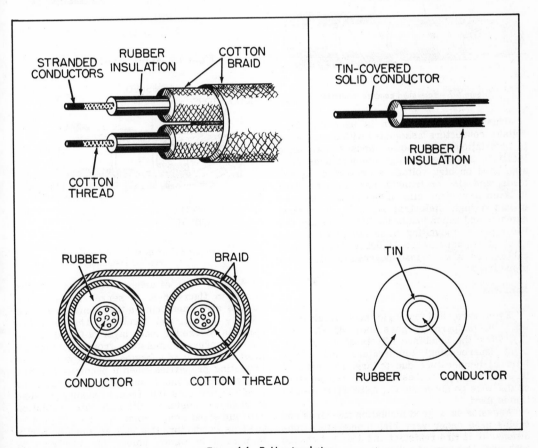

Figure 6-6.—Rubber insulation.

and crack. VARNISHED CAMBRIC insulation will stand much higher temperatures than rubber insulation. Varnished cambric is cotton cloth that has been coated with an insulating varnish. Figure 6-7 shows some of the detail of a cable covered with varnished cambric insulation. The varnished cambric is in tape form and is wound around the conductor in layers. An oily compound is applied between each layer of the tape. This compound prevents water from seeping through the insulation. It also acts as a lubricant between the layers of tape, so they will slide over each other when the cable is bent.

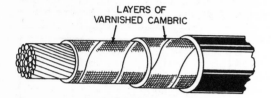

Figure 6-7.—Varnished cambric insulation.

This type of insulation is used on high-voltage conductors associated with switch gear in substations and power houses and other locations subjected to high temperatures. It is also used on high-voltage generator coils and leads, and also on transformer leads because it is unaffected by oils or grease and because it has a high dielectric strength. Varnished cambric and paper insulation for cables are the two types of insulating materials most widely used at voltages above 15,000 volts, but such cables are always lead-covered to keep the moisture out.

Asbestos

Even varnished cambric may break down when the temperature goes above 85° C., (185° F.). When the combined effects of a high ambient (surrounding) temperature and a high internal temperature due to large current flow through the wire makes the total temperature of the wire go above 85° C., ASBESTOS insulation is used.

Asbestos is a good insulation for wires and cables used under very high temperature conditions. It is fire resistant and does not change with age. One type of asbestos-covered wire is

shown in figure 6-8. It consists of a stranded copper conductor covered with felted asbestos, which is, in turn, covered with asbestos braid. This type of wire is used in motion-picture projectors, arc lamps, spotlights, heating element leads, and so forth.

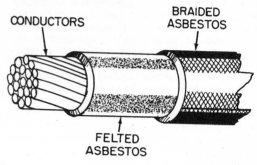

Figure 6-8.—Asbestos insulation.

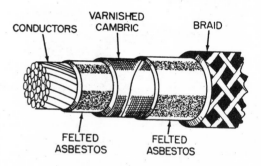

Figure 6-9.—Asbestos and varnished cambric insulation.

Another type of asbestos-covered cable is shown in figure 6-9. It serves as leads for motors and transformers that sometimes must operate in hot, wet locations. The varnished cambric covers the inner layer of felted asbestos and prevents moisture from reaching the innermost layer of asbestos. Asbestos loses its insulating properties when it becomes wet, and will in fact become a conductor. The varnished cambric prevents this from happening because it resists moisture. Although this insulation will withstand some moisture, it should not be used on conductors that may at times be partly immersed in water, unless the insulation is protected with an outer lead sheath.

Paper

Paper has little insulation value alone, but when impregnated with a high grade of mineral oil, it serves as a satisfactory insulation for high-voltage cables. The oil has a high dielectric strength, and tends to prevent breakdown of paper insulation when the paper is thoroughly saturated with it. The thin paper tape is wrapped in many layers around the conductors, and it is then soaked with oil.

The 3-conductor cable shown in figure 6-10 consists of paper insulation on each conductor with a spirally wrapped nonmagnetic metallic tape over the insulation. The space between conductors is filled with a suitable spacer to round out the cable and another nonmagnetic metal tape is used to secure the entire cable, and then a lead sheath is applied over all. This type of cable is used on voltages from 10,000 volts to 35,000 volts.

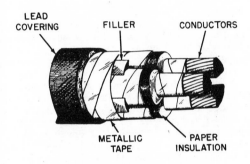

Figure 6-10.—Paper-insulated power cables.

Silk and Cotton

In certain types of circuits—for example, communications circuits—a large number of conductors are needed, perhaps as many as several hundred. Figure 6-11 shows a cable containing many conductors, each insulated from the others by silk and cotton threads.

The use of silk and cotton as insulation keeps the size of the cable small enough to be handled easily. The silk and cotton threads are wrapped around the individual conductors in reverse directions, and the covering is then impregnated with a special wax compound.

Because the insulation in this type of cable is not subjected to high voltage, thin layers of silk and cotton are used.

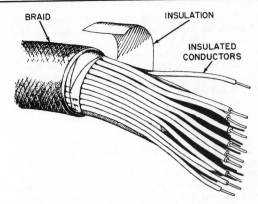

Figure 6-11.—Silk and cotton insulation.

Enamel

The wire used on the coils of meters, relays, small transformers, and so forth, is called MAGNET WIRE. This wire is insulated with an enamel coating. The enamel is a synthetic compound of cellulose acetate (wood pulp and magnesium). In the manufacture, the bare wire is passed through a solution of the hot enamel and then cooled. This process is repeated until the wire acquires from 6 to 10 coatings. Enamel has a higher dielectric strength than rubber for equal thickness. It is not practical for large wires because of the expense and because the insulation is readily fractured when large wires are bent.

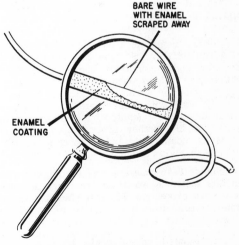

Figure 6-12.—Enamel insulation.

Figure 6-12 shows an enamel-coated wire. Enamel is the thinnest insulating coating that can be applied to wires. Hence, enamel-insulated magnet wire makes smaller coils. Enameled wire is sometimes covered with one or more layers of cotton covering to protect the enamel from nicks, cuts, or abrasions.

CONDUCTOR PROTECTION

Wires and cables are generally subject to abuse. The type and amount of abuse depends on how and where they are installed and the manner in which they are used. Cables buried directly in the ground must resist moisture, chemical action, and abrasion. Wires installed in buildings must be protected against mechanical injury and overloading. Wires strung on crossarms on poles are kept far enough apart so that they do not touch; but snow, ice, and strong winds necessitate the use of conductors having high tensile strength and substantial supporting frame structures.

Generally, except for overload transmission lines, wires or cables are protected by some form of covering. The covering may be some type of insulator like rubber or plastic. Over this an outer covering of fibrous braid may be applied. If conditions require, a metallic outer covering may be used. The type of outer covering used depends on how and where the wire or cable is to be used.

Fibrous Braid

Cotton, linen, silk, rayon, and jute are types of FIBROUS BRAIDS. They are used for outer covering under conditions where the wires or cables are not exposed to heavy mechanical injury. Interior wiring for lights or power is usually done with impregnated cotton, braid-covered, rubber-insulated wire. Generally, the wire will be further protected by a flame-resistant nonmetallic outer covering or by a flexible or rigid conduit.

Figure 6-13 shows a typical building wire. In this instance two braid coverings are used for extra protection. The outer braid is soaked with a compound that resists moisture and flame.

Impregnated cotton braid is used as a covering for outdoor overhead conductors to

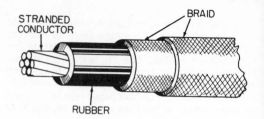

Figure 6-13.—Fibrous braid covering.

afford protection against abrasion. For example, the service wires from the transformer secondary mains to the service entrance and also the high-voltage primary mains to the transformer are protected in this manner.

Lead Sheath

Subway-type cables or wires that are continually subjected to water must be protected by a watertight cover. This watertight cover is made either of a continuous lead jacket or a rubber sheath molded around the cable.

Figure 6-14 is an example of a lead-sheathed cable used in power work. The cable shown is a stranded 3-conductor type. Each conductor is insulated with rubber and then wrapped with a layer of rubberized tape. The conductors are twisted together and fillers or rope are added to form a rounded core. Over this is wrapped a second layer of tape called the SERVING, and finally the lead sheath is molded around the cable.

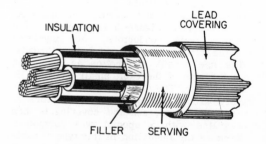

Figure 6-14.—Lead sheathed cable.

106

Metallic Armor

Metallic armor provides a tough protective covering for wires or cables. The type, thickness, and kind of metal used to make the armor depend on the use of the conductors, the circumstances under which the conductors are to be used, and on the amount of rough treatment that is to be expected.

Four types of metallic armor for cables are shown in figure 6-15.

Wire braid armor is used wherever light, flexible protection is needed. This type of armor is used almost exclusively aboard ship. The individual wires that are woven together to form the metal braid may be made of steel, copper, bronze, or aluminum. Besides mechanical protection, the wire braid also presents a static shield. This is important in radio work aboard ship to prevent interference from stray fields.

When cables are buried directly in the ground, they might be injured from two sources —moisture, and abrasion. They are protected from moisture by a lead sheath, and from abrasion by steel tape or interlocking armor covers. The steel tape covering, as shown in figure 6-15, is wrapped around the cable and then covered with a serving of jute. It is known as Parkway cable. The interlocking armor covering can withstand impacts better than steel tape. Interlocking armor has other uses besides underground work. In wiring the interior of buildings, interlocking armor-covered wire (BX cable) without the lead sheath is frequently used.

Armor wire is the best type of covering to withstand severe wear and tear. Underwater leaded cable usually has an outer armor wire cover.

All wires and cables do not have the same type of protective covering. Some coverings are designed to withstand moisture, others to withstand mechanical strain, and so forth. A cable may have a combination of each type, each doing its own job.

CONDUCTOR SPLICES AND TERMINAL CONNECTIONS

Conductor splices and connections are an essential part of any electric circuit. When

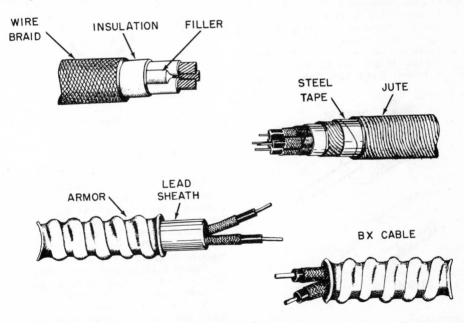

Figure 6-15.—Metallic armor.

107

conductors join each other, or connect to a load, splices or terminals must be used. It is important that they be properly made, since any electric circuit is only as good as its weakest link. The basic requirement of any splice or connection is that it be both mechanically and electrically as strong as the conductor or device with which it is used. High-quality workmanship and materials must be employed to insure lasting electrical contact, physical strength, and insulation (if required). The most common methods of making splices and connections in electric cables will now be discussed.

Preparing Conductors for Splices and Terminals

The first step in making a splice is preparing the wires or conductor. Insulation must be removed from the end of the conductor and the exposed metal cleaned. In removing the insulation from the wire, a sharp knife is used in much the same manner as in sharpening a pencil. That is, the knife blade is moved at a small angle with the wire to avoid "nicking" the wire. This produces a taper on the cut insulation, as shown in figure 6-16. The insulation may also be removed by using a plier-like hand-operated cable stripper. After the insulation is removed, the bare wire ends should then be scraped bright with the back of a knife blade or rubbed clean with fine sandpaper.

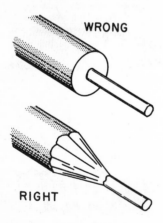

Figure 6-16.—Removing insulation from a wire.

Western Union Splice

Small, solid conductors may be joined together by a simple connection known as the WESTERN UNION SPLICE. In most instances the wires may be twisted together with the fingers and the ends clamped into position with a pair of pliers.

Figure 6-17 shows the steps in making a Western Union splice. First, the wires are prepared for splicing by removing sufficient insulation and cleaning the conductor. Next, the wires are brought to a crossed position and a long twist or bend is made in each wire. Then one of the wire ends is wrapped four of five times around the straight portion of the wire. The other end wire is wrapped in a similar manner. Finally, the ends of the wires should be pressed down as close as possible to the straight portion of the wire. This prevents the sharp ends from puncturing the tape covering that is wrapped over the splice.

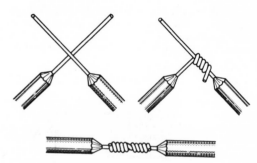

Figure 6-17.—Western Union splice.

Staggered Splice

Joining small, multiconductor cables together presents somewhat of a problem. Each conductor must be spliced and taped; and if the splices are directly opposite each other, the overall size of the joint becomes large and bulky. A smoother and less bulky joint may be made by staggering the splices.

Figure 6-18 shows how a 2-conductor cable is joined to a similar cable by means of the staggered splice. Care should be exercised to ensure that a short wire is connected to a long wire, and that the sharp ends are clamped firmly down on the conductor.

STAGGERED SPLICE

Figure 6-18.—Staggered splice.

Rattail Joint

Wiring that is installed in buildings is usually placed inside long lengths of steel pipe (conduit). Whenever branch circuits are required, junction or pull boxes are inserted in the conduit. One type of splice that is used for branch circuits is the rattail joint shown in figure 6-19.

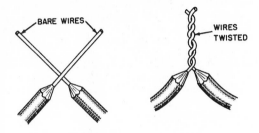

Figure 6-19.—Rattail joint.

The ends of the conductors to be joined are stripped of insulation. The wires are then twisted to form the rattail effect.

Fixture Joint

A fixture joint is used to connect a light fixture to the branch circuit of an electrical system where the fixture wire is smaller in diameter than the branch wire. Like the rattail joint, it will not stand much mechanical strain.

The first step is to remove the insulation from the wires to be joined. Figure 6-20 shows the steps in making a fixture joint.

After the wires are prepared, the fixture wire is wrapped a few times around the branch wire, as shown in the figure. The wires are not twisted, as in the rattail joint. The end of the branch wire is then bent over the completed turns. The remainder of the bare fixture wire is then wrapped over the bent branch wire. Soldering and taping completes the job.

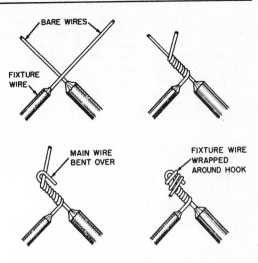

Figure 6-20.—Fixture joint.

Knotted Tap Joint

All of the splices considered up to this point are known as BUTTED splices. Each was made by joining the FREE ends of the conductors together. Sometimes, however, it is necessary to join a conductor to a CONTINUOUS wire, and such a junction is called a TAP joint.

The main wire, to which the branch wire is to be tapped, has about one inch of insulation removed. The branch wire is stripped of about three inches of insulation. The steps in making the tap are shown in figure 6-21.

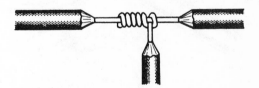

KNOTTED TAP JOINT

Figure 6-21.—Knotted tap joint.

The branch wire is crossed over the main wire, as shown in the figure, with about three-fourths of the bare portion of the branch wire

109

extending above the main wire. The end of the branch wire is bent over the main wire, brought under the main wire, around the branch wire, and then over the main wire to form a knot. It is then wrapped around the main conductor in short, tight turns and the end is trimmed off.

The knotted tap is used where the splice is subject to strain or slip. When there is no mechanical strain, the knot may be eliminated.

SOLDERING EQUIPMENT

The various splices and joints commonly used are not completed until they are properly soldered and insulated.

Solder

Solder is a metallic alloy with a low melting point; it is used to join metallic surfaces. Solder used in electrical work comes in two forms —solid solder bars, and the rosin core type,

resembling wire wound on spools. Figure 6-22 illustrates the two types.

The rosin core type solder is most commonly used. The rosin core of the solder, when melted, flows on the surfaces of the splice or joint, preventing their contact with air and thus preventing oxidation. Without oxidation, the solder and surfaces will cohere strongly.

Soldering Iron

The soldering iron is a handtool that is used to heat the wire splice or joint to a temperature that will cause the solder to melt and flow freely over the splice or joint. Electric soldering irons are rated in watts, from 25 to 500. The size of the conductors being soldered will determine the size of soldering iron to be used. All high quality irons operate in a temperature range of 500° to 600° F. Even the little 25-watt midget iron produces this temperature. The important difference in iron sizes is not temperature, but the capacity of the iron

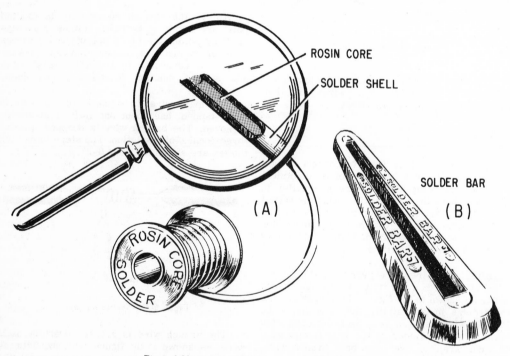

Figure 6-22.—Solder: (A) Rosin core; (B) solid bars.

to generate and maintain a satisfactory solder-ing temperature while giving up heat to the joint to be soldered.

Some irons have built-in thermostats. Others are provided with thermostatically controlled stands. One type of iron is equipped with several different tips that range from 1/4 inch to 1/2 inch is size (diameter) and are of various shapes. This feature makes the iron adaptable to a variety of jobs. Figure 6-23 shows several different type soldering irons.

ELECTRIC HEATING ELEMENT SOLDERING IRON

Figure 6-23 (A) shows three common sizes of the electric heating element soldering iron. This is the most commonly used type iron. A cylindrical electric heating element is mounted in its body. About half of the copper tip is inserted and secured within the cylindrical element, obtaining heat by physical contact. Heat is conducted to the protruding half, to be used in melting solder.

INDUCTION-TYPE SOLDERING IRON

This soldering iron (most often referred to as "soldering gun") is shown in figure 6-23 (B). It contains a stepdown transformer in its body. The transformer secondary output cur-rent flows through the tip, causing it to heat. The tip heats only when the trigger is de-pressed, and then very rapidly. This type iron affords easy access to cramped quarters, be-cause of its small tip. It usually has a small light which is focused on the tip working area. The soldering tip is replaceable.

ELECTRIC RESISTANCE SOLDERING IRON

This iron is shown in figure 6-23 (C). When the contact jaws are clamped on the work, current flows between the jaws through the work. The contact resistance causes heating, thus melting the solder.

TORCH-HEATED SOLDERING IRON

As shown in figure 6-23 (D), this type iron is heated directly by a blowtorch or other heat source. It is then held against the soldering work to transfer its heat. After cooling to an unusable temperature, it is reheated. This iron is usually used where electric power is not available and an open flame is permissible.

Care of Soldering Iron

Soldering irons require more care in both use and maintenance than most handtools. A typical electric iron has a heating element, a power cord, a wooden handle, and a copper tip.

The copper tip generally requires the most care and maintenance. Also, to prevent damage to the heating element, the iron should not be subjected to heavy mechanical abuse. For in-stance, if the iron is dropped, or used as a hammer, the heating element may be broken or shorted. Always make certain that the cord does not come in contact with the iron tip, where it can be burned.

The copper tip should be removed occasion-ally to permit cleaning away the oxide scale which forms between the tip and metal housing. Removal of this oxide increases the heating efficiency of the iron.

Before a soldering iron can be used for soldering, the pointed end of the copper tip must be tinned. Unless the tip is tinned the iron will not readily transfer heat from the copper tip to the connection to be soldered. Tinning the end of the tip means covering it with a thin coating of solder. After heating, all of the tip except the tinned portion becomes covered with an oxide film. This film does not readily conduct heat. Only the tinned portion of the tip will give off enough heat to melt solder readily. An iron which needs tinning does not produce satisfactory results when making solder con-nections. After an iron has been used for a period of time, the solder on the tip burns off and the iron needs retinning.

The action of the heat and solder causes pitting and corroding of the tip. Consequently, it not only needs retinning occasionally, but also needs occasional reshaping. Tips usually either have a 4-sided taper point or a 2-sided chisel point. Regardless of the tip size or shape, the same tinning procedure is used.

To reshape the tip, first remove it from the iron, either by unscrewing it from the housing or loosening a setscrew, depending on the type of iron. Place the tip in a vise with the point in such a position that the side to be tinned can be filed. Do not tighten the vise too tightly, as the copper tip is soft and bends easily. Using flat strokes, file the sides of the point until all of

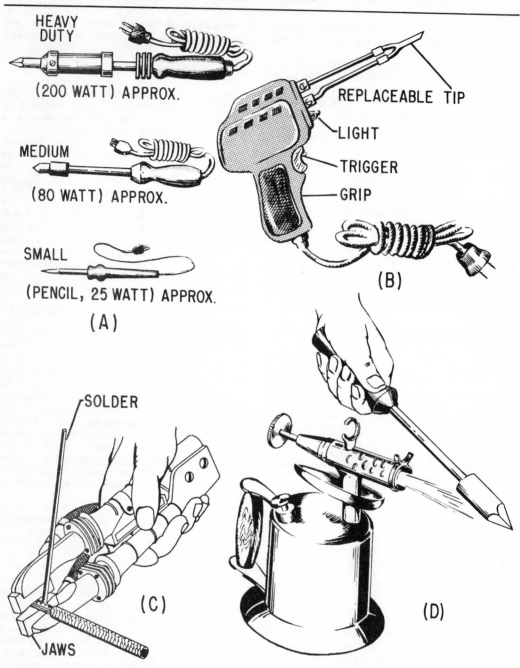

HEAVY DUTY

(200 WATT) APPROX.

MEDIUM

(80 WATT) APPROX.

SMALL

(PENCIL, 25 WATT) APPROX.

(A)

REPLACEABLE TIP

LIGHT

TRIGGER

GRIP

(B)

SOLDER

(C)

JAWS

(D)

Figure 6-23.—Soldering irons.

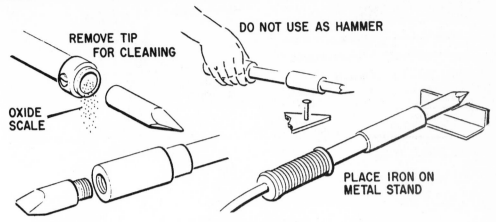

REMOVE TIP FOR CLEANING

DO NOT USE AS HAMMER

OXIDE SCALE

PLACE IRON ON METAL STAND

Figure 6-24.—Caring for the soldering iron.

the pits, oxide, and old tinning are removed. Always file the tip to the original taper, making certain that you do not round off the sides of the point.

Replace the filed tip in the iron housing. Holding the iron with the tip upward, plug the cord into a power outlet. As the iron heats, touch rosin core solder to the cleaned sides of the tip at intervals until the iron first begins to melt the solder. Then quickly melt solder onto all of the cleaned portion of the tip, applying as much solder as will melt onto each side. With a dry cloth or piece of steel wool, lightly brush the excess solder from the tinned sides of the tip. The iron is now ready to use for soldering. Heated irons, when not in actual use, should be placed on a metal iron rest or some other appropriate holder.

To solder an electrical connection, the tinned portion of the iron tip is held flat against the connection, as shown in figure 6-25. Touch solder to the connection until the entire connection is covered with molten solder. Remove the solder, but continue to apply heat for a moment; then remove the iron and allow the solder to harden. The solder should always be melted by the heated wire and not by the iron. Melting the solder onto the iron and then transferring it to the connection often results in a cold solder joint, with the solder not actually holding to the wire or connection. Only enough solder to fill all crevices and spaces in the joint should be used.

TAPING A SPLICE

The final step in completing a splice or joint is the placing of insulation over the bare wire. The insulation should be of the same basic substance as the original insulation. Usually a rubber splicing compound is used.

Rubber Tape

Latex (rubber) tape is a splicing compound. It is used where the original insulation was rubber. The tape is applied to the splice with a light tension so that each layer presses tightly against the one underneath it. This pressure causes the rubber tape to blend into a solid mass. When the application is completed, an insulation similar to the original has been restored.

Between each layer of latex tape, when it is in roll form, there is a layer of paper or treated cloth. This layer prevents the latex from fusing while still on the roll. The paper or cloth is peeled off and discarded before the tape is applied to the splice.

Figure 6-26 shows the correct way to cover a splice with rubber insulation. The rubber splicing tape should be applied smoothly and under tension so that there will be no air spaces between the layers. In putting on the first layer, start near the middle of the joint instead of the end. The diameter of the completed insulated joint should be somewhat greater that

113

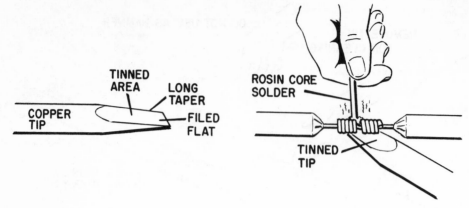

Figure 6-25.—Soldering a splice.

the overall diameter of the original cable, including the insulation.

Figure 6-26.—Applying rubber tape.

Friction Tape

Putting rubber tape over the splice means that the insulation has been restored to a great degree. It is also necessary to restore the protective covering. Friction tape is used for this purpose; it also affords a minor degree of electrical insulation.

Friction tape is a cotton cloth that has been treated with a sticky rubber compound. It comes in rolls similar to rubber tape except that no paper or cloth separator is used. Friction tape is applied like rubber tape; however, it does not stretch.

The friction tape should be started slightly back on the original braid covering. Wind the tape so that each turn overlaps the one before it; and extend the tape over onto the braid covering at the other end of the splice. From this point a second layer is wound back along the splice until the original starting point is reached. Cutting the tape and firmly pressing down the end complete the job. When proper care is taken, the splice can take as much abuse as the rest of the wire.

Weatherproof wire has no rubber insulation, just a braid covering. In that case, no rubber tape is necessary, only friction tape need be used.

Plastic Electrical Tape

Plastic electrical tape has come into wide use in recent years. It has certain advantages over rubber and friction tape. For example, it will withstand higher voltages for a given thickness. Single thin layers of certain commercially available plastic tape will stand several thousand volts without breaking down. However, to provide an extra margin of safety several layers are usually wound over the splice. Because the tape is very thin, the extra

114

layers add only a very small amount of bulk; but at the same time the added protection, normally furnished by friction tape, is provided by the additional layers of plastic tape. In the choice of plastic tape, the factor of expense must be balanced against the other factors involved.

Plastic electric tape normally has a certain amount of stretch so that it easily conforms to the contour of the splice without adding unnecessary bulk. The lack of bulkiness is especially important in some junction boxes where space is at a premium.

For high temperatures—for example, above 175° F.—a special type of tape backed with glass cloth is used.

SOLDER CONNECTORS

In some cases, splices and joints cannot readily be made by twisting and soldering conductors. For instance, it would be quite difficult to twist conductors together neatly if each consisted of many small strands. Stranded conductors are usually spliced by using special hardware designed for that purpose. Some of these devices use solder, while others do not.

Solder Splicers

The solder-type splicer is essentially a short piece of metal tube. Its inside diameter is just large enough to allow the tip of a stranded conductor to be inserted in either end, after the conductor tip has been stripped of insulation. This type of splicer is shown in figure 6-27.

The splicer is first heated and filled with solder. While still molten, the solder is then poured out, leaving the inner surfaces tinned. When the conductor tips are stripped, the length of exposed strands should be long enough so that the insulation butts against the splicer when the conductors are tinned and fully inserted. (See fig. 6-27 (B).) When heat is applied to the connection and the solder melts, excess solder will be squeezed out through the vents. This must be cleaned away. After the splice has cooled, insulating material must be wrapped or tied over the joint.

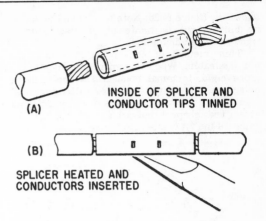

(A)   INSIDE OF SPLICER AND CONDUCTOR TIPS TINNED

(B)   SPLICER HEATED AND CONDUCTORS INSERTED

Figure 6-27.—Steps in using solder splicer.

Solder Terminal Lugs

In addition to being joined or spliced to one another, conducts are often connected to other objects, such as motors and switches. Since this is where a length of conductor ends (terminates), such connections are referred to as terminal points. In some cases, it is allowable to bend the end of the conductor into a small "eye" and put it around a terminal binding post. Where a mounting screw is used, the screw is passed through the eye. The conductor tip which forms the eye should be bent as

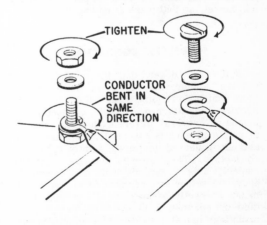

TIGHTEN

CONDUCTOR BENT IN SAME DIRECTION

Figure 6-28.—Conductor terminal connection.

115

shown in figure 6-28. Note that when the screw or binding nut is tightened, it also tends to tighten the conductor eye.

This method of connection is sometimes not desirable. When design requirements are more rigid, terminal connections are made by using special hardware devices called terminal lugs. There are terminal lugs of many different sizes and shapes, but all are essentially the same as the type shown in figure 6-29.

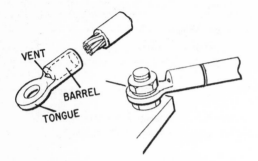

Figure 6-29.—Solder-type terminal lug.

Each type of lug has a barrel (sleeve) which is wedged, crimped, or soldered to its conductor. There is also a tongue with a hold or slot in it to receive the terminal post or screw. When mounting a solder-type terminal lug to a conductor, first tin the inside of the barrel. The conductor tip is stripped and also tinned, then inserted in the preheated lug. When mounted, the conductor insulation should butt against the lug barrel, so that there is no exposed conductor.

SOLDERLESS CONNECTORS

Splicers and terminal lugs which do not require solder are more widely used than those which do require solder. Solderless connectors are attached to their conductors by means of several different devices, but the principle of each is essentially the same. They are all squeezed (crimped) tightly onto their conductors. They afford adequate electrical contact, plus great mechanical strength. In addition, solderless connectors are easier to mount correctly because they are free from the most common problems of solder connector mounting; namely, cold solder joints, burned insulation, and so forth.

Solderless connectors are made in a great variety of sizes and shapes, and for many different purposes. Only a few are discussed here.

Solderless Splicers

Three of the most common type solderless splicers, classified according to their methods of mounting, are the split-sleeve, split-tapered-sleeve, and crimp-on splicers.

SPLIT-SLEEVE SPLICER

A split-sleeve splicer is shown in figure 6-30. To connect this splicer to its conductor, the stripped conductor tip is first inserted between the split-sleeve jaws. Using a tool designed for that purpose, the slide ring is forced toward the end of the sleeve. The sleeve jaws are closed tightly on the conductor, and the slide ring holds them securely.

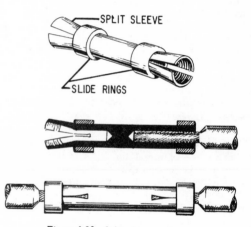

Figure 6-30.—Split-sleeve splicer.

SPLIT-TAPERED-SLEEVE SPLICER

A cross-sectional view of a split-tapered-sleeve splicer is shown in figure 6-31 (A). To mount this type of splicer, the conductor is stripped and inserted in the split-tapered sleeve. The threaded sleeve is turned or screwed into the tapered bore of the body. As the sleeve is turned in, the split segments are squeezed tightly around the conductor by the narrowing bore. The finished splice (fig. 6-31 (B)), must be covered with insulation.

116

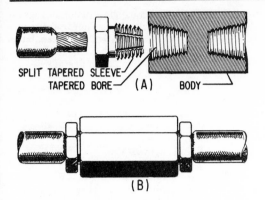

SPLIT TAPERED SLEEVE
TAPERED BORE (A) BODY

(B)

Figure 6-31.—Split-tapered-sleeve splice.

CRIMP-ON SPLICER

The crimp-on splicer (fig. 6-32) is the simplest of the splicers discussed. The type shown is preinsulated, though uninsulated types are manufactured. These splicers are mounted with a special plier-like hand-crimping tool designed for that purpose. The stripped conductor tips are inserted in the splicer, which is then squeezed tightly closed. The insulating sleeve grips the outer insulated conductor, and the metallic internal splicer grips the bare conductor strands.

Solderless Terminal Lugs

Solderless terminal lugs are used more widely than solder terminal lugs. They afford adequate electrical contact, plus great mechanical strength. In addition, solderless lugs are easier to attach correctly, because they are free from the most common problems of solder terminal lugs; namely, cold solder joints, burned insulation, and so forth. There are many sizes and shapes of these lugs, each intended for a different type of service of conductor size. Only a few are discussed here.

These are classified according to their method of mounting. They are the split-tapered-sleeve (wedge-type), split-tapered-sleeve (threaded-type), and crimp-on.

SPLIT-TAPERED-SLEEVE
TERMINAL LUG (WEDGE)

This type lug is shown in figure 6-33. It is commonly referred to as a "wedge-on," because of the manner in which it is secured to a conductor. The stripped conductor is inserted through the hole in the split sleeve. When the sleeve is forced or "wedged" down into the barrel, its tapered segments are squeezed tightly around the conductor.

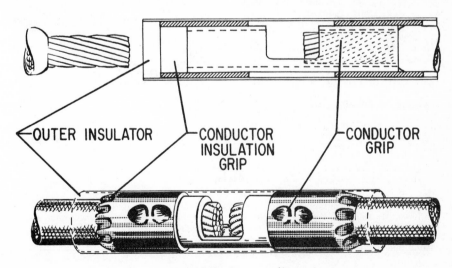

OUTER INSULATOR   CONDUCTOR INSULATION GRIP   CONDUCTOR GRIP

Figure 6-32.—Crimp-on splicer.

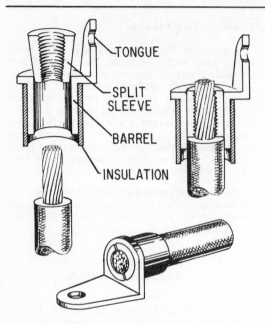

Figure 6-33.—Split-tapered-sleeve terminal lug (wedge type).

SPLIT-TAPERED-SLEEVE TERMINAL LUG (THREADED)

This lug (fig. 6-34) is attached to a conductor in exactly the same manner as a split-sleeve splicer. The segments of the threaded split sleeve squeezes tightly around the conductor as it is turned into the tapered bore of the barrel. For this reason, the lug is commonly referred to as a "screw-wedge."

CRIMP-ON TERMINAL LUG

The crimp-on lug is shown in figure 6-35. This lug is simply squeezed or "crimped"

tightly onto a conductor. This is done by using the same tool used with the crimp-on splicer. The lug shown is preinsulated, but uninsulated types are manufactured. When mounted, both the conductor and its insulation are gripped by the lug.

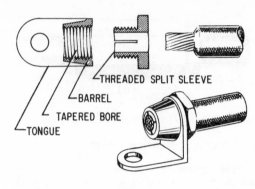

Figure 6-34.—Split-tapered-sleeve terminal lug (threaded).

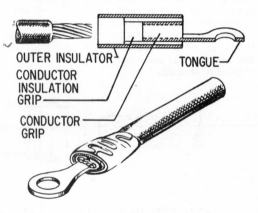

Figure 6-35.—Crimp-on terminal lug.

QUIZ

1. A mil is what part of an inch?
   a. 1/10
   b. 1/100
   c. 1/1000
   d. 1/1,000,000

2. The discharge (electrical leakage) that might occur from a wire carrying a high potential is called
   a. arcing
   b. sparking
   c. static discharge
   d. corona

3. Bare wire ends are spliced by the
   a. western union method
   b. rat-tail joint method
   c. fixture joint method
   d. all of the above

4. What is a unit conductor called that has a length of one foot and a cross-sectional area of one circular mil?
   a. Square mil
   b. Circular mil
   c. Circular mil foot
   d. Square mil foot

5. The induction-type soldering iron is commonly known as the
   a. soldering copper
   b. pencil iron
   c. soldering gun
   d. resistance gun

6. All good quality soldering irons operate at what temperature?
   a. 400 - 500° F.
   b. 500 - 600° F.
   c. 600 - 700° F.
   d. 300 - 600° F.

7. A No. 12 wire has a diameter of 80.81 mils. What is the area in circular mils?
   a. 6,530 cm.
   b. 5,630 cm.
   c. 4,530 cm.
   d. 3,560 cm.

8. Dielectric strength is the
   a. opposite of potential difference
   b. ability of a conductor to carry large amounts of current
   c. ability of an insulator to withstand a potential difference
   d. strength of a magnetic field

9. To readily transfer the heat from the soldering iron tip, it first should be
   a. tinned with solder
   b. allowed to form an oxide film
   c. cleaned with carbon tet
   d. allowed to heat for 25 minutes

10. A No. 12 wire has a diameter of 80.81 mils. What is the area in square mils?
    a. 2,516.8 square mils
    b. 5,128.6 square mils
    c. 6,530 square mils
    d. 8,512.6 square mils

11. Varnished cambric insulation is used to cover conductors carrying voltages above
    a. 1,000 volts
    b. 1,500 volts
    c. 15,000 volts
    d. 5,000 volts

12. The solder splicer is used to
    a. prevent the waste of rosin core solder
    b. connect together small lengths of solder
    c. connect two conductors together
    d. none of the above

13. The conductance of a conductor is the ease with which current will flow through it. It is measured in
    a. ohms
    b. mhos
    c. henrys
    d. amperes

14. Asbestos insulation loses its insulating properties when it becomes
    a. overaged
    b. overheated
    c. used over a long period of time
    d. wet

15. How are solderless connectors installed on conductors?
    a. Bolted on
    b. Chemical compound
    c. Crimped on
    d. All of the above

16. The factor(s) governing the selection of wire size is/are
    a. (I^2R loss) in the line
    b. (IR drop) in the line
    c. current-carrying ability of the line
    d. all of the above

17. Enamel insulated conductors are usually called
    a. magnet wire
    b. high voltage wire
    c. low voltage wire
    d. transmission lines

18. The advantage of solderless connectors over soldered type connectors is that they are
    a. mechanically stronger
    b. easier to install
    c. free of corrosion
    d. all of the above

19. The basic requirement of any splice is that it be
    a. soldered
    b. mechanically and electrically as strong as the conductor that is spliced
    c. made with a splicer
    d. taped

20. The type of tape that is used for electrical circuits having a temperature of 175° F. or above is
    a. glass cloth
    b. plastic
    c. synthetic rubber compound
    d. impregnated cloth

119

CHAPTER 7

ELECTROMAGNETISM AND MAGNETIC CIRCUITS

The fundamental theories concerning simple magnets and magnetism were discussed in chapter 1 of this course. Those discussions dealt mainly with forms of magnetism that were not related directly to electricity—permanent magnets for instance. Only brief mention was made of those forms of magnetism having direct relation to electricity (such as "producing electricity with magnetism"). This chapter resumes the study of magnetism where chapter 1 left off. Therefore, it may be necessary for you to review parts of chapter 1 from time to time. This chapter begins the more advanced study of MAGNETISM AS IT IS AFFECTED BY ELECTRIC CURRENT FLOW, and the closely related study of ELECTRICITY AS IT IS AFFECTED BY MAGNETISM. This general subject area is most often referred to as ELECTROMAGNETISM.

Magnetism and basic electricity are so closely related that one cannot be studied at length without involving the other. This close fundamental relationship will be continually borne out in other chapters of this course, such as in the study of generators, transformers, and motors. You will become familiar with many of the most general relationships between magnetism and electricity, such as the following:

1. Electric current flow will ALWAYS produce some form of magnetism.

2. Magnetism is by far the most commonly used means for producing or using electricity.

3. The peculiar behavior of electricity under certain conditions is caused by magnetic influences.

Magnetic Field Around a Current-Carrying Conductor

In 1819 Hans Christian Oersted, a Danish physicist, found that a definite relation exists between magnetism and electricity. He discovered that an electric current is accompanied by certain magnetic effects and that these effects obey definite laws. If a compass is placed in the vicinity of a current-carrying conductor, the needle alines itself at right angles to the conductor, thus indicating the presence of a magnetic force. The presence of this force can be demonstrated by passing an electric current through a vertical conductor which passes through a horizontal piece of cardboard, as illustrated in figure 7-1. The magnitude and direction of the force are determined by setting a compass at various points on the cardboard and noting the deflection.

The direction of the force is assumed to be the direction the north pole of the compass points. These deflections show that a magnetic field exists in circular form around the conductor. When the current flows upward, the field direction is clockwise, as viewed from the top, but if the polarity of the supply is reversed so that the current flows downward, the direction of the field is counterclockwise.

The relation between the direction of the magnetic lines of force around a conductor and the direction of current flow along the conductor may be determined by means of the LEFT-HAND RULE FOR A CONDUCTOR. If the conductor is grasped in the left hand with the thumb extended in the direction of electron flow (- to +), the fingers will point in the direction of the magnetic lines of force. This is the same direction in which the north pole of a compass would point if the compass was placed in the magnetic field.

Arrows generally are used in electric diagrams to denote the direction of current flow along the length of wire. Where cross sections of wire are shown, a special view of the arrow

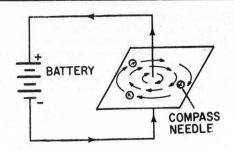

Figure 7-1.—Magnetic field around a current-carrying conductor.

is used. A cross-sectional view of a conductor that is carrying current toward the observer is illustrated in figure 7-2 (A). The direction of current is indicated by a dot, which represents the head of the arrow. A conductor that is carrying current away from the observer is illustrated in figure 7-2 (B). The direction of current is indicated by a cross, which represents the tail of the arrow.

When two parallel conductors carry current in the same direction, the magnetic fields tend to encircle both conductors, drawing them together with a force of attraction, as shown in figure 7-3 (A). Two parallel conductors carrying currents in opposite directions are shown in figure 7-3 (B). The field around one conductor is opposite in direction to the field around the other conductor. The resulting lines of force are crowded together in the space between the wires, and tend to push the wires apart. Therefore, two parallel adjacent conductors carrying currents in the same direction attract each other and two parallel conductors carrying currents in opposite directions repel each other.

Magnetic Field of a Coil

The magnetic field around a current-carrying wire exists at all points along its length. The field consists of concentric circles in a plane perpendicular to the wire. (See fig. 7-1.) When this straight wire is wound around a core, as shown in figure 7-4 (A), it becomes a coil and the magnetic field assumes a different shape. Part (A) is a partial cutaway view which shows the construction of a simple coil. Part (B) is a complete cross-sectional view of the same coil. The two ends of the coil are identified as *a* and *b*. When current is passed through the coiled conductor, as indicated, the magnetic field of each

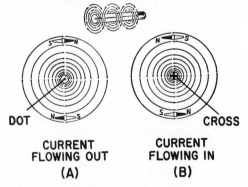

Figure 7-2.—Magnetic field around a current-carrying conductor, detailed view.

turn of wire links with the fields of adjacent turns, as explained in connection with figure 7-3 (A). The combined influence of all the turns produces a two-pole field similar to that of a simple bar magnet. One end of the coil will be a north pole and the other end will be a south pole.

POLARITY OF AN ELECTROMAGNETIC COIL

In figure 7-2, it was shown that the direction of the magnetic field around a straight conductor depends on the direction of current flow through that conductor. Thus, a reversal of current flow through a conductor causes a reversal in the direction of the magnetic field that is produced. It follows that a reversal of the current flow through a coil also causes a reversal of its two-pole field. This is true because that field is the product of the linkage between the individual turns of wire on the coil. Therefore, if the field of each turn is reversed, it follows that the total field (coil's field) is also reversed.

When the direction of electron flow through a coil is known, its polarity may be determined by use of the LEFT-HAND RULE FOR COILS. This rule is illustrated in figure 7-5, and is stated as follows: GRASPING THE COIL IN THE LEFT HAND, WITH THE FINGERS "WRAPPED AROUND" IN THE DIRECTION OF ELECTRON

121

FLOW, THE THUMB WILL POINT TOWARD THE NORTH POLE.

STRENGTH OF AN ELECTROMAGNETIC FIELD

The strength, or intensity, of a coil's field depends on a number of factors. The major factors are listed below. All of these factors are discussed under headings that follow.

1. The number of turns of conductor.
2. The amount of current flow through the coil.
3. The ratio of the coil's length to its width.
4. The type of material in the core.

Magnetic Circuits

Many electrical devices depend upon magnetism in one or more forms for their operation. To have these devices function efficiently, engineers work out intricate designs for the required magnetic conditions. The magnets designed to do a particular job must have the required strength, and must be provided with paths, or circuits, of suitable shapes and materials.

A magnetic circuit is defined as the path (or paths) taken by the magnetic lines of force leaving a north pole, passing through the entire circuit and returning to the south pole. A magnetic circuit may be a series or parallel circuit or any combination.

Ohm's Law Equivalent for Magnetic Circuits

The law of current flow in the electric circuit is similar to the law for the establishing of flux in the magnetic circuit.

Ohm's law for ELECTRIC circuits states that the current is directly proportional to the applied voltage and inversely proportional to the resistance offered by the circuit. Expressed mathematically,

$$I = \frac{E}{R}.$$

Rowland's law for MAGNETIC circuits states, in effect, that the number of lines of magnetic flux in maxwells (Φ) is directly proportional to the magnetomotive force in gilberts (F) and inversely proportional to the reluctance ($\mathfrak{R}$) offered by the circuit. The unit of reluctance sometimes used is the REL, $\mathfrak{R}$. Expressed mathematically,

$$\Phi = \frac{F}{\mathfrak{R}}.$$

The similarity of Ohm's law and Rowland's law is apparent. However, the units used in the expression for Rowland's law need to be explained.

The MAGNETIC FLUX, Φ, (phi) is similar to current in the Ohm's law formula, and comprises the total number of lines of force existing in the magnetic circuit. The MAXWELL is the unit of flux—that is, 1 line of force is equal to 1 maxwell. However, the maxwell is often referred to as simply a LINE OF FORCE, LINE OF INDUCTION or LINE.

The MAGNETOMOTIVE FORCE, F, or m. m. f., comparable to electromotive force in the Ohm's law formula, is the force that produces the flux in the magnetic circuit. The practical unit of magnetomotive force is the AMPERE-TURN. Another unit of magnetomotive force sometimes used is the GILBERT, designated by the capital letter, F. The gilbert is the magnetomotive force required to establish 1 maxwell in a magnetic circuit having 1 unit of reluctance (1 rel). The magnetomotive force in gilberts is expressed in terms of ampere-turns as

$$F = 1.257\,IN,$$

where F is in gilberts, I is in amperes, and N is the number of complete turns of wire encircling the circuit.

The UNIT OF INTENSITY of magnetizing force per unit of length is designated as H, and is sometimes expressed as gilberts per centimeter of length. Expressed mathematically,

$$H = \frac{1.257\,IN}{l},$$

where l is the length in centimeters.

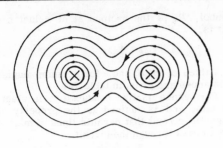

CURRENTS FLOWING IN THE SAME DIRECTION

(A)

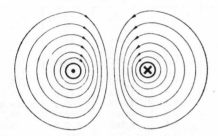

CURRENTS FLOWING IN OPPOSITE DIRECTIONS

(B)

Figure 7-3.—Magnetic field around two parallel conductors.

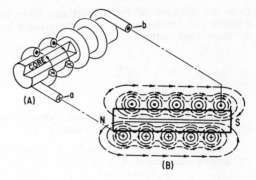

(A)

(B)

Figure 7-4.—Magnetic field produced by a current-carrying coil.

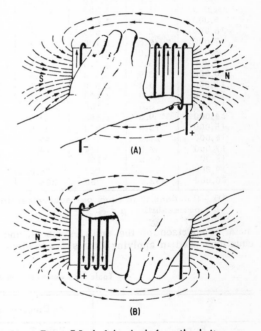

Figure 7-5.—Left-hand rule for coil polarity.

The RELUCTANCE, $\mathscr{R}$, similar to resistance in the Ohm's law formula, is the opposition offered by the magnetic circuit to the passage of magnetic flux. The unit of reluctance has not been named officially. However, the REL has been proposed, and the symbol $\mathscr{R}$ is commonly used. The unit of reluctance is the reluctance of 1 centimeter-cube of air. The reluctance of a magnetic substance varies directly as the length of the flux path and inversely as the cross-sectional area and the permeability, μ, of the substance. Expressed mathematically,

$$\mathscr{R} = \frac{l}{\mu A},$$

where l is the length in centimeters, and A is the cross-sectional area in square centimeters.

PERMEABILITY, designated by the Greek letter mu, μ, is treated under a separate heading.

However, it is defined here to permit a fuller interpretation of Rowland's law and also a practical application of this law. Permeability is a measure of the relative ability of a substance to conduct magnetic lines of force as compared with air. The permeability of air is taken as 1. Permeability is indicated as the ratio of the flux density in lines per square centimeter (gauss,

B) to the intensity of the magnetizing force in gilberts per centimeter of length, indicated by H. Expressed mathematically,

$$\mu = \frac{B}{H}.$$

Another term used in magnetic circuits is PERMEANCE. Permeance, indicated by the symbol, P, is the reciprocal of reluctance—that is,

$$P = \frac{1}{\mathcal{R}}.$$

Values of B, H, and μ for common magnetic substances are given in table 7-1.

Permeance is like conductance in electric circuits, and is defined as the property of a magnetic circuit that permits lines of magnetic flux to pass through the circuit.

Table 7-1.–B, H, and μ for common magnetic material.*

B	Sheet steel		Cast steel		Wrought iron		Cast iron	
	H	μ	H	μ	H	μ	H	μ
3,000	1.3	2,310	2.8	1,070	2.0	1,500	5.0	600
4,000	1.6	2,500	3.4	1,177	2.5	1,600	8.5	471
5,000	1.9	2,630	3.9	1,281	3.0	1,666	14.5	347
6,000	2.3	2,605	4.5	1,332	3.5	1,716	24.0	250
7,000	2.6	2,700	5.1	1,371	4.0	1,750	38.5	182
8,000	3.0	2,666	5.8	1,380	4.5	1,778	60.0	133
9,000	3.5	2,570	6.5	1,382	5.0	1,800	89.0	101
10,000	3.9	2,560	7.5	1,332	5.6	1,782	124.0	80.6
11,000	4.4	2,500	9.0	1,222	6.5	1,692	166.0	66.4
12,000	5.0	2,400	11.5	1,042	7.9	1,520	222.0	54.1
13,000	6.0	2,166	16.0	813	10.0	1,300	290.0	44.8
14,000	9.0	1,558	21.5	651	15.0	934	369.0	38.0
15,000	15.5	970	32.0	469	25.0	600	....	...
16,000	27.0	594	49.0	327	49.0	327	....	...
17,000	52.5	324	74.0	230	93.0	183	....	...
18,000	92.0	196	115.0	156	152.0	118	....	...
19,000	149.0	127	175.0	108	229.0	83	....	...
20,000	232.0	86	285.0	70	....	....	....	...

*B = flux density in lines per square centimeter; H = gilberts per centimeter of length; μ = permeability; $\mu = \frac{B}{H}$.

A comparison of the units, symbols, and equations used in applying Ohm's law to electric circuits and Rowland's law to magnetic circuits is given in table 7-2.

Table 7-2.—Comparison of electric and magnetic circuits.

	Electric circuit	Magnetic circuit
Force.........	Volt, E, or e.m.f.	Gilberts, F, or m.m.f.
Flow	Ampere, I	Flux, Φ, in maxwells
Opposition......	Ohms, R	Reluctance, $\mathcal{R}$, or rels
Law..........	Ohm's law, $I = \frac{E}{R}$	Rowland's law, $\Phi = \frac{F}{\mathcal{R}}$
Intensity of force .	Volts per cm. of length	$H = \frac{1.257IN}{\ell}$, gilberts per centimeter of length.
Density........	Current density— for example, amperes per cm.^{2}.	Flux density—for example, lines per cm.^{2}, or gausses.

As a practical application of Rowland's law, let it be required to find the ampere-turns *(IN)* necessary to produce 20,000 lines of flux in a CAST STEEL ring having a cross-sectional area of 4 square centimeters and an average length of 20 centimeters, as shown in figure 7-6.

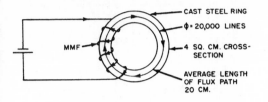

Figure 7-6.—Determining ampere-turns in a magnetic circuit.

Flux density B is expressed as

$$B = \frac{\Phi}{A} = \frac{200,000}{4} = 5,000 \text{ lines/cm.}^2,$$

and from table 7-1 the corresponding value of H for cast steel is 3.9. The formula for H has previously been given as

$$H = \frac{1.257\,IN}{l},$$

from which

$$IN = \frac{Hl}{1.257}.$$

Substituting 3.9 for H and 20 for l in the preceding equation,

$$IN = \frac{3.9 \times 20}{1.257} = 62 \text{ ampere-turns.}$$

Properties of Magnetic Materials

PERMEABILITY

When an annealed sheet steel core is used in an electromagnet it produces a stronger magnet than if a cast iron core is used. This is true because annealed sheet steel is more readily acted upon by the magnetizing force of the coil than is hard cast iron. In other words, soft sheet steel is said to have greater permeability because the magnetic lines are established more easily in it than in cast iron. The ratio of the flux produced by a coil when the core is iron (or some other substance) to the flux produced when the core is air is called the PERMEABILITY of the iron (or whatever substance is used), the current in the coil being the same in each case. The permeability of a substance is thus a measure of the relative ability to conduct magnetic lines of force, or its magnetic conductivity. The permeability of air is 1. The permeability of nonmagnetic materials, such as wood, aluminum, copper, and brass is essentially unity, or the same as for air.

Magnetization curves for the four magnetic materials listed in table 7-1 are given in figure 7-7.

The permeability of magnetic materials varies with the degree of magnetization, being smaller for high values of flux density, as is indicated in table 7-1 and figure 7-8.

HYSTERESIS

The simplest method of illustrating the property of hysteresis is by graphical means such as the hysteresis loop shown in figure 7-9.

In this figure the magnetizing force is indicated in gilberts per centimeter of length along the plus and minus H axis, and the flux density is indicated in gausses along the plus and minus B axis. The intensity of the magnetizing force, H, applied by means of a current-carrying coil of wire around the sample of magnetic material, is varied uniformly through one cycle of operation, starting at zero. The force, H, is increased in the positive direction (current flowing in a given direction through the coil) to 11 gilberts per centimeter. During this time the flux density, B, increases from zero to 14,000 at point A. If H is decreased to zero, the descending curve of flux density does not return to zero via its rise path. Instead, it returns to point B, where the flux density is 13,000. The magnetic flux indicated by the length of line OB represents the RETENTIVITY of the magnetic substance.

Retentivity is the ability of a magnetic substance to retain its magnetism after the magnetizing force has been removed. Retentivity is most apparent in hard steel and is least apparent in soft iron.

The value of the RESIDUAL, or remaining, MAGNETISM when H has been reduced to zero, depends on the substance used and the degree

125

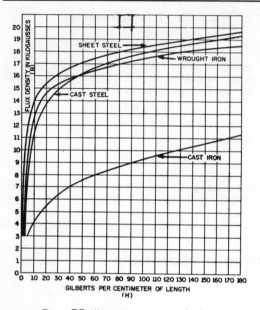

Figure 7-7.—Magnetization curves for four
magnetic materials.

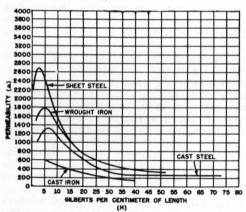

Figure 7-8.—Permeability curves.

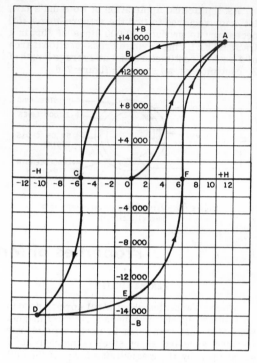

Figure 7-9.—Hysteresis loop.

the residual magnetism to zero is called the
COERCIVE FORCE. In this example the coercive
force is **6 gilberts** per centimeter.

If the **magnetizing force** is continued to -11
gilberts per centimeter, the curve descends from
C to D, magnetizing the sample of magnetic
material with the opposite polarity. If the magnetizing force is reduced again to zero, the flux
density is reduced to point E. The magnetic flux
indicated by the length of line OE represents
the retentivity of the magnetic substance, as did
line OB. The residual magnetism is again 13,000
gausses.

If the current through the coil is again reversed (sent through in the original direction),
the magnetization curve moves to zero when the
magnetizing force is increased to point F.

Thus, when the magnetizing force goes
through a complete cycle, the resulting magnetization likewise goes through a complete **cycle**.

From the foregoing analysis it is apparent
that hysteresis is the property of a **magnetic**

of flux density attained. In this example the
residual magnetism is 13,000 gausses.

If current is now sent through the coil in
the opposite direction, so that the intensity of
the magnetizing force becomes -H, the force
will have to be increased to point C before the
residual magnetism is reduced to zero. The
magnetizing force, OC, necessary to reduce

substance that causes the magnetization to lag behind the force that produces it. The lag of magnetization behind the force that produces it is caused by molecular friction. Energy is needed to move the molecules (or domains) through a cycle of magnetization. If the magnetization is reversed slowly, the energy loss may be negligible. However, if the magnetization is reversed rapidly, as when commercial alternating current is used, considerable energy may be dissipated. If the molecular friction is great, as when hard steel is used, the losses may be very great. Another factor that determines hysteresis loss is the maximum density of the flux established in the magnetic material.

A comparison of the hysteresis loops for annealed steel and hard steel is shown in figure 7-10. The area within each loop is a measure of the hysteresis energy loss per cycle of operation. Thus, as shown in the figure, more energy is dissipated in molecular friction in hard steel than in annealed steel. It is therefore important that substances having low hysteresis loss be used for transformer cores and similar a-c applications.

Electromagnets

An electromagnet is composed of a coil of wire wound around a core of soft iron. When direct current flows through the coil the core will become magnetized with the same polarity that the coil (solenoid) would have without the core. If the current is reversed, the polarity of both the coil and the soft-iron core is reversed.

The polarity of the electromagnet is determined by the left-hand rule in the same manner that the polarity of the solenoid in figure 7-5 was determined. If the coil is grasped in the left hand in such a way that the fingers curve around the coil in the direction of electron flow (- to +), the thumb will point in the direction of the north pole.

The addition of the soft-iron core does two things for the current-carrying coil, or solenoid. First, the magnetic flux is increased because the soft-iron core is more permeable than the air core; second, the flux is more highly concentrated. The permeability of soft iron is many times that of air, and therefore the flux density is increased considerably when a soft-iron core is inserted in the coil.

The magnetic field around the turns of wire making up the coil influences the molecules in the iron bar causing, in effect, the individual molecular magnets, or domains, to line up in the direction of the field established by the coil. Essentially the same effect is produced in a soft-iron bar when it is under the influence of a permanent magnet.

The magnetomotive force resulting from the current flow around the coil does not increase the magnetism that is inherent in the iron core, it merely reorientates the "atomic" magnets that were present before the magnetizing force was applied. If substantial numbers of the tiny magnets are orientated in the same direction, the core is said to be magnetized.

When soft iron is used, most of the atomic magnets return to what amounts to a miscellaneous orientation upon removal of the magnetizing current, and the iron is said to be demagnetized. If hard steel is used, more of them will remain in alinement with the direction of the flux produced by the flow of current through the coil, and the metal is said to be a permanent magnet. Soft iron and other magnetic materials having high permeability and low retentivity are generally used in electromagnets.

It is known from experience that a piece of soft iron is attracted to either pole of a permanent magnet. A soft-iron bar is likewise attracted by a current-carrying coil, if the coil and bar are orientated as in figure 7-11. As shown in the figure, the lines of force extend through the soft iron and magnetize it. Because unlike poles attract, the iron bar is pulled toward the coil. If the bar is free to move, it will be drawn into the coil to a position near the center where the field is the strongest.

The SOLENOID-AND-PLUNGER TYPE of magnet in various forms is employed extensively aboard ships and aircraft. These are used to operate the feeding mechanism of carbon-arc searchlights; to open circuit-breakers automatically when the load current becomes excessive; to close switches for motorboat starting; to fire guns; and to operate flood valves, magnetic brakes, and many other devices.

The ARMATURE-TYPE of electromagnet also has extensive applications. In this type of magnet the coil is wound on and insulated from the iron core. The core is not movable. When

127

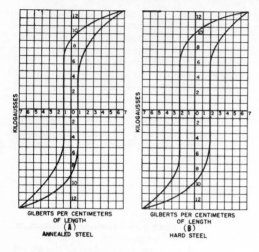

GILBERTS PER CENTIMETERS OF LENGTH
(A)
ANNEALED STEEL

GILBERTS PER CENTIMETERS OF LENGTH
(B)
HARD STEEL

Figure 7-10.—Comparison of hysteresis loops.

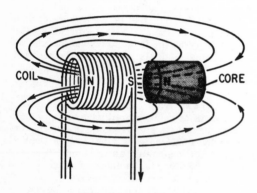

COIL — N S — CORE

Figure 7-11.—Solenoid with iron core.

current flows through the coil the iron core becomes magnetized and causes a pivoted soft-iron armature located near the electromagnet, to be attracted toward it. This type of magnet is used in door bells, relays, circuit breakers, telephone receivers, and so forth.

APPLICATIONS OF ELECTROMAGNETS

Electric Bell

The electric bell is one of the most common devices employing the electromagnet. A simple

electric bell is shown in figure 7-12. Its operation is explained as follows:

1. When the switch is closed, current flows from the negative terminal of the battery, through the contact points, the spring, the two coils, and back to the positive terminal of the battery.

2. The cores are magnetized, and the soft-iron armature (magnetized by induction) is pulled down, thus causing the hammer to strike the bell.

3. At the instant the armature is pulled down, the contact is broken, and the electromagnet loses its magnetism. The spring pulls the armature up so that contact is reestablished, and the operation is repeated. The speed with which the hammer is moved up and down depends on the stiffness of the spring and the mass of the moving element.

The magnetomotive forces of the two coils are in series aiding and therefore the magnetization of the core is increased over that produced by one coil alone.

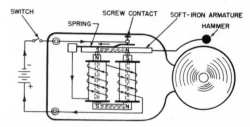

Figure 7-12.—Electric bell.

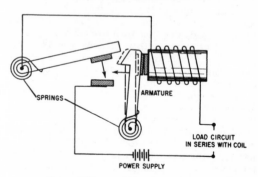

Figure 7-13.—Magnetic circuit breaker.

Circuit Breaker

A circuit breaker, like a fuse, protects a circuit against short circuits and overloading. In this device the winding of an electromagnet is

128

connected in series with the load circuit to be protected and with the switch contact points. The principle of operation is shown in figure 7-13. Excessive current through the magnet winding causes the switch to be tripped, and the circuit to both breaker and load is opened by a spring. When the circuit fault has been cleared, the circuit is closed again by manually resetting the circuit breaker.

Many more applications of electromagnets are discussed throughout this course. Their applications to generators, motors, voltage regulators, reverse current relays, and servo-mechanisms will be covered.

QUIZ

1. Reversing the current flow through a coil
   a. reduces the amount of flux produced
   b. reverses its two-pole field
   c. reduces power consumed
   d. reduces eddy currents

2. The unit of magnetic flux is
   a. ampere-turn
   b. gilbert
   c. intensity
   d. maxwell

3. Flux in a magnetic circuit compares in an electrical circuit with
   a. voltage
   b. current
   c. resistance
   d. opposition

4. If a compass is placed in the vicinity of a conductor carrying d.c., the needle alines itself
   a. in the direction of current flow in the conductor
   b. at the right angles to the conductor
   c. in the general direction of the north pole
   d. in the general direction of the south pole

5. The left-hand rule for coils states: Grasping the
   a. coil with the left hand, with fingers pointing in the direction of the magnetic field, the middle finger will point to the north pole
   b. coil with the left hand, thumb pointing in the direction of the conductor movement, the fingers will point in the direction of the magnetic field
   c. conductor with the left hand, fingers pointing in the direction of the north pole, the thumb will indicate current flow
   d. coil in the left hand, fingers wrapped around in the direction of electron flow, the thumb will point towards north pole

6. The word permeability indicates the
   a. amount of reluctance of one centimeter-cube of air
   b. number of turns of an air core
   c. ability of a substance to conduct magnetic lines of force
   d. m.m.f. required to produce one gilbert

7. If an iron core is inserted part way into a coil and current is applied to the coil, the core will be drawn into the coil in an effort to
   a. increase reluctance of the magnetic circuit
   b. decrease the length of the magnetic circuit
   c. reduce the permeability of the circuit
   d. increase the residual effect

8. Current flow in a straight conductor produces
   a. hysteresis
   b. magnetic lines of force
   c. a north pole
   d. permeability

9. The inductance of a coil depends upon the
   a. number of turns, current flow, type of core material, and ratio of coil's length to its width
   b. current, flux, and core material
   c. direction of rotation, flux, and speed
   d. permeability, reluctance, gausses, and maxwells

10. The ability of a magnetic substance to hold its magnetism after the magnetizing force has been removed is
    a. residual
    b. retentivity
    c. hysteresis
    d. permeability

11. The solenoid and plunger type of magnet is employed in various forms to control
    a. electrical equipment
    b. hysteresis losses
    c. permeability
    d. all of the above

12. When using the left-hand rule for a conductor
    a. grasp the conductor with fingers pointing in the direction of current flow and thumb will indicate direction of field
    b. the compass will point in the direction of current flow and fingers will indicate direction of magnetic field
    c. grasp the conductor with the thumb extended in the direction of electron flow, the fingers will point in the direction of the magnetic lines of force
    d. reverse the current flow and thumb will point in direction of the magnetic field

13. The magnetic circuit is determined by
    a. lines of force leaving the south pole and entering the north pole externally
    b. permeability to current and the north pole
    c. maxwells to length in centimeters and the south pole
    d. the complete path taken by magnetic lines leaving the north pole, and returning to the north pole

14. In what material is retentivity most apparent?
    a. Hard steel
    b. Soft iron
    c. Copper
    d. Wood

15. The armature type of electromagnet
    a. has a movable iron bar in its magnetic circuit
    b. uses a permanent magnet core
    c. has a hard steel core and a pivoted bar of copper
    d. has a movable iron core

16. When two parallel conductors carrying current in the same direction are placed side by side, the fields produced by both
    a. cancel each other's field
    b. push each other apart
    c. form a north pole
    d. encircle each other, drawing the conductors together

17. The equivalent Ohm's law formula for magnetic circuits is

    a. $I = \dfrac{e}{r}$

    b. $R = \dfrac{I}{E}$

    c. $\Phi = \dfrac{E}{R}$

    d. $P = \dfrac{I}{E}$

18. Which of the following materials incurs low hysteresis loss when used for transformer cores and similar applications?
    a. Hard steel
    b. Annealed steel
    c. Soft iron
    d. Cast steel

19. The magnetic field around a current-carrying wire
    a. is parallel to the current flow in the conductor
    b. exists at all points along its length
    c. exists only at the beginning of electron movement
    d. moves in the direction of current flow

20. Direct current flows through a coil of wire which has an iron core. When the iron core is removed and all other factors remain unchanged, the total number of lines of force through the coil will change because
    a. changing the core material affects m.m.f.
    b. permeance has been increased
    c. reluctance has been increased
    d. the permeability of the magnetic circuit has been increased

21. When loops of wire are formed into a coil and current is passed through this coil
    a. the result is a permanent magnet
    b. each turn will cancel the magnetic field of each adjacent turn
    c. the magnetic field of each turn of wire links with the fields of adjacent turns
    d. permeability decreases to minimum

130

CHAPTER 8

INTRODUCTION TO ALTERNATING-CURRENT ELECTRICITY

In the study of batteries you learned that electrons flow continually in one direction—from the negative terminal to the positive terminal, via the load.

In the case of alternating current, electrons are made to move first in one direction and then in the other. The direction of current flow reverses periodically.

Basic A-C Generator

An alternating-current generator converts mechanical energy into electrical energy. It does this by utilizing the principle of electromagnetic induction. In the study of magnetism, it was shown that a current-carrying conductor produces a magnetic field around itself. It is also true that a changing magnetic field may produce an e.m.f. in a conductor. If a conductor lies in a magnetic field, and either the field or conductor moves, an e.m.f. is induced in the conductor. This effect is called electromagnetic induction.

CYCLE

Figure 8-1 shows a suspended loop of wire (conductor) being rotated (moved) in a counterclockwise direction through the magnetic field between the poles of a permanent magnet. For ease of explanation, the loop has been divided into a dark and a light half. Notice that in part (A), the dark half is moving along (parallel to) the lines of force. Consequently, it is cutting none of these lines. The same is true of the light half, moving in the opposite direction. Since the conductors are cutting no lines of force, no e.m.f. is induced. As the loop rotates toward the position shown in part (B), it cuts more and more lines of force per second because it is cutting more directly across the field (lines of force) as it approaches the position shown in (B). At position (B) the induced voltage is greatest because the conductor is cutting directly across the field.

As the loop continues to be rotated toward the position shown in part (C), it cuts fewer and fewer lines of force per second. The induced voltage decreases from its peak value. Eventually, the loop is once again moving in a plane parallel to the magnetic field, and no voltage (zero voltage) is induced. The loop has now been rotated through half a circle (one alternation, or 180°). The sine curve shown in the lower part of the figure shows the induced voltage at every instant of rotation of the loop. Notice that this curve contains 360°, or two alternations. Two alternations represent one complete cycle of rotation.

The direction of current flow during the rotation from (B) to (C), when a closed path is provided across the ends of the conductor loop, can be determined by using the LEFT-HAND RULE FOR GENERATORS. The left-hand rule is applied as follows: Extend the left hand so that the THUMB points in the direction of conductor movement, and the FOREFINGER points in the direction of magnetic flux (north to south). By pointing the MIDDLE FINGER 90 degrees from the forefinger, it will point in the direction of current flow within the conductor.

Applying the left-hand rule to the dark half of the loop in part (B), you will find that the direction of current flow is as shown by the heavy arrow. Similarly, you can determine the direction of current flow through the light half of the loop. The two induced voltages add together to form one total e.m.f. When the loop is further rotated to the position shown in part (D), the action is reversed. The dark half is moving

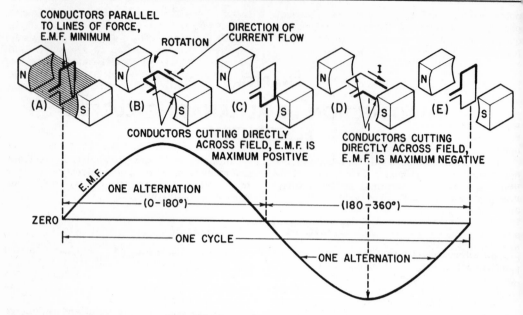

Figure 8-1.—Basic alternating-current generator.

up instead of down, and the light half is moving down instead of up. By applying the left-hand rule once again, you will find that the direction of the induced e.m.f. and its resulting current have reversed. The voltage builds up to maximum in this new direction, as shown by the sine-wave tracing. The loop finally returns to its original position (part E), at which point voltage is again zero. The wave of induced voltage has gone through one complete cycle.

If the loop is rotated at a steady rate, and if the strength of the magnetic field is uniform, the number of cycles per second and the voltage will remain at fixed values. Continuous rotation will produce a series of sine-wave voltage cycles, or, in other words, an a-c voltage. In this way mechanical energy is converted into electrical energy.

The rotating loop in figure 8-1 is called an armature. The armature may have any number of loops or coils.

FREQUENCY

The frequency of an alternating current or voltage is the number of complete cycles occurring in each second of time. Hence, the speed of rotation of the loop determines the frequency. For a single loop rotating in a two-pole field you can see that each time the loop makes one complete revolution the current reverses direction twice. A single cycle of a-c per second will result if the loop makes one revolution each second. If it makes two revolutions per second, the output frequency will be two cycles per second. In other words, the frequency of a two-pole generator happens to be the same as the number of revolutions per second. As the speed is increased, the frequency is increased.

If an alternating-current generator has four pole pieces, as in figure 8-2, every complete mechanical revolution of the armature will produce TWO a-c cycles. When the dark half of the loop passes between poles S1 and N2, a voltage is induced which causes current to flow into the dark slipring attached to the end of the loop.

When the dark half passes between N2 and S2, the induced voltage reverses direction. Another reversal occurs when it passes between S2 and N1. The voltage at the sliprings reverses direction FOUR TIMES during each revolution. In other words, two cycles of a-c voltage are generated for each mechanical revolution. If each revolution lasts one second, the frequency of the output is two cycles per second. The more

132

poles that are added, the higher the frequency per revolution becomes. To find the output frequency of any a-c generator, the following formula can be used:

$$f = \frac{P \times r.p.m.}{120}$$

where f is frequency in cycles per second, r.p.m. is revolutions per minute, and P is the number of poles.

A generator made to deliver 60 cycles per second (c.p.s.), having two field poles, would need an armature designed to rotate at 3,600 r.p.m. If it had four field poles, it would need an armature designed to rotate at 1,800 r.p.m. In either case, frequency would be the same. In actual practice, a generator designed for low-speed operation generally has a greater number of pole pieces, while a high-speed machine will have relatively fewer pole pieces, if both are to deliver power at the same frequency.

PERIOD

The period of an a-c voltage or current of sine waveform is the time for one complete cycle, or $1/f$. For example, the period of a 60-cycle voltage is 1/60 of a second; that of a 50-cycle voltage is 1/50 second.

GENERATED VOLTAGE

Alternating-current generators are usually constant-potential machines because they are driven at constant speed and have fixed magnetic field strength for a given load. The effective voltage, E, generated by a single-winding (phase) a-c generator is related to the total field strength per pole, Φ; the frequency, f; and the total number of active conductors, N, in the armature winding; as indicated in the following equation:

$$E = 2.22 \, \Phi f N 10^{-8}$$

For example, if $\Phi = 2.5 \times 10^6$, $f = 60$ cycles per second, and $N = 96$ conductors, the voltage generated is

$$E = 2.22 \times 2.5 \times 10^6 \times 60 \times 96 \times 10^{-8}$$

$$E = 320 \text{ volts.}$$

(The factors of poles (P) and speed (S in r.p.m.), which appear in the equation for generated voltage in multipolar series-wound d-c generators, do not appear in the formula for the voltage generated in each phase of the a-c generator. This is because they are replaced by the equivalent factor of frequency ($f = \frac{PS}{120}$).

The length of active conductor extending under a pole does not appear in the equation directly because it is included in the factor of total magnetic flux per pole. The longer the active conductor, the more flux there will be for each pole, since the pole length and conductor length are assumed to be the same. For example, if an active conductor length is doubled, the pole length is doubled, the flux per pole is doubled, and the generated voltage is doubled.

Analysis of Sine Wave of Voltage

VECTORS DEFINED

As mentioned previously, an alternating current or voltage is one in which the direction changes periodically. The electron movement is first in one direction, then in the other. The variation is of sine waveform. Straight lines drawn to scale, called VECTORS, are used in solving problems involving sine-wave currents and voltages.

A simple vector is a straight line used to denote the magnitude and direction of a given quantity. Magnitude is denoted by the length of the line, drawn to scale, and direction is indicated by an arrow at one end of the line, together with the angle that the vector makes with a horizontal reference vector.

For example, if a certain point B (fig. 8-3) lies 1 mile east of point A, the direction and distance from A to B can be shown as vector e by using a scale of approximately 1/2 inch = 1 mile.

Vectors may be rotated like the spokes of a wheel to generate angles. Positive rotation is counterclockwise and generates positive angles. Negative rotation is clockwise and generates negative angles.

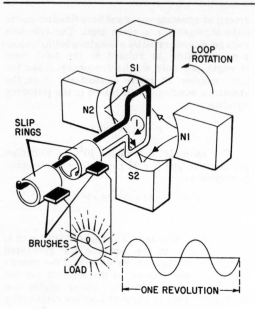

Figure 8-2.—Four-pole basic a-c generator.

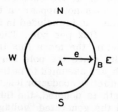

Figure 8-3.—Designating direction and distance by vectors.

The vertical projection (dotted line in fig. 8-4) of a ROTATING VECTOR may be used to represent the voltage at any instant. Vector E_m represents the maximum voltage induced in a conductor rotating at uniform speed in a 2-pole field (points 3 and 9). The vector is rotated counterclockwise through one complete revolution (360°). The point of the vector describes a circle. A line drawn from the point of the vector perpendicular to the horizontal diameter of the circle is the vertical projection of the vector.

The circle also describes the path of the conductor rotating in the bi-polar field. The vertical projection of the vector represents the voltage generated in the conductor at any instant

corresponding to the position of the rotating vector as indicated by angle θ. Angle θ represents selected instants at which the generated voltage is plotted. The sine curve plotted at the right of the figure represents successive values of the a-c voltage induced in the conductor as it moves at uniform speed through the 2-pole field because the instantaneous values of rotationally induced voltage are proportional to the sine of the angle θ that the rotating vector makes with the horizontal.

EQUATION OF SINE WAVE OF VOLTAGE

The sine curve is a graph of the equation

$$e = E_m \sin \theta,$$

where e is the instantaneous voltage, E_m is the maximum voltage, θ is the angle of the generator armature, and "sine" is one of the trigonometric functions shown in figure 8-4.

The instantaneous voltage, e, depends on the sine of the angle. It rises to a maximum positive value as the angle reaches 90°. This occurs because the conductor cuts directly across the flux at 90°. It falls to zero at 180°, because the conductor cuts no lines of flux at 180°. It reaches a negative peak at 270°, and becomes zero again at 360°. For example, when $\theta = 60°$ and $E_m = 100$ volts, $e = 100 \times \sin 60° = 86.6$ volts. When $\theta = 240°$, $e = 100 \sin 240° = -86.6$ volts.

Another form of the trigonometric equation for a sine wave of voltage involves the angular velocity of its rotating vector. The term "angular velocity" refers to the number of degrees (angles) through which a voltage vector rotates per second. Angular velocity is symbolized by the Greek letter omega (ω). In practice, ω is generally given in terms of RADIANS per second, rather than degrees per second. A radian is a segment of the circumference of a circle. This segment is always exactly equal in length to the RADIUS of that circle. There are π (3.14) radians in half a circle, and 2π (6.28) radians in the circumference of a complete circle. Therefore, when a voltage vector makes one complete revolution, describing one complete circle, it traverses 2π or 6.28 radians. In terms of degrees of rotation, one radian is 360°/6.28 or 57.32°.

The number of radians per second traversed by an alternating-voltage vector is

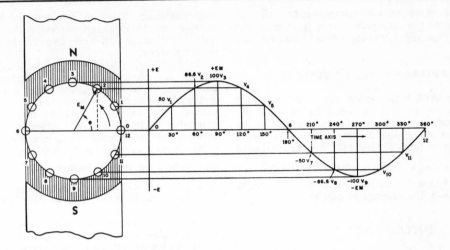

Figure 8-4—Generation of sine-wave voltage.

closely related to its frequency, because either may be used to express the other. Since one vector revolution equals one complete cycle, then each cycle equals 6.28 radians of vector travel. That is, an alternating voltage whose frequency is 60 cycles would be said to have an angular velocity of 6.28 x 60, or roughly 377 radians per second. Written as a formula, angular velocity is $\omega = 2\pi f$. Thus, in a formula involving angular velocity, the term $2\pi f$ may be replaced by the simpler symbol ω, if convenient. As previously stated, another form of the trigonometric equation for a sine wave of voltage involves the angular velocity of the generating vector.

The equation is

$$e = E_m \times \sin \omega t.$$

It is used to determine the voltage of a rotating vector at some given instant of time. The starting reference, or "time zero," is usually when the voltage vector is at a peak positive value. The equation time factor t is the elapsed time from time zero, and is the exact instant at which the voltage is to be determined. To determine the exact angular position at any instant, multiply the angular velocity (ω) of the vector by the time elapsed (t). By dividing elapsed time t by the period for one cycle, and multiplying by 360°, the angular position of the

voltage vector may be determined for any instant. Multiplying E_m by the sine of that instantaneous angle will yield the instantaneous voltage e.

For example, consider a 60-cycle voltage whose peak value is 100 volts. Assume you must determine the voltage 0.00139 second after the voltage has reached a positive peak.

$$\sin t = \sin 2\pi ft = \sin 360(60)(0.00139) = \sin 30° = 0.5$$

The instantaneous voltage e is

$$e = E_m \times \sin 30°$$

$$e = 100 \times 0.5$$

$$e = 50 \text{ volts.}$$

There are four important values associated with sine waves of voltage or current:

Instantaneous—designated as e or i; maximum—designated as E_m or I_m; average—designated as E_{avg} or I_{avg}; and effective—designated as E or I.

The INSTANTANEOUS value may be any value between zero and maximum depending on the instant chosen, as indicated by the equation $e = E_m \sin \omega t$.

The MAXIMUM value of voltage is reached twice each cycle and is the greatest value of instantaneous voltage generated during each cycle.

135

The ratio of the instantaneous value of voltage to the maximum value is equal to the sine of the angle corresponding to that instant.

AVERAGE VALUE OF VOLTAGE

The AVERAGE value of a sine wave of voltage or current is found by dividing the area under one alternation (half cycle) by the distance along the X axis between two successive instants (0° and 180°) corresponding to zero voltage. The average value is $\frac{2}{\pi}$, or 0.637, times the maximum. In the example in figure 8-5, the average voltage is

$$\frac{2}{\pi} \times 100, \text{ or } 63.7 \text{ volts.}$$

Thus,

$$E_{avg} = 0.637\, E_{max}$$

EFFECTIVE OR R.M.S. VALUE

The EFFECTIVE value of an a-c voltage or current of sine waveform is defined in terms of the equivalent heating effect of a direct current. Heating effect is INDEPENDENT of direction of electron flow and varies as the square of the instantaneous current. Thus, an alternating current of sine waveform having a maximum value of 14.14 amperes produces the same amount of heat in a circuit having a resistance of 1 ohm that a direct current of 10 amperes produces. The effective value of this alternating current is equal to 0.707 of the maximum value. Thus, $I_{eff} = 0.707\, I_{max}$, or 0.707 x 14.14 = 10 amperes. The effective value is also known as the ROOT-MEAN-SQUARE (r.m.s.) value because it is the square root of the average of the squared values between zero and maximum. Thus an effective, or r.m.s. current of 10 amperes produces the same heating in a given resistance as a direct current of 10 amperes.

In practice, r.m.s. values of voltage and current are more important than instantaneous, maximum, or average values. Most a-c voltmeters and ammeters are calibrated in r.m.s. values. For example, suppose that an a-c voltmeter indicates that the effective voltage between the two conductors in a cable is 440 volts. Twice in each cycle the insulation is subject to a voltage stress that is $\frac{E_m}{E} = \frac{1}{0.707}$, or 1.41 times 440 volts, or 620 volts; where E_m is the maximum voltage and E is the r.m.s. value.

Suppose an a-c ammeter in the same circuit indicates an effective current of 10 amperes. Twice in each cycle the current exceeds this value by 41 percent but the average heating effect is that which a direct current of 10 amperes would produce. Thus, the conductor size is based on the ammeter indication (r.m.s. current) rather than on the maximum value, even though the insulation stress is always 41 percent higher than the voltmeter indication.

The ratio of the effective value to the average value of a wave is called the FORM FACTOR and for all sine waves is equal to $\frac{0.707}{0.637}$ or 1.11. The form factor for waveforms such as flattop waves is less than 1.11. For waveforms such as peaked waves the form factor is greater than 1.11. If a waveform is not that of a sine wave the constants for effective and average values do not apply. Most electrical power and lighting circuits have sine-wave currents and voltages and the effective values indicated by voltmeters and ammeters are appropriate.

Combining A-C Voltages

Vectors may be used to combine a-c voltages of sine waveform and of the same frequency. The angle between the vectors indicates the time difference between their positive maximum values. The length of the vectors represents either the effective value or the positive maximum value, as desired.

The sine wave voltages generated in coils a and b of the simple generators (fig. 8-6(A)) are 90° out of phase because the coils are located 90° apart on the two-pole armatures. The armatures are on a common shaft. When coil a is cutting squarely across the field, coil b is moving parallel to the field and not

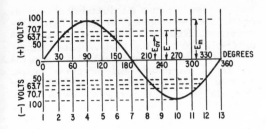

Figure 8-5.—Relative values of an a-c sine-wave voltage.

cutting through it. Thus, the voltage in coil a is maximum when the voltage in coil b is zero. If the frequency is 60 cycles per second, the time difference between the positive maximum values of these voltages is $\dfrac{90}{360} \times \dfrac{1}{60} = 0.00416$ second.

Vector E_a leads vector E_b by 90° in figure 8-6 (B) and sine wave a leads sine wave b by 90° in figure 8-6 (C). The curves are shown on separate axes to identify them with their respective generators; they are also projected on a common axis to show the relation between their instantaneous values. If coils a and b are connected in series and the maximum voltage generated in each coil is 10 volts, the total voltage is not 20 volts because the two maximum values of voltage do not occur at the same instant, but are separated one-fourth of a cycle. The voltages cannot be added arithmetically because they are out of phase. These values, however, can be added vectorially.

E_c in figure 8-6 (B) is the vector sum of E_a and E_b, and is the diagonal of the parallelogram, the sides of which are E_a and E_b. The effective voltage in each coil is 0.707 x 10 or 7.07 volts (where 10 volts is the maximum) and represents the length of the sides of the parallelogram. The effective voltage of the series combination is 7.07 x $\sqrt{2}$ or 10 volts and represents the length of the diagonal of the parallelogram.

Curve c in figure 8-6 (C) represents the sine wave variations of the total voltage E_c developed in the series circuit connecting coils a and b. Voltage E_a leads E_b by 90°. Voltage E_c lags E_a by 45°, and leads E_b by 45°.

Counterclockwise rotation of the vectors is considered positive rotation thus giving the sense of lead or lag. Thus, if E_a and E_b (fig. 8-6 (B)) are rotated counterclockwise, and their

movement observed from a fixed position, E_a will pass this position first, then 90° later E_b will pass the position. Thus E_b lags E_a by 90°. If the maximum voltage in each coil is 10 volts, the maximum value of the combined voltage will be 10 x$\sqrt{2}$ or 14.4 volts. (See fig. 8-6 (C)).

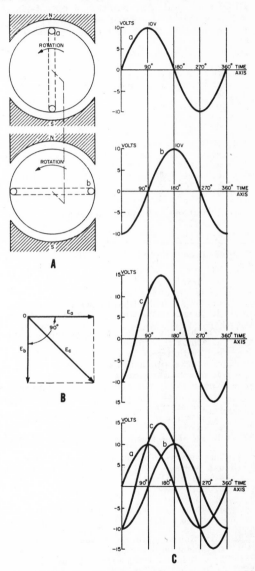

Figure 8-6.—Combining a-c voltages.

137

The important point to be made in this discussion is that two out-of-phase voltages may be resolved into a single resultant value by the use of vectors. Though generated voltages were used to illustrate the point in this case, the same rules apply to VOLTAGE DROPS as well. Any number of out-of-phase voltages may be combined vectorially, as long as they all have the same frequency; that is, as long as they remain a fixed number of degrees apart, like the two generator loops. Their magnitudes (LENGTH of their vectors) may be different. You will find vectors quite useful in the section of this course that deals with the effects of capacitors and inductors on a-c circuits. They are used to determine a-c impedances and currents, as well as voltages.

QUIZ

1. In formula form, angular velocity as applied to voltage or current is
   a. 2ω
   b. $2\pi\omega$
   c. $2\pi F$
   d. $2 F$

2. How much larger is the maximum voltage value than the effective voltage value?
   a. 1.414
   b. 1.111
   c. 0.707
   d. 0.637

3. How many radians are in a complete circle?
   a. 0.707
   b. 1.11
   c. 3.14
   d. 6.28

4. Magnitude of a vector is denoted by the
   a. time axis
   b. length of the line
   c. length of the line, drawn to scale
   d. length of the time axis, drawn to scale

5. Which of the following best defines a cycle?
   a. One alternation
   b. Two alternations
   c. Three alternations
   d. Four alternations

6. The most important value associated with sine waves of voltage or current are
   a. instantaneous
   b. maximum
   c. average
   d. all of the above

7. The maximum value of a single sine wave of a-c voltage is 141.4 volts. What is the effective value?
   a. 63.7 volts
   b. 70.7 volts
   c. 99.97 volts
   d. 141.4 volts

8. Direction of a simple vector
   a. cannot be determined
   b. will indicate the reference point
   c. is indicated by an arrow at one end of the line
   d. is indicated by the magnitude

9. Frequency as applied to alternating current or voltage is the number of
   a. r.p.m. per second of time
   b. cycles per second of time
   c. poles per second of time
   d. volts generated per second of time

10. The effective value of an a-c voltage or current of sine waveform is defined in terms of the equivalent d.c.
    a. "voltage effect"
    b. "current effect"
    c. "heating effect"
    d. "cooling effect"

11. The average value of a single sine wave of a-c current is 63.7 amps. What is the r.m.s. value?
    a. 63.7 amps
    b. 70.7 amps
    c. 141.4 amps
    d. 156.95 amps

12. The instantaneous value of induced voltage of a single-phase generator
    a. will never be zero
    b. depends on the sine of the angle
    c. will always be the same
    d. depends on the cosine of the angle

13. The period of a-c voltage of sine waveform is the time required for one complete
    a. r.p.m.
    b. alternation
    c. cycle
    d. degree

14. The "root-mean-square" value is also known as the
    a. average value
    b. peak value
    c. instantaneous value
    d. effective value

15. Two voltages of the same frequency "120 cycles per second" have their positive maximum values displaced by 90°. What is the time difference between the phases?
    a. 0.00208 sec.
    b. 0.00416 sec.
    c. 0.02080 sec.
    d. 0.04160 sec.

16. Positive rotation of a vector is
    a. clockwise
    b. counterclockwise
    c. either clockwise or counterclockwise
    d. neither clockwise nor counterclockwise

17. The effective generated voltage of a single-phase a-c generator may be obtained by the formula
    a. $E = 1.111 \; \Phi \; fD10^{-8}$
    b. $E = 2.22 \; \Phi \; fN-6$
    c. $E = 1.111 \; \Phi \; FD-6$
    d. $E = 2.22 \; \Phi \; fN10^{-8}$

18. Most a-c voltmeters and ammeters are calibrated in
    a. r.m.s. values
    b. average values
    c. peaks values
    d. instantaneous values

19. A radian is always equal to
    a. the circumference of the circle
    b. the radius of the circle
    c. pi
    d. 60 degrees

20. Angular velocity is symbolized by the Greek letter
    a. gamma γ
    b. mu μ
    c. omega ω
    d. beta β

21. If an active conductor's length is doubled, the
    a. pole length is cut in half
    b. flux per pole is cut in half
    c. generated voltage is doubled
    d. generated voltage is tripled

22. The "form factor" in most cases refers to the ratio of
    a. average value to maximum value
    b. instantaneous value to maximum value
    c. r.m.s. value to effective value
    d. r.m.s. value to average value

23. Conductor size in an a-c circuit is based on
    a. instantaneous current
    b. maximum current
    c. average current
    d. effective current

24. The term, "angular velocity," as applied to electricity refers to the number of
    a. radians per second a voltage vector rotates
    b. radians per minute a voltage vector rotates
    c. degrees averaged together
    d. degrees subtracted from the radians

25. Vectors indicate
    a. direction
    b. magnitude
    c. time, direction, and magnitude
    d. magnitude and direction

26. When voltages are out of phase, the total voltage can be found by adding
    a. arithmetically
    b. vectorially
    c. peaks values
    d. average values

27. The number of radians per second traversed by an alternating-voltage vector is closely related to its
    a. current sine wave
    b. voltage sine wave
    c. frequency
    d. none of the above

139

CHAPTER 9

INDUCTANCE AND CAPACITANCE

Inductance

Inductance is the property of an electric circuit that opposes any CHANGE IN THE CURRENT through that circuit. That is, if the current increases, a self-induced voltage opposes this change and delays the increase. If current decreases, a self-induced voltage tends to aid, or prolong the current flow, and delays the decrease. Thus, the most noticeable effect of inductance in a circuit is that current can neither increase nor decrease as fast in an inductive circuit as it can in a noninductive circuit.

The opposition to the current change is essentially an effect of electromagnetic induction, or induced e.m.f. In chapter 1 it was pointed out that a voltage is induced in a conductor whenever the conductor is moved across a magnetic field. The same thing also happens when the magnetic field is moved across the conductor. It is this relative motion between field and conductor that produces self-induced voltage in a conductor.

SELF-INDUCTANCE

Even a perfectly straight length of conductor has some inductance. As previously explained, current in a conductor always produces a magnetic field surrounding, or linking with, the conductor. When the current changes, the magnetic field changes, and an e.m.f. is induced in the conductor. This e.m.f. is called a SELF-INDUCED E.M.F. because it is induced in the conductor carrying the current. The direction of the induced e.m.f. has a definite relation to the direction in which the field that induces the e.m.f. varies. When the current in a circuit is increasing, the flux linking with the circuit is increasing. This flux cuts across the conductor and induces an e.m.f. in the conductor in such a direction as to oppose the increase in current

and flux. Likewise, when the current is decreasing, an e.m.f. is induced in the opposite direction and opposes the decrease in current. These effects are summarized by Lenz's law, which states that THE INDUCED E.M.F. IN ANY CIRCUIT IS ALWAYS IN A DIRECTION TO OPPOSE THE EFFECT THAT PRODUCED IT.

The inductance is increased by shaping a conductor so that the electromagnetic field around each portion of the conductor cuts across some other portion of the same conductor. This is shown in its simplest form in figure 9-1 (A). A length of conductor is looped so that two portions of the conductor lie adjacent and parallel to one another. These portions are labeled conductor 1 and conductor 2. When the switch is closed, electron flow through the conductor establishes a typical concentric field around ALL portions of the conductor. For simplicity, however, the field is shown in a single plane that is perpendicular to both conductors. Although the field originates simultaneously in both conductors it is considered as originating in conductor 1 and its effect on conductor 2 will be noted. With increasing current, the field expands outward, cutting across a portion of conductor 2. The resultant induced e.m.f. in conductor 2 is shown by the dashed arrow. Note that it is in OPPOSITION to the battery current and voltage, according to Lenz's law.

The direction of this induced voltage may be determined by applying the Left-Hand Rule for Generators. This rule is applied to a portion of conductor 2 that is "lifted" and enlarged for the purpose in part (A) of figure 9-1. In applying this rule, the thumb of the left hand points in the direction that a conductor is moved through a field. (In this case, the field is moving, or expanding, in one direction, which is the same as the conductor moving in the opposite direction.) The index finger points in the direction of the

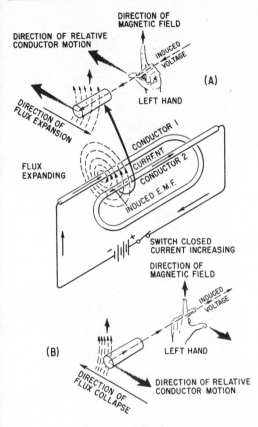

Figure 9-1.—Self-inductance.

UNIT OF INDUCTANCE

The unit for measuring inductance, L, is the HENRY, h. An inductor has an inductance of 1 henry if an e.m.f. of 1 volt is induced in the inductor when the current through the inductor is changing at the rate of 1 ampere per second. The relation between the induced voltage, inductance, and rate of change of current with respect to time is stated mathematically as

$$E = L \frac{\Delta I}{\Delta t},$$

where E is the induced e.m.f. in volts, L is the inductance in henrys, and ΔI is the change in current in amperes occurring in Δt seconds. (Delta, symbol Δ, means "a change in . . . . . ")

The henry is a large unit of inductance and is used with relatively large inductors. The unit employed with small inductors is the millihenry, mh. For still smaller inductors the unit of inductance is the microhenry, μh.

FACTORS AFFECTING SELF-INDUCTANCE

Many things affect the self-inductance of a circuit. An important factor is the degree of linkage between the circuit conductors and its electromagnetic flux. In a straight length of conductor, there is very little flux linkage between one part of the conductor and another. Therefore, its inductance is extremely small. Conductors become much more inductive when they are wound into coils, as shown in figure 9-2. This is true because there is maximum flux linkage between the conductor turns, which lie side by side in the coil.

Inductance is further affected by the manner in which a coil is wound. The coil in figure 9-2 (A) is a poor inductor if compared to the others in the figure, because its turns are widely spaced, thus decreasing the flux linkage between its turns. Also, its lateral flux movement, indicated by the dashed arrows, does not link effectively, because there is only one layer of turns. A more inductive coil is shown in part (B). The turns are closely spaced, and the two layers link each other with a greater number of flux loops during all lateral flux movements. Note that nearly all turns, such as (a) are directly adjacent to four other turns (shaded), thus affording increased flux linkage.

The coil is made still more inductive by winding it in three layers, and providing a highly

magnetic field. The middle finger, extended as shown, will now indicate the direction of induced (generated) voltage.

In part (B), the same section of conductor 2 is shown, but with the switch opened and the flux collapsing. Applying the left-hand rule in this case shows that the reversal of flux MOVEMENT has caused a reversal in the direction of the induced voltage. The most important thing to note, however, is that the voltage of self-induction opposes both CHANGES in current. It delays the initial buildup of current by opposing the battery voltage, and delays the breakdown of current by exerting an induced voltage in the same direction that the battery voltage acted.

permeable core, as in figure 9-2 (C). The increased number of layers (cross-sectional area) improves lateral flux linkage. Note that some turns, such as (b) lie directly adjacent to six other turns (shaded). The magnetic properties of the iron core increase the total coil flux strength many times that of an air core coil of the same number of turns.

From the foregoing, it can be seen that the primary factors controlling the inductance of a coil are (1) the number of turns of conductor, (2) the ratio of the cross-sectional area of the coil to its length, and (3) the permeability of its core material. The inductance of a coil is affected by the magnitude of current when the core is a magnetic material. When the core is air, the inductance is independent of the current.

Various formulas have been developed for calculating the self-inductance of inductors. For an inductor consisting of a single layer of wire, and having a length 10 or more times the diameter, the following formula is essentially correct:

$$L = \frac{0.4\pi\mu N^2 S}{10^8 l} ,$$

in which L is the self-inductance in henrys, N is the number of turns, π equals 3.14, μ is the permeability of the core (if nonmagnetic, $\mu = 1$), S is the cross-sectional area of the coil in cm.^{2} and l is the length of the coil in centimeters. Thus, it may be seen that the inductance is increased very rapidly as the number of turns is increased; also, the inductance increases as the coil is made shorter, the cross-sectional area is made larger, or the permeability of the core is increased.

For example, the inductance of a coil having a length of 20 cm., a diameter of 2 cm., a core permeability of 200, and 200 turns of wire is approximately

$$L = \frac{0.4\pi \times 200 \times 200^2 \times 0.7854 \times 2^2}{10^8 \times 20} = 0.0158 \text{ henry.}$$

GROWTH AND DECAY OF CURRENT IN AN R-L SERIES CIRCUIT

If a battery is connected across a pure inductance, the current builds up to its final value at a rate that is determined by the battery voltage and the internal resistance of the battery.

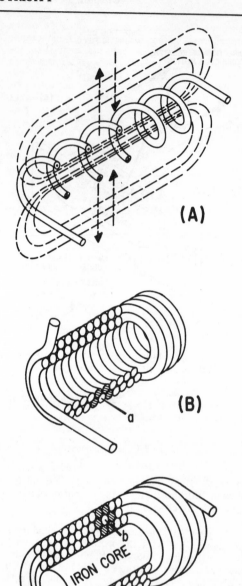

Figure 9-2.—Coils of various inductances.

The current buildup is gradual because of the counter e.m.f. generated by the self-inductance of the coil. When the current starts to flow, the magnetic lines of force move out, cut the turns of wire on the inductor, and build up a counter e.m.f. that opposes the e.m.f. of the battery. This opposition causes a delay in the time it takes the current to build up to steady value. When the battery is disconnected, the lines of force collapse, again cutting the turns of the inductor and building up an e.m.f. that tends to prolong the current flow.

A voltage divider containing resistance and inductance may be connected in a circuit by means of a special switch, as shown in figure 9-3 (A). Such a series arrangement is called an R-L series circuit.

If switch $S1$, is closed (as shown), a voltage, E, appears across the divider. A current attempts to flow, but the inductor opposes this current by building up a back e.m.f. that, at the initial instant, exactly equals the input voltage, E. Because no current can flow under this condition, there is no voltage across resistor R. Figure 9-3 (B) shows that all of the voltage is impressed across L and no voltage appears across R at the instant switch $S1$ is closed.

As current starts to flow, a voltage, e_r, appears across R, and e_L is reduced by the same amount. The fact that the voltage across L is reduced means that the growth current, i_g, is increasing and consequently e_r is increasing. Figure 9-3 (B) shows that e_L finally becomes zero when i_g stops increasing, while e_r builds up to the input voltage, E, as i_g reaches its maximum value. Under steady-state conditions, only the resistor limits the size of the current.

Electrical inductance is like mechanical inertia, and the growth of current in an inductive circuit can be likened to the acceleration of a boat on the surface of the water. The boat begins to move at the instant a constant force is applied to it. At this instant its rate of change of speed (acceleration) is greatest, and all the applied force is used to overcome the inertia of the boat. After a while the speed of the boat increases (its acceleration decreases) and the applied force is used up in overcoming the friction of the water against the hull. As the speed levels off and the acceleration becomes zero, the applied force equals the opposing friction force at this speed and the inertia effect disappears.

When the battery switch in the $R-L$ circuit of figure 9-3 (A) is closed, the rate of current

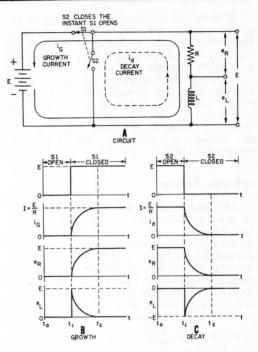

Figure 9-3.—Growth and decay of current in an R-L series circuit.

increase is maximum in the inductive circuit. At this instant all the battery voltage is used in overcoming the e.m.f. of self-induction which is a maximum because the rate of change of current is maximum. Thus the battery voltage is equal to the drop across the inductor and the voltage across the resistor is zero. As time goes on more of the battery voltage appears across the resistor and less across the inductor. The rate of change of current is less and the induced e.m.f. is less. As the steady-state condition of the current flow is approached the drop across the inductor approaches zero and all of the battery voltage is used to overcome the resistance of the circuit.

Thus the voltage across the inductor and resistor change in magnitudes during the period of growth of current the same way the force applied to the boat divides itself between the inertia and friction effects. In both examples, the force is developed first across the inertia-inductive effect and finally across the friction-resistive effect.

143

If switch $S2$ is closed (source voltage E removed from the circuit), the flux that has been established around L collapses through the windings and induces a voltage, e_L, in L that has a polarity opposite to E and essentially equal to it in magnitude. The induced voltage, e_L, causes current i_d to flow through R in the same direction that it was flowing when $S1$ was closed. A voltage, e_r, that is initially equal to E, is developed across R. It rapidly falls to zero as the voltage, e_L, across L, due to the collapsing flux, falls to zero.

L/R Time Constant

The time required for the current through an inductor to increase to 63 percent (actually, 63.2 percent) of the maximum current or to decrease to 37 percent (actually, 36.7 percent) is known as the TIME CONSTANT of the circuit. An R-L circuit and its charge and discharge graphs are shown in figure 9-4. The value of the time constant in seconds is equal to the inductance in henrys divided by the circuit resistance in ohms. One set of values is given in figure 9-4 (A). $\frac{L}{R}$ is the symbol used for this time constant.

Two useful relations used in calculating $\frac{L}{R}$ time constants are as follows:

$$\frac{L \text{ (in henrys)}}{R \text{ (in ohms)}} = t \text{ (in seconds)}.$$

$$\frac{L \text{ (in microhenrys)}}{R \text{ (in ohms)}} = t \text{ (in microseconds)}.$$

The time constant may also be defined as the time required for the current through the inductor to grow or decay to its final value IF it continued to grow or decay at its initial rate. As may be seen in figure 9-4 (B), the slope of the dotted tangent line, ox, indicates the initial rate of current growth with respect to time. At this rate, the current would reach its maximum value in $\frac{L}{R}$ seconds. Similarly, the slope of the dotted tangent line, YZ, indicates the initial rate of current decay with respect to time, and the decay would be completed in $\frac{L}{R}$ seconds.

The equation for the growth of current, i_L, through L is

$$i_L = \frac{E}{R}\left(1 - \frac{1}{2.718^{\frac{Rt}{L}}}\right),$$

where i_L is the instantaneous current through inductor L, E is the applied voltage (100 volts in this case), R is the resistance in ohms, t is the time in seconds, and L is the inductance in henrys. Figure 9-4 (B) shows a graph of this equation.

When $t = \frac{L}{R}$, the exponent $\frac{Rt}{L}$ in the preceding equation reduces to 1. Then $\frac{1}{2.718} = 0.368$. Therefore,

$$i_L = \frac{E}{R}(1 - 0.368) = 0.632\frac{E}{R}.$$

In other words, when $t = \frac{L}{R}$, i_L is equal to 63.2 percent of the ratio $\frac{E}{R}$, which is the maximum current. When the maximum current is 10 amperes ($E = 100$ and $R = 10$), the current through L grows to 6.32 amperes in $\frac{L}{R} = \frac{10}{10}$, or 1 second.

The equation for inductor voltage, e_L, on growth of current is

$$e_L = E\left(\frac{1}{2.718^{\frac{Rt}{L}}}\right).$$

The graph of this equation is also shown in figure 9-4 (B). When $t = \frac{L}{R}$, $e_L = 0.368E$; that is, $e_L = 0.368 \times 100 = 36.8$ volts.

Mutual Inductance

MUTUAL INDUCTANCE DEFINED

Whenever two coils are located so that the flux from one coil links with the turns of the other, a change of flux in one coil will cause an e.m.f. to be induced in the other coil. The two coils have MUTUAL INDUCTANCE. The amount of mutual inductance depends on the relative position of the two coils. If the coils are separated a considerable distance, the amount of flux common to both coils is small and the mutual inductance is low. Conversely, if the coils are close together so that nearly all the flux of one coil links the turns of the other the mutual inductance is high. The mutual inductance can be increased greatly by mounting the coils on a common iron core.

Two coils placed close together with their axes in the same plane are shown in figure 9-5. Coil A is connected to a battery through switch S, and coil B is connected to galvanometer G. When the switch is closed (fig. 9-5 (A)), the current that flows in coil A sets up a magnetic field that links coil B, causing an induced current and a momentary deflection of galvanometer G. When the current in coil A reaches a steady value, the galvanometer returns to zero. If the switch is opened (fig. 9-5 (B)), the galvanometer deflects momentarily in the opposite direction, indicating a momentary flow of current in the opposite direction in coil B. This flow of current in coil B is caused by the e.m.f. induced in coil B, which is produced by the collapsing flux of coil A.

When current flows through coil A the flux expands in coil A producing a north pole nearest coil B. Some of the flux, that expands from left to right, cuts the turns of coil B. This flux induces an e.m.f. and current in coil B that opposes the growth of current and flux in coil A. Thus the current in B tries to establish a north pole nearest coil A (like poles repel).

When the switch is opened, the magnetic field produced by coil A collapses. The collapse of the flux cuts the turns of coil B in the opposite direction and produces a south pole nearest coil A (unlike poles attract). This polarity aids the magnetism of coil A, tending to prevent the collapse of its field.

FACTORS AFFECTING MUTUAL INDUCTANCE

The mutual inductance of two adjacent coils is dependent upon the—(1) physical dimensions of the two coils, (2) number of turns in each coil, (3) distance between the two coils, (4) relative positions of the axes of the two coils, and (5) the permeability of the cores.

If the two coils are positioned so that all the flux of one coil cuts all the turns of the other, the mutual inductance can be expressed as follows:

$$M = \frac{0.4\pi\mu\, SN_1N_2}{10^8 l}$$

where M equals mutual inductance of coils in henrys

N_1 and N_2 equal the number of turns in coils 1 and 2 respectively

S equals area of core in square cm.

μ equals permeability of core

l equals length of core in cm.

If the two coils are so positioned with respect to each other that all the flux of one coil cuts all the turns of the other, the coils have UNITY COEFFICIENT OF COUPLING. If all of the flux produced by one of the coils cuts only one-half the turns of the other coil, the coefficient of coupling is 0.5. Coefficient of coupling is designated by the letter, K. The coefficient of coupling is equal to the percentage of flux originating in one coil that cuts the other coil. It is never exactly equal to unity but it approaches this value in certain shell-type transformers.

The mutual inductance between two coils, $L1$ and $L2$, may be expressed in terms of the inductance of each coil and the coefficient of coupling, K, as follows,

$$M = K \sqrt{L_1 L_2},$$

where M is in the same units of inductance as $L1$ and $L2$.

SERIES INDUCTORS WITHOUT MAGNETIC COUPLING

When inductors are well shielded, or located far enough apart to make the effects of mutual inductance negligible, the inductance of the various inductors are added in the same manner that the resistances of resistors are added. For example,

$$L_T = L_1 + L_2 + L_3 \ldots + L_N.$$

where L_t is the total inductance; L_1, L_2, L_3 are the inductances of $L1$, $L2$, $L3$; and L_N means that any number (N) of inductors may be used.

SERIES INDUCTORS WITH MAGNETIC COUPLING

When two inductors in series are so arranged that the field of one links the other, the combined inductance is determined as

$$L_T = L_1 + L_2 \pm 2M,$$

145

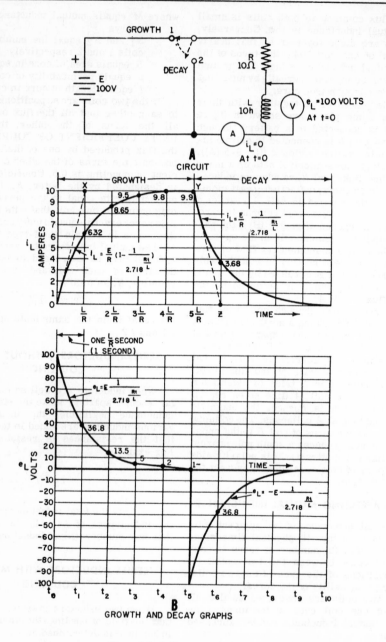

Figure 9-4.—L/R time constant.

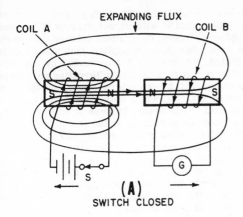

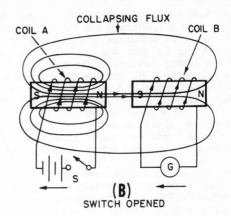

Figure 9-5.—Mutual inductance.

where L_T is the total inductance, L_1 and L_2 are the self inductances of $L1$ and $L2$ respectively, and M is the mutual inductance between the two inductors. The plus sign is used with M when the magnetomotive forces of the two inductors are aiding each other. The minus sign is used with M when the m.m.f.'s of the two inductors oppose each other. The factor 2 accounts for the influence of $L1$ on $L2$ and of $L2$ on $L1$.

If the coils are arranged so that one can be rotated relative to the other to cause a variation in the coefficient of coupling, the mutual inductance between them can be varied. The total inductance, L_T, may be varied by an amount equal to $4M$.

PARALLEL INDUCTORS WITHOUT MAGNETIC COUPLING

The total inductance, L_T, of inductors in parallel is calculated in the same manner that the total resistance of resistors in parallel is calculated, provided the coefficient of coupling between the coils is zero. For example,

$$\frac{1}{L_T} = \frac{1}{L_1} + \frac{1}{L_2} + \frac{1}{L_3} \ldots + \frac{1}{L_N},$$

where L_1, L_2, and L_3 are the respective inductances of inductors $L1$, $L2$, and $L3$; and L_N means that any number (N) of inductors may be used.

EFFECTS OF INDUCTANCE IN AN ELECTRIC CIRCUIT

Reaction of an Inductor to Flux Change

Up to this point, the effects of inductance in an electric circuit have been considered as being controlled only by the particular inductor considered in each case. For instance, the time required for the growth and decay of current in the circuit shown in figure 9-3 is determined only by the inherent properties of the inductor L, namely, the ratio of its inductance to its resistance. When permitted to change at this inherent, or natural rate, the shape of the L/R curve for any particular inductor will always remain the same. That is, it will always exhibit the same natural opposition to any change in current and flux, when left to its own tendencies. At this point, however, it must be pointed out that an inductor can be made to exhibit many different degrees of reaction. This is done by using external means to change the flux linking the inductor. These changes, such as variations in the applied frequency, usually do not occur at the same rate as the inductor's inherent rate. When the flux is changed RAPIDLY by some external means, the inductor's reaction is much greater than when the flux is changed gradually. That is, the inductor's self-induced e.m.f. is dependent on the RATE with respect to time at which the linking flux is changed.

The dependence of the induced voltage on the rate of change of flux with respect to time is shown by means of the simple apparatus in

147

figure 9-6. When the switch is closed, current builds up to a maximum, and the lamp glows with its normal brilliance. If the iron core is inserted rapidly into the coil, the flux increases rapidly (because of the increased inductance of the coil), and the induced voltage opposes, according to Lenz's law, the source voltage. Therefore, less current flows through the lamp, and it dims momentarily. If the core is withdrawn rapidly from the coil, a portion of the flux that was established around the coil collapses. The resulting induced voltage opposes the decrease (again, according to Lenz's law) by aiding the source voltage, and the coil current increases. Consequently, the lamp burns brighter momentarily. The faster the iron core is moved the greater is the flux change per unit of time and the more noticeable is the effect on the lamp.

effect is continuous and much greater than when it was supplied with direct current. For equal applied voltages, the current through the circuit is less when a. c. is applied than when d. c. is applied, as may be demonstrated by the circuits of figure 9-7. The alternating current is accompanied by an alternating magnetic field around the coil, which cuts through the turns of the coil. This action induces a voltage in the coil that always opposes the changing current. When the switch is in position ① the lamps burn brightly on direct current but in position ②, although the effective value of the applied a-c voltage is equal to the d-c value, the lamps burn dimly because of the opposition developed across the inductance. Most of the applied voltage appears across L, with little remaining for the lamps.

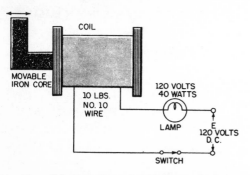

Figure 9-6.—Dependence of self-induced voltage on the rate of change of flux.

Effects of Inductance in an A-C Circuit

When a circuit containing a coil is energized with direct current, the coil's effect in the circuit is evident only when the circuit is energized, or when it is deenergized. For instance, when the switch in figure 9-7 is placed in position ①, the inductance of coil L will cause a delay in the time required for the lamps to attain normal brilliance. After they have attained normal brilliance, the inductance has no effect on the circuit as long as the switch remains closed. When the switch is opened, an electric spark will jump across the opening switch contacts. The e.m.f. which produces the spark is caused by the collapsing magnetic field cutting the turns of the inductor.

When the inductive circuit is supplied with alternating current, however, the inductor's

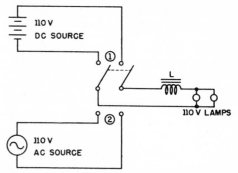

Figure 9-7.—Relative effects of inductance in d-c and a-c circuits.

Relation Between Induced Voltage and Current

As stated previously, any change in current, either a rise or a fall, in a coil causes a corresponding change of the magnetic flux around the coil (fig. 9-8, (A)). If the current is sinusoidal, the induced voltage will also have the form of a sine wave. Because the current changes at its maximum rate when it is going through its zero value at 0°, 180°, and 360° (fig. 9-8 (B)), the flux change is also greatest at those times. Consequently, the self-induced voltage in the coil is at its maximum value at these instants. According to Lenz's law, the induced voltage always opposes the change in current. Thus, when the current is rising in a positive direction at 0°, the induced e.m.f. is of opposite polarity to the impressed e.m.f. and opposes the rise

148

in current. Later, when the current is falling toward its zero value at 180°, the induced voltage is of the same polarity as the current and tends to keep the current from falling. Thus the induced voltage can be seen to lag the current by 90°. The resistance of the coil is small and the principal opposition to the current flow through the coil is the induced voltage, E_{ind}. The applied voltage, E, is slightly larger than E_{ind} and diametrically opposed to it, as indicated in the vector diagram (fig. 9-8 (C)).

The current lags the applied voltage in an inductive circuit by an angle of 90° and leads the induced voltage by 90°. The induced voltage is always of opposite polarity to the applied voltage and is called a COUNTER E.M.F. or a BACK E.M.F. because it always opposes the change of current.

Capacitance

Capacitance is the property of an electric circuit that resists, or opposes, any CHANGE OF VOLTAGE in the circuit. That is, if applied voltage is increased, capacitance opposes the change and delays the voltage increase across the circuit. If applied voltage is decreased, capacitance tends to maintain the higher original voltage across the circuit, thus delaying a decrease. Consequently, the most noticeable effect of capacitance in a circuit is that voltage can neither increase nor decrease as fast in a capacitive circuit as it can in a noncapacitive circuit. Capacitance is also defined as that property of a circuit that enables energy to be stored in an electric field.

THE CAPACITOR

Figure 9-9 depicts a capacitor in its simplest form. It consists of two metal plates separated by a thin layer of insulating material (dielectric). When connected to a voltage source (battery) as shown, the voltage forces electrons onto one plate, making it negative, and pulls them off the other, making it positive. Electrons cannot flow through the dielectric. Since it takes a definite quantity of electrons to "fill up," or charge, a capacitor, it is said to have a CAPACITY. This characteristic is referred to as CAPACITANCE.

The basic action of a capacitor is illustrated in figure 9-10. In part (A), the capacitor is in a balanced, or uncharged, condition. When the switch is set to position 1, in part (B), a surge of battery current immediately charges the capacitor. The natural tendency of the capacitor is to restore its own balance by discharging through the battery in a counterclockwise direction. This tendency is small at first, but grows as the capacitor is charging.

This characteristic is commonly referred to as a counter e.m.f., since it is actually a voltaic force. When the capacitor's counter e.m.f. has risen to equal the battery voltage, the capacitor is said to be charged, and current is zero. When the charge is completed, the switch is placed back to position 2, as shown in figure 9-10 (C).

In this condition, the capacitor is a source of potential energy, similar to a charged battery. Its charged plates exert a voltage between terminals 2 and 3 of the switch. In addition, an electrostatic field, or force, exists between the plates, acting through the dielectric. This is an actual physical force, evidenced by the mutual attraction of the unlike charges, and the dielectric must be structurally strong enough to withstand it. The dielectric must also have sufficient insulating qualities to withstand the potential differences. When the switch is placed in position 3, the capacitor discharges, thus rebalancing itself. As the potential difference of the plates goes to zero, their charges are equalized, and the electrostatic force is relaxed.

Two facts should be noted in connection with figure 9-10 (B):

1. After a momentary surge of electrons, direct current is completely stopped by the capacitor.

2. Free electrons do not pass from one plate to the other through the dielectric because the dielectric is a nonconductor.

The electrons are distributed on the negative plate and held there by the mutual attraction of the corresponding positive charges on the positive plate. The presence of the two polarities (plus and minus) establishes the electric field through the dielectric.

The electric lines of force (flux) originate on the negatively charged plate and terminate on the positively charged plate. In other words,

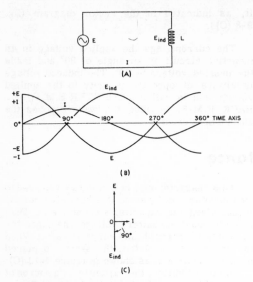

Figure 9-8.—Relation between induced voltage and current.

the lines are assumed to follow the same paths that UNIT NEGATIVE CHARGES would take if they were free to move. The lines of force would be present even if the plates were enclosed in a perfect vacuum. Electric lines of force cannot exist in a metallic conductor to any great extent, because equalizing currents are free to flow within the metal. If the force is to exist, two dissimilarly charged bodies must be separated by a nonconductor.

DIELECTRIC MATERIALS

Various materials differ in their ability to support electric flux or to serve as dielectric material for capacitors. This phenomenon is somewhat similar to permeability in magnetic circuits. Dielectric materials, or insulators are rated in their ability to support electric flux in terms of a figure called the DIELECTRIC CONSTANT. The higher the value of dielectric constant (other factors being equal), the better is the dielectric material.

Dry air is the standard dielectric for purposes of reference and is assigned the value of unity (or one). The dielectric constant of a dielectric material is also defined as the ratio of the capacitance of a capacitor having that particular material as the dielectric to the capacitance of the same capacitor having air as the dielectric. By way of comparison, the dielectric constant of pure water is 81; flint glass, 9.9; and paraffin paper, 3.5. The range of dielectric constants is much more restricted than is the range of permeabilities. Average dielectric constants for some common materials is given in the following list.

Material	Dielectric-constant (Average values)
Air............	1
Polystyrene	2.5
Paraffin paper	3.5
Mica...........	6
Flint glass.......	9.9
Methyl alcohol.....	35
Glycerin	56.2
Pure water.......	81

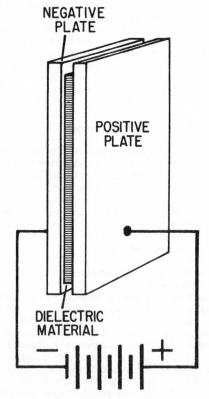

Figure 9-9.—Simple capacitor.

UNIT OF CAPACITANCE

The capacitance of a capacitor is proportional to the quantity of charge that can be stored in it for each volt applied across its plates. A capacitor possesses a capacitance of 1 FARAD when a quantity of charge of 1 coulomb imparted to it raises its potential 1 volt (1 coulomb is equal to 6.28×10^{18} electrons). The relation between capacitance, charge, and voltage is the basic formula of the capacitor, and may be stated as follows:

$$C = \frac{Q}{E},$$

where C is the capacitance in farads, Q the quantity of charge in coulombs, and E the difference in potential in volts.

A capacitor with a value of 1 farad would be of enormous dimensions. Hence, use of the farad as a unit is usually limited to definition and calculations. The practical units of capacitance are the microfarad (μf.) and the micromicrofarad ($\mu\mu$f.). A capacitor whose value is 1 microfarad is one in which a microcoulomb (6.28×10^{12} electrons) is stored when 1 volt is applied across its plates.

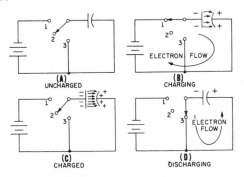

(A) UNCHARGED **(B)** CHARGING ELECTRON FLOW

(C) CHARGED **(D)** DISCHARGING ELECTRON FLOW

Figure 9-10.—Capacitor action.

FACTORS AFFECTING THE VALUE OF CAPACITANCE

The capacitance of a capacitor depends on the three following factors:
1. The area of the plates.
2. The distance between the plates.
3. The dielectric constant of the material between the plates.

These three factors are related to the capacitance of a parallel-plate capacitor consisting of two plates by the formula

$$C = 0.2249 \left(\frac{k A}{d} \right)$$

where C is in micromicrofarads, A is the area of one of the plates in square inches, d is the distance between the plates in inches, and k is the dielectric constant of the insulator separating the plates.

For example, the capacitance of a parallel-plate capacitor with an air dielectric and spacing of 0.0394 inch between the plates, each of which has an area of 15.5 square inches, is approximately

$$C = 0.225 \left(\frac{1 \times 15.5}{0.0394} \right) = 88.5 \text{ micromicrofarads.}$$

From this formula it may seen that the capacitance increases when the plates are increased in area; it decreases. if the spacing of the plates is increased; and it increases if the k-value is increased.

The dielectric constant, k, expresses the relative capacitance when materials other than air are used as the insulating material between the plates. For example, if mica is substituted for air as the dielectric, the capacitance increases 6 times because the dielectric constant of mica is 6 and that of air is 1.

If the capacitor is composed of more than two parallel plates, the capacitance is calculated by multiplying the preceding formula by $N - 1$, where N is the number of plates. The plates are interlaced as shown in figure 9-11, and the effect is that of increasing the capacitance of the two-plate capacitor by the factor $N - 1$. In the figure there are 11 plates, and the capacitance is 10 times that of a 2-plate capacitor of the same plate area, spacing, and dielectric material.

CHARGE AND DISCHARGE OF AN R-C SERIES CIRCUIT

Ohm's law states that the voltage across a resistance is equal to the current through it times the value of the resistance. This means that a voltage will be developed across a resistance ONLY WHEN CURRENT FLOWS through it.

A capacitor is capable of storing or holding a charge of electrons. When uncharged, both

151

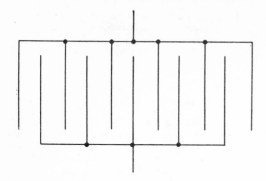

Figure 9-11.—Capacitor multiple-plate construction.

plates contain the same number of free electrons. When charged, one plate contains more free electrons than the other. The difference in the number of electrons is a measure of the charge on the capacitor. The accumulation of this charge builds up a voltage across the terminals of the capacitor, and the charge continues to increase until this voltage equals the applied voltage. The charge in a capacitor is related to the capacitance and voltage as follows:

$$Q = CE,$$

in which Q is the charge in coulombs, C the capacitance in farads, and E the difference in potential in volts. Thus, the greater the voltage, the greater the charge on the capacitor. Unless a discharge path is provided, a capacitor keeps its charge indefinitely. Any practical capacitor, however, has some leakage through the dielectric so that the charge will gradually leak off.

A voltage divider containing resistance and capacitance may be connected in a circuit by means of a switch, as shown in figure 9-12 (A). Such a series arrangement is called an R-C series circuit.

If $S1$ is closed, electrons flow counterclockwise around the circuit containing the battery, capacitor, and resistor. This flow of electrons ceases when C is charged to the battery voltage. At the instant current begins to flow, there is no voltage on the capacitor and the drop across R is equal to the battery voltage. The initial charging current, I, is therefore equal to $\frac{E_S}{R}$. Figure 9-12 (B) shows that at the instant the switch is closed, the

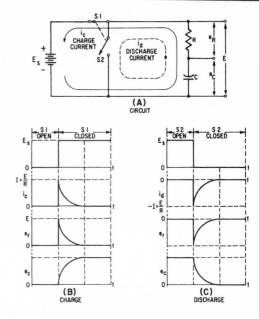

Figure 9-12.—Charge and discharge of an R-C series circuit.

entire input voltage, E_S, appears across R, and that the voltage across C is zero.

The current flowing in the circuit soon charges the capacitor. Because the voltage on the capacitor is proportional to its charge, a voltage, e_c, will appear across the capacitor. This voltage opposes the battery voltage—that is, these two voltages buck each other. As a result, the voltage e_r across the resistor is $E_S - e_c$, and this is equal to the voltage drop $(i_c R)$ across the resistor. Because E_S is fixed, i_c decreases as e_c increases.

The charging process continues until the capacitor is fully charged and the voltage across it is equal to the battery voltage. At this instant, the voltage across R is zero and no current flows through it. Figure 9-12 (B) shows the division of the battery voltage, E_S, between the resistance and capacitance at all times during the charging process.

If $S2$ is closed ($S1$ opened) in figure 9-12 (A), a discharge current, i_d, will discharge the capacitor. Because i_d is opposite in direction to i_c, the voltage across the resistor will have a polarity opposite to the polarity during the

152

charging time. However, this voltage will have the same magnitude and will vary in the same manner. During discharge the voltage across the capacitor is equal and opposite to the drop across the resistor, as shown in figure 9-12 (C). The voltage drops rapidly from its initial value and then approaches zero slowly, as indicated in the figure.

RC TIME CONSTANT

The time required to charge a capacitor to 63 percent (actually 63.2 percent) of maximum voltage or to discharge it to 37 percent (actually 36.8 percent) of its final voltage is known as the TIME CONSTANT of the circuit. An R-C circuit with its charge and discharge graphs is shown in figure 9-13. The value of the time constant in seconds is equal to the product of the circuit resistance in ohms and its capacitance in farads, one set of values of which is given in figure 9-13 (A). RC is the symbol used for this time constant.

Some useful relations used in calculating RC time constants are as follows:

R (ohms) × C (farads) = t (seconds).

R (megohms) × C (microfarads) = t (seconds).

R (ohms) × C (microfarads) = t (microseconds).

R (megohms) × C (micromicrofarads) = t (microseconds).

The time constant may also be defined as the time required to charge or discharge a capacitor completely IF it continues to charge or discharge at its initial rate. As may be seen in figure 9-13 (B), the slope of the dotted tangent line, OX, indicates the initial rate of charge. At this rate, the capacitor would be completely charged in RC seconds. Likewise, the slope of the dotted tangent line, YZ, indicates the initial rate of discharge with respect to time, and at this rate the capacitor would be completely discharged in RC seconds.

The equation for the rise in voltage, e_C, across the capacitor is

$$e_c = E \left(1 - \frac{1}{2.718^{\frac{t}{RC}}}\right),$$

where e_C, is the instantaneous voltage across the capacitor, E the applied voltage (100 volts in this case), t the time in seconds, R the resistance in ohms, C the capacitance in farads (0.000001 farad or 1μf. in this case), and the

number 2.718 the natural logarithm base. Figure 9-13 (B) shows a graph of this equation.

When $t = RC$, the exponent, $\frac{t}{RC}$, reduces to 1. Therefore,

$$e_c = E \left(1 - \frac{1}{2.718}\right) = 0.632\,E.$$

In other words, when $t = RC$, e_C is equal to 63.2 percent of E, the maximum value. When the maximum is 100 volts, as shown, the voltage across the capacitor increases to 63.2 volts in RC seconds—that is, in 10 microseconds.

The equation for the charging current, i_C, is

$$i_c = \frac{E}{R}\left(\frac{1}{2.718^{\frac{t}{RC}}}\right).$$

The graph of this equation is shown in figure 9-13 (B). When $t = RC$, $i_C = 0.368 \times \frac{E}{R}$; that is when $t = 10$ microseconds, $i_C = 0.368 \times \frac{100}{10} = 3.68$ amperes.

UNIVERSAL TIME CONSTANT CHART

Because the impressed voltage and the values of R and C or R and L usually will be known, a universal time constant chart (fig. 9-14) can be used. Curve A is a graph of the voltage across the capacitor on charge; it is also a graph of the inductor current and the voltage across the resistor in series with the inductor on the growth of current. Curve B is a graph of capacitor voltage on discharge, capacitor current on charge, inductor current on decay, or the voltage across the resistor in series with the capacitor on charge. The graphs of resistor voltage and current and inductor voltage on discharge are not shown because negative values would be involved.

The time scale (horizontal scale) is graduated in terms of the RC or $\frac{L}{R}$ time constants so that the curves may be used for any value of R and C or L and R. The voltage and current scales (vertical scales) are graduated in terms of the fraction of the maximum voltage or current so that the curves may be used for any value of voltage or current. If the time constant and the initial or final voltage for the circuit in question are known, the voltages across the various parts of the circuit can be obtained from the curves for any time after the switch

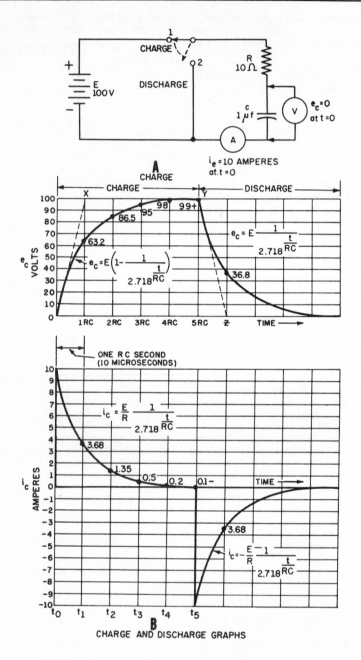

Figure 9-13.—R-C time constant.

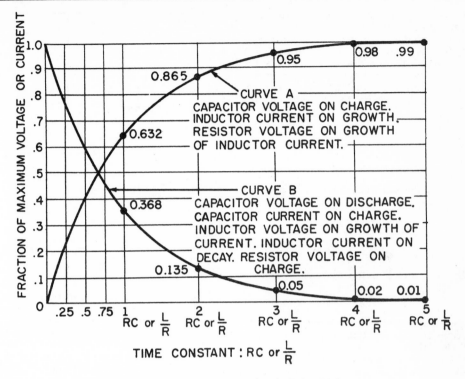

Figure 9-14.—Universal time constant chart for R-C and R-L circuits.

is closed, either on charge or discharge. The same reasoning is true of the current in the circuit.

The following problem illustrates how the universal time constant chart may be used.

A circuit is to be designed in which a capacitor must charge to one-fifth (0.2) of the maximum charging voltage in 100 microseconds (0.0001 second). Because of other considerations, the resistor must have a value of 20,000 ohms. What size of capacitor is needed? Curve A is first consulted to determine the RC time necessary to give 0.2 of the full voltage. The time is less than 0.25 RC, approximately 0.22 RC. If 0.22 RC must be equal to 100 microseconds, one complete RC must be equal to $\frac{100}{0.22}$ = 455 microseconds, or 0.000455 second. Therefore,

$$RC = 0.000455.$$

Substituting the known value of R and solving for C,

$$C = \frac{0.000455}{20,000} = 0.000000023 \text{ farad,}$$

or 0.023 microfarad.

The graphs shown in figure 9-13 are not entirely complete—that is, the charge or discharge (or the growth or decay) is not quite completed in 5 RC or $5\frac{L}{R}$ seconds. However, when the values reach 0.99 of the maximum (corresponding to 5 RC or $5\frac{L}{R}$) the graphs may be considered accurate enough for most purposes.

CAPACITORS IN PARALLEL AND IN SERIES

Capacitors may be combined in parallel or series to give equivalent values, which may be either the sum of the individual values (in parallel) or else a value less than that of the smallest capacitance (in series). Figure 9-15 shows the parallel and series connections.

In figure 9-15 (A) the voltage, E, is the same for all the capacitors and the total charge, Q_t, is the sum of all the individual charges, Q_1, Q_2, and Q_3. From the equation of the capacitor,

$$C = \frac{Q}{E}.$$

The total charge is

$$Q_t = C_t E,$$

where C_t is the total capacitance. In parallel, the total charge is

$$Q_t = Q_1 + Q_2 + Q_3$$

$$C_t E = C_1 E + C_2 E + C_3 E.$$

Dividing both sides of the equation by E gives

$$C_t = C_1 + C_2 + C_3.$$

The total capacitance of any number of capacitors connected in parallel is the sum of their individual values.

In the series arrangement (fig. 9-15 (B)), the current is the same in all parts of the circuit. Each capacitor develops a voltage during charge, and the sum of the voltages of all the capacitors must equal the applied voltage, E. By the capacitor equation, the applied voltage, E is equal to the total charge divided by the total capacitance, or

$$E = \frac{Q_t}{C_t}.$$

The total charge, C_t, is equal to the charge on any one of the capacitors because the same current flows in all for the same length of time, and because charge equals current times time in seconds ($Q = It$). Therefore,

$$Q_t = Q_1 = Q_2 = Q_3.$$

but

$$E = E_1 + E_2 + E_3,$$

where E_1, E_2, and E_3 are the voltages of the three capacitors. Then

$$\frac{Q_t}{C_t} = \frac{Q_t}{C_1} + \frac{Q_t}{C_2} + \frac{Q_t}{C_3}.$$

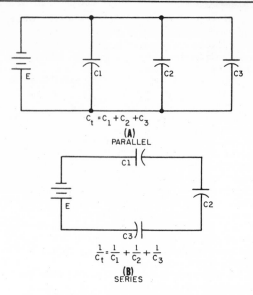

$$C_t = C_1 + C_2 + C_3$$
(A)
PARALLEL

$$\frac{1}{C_t} = \frac{1}{C_1} + \frac{1}{C_2} + \frac{1}{C_3}$$
(B)
SERIES

Figure 9-15.—Capacitors in parallel and in series.

Dividing both sides of the equation by Q_t gives

$$\frac{1}{C_t} = \frac{1}{C_1} + \frac{1}{C_2} + \frac{1}{C_3}.$$

The reciprocal of the total capacitance of any number of capacitors in series is equal to the sum of the reciprocals of the individual values.

Parallel capacitors combine by a rule similar to that for combining resistors in series. Series capacitors combine by a rule similar to that for combining parallel resistors.

In the series arrangement of two capacitors, C_1 and C_2, the total capacitance is given by the equation:

$$C_t = \frac{C_1 C_2}{C_1 + C_2}.$$

VOLTAGE RATING OF CAPACITORS

In selecting or substituting a capacitor for use in a particular circuit, you must consider (1) the value of capacitance desired, and (2) the amount of voltage to which the capacitor is to be subjected. If the voltage applied across the plates is too great, the dielectric will break down and arcing will occur between the

156

plates. The capacitor is then short-circuited and the possible flow of direct current through it can cause damage to other parts of the equipment. Capacitors have a voltage rating that should not be exceeded.

The working voltage of the capacitor is the maximum voltage that can be steadily applied without danger of arc-over. The working voltage depends on (1) the type of material used as the dielectric, and (2) the thickness of the dielectric.

The voltage rating of the capacitor is a factor in determining the capacitance because capacitance decreases as the thickness of the dielectric increases. A high-voltage capacitor that has a thick dielectric must have a larger plate area in order to have the same capacitance as a similar low-voltage capacitor having a thin dielectric. The voltage rating also depends on frequency because the losses, and the resultant heating effect, increase as the frequency increases.

A capacitor that may be safely charged to 500 volts d.c. cannot be safely subjected to alternating or pulsating direct voltages whose effective values are 500 volts. An alternating voltage of 500 volts (r.m.s.) has a peak voltage of 707 volts, and a capacitor to which it is applied should have a working voltage of at least 750 volts. The capacitor should be selected so that its working voltage is at least 50 percent greater than the highest voltage to be applied to it. Effective (r.m.s.) voltage and the action of capacitors in a-c circuits are described in a later chapter.

CAPACITOR TYPES

Capacitors may be divided into two major groups—fixed and variable.

Fixed Capacitors

Fixed Capacitors are constructed in such manner that they possess a fixed value of capacitance which cannot be adjusted. They may be classified according to the type of material used as the dielectric, such as paper, oil, mica, and electrolyte.

Paper Capacitors.—The plates of paper capacitors are made of strips of metal foil. These are separated by waxed paper. The capacitance of paper capacitors ranges from about 200 micromicrofarads to several microfarads. The strips of foil and paper are rolled together to form a cylindrical cartridge, which is then sealed in wax to keep out moisture and to prevent corrosion and leakage. Two metal leads are soldered to the plates, one extending from each end of the cylinder. Some paper capacitors may have one terminal (lead) marked GROUND, which means that this terminal connects to the outside foil of the capacitor.

Many different kinds of outer covering are used for paper capacitors, the simplest being a tubular cardboard. Some types of paper capacitors are encased in a mold of very hard plastic; these types are very rugged and may be used over a much wider temperature range than the cardboard-case type. Figure 9-16 (A) shows the construction of a tubular paper capacitor; part (B) shows a completed cardboard encased capacitor.

Bathtub-type capacitors consist of paper-capacitor cartridges hermetically sealed in metal containers. (See fig. 9-16 (C)). The container often serves as a common terminal for several enclosed capacitors. It always serves as a shield against electrical interference.

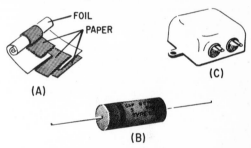

Figure 9-16.—Paper capacitor.

Oil Capacitors.—In radio and radar transmitters, voltages high enough to cause arcing, or breakdown, of paper dielectrics are often employed. Consequently, in these applications capacitors that have oil or oil-impregnated paper as the dielectric material are preferred. Capacitors of this type are considerably more expensive than ordinary paper capacitors and their use is generally restricted to radio and radar transmitting equipment.

Mica Capacitors.—The fixed mica capacitor is made of metal foil plates that are separated by sheets of mica, which form the dielectric. The whole assembly is covered in molded plastic. By molding the capacitor parts into a plastic case, corrosion and damage to the plates and dielectric are prevented in addition to making the capacitor mechanically strong. Various types of terminals are used to connect mica capacitors into circuits; these are also molded into the plastic case.

Mica is an excellent dielectric and will withstand higher voltages than paper without allowing arcing between the plates. Common values of mica capacitors range from approximately 50 micromicrofarads to about 0.02 microfarad. Some typical mica capacitors are shown in figure 9-17.

Figure 9-17.—Typical mica capacitors.

Electrolytic Capacitors.—For capacitances greater than a few microfarads, the physical size of a paper or a mica capacitor becomes excessive. Electrolytic capacitors are used for values of capacitance ranging from 1 to 1,500 microfarads. These capacitors provide large capacitance in small physical sizes. Unlike the other types, electrolytic capacitors are generally polarized, and should be subjected to direct voltage, or pulsating direct voltage only; however, a special type of electrolytic capacitor is made for use in alternating-current motors. Remember that unless an electrolytic is designed for use on a.c., it must always be connected in accordance with its polarity markings.

The electrolytic capacitor is widely used in electronic circuits, and consists of two metal plates separated by an electrolyte. The electrolyte, either in paste or liquid form, is in contact with the negative terminal and this combination comprises the negative electrode. The dielectric is an exceedingly thin film of oxide deposited on the positive electrode of the capacitor. The positive electrode is an aluminum sheet, and it is folded so as to achieve maximum area. The capacitor is subjected to a forming process during manufacture, in which current is passed through it. The flow of current results in the deposit of the thin coating of

oxide on the aluminum plate. The close spacing of the negative and positive electrodes gives rise to the comparatively high capacitance value. However, it allows greater possibility of voltage breakdown and leakage of electrons from one electrode to the other.

Two kinds of electrolytic capacitors are in use—wet-electrolytic and dry-electrolytic. In the former, the electrolyte is a liquid and the container must be leakproof. This type should always be mounted in a vertical position.

The electrolyte of the dry-electrolytic unit is a paste contained in a separator made of absorbent material such as gauze or paper. The separator serves to hold the electrolyte in place, and also prevents short-circuiting the plates. Dry-electrolytic capacitors are made in both cylindrical and rectangular form and may be contained either within cardboard or metal covers. Since the electrolyte cannot spill, the dry capacitor may be mounted in any convenient position. Some typical electrolytic capacitors are shown in figure 9-18.

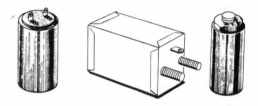

Figure 9-18.—Typical electrolytic capacitors.

Variable Capacitors

Variable capacitors are constructed in such manner that their value of capacitance can be varied. A typical variable capacitor (adjustable capacitor) is the rotor/stator type. It consists of two sets of metal plates that are arranged so that the rotor plates move between the stator plates. Air is the dielectric. As the position of the rotor is changed, the capacitance value is likewise changed. This is the type capacitor used for tuning most radio receivers and it is shown in figure 9-19 (A). Another type variable (trimmer) capacitor is shown in figure 9-19 (B); it consists of two plates separated by a sheet of mica. A screw adjustment is used to change the distance between the plates, thereby changing the capacitance.

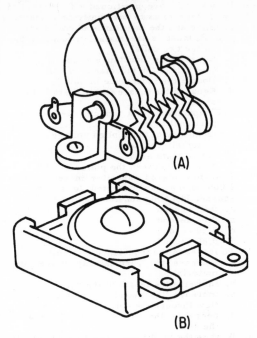

(A)

(B)

Figure 9-19.—Variable capacitors.

Ceramic Capacitors

A relatively new type capacitor that may be constructed as either fixed or variable is the ceramic. Ceramic capacitors usually range in value between 1 micromicrofarad and 0.01 microfarad. Ceramic is used as the dielectric and film deposits of silver are used for the plates. These capacitors are small in physical size and are constructed in various shapes. Typical capacitors are shown in figure 9-20.

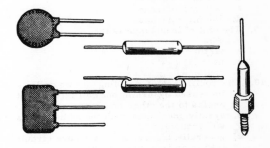

Figure 9-20.—Ceramic capacitors.

QUIZ

1. Inductance is the property of an electric circuit that
   a. opposes any change in the applied voltage through that circuit
   b. opposes any change in the current through that circuit
   c. aids any change in the applied voltage through that circuit
   d. aids any change in the current through that circuit
2. A coil has a resistance of 22 ohms, and in 0.1 second after the switch is closed, the current has reached 63.2% of its final value. The value of inductance (L) is
   a. 0.22 henries
   b. 0.44 henries
   c. 2.20 henries
   d. 4.40 henries
3. When a capacitor's counter e.m.f. has risen to equal the battery voltage, the current is
   a. maximum in the circuit
   b. at 63.2% of its maximum Ohm's law value in the circuit
   c. zero in the circuit
   d. at 36.8% of its maximum Ohm's law value in the circuit

4. The total capacitance of two 100-microfarad capacitors connected in series is
   a. 25 microfarads
   b. 50 microfarads
   c. 100 microfarads
   d. 200 microfarads
5. When the magnetic field is collapsing, the induced e.m.f.
   a. aids and tends to prolong the impressed current
   b. opposes the impressed current
   c. has no effect upon the impressed current
   d. causes the impressed current to go immediately to zero
6. To increase the time required for the current to reach its maximum Ohm's law value in a series resistance and inductance circuit, it is necessary to
   a. increase the resistance
   b. decrease the resistance
   c. decrease the inductance
   d. increase the applied voltage

159

7. In a simple capacitor (fig. 9-6), the plate area is 2 square inches, the dielectric material is mica, and the distance between the plates is 0.01 inch. To increase the capacitance
   a. increase the distance between the plates
   b. change dielectric material from mica to paraffin paper
   c. decrease the plate area
   d. change dielectric material from mica to flint glass
8. What is the total capacitance of two 200-microfarad capacitors connected in series with each other and both in parallel with a 50-microfarad capacitor?
   a. 50 microfarads
   b. 250 microfarads
   c. 100 microfarads
   d. 150 microfarads
9. The unit of inductance is the
   a. ohm
   b. farad
   c. henry
   d. coulomb
10. The coefficient of coupling of two coils is
    a. increased by turning one coil axis at right angles to the other coil axis
    b. greatly increased with the addition of a soft iron core
    c. generally higher in an air core circuit than in an iron core circuit
    d. almost unity on a diamagnetic core
11. Factors that determine the capacitance of parallel-electrode capacitors are
    a. area of the plates and the type of dielectric
    b. thickness of the plates, type and thickness of the dielectric
    c. type and thickness of the dielectric and the plate area
    d. thickness of the dielectric, area of the plate, and the direction of the current flow
12. The time constant of a resistance-capacitance circuit is
    a. The time required to discharge a capacitor to 36.8% of its final voltage
    b. the time required to charge a capacitor to 36.8% of its maximum voltage
    c. equal to the circuit capacitance divided by the circuit resistance
    d. equal to the circuit resistance divided by the circuit capacitance
13. The voltage due to self-induction
    a. can only occur when the conductor is wound in the form of a coil
    b. is produced when the strength of the magnetic field changes
    c. is produced by moving a conductor through a magnetic field
    d. cannot occur in a direct-current circuit

14. If two coils are positioned with respect to each other so as to have unity coefficient of coupling and the inductance of coil A equals coil B, what is the mutual inductance between the two coils?
    a. Equal to the inductance of coil A.
    b. One half of the inductance of coil A.
    c. Double the inductance of coil A.
    d. Equal to the square root of the inductance of coil A.
15. The capacitance of a capacitor is inversely proportional to the
    a. frequency of the applied voltage
    b. dielectric constant
    c. active plate area
    d. distance between the plates
16. A 40-microfarad capacitor in series with 2,000 ohms is connected to a 200-volt source. The time constant is
    a. 0.05 second
    b. 0.08 second
    c. 0.50 second
    d. 0.80 second
17. To increase the inductance of a coil
    a. increase the permeability of the core material
    b. increase the length of the coil
    c. increase the magnitude of the current flow through the coil
    d. decrease the cross-sectional area of the coil
18. What is the total inductance (L_t) of two coils connected in parallel when the coefficient of coupling is zero?
    a. $L_t = L_1 + L_2$
    b. $L_t = L_1$
    c. $L_t = \frac{1}{L_1} + \frac{1}{L_2}$
    d. $L_t = \frac{L_1 \quad L_2}{L_1 + L_2}$
19. The charge that is stored in a capacitor depends upon
    a. voltage divided by the capacitance
    b. voltage multiplied by the capacitance
    c. capacitance divided by the voltage
    d. capacitance multiplied by the resistance
20. When selecting a capacitor for use in a circuit, its working voltage should be at least
    a. 10% greater than the highest voltage to be applied to it
    b. equal to the highest voltage to be applied to it
    c. 30% greater than the highest voltage to be applied to it
    d. 50% greater than the highest voltage to be applied to it

21. A battery, a switch, a resistor, and a coil are connected in series. What happens at the instant the switch is closed?
    a. The voltage across the resistor is maximum
    b. The voltage across the coil is maximum
    c. The current in the circuit is maximum
    d. The voltage across the resistor and the coil are minimum

22. Capacitance is the property of an electric circuit that
    a. opposes any change of current in the circuit
    b. opposes any change of voltage in the circuit
    c. is not affected by a change of voltage
    d. aids any change of current in the circuit

23. When capacitors are connected in parallel, the resulting capacitance is the
    a. sum of the individual capacitances
    b. reciprocal of the sum of reciprocals of the individual capacitors
    c. sum of the individual reciprocals of the capacitors
    d. reciprocal of the sum of capacitances

24. The time constant of an inductive-resistive circuit is
    a. that time required for a direct current to rise one-half of its maximum value
    b. a method of determining how much current would flow at the end of one second
    c. the product of the resistance and the inductance of a circuit
    d. the time in seconds required for the current to rise to 63.2% of its final Ohm's law value

25. When capacitors are connected in series, the resulting capacitance is found by

    a. a rule similar to that for combining parallel resistors
    b. a rule similar to that for combining resistors in series
    c. dividing the applied voltage by the total resistance of series circuit
    d. multiplying the applied voltage by the total resistance of series circuit

CHAPTER 10

INDUCTIVE AND CAPACITIVE REACTANCE

Inductive Reactance

FACTORS AFFECTING INDUCTIVE REACTANCE

In the preceding chapter, it was shown that when an alternating voltage is applied to an inductor, the inductor reacts in such a way as to oppose alternating-current flow. This opposition is thus referred to in general as an inductive reactance. The amount of opposition exhibited by a coil depends on the magnitude of its self-induced voltage, E_{ind}. The effective value of this self-induced voltage, or counter e.m.f. in volts, is

$$E_{ind} = 2\pi f L I,$$

where 2π is a constant, I is in effective amperes, L is in henrys, and f is in cycles per second. The induced voltage varies directly with the frequency, the inductance, and the current.

The amount of opposition to current flow offered by an inductor is referred to as its inductive reactance. This reactance is expressed as the ratio of the inductor's counter e.m.f. to the current through the inductor, or

$$X_L = \frac{E_{ind}}{I}$$

where X_L is the inductor's opposition to current flow measured in ohms, E_{ind} is the inductor's counter e.m.f. in volts, and I is the inductor current in amperes. Assuming the current and counter voltage have sine waveforms, the inductive reactance X_L, in ohms, is

$$X_L = 2\pi f L$$

Since the inductive reactance of a coil and its counter e.m.f. are closely related, anything which influences one must also influence the other. It has been shown that the counter e.m.f.

of a coil depends on its inductance and the rate of flux change around the coil. Consequently, the inductive reactance must also be affected by the same influences. The rate of flux change per unit of time depends on the FREQUENCY of the inductor current. Flux must change more rapidly at high frequencies than at low frequencies. From the foregoing it can be seen that the inductive reactance of a coil depends primarily on (1) the coil's INDUCTANCE and (2) the FREQUENCY of the current flowing through the coil.

If frequency or inductance varies, inductive reactance must also vary. A coil's inductance does not vary appreciably after the coil is manufactured, unless it is designed as a variable inductor. Thus, frequency is generally the only variable factor affecting the inductive reactance of a coil. The coil's inductive reactance will vary directly with the applied frequency.

POWER IN AN INDUCTIVE CIRCUIT

The power in a d-c circuit is equal to the product of volts and amperes, but in an a-c circuit this is true only when the load is resistive, and has no reactance.

In a circuit possessing inductance only, the true power is zero (fig. 10-1). The current lags the applied voltage by 90°. The TRUE POWER is the average power actually consumed by the circuit, the average being taken over one complete cycle of alternating current. The APPARENT POWER is the product of r.m.s. volts and r.m.s. amperes. Thus, in figure 10-1 (A), the apparent power is 100 x 10 = 1,000 volt-amperes. However, the power absorbed by the coil during the time the current is rising (fig. 10-1 (B)), is returned to the source during the

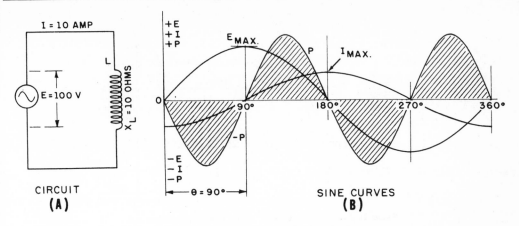

Figure 10-1.—Power in an inductive circuit.

time the current is falling, so that the average power is zero.

The product of instantaneous values of current and voltage yield the double frequency power curve P. (See fig. 10-1 (B).) The shaded areas under this curve above the X axis represent positive energy and the shaded areas below the X axis represent negative energy.

From 0 degrees to 90 degrees current is negative and falling; the magnetic field is collapsing and the energy in the field is being returned to the source (negative energy). The product of negative current and positive voltage is negative power.

From 90 degrees to 180 degrees the current is positive and rising; energy from the source is being stored in the rising magnetic field (positive energy). The product of positive current and positive voltage is equal to positive power.

From 180 degrees to 270 degrees current is positive and falling. Again energy is being returned to the source; the product of positive current and negative voltage is negative power.

From 270 degrees to 360 degrees current is negative and rising. Energy (positive) is being supplied by the source and stored in the magnetic field. The product of negative current and negative voltage is positive power.

Thus when current is rising, power is being supplied by the source and stored in the magnetic field; when current is falling, power is being returned to the source from the collapsing magnetic field. In the theoretically pure inductance shown in figure 10-1 the supplied power is equal to the returned power. Thus, average power used (true power) is zero.

The ratio of the true power to the apparent power in an a-c circuit is called the POWER FACTOR. It may be expressed as a percent or as a decimal. In the inductor of figure 10-1 (A), the power factor is $\frac{0}{1,000} = 0$. The power factor is also equal to the $\cos \theta$, where θ is the phase angle between the current and voltage. The phase angle between E and I in the inductor is $\theta = 90°$. Thus the power factor of an inductor of negligible losses is $\cos 90° = 0$. The apparent power in a purely inductive circuit is called REACTIVE POWER and the unit of reactive power is called the VAR. This unit is derived from the first 'letters of the words volt-ampere-reactive.

RESISTANCE IN AN A-C CIRCUIT

In an a-c circuit containing only resistance, the current and voltage are always in phase ($\theta = 0°$). (See fig. 10-2.) The true power dissipated in heat in a resistor in an a-c circuit when sine waveforms of voltage and current are applied is equal to the product of the r.m.s. volts and the r.m.s. amperes. In the circuit of figure 10-2 (A) the power absorbed by the resistor is $P = EI = 100 \times 10 = 1,000$ watts. The product of the instantaneous values of current and voltage (fig. 10-2 (B)) gives the power curve, P, the axis of which is displaced above

163

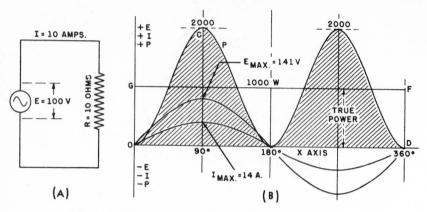

Figure 10-2.—Relation between E, I, and P in a resistive circuit.

the X axis by an amount that is proportional to 1,000 watts.

The true average power is

$$P = \frac{E_{max} \times I_{max}}{2} = E_{eff} \times I_{eff}.$$

The power factor of a resistive circuit is cos $0° = 1$, or 100 percent. The apparent power in the resistor is also equal to the true power. The reactive power in the resistive circuit is zero.

RESISTANCE AND INDUCTIVE REACTANCE IN SERIES

Because any practical inductor must be wound with wire that has resistance, it is not possible to obtain a coil without some resistance. The resistance associated with a coil may be considered as a separate resistor, R, in the series with an inductor, L, which is purely inductive and contains only inductive reactance (fig. 10-3 (A)). The resistance has been exaggerated in this example to be of the same order of magnitude as the inductive reactance of the inductor in order to simplify the trigonometric solution.

If an alternating current, I_O, flows through the inductor a voltage drop occurs across both the resistor and the inductor. The voltage, E_γ, across the resistor is in phase with the current, and the voltage drop, E_L, across the inductor leads the current by 90° (fig. 10-3 (B)). The voltage across the resistor is assumed to be 50

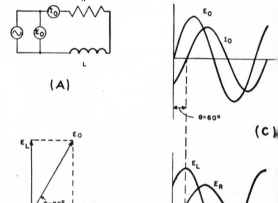

Figure 10-3.—Resistance and inductive reactance in series.

volts and the voltage across the inductor, 86.6 volts. These two voltages are 90° out of phase, as indicated in the figure. The applied voltage, E_O, is the hypotenuse of a right triangle, the sides of which are 50 and 86.6, respectively. Thus,

$$E_O = \sqrt{50^2 + 86.6^2} = 100 \text{ volts.}$$

The sine curves of circuit current, I_O, applied voltage, E_O, the voltage across the coil, E_L, and the voltage across the resistor, E_γ, are shown in figure 10-3 (C).

Impedance

Impedance is the total opposition to the flow of alternating current in a circuit that contains resistance and reactance. In the case of pure inductance, inductive reactance, X_L is the total opposition to the flow of current through it. In the case of pure resistance, R represents the total opposition. The combined opposition of R and X_L in series or in parallel to current flow is called IMPEDANCE. The symbol for impedance is Z.

The impedance of resistance in series with inductance is

$$Z = \sqrt{R^2 + X_L^2} \, ,$$

where Z, R, and X_L are the hypotenuse, base, and altitude respectively of a right triangle in which $\cos \theta = \dfrac{R}{Z}$, $\sin \theta = \dfrac{X_L}{Z}$, and $\tan \theta = \dfrac{X_L}{R}$. As mentioned before, $\cos \theta$ is equal to the circuit power factor; $\sin \theta$ is sometimes referred to as the reactive factor; and $\tan \theta$ is referred to as the quality, or Q, of a circuit or a circuit component. The trigonometric functions including the sine, cosine, and tangent of angles between $0°$ and $90°$ are given in appendix VI at the end of this training manual.

Power in a Series Circuit Containing R and X_L

The true power in any circuit is the product of the applied voltage, the circuit current, and the cosine of the phase angle between them. Thus, in figure 10-4, the true power is

$$P = EI \cos \theta = 100 \times 7.07 \, (\cos 45° = 0.707) = 500 \text{ watts.}$$

The power curve is partly above the X axis (fig. 10-4 (B)) and partly below it. The axis of the power curve is displaced above the X axis an amount proportional to the true power, $EI \cos \theta$. The apparent power in this circuit is

$$100 \times 7.07 = 707 \text{ volt-amperes.}$$

The power factor is

$$\cos \theta = \frac{\text{true power}}{\text{apparent power}} = \frac{500}{707} = 0.707, \text{ or } 70.7 \text{ percent}.$$

The reactive power in the L-R circuit is the product of $EI \sin \theta$ where $\sin \theta$ is the reactive factor. Thus the reactive power is

$$100 \times 7.07 \, (\sin 45° = 0.707) = 500 \text{ VARS (lagging).}$$

Summary of E, Z, and P Relations in L-R Circuit

The relation between voltage, impedance, and power in a series L-R circuit with sine waveforms applied is summarized in figure 10-5. In this example the circuit contains 12 ohms of resistance in series with 16 ohms of inductive reactance (fig. 10-5 (A)). The phase relations between the applied voltage; the voltage across the resistance, R; and the voltage across the inductance, L; are shown in figure 10-5 (B). The IR drop across R is 5 x 12 = 60 volts and forms the base of the right triangle. The altitude is the IX_L drop, or 5 x 16 = 80 volts, across L. The applied voltage represents the vector sum of the IR drop and the IX_L drop and is the hypotenuse of the right triangle. Its magnitude is 100 volts. All voltages are effective values.

The relation between resistance, inductive reactance, and impedance is shown by the vectors of figure 10-5 (C). The resistance of 12 ohms forms the base of the right triangle. The altitude of this triangle represents the inductive reactance of the coil and has a magnitude of 16 ohms. The combined impedance of the circuit is $Z = \sqrt{12^2 + 16^2} = 20$ ohms. In this triangle $\cos \theta = \dfrac{R}{Z}$. Thus $\cos \theta = \dfrac{12}{20} = 0.6$, from which $\theta = 53.1°$.

The relation between apparent power, true power, and reactive power is shown in figure 10-5 (D). The hypotenuse represents the apparent power and is equal to EI, or 100 x 5 = 500 volt-amperes. The base represents true power and is equal to $EI \cos \theta$, or 100 x 5 x 0.6 = 300 watts, where 0.6 = $\cos 53.1°$. The altitude represents reactive power and is equal to $EI \sin \theta$, or 100 x 5 x 0.8 = 400 VARS, where 0.8 = $\sin 53.1°$.

In all three vector diagrams the right triangles are similar. The common factor of current, I, makes their corresponding sides proportional. Thus the voltage triangle of figure 10-5 (B), is obtained by multiplying the corresponding sides of the impedance triangle of figure 10-5 (C), by I. The hypotenuse is equal to the applied voltage, or $IZ = 5 \times 20 = 100$ volts. The base is equal to the voltage across R, or $IR = 5 \times 12 = 60$ volts. The altitude is equal to

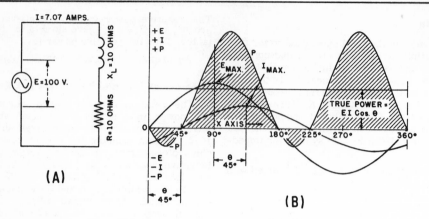

Figure 10-4.—Power in a circuit containing L and R in series.

the voltage across L, or IX_L = 5 x 16 = 80 volts.

Multiplying corresponding sides of the voltage triangle by I gives the power triangle of figure 10-5 (D). The hypotenuse is IZ times I, or $I^2Z = 5^2$ x 20 = 500 volt-amperes of apparent power. The base is IR times I, or $I^2R = 5^2$ x 12 = 300 watts of true power. The altitude is IX_L times I, or $I^2X_L = 5^2$ x 16 = 400 VARS of reactive power.

In the three vector diagrams, the circuit power factor is equal to the following ratios: In the voltage diagram,

$$\cos \theta = \frac{IR}{IZ} = \frac{60}{100} = 0.6.$$

In the impedance diagram,

$$\cos \theta = \frac{R}{Z} = \frac{12}{20} = 0.6.$$

In the power diagram,

$$\cos \theta = \frac{I^2R}{I^2Z} = \frac{300}{500} = 0.6.$$

In all three diagrams θ = 53.1° and the power factor is 60 percent.

Capacitive Reactance

Capacitance was defined in chapter 9 as that quality of a circuit that enables energy to be stored in an electric field. A capacitor is a device that possesses the quality of capacitance. In simple form it has been shown to consist of two parallel metal plates separated by an insulator, called a DIELECTRIC. The electric field consists of parallel lines of electric force which terminate in a positive charge on one plate and a negative charge on the other. The positive and negative charges on the plates establish the electric field in the dielectric because the dielectric prevents these charges from neutralizing each other.

CURRENT FLOW IN A CAPACITIVE CIRCUIT

A capacitor that is initially uncharged tends to draw a large current when a d-c voltage is first applied. During the charging period, the capacitor voltage rises. After the capacitor has received sufficient charge the capacitor voltage equals the applied voltage and the current flow ceases. If a sine-wave a-c voltage is applied to a pure capacitance the current is a maximum when the voltage begins to rise from zero, and the current is zero when the voltage across the capacitor is a maximum (fig. 10-6 (A)). The current leads the applied voltage by 90°, as indicated in the vector diagram of figure 10-6 (B).

ACTORS THAT CONTROL CHARGING CURRENT

Because a capacitor of large capacitance can store more energy than one of small capacitance, a larger current must flow to charge

166

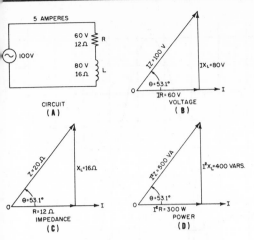

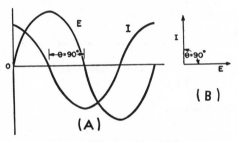

Figure 10-5.—Summary of relation between E, Z, and P in a series L-R circuit.

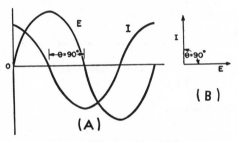

Figure 10-6.—Phase relation between E and I in a capacitive circuit.

a large capacitor than to charge a small one, assuming the same time interval in both cases. Also, because the current flow depends on the rate of charge and discharge, the higher the frequency, the greater is the current flow per unit time.

The charging current in a purely capacitive circuit varies directly with the capacitance, voltage, and frequency—

$$I = 2\pi f C E$$

where I is effective current in amperes, f is in cycles per second, C is the capacitance in farads, and E is in effective volts.

FORMULA FOR CAPACITIVE REACTANCE

The ratio of the effective voltage across the capacitor to the effective current is called the

CAPACITIVE REACTANCE, X_C, and represents the opposition to current flow in a capacitive circuit of zero losses—

$$X_c = \frac{1}{2\pi f C}$$

When f is in cycles per second, and C is in farads, then X_c is in ohms.

Example: What is the capacitive reactance of a capacitor operating at a frequency of 60 cycles per second and having a capacitance of 133 microfarads, or 1.33×10^{-4} farads?

$$X_c = \frac{1}{2\pi f C} = \frac{1}{6.28 \times 60 \times 1.33 \times 10^{-4}} = 20 \text{ ohms.}$$

POWER IN A CAPACITIVE CIRCUIT

With no voltage or charge, the electrons in the dielectric between the capacitor plates rotate around their respective nuclei in normally circular orbits. When the capacitor receives a charge the positive plate repels the positive nuclei and at the same time the electrons in the dielectric are strained toward the positive plate and repelled away from the negative plate. This distorts the orbits of the electrons in the direction of the positive charge. During the time the electron orbits are changing from normal to the strained position there is a movement of electrons in the direction of the positive charge. This movement constitutes the DISPLACEMENT CURRENT in the dielectric. When the polarity of the plates reverses, the electron strain is reversed. If a sine-wave voltage is applied across the capacitor plates the electrons will oscillate back and forth in a direction parallel to the electrostatic lines of force. DISPLACEMENT CURRENT is a result of the movement of bound electrons, whereas CONDUCTION CURRENT represents the movement of free electrons.

Figure 10-7 (A) shows a capacitive circuit and figure 10-7 (B) indicates the sine waveform of charging current, applied voltage, and instantaneous power. The effective voltage is 70.7 volts. The effective current is 7.07 amperes. Because the losses are neglected, the phase angle between current and voltage is assumed to be 90°. The true power is zero, as indicated by the expression

$$P = EI \cos \theta$$
$$= 70.7 \times 7.07 \ (\cos 90° = 0) = 0 \text{ watt.}$$

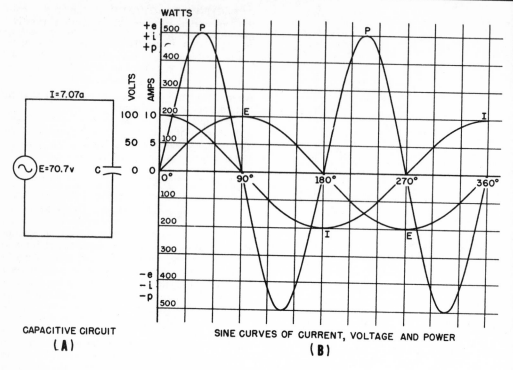

CAPACITIVE CIRCUIT
(A)

SINE CURVES OF CURRENT, VOLTAGE AND POWER
(B)

Figure 10-7.—Power in a capacitive circuit.

Multiplying instantaneous values of current and voltage over one cycle, or 360°, gives the power curve, P. During the first quarter cycle (from 0° to 90°) the applied voltage rises from zero to a maximum and the capacitor is receiving a charge. The power curve is positive during this period and represents energy stored in the capacitor. From 90° to 180° the applied voltage is falling from maximum to zero and the capacitor is discharging. The corresponding power curve is negative and represents energy returned to the circuit during this interval. The third quarter cycle represents a period of charging the capacitor and the fourth quarter cycle represents a discharge period. Thus, the average power absorbed by the capacitor is zero. The action is like the elasticity of a spring. Storing a charge in the capacitor is like compressing the spring. Discharging the capacitor is like releasing the pressure on the spring, thus allowing it to return the energy that was stored within it on compression.

The apparent power in the capacitor is EI = 70.7 x 7.07 = 500 volt-amperes. The reactive power in the capacitor is

$EI \sin \theta = 70.7 \times 7.07 \times (\sin 90° = 1) = 500$ VARS (leading).

CAPACITIVE REACTANCE AND RESISTANCE IN SERIES

Losses that appear in capacitive circuits may be lumped in a resistor connected in series with the capacitor, as indicated in figure 10-8. In this example a 39.8-microfarad capacitor is connected in series with a 20-ohm resistor (fig. 10-8 (A)). The applied voltage across the R-C series circuit is 134 volts and the frequency is 100 cycles per second.

The capacitive reactance at this frequency is

$$X_c = \frac{1}{2\pi f C} = \frac{1}{6.28 \times 100 \times 39.8 \times 10^{-6}} = 40 \text{ ohms}.$$

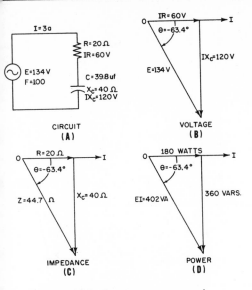

Figure 10-8.—Capacitive reactance and resistance in series.

The impedance diagram is indicated in figure 10-8 (C). The base of the triangle represents the resistance, R, of the circuit and has a magnitude of 20 ohms. The capacitive reactance, X_c is represented as the altitude of the triangle and has a magnitude of 40 ohms. The total impedance may be represented as the hypotenuse of the triangle and has a magnitude of $\sqrt{20^2 + 40^2}$ = 44.7 ohms, which is also the ratio of the applied voltage to the circuit current. The impedance diagram is a right triangle that is similar to the triangle representing the voltage relation in figure 10-8 (B).

Power

The power relations are indicated in the vector diagram of figure 10-8 (D). This diagram is also a right triangle similar to the other two. The base represents the true power absorbed by the circuit resistance and has a magnitude of $I^2R = 3^2$ x 20 = 180 watts. The altitude represents the reactive volt-ampere (leading) and has a magnitude of $I^2X_c = 3^2$ x 40 = 360 VARS. The total apparent power is

$$EI = 134. \times 3 = 402 \text{ volt-amperes.}$$

Voltage Relation

The voltages across R and C are 90° out of phase and equal to 60 volts and 120 volts respectively, as shown in the vector diagram of figure 10-8 (B). The voltage across C is represented as IX_c and is plotted vertically downward from the horizontal in order in indicate that the current leads the voltage across the capacitor by 90°. Angle θ between the voltage across the capacitor and the circuit current is represented as -90° because it is measured clockwise from the horizontal reference vector, OI. The total voltage is equal to the vector sum of IR and IX_c and is represented in the figure as the hypotenuse of a right triangle the base of which represents the voltage across R, having an effective value of 60 volts and the voltage drop across C, having an effective value of 120 volts. The total (applied) voltage is $60^2 - 120^2 - 134$ volts.

Impedance

The total impedance, Z, of the series circuit is

$$Z = \frac{E}{I} = \frac{134}{3} = 44.7 \text{ ohms.}$$

Summary of E, Z, and P Relations in R-C Circuits

As mentioned previously, all three triangles are similar; and the phase angle, θ, between E and I is equal to the same value in all three diagrams. Thus, the circuit power factor is equal to

$$\cos \theta = \frac{IR}{IZ} = \frac{60}{134} = 0.446 \text{ (fig. 10-8, B)}$$

$$\cos \theta = \frac{R}{Z} = \frac{20}{44.7} = 0.446 \text{ (fig. 10-9, C)}$$

$$\cos \theta = \frac{I^2R}{I^2Z} = \frac{180}{402} = 0.446 \text{ (fig. 10-8, D)}$$

and angle $\theta = 63.4°$ in all three triangles.
The true power is

$$EI \cos \theta = 134 \times 3 \times (\cos 63.4° = 0.446) = 180 \text{ watts.}$$

The reactive power is

$$EI \sin \theta = 134 \times 3 \times (\sin 63.4° = 0.894) = 360 \text{ VARS.}$$

The apparent power is

$$EI = 134 \times 3 = 402 \text{ volt-amperes.}$$

169

QUIZ

1. When frequency is increased in an inductive circuit, the current flow will
   a. increase because of greater inductive voltage
   b. increase because of less inductive voltage
   c. decrease because of greater inductive voltage
   d. decrease because of less inductive voltage

2. The unit of measurement for reactive power is the
   a. Volt Amp (VA)
   b. Volt Amp Wattage (VAW)
   c. Volt Amp Reactive (VAR)
   d. Volt Amp Kilo Watt (KVAW)

3. The prime factors that determine inductive reactance are
   a. frequency and current
   b. frequency and induced voltage
   c. inductance and frequency
   d. inductance and voltage

4. What are the prime factors affecting capacitive reactance?
   a. Frequency and capacitance
   b. Frequency and inductance
   c. Frequency and resistance
   d. Frequency squared

5. The reaction of an inductor to any change in current is known as inductive
   a. reactance
   b. voltage
   c. current
   d. resistance

6. What two quantities comprise the total power of an a-c circuit?
   a. Apparent power and VARS
   b. True power and VARS
   c. True power and VAWS
   d. True power and power factor

7. Power factor is the
   a. percentage of apparent power expended in heat
   b. amount of apparent power in an a-c circuit
   c. amount of apparent power plus true power
   d. efficiency of a circuit expressed as an angle

8. The unit of measurement for inductive reactance is the
   a. ohm
   b. volt
   c. ampere
   d. henry

9. What is the power factor of a pure capacitive circuit?
   a. 70.7%
   b. 86.6%
   c. 100%
   d. 0%

10. The self-induced voltage in a coil depends on the
    a. voltage applied
    b. inductive reactance
    c. c.e.m.f.
    d. current change in the coil

11. What is the path for current flow through a capacitor?
    a. Does not actually flow through
    b. From negative plate to positive plate
    c. From positive plate to negative plate
    d. From dielectric to plates

12. Power is described as the rate at which
    a. work is being done
    b. energy is being used
    c. energy is being expended
    d. all of the above are correct

13. What is the power characteristic of a pure inductive circuit?
    a. Positive power is the largest
    b. Positive and negative power are equal
    c. Negative power is the largest
    d. Negative power is the smallest

14. The vector sum of X_C and R in a series R-C circuit is the total
    a. opposition to voltage in the circuit
    b. capacitive reactance in the circuit
    c. resistance in the circuit
    d. opposition to current flow in the circuit

15. Self-induced voltage in an inductor will always oppose
    a. the applied voltage by 180 degrees
    b. circuit current
    c. the applied voltage by 90 degrees
    d. the circuit current by 180 degrees

16. What is the value of apparent current flow in a capacitive circuit when it is first energized?
    a. No current flow in a capacitive circuit
    b. Minimum
    c. Maximum
    d. Zero

17. What is the phase relationship between current and voltage in a resistive circuit?
    a. 90° phase difference
    b. 0° phase difference
    c. Out of phase
    d. Cannot be determined without numerical value of R

8. Voltage and current are considered to be out of phase with each other in a pure inductive circuit by what amount?
   a. Current leads voltage by 90 degrees
   b. Current lags voltage by 90 degrees
   c. Current leads voltage by 180 degrees
   d. Current lags voltage by 180 degrees

9. What is the phase relationship between current and voltage in a pure capacitive circuit?
   a. No phase angle
   b. Current lags voltage by 90 degrees
   c. Voltage leads current by 90 degrees
   d. Voltage lags current by 90 degrees

0. The phase angle between current and voltage in a circuit containing both resistive and inductive elements is
   a. greater than 0° but less than 90°
   b. a constant 45°
   c. 90° at all times
   d. 0° because X_L and R are equal

21. In the formula for capacitive reactance, the symbol "C" represents capacitance in
   a. farads
   b. micromicrofarads
   c. microfarads
   d. ohms

22. What is the effect on capacitor voltage when frequency is increased?
   a. Voltage increases
   b. Voltage decreases
   c. Voltage not affected
   d. Voltage is minimum

23. What is impedance?
   a. Opposition to current flow in an a-c circuit created by resistance and reactances
   b. Resistance of an a-c circuit
   c. Vector sum of voltage drops in an a-c circuit
   d. Current divided by voltage in an a-c circuit

CHAPTER 11

FUNDAMENTAL ALTERNATING-CURRENT CIRCUIT THEORY

In the preceding chapter, terms were clarified, a-c reactance was explained, and the effects of individual inductors and capacitors were described. To do this, only the simplest two-element R-L and R-C series circuits were employed. In this chapter, the subject coverage will be expanded to include more complex reactive circuits.

RESISTANCE, INDUCTANCE, AND CAPACITANCE IN SERIES

Relation of Voltages and Current in an R-L-C Series Circuit

When resistive, inductive, and capacitive elements are connected in series, their INDIVIDUAL characteristics are unchanged. That is, the current through and the voltage drop across the resistor are in phase while the voltage drops across the reactive components (assuming pure reactances) and the current through them are 90 degrees out of phase. However, a new relation must be recognized with the introduction of the three-element circuit. This pertains to the effect on total line voltage and current when connecting reactive elements in series, whose individual characteristics are opposite in nature, such as inductance and capacitance. Such a circuit is shown in figure 11-1.

In the figure, note first that CURRENT is the common reference for all three element voltages, because there is only one current in a series circuit, and it is common to all elements. The common series current is represented by the dashed line in figure 11-1 (A). The voltage vector for each element, showing its individual relation to the common current, is drawn above each respective element. The

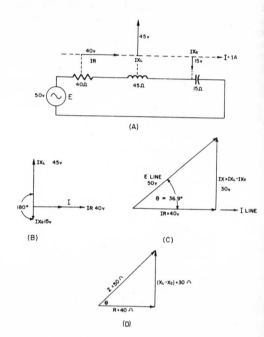

Figure 11-1.—Resistance, inductance, and capacitance connected in series.

total source voltage E is the vector sum of the individual voltages of IR, IX_L, and IX_C.

The three element voltages are arranged for summation in part (B). Since IX_L and IX_C are each 90° away from I, they are therefore 180° from each other. Vectors in direct opposition (180° out of phase) may be subtracted directly. The total reactive voltage E_X is the difference of IX_L and IX_C. Or, $E_X = IX_L - IX_C = 45 - 15 = 30$ volts. The final relationship of line voltage and current, as seen from the source, is shown in

172

part (C). Had X_C been larger than X_L, the voltage would lag, rather than lead. When X_C and X_L are of equal values, line voltage and current will be in phase.

Impedance of R-L-C Series Circuits

The impedance of an R-L-C (three-element) series circuit is computed in exactly the same manner described for the two-element circuits in the preceding chapter. However, there is one additional operation to be performed. That is, the DIFFERENCE of X_L and X_C must be determined prior to computing total impedance. When employing the Pythagorean Theorem-based formula for determining series impedance, the net reactance of the circuit is represented by the quantity in parenthesis $(X_L - X_C)$. Applying this formula to the circuit in figure 11-1, the impedance is

$$Z = \sqrt{R^2 + (X_L - X_C)^2}$$

$$= \sqrt{40^2 + (45 - 15)^2}$$

$$= \sqrt{1,600 + 900}$$

$$= \sqrt{2,500}$$

$$Z = 50\,\Omega.$$

Series impedance may also be determined by the use of vectorial layout, or triangulation. In an impedance triangle (fig. 11-1 (D)) for a series circuit, the base always represents the series resistance, the altitude represents the NET reactance $(X_L - X_C)$, and the hypotenuse represents total impedance.

It should be noted that as the DIFFERENCE of X_L and X_C becomes greater, total impedance also increases. Conversely, when X_L and X_C are equal, their effects cancel each other, and impedance is minimum, equal only to the series resistance. When X_L and X_C are equal, their INDIVIDUAL voltages are 90° out of phase with current, but their COLLECTIVE effect is zero, because they are equal and opposite in nature. Therefore, when X_L and X_C are equal, line voltage and current are in phase. This condition is the same as if there were only resistance and no reactances in the circuit. A circuit in this condition is said to be at RESONANCE.

Power in an R-L-C Series Circuit

Total true power in an R-L-C series circuit is the product of line voltage and current, times the cosine of the angle between them. When X_L and X_C are equal, total impedance is at a minimum, and thus current is maximum. When maximum current flows, the series resistor dissipates maximum power. When X_L and X_C are made unequal, total impedance increases, line current decreases, and moves out of phase with line voltage. Both the decrease in current and the creation of a phase difference cause a decrease in true power.

INDUCTANCE AND RESISTANCE IN PARALLEL

If the voltage applied across a resistor and inductor in parallel has a sine waveform, the currents in the branches will also have sine waveforms. In the parallel circuit of figure 11-2 (A), the applied voltage, E, has a magnitude of 100 volts (r.m.s.). Branch ① contains a 20-ohm resistor, and the current, I_1, is equal to $\frac{100}{20}$, or 5 amperes (r.m.s.). This current is in phase with E. Branch ② contains an inductance of 0.053 henry. The line frequency is 60 cycles and the INDUCTIVE REACTANCE is

$$X_L = 2\pi f L = 6.28 \times 60 \times 0.053 = 20 \text{ ohms.}$$

The true power losses associated with the inductor in this example are considered negligible. Therefore, current I_2 is equal to $\frac{100}{20}$, or 5 amperes. This current lags E by an angle of 90°. (In an inductive circuit the current always lags the voltage by some angle.)

The sine waveforms of applied voltage and current are shown in figure 11-2 (B). I_1 is in phase with E. I_2 lags E by an angle of 90°. The total current, I_t, lags E by an angle of 45°.

Current Vectors

A polar-vector diagram representing the three currents and the applied voltage is shown in figure 11-2 (C). Vector OE represents the effective value of the applied voltage and is the horizontal reference vector for both branches because it is common to both branches. Vector

I_1 is the effective current of 5 amperes in branch ①. This vector is in the same line as vector OE because the current and voltage in the resistive circuit are in phase. Vector I_2 is the effective current of 5 amperes in branch ② and lags vector OE by an angle of 90°. I_1 is called the ENERGY COMPONENT of the circuit current. It flows in the resistive branch in which true power is absorbed from the source and is dissipated as heat. I_2 is called the NON-ENERGY COMPONENT of the circuit current. This current flows in the inductive branch where the true power is zero, and the reactive power is exchanged with the source twice during each cycle of applied voltage.

The total circuit current, I_t, is represented as the diagonal of the parallelogram, the sides of which are I_1 and I_2 (fig. 11-2 (C)). In this example, the sides are 5 amperes (r.m.s.) each and the diagonal is 7.07 amperes (r.m.s.).

A topographic-vector diagram representing the three currents and the applied voltage is shown in figure 11-2 (D). As in the polar diagram, OE is the reference vector. I_1, in phase with OE, is the base of the triangle. I_2, 90° out of phase with OE, is the altitude of the triangle, and is plotted downward to indicate lag. The resultant current, I_t, is the hypotenuse of the triangle. The hypotenuse is equal to the square root of the sum of the squares of the other two sides. Thus,

$$I_t = \sqrt{I_1^2 + I_2^2} = \sqrt{5^2 + 5^2} = 7.07 \text{ amperes.}$$

The phase angle between I_t and E is the angle whose cosine is

$$\frac{I_1}{I_t} = \frac{5}{7.07} = 0.707.$$

This angle is 45°.

Power and Power Factor

The apparent power, true power, and reactive power in the parallel circuit are related as the hypotenuse, base, and altitude, respectively, of a right triangle in a similar manner to that described in the preceding chapter.

The relation between apparent power, true power, and reactive power is shown in figure 11-2 (E). The hypotenuse of the right triangle represents the apparent power and is equal to EI_t, or 100 x 7.07 = 707 volt-amperes. The base of the triangle represents the true power and is equal to $EI_t \cos \theta t$, or 100 x 7.07 x 0.707 = 500 watts, where 0.707 = cos 45°. The altitude represents the reactive power and is equal to $EI_t \sin \theta t$, or 100 x 7.07 x 0.707 = 500 vars, where 0.707 = sin 45°. The power triangle is similar to the current triangle and is related to it by the common factor of voltage (the voltage is the same across both branches of the parallel circuit).

Because branch ① (fig. 11-2 (A)) is purely resistive and branch ② is purely inductive, the true power of the circuit is absorbed in branch ① and the reactive power is developed in branch ②. In branch ① the true power is $EI_1 \cos \theta_1$, or 100 x 5 x 1 = 500 watts, where 1 = cos 0°. In branch ② the reactive power is $EI_2 \sin \theta_2$, or 100 x 5 x 1 = 500 vars, where 1 = sin 90°.

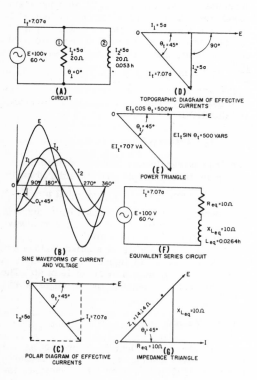

Figure 11-2.—Resistance and inductance in parallel.

The true power in branch ① may also be calculated as $I_1{}^2 R_1$, or $5^2 \times 20 = 500$ watts. The reactive power in branch ② may be calculated as $I_2{}^2 X_{L2}$, or $5^2 \times 20 = 500$ vars. The total circuit power factor is $\cos \theta_t = \dfrac{\text{true power}}{\text{apparent power}} = \dfrac{500}{707} = 0.707$. The power factor of branch ① is $\cos \theta_1 = \cos 0° = 1$, and the power factor of branch②is $\cos \theta_2 = \cos 90° = 0$.

Equivalent Series-Circuit Impedance

The combined impedance of the parallel circuit is

$$Z_t = \frac{E}{I_t} = \frac{100}{7.07} = 14.14 \text{ ohms.}$$

The combined impedance is also called the impedance of the equivalent series circuit. The equivalent series circuit (fig. 11-2 (F)) contains a resistor and an inductor in series that combine to give the same impedance as the total impedance, of the given parallel circuit. Thus, the current in the equivalent series circuit is equal to the total circuit current in the parallel circuit when rated voltage and frequency are applied to the circuits.

In figure 11-2 (G), the hypotenuse, Z_t, of the impedance triangle is 14.14 ohms and the phase angle, θ_t, between total current and line voltage, is 45°. The equivalent series RESISTANCE, R_{eq}, is the base of the impedance triangle and is equal to $Z_t \cos \theta$, or 14.14 x $\cos 45° = 10$ ohms. The equivalent series REACTANCE, X_{Leq}, is the altitude of the impedance triangle and is equal to $Z_t \sin \theta_t$, or 14.14 x $\sin 45° = 10$ ohms.

The inductance of the equivalent series circuit is

$$L_{eq} = \frac{X_L}{2\pi f} = \frac{10}{6.28 \times 60} = 0.0264 \text{ henry.}$$

Thus, in this example, the 20-ohm resistor in branch ① shunts the 0.053-henry inductor in branch②, and the source "sees" an equivalent resistor of 10 ohms in series with an equivalent inductor of 0.0264 henry.

Equivalent Circuit of a Low-Loss Inductor

The losses in air-core inductor occur in the wire with which the inductor is wound. If the losses are small, the resistance of the wire will be small compared with the inductive reactance developed at the operating frequency. The coil resistance acts in series with the coil reactance.

An equivalent parallel circuit for a low-loss coil can be established by substituting an equivalent coil of zero losses, but having the same inductance as the given coil for one branch and a resistor for the other branch. The resistor is of such a magnitude that the same losses will occur in this branch as occur in the given coil when rated voltage and frequency are applied.

In the following example a low-loss circuit is established and then the equivalent parallel circuit is derived. A low-loss coil is indicated in figure 11-3 (A). It has an inductance of 1.59 henry and a d-c resistance of 10 ohms at an operating frequency of 100 c.p.s. The INDUCTIVE REACTANCE is

$$X_L = 2\pi f L = 6.28 \times 100 \times 1.59 = 1,000 \text{ ohms.}$$

The equivalent series circuit (fig. 11-3 (B)) is shown with 10 ohms of resistance acting in series with 1,000 ohms of inductive reactance. The impedance triangle is shown in figure 11-3 (C).

A low-loss coil has a low power factor. Thus, in the impedance triangle, $\cos \theta = \dfrac{R_{se}}{Z} = \dfrac{10}{1,000} = 0.01$, or 1 percent. As can be seen in this example, Z is approximately equal to X_L, and $\cos \theta = \dfrac{R_{se}}{X_L}$. Since $\tan \theta = \dfrac{X_L}{R_{se}}$, it follows that in this case $\cos \theta = \dfrac{1}{\tan \theta}$. Thus $\tan \theta = \dfrac{1,000}{10} = 100$, and the POWER FACTOR $= \dfrac{10}{1,000}$, or 0.01, or 1 percent.

A useful relationship for finding angle θ in low-loss circuits is shown in figure 11-3 (D). This concept involves the relation between $\cos \theta$, expressed decimally, and the complementary angle, 90 - θ, expressed in radians. The figure indicates a unit-radius circle in which any length of arc BC measures the corresponding angle (90 - θ) which it subtends. The length of arc is equal to the angle in radians. Since 2π radians are equal to 360° it follows that 1 radian is approximately equal to $\dfrac{360°}{2\pi}$, or 57.3°. Thus, from a knowledge of the angle in radians, the equivalent angle θ, in degrees, is $\theta = 57.3$ x angle in radians.

175

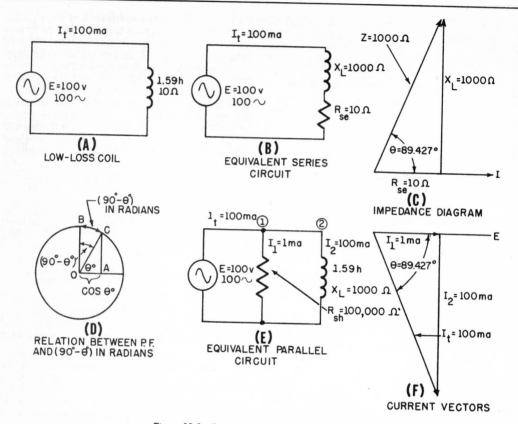

Figure 11-3.—Equivalent circuits of a low-loss coil.

For angles greater than 84.3°, tan θ is greater than 10 and cos θ—which equals OA, in figure 11-3 (D)—is approximately equal to arc BC. Arc BC is a measure of the complementary angle 90 - θ and is expressed in radians. Thus, cos θ is approximately equal to the angle in radians by which the current fails to be exactly 90° out of phase with the voltage. In this example, the power factor is 0.01 and therefore the angle by which the current fails to be 90° out of phase with the voltage (complementary angle) is 0.01 radian. This angle, in degrees, becomes 57.3° x 0.01, or 0.573°. Therefore, θ is equal to 90° - 0.573°, or 89.427°, and cos 89.427° = 0.01.

The relationship described in the preceding example is expressed in general terms as follows: The complementary angle, (90 - θ) in

radians, is equal to the power factor, cos θ, expressed decimally, where tan θ is numerically equal to or greater than 10. From this relationship it is possible to estimate quickly the phase angle between current and voltage in low power-factor (low-loss) circuits.

The equivalent parallel circuit for the 1.59-henry coil discussed in this example is shown in figure 11-3 (E). The equivalent shunt resistor, R_{sh}, has a resistance of 100,000 ohms (to be derived later), and this resistor is connected in parallel with a 1.59-henry inductor having zero losses. With rated voltage and frequency applied, the input current to the parallel circuit has the same magnitude and phase with respect to the applied voltage as in the original coil.

176

The current in the resistive branch is $\frac{100}{100,000}$ = 0.001 ampere, or 1 milliampere, and is the base of the current triangle (fig. 11-3 (F)). The current in the inductive branch is $\frac{100}{1,000}$ = 0.1 ampere, or 100 ma., and is the altitude of the current triangle. The total current in the parallel circuit is equal to $\sqrt{1^2 + 100^2}$ = 100 milliamperes (approx.), and is the hypotenuse of the current triangle. This current lags the line voltage by an angle of $90° - (57.3° \times 0.01)$, or 89.427°.

The equivalent series-circuit impedance triangle (fig. 11-3 (C)) is similar to the current triangle (fig. 11-3 (F)). From the impedance triangle, $\cos \theta \approx \frac{R_{se}}{X_L}$; and from the current triangle, $\cos \theta \approx \frac{I_1}{I_2}$, where I_1 is the energy current and I_2 is the nonenergy current. Therefore,

$$\frac{I_1}{I_2} = \frac{R_{se}}{X_L} . \qquad (11\text{-}1)$$

For the resistive branch,

$$I_1 = \frac{E}{R_{sh}}, \qquad (11\text{-}2)$$

and for the inductive branch,

$$I_2 = \frac{E}{X_L}. \qquad (11\text{-}3)$$

Substituting equations 11-2 and 11-3 in equation 11-1,

$$\frac{\frac{E}{R_{sh}}}{\frac{E}{X_L}} = \frac{R_{se}}{X_L} . \qquad (11\text{-}4)$$

Canceling E and transposing equation 11-4,

$$R_{sh} = \frac{X_L^2}{R_{se}} . \qquad (11\text{-}5)$$

In the example of figure 11-3, R_{se} = 10 ohms, X_L = 1,000 ohms, and $R_{sh} = \frac{(1,000)^2}{10}$ = 100,000 ohms.

The preceding relations are sufficiently accurate for low-loss inductive circuits in which θ is 84.3° or higher, and $\tan \theta$ is 10 or higher.

Combining Currents at Acute Angles

Figure 11-4 (A) represents a 2-branch parallel circuit in which branch① has a power factor of 0.50 and branch② has a power factor of 0.866. The current in branch① lags the applied voltage by an angle of 60° and the current in branch② lags the applied voltage by an angle of 30°. The series resistance, R_1, of branch① is 10 ohms, the series inductive reactance, X_{L1}, is 17.32 ohms, and the impedance, Z_1, is $\sqrt{10^2 + (17.32)^2}$ = 20 ohms. The series resistance, R_2, of branch② is 17.32 ohms, the series inductive reactance, X_{L2}, is 10 ohms, and the impedance, Z_2, is

$$\sqrt{(17.32)^2 + 10^2} = 20 \text{ ohms.}$$

A topographic-vector diagram of the currents in the two branches and the total circuit current is shown in figure 11-4 (B). The current in branch ① is $I_1 = \frac{100}{20}$ = 5 amperes and is the hypotenuse of the right triangle of which the base (energy component) is 5 cos 60° = 2.5 amperes and the altitude (nonenergy component) is 5 sin 60° = 4.33 amperes. The current in branch ② is $I_2 = \frac{100}{20}$ = 5 amperes and is the hypotenuse of the right angle of which the base (energy component) is 5 cos 30° = 4.33 amperes and the altitude (nonenergy component) is 5 sin 30° = 2.5 amperes. The total circuit current is the vector sum of I_1 and I_2, and is the hypotenuse of the resultant right triangle, the base of which is the sum of the energy components of both branches, 2.5 + 4.33 = 6.83 amperes, and the altitude of which is the sum of the nonenergy components of both branches, 4.33 + 2.5 = 6.83 amperes. Thus,

$$I_t = \sqrt{(2.5 + 4.33)^2 + (4.33 + 2.5)^2} = 9.66 \text{ amperes.}$$

The circuit power factor is $\cos \theta_t = \frac{2.5 + 4.33}{9.66} = 0.707$, and $\theta_t = 45°$.

The power relations for this circuit are shown in figure 11-4 (C). The apparent power in branch ① is EI_1 = 100 x 5 = 500 volt-amperes and is the hypotenuse of the right triangle, the base of which is $EI_1 \cos \theta_1$ = 100 x 5 x cos 60° = 250 watts of true power, and the altitude of which is $EI_1 \sin \theta_1$ = 100 x 5 x sin 60° = 433 VARS of reactive power.

The apparent power in branch ② is EI_2 = 100 x 5 = 500 volt-amperes and is the hypotenuse of the right triangle, the base of which is $EI_2 \cos \theta_2 = 100 \times 5 \times \cos 30° = 433$ watts of true power, and the altitude of which is $EI_2 \sin \theta_2 = 100 \times 5 \times \sin 30° = 250$ VARS of reactive power.

The total apparent power of the combined parallel circuit is the hypotenuse of the resultant triangle, the base of which is equal to the sum of the true power components in both branches, and the altitude of which is equal to the sum of the reactive power components in both branches. Thus, the total apparent power

$$= \sqrt{(250+433)^2 + (433+250)^2} = 966 \text{ volt-amperes.}$$

The equivalent series circuit (fig. 11-4 (D)), representing the combined impedance of the given parallel circuit, has a total impedance, Z_t, that is determined by dividing the applied voltage, E, by the total circuit current, I_t.

$$Z_t = \frac{E}{I_t} = \frac{100}{9.66} = 10.35 \text{ ohms.}$$

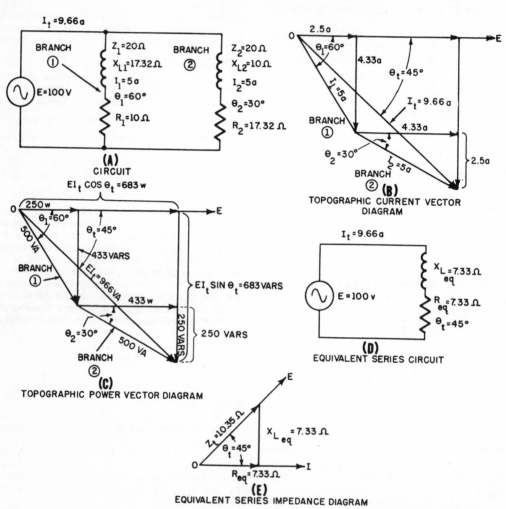

Figure 11-4.—Two-branch L-R circuit with currents 30° out of phase.

178

he hypotenuse of the impedance triangle (fig. 1-4 (E)) is 10.35 ohms. The impedance triangle is similar to the resultant-current right ·iangle (fig. 11-4 (B)), and angle θ_t has the ame magnitude in both triangles. This angle is qual to 45°, as determined in the current-·iangle calculations.

The equivalent series resistance, R_{eq}, is the ase of the impedance triangle and is equal to $_t$ cos θ_t, or 10.35 x cos 45°, = 7.33 ohms.

The equivalent series reactance, $X_{L_{eq}}$, is the ltitude of the impedance triangle and is equal to $_t$ sin θ_t or 10.35 x sin 45°=7.33 ohms.

The impedance triangle is also similar to the ·esultant power triangle for the combined paral-el circuit (fig. 11-4 (C)). The common factor ·etween the two triangles is the square of the ·otal circuit current, I_t^2. The base of the re-ultant power triangle is $I_t^2 R_{eq}$ = (9.66)^2 x 7.33= ·83 watts of true power. This product may be ·hecked by adding the true power components in ·ranches①and②.Thus, 250 + 433 = 683 watts of ·rue power.

The altitude of the resultant power triangle s $I_t^2 X_{L_{eq}}$ = (9.66)^2 x 7.33 = 683 VARS of reac-ive power. This product may be checked by add-ng the reactive VAR components in branches ① and ②. Thus, 433+250 = 683 VARS of reactive ·ower.

The hypotenuse of the resultant power tri-.ngle is $I_t^2 Z_t$ = (9.66)^2 x 10.35= 966 volt-.mperes of apparent power. This product may be ·hecked by adding vectorially the apparent power ·n branch①and the apparent power in branch② This product is equal to the hypotenuse of the ·esultant power triangle (fig. 11-4 (C)). This ·roduct CANNOT be checked accurately by .dding arithmetically the apparent power in ·ranch ① to the apparent power in branch②be-·ause these quantities are not in phase with each ·ther.

:APACITANCE AND RESISTANCE IN PARALLEL

The action of a capacitor in an a-c series ·ircuit was described in chapter 10 and is am-lified further at this time as an introduction to ·he a-c parallel R-C circuit. In figure 11-5 (A), ·n a-c voltage of sine waveform is applied across · capacitor and a charging current of sine wave-·orm flows around the circuit in a manner some-·hing like that of the flow of water in the hydraulic .nalogy shown in figure 11-5 (B). The pump at ·he left corresponds to the a-c source and the ·ylinder at the right corresponds to the capa-

citor. If the pump piston is driven by means of a crank turning at uniform speed, the resulting motion of the water will be sinusoidal. The motion of the water is transmitted through the flexible diaphragm in the cylinder and the re-sulting motion, first in one direction and then in the other, corresponds to the electron flow in the wires connecting the capacitor to the a-c source.

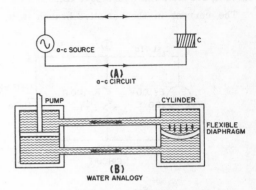

(A)
a-c CIRCUIT

(B)
WATER ANALOGY

Figure 11-5.—Water analogy of a capacitor in an a-c circuit.

The mechanical stress in the diaphragm in the cylinder corresponds to the electric stress in the dielectric between the plates of the capacitor. Electron flow does not occur through the di-electric in the same way that water would flow through the flexible diaphragm if a hole were punctured in it. Instead, the electrons flow around the capacitor circuit on one alternation causing a negative charge to build up on one plate, and a corresponding positive charge on the other, and on the next alternation causing a reversal of the polarity of the charges on the plates. Thus, the effective impedance which the capacitor offers to the flow of ALTERNATING CURRENT can be relatively low at the same time that the insulation resistance which the dielectric offers to the flow of DIRECT CUR-RENT is extremely high.

In the example of figure 11-6, a 2-branch circuit consists of a 100-ohm resistor and a 15.9-microfarad capacitor of negligible losses in parallel with a 100-volt a-c source. The fre-quency of the source voltage is 100 c.p.s. and the voltage is assumed to have a sine waveform.

The current in branch ① is $\frac{100}{100}$ = 1 ampere (r.m.s)

The impedance of branch ② is composed of

179

capacitive reactance; its resistance component is neglected. In branch ② $X_C = \frac{1}{2\pi fC} = \frac{1}{6.28 \times 100 \times 15.9 \times 10^{-6}} = 100$ ohms. The current in branch ② is $\frac{100}{100} = 1$ ampere (r.m.s.). The sine waveform of the branch currents and the applied voltage, together with the resultant line current, are shown in figure 13-6 (B).

The current in the resistive branch is in phase with the applied voltage and has a peak value of $\frac{1}{0.707} = 1.41$ amperes. The current in the capacitor branch leads the applied voltage by an angle of 90° and has a peak value of $\frac{1}{0.707} = 1.41$ amperes. The resultant line current is the algebraic sum of the instantaneous values of the currents in the two branches and has a peak value of 2 amperes. The resultant line current, I_t, leads the applied voltage by an angle of 45°

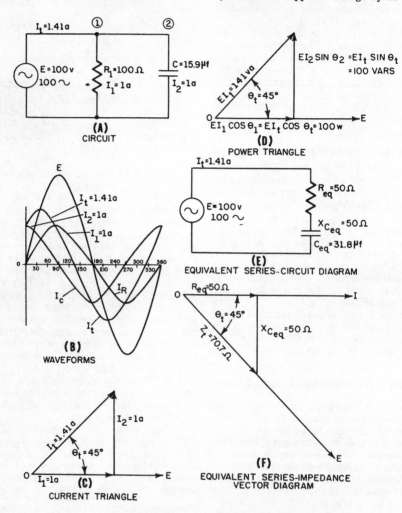

Figure 11-6.—Parallel R-C circuit analysis.

ırrent Vectors

A topographic-vector diagram of the EF-ECTIVE VALUES of these currents is shown figure 11-6 (C). The base of the current tri-ıgle is 1 ampere and represents the current in ranch ①. This current is in phase with the ap-.ied voltage and represents the energy com-ınent of the total line current.

The altitude of the current triangle is 1 am-ıre and represents the current in branch ②. his current leads the applied voltage by 90° and ıpresents the nonenergy component of the total ne current.

The hypotenuse of the triangle is 1.41 am-ıres and represents the total line current.

The reference vector, OE, for the current ʻiangle is the line voltage, and in the R-C paral-ıl circuit, the altitude extends above the re-ırence vector to indicate the sense of lead. his direction is opposite to that of the altitude f the current triangle for the R-L parallel cir-ıit in figure 11-2 (D). In both figures the vectors ıre assumed to rotate in a counterclockwise ırection to indicate the sense of lead or lag of ıe currents with respect to the line voltage. In ll single-phase circuits such as these, the cur-ent vectors are considered in their relative ıase by angles that never exceed 90° with re-ıect to their common reference voltage vector.

In figure 11-2 (D), the line current lags the ıne voltage by an angle of 45°, and in figure 1-6 (C), the line current leads the line voltage y an angle of 45°. If both inductance and capaci-ance exist in the same parallel circuit as eparate branches, the currents in these ʻranches will be 180° out of phase with each ther, but the current in the inductive branch will ever lag the line voltage by an angle in excess f 90°, and the current in the capacitive branch vill never lead the line voltage by an angle in xcess of 90°

ower and Power Factor

The power triangle for the parallel R-C cir-uit is shown in figure 11-6 (D). The TRUE power ı branch ① is

$$EI_1 \cos \theta_1 = 100 \times 1 \times (\cos 0° = 1) = 100 \text{ watts,}$$

ınd forms the base of the triangle in line with he voltage vector, OE. The REACTIVE power ı branch ② is

$$EI_2 \sin \theta_2 = 100 \times 1 \,(\sin 90° = 1) = 100 \text{ VARS,}$$

and is the altitude of the power triangle, per-pendicular to OE. The REACTIVE power in branch ① is

$$EI_1 \sin \theta_1 = 100 \times 1 \,(\sin 0° = 0) = 0 \text{ VAR,}$$

and the TRUE power in branch ② is

$$EI_2 \cos \theta_2 = 100 \times 1 \,(\cos 90° = 0) = 0 \text{ watt.}$$

The APPARENT power of the parallel R-C circuit is

$$EI_t = 100 \times 1.41 = 141 \text{ volt-amperes}$$

and is the hypotenuse of the power triangle.

The power triangle (fig. 11-6 (D)) is simi-lar to the current triangle (fig. 11-6 (C)), since θ_t has the same magnitude in both triangles. The total circuit power factor, as determined from the current triangle, is

$$\cos \theta_t = \frac{I_1}{I_t} = \frac{1}{1.41} = 0.707.$$

The total circuit power factor, as determined from the power triangle, is

$$\cos \theta_t = \frac{\text{true power}}{\text{apparent power}} = \frac{100}{141} = 0.707.$$

The TRUE power of the total circuit, as determined from the power triangle, is

$$EI_t \cos \theta_t = 100 \times 1.41 \,(\cos 45° = 0.707) = 100 \text{ watts.}$$

This value is equal to the true power in branch ①.

The REACTIVE power of the total circuit, as determined from the power triangle, is

$$EI_t \sin \theta_t = 100 \times 1.41 \,(\sin 45° = 0.707) = 100 \text{ VARS.}$$

This value is equal to the reactive power in branch ②.

Equivalent Series Impedance

The total impedance of the parallel R-C cir-cuit is

$$Z_t = \frac{E}{I_t} = \frac{100}{1.41} = 70.7 \text{ ohms.}$$

181

As mentioned previously, the total impedance is also the impedance of the equivalent series circuit (fig. 11-6 (E)). In figure 11-6 (F), the hypotenuse, Z_t, of the impedance triangle is 70.7 ohms and the phase angle, θ_t, between total current and line voltage is 45°. The equivalent series resistance, R_{eq}, is the base of the impedance triangle and has a magnitude of

$$R_{eq} = Z_t \cos \theta_t = 70.7 \, (\cos 45° = 0.707) = 50 \text{ ohms.}$$

The equivalent series reactance, $X_{C_{eq}}$, is the altitude of the impedance triangle and has a magnitude of $Z_t \sin \theta_t = 70.7 \, (\sin 45° = 0.707) = 50$ ohms. The altitude is extended downward, in contrast to the upward direction of the altitude of the current triangle in figure 11-6 (C), to maintain the sense of current lead for counterclockwise vector rotation. The line voltage is the horizontal reference vector, OE (fig. 11-6 (C)), and the line current is the horizontal reference vector, OI (fig. 11-6 (F)).

The capacitance in microfarads of the equivalent series impedance is

$$C_{eq} = \frac{10^6}{2\pi f X_{C_{eq}}} = \frac{10^6}{6.28 \times 100 \times 50} = 31.8 \text{ microfarads.}$$

Thus, in this example, the 100-ohm resistor in branch ① shunts the 15.9-microfarad capacitor in branch ② and the source "sees" an equivalent resistor of 50 ohms in series with an equivalent capacitor of 31.8 microfarads (fig. 11-6 (E)).

Equivalent Circuit of a Low-Loss Capacitor

The action of a capacitor in an a-c circuit was described as being like the flow of water in a cylinder having a flexible diaphragm. The diaphragm corresponds to the dielectric in a capacitor and the mechanical stresses in the diaphragm correspond to the electric stress in the dielectric.

Most of the heating produced in a capacitor is due to the loss in the dielectric. The movement of the electrons in the atoms of a solid dielectric is pictured in figure 11-7. The capacitor is connected to a source of a-c voltage of sine waveform and the conditions are indicated for three successive instants in the cycle of applied a-c voltage.

In figure 11-7 (A), the voltage across the capacitor plates is positive maximum and the capacitor is charged. The atoms in the dielectric are subjected to electric stress that cause their orbital electrons to move in paths that are changed from circular to elliptical patterns. The elliptical pattern forms as a result of the attractive force of the negatively charged plate on the positive nucleus and the simultaneous repulsion of the positively charged plate on the nucleus. At the same time the positive plate attracts the orbital electrons, the negative plate repels them.

In figure 11-7 (B), the charge on the plate is zero and the electric stress is removed from the dielectric. In this case the orbital electron travel in circular paths about the nucleus with no external forces applied to them.

In figure 11-7 (C), the charges on the plate are reversed and the orbital electrons are again caused to move in elliptical paths. In this case the protons (entire nucleus) are moved toward the upper plate, the forces being opposite to those developed in figure 11-7 (A).

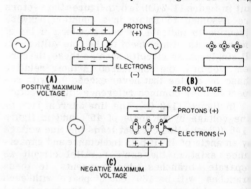

Figure 11-7.—Capacitor dielectric losses.

The rapid reversals of applied voltage accompanied by the change of the orbital electron paths from circular to elliptical and back to circular patterns cause heat to be developed in the dielectric. The change in pattern of the electron orbits constitutes a dielectric displacement current. This current is considered to be made up of two components, one leading the voltage by 90°, the other an energy component in phase with the applied voltage. Factors that determine the dielectric loss are the applied voltage, the dielectric constant, the capacitor power factor, and the frequency of the applied voltage. An air-dielectric capacitor has no appreciable loss, and the power factor is 0. A mica capacitor, having a dielectric constant of 7 and a power factor of 0.0001, has relatively low loss and low dielectric heating at high voltages and high frequencies.

The product of the dielectric constant and the power factor is called the LOSS FACTOR. The loss factor is low for good dielectrics that operate without much dielectric heating. The loss factor is the best indication of the ability of a material to withstand high voltages at high frequencies. The loss factor for the previously mentioned mica capacitor is 7 x 0.0001 = 0.0007. The loss factor for air dielectric is zero because the power factor is zero.

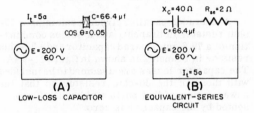

(A)
LOW-LOSS CAPACITOR

(B)
EQUIVALENT—SERIES CIRCUIT

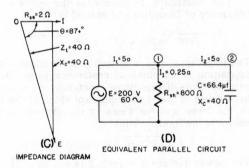

(C)
IMPEDANCE DIAGRAM

(D)
EQUIVALENT PARALLEL CIRCUIT

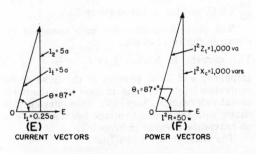

(E)
CURRENT VECTORS

(F)
POWER VECTORS

Figure 11-8.—Equivalent circuits of a low-loss capacitor.

The equivalent circuits of a low power-factor capacitor are represented in figure 11-8. The circuits are derived by assuming a capacitor of the same capacitance as that of the original capacitor, but having no losses (zero power factor), to be connected (1) in SERIES with a resistor that develops the same true power loss as in the original capacitor; and (2) a capacitor of the same capacitance as that of the original capacitor, but having no losses (zero power factor), to be connected in SHUNT with a resistor that develops the same true power loss as in the original capacitor. The capacitance of the capacitor in this example is 66.4 microfarads. The power factor of the capacitor is cos θ = 0.05. The effective voltage is 200 volts and the capacitor current is 5 amperes.

The equivalent series circuit is shown in figure 11-8 (B). At the operating frequency of 60 cycles per second the capacitive reactance of the capacitor is

$$X_C = \frac{1}{2\pi f C} = \frac{1}{6.28 \times 60 \times 66.4 \times 10^{-6}} = 40 \text{ ohms approximately.}$$

The impedance of the series circuit is

$$Z_t = \frac{E}{I_t} = \frac{200}{5} = 40 \text{ ohms.}$$

The equivalent series resistance is

$$R_{se} = Z_t \cos \theta_t = 40 \times 0.05 = 2 \text{ ohms,}$$

(fig. 11-8 (B)). The base of the impedance triangle is 2 ohms of resistance (fig. 11-8 (C)), the altitude of the impedance triangle is 40 ohms of capacitive reactance, and the hypotenuse is approximately 40 ohms of impedance.

The power factor of this circuit is cos θ_t = $\frac{R_{se}}{Z_t}$ = $\frac{2}{40}$ = 0.05, or 5 percent. In this example, as in the low-loss inductor of figure 11-3, Z_t is approximately equal to X_C, and cos $\theta_t = \frac{R_{se}}{X_C}$. Since tan $\theta_t = \frac{X_C}{R_{se}} = \frac{40}{2} = 20$, it follows that cos $\theta_t = \frac{1}{\tan \theta}$, and the power factor of the capacitor is $\frac{2}{40}$, or 0.05.

The angle whose cosine is 0.05 may be closely approximated by the previously described relation between the power factor and the complementary angle in radians. In this example, the complementary angle by which the

183

current fails to be 90° out of phase with the voltage is 0.05 radian, or $0.05 \times 57.3 = 2.865°$, and $\theta = 90° - 2.865° = 87.135°$. This angle is indicated in all of the vector diagrams of figure 11-8 as 87+°

The equivalent parallel circuit for the 66.4-microfarad capacitor discussed in this example is shown in figure 11-8 (D). The equivalent series resistance and the equivalent shunt resistance are related in the equivalent capacitor circuits in the same way that R_{se} and R_{sh} are related in the low-loss inductor circuits of figure 11-3. This relation was stated in equation 11-5. Thus, in the capacitor circuits,

$$R_{sh} = \frac{(X_C)^2}{R_{se}} = \frac{(40)^2}{2} = 800 \text{ ohms.}$$

The equivalent shunt resistance of 800 ohms is connected in parallel with a 66.4-microfarad capacitor of zero losses. With rated voltage and frequency applied, the input current to the parallel circuit will have the same magnitude and phase with respect to the applied voltage as in the original capacitor.

The energy current in the resistive branch is $I_1 = \dfrac{E}{R_{sh}} = \dfrac{200}{800} = 0.25$ ampere and is the base of the current triangle (fig. 11-8 (E)). The non-energy current in the capacitive branch is $I_2 = \dfrac{E}{X_C} = \dfrac{200}{40} = 5$ amperes and is the altitude of the current triangle. The total current in the parallel circuit is equal to $\sqrt{(0.25)^2 + (5)^2} = 5$ amperes (approx.) and is the hypotenuse of the current triangle. This current leads the voltage by an angle of 87.135°.

The power relations are shown in figure 11-8 (F). The true power of the circuit may be found in a number of ways. Three methods are listed as follows:

1. $P = EI_t \cos \theta_t = 200 \times 5 \times 0.05 = 50$ watts (fig. 11-8 (A)).
2. $P = I_t^2 R_{se} = 5^2 \times 2 = 50$ watts (fig. 11-8 (B)).
3. $P = I_1^2 R_{sh} = (0.25)^2 \times 800 = 50$ watts (fig. 11-8 (D)).

The true power of 50 watts is the base of the power triangle (fig. 11-8 (F)).

The reactive power may be calculated in a number of ways. Three methods are indicated as follows:

1. $\text{VARS} = E_t I_t \sin \theta_t = 200 \times 5 \times (\sin 87+° = 1 \text{ approx.}) = 1,000$ VARS (fig. 11-8 (A)).
2. $\text{VARS} = I_t^2 X_C = 5^2 \times 40 = 1,000$ VARS (fig. 11-8 (B)).
3. $\text{VARS} = I_2^2 X_C = 5^2 \times 40 = 1,000$ VARS (fig. 11-8 (D)).

The reactive power of 1,000 VARS is the altitude of the power triangle (fig. 11-8 (F)).

The apparent power of the capacitor may be calculated as:

1. Apparent power $= EI_t = 200 \times 5 = 1,000$ VA (fig. 11-8 (A)).
2. Apparent power $= I_t^2 Z_t = 5^2 \times 40 = 1,000$ VA (fig. 11-7 (B)).

The apparent power of 1,000 volt-amperes is the hypotenuse of the power triangle (fig. 11-8 (F)).

Combining Currents at Acute Angles

A 2-branch parallel circuit containing a 75-ohm resistor in branch①and a series combination of a 79.6-microfarad capacitor and a 30-ohm resistor in branch②is shown in figure 11-9 (A). The capacitor losses are assumed to be included with those of the 30-ohm resistor so that the power factor of that portion of branch②represented by the capacitor is zero.

The capacitive reactance at the operating frequency of 50 cycles per second is

$$X_C = \frac{1}{2\pi f C} = \frac{1}{6.28 \times 50 \times 79.6 \times 10^{-6}} = 40 \text{ ohms.}$$

The impedance, Z_2, of branch②is the combined opposition of 30 ohms of resistance in series with 40 ohms of capacitive reactance and is the hypotenuse of the right triangle of which 30 ohms is the base and 40 ohms is the altitude (not shown in the figure). Thus,

$$Z_2 = \sqrt{30^2 + 40^2} = 50 \text{ ohms.}$$

The power factor of branch②is $\cos \theta_2 = \dfrac{R_2}{Z_2} = \dfrac{30}{50} = 0.60$ and the phase angle is 53.1°.

The current vectors for both branches are shown in figure 11-9 (B).

The current in branch①is $I_1 = \dfrac{E}{Z_1} = \dfrac{150}{75} = 2$ amperes, and is a portion of the base of the equivalent right triangle in line with the horizontal reference voltage, OE. This current is in phase with the applied voltage because there is no reactance present in branch①

The current in branch②is

$$I_2 = \frac{E}{Z_2} = \frac{150}{50} = 3 \text{ amperes,}$$

and is the hypotenuse of the right triangle, the base of which is $I_2 \cos \theta_2 = 3$ (cos 53.1 = 0.6) = 1.8 amperes (energy current) and the altitude of which is $I_2 \sin \theta_2 = 3$ (sin 53.1 = 0.8) = 2.4 amperes (nonenergy current). The total current is the vector sum of I_1 and I_2 and is the hypotenuse of the equivalent right triangle, the base of which is the arithmetic sum of the current in branch①and the energy component of current in branch②, or 2 + 1.8 = 3.8 amperes. The altitude of the equivalent right triangle is equal to the nonenergy current in branch② or 2.4 amperes. The total current in the parallel circuit is

$$I_t = \sqrt{(3.8)^2 + (2.4)^2} = 4.5 \text{ amperes.}$$

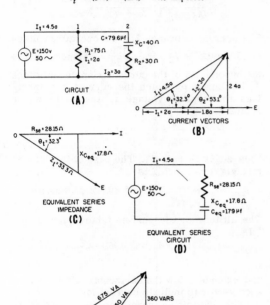

CIRCUIT
(A)

CURRENT VECTORS
(B)

EQUIVALENT SERIES IMPEDANCE
(C)

EQUIVALENT SERIES CIRCUIT
(D)

POWER VECTORS
(E)

Figure 11-9.—Two-branch R-C circuit with currents out of phase by an angle of 53.1°.

The phase angle, θ_t between the total circuit current and the applied voltage is the angle whose cosine is $\frac{3.8}{4.5} = 0.845$. This angle is approximately 32.3°. Thus, the total current leads the applied voltage by an angle of 32.3°.

The total impedance of the parallel circuit is

$$Z_t = \frac{E}{I_t} = \frac{150}{4.5} = 33.3 \text{ ohms}$$

and is the hypotenuse of the impedance triangle (fig. 11-9 (C)). The base of the triangle is

$$R_{se} = Z_t \cos \theta_t = 33.3 \text{ (cos } 32.3° = 0.845) = 28.15 \text{ ohms}$$

of resistance and is in line with the horizontal current reference vector for the equivalent series circuit (fig. 11-9 (D)). The altitude of the triangle is

$$X_{C_{eq}} = Z_t \sin \theta_t = 33.3 \text{ (sin } 32.3° = 0.534) = 17.8 \text{ ohms}$$

of capacitive reactance. The capacitance of the equivalent series circuit at the operating frequency of 50 cycles per second is

$$C_{eq} = \frac{10^6}{2\pi f X_C} = \frac{10^6}{6.28 \times 50 \times 17.8} = 179 \text{ microfarads.}$$

The power relations are indicated in the triangles of figure 11-9 (E). The apparent power of the total circuit is $EI_t = 150 \times 4.5 = 675$ volt-amperes and is the hypotenuse of the equivalent right triangle representing the total parallel circuit.

The true power in branch①is

$$I_1^2 R_1 = 2^2 \times 75 = 300 \text{ watts.}$$

The true power in branch②is

$$I_2^2 R_2 = 3^2 \times 30 = 270 \text{ watts.}$$

The total true power is

$$300 + 270 = 570 \text{ watts,}$$

and is the base of the equivalent right triangle for the entire circuit. The reactive power in the total circuit—that is, the reactive power of branch②—is

$$I_2^2 X_C = 3^2 \times 40 = 360 \text{ VARS,}$$

and is the altitude of the equivalent triangle. The apparent power in branch①is equal to the true power because the power factor is unity. The apparent power in branch②is $EI_2 = 150 \times 3 = 450$ volt-amperes and is the hypotenuse of the power triangle for this branch. The true power of 270 watts in branch②is the base of this triangle. The reactive power of 360 VARS in branch ② is the altitude of the triangle. The power factor for branch ② is $\cos \theta_2 = \dfrac{\text{true power}}{\text{apparent power}} = \dfrac{270}{450} = 0.60$, and the phase angle for branch ② is $\theta_2 = 53.1°$.

PARALLEL CIRCUITS CONTAINING L, R, AND C

Inductance in an a-c circuit causes the current to lag behind the applied voltage. Transformers and induction motors are essentially inductive in nature and the power factor, especially on light loads (as contrasted with full loads), is relatively low.

Most circuits that supply electric power from the source to the consumer transmit the power at relatively high voltage and low current in order to keep the I^2R loss in the transmission lines satisfactorily low. Transformers at the point of utilization reduce the voltage to the proper value to operate the equipment.

Capacitance in a-c circuits causes the current to lead the applied voltage and when placed in parallel with inductive components can produce a neutralizing effect so that lagging currents can be brought into phase with the applied voltage or may be made to lead the applied voltage, depending on the relative magnitude of the capacitance and inductance in parallel.

The true power of a circuit is $P = EI \cos \theta$; and for any given amount of power to be transmitted, the current, I, varies inversely with the power factor, $\cos \theta$. Thus, the addition of capacitance in parallel with inductance will, under the proper conditions, improve the power factor (make nearer unity power factor) of the circuit and make possible the transmission of electric power with reduced line loss and improved voltage regulation.

Current Vectors

In the example of figure 11-10, the parallel circuit contains three branches. Branch ① contains a 30-ohm resistor. Branch ② consists of an inductor of 0.0612 henry and a resistor of 6.6 ohms. Branch ③ contains a capacitance of 44.3 microfarads having negligible losses. The parallel circuit is shown in figure 11-10 (A). The current vectors are shown in figure 11-10 (B).

The current in branch ① is

$$I_{1\text{en}} = \frac{E}{R_1} = \frac{120}{30} = 4 \text{ amperes.}$$

The corresponding 4-ampere vector in figure 11-10 (B), is drawn in the same horizontal reference line as the voltage vector because the phase angle between the current and voltage in this branch is zero.

The inductive reactance of branch ② at the operating frequency of 60 cycles per second is

$$X_L = 2\pi f L = 6.28 \times 60 \times 0.0612 = 23.1 \text{ ohms.}$$

The impedance of branch ② is

$$Z_2 = \sqrt{R_2^2 + X_L^2} = \sqrt{(6.6)^2 + (23.1)^2} = 24 \text{ ohms.}$$

The current in branch ② at the operating voltage of 120 volts, is $I_2 = \dfrac{E}{Z_2} = \dfrac{120}{24} = 5$ amperes and is the hypotenuse of the current triangle for branch ②. The angle by which the current in branch ② lags the applied voltage is the angle whose cosine is

$$\frac{R_2}{Z_2} = \frac{6.6}{24} = 0.275.$$

This angle is $\theta_2 = 74°$. The base of the current triangle for branch ② is

$$I_{2\text{ en}} = I_2 \cos 74° = 5 (\cos 74° = 0.275) = 1.38 \text{ amperes.}$$

The altitude of the current triangle for branch ② is

$$I_{2\text{ nonen}} = I_2 \sin 74° = 5(\sin 74° = 0.962) = 4.8 \text{ (approx.) amperes}$$

and extends below the horizontal voltage reference vector to indicate current lag.

The capacitive reactance in branch ③ is

$$X_c = \frac{1}{2\pi f C} = \frac{1}{6.28 \times 60 \times 44.3 \times 10^{-6}} = 60 \text{ ohms,}$$

and with negligible losses, the impedance, Z_3, is also 60 ohms. The current in branch ③ is

$$I_{3\text{ nonen}} = \frac{E}{Z_3} = \frac{120}{60} = 2 \text{ amperes.}$$

The current in the capacitor branch leads the applied voltage by an angle of 90°. The non-energy component of the current in the inductive branch lags the applied voltage by an angle of 90°. Therefore, these two currents are 180° out of phase with each other, and the capacity current vector, I_3, extends upward

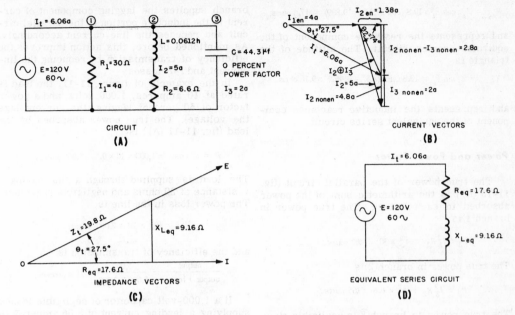

Figure 11-10.—Parallel circuit containing L, R, and C.

from the lower extremity of the vector representing the nonenergy component of current in branch②.

The total current, I_t, in the parallel circuit is the vector sum of the currents in the three branches and is the hypotenuse of the equivalent current triangle, the base of which is the arithmetic sum of the energy components of the currents and the altitude of which is the algebraic sum of the nonenergy components of the currents. Thus, the total current is

$$I_t = \sqrt{(I_{1en} + I_{2en})^2 + (I_{2nonen} - I_{3nonen})^2}$$

$$= \sqrt{4 + (1.38)^2 + (4.8 - 2)^2}$$

$$= 6.06 \text{ amperes.}$$

The phase angle, θ_t, between the total current and the applied voltage is the angle whose cosine is the ratio of the sum of the energy components of the currents in all the branches to the total current. Thus,

$$\cos \theta_t = \frac{4 + 1.38}{6.06} = 0.888.$$

$$\theta_t = 27.5°,$$

and the total circuit current lags the applied voltage by an angle of 27.5°.

Equivalent Series Impedance

The total impedance of the parallel circuit (fig. 11-10 (A)) is equal to the total circuit voltage divided by the total circuit current, or

$$Z_t = \frac{E}{I_t} = \frac{120}{6.06} = 19.8 \text{ ohms,}$$

and is the hypotenuse of the impedance triangle (fig. 11-10 (C)). This triangle represents the impedance relations existing in the equivalent series circuit (fig. 11-10 (D)). The phase angle, θ_t, of the equivalent series circuit has the same magnitude as the phase angle between the total circuit current and the applied voltage across the parallel circuit. The impedance of the equivalent series circuit has the same magnitude as the total impedance of the parallel circuit. The base of the triangle is

187

$R_{eq} = Z_t \cos \theta_t = 19.8 \, (\cos 27.5° = 0.889) = 17.6 \text{ ohms},$

and represents the resistive component of the equivalent series circuit. The altitude of the triangle is

$X_{L_{eq}} = Z_t \sin \theta_t = 19.8 \, (\sin 27.5° = 0.462) = 9.16 \text{ ohms},$

and represents the inductive reactance component of the equivalent series circuit.

Power and Power Factor

The true power of the parallel circuit (fig. 11-10 (A)) is the arithmetic sum of the power absorbed in each branch. The true power in branch①is

$P_1 = I_1^2 R_1 = 4^2 \times 30 = 480 \text{ watts}.$

The true power in branch②is

$P_2 = I_2^2 R_2 = 5^2 \times 6.6 = 165 \text{ watts}.$

The true power in branch③is negligible since the power factor of the capacitor is assumed to be zero. The total true power is

$$480 + 165 = 645 \text{ watts}.$$

The total apparent power of the parallel circuit is the product of the total circuit current and the applied voltage. Thus, the apparent power is

$EI_t = 120 \times 6.06 = 727.2 \text{ volt-amperes}.$

The parallel circuit power factor is the ratio of the total true power to the total apparent power. Thus, the circuit power factor is

$\cos \theta_t = \dfrac{\text{true power}}{\text{apparent power}} = \dfrac{645}{727.2} = 0.888.$

Power-Factor Correction

Power-factor correction in parallel circuits is accomplished by placing a capacitor of the proper size in parallel with the circuit at the point where the power-factor correction is to be effected. The leading current of the capacitor branch supplies the lagging component of current in the inductive portion of the parallel circuit and reduces the line current accordingly. As mentioned before, this action improves the efficiency of transmission by reducing the line current and I^2R losses.

In the example of figure 11-11, the load is rated at 10 amperes, 1,000 volts, and a power factor of 50 percent lagging (the current lags the voltage). The true power absorbed by the load (fig. 11-11 (A)) is

$P = EI \cos \theta = 1,000 \times 10 \times 0.5 = 5,000 \text{ watts}.$

The load is supplied through a line having a resistance of 20 ohms and negligible reactance. The power loss in the line is

$I^2R = 10^2 \times 20 = 2,000 \text{ watts},$

and the efficiency of transmission is

$\dfrac{\text{output}}{\text{output + losses}} = \dfrac{5,000}{5,000 + 2,000} = 71.4 \text{ percent}.$

If a 1,000-volt capacitor of negligible losses supplying a leading current of 8.66 amperes is placed in parallel with the inductive load (fig. 11-11 (B)), the total line current will be reduced from 10 amperes to 5 amperes.

The current vectors are shown in figure 11-11 (C). The nonenergy component of the current in the inductive branch is $I_{nonen} = I \sin \theta = 10 \, (\sin 60° = 0.866) = 8.66$ amperes (lagging) and is 180° out of phase with the capacitor current of 8.66 amperes (leading). These currents circulate between the capacitor and the inductive load and do not enter the line. The vector sum of the capacitor current and the total inductive load current is equal to the line current ($I_t = 5$ amperes), and in the vector diagram is represented as the diagonal of the parallelogram of which the 2 branch currents are the sides. The line current vector, I_t, is in the same horizontal reference as the load voltage vector, indicating that the line current is in phase with the voltage applied to the parallel combination of the inductive load and the capacitor.

The reduction in line current from 10 to 5 amperes reduces the line loss from 2,000 watts to $5^2 \times 20 = 500$ watts and increases the efficiency of transmission from 71.4 percent to $\dfrac{5,000}{5,000 + 500} = 91$ percent. Thus, the improvement in efficiency of operation of the line and load is

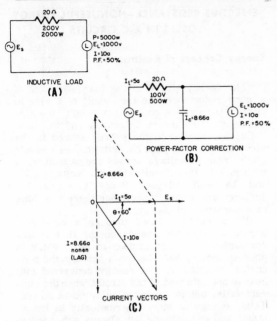

INDUCTIVE LOAD
(A)

POWER-FACTOR CORRECTION
(B)

CURRENT VECTORS
(C)

Figure 11-11.—Power-factor correction.

VOLTAGE REDUCTION WITH INDUCTANCE

In figure 11-12 (B), the voltage applied to the load is reduced to 50 volts through the action of the series inductor. Neglecting the relatively small losses in the inductor, the circuit efficiency remains high compared to the efficiency of the previous circuit, but the series inductor lowers the power factor from unity (100 percent) to 50 percent. The circuit current is still 10 amperes, and the accompanying line loss between the source and the inductor unnecessarily high.

The voltage vectors for the L-R circuit are shown in figure 11-12 (C). The load voltage of 50 volts is the base of the right triangle and is in phase with the load current. The voltage drop across the inductor is 86.6 volts and is the altitude of the voltage triangle. The source voltage, E_S = 100 volts, is the vector sum of the load voltage and the inductor voltage and is the hypotenuse of the voltage triangle. The circuit power factor is

$$\cos \theta = \frac{E_{\text{load}}}{E_{\text{source}}} = \frac{50}{100} = 0.5,$$

and

$$\theta = 60°.$$

In figure 11-12 (D), the circuit power factor is improved to unity by the addition of a capacitor of negligible losses which supplies a leading current of 8.66 amperes. This current supplies the nonenergy component of the current in the branch containing the inductor and load, and reduces the line current from 10 amperes to 5 amperes.

The current vectors are shown in figure 11-12 (E). The capacitor current of 8.66 amperes is represented by the vector extending above the horizontal voltage reference vector to indicate a lead of 90°. The inductor branch (load) current extends below the horizontal at an angle of 60° to indicate lag. The vector sum of these currents is the diagonal of the parallelogram of which the branch currents are the sides, and is a horizontal vector of 5 amperes in phase with the source voltage. Thus, the power factor of the parallel circuit is unity and the line current is reduced from 10 amperes to 5 amperes.

demonstrated. The condition represented involves an interchange of energy between the inductive and capacitive branches known as parallel resonance and is described in the training manual, *Basic Electronics*, NavPers 10087, chapter 1, on the subject of resonance in L-R-C circuits.

VOLTAGE REDUCTION WITH RESISTANCE

The example of figure 11-12 illustrates the advantages and disadvantages of controlling the voltage on a load by means of resistance and inductance and also the effect of power-factor correction on the circuit efficiency.

In figure 11-12 (A), the voltage applied to the load is reduced from 100 volts to 50 volts through the action of the dropping resistor. The circuit current is 10 amperes, and the voltage across the dropping resistor is 50 volts. With this arrangement, the input power to the circuit is divided equally between the resistor and the load, and the circuit efficiency ($\frac{\text{output}}{\text{output} + \text{losses}}$ x 100) is $\frac{500}{500 + 500}$ x 100 = 50 percent. This arrangement represents an inefficient method of voltage reduction.

ADVANTAGES OF INDUCTIVE ARRANGEMENT WITH POWER-FACTOR CORRECTION

In the example under consideration, voltage reduction with a series inductor and a shunt capacitor provides a means of supplying a 50-volt 10-ampere load from a 100-volt source with only the small losses associated with the reactive components. The line current is kept to the minimum value required to supply the 500-watt load, and the circuit efficiency is high. Inductive control alone provides a means of reducing the load voltage by changing the phase of the applied voltage with respect to the load voltage. The addition of the capacitor reduces the current in the line without altering the load current, and thus reduces the line losses; at the same time the circuit power factor is increased to unity. In most circuits it is not economical to improve the power factor to unity, but to improve it, for example, from 50 percent lagging to 85 percent lagging. The reduction in line losses is most pronounced in this range and any further reduction in losses may not justify the added expense of the capacitance required to further improve the power factor in the range from 85 percent lagging to unity.

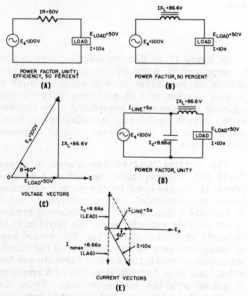

Figure 11-12.—Voltage reduction and power-factor correction.

EFFECTIVE RESISTANCE—NONUSEFUL ENERGY LOSSES IN A-C CIRCUITS

Energy Concept of Resistance

The energy stored in the magnetic field of a pure inductance, as the result of a rise in current through the coil, is returned to the circuit when the current decreases and the field collapses. Similarly, the energy stored in the electric field of a pure capacitance, as a result of the rise in voltage across the capacitor, is returned to the circuit when the voltage falls and the field collapses. Hence, in a pure inductance and a pure capacitance there is no loss or expenditure of energy.

When current flows through a conductor having appreciable resistance the flow is accompanied by the generation of heat. Work is done in moving the electrons through the conductor resistance. The energy converted into heat is not returned to the circuit when the current falls, but is expended rather than stored. Thus, energy is stored periodically in inductance and capacitance but always expended in resistance.

Because resistance is the only circuit quality capable of expending electrical energy, all energy expended in any circuit can be identified in electrical terms, one factor of which is effective resistance. The effective resistance, R_{ac}, of any circuit may be defined as the ratio of the true power absorbed by the circuit to the square of the effective current flowing in the circuit, or $R_{ac} = \dfrac{P}{I^2}$. When the power is expressed in watts and the current is expressed in amperes, the effective resistance will be in ohms. The d-c circuit resistance as measured by an ohmmeter or d-c bridge may be considerably lower than the effective a-c resistance as calculated from the readings on a wattmeter and an ammeter.

For example, assume that a motor draws 1 kilowatt from a 110-volt source. The input current is 10 amperes. The effective resistance between the motor terminals is

$$R_{ac} = \frac{P}{I^2} = \frac{1,000}{(10)^2} = 10 \text{ ohms.}$$

The d-c resistance measured between the motor terminals, for example with an ohmmeter, is

190

0.5 ohm. Thus, in this example the effective a-c resistance is $\frac{10}{0.5}$, or 20 times the d-c resistance. Most of the energy taken from the line is converted into mechanical energy and is not returnable to the electric circuit; hence, it is represented electrically as being expended in an effective a-c resistance of 10 ohms.

The source of power for the motor is unaware of the manner in which the motor expends the electrical energy. To the source, the motor appears as an impedance, $Z = \frac{E}{I} = \frac{110}{10} = 11$ ohms, having a resistive component of 10 ohms. The nature of the various energy conversions taking place inside the motor is important only when the motor itself is being analyzed. From this point of view a motor, electric light, loudspeaker, electron tube, or any other electrical device can be pictured as an equivalent electric circuit containing the fundamental components of inductance, capacitance, and resistance. The energy expended in the circuit is always interpreted in terms of the effective resistance component.

The energy expended in any electrical device may be divided into two parts: (1) That which is converted into useful form; and (2) that which is not useful. No machine has been built that is capable of perfect conversion—that is, one in which there are no losses. In the motor, for example, there are friction losses in the bearings and heat losses in the windings as a result of the current flow through the resistance which they possess.

The number of possible nonuseful losses in a-c circuits is much greater than in d-c circuits. These include: (1) ohmic-resistance loss, (2) skin-effect loss, (3) eddy-current loss, (4) dielectric loss, (5) magnetic-hysteresis loss, (6) corona loss, and (7) radiation loss.

Effective Resistance of Conductors

The effective (a-c) resistance of electrical conductors is frequently higher than their d-c resistance especially when they are embedded in iron slots, as in the case of motor and generator armatures; and when they are being used in high-frequency circuits, as in radio transmitters and receivers.

Direct current is distributed uniformly throughout the cross-sectional area of a homogeneous conductor. For example, if a conductor having a cross-sectional area of 1,000 circular mils is carrying one ampere of direct current then one-thousandth of an ampere (one milliampere) is flowing in each circular mil of cross-sectional area. However, when the current in the conductor varies in amplitude, this uniform distribution throughout the conductor cross section is no longer obtained. The accompanying magnetic field is strongest near the center of the conductor and weaker at the circumference. The varying field induces a voltage in the conductor that opposes the change in current. The voltage induced in that portion of the conductor near the center is greater than the voltage induced in the outer surface of the conductor. The total opposition to the current flow includes the effect of this induced e.m.f. and is greater near the center of the conductor than at the surface. Therefore, the current divides inversely with the opposition—more of the current flowing near the circumference, and less near the center of the conductor.

The overall result of this action is a decrease in the available area of cross section to conduct the current and an increase in conductor resistance. The decrease in area and increase in resistance become pronounced at high frequencies, at high current densities, and at high magnetic flux densities. This action is called SKIN EFFECT. It represents the tendency of a-c conductors to carry the circuit current on the surface, or skin, of the conductors rather than uniformly throughout their cross section. As a result of this tendency, many electrical conductors are made of hollow tubing in order to save the added weight and expense of the unused central portion of the solid conductor. The effective a-c resistance of an isolated circular conductor varies approximately as the product of the square root of the frequency and the length of the conductor, and inversely as the conductor diameter.

Effective Resistance of Inductors

When a conductor is wound in the form of a coil, the current is concentrated on the inner sides of the turns and into an area much smaller than would be the case in an isolated straight conductor. This action results in a large increase in effective resistance. The area in which the current is concentrated decreases as the frequency increases, hence, effective resistance will increase with frequency. When two or more conductors carrying alternating current are so placed that the magnetic field of one reacts with the field of the other, the resultant field around each conductor is no longer uniform. The change in current distribution in a conductor due to the action of an alternating current in a nearby conductor is called PROXIMITY EFFECT.

The proximity effect decreases as the separation between conductors increases. Thus, to lower the effective resistance of radio frequency inductance coils, it is common practice to space the turns a distance equal to the diameter of the conductor. This decreases the reaction between magnetic fields of adjacent turns and permits the current to distribute itself over a larger area in the cross section of each turn.

The inductance of a hollow-core coil operating at a frequency of 60 cycles per second is increased many fold when a laminated core of soft silicon steel is inserted in the coil. This increase is due to the high permeability of the transformer-iron laminations. Thus, the skin effect is also increased due to the increased field strength. In addition to the increased skin effect in the coil, the effective a-c resistance is further increased because of the magnetic hysteresis loss in the iron. Thus, if the coil is connected to a constant-potential a-c source, the current in the coil will decrease when the iron core is inserted because of a small increase in effective resistance and a large increase in the coil reactance. If the laminated steel core is removed and a piece of steel shafting is inserted in the coil, the effective resistance is further increased due to the eddy-current losses and the larger hysteresis losses in the steel shaft. A wattmeter inserted in the coil circuit will indicate this increase in effective resistance by an increased deflection when the solid steel core is inserted in place of the laminated core.

Powdered iron cores are used in certain types of coils on frequencies as high as 100 megacycles in order to limit the effective resistance of the coil to a satisfactorily low value. The iron particles are separated from each other by an insulated coating and when compressed into cylindrical form and inserted in the coil the induced voltage in each iron particle is so small in relation to the resistance to the path for eddy currents that the accompanying heat loss is negligible. Eddy-current losses are reduced in generator and motor armature conductors of large size by laminating the conductors and insulating the adjacent laminations in a manner similar to that in which the iron of the armature core itself is laminated. Thus, the effective resistance of the armature conductors is reduced.

Effective Resistance of Capacitors

The equivalent circuits of a low-loss capacitor were described earlier in this chapter and the factors affecting the equivalent series resistance noted. The effective a-c resistance of a capacitor is equal to its equivalent series resistance and represents the factor which when multiplied by the square of the effective capacitor charging current will equal the power expended in heat in the capacitor circuit.

As mentioned previously, most of the heating is produced in solid dielectrics, and only a negligible amount is produced in the capacitor plates themselves. The dielectric heating is produced by dielectric displacement currents described in connection with figure 11-7. In most electrical circuits, dielectric heating is a nonuseful loss. However, in one commercial application, dielectric heating has been put to good use—that of facilitating the gluing together of stacks of laminated plywood. The plywood laminations are stacked between the plates of a capacitor and a moderately high-frequency voltage is applied across the plates. The resulting dielectric displacement currents heat the stack from the inside and the glue is quickly set—much more rapidly than in processes involving the external application of steam heat.

Corona Loss

Corona loss occurs as the result of the emission of electrons from the surface of electrical conductors at high potentials. It is dependent upon the curvature of the conductor surface, with most emission occurring from sharp points and the least emission occurring from surfaces having a large radius of curvature. Corona loss is frequently accompanied by a visual blue glow and an audible hissing sound as the electrons leak off the conductor surface into the atmosphere. Corona loss increases with voltage increase and decreases with increase in atmospheric pressure. This loss is held to a satisfactorily low value by (1) the use of large-diameter conductors, (2) not excessively high voltages, (3) smooth polished surfaces, (4) avoiding sharp points, bends, or turns, and (5) in some devices, for example, high-voltage capacitors, by the use of a compressed gas to retard the electron emission.

Radiation Loss

Radiation loss is not appreciable at power line frequencies, but in the field of communications this loss may become excessive. Power is radiated from transmitting antennas in the form of electric and magnetic fields, and its magnitude varies as the square of the antenna input current and as the so-called radiation resistance of the antenna. The transmission line that connects the transmitter and the antenna may, under certain circumstances, develop a radiation loss. This loss is discussed in chapter 10 of *Basic Electronics*, NavPers 10087, in connection with various types of transmission lines.

QUIZ

1. When resistive, inductive, and capacitive elements are connected in series,
   a. they lose their individual characteristics
   b. their individual characteristics remain unchanged
   c. the inductance component is always the largest
   d. the capacitive component is always the largest

2. In a circuit containing both X_C and X_L, if the difference between X_C and X_L increases, the total
   a. impedance decreases
   b. impedance increases
   c. impedance remains the same
   d. resistance increases

3. In a 60-cycle a-c circuit, with an inductor of 0.053 microhenry and a resistance of 50 ohms connected in series, the impedance would be
   a. 539 ohms
   b. 5.39 ohms
   c. 53.9 ohms
   d. 19.97 ohms

4. The effective resistance of a circuit may be defined as the ratio of the
   a. true power absorbed by the circuit to the square of the effective current flowing
   b. apparent power absorbed by the circuit to the square of the effective current flowing
   c. true power absorbed by the circuit to the square of the total resistance in the circuit
   d. apparent power absorbed by the circuit to the square of the total resistance in the circuit

5. In a series circuit, when X_C and X_L are equal,
   a. line voltage leads line current by an unknown $/\theta$
   b. line current leads line voltage by an unknown $/\theta$
   c. total impedance is minimum
   d. total impedance is maximum

6. To find true power, use the formula
   a. $T.P. = E \times I$
   b. $T.P. = E \times I \times \cos /\theta$
   .c. $T.P. = E^2 \div I \times \cos /\theta$
   d. $T.P. = E \times I \times \sin /\theta$

7. A low-loss inductor has a low
   a. X_L at high frequencies
   b. current at low frequencies
   c. inductance
   d. resistance

8. The most inefficient method of voltage reduction, from the standpoint of power loss, is a/an
   a. capacitor in series with the load
   b. inductor in series with the load
   c. capacitor and an inductor in series with the load
   d. resistor in series with the load

9. The formula for finding the loss factor of a capacitor is the dielectric constant
   a. times the power factor
   b. divided by the power factor
   c. times the apparent power
   d. times the true power

10. A phase difference between E and I causes
    a. true power to increase
    b. apparent power to increase
    c. true power to decrease
    d. apparent power to decrease

11. The energy component of a current flowing in an R-L circuit is the current flowing through the
    a. inductor and resistor
    b. inductor
    c. resistor
    d. power source

12. Corona loss is the result of
    a. emission of electrons from the surface of a conductor
    b. electron collision inside a conductor
    c. overheating a high-frequency conductor
    d. none of the above

13. To find total true power in a parallel circuit, first find the true power in each branch and then
    a. add the power in all branches arithmetically
    b. add the power in all branches using the parallelogram method
    c. multiply the voltage times the current
    d. multiply the square of the current times the resistance

14. The hypotenuse of the power triangle represents
    a. true power
    b. VARS
    c. apparent power
    d. none of the above

15. To find a circuit's power factor in percent, use the formula
    a. $P.F. = \dfrac{AP}{TP} \times 100$
    b. $P.F. = \cos \angle\theta$
    c. $P.F. =$ angle in degrees x 100
    d. $P.F. = \dfrac{E \times I \times \cos \angle\theta}{E \times I} \times 100$

16. Corona loss can be held to a satisfactory low value by
    a. avoiding sharp points, bends, and turns
    b. using low voltages
    c. using large diameter conductors
    d. all of the above

17. In a parallel circuit with a lagging power factor, to improve the power factor
    a. increase the inductance
    b. put an inductor in parallel with the rest of the circuit
    c. put a capacitor in parallel with the rest of the circuit
    d. decrease the resistance

18. The nonenergy component of an a-c circuit is
    a. true power
    b. reactive power
    c. apparent power
    d. none of the above

19. The formula for computing R-L-C in series is
    a. $Z = R_T + X_L + X_C$
    b. $Z = R + X_L - X_C$
    c. $Z^2 = R^2 + (X_L^2 - X_C^2)$
    d. $Z = R^2 + (X_L^2 - X_C^2)$

20. One radian is equal to
    a. $\dfrac{180}{2\pi}$
    b. 2π
    c. 1.414
    d. $\dfrac{360}{2\pi}$

21. Skin effect describes the tendency of
    a. d-c conductors to carry the circuit current on their surfaces
    b. a-c conductors to carry the circuit current on their surfaces
    c. both a-c and d-c conductors to carry the circuit current on their surfaces
    d. none of the above

22. The current in an a-c parallel circuit varies
    a. inversely with the $\cos \angle\theta$
    b. directly with the $\cos \angle\theta$
    c. inversely with the sine $\angle\theta$
    d. directly with the sine $\angle\theta$

23. In a circuit containing X_C and X_L, if X_C is larger,
    a. the voltage would lead the current
    b. the current would lead the voltage
    c. there would be no phase difference
    d. true power is maximum

24. The effective resistance of a capacitor is dissipated in heat in the
    a. positive capacitor plate
    b. negative capacitor plate
    c. dielectric
    d. leads connecting the capacitor in the circuit

CHAPTER 12

BASIC ELECTRICAL INDICATING INSTRUMENTS

In the field of electricity, as in all the other physical sciences, accurate quantitative measurements are essential. This involves two important items—numbers and units. Simple arithmetic is used in most cases, and the units are well-defined and easily understood. The standard units of current, voltage, and resistance as well as other units are defined by the National Bureau of Standards. At the factory, various instruments are calibrated by comparing them with established standards.

The technician commonly works with ammeters, voltmeters, ohmmeters, and electron-tube analyzers; but he may also have many occasions to use wattmeters, watt-hour meters, power-factor meters, synchroscopes, frequency meters, and capacitance-resistance-inductance bridges.

Electrical equipments are designed to operate at certain efficiency levels. To aid the technician in maintaining the equipment, technical instruction books and sheets containing optimum performance data, such as voltages and resistances, are prepared for each Navy equipment.

To the technician, a good understanding of the functional design and operation of electrical instruments is important. In electrical service work one or more of the following methods are commonly used to determine if the circuits of an equipment are operating properly.

1. Use an ammeter to measure the amount of current flowing in a circuit.

2. Use a voltmeter to determine the voltage existing between two points in a circuit.

3. Use an ohmmeter or megger (megohm-meter) to measure circuit continuity and total or partial circuit resistance.

The technician may also find it necessary to employ a wattmeter to determine the total POWER being consumed by certain equipments. If he wishes to measure the ENERGY consumed by certain equipments or certain circuits, a watt-hour of kilowatt-hour meter is used.

For measuring other quantities such as power factor and frequency, which will be treated in a later chapter, the technician employs the appropriate instruments. In each case the instrument indicates the value of the quantity measured, and the technician interprets the information in a manner that will help him understand the way the circuit is operating. Occasionally the technician will need to determine the value of a capacitor or an inductor. Inductance or capacitance bridges may be employed for this purpose.

Although in this chapter the discussion is confined largely to d-c instruments, some of the instruments discussed may be used with alternating as well as direct current. Alternating-current instruments are treated in chapter 17.

A thorough understanding of the construction, operation, and limitations of the basic types of electrical measuring instruments, coupled with the theory of circuit operation, is most essential in servicing and maintaining electrical equipment.

D'Arsonval Meter

CONSTRUCTION

The stationary permanent-magnet moving-coil meter is the basic movement used in most measuring instruments for servicing electrical,

especially d-c, equipment. This type of movement is commonly called the D'Arsonval movement because it was first employed by the Frenchman D'Arsonval in making electrical measurements.

The basic D'Arsonval movement consists of a stationary permanent magnet and a movable coil. When current flows through the coil the resulting magnetic field reacts with the magnetic field of the permanent magnet and causes the coil to rotate. The greater the amount of current flow through the coil the stronger the magnetic field produced and the stronger this field the greater the rotation of the coil. In order to determine the amount of current flow a means must be provided to indicate the amount of coil rotation. Either of two methods may be used—(1) the pointer arrangement, and (2) the light and mirror arrangement. In the pointer arrangement, one end of the pointer is fastened to the rotating coil and as the coil turns the pointer also turns. The other end of the pointer moves across a graduated scale and indicates the amount of current flow. A disadvantage of the pointer arrangement is that it introduces the problem of coil balance, especially if the pointer is long. An advantage of this arrangement is that it permits overall simplicity. The use of a mirror and a beam of light simplifies the problem of coil balance. When this arrangement is used to measure the turning of the coil, a small mirror is mounted on the supporting ribbon (fig. 12-1) and turns with the coil. An internal light source is directed to the mirror, and then reflected to the scale of the meter. As the moving coil turns, so does the mirror, causing the light reflection to move over the scale of the meter. The movement of the reflection is proportional to the movement of the coil, thus the amount of current being measured by the meter is indicated.

A simplified diagram of one type of stationary permanent-magnet moving-coil instrument is shown in figure 12-1. Such an instrument is commonly called a GALVANOMETER. The galvanometer indicates very small amounts (or the relative amounts) of current or voltage, and is distinguished from other instruments used for the same purpose in that the movable coil is suspended by means of metal ribbons instead of by means of a shaft and jewel bearings.

The movable coil of the galvanometer in figure 12-1 is suspended between the poles of the magnet by means of thin flat ribbons of phospher bronze. These ribbons provide the conducting path for the current between the circuit under test and the movable coil. They also provide the restoring force for the coil. The restoring force, exerted by the twist in the ribbons, is the force against which the driving force of the coil's magnetic field (to be described later) is balanced in order to obtain a measurement of the current strength. The ribbons thus tend

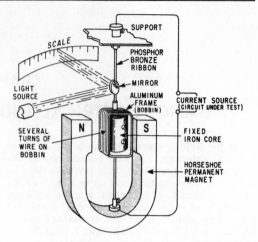

Figure 12-1.—Simplified diagram of a galvanometer.

to oppose the motion of the coil, and will twist through an angle that is proportional to the force applied to the coil by the action of the coil's magnetic field against the permanent field. The ribbons thus restrain or provide a counter force, for the magnetic force acting on the coil. When the driving force of the coil current is removed, the restoring force returns the coil to its zero position.

If a beam of light and mirrors are used, the beam of light is swept to the right or left across a central-zero translucent screen (scale) having uniform divisions. If a pointer is used, the pointer is moved in a horizontal plane to the right or left across a central-zero scale having uniform divisions. The direction in which the beam of light or the pointer moves depends on the direction of current through the coil.

This instrument is used to measure minute current as, for example, in bridge circuits. In modified form, the basic D'Arsonval movement has the highest sensitivity of any of the various types of meters in use today.

OPERATING PRINCIPLE

In order to understand the operating principle of the D'Arsonval meter it is first necessary to consider the force acting on a current-carrying conductor placed in a magnetic field. The magnitude of the force is proportional to the product of the magnitudes of the current and the field strength. The field is established between the poles of a U-shaped permanent magnet and is concentrated through the conductor by means of a soft-iron stationary member mounted between the poles to complete the magnetic circuit. The conductor is made movable by shaping it in the form of a closed loop and mounting it between fixed pivots so that it is free to swing about the fixed iron member between the poles of the magnets. A convenient method of determining the direction of motion of the conductor is by the use of the RIGHT-HAND MOTOR RULE FOR ELEC-TRON FLOW (fig. 12-2).

To find the direction of motion of a conductor, the thumb, first finger, and second finger of the right hand are extended at right angles to each other, as shown. The first finger is pointed in the direction of the flux (toward the south pole) and the second finger is pointed in the direction of electron flow in the conductor. The thumb then points in the direction of motion of the conductor with respect to the field. The conductor, the field, and the force are mutually perpendicular to each other.

The force acting on a current-carrying conductor in a magnetic field is directly proportional to the field strength of the magnet, the active length of the conductor, and the intensity of the electron flow through it. Thus,

$$F = \frac{8.85 \times BLI}{10^8},$$

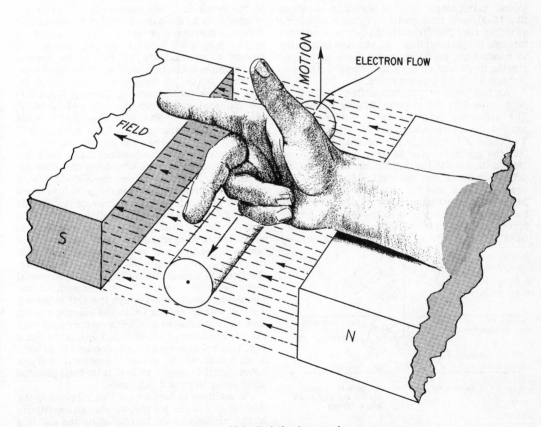

Figure 12-2.—Right-hand motor rule.

where F is the force in pounds, B the flux density in lines per square inch, L the active length of the conductor in inches, and I the current in amperes.

In the D'Arsonval-type meter, the length of the conductor is fixed and the strength of the field between the poles of the magnet is fixed. Therefore, any change in I causes a proportionate change in the force acting on the coil.

The principle of the D'Arsonval movement may be more clearly shown by the use of the simplified diagram (fig. 12-3) of the D'Arsonval movement commonly used in d-c instruments. In the diagram, only one turn of wire is shown; however, in an actual meter movement many turns of fine wire would be used, each turn adding more effective length to the coil. The coil is wound on an aluminum frame or bobbin, to which the pointer is attached. Oppositely wound hairsprings (one of which is shown in fig. 12-3), are also attached to the bobbin, one at either end. The circuit to the coil is completed through the hairsprings. In addition to serving as conductors, the hairsprings serve as the restoring force that returns the pointer to the zero position when no current flows.

As has been stated, the deflecting force is proportional to the current flowing in the coil. The deflecting force tends to rotate the coil against the restraining force of the hairspring. The angle of rotation is proportional to the force that the spring exerts against the moving coil (within the elastic limit of the spring). When the deflecting force and the restraining force are equal, the coil and the pointer cease to move. Because the restoring force is proportional to the angle of deflection, it follows that the driving force, and the current in the coil, are proportional to the angle of deflection. When current

ceases to flow in the coil, the driving force ceases, and the restoring force of the springs returns the pointer to the zero position.

If the current through the single turn of wire is in the direction indicated (away from the observer on the right-hand side and toward the observer on the left-hand side), the direction of force, by the application of the right-hand motor rule, is upward on the left-hand side and downward on the right-hand side. The direction of motion of the coil and pointer is clockwise. If the current is reversed in the wire, the direction of motion of the coil and pointer is reversed.

A detailed view of the basic D'Arsonval movement, as commonly employed in ammeters and voltmeters, is shown in figure 12-4. This instrument is essentially a MICROAMMETER because the current necessary to activate it is of the order of 1 microampere. The principle of operation is the same as that of the simplified versions discussed previously. The iron core is rigidly supported between the pole pieces and serves to concentrate the flux in the narrow space between the iron core and the pole piece—in other words, in the space through which coil and the bobbin moves. Current flows into one hairspring, through the coil, and out of other hairspring. The restoring force of the spiral springs returns the pointer to the normal, or zero, position when the current through the coil is interrupted. Conductors connect the hairsprings with the outside terminals of the meter.

If the instrument is not damped—that is, if viscous friction or some other type of loss is not introduced to absorb the energy of the moving element—the pointer will oscillate for a long time about its final position before coming to rest. This action makes it nearly impossible to obtain a reading and some form of damping is necessary to make the meter practicable. Damping is accomplished in many D'Arsonval movements by means of the motion of the aluminum bobbin upon which the coil is wound. As the bobbin oscillates in the magnetic field, an e.m.f. is induced in it because it cuts through the lines of force. Therefore, according to Lenz's law, induced currents flow in the bobbin in such a direction as to oppose the motion, and the bobbin quickly comes to rest in the final position after going beyond it only once.

In addition to factors such as increasing the flux density in the air gap, the overall sensitivity of the meter can be increased by the use of a lightweight rotating assembly (bobbin, coil, and

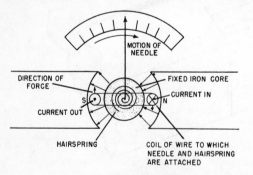

Figure 12-3.—D'Arsonval movement.

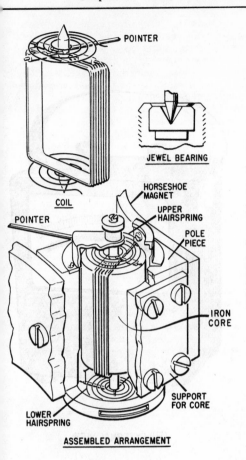

POINTER

JEWEL BEARING

COIL

POINTER

HORSESHOE MAGNET

UPPER HAIRSPRING

POLE PIECE

IRON CORE

SUPPORT FOR CORE

LOWER HAIRSPRING

ASSEMBLED ARRANGEMENT

Figure 12-4.—Detailed view of basic D'Arsonval movement.

pointer) and by the use of jewel bearings as shown.

While D'Arsonval-type galvanometers are useful in the laboratory for measurements of extremely small currents, they are not portable, compact or rugged enough for use in the maintenance of military equipment. The Weston meter movement is used instead.

The Weston meter uses the principles of the D'Arsonval galvanometer, but it is portable, compact, rugged and easy to read. In the Weston meter the coil is mounted on a shaft fitted between two permanently mounted jewel bearings. A lightweight pointer is attached to and turns with the coil; the pointer indicates the amount of current flow. Figure 12-5 (A) illustrates this movement.

Balance springs on each end of the shaft exert opposite turning forces on the coil. By adjusting the tension of one spring, the meter pointer may be adjusted to read zero on the meter scale. Since temperature change affects both coil springs equally, this factor can be discounted. As the meter coil turns, one spring tightens to provide a restoring force; at the same time the other spring releases its tension. In addition to providing tension, the springs are also used as conductors to carry current from the meter terminals to the moving coil.

In order that the turning force will increase uniformly as the current increases, the horseshoe magnet poles are shaped to form semicircles. The amount of current required to turn the meter pointer to full-scale deflection depends upon the magnet's strength and the number of turns of wire in the moving coil. This amount of current is the ammeter's MAXIMUM ALLOWABLE AMOUNT. A further increase of meter current would damage the meter.

Ammeter

CONSTRUCTION

The small size of the wire with which an ammeter's movable coil is wound places severe limits on the current that may be passed through the coil. Consequently, the basic D'Arsonval movement discussed thus far may be used to indicate or measure only very small currents—for example, microamperes (10^{-6} amperes) or milliamperes (10^{-3} amperes), depending on meter sensitivity.

To measure a larger current, a shunt must be used with the meter. A shunt is a heavy low-resistance conductor connected across the meter terminals to carry most of the load current. This shunt has the correct amount of resistance to cause only a small part of the total circuit current to flow through the meter coil. The meter current is proportional to the load current. If the shunt is of such a value that the meter is calibrated in milliamperes, the instrument is called a MILLIAMMETER. If the shunt is of such

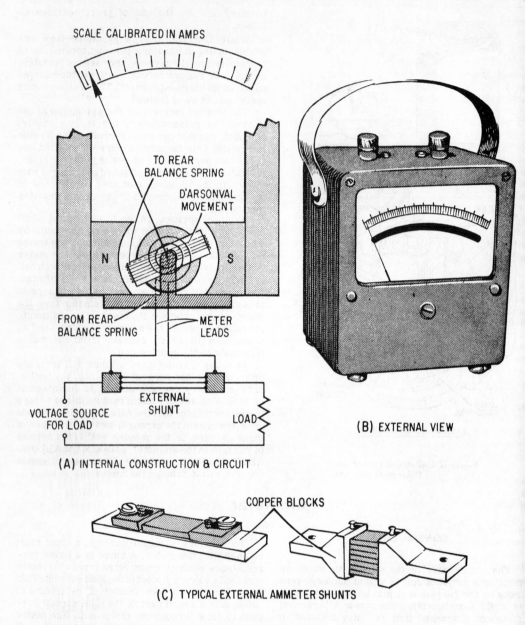

SCALE CALIBRATED IN AMPS

TO REAR
BALANCE SPRING

D'ARSONVAL
MOVEMENT

N   S

FROM REAR
BALANCE SPRING

METER
LEADS

EXTERNAL
SHUNT

VOLTAGE SOURCE
FOR LOAD

LOAD

(A) INTERNAL CONSTRUCTION & CIRCUIT

(B) EXTERNAL VIEW

COPPER BLOCKS

(C) TYPICAL EXTERNAL AMMETER SHUNTS

Figure 12-5.—Weston ammeter employing D'Arsonval principle in its movement.

value that the meter is calibrated in amperes, is called an AMMETER.

A single type of standard meter movement is generally used in all ammeters, no matter what the range of a particular meter. For example, meters with working ranges of zero to 10 amperes, zero to 5 amperes, or zero to 1 ampere all use the same galvanometer movement. The designer of the ammeter simply calculates the correct shunt resistance required to extend the range of the one-milliampere meter movement to measure any desired amount of current. This shunt is then connected across the meter terminals. Shunts may be located inside the meter case (internal shunt) or somewhere away from the meter (external shunt), with leads going to the meter. An external shunt arrangement is shown in figure 12-5 (A). Some typical external shunts are shown in part (C).

The shunt strips are usually made of manganin; an alloy having an almost zero temperature coefficient of resistance. The ends of the shunt strips are embedded in heavy copper blocks to which are attached the meter coil leads and the line terminals. To insure accurate readings, the meter leads for a particular ammeter should not be used interchangeably with those for a meter of a different range. Slight changes in lead length and size may vary the resistance of the meter circuit and thus its current, and may cause an incorrect meter reading. External shunts are generally used where currents greater than 50 amperes must be measured.

It is important to select a suitable shunt when using an external shunt ammeter so that the scale indication is easily read. For example, if the scale has 150 divisions and the load current to be measured is known to be between 50 and 100 amperes, a 150-ampere shunt is suitable. If the scale deflection is 75 divisions, the load current is 75 amperes, the needle will deflect half-scale when using the same 150-ampere shunt.

A shunt having exactly the same current rating as the estimated normal load current should never be selected because any abnormally high load would drive the pointer off scale and might damage the movement. A good choice would bring the needle somewhere near the mid-scale indication, when the load is normal.

EXTENDING THE RANGE BY USE OF INTERNAL SHUNTS

For limited current ranges (below 50 amperes), internal shunts are most often employed. In this manner the range of the meter may be easily changed by selecting the correct internal shunt having the necessary current rating. Before the required resistance of the shunt for each range can be calculated, the resistance of the meter movement must be known.

For example, suppose it is desired to use a 100-microampere D'Arsonval meter having a resistance of 100 ohms to measure line currents up to 1 ampere. The meter deflects full scale when the current through the 100-ohm coil is 100 microamperes. Therefore, the voltage drop across the meter coil is IR, or

$$0.0001 \times 100 = 0.01 \text{ volt.}$$

Because the shunt and coil are in parallel, the shunt must also have a voltage drop of 0.01 volt. The current that flows through the shunt is the difference between the full-scale meter current and the line current. In this case, the meter current is 100×10^{-6}, or 0.0001 ampere. This current is negligible compared with the line (shunt) current, so the shunt current is approximately 1 ampere. The resistance, R_S, of the shunt is therefore

$$R_s = \frac{E}{I} = \frac{0.01}{1} = 0.01 \text{ ohm (approx.)},$$

and the range of the 100-microampere meter has been increased to 1 ampere by paralleling it with the 0.01-ohm shunt.

The 100-microampere instrument may also be converted to a 10-ampere meter by the use of a proper shunt. For full-scale deflection of the meter the voltage drop, E, across the shunt (and across the meter) is still 0.01 volt. The meter current is again considered negligible, and the shunt current is now approximately 10 amperes. The resistance, R_S, of the shunt is therefore

$$R_s = \frac{E}{I} = \frac{0.01}{10} = 0.01 \text{ ohm.}$$

The same instrument may likewise be converted to a 50-ampere meter by the use of the

201

proper type of shunt. The current, I_S, through the shunt is approximately 50 amperes and the resistance, R_S, of the shunt is

$$R_s = \frac{E}{I_s} = \frac{0.01}{50} = 0.0002 \text{ ohm.}$$

Various values of shunt resistance may be used, by means of a suitable switching arrangement, to increase the number of current ranges that may be covered by the meter. Two switching arrangements are shown in figure 12-6. Figure 12-6 (A), is the simpler of the two arrangements from the point of view of calculating the value of the shunt resistors when a number of shunts are used. However, it has two disadvantages:

1. When the switch is moved from one shunt resistor to another the shunt is momentarily removed from the meter and the line current then flows through the meter coil. Even a momentary surge of current could easily damage the coil.

2. The contact resistance—that is, the resistance between the blades of the switch when they are in contact—is in series with the shunt but not with the meter coil. In shunts that must

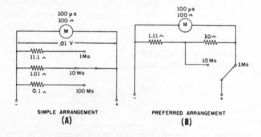

SIMPLE ARRANGEMENT
(A)

PREFERRED ARRANGEMENT
(B)

Figure 12-6.—Ways of connecting internal shunts.

pass high currents the contact resistance becomes an appreciable part of the total shunt resistance. Because the contact resistance is of a variable nature, the ammeter indication may not be accurate.

A more generally accepted method of range switching is shown in figure 12-6 (B). Although only two ranges are shown, as many ranges as needed can be used. In this type of circuit the range selector switch contact resistance is external to the shunt and meter in each range position, and therefore has no effect on the accuracy of the current measurement.

CURRENT-MEASURING INSTRUMENT MUST ALWAYS BE CONNECTED IN SERIES WITH A CIRCUIT AND NEVER IN PARALLEL WITH IT. If an ammeter were connected across a constant-potential source of appreciable voltage the shunt would become a short circuit, and the meter would burn out.

If the approximate value of current in a circuit is not known, it is best to start with the highest range of the ammeter and switch to progressively lower ranges until a suitable reading is obtained.

Most ammeter needles indicate the magnitude of the current by being deflected from left to right. If the meter is connected with reverse polarity, the needle will be deflected backwards, and this action may damage the movement. Hence the proper polarity should be observed in connecting the meter in the circuit. That is, the meter should always be connected so that the electron flow will be into the negative terminal and out of the positive terminal.

Figure 12-7 shows various circuit arrangements; the ammeter or ammeters are properly connected for measuring current in various portions of the circuits.

Voltmeter

CONSTRUCTION

The 100-microampere D'Arsonval meter used as the basic meter for the ammeter may also be used to measure voltage if a high resistance is placed in series with the moving coil of the meter. For low-range instruments, this resistance is mounted inside the case with the D'Arsonval movement and typically consists of resistance wire having a low temperature coefficient and wound either on spools or card frames. For higher voltage ranges, the series

resistance may be connected externally. When this is done the unit containing the resistance is commonly called a MULTIPLIER.

A simplified diagram of a voltmeter is shown in figure 12-8 (A). The resistance coils are treated in such a way that a minimum amount of moisture will be absorbed by the insulation. Moisture reduces the insulation resistance and increases leakage currents, which cause incorrect readings. Leakage currents through the insulation increase with length of resistance wire and become a factor that limits the magnitude

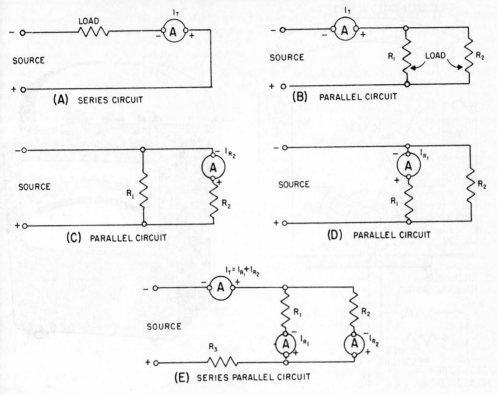

Figure 12-7.—Proper ammeter connections.

of voltage that may be measured. An external view of a voltmeter is shown in figure 12-8 (B).

EXTENDING THE RANGE

The value of the necessary series resistance is determined by the current required for full-scale deflection of the meter and by the range of voltage to be measured. Because the current through the meter circuit is directly proportional to the applied voltage, the meter scale can be calibrated directly in volts for a fixed series resistance.

For example, assume that the basic meter (microammeter) is to be made into a voltmeter with a full-scale reading of 1 volt. The coil resistance of the basic meter is 100 ohms, and 0.0001 ampere (100 microamperes) causes a full-scale deflection. The total resistance, R, of the meter coil and the series resistance is

$$R = \frac{E}{I} = \frac{1}{0.0001} = 10,000 \text{ ohms,}$$

and the series resistance alone is

$$R_s = 10,000 - 100 = 9,900 \text{ ohms.}$$

Multirange voltmeters utilize one meter movement with the required resistances connected in series with the meter by a convenient switching arrangement. A multirange voltmeter with three ranges is shown in figure 12-9. The total circuit resistance for each of the three ranges beginning with the 1-volt range is:

$$R = \frac{E}{I} = \frac{1}{100} = 0.01 \text{ megohm,}$$

$$= \frac{100}{100} = 1 \text{ megohm,}$$

$$= \frac{1,000}{100} = 10 \text{ megohms.}$$

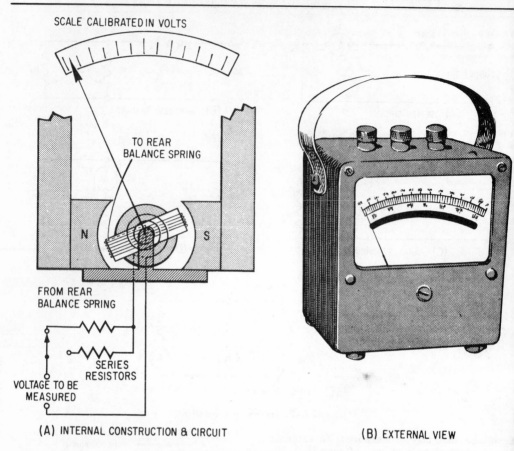

SCALE CALIBRATED IN VOLTS

TO REAR
BALANCE SPRING

N   S

FROM REAR
BALANCE SPRING

SERIES
RESISTORS

VOLTAGE TO BE
MEASURED

(A) INTERNAL CONSTRUCTION & CIRCUIT

(B) EXTERNAL VIEW

Figure 12-8.—Simplified voltmeter circuit.

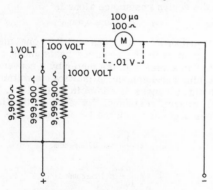

Figure 12-9.—Multirange voltmeter.

VOLTAGE-MEASURING INSTRUMENT
ARE CONNECTED ACROSS (IN PARALLE
WITH) A CIRCUIT. If the approximate value o
the voltage to be measured is not known, it i
best to start with the highest range of the volt
meter and progressively lower the range unti
a suitable reading is obtained.

In many cases, the voltmeter is not a central
zero indicating instrument. Thus, it is necessar
to observe the proper polarity when connectin
the instrument to the circuit, as is the case i
connecting the d-c ammeter. The positive ter
minal of the voltmeter is always connected to th
positive terminal of the source, and the negativ
terminal to the negative terminal of the sourc
when the source voltage is being measured. I

204

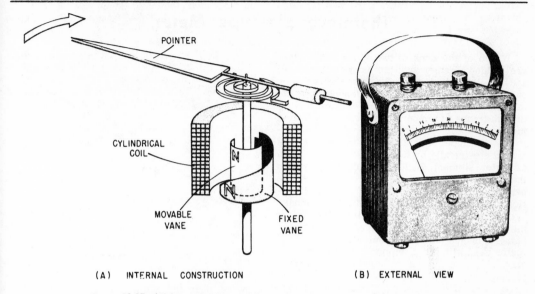

(A)   INTERNAL   CONSTRUCTION   (B) EXTERNAL   VIEW

Figure 12-17.–(A) Simplified diagram of a moving iron-vane meter, (B) external view.

Inclined-Coil Iron-Vane Meter

The principle of the moving iron-vane mechanism is applied to the inclined-coil type of meter shown in figure 12-18. The inclined-coil iron-vane meter has a coil mounted at an angle to the shaft. Attached obliquely to the shaft, and located inside the coil, are two soft-iron vanes. When no current flows through the coil, a control spring holds the pointer at zero and the iron vanes lie in planes parallel to the plane of the coil. When current flows through the coil, the vanes tend to line up with magnetic lines passing through the center of the coil at right angles to the plane of the coil. Thus the vanes rotate against the spring action to move the pointer over the scale.

The iron vanes tend to line up with the magnetic lines regardless of the direction of current flow through the coil. Therefore, the inclined-coil iron-vane meter can be used to measure either alternating current or direct current. The aluminum disk and the drag magnets provide electromagnetic damping.

Like the moving iron-vane meter, the inclined-coil type requires a relatively large

amount of current for full-scale deflection and hence is seldom used in high-resistance low-power circuits.

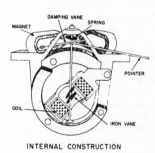

INTERNAL CONSTRUCTION

Figure 12-18.–Inclined-coil iron-vane meter.

As in the moving iron-vane instrument, the inclined-coil instrument is wound with few turns of relatively large wire when used as an ammeter and with many turns of small wire when used as a voltmeter.

Thermocouple-Type Meter

If two of the ends of two dissimilar metals are welded together and this junction is heated, a d-c voltage is developed across the two open ends. The voltage developed depends on the material of which the wires are made and on the difference in temperature between the heated junction and the open ends.

In one type of instrument, the junction is heated electrically by the flow of current through a heater element. It does not matter whether the current is alternating or direct because the heating effect is independent of current direction. The maximum current that may be measured depends on the current rating of the heater, the heat that the thermocouple can stand without being damaged, and on the current rating of the meter used with the thermocouple. Voltage may also be measured if a suitable resistor is placed in series with the heater.

A simplified schematic diagram of one type of thermocouple is shown in figure 12-19. The input current flows through the heater strip via the terminal blocks. The function of the heater strip is to heat the thermocouple, which is composed of a junction of two dissimilar wires welded to the heater strip. The open ends of these wires are connected to the center of two copper compensating strips. The function of these strips is to radiate heat so that the open ends of the wires will be much cooler than the junction end of the wires; thus permitting a higher voltage to be developed across the open ends of the thermocouple. The compensating strips are thermally and electrically insulated from the terminal blocks.

The heat produced by the flow of line current through the heater strip is proportional to the square of the heating current $(P = I^2R)$. Because the voltage appearing across the two open terminals is proportional to the temperature, the movement of the meter element connected across these terminals is proportional to the square of the current flowing through the heater element. The scale of the meter is crowded near the zero end, and is progressively less

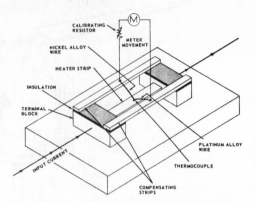

Figure 12-19.—Simplified schematic of one type of thermocouple.

crowded near the maximum end of the scale. Because the lower portion of the scale is crowded the reading is necessarily less accurate. For the sake of accuracy in making a given measurement, it is desirable to choose a meter in which the deflection will extend at least to the more open portion of the scale.

The meter used with the thermocouple should have low resistance to match the low resistance of the thermocouple, and it must deflect full scale when rated current flows through the heater. Because the resistance must be low and the sensitivity high, the moving element must be light.

A more nearly uniform meter scale may be obtained if the permanent magnet of the meter is constructed so that as the coil rotates (needle moves up scale), it moves into a magnetic field of less and less density. The torque then increases approximately as the first power of the current instead of as the square of the current, and a more linear scale is achieved.

If the thermocouple is burned out by excessive current through the heater strip, it may be replaced and the meter recalibrated by means of the calibrating variable resistor.

214

QUIZ

1. In a D'Arsonval type meter, the primary purpose of the iron core is to
   a. dampen coil movement
   b. concentrate the flux between the core and the pole piece
   c. concentrate the flux between the core and the hairsprings
   d. weaken the flux between the core and the pole piece

2. The D'Arsonval movement operates on the principle of
   a. mutual induction
   b. repulsion
   c. magnetic repulsion and attraction
   d. magnetic attraction

3. In order to measure large currents with the D'Arsonval ammeter,
   a. the meter must be made more rugged
   b. an increased number of turns must be put on the moving coil
   c. shunts are used
   d. the pointer must be lengthened

4. The primary purpose of the megger is to measure
   a. milliohms
   b. kilohms
   c. megohms
   d. microhms

5. A moving iron-vane meter works on the principle of
   a. induction
   b. repulsion
   c. conduction
   d. attraction

6. When hairsprings are used in a D'Arsonval type meter, they
   a. serve as conductors
   b. are wound oppositely and provide restoring forces
   c. are attached to the ends of the bobbin
   d. all of the above are true

7. The metal ribbons attached to the moving coil in the galvanometer have no force on them when the
   a. north pole of the moving coil is close to the south pole of the horseshoe magnet
   b. north pole of the moving coil is as close as possible to the north pole of the horseshoe magnet
   c. north pole of the moving coil is 90° from the north pole of the horseshoe magnet
   d. none of the above

8. When shunts are used with an ammeter they
   a. must be located within the case
   b. must be located outside the case
   c. may be located either inside or outside the case
   d. reduce the accuracy of the movement

9. The power supply for a megger comes from
   a. two flashlight batteries
   b. a hand-driven generator
   c. any 115 v. wall plug
   d. the aircraft battery

10. The iron-vane meter can be used on
    a. a.c. only
    b. a.c. and d.c.
    c. d.c. only
    d. rectified a.c.

11. The Weston meter uses the principle of operation of the
    a. D'Arsonval galvanometer
    b. Thompson incline coil
    c. iron vane
    d. V. T. V. M.

12. Current-measuring instruments must always be connected in
    a. parallel with a circuit
    b. series with a circuit
    c. series-parallel with a circuit
    d. delta with the shunt

13. If the pointer fails to come back to zero when the megger is not in use,
    a. the megger is out of calibration
    b. this is normal operation
    c. the hairsprings are burned out
    d. the pointer is stuck

14. When using ammeters,
    a. reverse polarity must be used
    b. + or - polarity can be used
    c. polarity should be observed
    d. regardless of polarity, the instrument cannot be damaged because it is grounded

15. For measuring resistances of multimillions of ohms, use a/an
    a. TS 297 multimeter
    b. ohmmeter with high scales
    c. megger
    d. combustion volt ammeter

16. Dampening is accomplished in the iron-vane meter by
    a. hairsprings
    b. the hermetically sealed case
    c. an aluminum bobbin
    d. an aluminum vane

17. Balance springs on each end of the shaft of the Weston ammeter
    a. are used to carry current to the moving coil
    b. are not balanced due to temperature change
    c. provide a turning force for the pointer
    d. are factory adjusted and must not be readjusted

215

18. The electrodynamometer-type meter employs
    a. two permanent magnets
    b. one permanent magnet and one electromagnet
    c. two fixed coils and one movable permanent magnet
    d. none of the above
19. With the ohmmeter setting on R x 1, it takes 0.01 ma. to deflect the pointer to half scale. If the meter was set on R x 100, how much would it take to deflect the pointer to half scale?
    a. 0.1 ma.
    b. 0.01 ma.
    c. 0.001 ma.
    d. 1.0 ma.
20. Electrodynamometer-type meters
    a. never utilize shunts
    b. utilize four coils, all of which are movable
    c. are seldom used in the laboratory because they are not accurate enough
    d. are not as sensitive as the D'Arsonval meter

21. Meggers provided aboard ships are usually rated at
    a. 250 volts
    b. 500 volts
    c. 750 volts
    d. 1,000 volts
22. The voltage developed in the thermocouple-type meter depends on the
    a. material of which the wires are made
    b. direction of current flow
    c. frequency of the heater voltage
    d. the type of meter movement
23. A multimeter contains a
    a. voltmeter and wattmeter
    b. voltmeter and frequency meter
    c. voltmeter, ohmmeter, and milliammeter
    d. voltmeter, ammeter, and ohmmeter

PART 2

PART 2

CHAPTER 13

GENERATORS AND TRANSFORMERS
ALTERNATING-CURRENT

A-C Generators

Most of the electric power for use aboard ship and ashore is generated by alternating-current generators. A-c generators are also finding increased use in aircraft, and even automobiles.

A-c generators are made in many different sizes, depending on their intended use. For example, any one of the generators at Boulder Dam can produce millions of volt-amperes, while generators used on aircraft produce only a few thousand volt-amperes.

Regardless of size, however, all generators operate on the same basic principle—a magnetic field cutting through conductors, or conductors passing through a magnetic field. Thus, all generators will have at least two distinct sets of conductors. They are (1) a group of conductors in which the output voltage is generated, and (2) a second group of conductors through which DIRECT CURRENT is passed to obtain an electromagnetic field of fixed direction. The conductors in which the output voltage is generated are always referred to as the ARMATURE WINDINGS. The conductors in which the electromagnetic field originates are always referred to as the FIELD WINDINGS.

In addition to the armature and field, there must also be MOTION between the two. To provide this, a-c generators are built in two major assemblies, the STATOR and the ROTOR. The rotor rotates inside the stator. It may be driven by any one of a number of commonly used power sources, such as gas or hydraulic turbines, electric motors, and steam or internal-combustion engines.

TYPES OF A-C GENERATORS

Revolving Armature

In the revolving-armature a-c generator, the stator provides a stationary electromagnetic field. The rotor, acting as the armature, revolves in the field, cutting the lines of force, producing the desired output voltage. In this generator, the armature output is taken through sliprings and thus retains its alternating characteristic.

For a number of reasons, the revolving-armature a-c generator is seldom used. Its primary limitation is the fact that its output power is conducted through sliding contacts (sliprings and brushes). These contacts are subject to frictional wear and sparking. In addition, they are exposed, and thus liable to arc-over at high voltages. Consequently, revolving-armature generators are limited to low-power low-voltage applications.

Revolving Field

The revolving-field a-c generator (fig. 13-1) is by far the most widely used type. In this type of generator, direct current from a separate source is passed through windings on the rotor by means of sliprings and brushes. This maintains a rotating electromagnetic field of fixed polarity (similar to a rotating bar magnet). The rotating magnetic field, following the rotor, extends outward and cuts through the armature windings imbedded in the surrounding stator. As the rotor turns, alternating voltages are induced in the windings since magnetic fields of first one polarity and then the other cut through them. Since the output power is taken from stationary windings, the output may be connected through fixed terminals directly to the external loads, as through terminals $T1$ and $T2$ in figure 13-1. This is advantageous, in that there are no sliding contacts, and the whole output circuit is continuously insulated, thus minimizing the danger of arc-over.

Sliprings and brushes are still used on the rotor to supply d.c. to the field; they are adequate for this purpose, because the power level in the field is much lower than in the armature circuit.

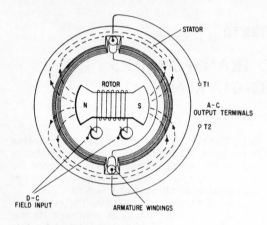

Figure 13-1.—Essential parts of rotating-field a-c generator.

RATING OF A-C GENERATORS

The RATING of an a-c generator pertains to the load it is capable of supplying. The normal-load rating is the load it can carry continuously. Its overload rating is the above-normal load which it can carry for specified lengths of time only. The load rating of a particular generator is determined by the internal heat it can withstand. Since heating is caused mainly by current flow, the generator's rating is identified very closely with its CURRENT capacity.

The maximum current that can be supplied by an a-c generator depends upon (1) the maximum heating loss (I^2R power loss) that can be sustained in the armature and (2) the maximum heating loss that can be sustained in the field. The armature current varies with the load. This action is similar to that of d-c generators. In a-c generators, however, lagging power-factor loads tend to demagnetize the field, and terminal voltage is maintained only by increasing the d-c field current. Therefore, a-c generators are rated in terms of armature load current and voltage output, or kilovolt-ampere (kv.-a.) output, at a specified frequency and power factor. The specified power factor is usually 80 percent lagging. For example, a single-phase a-c generator designed to deliver 100 amperes at 1,000 volts is rated at 100 kv.-a. This machine would supply a 100-kw. load at unity power factor or an 80-kw. load at 80 percent power factor. If, however, the a-c generator supplied a 100 kv.a. load at 20 percent power factor, the required increase in d-c field current needed to maintain the desired terminal voltage would cause excessive heating in the field.

Basic Functions of Generator Parts

Almost all rotating-field a-c generators used in the Navy are actually two generators in one. A typical machine consists of the a-c generator and a smaller d-c generator built in a single unit. The output of the a-c generator section supplies alternating current to the load for which the generator was designed. The d-c generator's only purpose is to supply the direct current required to maintain the a-c generator field. This d-c generator is referred to as the EXCITER. A typical a-c generator is shown in figure 13-2 (A); figure 13-2 (B) is a simplified schematic of the generator.

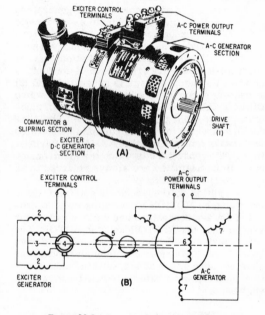

Figure 13-2.—A-c generator and schematic.

Any rotary generator requires a prime moving force (1, fig. 13-2) to rotate the a-c field and exciter armature. This rotary force is transmitted to the generator through the rotor drive shaft and is usually furnished by a combustion engine, turbine, or electric motor. The EXCITER SHUNT FIELD (2) creates an area of intense magnetic flux between its poles. When the EXCITER ARMATURE (3) is rotated in the exciter field flux, voltage is induced into the exciter armature windings. The EXCITER OUTPUT COMMUTATOR and BRUSHES (4) connects the exciter output directly to the A-C GENERATOR FIELD INPUT SLIPRINGS and BRUSHES (5). Since these sliprings, rather than a commutator, are used to supply current through the A-C GENERATOR FIELD (6), current will always flow in one direction only through these windings. Thus, a FIXED POLARITY magnetic field is maintained at all times in the a-c generator field windings. When the a-c generator field is rotated, its magnetic flux is passed through and across the A-C GENERATOR ARMATURE WINDINGS (7). Remember, a voltage is induced into a conductor if it is stationary and a magnetic field is passed across the conductor, the same as if the field is stationary and the conductor is moved. The alternating voltage induced in the a-c generator armature windings is connected through fixed terminals to the a-c load.

Construction

A-c generators used in the Navy are divided into three classes according to the type of prime mover—(1) low-speed engine-driven, (2) high-speed turbine-driven, and (3) aircraft engine-driven high-speed, 4,000 and 8,000 r.p.m.

The stator, or armature, of the revolving-field a-c generator is built up from steel punchings, or laminations. The laminations on an a-c generator stator form a steel ring that is keyed or bolted to the inside circumference of a steel frame. The inner surface of the laminated ring has slots in which the stator winding is placed.

The low-speed engine-driven a-c generator (fig. 13-3) has a large diameter revolving field with many poles, and a stationary armature relatively short in axial length. The stator (fig. 13-3 (A)) contains the armature windings, and the rotor (fig. 13-3 (B)) consists of salient poles, on which are mounted the d-c field windings. The exciter armature is the smaller unit shown in the foreground and mounted on an extension of the a-c generator shaft.

The high-speed turbine-driven a-c generator (fig. 13-4) is connected either directly or through gears to a steam turbine. The enclosed metal

structure is a part of a forced ventilation system that carries away the heat by circulation of the air through the stator (fig. 13-4 (A)) and rotor (fig. 13-4 (B)). The exciter is a separate unit (not shown). The enclosed stator directs the paths of the circulating air-cooling currents and also reduces windage noise.

The aircraft a-c generator (fig. 13-5) may be driven directly by the aircraft engine, a hydraulic constant-speed drive, or an air turbine.

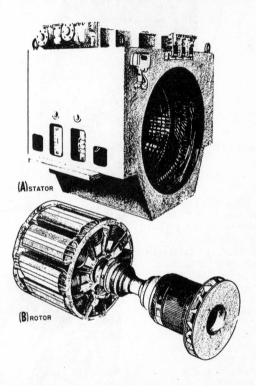

(A) STATOR

(B) ROTOR

Figure 13-3.—Low-speed engine-driven a-c generator.

SINGLE-PHASE GENERATORS

A single-phase a-c generator has a stator made up of a number of windings in series, which form a single circuit in which an output voltage is generated. The principle of the single-phase a-c generator is described first, and the polyphase a-c generator is described later.

Figure 13-6 illustrates a schematic diagram of a single-phase a-c generator having four poles. The stator has four polar groups evenly

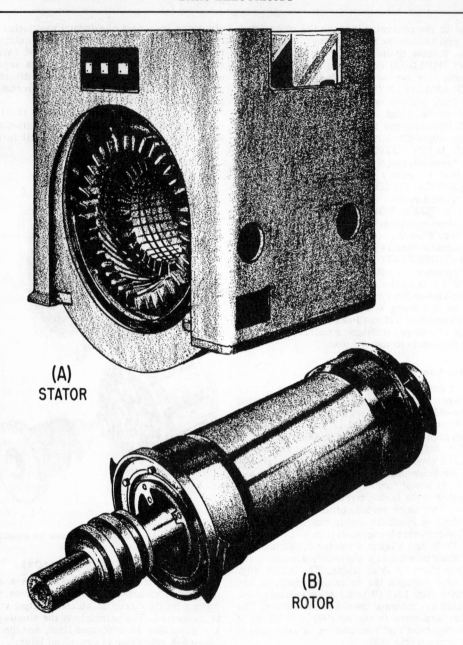

**(A)
STATOR**

**(B)
ROTOR**

Figure 13-4.—High-speed turbine-driven a-c generator.

220

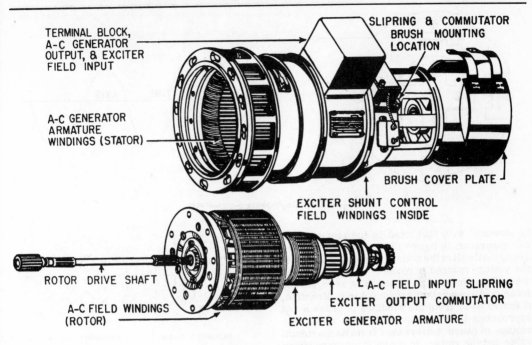

TERMINAL BLOCK,
A-C GENERATOR
OUTPUT, & EXCITER
FIELD INPUT

SLIPRING & COMMUTATOR
BRUSH MOUNTING
LOCATION

A-C GENERATOR
ARMATURE
WINDINGS (STATOR)

BRUSH COVER PLATE

EXCITER SHUNT CONTROL
FIELD WINDINGS INSIDE

ROTOR DRIVE SHAFT

A-C FIELD INPUT SLIPRING

A-C FIELD WINDINGS
(ROTOR)

EXCITER OUTPUT COMMUTATOR

EXCITER GENERATOR ARMATURE

Figure 13-5.—Aircraft a-c generator.

spaced around the stator frame. The rotor has
four poles, with adjacent poles of opposite polarity. As the rotor revolves, a-c voltages are
induced in the stator windings. Since one rotor
pole is in the same position relative to a stator
winding as any other rotor pole, all stator polar
groups are cut by equal amounts of magnetic
lines of force at any given time. As a result, the
voltages induced in all the windings have the
same amplitude, or value, at any given instant.
The four stator windings are connected to each
other so that the a-c voltages are in phase, or
"series aiding." Assume that rotor pole 1, a
south pole, induces a voltage in the direction
indicated by the arrow in stator winding 1. Since
rotor pole 2 is a north pole, it will induce a voltage in the opposite direction in stator coil 2 with
respect to that in coil 1.

In order that the two induced voltages be in
series addition, the two coils are connected as
shown. Applying the same reasoning, the voltage
induced in stator coil 3 (clockwise rotation of
the field) is in the same direction (counterclockwise) as the voltage induced in coil 1. Similarly,
the direction of the voltage induced in winding 4

is opposite to the direction of the voltage induced
in coil 1. All four stator coil groups are connected in series so that the voltages induced in
each winding add to give a total voltage that is
four times the voltage in any one winding.

TWO-PHASE GENERATORS

Multiphase or polyphase a-c generators have
two or more single-phase windings symmetrically spaced around the stator. In a 2-phase a-c
generator there are two single-phase windings
physically spaced so that the a-c voltage induced
in one is 90° out of phase with the voltage induced in the other. The windings are electrically
separate from each other. When one winding is
being cut by maximum flux, the other is being
cut by no flux. This condition establishes the 90°
relation between the two phases.

Figure 13-7 is a schematic diagram of a
2-phase 4-pole a-c generator. The stator consists of two single-phase windings (phases) completely separated from each other. Each phase
is made up of four windings, which are connected
in series so that their voltages add. The rotor

221

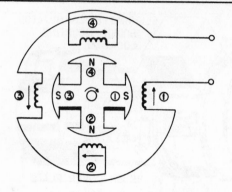

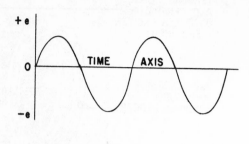

Figure 13-6.—Single-phase a-c generator.

is identical with that used in the single-phase a-c generator. In figure 13-7 (A), the rotor poles are opposite all of the coils of phase A. Therefore, the voltage induced in phase A is maximum and the voltage induced in phase B is zero. As the rotor continues rotating in a clockwise direction, it moves away from the windings of phase A and approaches those of phase B. As a result, the voltage in phase A decreases from its maximum value and the voltage in phase B increased from zero. In figure 13-7 (B), the rotor poles are opposite the windings of phase B. Now the voltage induced in phase B is maximum; whereas the voltage induced in phase A has dropped to zero. Notice that in the 4-pole a-c generator a 45° mechanical rotation of the rotor corresponds electrically to one quarter cycle, or 90 electrical degrees. Figure 13-7 (C) illustrates the waveforms of the voltage generated in each of the two phases. Both are sine curves, and A leads B by 90°. Figure 13-7 (D) illustrates the vectors representing the 2-phase voltages. Vector A leads vector B by 90°.

The two phases of a 2-phase a-c generator can be connected to each other as shown in figure 13-8, so that only three leads are brought out to the load. The a-c generator is then called a 2-phase 3-wire a-c generator. The two phases for a 4-pole a-c generator are shown in figure 13-8 (A). A simplified schematic diagram is shown in figure 13-8 (B), in which the rotor is omitted and each phase is indicated as a single coil. The two coils are drawn at right angles to each other to represent the 90° phase displacement between their respective voltages. The three wires make possible three different load connections—*(A)* and *(B)* across phases A and

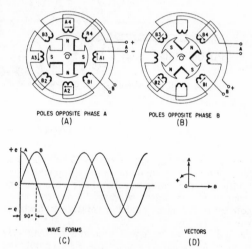

Figure 13-7.—Two-phase four-pole a-c generator.

B, respectively, and *(C)* across both phases in series. The third voltage *(C)* is displaced 45° from the A and B phase voltages and is their vector sum. If each phase voltage has an effective value of 100 volts, the vector sum of these voltages will be the hypotenuse of a right triangle, the base and altitude of which are each 100 volts. This hypotenuse is equal to

$$\frac{100}{\cos 45°}, \text{ or } \frac{100}{0.707} \text{ 141 volts.}$$

222

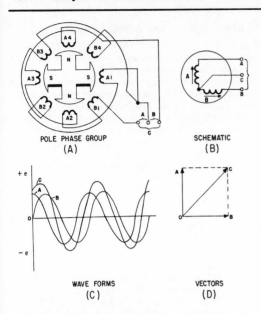

POLE PHASE GROUP
(A)

SCHEMATIC
(B)

WAVE FORMS
(C)

VECTORS
(D)

Figure 13-8. Two-phase three-wire a-c generator.

THREE-PHASE GENERATORS

The 3-phase a-c generator, as the name implies, has three single-phase windings spaced so that the voltage induced in each winding is 120° out of phase with the voltages in the other two windings. A schematic diagram of a 3-phase stator showing all the coils becomes complex, and it is difficult to see what is actually happening. A simplified schematic diagram, showing all the windings of a single phase lumped together as one winding, is illustrated in figure 13-9 (A). The rotor is omitted for simplicity. The waveforms of voltage are shown to the right of the schematic. The three voltages are 120° apart and are similar to the voltages that would be generated by three single-phase a-c generators whose voltages are out of phase by angles of 120°. The three phases are independent of each other.

The Wye Connection

Rather than have six leads come out of the 3-phase a-c generator, one of the leads from each phase may be connected to form a common junction. The stator is then called WYE, or STAR, connected. The common lead may or may not be

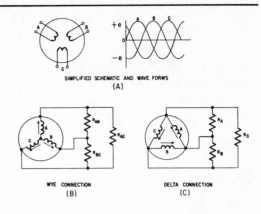

SIMPLIFIED SCHEMATIC AND WAVE FORMS
(A)

WYE CONNECTION
(B)

DELTA CONNECTION
(C)

Figure 13-9.—Three-phase a-c generator.

brought out of the machine. If it is brought out, it is called the NEUTRAL. The simplified schematic (fig. 13-9(B)) shows a wye-connected stator with the common lead not brought out. Each load is connected across two phases in series. Thus, R_{ab} is connected across phases A and B in series, R_{ac} is connected across phases A and C in series, and R_{bc} is connected across phases B and C in series. Thus, the voltage across each load is larger than the voltage across a single phase. In a wye-connected a-c generator the three start ends of each single-phase winding are connected together to a common neutral point and the opposite, or finish, ends are connected to the line terminals A, B, and C. These letters are always used to designate the three phases of a 3-phase system, or the three line wires to which the a-c generator phases connect. A 3-phase wye-connected a-c generator supplying three separate loads is shown in figure 13-10 (A). When unbalanced loads are used, a neutral may be added as shown in the figure by the broken line between the common neutral point and the loads. The neutral wire serves as a common return circuit for all three phases and maintains a voltage balance across the loads. No current flows in the neutral wire when the loads are balanced. This system is a 3-phase 4-wire circuit and is used to distribute 3-phase power to shore-based installations. The 3-phase 4-wire system is not used aboard ship, but is widely used in industry and for aircraft a-c power systems.

The phase relations in a 3-wire 3-phase wye-connected system are shown in figure 13-10 (B). In constructing vector diagrams of 3-phase

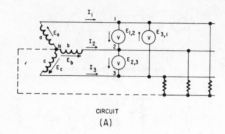

CIRCUIT

(A)

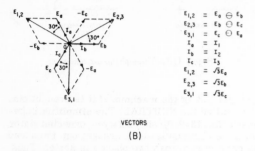

$$E_{1,2} = E_a \ominus E_b$$
$$E_{2,3} = E_b \ominus E_c$$
$$E_{3,1} = E_c \ominus E_a$$
$$I_a = I_1$$
$$I_b = I_2$$
$$I_c = I_3$$
$$E_{1,2} = \sqrt{3}E_a$$
$$E_{2,3} = \sqrt{3}E_b$$
$$E_{3,1} = \sqrt{3}E_c$$

VECTORS

(B)

Figure 13-10.—Three-phase wye-connected system.

circuits, a counterclockwise rotation is assumed in order to maintain the correct phase relation between line voltages and currents. Thus, the a-c generator is assumed to rotate in such a direction as to generate the three phase voltages in the order, E_a, E_b, E_c.

The voltage in phase b, or E_b, lags the voltage in phase a, or E_a, by 120°. Likewise, E_c lags E_b by 120°, and E_a lags E_c by 120°. In figure 13-10 (A), the arrows E_a, E_b, and E_c, represent the positive direction of generated voltage in the wye-connected a-c generator. The arrows I_1, I_2, and I_3 represent the positive direction of phase and line currents supplied to balanced unity power-factor loads connected in wye. The three voltmeters connected between lines 1-2, 2-3, and 3-1, respectively, indicate effective values of line voltage. The line voltage is greater than the voltage of a phase in the wye-connected circuit because there are two phases connected in series between each pair of line wires, and their voltages combine. Line voltage is not twice the value of phase voltage, however, because the phase voltages are not in phase with each other. The relation between phase and line voltages is shown in the vector diagram. Effective values

of phase voltage are indicated by vectors, E_a, E_b, and E_c. Effective values of line and phase current are indicated by vectors I_a, I_b, and I_c. Because there is only one path for current between any given phase and the line wire to which it is connected, the phase current is equal to the line current. The respective phase currents have equal values because the load is assumed to be balanced. For the same reason, the respective line currents have equal values. When the load has unity power factor, the phase currents are in phase with their respective phase voltages.

In combining a-c voltages it is necessary to know the DIRECTION in which the positive maximum values of the voltages act in the circuit as well as the MAGNITUDES of the voltages. For example, in figure 13-11 (A), the positive maximum voltage generated in coils A and B act in the direction of the arrows, and B leads A by 120°. This arrangement may be obtained by assuming coils A and B to be two armature windings located 120° apart. If each voltage has an effective value of 100 volts, the total voltage is $E_\gamma = 100$ volts, as shown by the polar vectors in figure 13-11 (B).

If the connections of coil B are reversed (fig. 13-11 (C)) with respect to their original connections, the two voltages will be in opposition, as will be seen by tracing around the circuit in the direction of the arrow in coil A. The positive direction of the voltage in coil B is opposite to the direction of the trace; the positive direction of the voltage generated in coil A is the same as that of the trace; hence, the two voltages are in opposition. This effect is the same as though the positive maximum value of E_b were 60° out of phase with that of E_a, and E_b acted in the same direction as E_a when the circuit trace was made (fig. 13-11 (D)) to vector E_a is accomplished by reversing the position of E_b from that shown in figure 13-11 (B) to the position shown in figure 13-11 (D) and completing the parallelogram. If E_a and E_b are each 100 volts, $E_\gamma = \sqrt{3} \times 100$, or 173 volts. The value of E_γ may be derived in the following manner: Erecting a perpendicular to E_γ divides the isosceles triangle into two equal right triangles each having a hypotenuse of 100 volts and a base of 100 cos 30°, or 86.6 volts. The total length of E_γ is 2 x 86.6, or 173.2 volts.

224

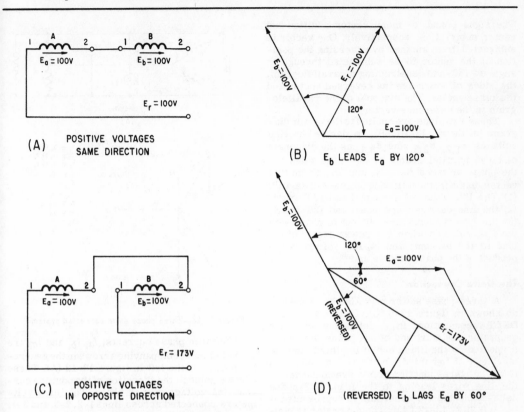

(A) POSITIVE VOLTAGES SAME DIRECTION

(B) E_b LEADS E_a BY 120°

(C) POSITIVE VOLTAGES IN OPPOSITE DIRECTION

(D) (REVERSED) E_b LAGS E_a BY 60°

Figure 13-11.—Vector analysis of voltages in series aiding and opposing.

To construct the line voltage vectors $E_{1,2}$, $E_{2,3}$, and $E_{3,1}$, in figure 13-10, it is first necessary to trace a path around the closed circuit which includes the line wires, armature windings, and one of the three voltmeters. For example, in figure 13-10 (A), consider the circuit that includes the upper and middle wires, the voltmeter connected across them, and the a-c generator phases a and b. The circuit trace is started at the center of the wye, proceeds through phase a of the a-c generator, out line 1, down through the voltmeter from line 1 to line 2, and through phase b of the a-c generator back to the starting point. Voltage drops along line wires are disregarded. The voltmeter indicates an effective value equal to the vector sum of the effective value of voltage in phases a and b. This value is the line voltage, $E_{1,2}$. According to Kirchhoff's law, the source voltage between lines

1 and 2 equals the voltage drop across the voltmeter connected to these lines.

If the direction of the path traced through the GENERATOR is the SAME as that of the arrow, the sign of the voltage is PLUS; if the direction of the trace is OPPOSITE to the arrow, the sign of the voltage is MINUS. If the direction of the path traced through the VOLTMETER is the SAME as that of the arrow, the sign of the voltage is MINUS; if the direction of the trace is OPPOSITE to that of the arrow, the sign of the voltage is PLUS.

The following equations for voltage are based on the preceding rules:

$$E_a \oplus (-E_b) = E_{1,2}, \text{ or } E_{1,2} = E_a \ominus E_b.$$

$$E_b \oplus (-E_c) = E_{2,3}, \text{ or } E_{2,3} = E_b \ominus E_c.$$

$$E_c \oplus (-E_a) = E_{3,1}, \text{ or } E_{3,1} = E_c \ominus E_a.$$

The signs ⊕ and ⊖ mean vector addition and vector subtraction, respectively. One vector is subtracted from another by reversing the position of the vector to be subtracted through an angle of 180° and constructing a parallelogram, the sides of which are the reversed vector and the other vector. The diagonal of the parallelogram is the difference vector.

These equations are applied to the vector diagram of figure 13-10 (B), to derive the line voltages $E_{1,2}$, $E_{2,3}$, and $E_{3,1}$, as the diagonals of three parallelograms of which the sides are the phase voltages E_a, E_b, and E_c. From this vector diagram, the following facts are observed: (1) The line voltages are equal and 120° apart; (2) the line currents are equal and 120° apart; (3) the line currents are 30° out of phase with the line voltages when the power factor of the load is 100 percent; and (4) line voltage is the product of the phase voltage and $\sqrt{3}$.

The Delta Connection

A three-phase stator may also be connected as shown in figure 13-9 (C). This is called the DELTA connection. In a delta-connected a-c generator, the start end of one phase winding is connected to the finish end of the third; and the start end of the third, to the finish end of the first. The three junction points are connected to the line wires leading to the load. A 3-phase delta-connected a-c generator is represented at the left (fig. 13-12 (A)). The generator is connected to a 3-phase 3-wire circuit which supplies a 3-phase delta-connected load at the right-hand end of the 3-phase line. Because the phases are connected directly across the line wires, phase voltage is equal to line voltage. When the generator phases are properly connected in delta, no appreciable current flows within the delta loop when there is no external load connected to the generator. If any one of the phases is reversed with respect to its correct connection, a short-circuit current will flow within the windings on no load, causing damage to the windings.

To avoid connecting a phase in reverse it is necessary to test the circuit before closing the delta. This may be done by connecting a voltmeter or fuse wire between the two ends of the delta loop before closing the delta. The two ends of the delta loop should never be connected if there is an indication of any appreciable current or voltage between them when no load is connected to the generator.

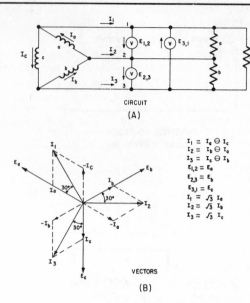

Figure 13-12.—Three-phase delta-connected system.

The three phase currents, I_a, I_b, and I_c, are indicated by accompanying arrows in the generator phases at the left in figure 13-12 (A). These arrows point in the direction of the positive current and voltage of each phase. The three voltmeters connected across lines 1-2, 2-3, and 3-1, respectively, indicate effective values of line and phase voltage. Line current I_1 is supplied by phases a and c, which are connected to line 1. Line current is greater than phase current, but not twice as great because the phase currents are not in phase with each other. The relation between line currents and phase currents is shown in figure 13-12 (B).

Effective values of line and phase voltages are indicated by vectors E_a, E_b, and E_c. Note that the vector sum of E_a, E_b, and E_c is zero. The phase currents are equal to each other because the loads are balanced. The line currents are equal to each other for the same reason. At unity-power-factor loads, the phase current and phase voltage have a 0° angle between them.

To construct the line current vectors it is first necessary to consider the direction of currents at the junctions of the line wires and the generator phases. Consider the junction formed by phase a, phase c, and line 1. According to Kirchhoff's law, line current I_1 is equal to the vector difference between I_a and I_c. In figure 13-12 (B), current vector I_a is in the same general direction as current vector I_1 (less than 90° displaced from I_1), and current vector I_c is in opposition to vector I_1 (more than 90° displaced from it). I_1 is the vector sum of I_a and $-I_c$. These are two equal values of phase current and they are 60° out of phase with each other. The vector sum of all the currents entering and leaving the junction is zero. Current arrows that point toward the junction are considered to represent positive currents. Current arrows that point away from the junction are considered to represent negative currents. The following equations for current are based on the preceding rules:

$$I_a \oplus (-I_c) = I_1, \text{ or } I_1 = I_a \ominus I_c.$$

$$I_b \oplus (-I_a) = I_2, \text{ or } I_2 = I_b \ominus I_a.$$

$$I_c \oplus (-I_b) = I_3, \text{ or } I_3 = I_c \ominus I_b.$$

Here also, the signs $\oplus$ and θ mean vector addition and vector subtraction, respectively. Vector subtraction is accomplished again by reversing the vector being subtracted through an angle of 180° and combining it with the other vector by the parallelogram method to form the diagonal which is the vector difference.

If the current equations are applied to the vector diagram of figure 13-12 (B), the line current I_1, I_2, and I_3 are derived as diagonals of the three parallelograms in which the sides are the phase currents I_a, I_b, and I_c. From this diagram the following facts are observed: (1) The line currents are equal and 120° apart; (2) the line voltages are equal and 120° apart; (3) the line currents are 30° out of phase with the line voltages when the power factor of the load is unity; and (4) the line current is equal to the product of the phase current and $\sqrt{3}$.

The power delivered by a balanced 3-phase wye-connected system is equal to three times the power delivered by each phase. The total true power is

$$P_t = 3E_{phase}I_{phase} \cos \theta$$

Because $E_{phase} = \dfrac{E_{line}}{\sqrt{3}}$ and $I_{phase} = I_{line}$,

the total true power is

$$P_t = 3\frac{E_{line}}{\sqrt{3}}I_{line} \cos \theta,$$

$$= \sqrt{3} \, E_{line} \, I_{line} \cos \theta.$$

The power delivered by a balanced 3-phase delta-connected system is also three times the power delivered by each phase.

Because $E_{phase} = E_{line}$ and $I_{phase} = \dfrac{I_{line}}{\sqrt{3}}$

the total true power is

$$P_t = 3E_{line} \frac{I_{line}}{\sqrt{3}} \cos \theta,$$

$$= \sqrt{3}E_{line} I_{line} \cos \theta.$$

Thus, the expression for 3-phase power delivered by a balanced delta-connected system is the same as the expression for 3-phase power delivered by a balanced wye-connected system. Two examples are given to illustrate the phase relations between current, voltage, and power in (1) a 3-phase wye-connected system and (2) a 3-phase delta-connected system.

Example 1: A 3-phase wye-connected a-c generator has a terminal voltage of 450 volts and delivers a full-load current of 300 amperes per terminal at a power factor of 80 percent. Find (a) the phase voltage, (b) the full-load current per phase, (c) the kilovolt-ampere, or apparent power, rating, and (d) the true power output.

(a) $E_{phase} = \dfrac{E_{line}}{\sqrt{3}} = \dfrac{450}{\sqrt{3}} = 260$ volts.

(b) $I_{phase} = I_{line} = 300$ amperes.

(c) Apparent power $= \sqrt{3} \, E_{line} \, I_{line}$

$\qquad = \sqrt{3} \times 450 \times 300 = 233{,}600$ va., or 233.6 kv.-a.

(d) True power $= \sqrt{3} \, E_{line} \, I_{line} \cos \theta$

$\qquad = \sqrt{3} \times 450 \times 300 \times 0.8$

$\qquad = 186{,}000$ watts, or 186.8 kw.

227

Example 2: A 3-phase delta-connected a-c generator has a terminal voltage of 450 volts and the current in each phase is 200 amperes. The power factor of the load is 75 percent. Find (a) the line voltage, (b) the line current, (c) the apparent power, and (d) the true power.

(a) $E_{\text{phase}} = E_{\text{line}} = 450$ volts.

(b) $I_{\text{line}} = \sqrt{3}\, I_{\text{phase}} = 1.732 \times 200 = 346$ amperes.

(c) Apparent power $= \sqrt{3}\, E_{\text{line}} I_{\text{line}}$
$= 1.732 \times 450 \times 346 = 269,000$ va., or 269 kv.-a.

(d) True power $= \sqrt{3}\, E_{\text{line}} I_{\text{line}} \cos \theta$

$= 1.732 \times 450 \times 346 \times 0.75$

$= 201,700$ watts, or 201.7 kw.

MEASUREMENT OF POWER

The wattmeter connections for measuring the true power in a 3-phase system are shown in figure 13-13. The method shown in figure 13-13 (A) uses three wattmeters with their current coils inserted in series with the line wires and their potential coils connected between line and neutral wires. The total true power is equal to the arithmetic sum of the three wattmeter readings.

The method shown in figure 13-13 (B) uses two wattmeters with their current coils connected in series with two line wires and their potential coils connected between these line wires and the common, or third, wire that does not contain the current coils. The total true power is equal to the algebraic sum of the two wattmeter readings. If one meter reads backward, its potential coil connections are first reversed to make the meter read up-scale and the total true power is then equal to the difference in the two wattmeter readings. If the load power factor is less than 0.5 and the loads are balanced, the total true power will be equal to the difference in the two wattmeter readings. If the load power factor is 0.5, one meter will indicate the total true power and the other will indicate zero. If the load power factor is above 0.5, the total true power is equal to the sum of the two wattmeter readings.

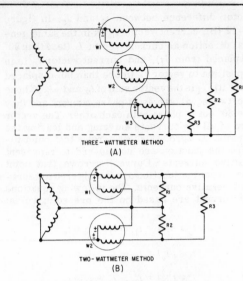

THREE—WATTMETER METHOD
(A)

TWO—WATTMETER METHOD
(B)

Figure 13-13.—Wattmeter connection for measurement of power in a 3-phase system.

FREQUENCY

The frequency of the a-c generator voltage depends upon the speed of rotation of the rotor and the number of poles. The faster the speed, the higher the frequency will be; and the lower the speed, the lower the frequency becomes. The more poles there are on the rotor, the higher the frequency will be for a given speed. When a rotor has rotated through an angle such that two adjacent rotor poles (a north and a south pole) have passed one winding, the voltage induced in that winding will have varied through one complete cycle. For a given frequency, the more pairs of poles there are, the lower will be the speed of rotation. A 2-pole generator rotates at twice the speed of a 4-pole generator for the same frequency of generated voltage. The frequency of the generator in cycles per second is related to the number of poles and the speed, as expressed by the equation

$$f = \frac{P}{2} \times \frac{N}{60} = \frac{PN}{120}$$

where P is the number of poles and N the speed in r.p.m. For example, a 2-pole 3,600 r.p.m. generator has a frequency of $\dfrac{2 \times 3,600}{120} = 60$

cycles per second; a 4-pole 1,800-r.p.m. generator has the same frequency; and a 6-pole 500-r.p.m. generator has a frequency of $\frac{6 \times 500}{120}$ = 25 cycles per second, and a 12-pole 4,000 r.p.m. generator has a frequency of $\frac{12 \times 4,000}{120}$ = 400 cycles per second.

GENERATED VOLTAGE

Once the machine has been designed and built, the generated voltage of an a-c generator is controlled, in practice, by varying the d-c excitation voltage applied to the field winding.

In the design, however, many factors must be taken into account, as the following text illustrates.

As mentioned before, the conductors in a generator armature are arranged in one or more groups called phases, according to whether the machine is designed to deliver single-phase, 2-phase, or 3-phase voltages. The effective voltage, E, per phase is

$$E = 2.22 \ \Phi Z f \ 10^{-8} \ K_b K_p,$$

where Φ is the number of magnetic lines of flux per pole, Z the number of conductors in series per phase, f the frequency in cycles per second, K_b a breadth (or belt) factor, and K_p a pitch factor.

Generally, the coils of each phase are distributed uniformly around the stator. The voltages generated in the various coils are not in time phase with each other because of the displacement of the coils. A breadth, or belt, factor K_b takes the displacement into account and reduces the total generated voltage per phase below the voltage that would be generated if all the active conductors were in the form of a concentrated winding. Also, if the two halves of a coil are less than 180 electrical degrees apart, the voltage generated in the coil is less than it would be if the coil pitch were a full 180 electrical degrees. The pitch factor, K_p, accounts for this reduction in voltage.

For example, a certain 3-phase, 60-cycle generator has 96 conductors in series per phase and a field pole flux of 2.54×10^6 lines per pole. The breadth factor is 0.958, and the pitch factor is 0.966. The effective voltage per phase is

$$E = \frac{2.22 \times 2.54 \times 10^6 \times 96 \times 60 \times 0.958 \times 0.966}{10^8} = 300 \text{ volts.}$$

CHARACTERISTICS

When the load on a generator is changed, the terminal voltage varies with the load. The amount of variation depends on the design of the generator and the power factor of the load. With a load having a lagging power factor, the drop in terminal voltage with increased load is greater than for unity power factor. With a load having a leading power factor, the terminal voltage tends to rise. The causes of a change in terminal voltage with load change are (1) armature resistance, (2) armature reactance, and (3) armature reaction.

Armature Resistance

When current flows through a generator armature winding, there is an IR drop due to the resistance of the winding. This drop increases with load, and the terminal voltage is reduced. The armature resistance drop is small because the resistance is low.

Armature Reactance

The armature current of an a-c generator varies approximately as a sine wave. The continuously varying current in the generator armature is accompanied by an IX_L voltage drop in addition to the IR drop. Armature reactance in an a-c generator may be from 30 to 50 times the value of armature resistance because of the relatively large inductance of the coils compared with their resistance.

A simplified series equivalent circuit of one phase of an a-c generator is shown in figure 13-14. The voltage generated in the phase winding is equal to the vector sum of the terminal voltage for the phase and the internal voltage loss in the armature resistance, R, and the armature reactance, X_L, associated with that phase. The voltage vectors for a unity power-factor load are shown in figure 13-14 (A). The armature IR drop is in phase with the current, I, and the terminal voltage, E_t. Because the armature IX_L drop is 90° out of phase with the current, the terminal voltage is approximately equal to the generated voltage, less the IR drop in the armature.

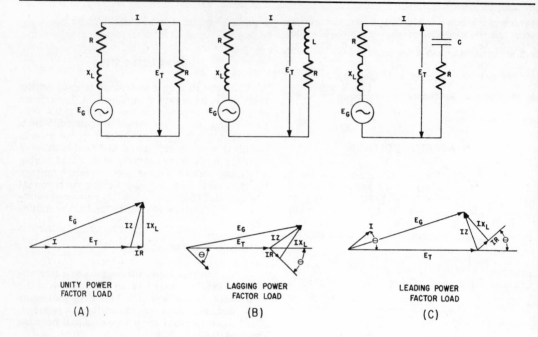

UNITY POWER
FACTOR LOAD

(A)

LAGGING POWER
FACTOR LOAD

(B)

LEADING POWER
FACTOR LOAD

(C)

Figure 13-14.—A-c generator voltage characteristics.

The voltage vectors for a lagging power-factor load are shown in figure 13-14 (B). The load current and IR drop lag the terminal voltage by angle θ. In this example, the armature IZ drop is more nearly in phase with the terminal voltage and the generated voltage. Hence, the terminal voltage is approximately equal to the generated voltage, less the armature IZ drop. Because the IZ drop is much greater than the IR drop, the terminal voltage is reduced that much more. The voltage vectors for a leading power-factor load are shown in figure 13-14 (C). The load current and IR drop lead the terminal voltage by angle θ. This condition results in an increase in terminal voltage above the value of E_g. The total available voltage of the a-c generator phase is the combined effect of E_g (rotationally induced) and the self-induced voltage (not shown in the vectors). The self-induced voltage, as in any a-c circuit, is caused by the varying field (accompanying the varying armature current) linking the armature conductors. The self-induced voltage always lags the current by 90°; hence, when I leads E_t, the self-induced voltage aids E_g, and E_t increases.

Armature Reaction

When an a-c generator supplies no load, the d-c field flux is distributed uniformly across the air gap. When an a-c generator supplies a reactive load, however, the current flowing through the armature conductors produces an armature magnetomotive force (m.m.f.) that influences the terminal voltage by changing the magnitude of the field flux across the air gap. When the load is inductive, the armature m.m.f. opposes the d-c field and weakens it, thus lowering the terminal voltage. When a leading current flows in the armature, the d-c field is aided by the armature m.m.f. and the flux across the air gap is increased, thus increasing the terminal voltage.

VOLTAGE REGULATION

The voltage regulation of an a-c generator is the change of voltage from full load to no load, expressed in percentage of full-load volts, when the speed and d-c field current are held constant.

$$\text{Percent regulation } = \frac{E_{NL} - E_{fL}}{E_{fL}} \times 100.$$

For example, the no-load voltage of a certain generator is 250 volts and the full-load voltage is 220 volts. The percent regulation is

$$\frac{250 - 220}{220} \times 100 = 13.6 \text{ percent.}$$

PRINCIPLES OF A-C VOLTAGE CONTROL

In an a-c generator, an alternating voltage is induced into the armature windings when magnetic fields of alternating polarity are passed across these windings. The amount of voltage induced into the a-c generator windings depends mainly on three things: the number of conductors in series per winding, the speed at which the magnetic field passes across the winding (generator r.p.m.), and the strength of the magnetic field. Any of these three could conceivably be used to control the amount of voltage induced into the a-c generator windings.

The number of windings, of course, is fixed when the generator is manufactured. Also, if the frequency of a generator's output is required to be of a constant value, then the speed of the rotating field must be held constant. This prevents the use of the generator r.p.m. as a means of controlling the voltage output. Thus, the only practical remaining method for obtaining voltage control is to control the strength of the rotating magnetic field. In some specialized applications, the field is furnished by a permanent magnet. The a-c generator in figure 13-2 uses an electromagnetic field rather than a permanent magnetic type field. The strength of this electromagnetic field may be varied by changing the amount of current flowing through the coil. This is done by varying the amount of voltage applied across the coil. It can be seen that by varying the exciter armature d-c output voltage, the a-c generator field strength is also varied. Thus, the magnitude of the generated a-c voltage depends directly on the value of the exciter output voltage. This relationship allows a relatively large a-c voltage to be controlled by a much smaller d-c voltage.

The next function of the a-c generator that you should understand is how the d-c exciter output voltage is controlled. Voltage control in a d-c generator is obtained by varying the strength of the d-c generator shunt field. This is done by using any of a number of different types of voltage regulators. A device which will vary the exciter shunt field current in accordance with changes in the a-c generator voltage is called an a-c generator voltage regulator. This regulator must also maintain the correct value of exciter shunt field current when no a-c voltage corrective action is required (steady state output). In figure 13-15, note that a pair of connections labeled A-C SENSING INPUT feeds a voltage proportional to the a-c generator output voltage to the A-C VOLTAGE REGULATOR. Note also that a portion of the exciter armature output is connected through the exciter's field rheostat, RX, then through the exciter shunt field windings, and finally back to the exciter armature. Obviously, the exciter supplies direct current to its own control field, in addition to the a-c generator field, as determined by the setting of RX. The setting of RX is controlled by the magnetic strength of the control coil L. The magnetic strength of L is, in turn, controlled by the voltage across resistor R. The voltage across R is rectified d. c., and is proportional to the a-c line voltage. (Rectifiers are devices that change a.c. to d.c.)

Thus, the essential function of the voltage regulator is to use the a-c output voltage, which it is designed to control, as a sensing influence to control the amount of current the exciter supplies to its own control field. A drop in the output a-c voltage will change the setting of RX in one direction and cause a rise in the exciter control field current. A rise in the output a-c voltage will change the setting of RX in the opposite direction and cause a drop in the exciter control field current. These latter two characteristics are caused by actions within the voltage regulator. These characteristics are common to both the resistive and magnetic (magnetic amplifier) types of a-c voltage regulators. Both types of regulators perform the same functions, but accomplish them through different operating principles. A detailed description of the construction and operating principles of any particular type of voltage regulator is best left to courses concerning specific ratings, such as the EM and AE courses.

PARALLEL OPERATION OF A-C GENERATORS

A-c generators are connected in parallel to (1) increase the plant capacity beyond that of a single unit, (2) serve as additional reserve power

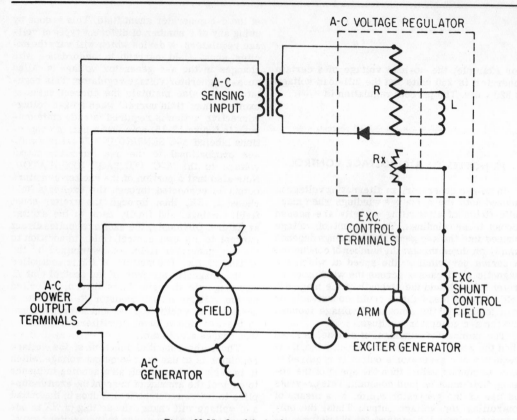

Figure 13-15.—Simplified voltage regulator circuit.

for expected demands, or (3) permit shutting down one machine and cutting in a standby machine without interrupting the power supply. When a-c generators are of sufficient size, and are operating at unequal frequencies and terminal voltages, severe damage may result if they are suddenly connected to each other through a common bus. To avoid this, the generators must be synchronized as closely as possible BEFORE connecting them together. This is done by connecting one generator to the bus (referred to as the BUS GENERATOR), and then sychronizing the other (INCOMING generator) to it before closing the incoming generator's main power contactor. The generators are synchronized when the following conditions are set:

1. Equal terminal voltages. This is obtained by adjustment of the incoming generator's field strength.

2. Equal frequency. This is obtained by adjustment of the incoming generator's prime mover speed.

3. Phase voltages in proper phase relation. (Connecting phase voltages must reach peak values of the same polarity at the same instant.) The generators could have the same frequency, and still not be IN STEP. That is, if the two generators have the same frequency, but one is lagging the other, the lagging generator will remain a fixed number of degrees behind the leading generator, until it is accelerated slightly to CATCH UP.

4. Phases connected in proper sequence. One pair of phases may be properly connected, while the other two pairs may be crossed. In this case, the phase sequence of one generator may be ACB, while the other is ABC.

Synchronizing, A-C Generators

All of the foregoing conditions may be set by the following methods:

Equal voltages may be checked by using a voltmeter. The remaining conditions, equal frequency, phase relations, and phase sequence, are checked by using either synchronizing lamps or a synchroscope. There are a number of ways in which synchronizing lamps may be connected, but the most satisfactory arrangement is the TWO-BRIGHT ONE-DARK method. This connective arrangement is shown in figure 13-16. Note that the lamps are connected directly between the incoming generator's output and the buses. In this way, the two a-c sources may be synchronized before the incoming generator's main power contactor is closed. At the instant the two generators are to be paralleled $L2$ and $L3$ will glow with maximum brilliance and $L1$ will be dark.

Assume that the incoming generator is far out of synchronism—lagging. All three lamps will appear to glow steadily, because the frequency of the voltage across them is the DIFFERENCE in the frequencies of the two generators, and thus is too high for individual alterations to be observed. As the lagging generator is accelerated, however, the lamp (differential) frequency decreases until their light flickers visibly. Their flickering will have a rotating sequence, if connections are correct, and will indicate which generator is faster.

At a point approaching synchronism, lamp $L1$ will be dark because it is connected between like phases. That is, the two phase C voltages will be so nearly synchronized that their differential voltage across $L1$ will be insufficient to make it glow visibly. However, this differential may still be of sufficient magnitude to damage the generators should they be connected at this time. The reason for cross-connecting $L2$ and $L3$ is now indicated. Under perfectly synchronized conditions, the phase voltages across $L2$ and $L3$ are both 120° apart, because of their cross-connec-

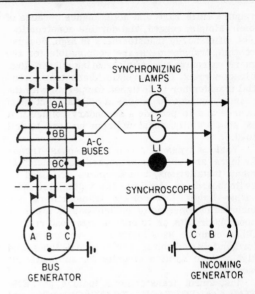

Figure 13-16.—Synchronizing lamp connection for TWO-BRIGHT ONE-DARK method.

tion, and both glow with equal brilliance. However, if the generators are not in complete synchronism, but only very near it, one of the bright lamps would be increasing in voltage as the other was decreasing. This action would cause a visible difference in the brilliance of $L2$ and $L3$. Thus, by adjusting the incoming generator's frequency so that no visible difference of brilliance exists between $L2$ and $L3$, the exact point of synchronism can be approached very closely before paralleling the incoming generator with the generator on the bus.

When the lamps have been used to get the generators as nearly synchronized as is visibly possible, the synchroscope is used to make the final FINE adjustment to the incoming generator's frequency. A synchroscope is a highly sensitive instrument used to detect a difference in frequency between two a-c sources.

Transformers

A transformer is a device that has no moving parts and that transfers energy from one circuit to another by electromagnetic induction. The energy is always transferred without a change in frequency, but usually with changes in voltage and current. A step-up transformer receives electrical energy at one voltage and delivers it at a higher voltage. Conversely, a stepdown transformer receives energy at one voltage and delivers it at a lower voltage. Transformers

233

require little care and maintenance because of their simple, rugged, and durable construction. The efficiency of transformers is high. Because of this, transformers are responsible for the more extensive use of alternating current than direct current. The conventional constant-potential transformer is designed to operate with the primary connected across a constant-potential source and to provide a secondary voltage that is substantially constant from no load to full load.

Various types of small single-phase transformers are used as shipboard equipment. In many installations, transformers are used on switchboards to stepdown the voltage for indicating lights. Low-voltage transformers are included in some motor control panels to supply control circuits or to operate overload relays. Other common uses include low-voltage supply for gunfiring circuits, special signal lights, and high-voltage ignition circuits for automatic oil burners.

Instrument transformers include POTENTIAL, or VOLTAGE, TRANSFORMERS and CURRENT TRANSFORMERS. Instrument transformers are commonly used with a-c instruments when high voltages or large currents are to be measured.

Electronic circuits and devices employ many types of transformers to provide necessary voltages for proper electron-tube operation, interstage coupling, signal amplification, and so forth. The physical construction of these transformers differs widely.

The POWER-SUPPLY TRANSFORMER used in electronic circuits is a single-phase constant-potential transformer with one or more secondary windings, or a single secondary with several tap connections. These transformers have a low volt-ampere capacity and are less efficient than large constant-potential power transformers. Most power-supply transformers for electronic equipment aboard ship are designed to operate at a frequency of 50 to 60 cycles per second. Aircraft power-supply transformers are designed for a frequency of 400 cycles per second. The higher frequencies permit a saving in size and weight of transformers and associated equipment.

CONSTRUCTION

The typical transformer has two windings insulated electrically from each other. These windings are wound on a common magnetic circuit made of laminated sheet steel. The principal parts are: (1) The CORE, which provides a circuit of low reluctance for the magnetic flux; (2) the PRIMARY WINDING, which receives the energy from the a-c source; (3) the SECONDARY WINDING, which receives the energy by mutual induction from the primary and delivers it to the load, and (4) the ENCLOSURE.

When a transformer is used to step up the voltage, the low-voltage winding is the primary. Conversely, when a transformer is used to step down the voltage, the high-voltage winding is the primary. The primary is always connected to the source of the power; the secondary is always connected to the load. It is common practice to refer to the windings as the primary and secondary rather than the high-voltage and low-voltage windings.

The principal types of transformer construction are the core type and the shell type, as illustrated respectively in figure 13-17 (A) and (B). The cores are built of thin stampings of silicon steel. Eddy currents, generated in the core by the alternating flux as it cuts through the iron, are minimized by using thin laminations and by insulating adjacent laminations with insulating varnish. Hysteresis losses, caused by the friction developed between magnetic particles as they are rotated through each cycle of magnetization, are minimized by using a special grade of heat-treated grain-oriented silicon-steel laminations.

In the core-type transformer, the copper windings surround the laminated iron core. In the shell-type transformer the iron core surrounds the copper windings. Distribution transformers are generally of the core type; whereas some of the largest power transformers are of the shell type.

If the windings of a core-type transformer were placed on separate legs of the core, a relatively large amount of the flux produced by the primary winding would fail to link the secondary winding and a large leakage flux would result. The effect of the leakage flux would be to increase the leakage reactance drop, IX_L, in both windings. To reduce the leakage flux and reactance drop, the windings are subdivided and half of each winding is placed on each leg of the core. The windings may be cylindrical in form and placed one inside the other with the necessary insulation, as shown in figure 13-17 (A). The low-voltage winding is placed with a large part

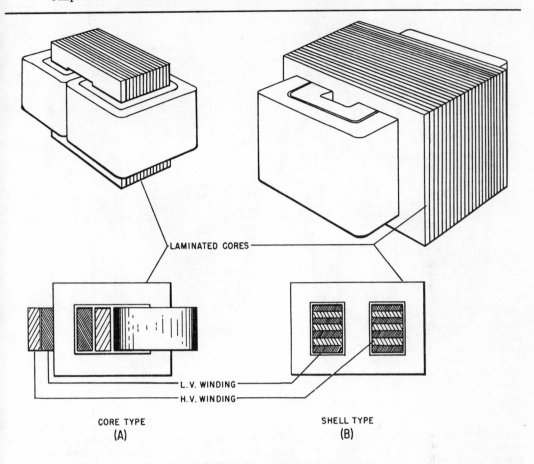

LAMINATED CORES

L.V. WINDING

H.V. WINDING

CORE TYPE
(A)

SHELL TYPE
(B)

Figure 13-17.—Types of transformer construction.

of its surface area next to the core, and the high-voltage winding is placed outside the low-voltage winding in order to reduce the insulation requirements of the two windings. If the high-voltage winding were placed next to the core, two layers of high-voltage insulation would be required, one next to the core and the other between the two windings.

In another method, the windings are built up in thin flat sections called pancake coils. These pancake coils are sandwiched together, with the required insulation between them, as shown in figure 13-17 (B).

The complete core and coil assembly (fig. 13-18 (A)) is placed in a steel tank. In commercial transformers the complete assembly is usu-ally immersed in a special mineral oil to provide a means of insulation and cooling. No oil is used in the transformer enclosures on naval vessels. Transformer banks installed in these vessels normally consist of single-phase air-cooled transformers mounted in drip-proof enclosures as shown in figure 13-18 (B).

Transformers are built in both single-phase and polyphase units. A 3-phase transformer consists of separate insulated windings for the different phases, wound on a 3-legged core capable of establishing three magnetic fluxes displaced 120° in time phase. Three-phase transformers are not installed aboard ship because the loss of a composite unit would result in an interruption to service. To insure continuity of

235

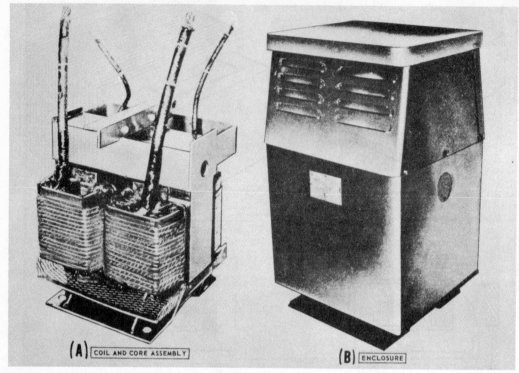

Figure 13-18.—Single-phase transformer for shipboard use.

service, three separate single-phase delta-connected transformers are installed to supply low-voltage service. If one transformer is damaged in such a system, it can be removed and the remaining two transformers can be operated in the open delta to supply the 3-phase service, but at a reduction in the original load capacity of the transformer bank. Because of the saving in space and weight, 3-phase transformers are often used in high-power airborne radar sets, and these are sometimes immersed in oil.

VOLTAGE AND CURRENT RELATIONS

The operation of the transformer is based on the principle that electrical energy can be transferred efficiently by mutual induction from one winding to another. When the primary winding is energized from an a-c source, an alternating magnetic flux is established in the transformer core. This flux links the turns of both primary and secondary, thereby inducing voltages in them. Because the same flux cuts both windings, the same voltage is induced in each turn of both windings. Hence, the total induced voltage in each winding is proportional to the number of turns in that winding. That is,

$$\frac{E_1}{E_2} = \frac{N_1}{N_2},$$

where E_1 and E_2 are the induced voltages in the primary and secondary windings, respectively, and N_1 and N_2 are the number of turns in the primary and secondary windings, respectively. In ordinary transformers the induced primary voltage is almost equal to the applied primary voltage; hence, the applied primary voltage and the secondary induced voltage are approximately proportional to the respective number of turns in the two windings.

A constant-potential single-phase transformer is represented by the schematic diagram in figure 13-19 (A). For simplicity, the primary winding is shown as being on one leg of the core and the secondary winding on the other leg. The equation for the voltage induced in one winding of the transformer is

$$E = \frac{4.44 \ BSfN,}{10^8}$$

where E is the r.m.s. voltage, B the maximum value of the magnetic flux density in lines per square inch in the core, S the cross-sectional area of the core in square inches, f the frequency in cycles per second, and N the number of complete turns in the winding.

For example, if the maximum flux density is 90,000 lines per square inch, the cross-sectional area of the core is 4.18 square inches, the frequency is 60 cycles per second, and the number of turns in the high-voltage winding is 1,100, the voltage rating of this winding is

$$E_1 = \frac{4.44 \times 90,000 \times 4.18 \times 60 \times 1,100}{10^8} = 1,100 \text{ volts.}$$

If the primary-to-secondary turns ratio of this transformer is 10 to 1, the number of turns in the low-voltage winding will be

$$\frac{1,100}{10} = 110 \text{ turns,}$$

and the voltage induced in the secondary will be

$$E_2 = \frac{1,100}{10} = 110 \text{ volts.}$$

The waveforms of the ideal transformer with no load are shown in figure 13-19 (B). When E_1 is applied to the primary winding, N_1, with the switch, S, open, the resulting current, I_0, is small and lags E_1 by almost 90° because the circuit is highly inductive. This no-load current is called the EXCITING, or MAGNETIZING, CURRENT because it supplies the magnetomotive force that produces the transformer core flux Φ. The flux produced by I_0 cuts the primary winding, N_1,

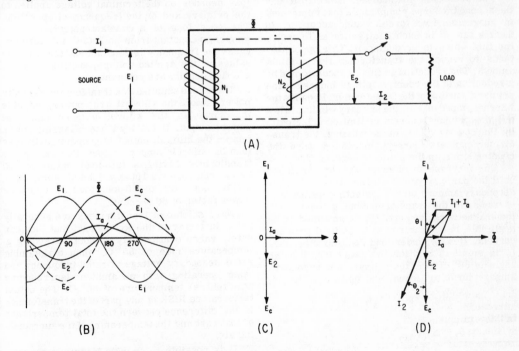

(A)

(B)   (C)   (D)

Figure 13-19.—Constant-potential transformer.

237

and induces a counter voltage E_c 180° out of phase with E_1, in this winding. The voltage, E_2, induced in the secondary winding is in phase with the induced (counter) voltage, E_c, in the primary winding, and both lag the exciting current and flux, whose variations produce them, by an angle of 90°. These relations are shown in vector form in figure 13-19 (C). The values are only approximate and are not drawn exactly to scale.

When a load is connected to the secondary by closing switch S (fig. 13-19 (A)), the secondary current I_2, depends upon the magnitude of the secondary voltage, E_2, and the load impedance, Z. For example, if E_2 is equal to 110 volts and the load impedance is 22 ohms, the secondary current will be

$$I_2 = \frac{E_2}{Z_2} = \frac{110}{22} = 5 \text{ amperes.}$$

If the secondary power factor is 86.6 percent, the phase angle, θ_2, between secondary current and voltage will be the angle whose cosine is 0.866, or 30°.

The secondary load current flowing through the secondary turns comprises a load component of magnetomotive force, which according to Lenz's law is in such a direction as to oppose the flux which is producing it. This opposition tends to reduce the transformer flux a slight amount. The reduction in flux is accompanied by a reduction in the counter voltage induced in the primary winding of the transformer. Because the internal impedance of the primary winding is low and the primary current is limited principally by the counter e.m.f. in the winding, the transformer primary current increases when the counter e.m.f. in the primary is reduced.

The increase in primary current continues until the primary ampere turns are equal to the secondary ampere turns, neglecting losses. For example, in the transformer being considered, the magnetizing current, I_0, is assumed to be negligible in comparison with the total primary current, $I_1 + I_0$, under load conditions because I_0 is small in relation to I_1 and lags it by an angle of 60°. Hence, the primary and secondary ampere turns are equal and opposite. That is,

$$N_1 I_1 = N_2 I_2.$$

In this example,

$$I_1 = \frac{N_2}{N_1} I_2 = \frac{110}{1,100} \times 5 = 0.5 \text{ ampere.}$$

Neglecting losses, the power delivered to the primary is equal to the power supplied by the secondary to the load. If the load power is P_2 = $E_2 I_2 \cos \theta_2$, or 110 x 5 (cos 30 = 0.866) = 476 watts, the power supplied to the primary is approximately $P_1 = E_1 I_1 \cos \theta$, or 110 x 0.5 (cos 30° = 0.866) = 476 watts.

The load component of primary current, I_1, increases with secondary load and maintains the transformer core flux at nearly its initial value. This action enables the transformer primary to take power from the source in proportion to the load demand, and to maintain the terminal voltage approximately constant. The lagging-power-factor load vectors are shown in figure 13-19 (D). Note that the load power factor is transferred through the transformer to the primary and that θ_2 is approximately equal to θ_1, the only difference being that θ_1 is slightly larger than θ_2 because of the presence of the exciting current which flows in the primary winding but not in the secondary.

The copper loss of a transformer varies as the square of the load current; whereas the core loss depends on the terminal voltage applied to the primary and on the frequency of operation. The core loss of a constant-potential transformer is constant from no load to full load because the frequency is constant and the effective values of the applied voltage, exciting current, and flux density are constant.

If the load supplied by a transformer has unity power factor, the kilowatt (true power) output is the same as the kilovolt-ampere (apparent power) output. If the load has a lagging power factor, the kilowatt output is proportionally less than the kilovolt-ampere output. For example, a transformer having a full-load rating of 100 kv.-a. can supply a 100-kw. load at unity power factor, but only an 80-kw. load at a lagging power factor of 80 percent.

Navy shipboard transformers are generally rated in terms of the kv.-a. load that they can safely carry continuously without exceeding a temperature rise of 80° C. when maintaining rated secondary voltage at rated frequency and when operating with an ambient (surrounding atmosphere) temperature of 40° C. The actual temperature RISE of any part of the transformer is the difference between the total temperature of that part and the temperature of the surrounding air.

It is possible to operate transformers on a higher frequency than that for which they are designed, but it is not permissable to operate them at more than 10 percent below their rated frequency, because of the resulting overheating. The exciting current in the primary varies directly with the applied voltage and, like any impedance containing inductive reactance, the exciting current varies inversely with the frequency. Thus, at reduced frequency, the exciting current becomes excessively large and the accompanying heating may damage the insulation and the windings.

EFFICIENCY

The efficiency of a transformer is the ratio of the output power at the secondary terminals to the input power at the primary terminals. It is also equal to the ratio of the output to the output plus losses. That is,

$$\text{efficiency} = \frac{\text{output}}{\text{input}} = $$

$$\frac{\text{output}}{\text{output + copper loss + core loss}}$$

The ordinary power transformer has an efficiency of 97 to 99 percent. The losses are due to the copper losses in both windings and the hysteresis and eddy-current losses in the iron core.

The copper losses vary as the square of the current in the windings and as the winding resistance. In the transformer being considered, if the primary has 1,100 turns of number 23 copper wire, having a length of 1,320 feet, the resistance of the primary winding is 26.9 ohms.

If the load current in the primary is 0.5 ampere, the primary copper loss is $(0.5)^2 \times 26.9 = 6.725$ watts. Similarly, if the secondary winding contains 110 turns of number 13 copper wire, having a length of approximately 132 feet, the secondary resistance will be 0.269 ohm. The secondary copper loss is $I_2^2 R_2$, or $(5)^2 \times 0.269 = 6.725$ watts, and the total copper loss is 6.725 x 2 = 13.45 watts.

The core losses, consisting of the hysteresis and eddy-current losses, caused by the alternating magnetic flux in the core are approximately constant from no load to full load, with rated voltage applied to the primary.

In the transformer of figure 13-19 (A), if the core loss is 10.6 watts and the copper loss is 13.4 watts, the efficiency is

$$\frac{\text{output}}{\text{output + copper loss + core loss}} = $$

$$\frac{476}{476 + 13.4 + 10.6} = \frac{476}{500} = 0.952,$$

or 95.2 percent. The rating of the transformer is

$$\frac{E_1 I_1}{1,000} = \frac{1,100 \times 0.5}{1,000} = 0.55 \text{ kv.-a.}$$

The efficiency of this transformer is relatively low because it is a small transformer and the losses are disproportionately large.

POLARITY MARKING OF TRANSFORMERS

Standard polarity markings and transformer lead color coding are covered in chapter 20 of this course.

SINGLE-PHASE CONNECTIONS

Single-phase distribution transformers usually have their windings divided into two or more sections, as shown in figure 13-20. When the two secondary windings are connected in series (fig. 13-20 (A)), their voltages add. In figure 13-20 (B), the two secondary windings are connected in parallel, and their currents add. For example, if each secondary winding is rated at 115 volts and 100 amperes, the series-connection output rating will be 230 volts at 100 amperes, or 23 kv.-a.; the parallel-connection output rating will be 115 volts at 200 amperes, or 23 kv.-a.

In the series connection, care must be taken to connect the coils so that their voltages add. The proper arrangement is indicated in the figure. A trace made through the secondary circuits from X_1 to X_4 is in the same direction as that of the arrows representing the maximum positive voltages.

In the parallel connection, care must be taken to connect the coils so that their voltages are in opposition. The correct connection is indicated in the figure. The direction of a trace made through the secondary windings from X_1 to X_2 to X_4 to X_3 and returning to X_1 is the same as that of the arrow in the right-hand winding. This condition indicates that the secondary voltages have their positive maximum values in directions opposite to each other in the closed circuit, which is formed by paralleling the two secondary windings. Thus, no circulating current will flow in these windings on no load. If either winding were reversed, a short-circuit current would flow in the secondary, and this would cause the primary to draw a short-circuit current from the source. This action would, of course, damage the transformer as well as the source.

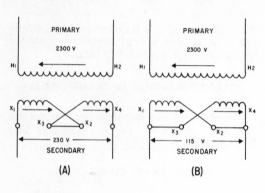

Figure 13-20.—Single-phase transformer secondary connections.

THREE-PHASE CONNECTIONS

Power may be supplied through 3-phase circuits containing transformers in which the primaries and secondaries are connected in various wye and delta combinations. For example, three single-phase transformers may supply 3-phase power with four possible combinations of their primaries and secondaries. These connections are: (1) primaries in delta and secondaries in delta, (2) primaries in wye and secondaries in wye, (3) primaries in wye and secondaries in delta, (4) primaries in delta and secondaries in wye.

Delta and wye connections were described earlier in this chapter under the subject "Three-Phase Generators," and the relations between line and phase voltages and currents were also described. These relations apply to transformers as well as to a-c generators.

If the primaries of three single-phase transformers are properly connected (either in wye or delta) to a 3-phase source, the secondaries may be connected in delta, as shown in figure 13-21. A topographic vector diagram of the 3-phase secondary voltages is shown in figure

13-21 (A). The vector sum of these three voltages is zero. This may be seen by combining any two vectors, for example, E_A and E_B, and noting that their sum is equal and opposite to the 3rd vector, E_C. A voltmeter inserted within the delta will indicate zero voltage, as shown in figure 13-21 (B), when the windings are connected properly.

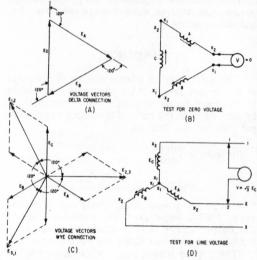

Figure 13-21.—Delta-connected transformer secondaries.

Assuming all three transformers have the same polarity, the delta connection consists in connecting the X_2 lead of winding A to the X_1 lead of B, the X_2 lead of B to X_1 of C, and the X_2 lead of C to X_1 of A. If any one of the three windings is reversed with respect to the other two windings, the total voltage within the delta will equal twice the value of one phase; and if the delta is closed on itself, the resulting current will be of short-circuit magnitude, with resulting damage to the transformer windings and cores. The delta should never be closed until a test is first made to determine that the voltage within the delta is zero or nearly zero. This may be done with a voltmeter, fuse wire, or test lamp. In the figure, when the voltmeter is inserted between the X_2 lead of A and the X_1 lead of B, the delta circuit is completed through the voltmeter, and the indication should be approximately zero. Then the delta is completed by connecting the X_2 lead of A to the X_1 lead of B.

If the three secondaries of an energized transformer bank are properly connected in delta

240

and are supplying a balanced 3-phase load, the line current will be equal to 1.73 times the phase current. If the rated current of a phase (winding) is 100 amperes, the rated line current will be 173 amperes. If the rated voltage of a phase is 120 volts, the voltage between any two line wires will be 120 volts.

The three secondaries of the transformer bank may be reconnected in wye in order to increase the output voltage. The voltage vectors are shown in figure 13-21 (C). If the phase voltage is 120 volts, the line voltage will be 1.73 x 120 = 208 volts. The line voltages are represented by vectors, $E_{1,2}$, $E_{2,3}$, and $E_{3,1}$. A voltmeter test for the line voltage is represented in figure 13-21 (D). If the three transformers have the same polarity, the proper connections for a wye-connected secondary bank are indicated in the figure. The X_1 leads are connected to form a common or neutral connection and the X_2 leads of the three secondaries are brought out to the line leads. If the connections of any one winding are reversed, the voltages between the 3 line wires will become unbalanced, and the loads will not receive their proper magnitude of load current. Also the phase angle between the line currents will be changed, and they will no longer be 120° out of phase with each other. Therefore, it is important to properly connect the transformer secondaries in order to preserve the symmetry of the line voltages and currents.

Transformer installations aboard naval vessels usually consist of 450/117-volt delta-connected banks to supply the general lighting circuits and service for the interior-communications and fire control circuits. Some ships also include 450/230-volt delta-connected banks to supply the galley equipment. Power is distributed over an ungrounded 3-wire, 3-phase, 450-volt system.

Three single-phase transformers with both primary and secondary windings delta connected are shown in figure 13-22. The H_1 lead of one phase is always connected to the H_2 lead of an adjacent phase, the X_1 lead is connected to the X_2 terminal of the corresponding adjacent phase, and so on; and the line connections are made at these junctions. This arrangement is based on the assumption that the three transformers have the same polarity.

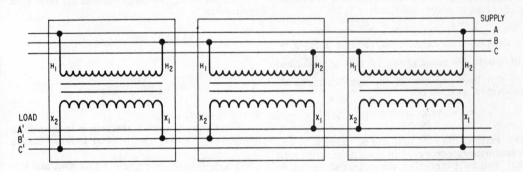

Figure 13-22.—Delta-delta transformer connections.

An open-delta connection results when any one of the three transformers is removed from the delta-connected transformer bank without disturbing the 3-wire 3-phase connections to the remaining two transformers. These transformers will maintain the correct voltage and phase relations on the secondary to supply a balanced 3-phase load. An open-delta connection is shown in figure 13-23. The 3-phase source supplies the primaries of the two transformers, and the secondaries supply a 3-phase voltage to the load.

The LINE CURRENT is equal to the transformer PHASE CURRENT in the open-delta connection. In the closed-delta connection, the transformer phase current, $I_{phase} = \dfrac{I_{line}}{\sqrt{3}}$. Thus, when one transformer is removed from a delta-connected bank of three transformers, the remaining two transformers will carry a current equal to $\sqrt{3}\ I_{phase}$. This value amounts to an overload current on each transformer of 1.73 times the rated current, or an overload of 73.2 percent.

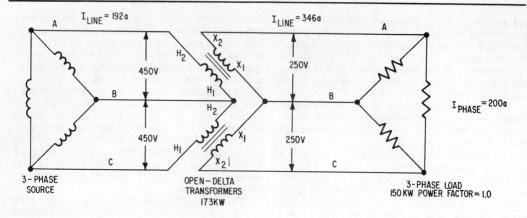

Figure 13-23.—Open-delta transformer connection.

Thus, in an open-delta connection, the line current must be reduced so as not to exceed the rated current of the individual transformers if they are not to be overloaded. The open-delta connection therefore results in a reduction in system capacity. The full-load capacity in a delta connection at unity power factor is

$$P_\Delta = 3I_{phase} E_{phase} = \sqrt{3}E_{line} I_{line}.$$

In an open-delta connection, the line current is limited to the rated phase current of $\frac{I_{line}}{\sqrt{3}}$, and the full-load capacity of the open-delta, or V-connected, system is

$$P_v = \sqrt{3}E_{line} \frac{I_{line}}{\sqrt{3}} = E_{line} I_{line}.$$

The ratio of the load that can be carried by two transformers connected in open delta to the load that can be carried by three transformers in closed delta is

$$\frac{P_v}{P_\Delta} = \frac{E_{line} I_{line}}{\sqrt{3}E_{line} I_{line}} = \frac{1}{\sqrt{3}} = 0.577, \text{ or } 57.7 \text{ percent}$$

of the closed-delta rating.

For example, a 150-kw. 3-phase balanced load operating at unity power factor is supplied at 250 volts. The rating of each of three transformers in closed delta is $\frac{150}{3}$ = 50 kw., and the phase current is $\frac{50,000}{250}$ = 200 amperes. The line current is 200$\sqrt{3}$=346 amperes. If one transformer is removed from the bank, the remaining

two transformers would be overloaded 346 - 200 =146 amperes, or $\frac{146}{200}$ x 100 =73 percent. To prevent overload on the remaining two transformers, the line current must be reduced from 346 amperes to 200 amperes and the total load reduced to

$$\frac{\sqrt{3} \times 250 \times 200}{1,000} = 86.6 \text{ kw.,}$$

or

$$\frac{86.6}{150} \times 100 = 57.7 \text{ percent}$$

of the original load.

The rating of each transformer in open delta necessary to supply the original 150-kw. load is $\frac{E_{phase} I_{phase}}{1,000}$, or $\frac{250 \times 346}{1,000}$ = 86.6 kw., and two transformers require a total rating of 2 x 86.6 = 173.2 kw., compared with 150 kw. for three transformers in closed delta. The required increase in transformer capacity is 173.2 - 150 =23.2 kw., or $\frac{23.2}{150}$ x 100 = 15.5 percent, when two transformers are used in open delta to supply the same load as three 50-kw. transformers in closed delta.

Three single-phase transformers with both primary and secondary windings wye connected are shown in figure 13-24. Only 57.7 percent of the line voltage ($\frac{E_{line}}{\sqrt{3}}$) is impressed across each

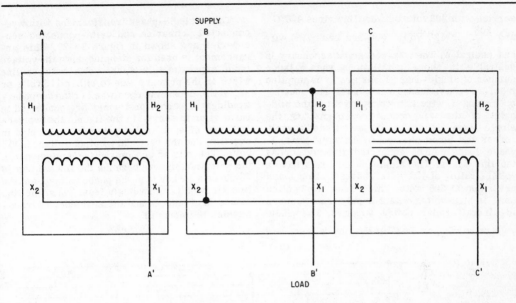

Figure 13-24.—Wye-wye transformer connections.

winding, but full-line current flows in each transformer winding. Although the wye-wye connection is never used aboard ship, it is frequently used in Navy shore installations.

Three single-phase transformers delta connected to the primary circuit and wye connected to the secondary circuit are shown in figure 13-25. This connection provides 4-wire, 3-phase

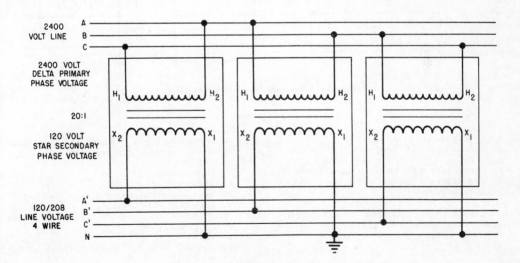

Figure 13-25.—Delta-wye transformer connections.

service with 208 volts between line wires $A'B'C'$, and $\frac{208}{\sqrt{3}}$, or 120 volts, between each line wire and neutral N. The wye-connected secondary is desirable in shore installations when a large number of single-phase loads are to be supplied from a 3-phase transformer bank. The neutral, or grounded, wire is brought out from the midpoint of the wye connection, permitting the single-phase loads to be distributed evenly across the three phases. At the same time, 3-phase loads can be connected directly across the line wires. The single-phase loads have a voltage rating of 120 volts, and the 3-phase loads are rated at 208 volts. This connection is often used in high-voltage plate-supply transformers in aircraft radar power supplies. The phase voltage is $\frac{1}{1.73}$, or 0.577 of the line voltage.

Three single-phase transformers with wye-connected primaries and delta-connected secondaries are shown in figure 13-26. This arrangement is used for stepping down the voltage from approximately 4,000 volts between line wires on the primary side to either 115 volts or 230 volts, depending upon whether the secondary windings of each transformer are connected in parallel or in series. In the figure, the two secondaries of each transformer are connected in parallel, and the secondary output voltage is 115 volts. There is an economy in transmission with the primaries in wye because the line voltage is 73 percent higher than the phase voltage, and the line current is accordingly less. Thus, the line losses are reduced and the efficiency of transmission is improved.

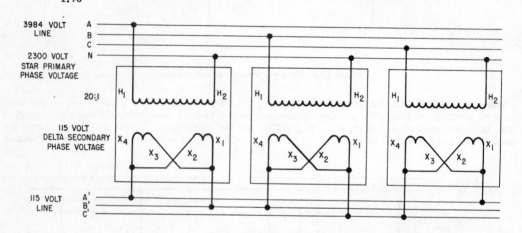

Figure 13-26.—Wye-delta transformer connections.

QUIZ

1. An a-c armature is always the
   a. rotating part of the generator
   b. stationary part of the generator
   c. conductors into which voltage is induced
   d. conductors through which d-c exciter current flows

2. The armature windings of a 2-phase a-c generator are physically placed so that the induced voltages are out of phase by
   a. 30°
   b. 60°
   c. 90°
   d. 120°

3. When connecting a 3-phase a-c generator for delta operation, the delta closure voltage should be
   a. line voltage
   b. phase voltage
   c. approximately zero volts
   d. less than phase voltage

4. With no load on the secondary, the current in the primary is
   a. zero
   b. limited only by the resistance of the winding
   c. determined by c.e.m.f. of secondary
   d. determined by c.e.m.f. of primary

5. The a-c field is always the
a. rotating part of the generator
b. stationary part of the generator
c. conductors into which voltage is induced
d. conductors through which d-c exciter current flows

6. The voltage induced into the armature windings is maximum when the field poles are
a. in the neutral plane
b. opposite the armature poles
c. between the armature poles
d. rotating at a high speed

7. The output frequency of an a-c generator is dependent upon the
a. number of poles and phases
b. rotor speed and phases
c. number of poles and the speed of the prime mover
d. number of poles and the rotor speed

8. The load rating of an a-c generator is determined by the
a. internal heat it can withstand
b. load it can carry continuously
c. load it is capable of supplying
d. overload it can carry for a specified time only

9. In a 2-phase 3-wire a-c generator, the formula for line voltage is
a. $E_L = \dfrac{E_p}{\cos 45°}$

b. $E_L = \dfrac{E_p}{\tan 45°}$

c. $E_L = E_p \times 0.707$

d. $E_L = E_p \times 1.73$

10. The voltage output of an a-c generator is controlled by
a. regulating the speed of the prime mover
b. varying the d-c exciter voltage
c. varying the reluctance of the air gap
d. shorting out part of the armature windings

11. The primary reason for connecting transformers wye-wye is to
a. double the input voltage
b. double the primary current
c. invert the frequency
d. decrease line losses by high voltage with low current in the line

12. The purpose of the d-c generator is to excite the
a. a-c armature
b. a-c field
c. d-c armature
d. a-c and d-c field

13. A 3-phase wye-connected a-c generator is used to produce
a. high current, low voltage
b. low current, low voltage
c. low current, high voltage
d. high current, high voltage

14. Two types of instrument transformers are
a. step-up and step-down
b. potential and high voltage
c. potential and current
d. auto and power

15. The output of a rotating field a-c generator is taken from
a. sliprings and brushes
b. commutator bars and brushes
c. fixed terminals
d. none of the above

16. Aircraft transformers are designed for 400 c.p.s. because
a. of the 400-c.p.s. supply available in the aircraft
b. the higher frequency permits savings of size and weight
c. it is more stable than lower frequencies
d. it has a higher average current flow

17. The closure voltage of a delta-connected transformer secondary is
a. 0 volts
b. phase voltage
c. line voltage
d. line voltage x 1.73

18. The revolving field type a-c generator is most widely used because of
a. low armature current
b. improved safety features
c. low field current through fixed terminals
d. high power from armature through sliprings

19. When using an a-c generator on a 3-phase 4-wire system, the neutral wire
a. maintains equal current in each phase
b. maintains equal power in each phase
c. maintains equal voltage in each phase
d. has no current flow when the loads are unbalanced

20. The three principal parts of a transformer are its
a. core, primary windings, and secondary windings
b. primary, load, and magnetic flux
c. primary windings, secondary windings, and magnetic flux
d. mutual induction, magnetic flux, and windings

21. A-c generators are classified
a. as to construction
b. as to power output
c. according to type of prime mover
d. according to load connections

22. The principle of operation of a transformer is
a. electromagnetic induction
b. varying a conductor in a magnetic field
c. mutual induction
d. thermionic emission

CHAPTER 14

ALTERNATING-CURRENT MOTORS

Most of the power generating systems ashore and afloat produce alternating current. Thus, it follows that a great majority of the motors used throughout the Navy are designed to operate on alternating current. However, there are other advantages in the use of a-c motors besides the wide availability of a-c power. In general, a-c motors are less expensive than d-c motors. Some types of a-c motors do not employ brushes and commutators. This eliminates many problems of maintenance and wear; in addition, it eliminates the problem of dangerous sparking.

D-c motors are best suited for some uses, such as applications that require variable-speed motors. However, in the great majority of applications, the a-c motor is best.

A-c motors are manufactured in many different sizes, shapes, and ratings, for use on an even greater number of jobs. They are designed for use with either polyphase or single-phase power systems.

This chapter cannot possibly cover all aspects of the subject of a-c motors. Consequently, it will deal mainly with the operating principles of only the two most common types—the rotating-field induction motor and the synchronous motor.

The Rotating Field

The rotating field is set up by out-of-phase currents in the stator windings. Figure 14-1 illustrates the manner in which a rotating field is produced by stationary coils, or windings, when they are supplied by a 3-phase current source. For purpose of explanation, rotation of the field is developed in the figure by "stopping" it at six selected positions, or instants. These instants are marked off at 60 degree intervals on the sine waves representing currents in the three phases A, B, and C.

At instant 1 the current in phase B is maximum positive. (Assume plus 10 amperes in this example.) Current is considered to be positive when it is flowing out from a motor terminal, and negative when it flows into a motor terminal. At the same time (instant 1) current flows into the A and C terminals at half value (minus 5 amperes each in this case). These currents combine at the neutral (common connection) to supply plus 10 amperes out through the B phase.

The resulting field at instant 1 is established downward and to the right as shown by the arrow NS. The major portion of this field is produced by the B phase (full strength at this time) and is aided by the adjacent phases A and C (half strength). The weaker portions of the field are indicated by the letters "n" and "s". The field is a two-pole field extending across the space that would normally contain the rotor.

At instant 2 the current in phase B is reduced to half value (plus 5 amperes in this example). The current in phase C has reversed its flow from minus 5 amperes to plus 5 amperes, and the current in phase A has increased from minus 5 to minus 10 amperes.

The resulting field at instant 2 is now established upward and to the right as shown by arrow NS. The major portion of the field is produced by phase A (full strength) and the weaker portions by phases B and C (half strength).

At instant 3 the current in phase C is plus 10 amperes and the field extends vertically upward; at instant 4 the current in phase B becomes minus 10 amperes and the field extends upward and to the left; at instant 5 the current in phase A becomes plus 10 amperes and the field extends downward and to the left; at instant 6 the current in phase C is minus 10 amperes and the field extends vertically downward. Instant 7 (not shown) corresponds to instant 1 when the field again extends downward and to the right.

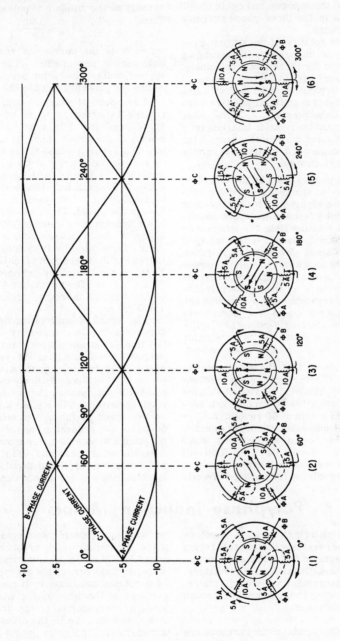

Figure 14-1.—Development of a rotating field.

Thus a full rotation of the two-pole field has been accomplished through one full cycle of 360 electrical degrees of the three-phase currents flowing in the windings.

The direction of rotation of the magnetic revolving field may be changed by interchanging any two line leads to the three motor terminals. For example, in figure 14-2 (A), if line 1 connects to phase a, line 2 to phase b, and line 3 to phase c, and the line currents reach their positive maximum values in the sequence 1, 2, 3, the phase sequence is a, b, c and the rotation is arbitrarily clockwise. If lines 1 and 2 are interchanged, the phase sequence becomes b, a, c, and the revolving field turns counterclockwise.

Most induction motors used by the Navy are designed to operate on single-phase power supplies, or the 3-phase supply used in the preceding discussion. The out-of-phase currents necessary to produce a rotating field are inherent in the 2-phase power supply, since 2-phase voltages are generated 90° apart. When a single-phase supply is used, it is necessary to split the power supply into two separate coil groups. The required phase difference is then generally obtained by inserting capacitance in series with one of the groups (other methods are sometimes used). This causes the single-phase or ''split-phase'' motor to have characteristics similar in many respects to the true 2-phase motor.

In figure 14-1, note that the sine waves of current traversed 300° through the six positions shown. Accordingly, the field rotated 300°. If the supplied current completes 60 cycles each second, the field would rotate at 60 revolutions per second (60 x 60 = 3,600 revolutions per minute). However, if the number of stator coils were doubled, producing a 4-pole field, the field will rotate only half as fast. Thus, it can be seen that the speed of the revolving field varies directly

as the frequency of the applied voltage and inversely as the number of poles.

Thus,

$$N = \frac{120f}{P},$$

where N is the number of revolutions that the field makes per minute, f the frequency of the applied voltage in cycles per second, and P the number of poles produced by the 3-phase winding.

The speed at which an induction motor field rotates is referred to as its SYNCHRONOUS speed, because it is synchronized to the frequency of the power supply at all times. A motor having a 2-pole 3-phase stator winding connected to a 60-cycle source has a synchronous speed (magnetic revolving field speed) of 3,600 r.p.m. A 2-pole 25-cycle motor has a synchronous speed of 1,500 r.p.m. Increasing the number of poles lowers the speed. Thus, a 4-pole 25-cycle motor has a synchronous speed of 750 r.p.m. A 12-pole 60-cycle motor has a synchronous speed of 600 r.p.m. Increasing the frequency of the line supply increases the speed with which the field revolves. Thus, if the frequency is increased from 50 to 60 cycles, and the motor has 4 poles, the speed of the field is increased from 1,500 r.p.m. to 1,800 r.p.m.

The speed of the rotating field is always independent of load changes on the motor, provided the line frequency is maintained constant. The magnetic revolving field always runs at the same speed, pole for pole, as the a-c generator supplying it. If a 2-pole 60-cycle a-c generator supplies a 2-pole motor, the motor has a synchronous speed of 3,600 r.p.m. which is the same as the speed of the a-c generator. If a 4-pole 60-cycle a-c generator runs at 1,800 r.p.m. and supplies a 4-pole 60-cycle motor, the motor has a synchronous speed of 1,800 r.p.m. If this same a-c generator supplies an 8-pole 60-cycle motor, the motor has a synchronous speed of 900 r.p.m.

Polyphase Induction Motors

The driving torque of both d-c and a-c motors is derived from the reaction of current-carrying conductors in a magnetic field. In the d-c motor, the magnetic field is stationary and the armature, with its current-carrying conductors, rotates. The current is supplied to the armature through a commutator and brushes.

In induction motors, the rotor currents are supplied by electro-magnetic induction. The sta-

tor windings contain two or more out-of-time-phase currents, which produce corresponding m.m.f.'s. These m.m.f.'s establish a rotating magnetic field across the air gap. This magnetic field rotates continuously at constant speed regardless of the load on the motor. The stator winding corresponds to the armature winding of a d-c motor or to the primary winding of a transformer. The rotor is not connected electrically to the power supply. The induction motor

248

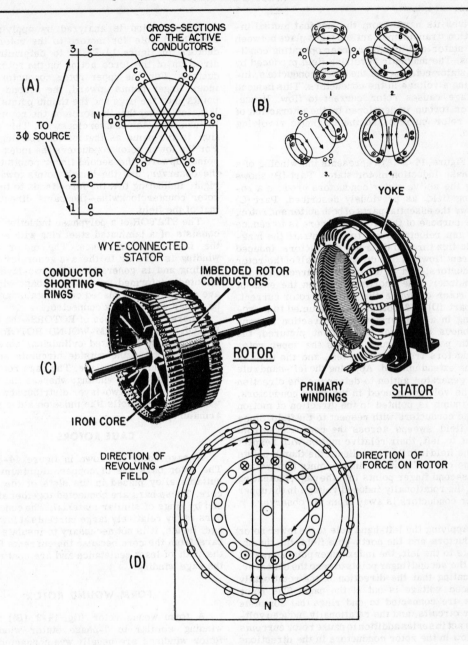

DIRECTION OF ROTATION
OF ROTOR AND FIELD

Figure 14-2.—Three-phase induction motor.

derives its name from the fact that mutual induction (transformer action) takes place between the stator and the rotor under operating conditions. The magnetic revolving field produced by the stator cuts across the rotor conductors, inducing a voltage in the conductors. This induced voltage causes rotor current to flow. Hence, motor torque is developed by the interaction of the rotor current and the magnetic revolving field.

Figure 14-2 (A) represents the winding of a 3-phase induction motor stator. Part (B) shows how the active stator conductors produce a rotating field, as previously described. Part (C) shows the essential parts of both stator and rotor. The purpose of the iron rotor core is to reduce air gap reluctance and to concentrate the magnetic flux through the rotor conductors. Induced current flows in one direction in half of the rotor conductors, and in the opposite direction in the remainder. The shorting rings on the ends of the rotor complete the path for rotor current. In part (D) a 2-pole field is assumed to be rotating in a counterclockwise direction at synchronous speed. At the instant pictured, the south pole field cuts across the upper rotor conductors from right to left, and the lines of force extend upward. Applying the left-hand rule for generator action to determine the direction of the voltage induced in the rotor conductors, the thumb is pointed in the direction of motion of the conductors with respect to the field. Since the field sweeps across the conductors from right to left, their relative motion with respect to the field is to the right. Hence the thumb points to the right. The index finger points upward and the second finger points into the page, indicating that the rotationally induced voltage in the upper rotor conductors is away from the observer.

Applying the left-hand rule to the lower rotor conductors and the north-pole field, the thumb points to the left, the index finger points upward, and the second finger points toward the observer, indicating that the direction of the rotationally induced voltage is out of the page. The rotor bars are connected to end rings that complete their circuits, and the rotationally induced voltages act in series addition to cause rotor currents to flow in the rotor conductors in the directions indicated. For simplification, the rotor currents are assumed to be in phase with the rotor voltages.

Motor action is analyzed by applying the right-hand rule for motors to the rotor conductors in figure 14-2 (D), to determine the direction of the force acting on the rotor conductors. For the upper rotor conductors, the index finger points upward, the second finger points into the page and the thumb points to the left, indicating that the force on the rotor tends to turn the rotor counterclockwise. This direction is the same as that of the rotating field. For the lower rotor conductors the index finger points upward, the second finger points toward the observer, and the thumb points toward the right, indicating that the force tends to turn the rotor counterclockwise—the same direction as that of the field.

The STATOR of a polyphase induction motor consists of a laminated steel ring with slots on the inside circumference. The motor stator winding is similar to the a-c generator stator winding and is generally of the two-layer distributed preformed type. Stator phase windings are symmetrically placed on the stator and may be either wye or delta connected.

There are two types of ROTORS—the CAGE ROTOR and the FORM-WOUND ROTOR. Both types have a laminated cylindrical core with parallel slots in the outside circumference to hold the windings in place. The cage rotor has an uninsulated bar winding; whereas the form-wound rotor has a two-layer distributed winding with preformed coils like those on a d-c motor armature.

CAGE ROTORS

A cage rotor is shown in figure 14-3 (A). The rotor bars are of copper, aluminum, or a suitable alloy placed in the slots of the rotor core. These bars are connected together at each end by rings of similar material. The conductor bars carry relatively large currents at low voltage. Hence, it is not necessary to insulate these bars from the core because the currents follow the path of least resistance and are confined to the cage winding.

FORM-WOUND ROTOR

A form-wound rotor (fig. 14-3 (B)) has a winding similar to 3-phase stator windings. Rotor windings are usually wye connected with the free ends of the winding connected to three slip rings mounted on the rotor shaft. An external variable wye-connected resistance (fig.

(A) CAGE ROTOR   (B) FORM-WOUND ROTOR

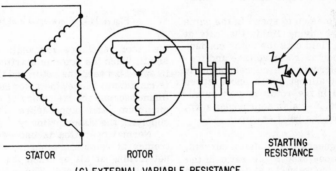

STATOR   ROTOR   STARTING RESISTANCE

(C) EXTERNAL VARIABLE RESISTANCE

Figure 14-3.—Induction motor rotors.

14-3 (C)) is connected to the rotor circuit through the sliprings. The variable resistance provides a means of increasing the rotor-circuit resistance during the starting period to produce a high starting torque. As the motor accelerates, the rheostat is cut out. When the motor reaches full speed, the sliprings are short-circuited and the operation is similar to that of the cage motor.

TORQUE

As previously described, the revolving field produced by the stator windings cuts the rotor conductors and induces voltages in the conductors. Rotor currents flow because the rotor end-rings provide continuous metallic circuits.

The resulting torque tends to turn the rotor in the direction of the rotating field. This torque is proportional to the product of the rotor current, the field strength, and the rotor power factor.

The simplified cross section of a 2-pole cage-rotor motor is shown in figure 14-4. The magnetic field is rotating in a clockwise direction. Applying the left-hand rule for generator action, note that in figure 14-4 (A), the induced currents flow outward in the upper half and inward in the lower half of the rotor conductors. Applying the right-hand rule for motor action, note that the force acting on the rotor conductors is to the right on the upper group and to the left on the lower group.

251

As previously stated, a d-c motor receives its armature current by means of conduction through the commutator and brushes; whereas an induction motor receives its rotor current by means of induction. In this respect the induction motor is like a transformer with a rotating secondary. The primary is the stator which produces the revolving field; the secondary is the rotor. At start, the frequency of the rotor current is that of the primary stator winding. The reactance of the rotor is relatively large compared with its resistance, and the power factor is low and lagging by almost 90°. The rotor current therefore lags the rotor voltage by approximately 90°, as shown in figure 14-4(B). Because almost half of the conductors under the south pole carry current outward and the remainder of the conductors carry current inward, the net torque on the rotor as a result of the interaction between the rotor and the rotating field is small.

As the rotor comes up to speed in the same direction as the revolving field, the rate at which the revolving field cuts the rotor conductors is reduced and the rotor voltage and frequency of rotor currents are correspondingly reduced. Hence, at almost synchronous speed the voltage induced in the rotor is very small. The rotor reactance, X_L, also approaches zero, as may be seen from the relationship

$$X_L = 2\pi f_o LS,$$

where f_o is the frequency of the stator current, L the rotor inductance, and S the ratio of the difference in speed (between the stator field and the rotor) to the synchronous speed—that is, the slip. Slip is expressed mathematically as

$$S = \frac{N_s - N_r}{N_s},$$

where N_s is the number of revolutions per minute of the stator field, and N_r the number of revolutions per minute of the rotor. The frequency of the induced rotor current is $f_o S$.

In figure 14-4 (A), the rotor current is nearly in phase with the rotor voltage, and the direction of flow under the south pole is the same in all conductors. The torque would be ideally high except for the very small rotor current, which is produced by the low rotor voltage. The rotor voltage is proportional to the difference in speed between the rotor and the rotating field —that is, proportional to the slip.

The frequency of the rotor current varies directly with the slip. Thus, when the slip and the frequency of rotor current are almost zero,

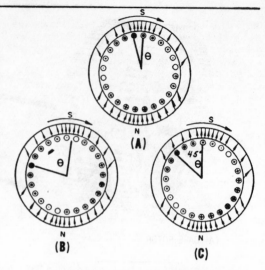

Figure 14-4.—Development of torque.

the rotor reactance and angle of lag are very small. When the rotor is starting, the difference in speed between the rotor and the rotating field is maximum; hence, the rotor reactance is maximum because the frequency of rotor current is maximum and approaches that of the line supplying the stator primary.

Normal operation is between these two extremes of rotor slip—that is, when the rotor is not turning at all or when it is turning almost at synchronous speed. The motor speed under normal load conditions is rarely more than 10 percent below synchronous speed. At the extreme of 100 percent slip, the rotor reactance is so high that the torque is low because of low power factor. At the other extreme of zero rotor slip, the torque is low because of low rotor current. The equation for torque, T, is

$$T = K \Phi I_r \cos \theta_r,$$

Where K is a constant, Φ the strength of the magnetic revolving field, I_r the rotor current, and $\cos \theta_r$ the power factor of the rotor current.

In the previous formula the product of rotor current and rotor power factor for a given strength of magnetic revolving field is a maximum value when the phase angle between rotor current and rotor induced voltage is 45° lagging, as indicated in figure 14-4, (C). In this case the reactance of the rotor equals the resistance of the rotor circuit, and the rotor power factor is 70.7 percent. This condition of operation is called the PULL-OUT POINT. Beyond this point, the motor speed falls off rapidly with added load, and the motor stalls.

Variations in applied stator voltage affect the motor torque. This applied voltage establishes m.m.f.'s which create the rotating field. The rotating field, in turn, establishes the rotor current. Because rotor torque varies as the product of these factors, the torque of an induction motor varies as the square of the voltage applied to the stator primary winding.

The rotating field also sweeps across the stator winding which produces it. This action induces a counter e.m.f. in the winding. The counter e.m.f. opposes the applied voltage and limits the stator currents. If the applied voltage is increased to magnetic saturation, the counter e.m.f. is limited, and the primary current becomes dangerously high.

SYNCHRONOUS SPEED AND SLIP

The speed, N, of the rotating field is called the SYNCHRONOUS SPEED of the motor. As previously stated, the torque on the rotor tends to turn the rotor in the same direction as the revolving field. If the motor is not driving a load, it will accelerate to nearly the same speed as the revolving field. During the starting period, the increase in rotor speed is accompanied by a decrease in induced rotor voltage because the relative motion between the rotating field and rotor conductors is less. If it were possible for the rotor to attain synchronous speed there would be no relative motion between the rotor and the rotating field. There would then be no induced e.m.f. in the rotor, no rotor current, and thus no torque.

It is obvious that an induction motor cannot run at exactly synchronous speed. Instead, the rotor always runs just enough below synchronous speed at no load to establish sufficient rotor current to produce a torque equal to the resisting torque that is caused by the rotor losses.

The frequency of the alternating voltage induced in the rotor depends on the speed of the revolving field with respect to the rotor. One cycle of alternating voltage is induced in the rotor when the stator field sweeps completely around the rotor once. The rotor frequency, f_r, is directly proportional to the percent slip—

$$f_r = \frac{Sf_s}{100}$$

where S is the percent slip and f_s is the frequency of the supply. For example, if the frequency of the supply is 60 cycles per second and the slip is 5 percent, the rotor frequency will be $\frac{5 \times 60}{100} = 3$ cycles per second. The frequency and magnitude of the induced rotor voltage decrease as the rotor speed increases. Both the rotor voltage and frequency would become zero if the rotor could attain synchronous speed.

LOSSES AND EFFICIENCY

The losses of an induction motor include (1) stator copper loss, $I_s^2 R_s$, and rotor copper loss, $I_r^2 R_r$; (2) stator and rotor core loss; and (3) friction and windage loss. For all practical purposes, the core, bearing friction, and windage losses are considered to be constant for all loads of an induction motor having a small slip. The power output may be measured on a mechanical brake or calculated from a knowledge of the input and the losses. The efficiency is equal to the ratio of the output power to input power; and at full load, it varies from about 85 percent for small motors to more than 90 percent for large motors.

CHARACTERISTICS OF THE CAGE-ROTOR MOTOR

As stated previously, the cage-rotor induction motor is comparable to a transformer with a rotating secondary. At no load, the magnetic revolving field produced by the primary stator winding cuts the turns of the stator winding. This action generates a counter e.m.f. in the stator winding, which limits the line current to a small value. This no-load value is called EXCITING CURRENT. Its function is to maintain the revolving field. Because the circuit is highly inductive, the power factor of the motor with no load is very poor. It may be as much as 30 percent lagging. Because there is no drag on the rotor, it runs at almost synchronous speed and the rotor current is quite small. Hence, the reaction of the rotor m.m.f. on the primary revolving field is small.

When load is added to the motor, the rotor slows down slightly; but the rotating field continues at synchronous speed. Therefore, the rotor current and slip increase. The motor torque increases more than the decrease in speed and the power output increases. The increased rotor m.m.f. opposes the primary field flux and lowers it slightly. The primary counter e.m.f. therefore decreases slightly and primary current increases. The load component of primary current maintains the rotating field and prevents its further weakening because of the rotor-current opposition. Because of the relatively low internal impedance of the motor windings, a small reduction in speed and counter e.m.f. in the primary may be accompanied by large increases in motor current, torque, and power output. Thus, the cage-rotor motor has essentially constant-speed variable-torque characteristics.

If the induction motor is stalled by overload, the resulting increased rotor current lowers the primary counter e.m.f. and causes excessive primary current. This excessive current may damage the motor winding. When the rotor of an induction motor is locked, the voltage applied to the primary winding should not exceed 50 percent of its rated voltage.

When the motor is operating at full load, the load component of stator current is more nearly in phase with the voltage across each stator phase because of the mechanical output (true power component) of the motor. The power factor is considerably improved over the no-load condition.

The torque and current curves for a 3-phase induction motor with cage rotor are shown in figure 14-5 (A). Rotor reactance increases with slip and increasingly affects the rotor current and power factor as the motor load is increased. The pull-out point on the torque curve occurs at about 25 percent slip. Maximum torque at this condition is about 3.5 times the normal full-load value, and, as previously mentioned, corresponds to a rotor power factor of 70.7 percent. Thus, for the pull-out condition, the rotor resistance equals the rotor reactance and the rotor power factor angle equals 45°. Any additional load on the motor beyond this point causes the rotor to pull out of its normal speed range and to stall quickly. At standstill, stator current is nearly 5 times normal; hence, constant-potential motor circuits like the one supplying this motor are equipped with time-delay automatic-overload protective devices. Sustained overload causes a circuit breaker to open and to protect both the motor and the circuit from damage.

The performance curves of a 4-pole 3-phase 450-volt 15-horsepower cage-rotor motor are shown in figure 14-5 (B). The full-load slip is only about 3.5 percent. At standstill, the rotor reactance of this type of motor is nearly 5 times as great as the rotor resistance. At full load,

however, the rotor reactance is much less than the rotor resistance. When the motor is running, the rotor current is determined principally by the rotor resistance. The torque increases up to the pull-out point as the slip increases. Beyond this point the torque decreases and the motor stalls. Because the change in speed from no load to full load is relatively small, the motor torque and the horsepower output are considered to be directly proportional.

The cage-rotor induction motor has a fixed rotor circuit. The resistance and inductance of the windings are determined when the motor is designed and cannot be changed after it is built. The standard cage-rotor motor is a general-purpose motor. It is used to drive loads that

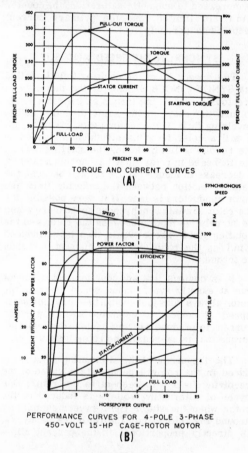

TORQUE AND CURRENT CURVES

(A)

PERFORMANCE CURVES FOR 4-POLE 3-PHASE
450-VOLT 15-HP CAGE-ROTOR MOTOR

(B)

Figure 14-5.—Characteristic curves of a cage-rotor motor.

require a variable torque at approximately constant speed with high full-load efficiency—such as blowers, centrifugal pumps, motor-generator sets, and various machine tools.

If the load requires special operating characteristics, such as high-starting torque, the cage rotor is designed to have high resistance. The starting current of a motor with a high-resistance rotor is less than that of a motor with a low-resistance rotor. The high-resistance rotor motor, like the cumulative compounded d-c motor, has wider speed variations than the low-resistance rotor motor. The high rotor resistance also increases the rotor copper losses, resulting in a lower efficiency than that of the low resistance type. These motors are used to drive cranes and elevators when high-starting torque and moderate-starting current are required and when it is desired to slow down the motor without drawing excessive currents.

CHARACTERISTICS OF WOUND-ROTOR MOTOR

The wound-rotor, or slipring, induction motor is used when it is necessary to vary the rotor resistance in order to limit the starting current or to vary the motor speed. As previously explained, the starting torque may be made equal to the pull-out torque by increasing the rotor resistance to the point where it equals the rotor reactance at standstill. Maximum torque at start can be obtained with a wound-rotor motor with about 1.15 times full-load current; whereas a cage-rotor motor may require 5 times full-load current to produce maximum torque at start. Because the rotor-circuit copper losses are largely external to the rotor winding, the wound-rotor motor is desirable for an application which requires frequent starts.

The advantages of the wound-rotor induction motor over the cage-rotor induction motor are: (1) high-starting torque with moderate starting current, (2) smooth acceleration under heavy loads, (3) no excessive heating during starting, (4) good running characteristics, and (5) adjustable speed. The chief disadvantage of the wound-rotor is that the initial and maintenance costs are greater than those of the cage-rotor motor.

Synchronous Motors

The synchronous motor differs from the induction motor in several ways. The synchronous motor requires a separate source of d-c for the field. It also requires special starting components. These include a salient-pole field with starting grid winding. The rotor of the conventional type synchronous motor is essentially the same as that of the salient-pole a-c generator. The stator windings of induction and synchronous motors are essentially the same. The stator of a synchronous motor is illustrated in figure 14-6 (A).

If supplied with proper voltage, a d-c generator operates satisfactorily as a d-c motor, and there is practically no difference in construction and rating between the two. Similarly, an a-c generator becomes à synchronous motor if electric power is supplied to its terminals from an external source. Synchronous-motor rotating fields are generally of the salient-pole type, as shown in figure 14-6 (B).

Assume, for example, that two a-c generators of the salient-pole type are operating in parallel and feeding the same bus. If the prime mover is disconnected from one of the generators, it will become a synchronous motor and

continue to run at the same speed, drawing its power from the other a-c generator.

With the exception of certain modifications to make its operation more efficient and also to make it self-starting, the synchronous motor is very similar to the salient-pole rotating-field a-c generator. The rotor fields of both are separately excited from a d-c source, and both run at synchronous speeds under varying load conditions. An 8-pole generator rotor revolving at 900 r.p.m. generates 60 cycles per second; likewise, an 8-pole synchronous motor supplied with 60-cycle current will rotate at 900 r.p.m.

PRINCIPLE OF OPERATION

A polyphase current is supplied to the stator winding of a synchronous motor and produces a rotating magnetic field the same as in an induction motor. A direct current is supplied to the rotor winding, thus producing a fixed polarity at each pole. If it could be assumed that the rotor had no inertia and that no load of any kind were applied, then the rotor would revolve in step with the revolving field as soon as power was applied to both of the windings. This, however,

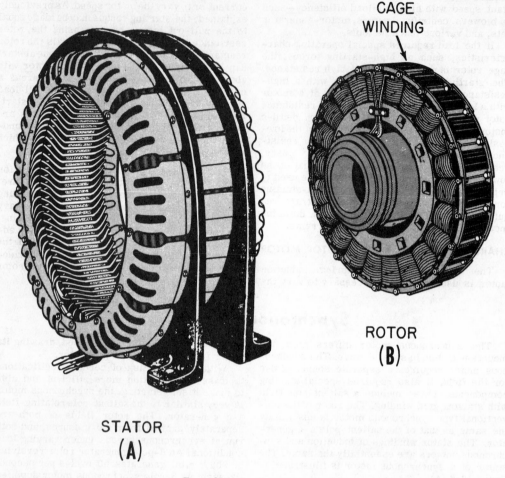

CAGE
WINDING

ROTOR
(B)

STATOR
(A)

Figure 14-6.—Synchronous motor.

is not the case. The rotor has inertia, and in addition there is a load.

The reason a synchronous motor has to be brought up to synchronous speed by special means, may be understood from a consideration of figure 14-7.

If the stator and rotor windings are energized, then as the poles of the rotating magnetic field approach rotor poles of opposite polarity (fig. 14-7 (A)), the attracting force tends to turn the rotor in the direction opposite to that of the rotating field. As the rotor starts in this direction, the rotating-field poles are leaving the rotor poles (fig. 14-7 (B)), and this tends to pull the rotor poles in the same direction as the rotating field. Thus, the rotating field tends to pull the rotor poles first in one direction and then in the other, with the result that the starting torque is zero.

STARTING

As has been explained, some type of starter must be used with the synchronous motor to bring the rotor up to synchronous speed. Although a small induction motor may be used to bring the rotor up to speed, this is not generally done.

256

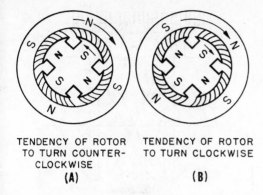

TENDENCY OF ROTOR
TO TURN COUNTER-
CLOCKWISE

(A)

TENDENCY OF ROTOR
TO TURN CLOCKWISE

(B)

Figure 14-7.—Operating principle of synchronous motor.

Sometimes, if direct current is available, a d-c motor coupled to the rotor shaft may be used to bring the rotor up to synchronous speed. After synchronous speed is attained, the d-c motor is converted to operate as a generator to supply the necessary direct current to the rotor of the synchronous motor.

In general, however, another method is used to start the synchronous motor. A cage-rotor winding is placed on the rotor of the synchronous motor to make the machine self-starting as an induction motor. At start, the d-c rotor field is deenergized and a reduced polyphase voltage is applied to the stator windings. Thus, the motor starts as an induction motor and comes up to a speed which is slightly less than synchronous speed. The rotor is then excited from the d-c supply (generally a d-c generator mounted on the shaft) and the field rheostat adjusted for minimum line current.

If the armature has the correct polarity at the instant synchronization is reached, the stator current will decrease when the excitation voltage is applied. If the armature has the incorrect polarity, the stator current will increase when the excitation voltage is applied. This is a transient condition, and if the excitation voltage is increased further the motor will slip a pole and then come into step with the revolving field of the stator.

If the rotor d-c field winding of the synchronous machine is open when the stator is energized, a high a-c voltage will be induced in it because the rotating field sweeps through the large number of turns at synchronous speed.

It is therefore necessary to connect a resistor of low resistance across the rotor d-c field winding during the starting period. During the starting period, the d-c field winding is disconnected from the source and the resistor is connected across the field terminals. This permits alternating current to flow in the d-c field winding. Because the impedance of this winding is high compared with the inserted external resistance, the internal voltage drop limits the terminal voltage to a safe value.

STARTING TORQUE

Both the alternating currents induced in the rotor field winding and the cage-rotor winding during starting are effective in producing the starting torque. The torques produced by the rotor d-c field winding and the cage-rotor winding at different speeds are shown by the curves T_r and T_S, respectively, of figure 14-8. Curve T is the sum of T_r and T_S and indicates the total torque at different speeds during the starting period. Note that T_r is very effective in producing torque as the rotor approaches synchronous speed, but that both windings contribute no torque at synchronous speed because the induced voltage is zero and no d-c excitation is yet applied to the d-c winding.

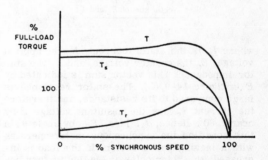

Figure 14-8.—Starting torque of a synchronous motor.

EFFECT OF VARYING LOAD AND FIELD STRENGTH

The power factor of an induction motor depends on the load and varies with it. The power factor of a synchronous motor carrying a definite load may be unity or less than unity, either lagging or leading, depending on the d-c field strength.

The induced (counter) e.m.f. in armature coil C, shown in figure 14-9 (A), is maximum when its sides are opposite the pole centers and minimum when its sides are midway between the pole tips; and it varies as indicated by the solid-line curve, E'_c. When the motor carries no load, the counter voltage E'_c is practically 180° out of phase with the applied voltage E_a (fig 14-9 (A) and (B)). If the field is adjusted so that E_c almost equals E_a, the stator current I_s is small and corresponds to the exciting current in a transformer.

When load is applied to the motor it causes the poles to be pulled α degrees behind their no-load position, as indicated by the broken curve in figure 14-9 (A), and the counter e.m.f. occurs α degrees later. This is indicated by curve E_c in figure 14-9 (A), and by vector E_c in figure 14-9(C). The resultant voltage, E, causes the stator current I_s, to lag behind E_a by angle θ.

In a d-c motor the armature current is determined from the equation

$$I_a = \frac{E_a - E_c}{R_a}.$$

Similarly, in a synchronous motor the stator current is determined as

$$I_s = \frac{\text{vector sum of } E_a \text{ and } E_c}{Z_s},$$

where I_s is the stator current, E_a the applied voltage, E_c the counter voltage, and Z_s the stator impedance. This vector sum is indicated by E in figure 14-9 (C). The stator reactance is large compared to its resistance, and therefore the current I_s lags the resultant voltage E by nearly 90°. Hence, I_s, lags, E_a, by angle θ. In this condition the synchronous motor operates with a lagging power factor. If the load is increased, the rotor poles are pulled further behind the stator poles, which causes E_c to lag further, and angle α to increase. This action causes the resultant voltage, E, and stator current, I_s, to increase.

Because the speed is constant, if the field excitation is decreased, the counter voltage, E_c, decreases; and the resultant voltage, E, becomes greater. The stator current becomes greater and lags the applied voltage, E_a, a greater amount. On the other hand, if the field

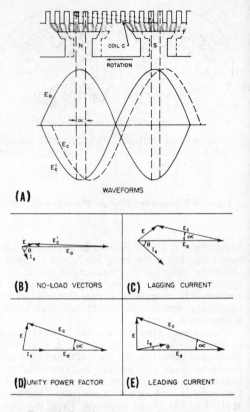

(A) WAVEFORMS

(B) NO-LOAD VECTORS

(C) LAGGING CURRENT

(D) UNITY POWER FACTOR

(E) LEADING CURRENT

Figure 14-9.-Effect of varying the load and field strength of a synchronous motor.

excitation is increased until the current, I_s, is in phase with the applied voltage, E_a, the power factor of the motor becomes unity for a given load (fig. 14-9 (D)). For a definite load at unity power factor, E and I_s are both at their minimum. If the field excitation is further increased, I_s increases and leads E_a (fig. 14-9 (E)). Thus, for a definite load, the power factor is governed by the field excitation—that is, a weak field produces lagging current and a strong field produces a leading current. Normal field excitation for a given load occurs when I_s is in phase with E_a.

The so-called synchronous motor V curves, which indicate the variations of current for a constant load and varied field excitation, are shown in figure 14-10. The corresponding variations of power factor are shown also.

258

Although synchronous motors are used as propulsion motors in practically all Navy vessels that have a-c electric propulsion systems, they have very few other uses in the Navy. However, a synchronous motor is frequently used in shore-based systems to change the power factor of the system to which it is paralleled by adjusting its field excitation. If operated without load, its power factor may be adjusted to a value as low as 10 percent leading. When operated under this condition, the motor is generally referred to as a synchronous condenser because it takes a leading current in the same manner as capacitors. In this case the synchronous condenser takes only enough true power from the line to supply its losses. At the same time, it supplies a high leading reactive power, which cancels the lagging reactive power taken by the parallel inductive loads, and the system power factor is thereby improved.

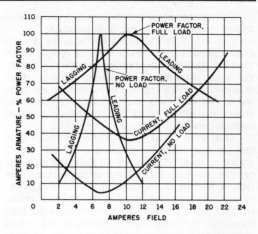

Figure 14-10.—V curves for a synchronous motor of 15 kv.-a.

Alternating-Current Motor Starters

As in the case of d-c motors, some type of starter (controller) may also be employed on a-c motors to limit the initial inrush of current.

ACROSS-THE-LINE starters are the most common form aboard ship because of their simplicity and because ships are generally equipped with sufficient generating capacity to handle the high starting currents of the motors. This type of starter throws the stator winding of the motor directly across the main supply line. This may be feasible if the motor is not too large (5 horsepower or less) and if the generating capacity of the a-c generator can take care of the added load.

PRIMARY RESISTOR starters insert a resistor in the PRIMARY circuit (the stator circuit) of the motor for starting, or for starting and speed control. This starter is used when it is necessary to limit the starting current of a large a-c motor so as not to put too great a load on the system. If the resistor is used only during starting, its rating is based on intermittent operation, in which case it is relatively small and operates at a higher temperature. If the resistor is used also for speed control of small motors, such as for ventilating fans, its rating is based on continuous operation. In this case the resistor is relatively large and operates at a lower temperature.

SECONDARY RESISTOR starters insert a resistor in the secondary circuit (the rotor circuit of the form-wound type of induction motor) for starting and speed control. This starter may be used to limit starting currents, but is usually found where speed control of a large a-c motor is required, in which case the resistors are rated for continuous duty. Examples are some elevators and hoists equipped with direct a-c electric drives.

COMPENSATOR, or AUTOTRANSFORMER, starters start the motor at reduced voltage through an autotransformer, and subsequently connect the motor to full voltage after acceleration. The compensator may be either of two types.

1. The OPEN-TRANSITION type, during the transition period of shifting the motor from the autotransformer to direct connection with the supply lines, disconnects the motor from all power for a short period of time during which, if the motor is of the synchronous type, it may coast and slip out of phase with the power supply. When the motor is then connected directly to the power lines, a high transition current may result.

2. The CLOSED-TRANSITION type keeps the motor connected to the power supply at all times during the transition period, thus not

permitting the motor to decelerate. Accordingly, no high transition current is developed.

The AUTOTRANSFORMER starter is the most common form of the reduced-voltage type used for limiting the starting current of a motor. The open-transition form has the disadvantage of allowing a high transition current to develop, which can cause circuit breakers to open. The closed-transition form is preferable because no high transition current is developed.

REACTOR STARTERS insert a reactor in the primary circuit of an a-c motor during starting, and subsequently short-circuit the reactor to apply full voltage to the motor. This type of starter is not very widely used at present, but is becoming more common for starting large motors because it does not have the high transition current problem of the open-transition compensator and is smaller than the closed-transition compensator.

A simplified schematic diagram of a compensator, or autotransformer, starter is shown in figure 14-11. Assume that the line voltage is 100 volts and that when the taps on the autotransformer are positioned as shown (in the starting position) 40 volts will be applied to the 3-phase motor stator. With the reduction in motor voltage, there is a corresponding reduction in starting current drawn from the line. At the same time, the motor current supplied by the secondary low-voltage windings is proportionately increased by the transformer action.

After the proper time interval, during which acceleration occurs, full-line voltage is applied to the motor.

A resistance starter could be used in place of autotransformer to lower the voltage applied to the stator. The power factor would be im-

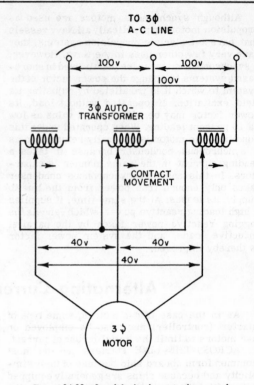

Figure 14-11.—Simplified schematic diagram of autotransformer starter.

proved, but the line current would be greater. The autotransformer has the advantage in permitting the motor to draw a relatively large starting current from the secondary with a relatively low line current.

Single-Phase Motors

Single-phase motors, as their name implies, operate on a single-phase power supply. These motors are used extensively in fractional horsepower sizes in the Navy and in commercial and domestic applications. The advantages of using single-phase motors in small sizes are that they are less expensive to manufacture than other types, and they eliminate the need for 3-phase a-c lines. Single-phase motors are used in interior communications equipment, fans, refrigerators, portable drills, grinders, and so forth.

A single-phase induction motor with only one stator winding and a cage rotor is like a 3-phase induction motor with a cage rotor except that the single-phase motor has no magnetic revolving field at start and hence no starting torque. However, if the rotor is brought up to speed by external means, the induced currents in the rotor will cooperate with the stator currents to produce a revolving field, which causes the rotor to continue to run in the direction in which it was started.

Several methods are used to provide the single-phase induction motor with starting torque. These methods identify the motor as split phase, capacitor, shaded pole, repulsion, and so forth.

Another class of single-phase motors is the a-c series (universal) type. Only the more commonly used types of single-phase motors are described. These include the (1) split-phase motor, (2) capacitor motor, (3) shaded-pole motor, (4) repulsion-start motor, and (5) a-c series motor.

SPLIT-PHASE MOTOR

The split-phase motor (fig. 14-12 (A)), has a stator composed of slotted laminations that contain an auxiliary (starting) winding and a running (main) winding. The axes of these two windings are displaced by an angle of 90 electrical degrees. The starting winding has fewer turns and smaller wire than the running winding, hence has higher resistance and less reactance. The main winding occupies the lower half of the slots and the starting winding occupies the upper half. The two windings are connected in parallel across the single-phase line supplying the motor. The motor derives its name from the action of the stator during the starting period. The single-phase stator is split into two windings (phases), which are displaced in space by 90°, and which contain currents displaced in time phase by an angle of approximately 15° (fig. 14-12 (B)). The current, I_S, in the starting winding lags the line voltage by about 30° and is less than the current in the main winding because of the higher impedance of the starting winding. The current, I_m, in the main winding lags the applied voltage by about 45°. The total current, I_{line}, during the starting period is the vector sum of I_S and I_m.

At start, these two windings produce a magnetic revolving field that rotates around the stator air gap at synchronous speed. As the rotating field moves around the air gap, it cuts across the rotor conductors and induces a voltage in them, which is maximum in the area of highest field intensity and therefore is in phase with the stator field. The rotor current lags the rotor voltage at start by an angle that approaches 90° because of the high rotor reactance. The interaction of the rotor currents and the stator field cause the rotor to accelerate in the direction in which the stator field is rotating. During acceleration, the rotor voltage, current, and reactance

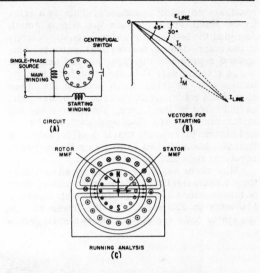

Figure 14-12.—Split-phase motor.

are reduced and the rotor currents come closer to an in-phase relation with the stator field.

When the rotor has come up to about 75 percent of synchronous speed, a centrifugally operated switch disconnects the starting winding from the line supply, and the motor continues to run on the main winding alone. Thereafter, the rotating field is maintained by the interaction of the rotor magnetomotive force and the stator magnetomotive force. These two m.m.f.'s are pictured as the vertical and horizontal vectors respectively in the schematic diagram of figure 14-12 (C).

The stator field is assumed to be rotating at synchronous speed in a clockwise direction, and the stator currents correspond to the instant that the field is horizontal and extending from left to right across the air gap. The left-hand rule for magnetic polarity of the stator indicates that the stator currents will produce an N pole on the left side of the stator and an S pole on the right side. The motor indicated in the figure is wound for two poles.

Applying the left-hand rule for induced voltage in the rotor (the thumb points in the direction of motion of the conductor with respect to the field), the direction of induced voltage is back on the left side of the rotor and forward on the right side. The rotor voltage causes a rotor current to flow, which lags the rotor voltage by an angle whose tangent is the ratio of rotor reactance to rotor resistance. This is a relatively small angle because the slip is small. Applying the left-hand rule for magnetic polarity to the rotor winding, the vertical vector pointing upward represents the direction and magnitude of the rotor m.m.f. This direction indicates the tendency to establish an N pole on the upper side of the rotor and an S pole on the lower side, as indicated in the figure. Thus, the rotor and stator m.m.f.'s are displaced in space by 90° and in time by an angle that is considerably less than 90°, but sufficient to maintain the magnetic revolving field and the rotor speed.

This motor has the constant-speed variable-torque characteristics of the shunt motor. Many of these motors are designed to operate on either 110 volts or 220 volts. For the lower voltage the stator coils are divided into two equal groups and these are connected in parallel. For the higher voltage the groups are connected in series. The starting torque is 150 to 200 percent of the full-load torque and the starting current is 6 to 8 times the full-load current. Fractional-horsepower split-phase motors are used in a variety of equipments such as washers, oil burners, and ventilating fans. The direction of rotation of the split-phase motor can be reversed by interchanging the starting winding leads.

CAPACITOR MOTOR

The capacitor motor is a modified form of split-phase motor, having a capacitor in series with the starting winding. An external view is shown in figure 14-13, with the capacitor located on top of the motor. The capacitor produces a

Figure 14-13.—Capacitor motor.

greater phase displacement of currents in the starting and running windings than is produced in the split-phase motor. The starting winding is made of many more turns of larger wire and is connected in series with the capacitor. The starting winding current is displaced approximately 90° from the running winding current. Since the axes of the two windings are also displaced by an angle of 90°, these conditions produce a higher starting torque than that of the split-phase motor. The starting torque of the capacitor motor may be as much as 350 percent of the full-load torque.

If the starting winding is cut out after the motor has increased in speed, the motor is called a CAPACITOR-START MOTOR. If the starting winding and capacitor are designed to be left in the circuit continuously, the motor is called a CAPACITOR MOTOR. Electrolytic capacitors for capacitor-start motors vary in size from about 80 microfarads for 1/8-horsepower motors to 400 microfarads for one-horsepower motors. Capacitor motors of both types are made in sizes ranging from small fractional horsepower motors up to about 10 horsepower. They are used to drive grinders, drill presses, refrigerator compressors, and other loads that require relatively high starting torque. The direction of rotation of the capacitor motor may be reversed by interchanging the starting winding leads.

SHADED-POLE MOTOR

The shaded-pole motor employs a salient-pole stator and a cage rotor. The projecting poles on the stator resemble those of d-c machines except that the entire magnetic circuit is laminated and a portion of each pole is split to accommodate a short-circuited copper strap called a SHADING COIL (fig. 14-14)). This motor is generally manufactured in very small sizes, up to 1/20 horsepower. A 4-pole motor of this type is illustrated in figure 14-14 (A). The shading coils are placed around the leading pole tip and the main pole winding is concentrated and wound around the entire pole. The 4 coils comprising the main winding are connected in series across the motor terminals. An inexpensive type of 2-pole motor employing shading coils is illustrated in figure 14-14 (B).

During that part of the cycle when the main pole flux is increasing, the shading coil is cut by the flux, and the resulting induced e.m.f. and current in the shading coil tend to prevent the flux from rising readily through it. Thus, the greater portion of the flux rises in that portion of the pole that is not in the vicinity of the shading coil. When the flux reaches its maximum value, the rate of change of flux is zero, and the voltage and current in the shading coil also are zero.

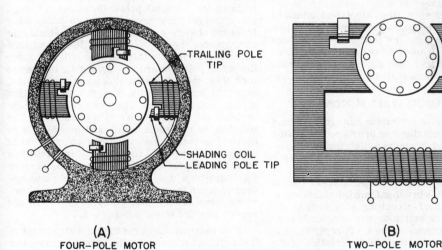

(A)
FOUR-POLE MOTOR

(B)
TWO-POLE MOTOR

Figure 14-14.—Shaded-pole motor.

At this time the flux is distributed more uniformly over the entire pole face. Then as the main flux decreases toward zero, the induced voltage and current in the shading coil reverse their polarity, and the resulting magnetomotive force tends to prevent the flux from collapsing through the iron in the region of the shading coil. The result is that the main flux first rises in the unshaded portion of the pole and later in the shaded portion. This action is equivalent to a sweeping movement of the field across the pole face in the direction of the shaded pole. The cage rotor conductors are cut by this moving field and the force exerted on them causes the rotor to turn in the direction of the sweeping field.

Most shaded-pole motors have only one edge of the pole split, and therefore the direction of rotation is not reversible. However, some shaded-pole motors used in fire control and interior communications circuits have both leading and trailing pole tips split to accommodate shading coils. The leading pole tip shading coils form one series group, and the trailing pole tip shading coils form another series group. Only the shading coils in one group are simultaneously active, while those in the other group are on open circuit.

The shaded-pole motor is similar in operating characteristics to the split-phase motor. It has the advantages of simple construction and low cost. It has no sliding electrical contacts and is reliable in operation. However, it has low starting torque, low efficiency, and high noise level. It is used to operate small fans. The shading coil and split pole are used in clock motors to make them self-starting.

REPULSION-START MOTOR

The repulsion-start motor has a form-wound rotor with commutator and brushes. The stator is laminated and contains a distributed single-phase winding. In its simplest form, the stator resembles that of the single-phase motor. In addition, the motor has a centrifugal device which removes the brushes from the commutator and places a short-circuiting ring around the commutator. This action occurs at about 75 percent of synchronous speed. Thereafter, the motor operates with the characteristics of the single-phase induction motor.

The starting torque of the repulsion-start induction motor is developed through the inter-

action of the rotor currents and the single-phase stator field. Unlike the split-phase motor, the stator field does not rotate at start, but alternates instead. The rotor currents are induced through transformer action. For example, in the 2-pole motor of figure 14-15 (A), the stator currents are shown for the instant when a north pole is established on the upper side of the stator, and a south pole on the lower side. The induced voltage in the rotor causes the rotor currents to flow in such a direction as to oppose the stator field. These currents flow in opposite directions under the left and right portions of the north pole and in similar manner under the south pole. Thus, the net force to turn the rotor is zero when the brushes are located in the positions shown.

In figure 14-15 (B), the brushes are moved 90° from their original positions, and again there is no rotor turning effort because in this case the rotor current is zero. There can be no rotor current in this position because the transformer induced voltages are equal and opposite to each other in the two halves (upper and lower) of the rotor winding.

In figure 14-15 (C), the brush axis is displaced from the stator polar axis by an angle of about 25°, and in this position maximum torque is developed.

The direction of the induced currents in the rotor under the north pole of the stator is toward the observer, and under the south pole, away from the observer. Applying the right-hand rule for motors, the force acting on the conductors under the north pole is toward the left, and under the south pole, toward the right, thus tending to turn the rotor in a counterclockwise direction. When the stator polarity reverses, the direction of the rotor current also reverses, thereby maintaining the same direction of rotation. The function of the commutator and brushes is to divide the rotor currents along an axis that is displaced from the axis of the stator field in a counterclockwise direction. The motor derives its name from the repulsion of like poles between the rotor and stator. Thus, the rotor currents establish the rotor poles $N'-S'$, which are repelled by the stator poles $N-S$.

The starting torque is 250 to 450 percent of the full-load torque, and the starting current is 375 percent of the full-load current. This motor is made in fractional horsepower sizes and in larger sizes up to 15 horsepower, but has been replaced in large parts by the cheaper and more rugged capacitor motor. The repulsion-start motor has higher pull-out torque (torque at which the motor stalls) than the capacitor-start motor, but the capacitor start motor can bring up to full speed loads that the repulsion motor can start but cannot accelerate.

A-C SERIES MOTOR

The a-c series motor will operate on either a-c or d-c circuits. It will be recalled that the direction of rotation of a d-c series motor is independent of the polarity of the applied voltage, provided the field and armature connections remain unchanged. Hence, if a d-c series motor is connected to an a-c source, a torque will be developed which tends to rotate the armature in one direction. However, a d-c series motor does not operate satisfactorily from an a-c supply for the following reasons:

1. The alternating flux sets up large eddy-current and hysteresis losses in the unlaminated portions of the magnetic circuit and causes excessive heating and reduced efficiency.

2. The self-induction of the field and armature windings causes a low power factor.

3. The alternating field flux establishes large currents in the coils that are short-circuited by the brushes; this action causes excessive sparking at the commutator.

To design a series motor for satisfactory operation on alternating current the following changes are made:

1. The eddy-current losses are reduced by laminating the field poles, yoke, and armature.

2. Hysteresis losses are minimized by using high-permeability transformer-type silicon-steel laminations.

3. The reactance of the field windings is kept satisfactorily low by using shallow pole pieces, few turns of wire, low frequency (usually 25 cycles for large motors), low flux density, and low reluctance (a short air gap).

4. The reactance of the armature is reduced by using a compensating winding embedded in the pole pieces. If the compensating winding is connected in series with the armature (fig. 14-16 (A)), the armature is CONDUCTIVELY compensated. If the compensating winding is short-circuited on itself (fig. 14-16 (B)), the armature is INDUCTIVELY compensated. If the motor is designed for operation on both d-c and a-c circuits, the compensating winding is connected in series with the armature. The axis of the compensating winding is displaced from the main field axis by an angle of 90°. This arrangement is similar to the compensating winding used in some d-c motors and generators to overcome armature reaction. The compensating winding establishes a counter magnetomotive force which neutralizes the effect of the armature magnetomotive force, thereby preventing distortion of the main field flux and reducing the armature reactance. The inductively compensated armature acts like the primary of a transformer, the secondary of which is the shorted compensating winding. The shorted secondary receives an induced voltage by the action of the alternating armature flux, and the resulting current flowing through the turns of the compensating winding establish the opposing magnetomotive force that neutralizes the armature reactance.

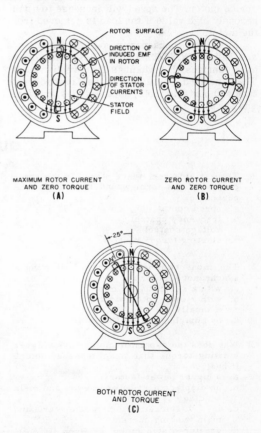

Figure 14-15.—Repulsion-start induction motor.

5. Sparking at the commutator is reduced by the use of PREVENTIVE LEADS P_1, P_2, P_3, and so forth (fig. 14-16 (C)). A ring armature is shown for simplicity. When coils at A and B are shorted by the brushes, the induced current is limited by the relatively high resistance of the leads. Preventive leads are used in some of the older type a-c series motors on electric locomotives. Sparking at the brushes is also reduced by using armature coils having only a single turn and multipolar fields. High torque is obtained by having a large number of armature conductors and a large-diameter armature. Thus, the commutator has a large number of commutator bars that are very thin, so that the armature voltage is limited to about 250 volts.

The operating characteristics of the a-c series motor are similar to those of the d-c series motor. The speed will increase to a dangerously high value if the load is removed from the motor.

Fractional horsepower a-c series motors are called UNIVERSAL MOTORS. They do not have compensating windings or preventive leads. They are used extensively in the Navy to operate fans and portable tools, such as drills, grinders, and saws.

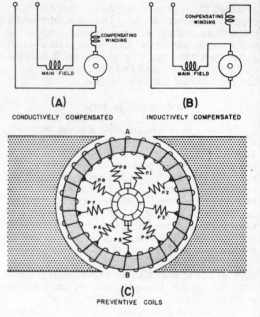

(A) CONDUCTIVELY COMPENSATED

(B) INDUCTIVELY COMPENSATED

(C) PREVENTIVE COILS

Figure 14-16.-A-c series motor.

QUIZ

1. The variable resistance placed in the rotor circuit of the form-wound rotor is for the purpose of
   a. speed control
   b. frequency control
   c. voltage control
   d. starting torque control

2. The most common method of starting a synchronous motor is
   a. with a separate d-c motor
   b. with a cage-rotor winding
   c. manually
   d. by applying d. c. to the rotor

3. Why does the capacitor motor have a higher starting torque than a split-phase motor? It has
   a. a higher power factor
   b. no displacement between start and main winding currents
   c. less displacement between start and main winding currents
   d. greater displacement between its start and main winding currents

4. The synchronous speed of an induction motor is the
   a. speed at which the rotor turns
   b. speed of the rotating field
   c. frequency of the rotor current
   d. slip in percent of rotor r.p.m.

5. Near synchronous speed, the
   a. voltage induced into the rotor is very small
   b. voltate induced into the rotor is large
   c. applied voltage on the stator is zero
   d. rotor frequency is maximum

6. What circumstances cause a lagging power factor?
   a. I_s lags resultant E by 90° - I_s lags E_a by angle θ
   b. I_s leads resultant E by 90° - I_s leads E_s by angle θ
   c. resultant E lags I_s by 90° - I_s lags E_a by angle ϕ
   d. E_c leads I_s by 90° - I_s leads E_a by angle ϕ

7. What is the direction of rotation of the shaded-pole motor in respect to the sweeping field?
   a. With the sweeping field
   b. Against the sweeping field
   c. Toward the unshaded tip
   d. Depends on direction motor was started
8. Increasing the number of poles in an induction motor
   a. increases the field speed
   b. decreases the field speed
   c. decreases the motor's rated torque
   d. causes the frequency of line E to drop
9. The rotor voltage is proportional to the
   a. strength of the magnetic field
   b. number of conductors on the stator
   c. angle at which lines of force are cut
   d. difference in rotor speed and the speed of the rotating field
10. The most common type of starter used on board ship for a-c motors is the
    a. autotransformer
    b. secondary capacitor
    c. primary resistor
    d. across-the-line
11. In the repulsion induction motor, what is the position of the brushes in relation to the stator polar axis for maximum torque?
    a. 15°
    b. 25°
    c. 45°
    d. 90°
12. Increasing the frequency of the voltage applied to an induction motor causes the
    a. field speed to decrease
    b. field speed to increase
    c. rotor torque to decrease
    d. stator current to increase
13. The purpose of the iron rotor core is to
    a. decrease motor weight
    b. produce eddy currents
    c. reduce air gap reluctance
    d. decrease permeability
14. The frequency of rotor current varies directly with
    a. applied voltage
    b. the resistance of the rotor
    c. the slip
    d. the number of windings on the stator
15. The efficiency of a motor is equal to the
    a. torque output at synchronous speed
    b. amount of current in the rotor
    c. horsepower of the motor
    d. ratio of its output power to its input power
16. The type of starter used when it is necessary to limit the starting current of an a-c motor is the
    a. autotransformer
    b. secondary resistor
    c. primary resistor
    d. primary capacitor

17. The type of starter used for speed control of an a-c motor is the
    a. secondary resistor
    b. open transition
    c. closed transition
    d. primary resistor
18. Motor action is best analyzed by applying
    a. Fleming's right-hand rule
    b. the magnetic laws of polarity
    c. Lenz's law for self-induced voltage
    d. the left-hand motor rule
19. A synchronous motor is not self-starting due to
    a. its lack of a rotating magnetic field
    b. inertia of the rotor
    c. magnetic locking action between rotor and stator fields
    d. its low power factor
20. The single-phase a-c motor is not self-starting because there is
    a. inertia in the rotor
    b. no high starting torque
    c. no revolving magnetic field
    d. a magnetic lock between the rotor and stator
21. In the a-c series motor, how are hysteresis losses minimized? By use of
    a. high frequency voltage
    b. laminations only
    c. hard iron
    d. silicone steel
22. The direction of rotation of an induction motor is
    a. opposite the rotating field direction
    b. same as direction of rotating field
    c. determined by the number of poles
    d. determined by the location of its brushes
23. A synchronous motor differs from an induction motor in that it
    a. is not self-starting
    b. requires an a-c and a d-c power supply
    c. may be used for power factor correction
    d. all of the above
24. How can the direction of rotation of a split-phase induction motor be reversed?
    a. Reverse leads of main winding
    b. Reverse leads of start windings
    c. Reverse leads of one phase
    d. Reverse any two leads
25. Fractional horsepower a-c series motors are called
    a. induction motors
    b. synchronous motors
    c. universal motors
    d. shaded-pole motors

CHAPTER 15

DIRECT-CURRENT GENERATORS

Generators can be designed to supply small amounts of power or they can be designed to supply many thousands of kilowatts of power. Also, generators may be designed to supply either direct current or alternating current. Direct-current generators are described in this chapter. Alternating-current generators were described in chapter 13.

A d-c generator is a rotating machine that converts mechanical energy into electrical energy. This conversion is accomplished by rotating an armature, which carries conductors, in a magnetic field, thus inducing an e.m.f. in the conductors. As stated before, in order for an e.m.f. to be induced in the conductors, a relative motion must always exist between the conductors and the magnetic field in such a manner that the conductors cut through the field. In most d-c generators the armature is the rotating member and the field is the stationary member. A mechanical force is applied to the shaft of the rotating member to cause the relative motion. Thus, when mechanical energy is put into the machine in the form of a mechanical force or twist on the shaft, causing the shaft to turn at a certain speed, electrical energy in the form of voltage and current is delivered to the external load circuit.

It should be understood that mechanical power must be applied to the shaft constantly so long as the generator is supplying electrical energy to the external load circuit.

The power source used to turn the armature is commonly called a PRIME MOVER. Many forms of prime movers are in use, such as steam turbines, diesel engines, gasoline engines, and steam engines. However, in the Navy, the principal sources of power aboard ship are steam turbines and diesel engines. Also, auxiliary power units containing d-c generators driven by gasoline engines are widely used in naval maintenance operations.

In naval aviation, aircraft engines function as prime movers for both a-c and d-c generating equipment.

A d-c generator consists essentially of (1) a steel frame or yoke containing the pole pieces and field windings, (2) an armature consisting of a group of copper conductors mounted in a slotted cylindrical core, made up of thin steel disks called LAMINATIONS, (3) a commutator for maintaining the current in one direction through the external circuit, and (4) brushes with brush holders to carry the current from the commutator to the external load circuit.

Though both contain the same essential parts, the shipboard d-c generator and the d-c generator used on aircraft are quite different in size, rating, and appearance. A typical generator used aboard ship is shown in figure 15-1 (A); an aircraft generator is shown in part (B). Shipboard generators may weigh thousands of pounds and be rated in the hundreds of kilowatts. Aircraft generators rarely exceed eighty pounds in weight or nine kilowatts in rating.

Construction

FRAME

The d-c generator field frame, or yoke, is usually made of annealed steel. The use of steel reduces the reluctance of the magnetic circuit to a low value and therefore reduces the necessary size of the field windings. The frame provides a mechanical support for the pole pieces and serves as a portion of the magnetic circuit to provide the necessary flux across the air gap.

The end bells are bolted to the frame structure and support the armature shaft bearings. One end bell also supports the brush rigging and extends over the commutator.

268

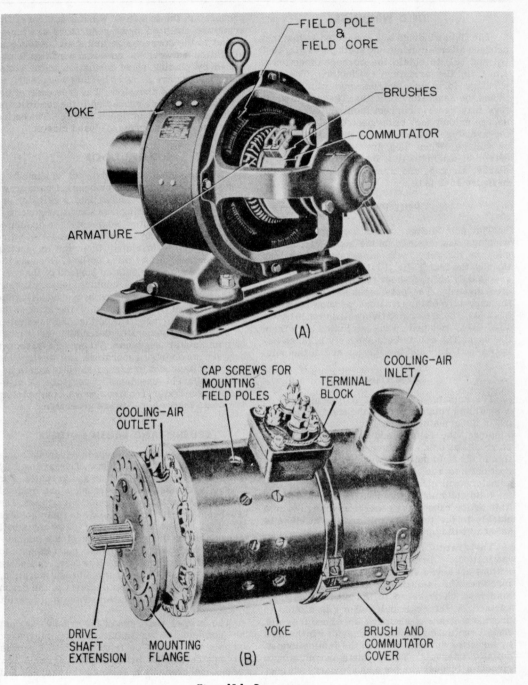

Figure 15-1.—D-c generators.

269

FIELD WINDINGS

The field windings are connected so that they produce alternate north and south poles (fig. 15-2 (A) and (F)) to obtain the correct direction of e.m.f. in the armature conductors. The field windings form an electromagnet which establishes the generator field flux. These field windings may receive current from an external d-c source or they may be connected directly across the armature, which then becomes the source of voltage. When they are so energized, they establish magnetic flux in the field yoke, pole pieces, air gap, and armature core, as shown in figure 15-2 (A).

POLE PIECES

The pole pieces, which support the field windings, are mounted on the inside circumference of the yoke, with capscrews that extend through the frame (fig. 15-1). These pole pieces are usually built of sheet steel laminations riveted together. The pole faces are shaped to fit the curvature of the armature, as shown in figure 15-2 (A). The preformed field coil shown in figure 15-2 (B) is mounted on the laminated core from the back. The coil is held securely in place between the frame and the flanged end of the pole.

ARMATURE

The armature (fig. 15-2 (C)) is mounted on a shaft and rotates through the field. If the output of the armature is connected across the field windings, the voltage and the field current at start will be small because of the small residual flux in the field poles. However, as the generator continues to run, the small voltage across the armature will circulate a small current through the field coils and the field will become stronger. This action causes the generator voltage to rise quickly to the proper value and the machine is said to "build up" its voltage.

The armature core is made of sheet steel laminations. In small machines these laminations are keyed directly to the shaft. In large machines the laminations are assembled on a spider which is keyed to the shaft. The outer surface of this cylindrical core is slotted to provide a means of securing the armature coils. Radial ventilating ducts are provided in the core by inserting spacers between the laminations at definite intervals. These ducts permit air to circulate through the core and to carry off heat

produced in the armature winding and core. The armature coils on most generators are formwound to the correct size and shape. Additional insulation between the core and windings is obtained by placing sheet insulation in the slots. The windings are secured by fiber wedges driven into the tops of the slots. The free ends of the armature coils are connected to the commutator riser, as indicated in figure 15-2 (C). The entire armature winding forms a closed circuit.

COMMUTATOR

The commutator consists of a number of wedge-shaped segments, or bars, of hard drawn copper that are assembled into a cylinder and held together by V-rings, as shown in figure 15-2 (D). The commutator segments are insulated from each other by sheet mica and the entire commutator is insulated from the supporting rings on the shaft by mica collars. Because the brushes bear on the outside surface of the commutator, better brush contact, less sparking, and less noise, are obtained by undercutting the mica to about 1/64 inch below the level of the commutator surface. The voltage and the number of poles in the generator determine the number of commutator segments. To prevent flashover between segments, generators are designed so that a voltage not to exceed 15 volts exists between adjacent segments. Therefore, a high-voltage generator requires more commutator segments than a low-voltage generator.

BRUSHES AND BRUSH HOLDERS

The brushes carry the current from the commutator to the external circuit. They are usually made of a mixture of carbon and graphite. For low-voltage machines the brushes are made of a mixture of graphite and a metallic powder. The brushes must be free to slide in their holders (fig. 15-2 (E)) so that they may follow any small irregularities in the curvature of the commutator. In addition, the brushes must be able to "feed in" as they wear. However, excessive play not only would encourage brush vibration, but also might cause misalinement of the brush with the axis of commutation. This would result in excessive sparking.

The proper pressure of the brushes against the commutator is maintained by means of springs and should be from 1-1/2 to 2 pounds per square inch of brush contact area. A low resistance connection between the brushes and

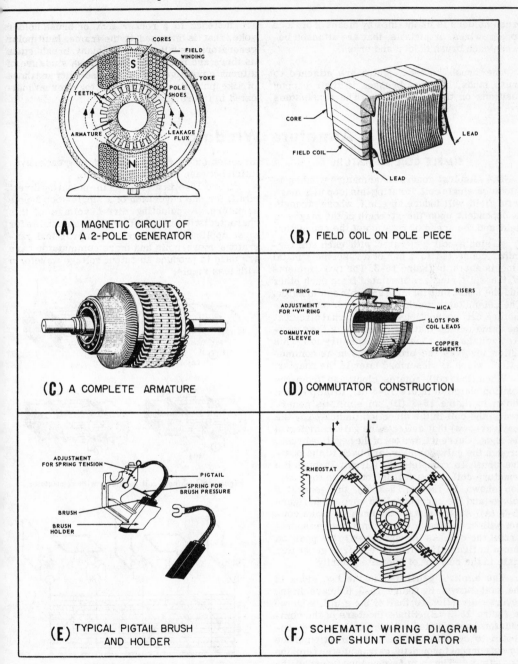

(A) MAGNETIC CIRCUIT OF A 2-POLE GENERATOR

(B) FIELD COIL ON POLE PIECE

(C) A COMPLETE ARMATURE

(D) COMMUTATOR CONSTRUCTION

(E) TYPICAL PIGTAIL BRUSH AND HOLDER

(F) SCHEMATIC WIRING DIAGRAM OF SHUNT GENERATOR

Figure 15-2.—D-c generator parts.

brush holders is maintained by means of braided copper wires, or pigtails, that are attached between each brush holder and brush.

The brush holders, which are attached to brush studs, hold the brushes in their proper positions on the commutator. The brush studs are fastened to a rocker arm, or brush holder yoke, that is attached to the frame. Multipolar generators usually have as many brush studs as there are main poles. The brush studs are of alternate positive and negative polarity and those of like polarity are connected together as indicated in figure 15-2 (F).

Armature Windings

SIMPLE COIL ARMATURE

The simplest generator armature winding is a loop or single coil. Rotating this loop in a magnetic field will induce an e.m.f. whose strength is dependent upon the strength of the magnetic field and the speed of rotation of the conductor.

A single-coil generator with each coil terminal connected to a bar of a 2-segment metal ring is shown in figure 15-3. The two segments of the split ring are insulated from each other and the shaft, thus forming a simple commutator. The commutator mechanically reverses the armature coil connections to the external circuit at the same instant that the direction of the generated voltage reverses in the armature coil. This action involves the process known as commutation, which is described later in the chapter.

When the coil rotates clockwise from the position shown in figure 15-3 (A), to the position shown in figure 15-3 (B), an e.m.f. is generated in the coil in the direction (indicated by the heavy arrows) that deflects the galvanometer to the right. Current flows out of the negative brush, through the galvanometer, and back to the positive brush to complete the circuit through the armature coil. If the coil is rotated to the position shown in figure 15-3 (C), the generated voltage and the current fall to zero, as in figure 15-3 (A). At this instant the brushes make contact with both bars of the commutator and short-circuit the coil. As the coil moves to the position shown in figure 15-3 (D), an e.m.f. is generated again in the coil but of opposite polarity.

The e.m.f.'s generated in the two sides of the coil shown in figure 15-3 (D), are in the reverse direction to that of the e.m.f.'s shown in figure 15-3 (B). Since the bars of the commutator have rotated with the coil and are connected to opposite brushes, the direction of the flow of current through the galvanometer remains the same. The e.m.f. developed across the brushes is pulsating and unidirectional (in one direction only), varying twice during each revolution between zero and maximum.

Figure 15-4 is a graph of the pulsating direct e.m.f. for one revolution of a single-loop 2-pole armature. A pulsating direct voltage of this characteristic (called RIPPLE) is unsuitable for most applications. Therefore, in practical generators more coils and more commutator bars are used to produce an output voltage waveform with less ripple.

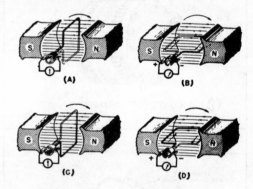

Figure 15-3.—Single-coil generator with commutator.

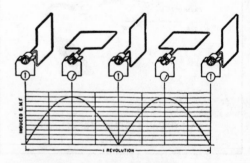

Figure 15-4.—Voltage from a single-coil armature.

EFFECT OF MORE COILS

Figure 15-5 shows the reduction in ripple component of the voltage obtained by the use of two coils instead of one. Since there are now four commutator segments in the commutator and only two brushes, the voltage cannot fall any lower than point A; Therefore, the ripple is limited to the rise and fall between points A and B. By adding still more armature coils, the ripple voltage can be reduced still more.

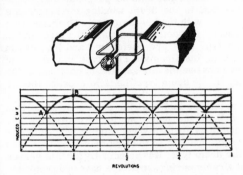

Figure 15-5.—Voltage from a two-coil armature.

GRAMME-RING WINDING

A Gramme-ring winding (fig. 15-6) is formed by winding insulated wire around a hollow iron ring and tapping it at regular intervals to the commutator bars. The portions of the windings on the inside of the ring cut practically no flux and act as connectors for the active portions of the conductors, which lie on the outer surface of the ring. Because only a small fraction of the conductor is used to generate voltage in such a winding, a relatively large amount of copper is required to produce a given voltage. The schematic wiring diagram of a Gramme-ring winding is frequently used as a simplified equivalent circuit for the practical but more complex drum armature wiring diagrams. The Gramme-ring winding is used in this discussion only to simplify the drum winding circuits.

In the 2-pole winding of figure 15-6 (A), there are two parallel paths for armature current between the brushes. One path is through the coils on the left side and the other is through the coils on the right side. The voltage between the brushes is the vector sum of the voltages generated in all the coils of each path. No circulating current flows between the two paths

because the generated voltages in the two paths are equal and in opposition. The polarity of the brushes may be determined by the left-hand rule for generator action. The negative terminal is the one from which electrons flow out to the load; the positive terminal is the one to which the electrons return from the load.

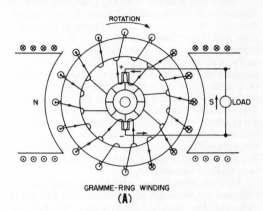

GRAMME-RING WINDING
(A)

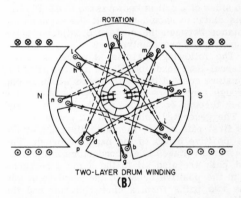

TWO-LAYER DRUM WINDING
(B)

Figure 15-6.—Basic d-c generator armature windings.

DRUM ARMATURE

In the basic drum winding shown in figure 15-6 (B), all the conductors lie in slots near the surface of the armature. The armature conductors are indicated in the figure as circles. Those on the left contain a dot to indicate that the direction of generated voltage is toward the observer; those on the right contain an x to show that the direction of the generated voltage is away from the observer. The dotted lines connecting the circles represent end connections on the back of the armature between the two halves of each coil. The solid lines between the commutator and the armature conductors represent the end connections on the front of the armature between the coils and commutator segments.

There are 8 coils, 8 slots, and 8 commutator segments in this simplified basic drum winding. One half of a coil lies in the upper portion of a slot and the other half of the coil lies in the lower portion of a slot that is approximately halfway around the armature. This arrangement permits the generated voltages in the two halves of a coil to be a maximum at almost the same instant, because the armature is rotating in a 2-pole field. The polarity of the brushes may be determined by the left-hand rule for generator action. The brushes are shown on the inside of the commutator surface to simplify the drawing. Normally, the brushes contact the outside surface of the commutator.

In drum armatures, with the exception of the coil-end connections, all of the copper is used to generate the e.m.f. The distance between the two sides of a coil is known as the COIL PITCH. This distance should be about the same as the distance between the centers of adjacent poles as mentioned previously.

The following analysis is made for a no-external-load condition. There are two paths for armature current through the drum winding—one through conductors a, b, c, d, e, f, g, and h; the other through conductors i, j, k, l, m, n, o, and p. The generated voltages in all conductors in the first path are in the same direction—from the positive brush to the negative brush. The generated voltages in all conductors in the second path are also all in the same direction—from the positive brush to the negative brush. The two paths form a closed circuit and the voltages of each path are equal and in opposition with respect to each other. Therefore no circulating current will flow.

Certain similarities exist in the Gramme-ring winding (fig. 15-6 (A)) and the drum winding (fig 15-6 (B)). The generated voltage distribution is the same. The number of paths for load current is the same. In both types, when a brush contacts two segments, a coil is short-circuited. In both types, the brushes are positioned so that only coils that are moving approximately parallel to the field are short-circuited. That is, a coil is short-circuited only at the exact instant that it has no voltage induced in it. Thus, sparking

is minimized. In both types, there are 8 commutator bars and 2 brushes and the armatures are wound for 2-pole fields. Also, in both types there are single-turn coils and 16 active conductors in which the voltage of the machine is generated.

The differences that exist in the two types of armatures are in the position of the brush axis, the method of mounting the coils, and the path for the magnetic field flux. In the Gramme-ring winding the brush axis is perpendicular to the field axis. In the drum winding the brush axis coincides with the field axis. In the Gramme-ring armature the coils are wound on a ring. In the drum type they are preformed and inserted in slots. In the Gramme-ring type the magnetic field crosses the air gap and is confined to the ring. In the drum type the field crosses the air gap and permeates the entire cross section of the armature including the outer slotted portion as well as the inner section. Finally, the end connections form a much higher percentage of the total winding in the Gramme-ring type than in the drum type. It is principally for this reason that Gramme-ring armatures have been replaced by the more efficient drum-type armature.

SIMPLEX LAP WINDING

As mentioned previously, direct-current armatures are generally wound with preformed coils, as shown in figure 15-7. The term "span" is the distance from one winding element of a coil to the other winding element of the same coil and is usually given in terms of the number of slots included between them. A winding element is a coil side consisting of one or more active (face) conductors in series and taped together to form that part of the coil that is inserted in the armature slot. The span of the armature coil should be about equal to the peripheral distance between the centers of adjacent field poles, so that the voltages generated in the two sides of the coil will be in series addition. This distance is called POLE PITCH. When the span of a coil is less than the pole pitch the winding is called a FRACTIONAL-PITCH WINDING. A fractional pitch coil can be as low as 0.8 pole pitch. Fractional pitch coils have reduced e.m.f. because the coil side voltages do not reach their maximum values at the same time. Ordinarily, the reduction in e.m.f. is small. The savings in copper, in shorter end-connections, warrants the loss.

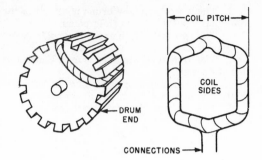

Figure 15-7.—Formed armature coil for 4-pole armature.

Direct-current armature windings are generally 2-layer windings. In this arrangement, the coils are placed on the armature with one side of a coil occupying the top of one slot and its other side occupying the bottom of another slot. The distance between the slots is approximately 1 pole span. Such an arrangement allows the windings to fit readily on the armature with an equal number of coils and slots. Thus each slot contains two layers of conductors in which voltages are generated as the armature rotates through the field. This arrangement is shown in the 2-layer drum winding of figure 15-6 (B).

A 4-pole simplex-lap winding is shown in figure 15-8. Starting with commutator bar 1, the circuit may be traced through the heavy black coil to the adjacent commutator bar 2. The trace may be continued through successive coils until the entire armature circuit has been traced from one end to the other. Upon reentering the starting commutator bar 1, the trace is completed. Thus, the circuit is seen to be a closed-circuit winding

There are four groups of coils generating the same voltage between brushes of opposite polarity in the example shown in figure 15-8. One group consists of coils occupying winding spaces 1, 12, 3, 14, 5, 16, 7, 18, 9, and 20. A second group consists of coils occupying winding spaces 11, 22, 13, 24, 15, 26, 17, 28, 19, and 30. A third group consists of coils occupying winding spaces 21, 32, 23, 34, 25, 36, 27, 38, 29, and 40. The fourth group consists of coils occupying winding spaces 31, 42, 33, 2, 35, 4, 37, 6, 39, 8, 41, and 10. These four groups of coils are placed in parallel by connecting the two positive brushes together and the two negative brushes together as indicated in the schematic diagram of figure 15-8 (B). No circulating current flows between these four parallel paths when no load is connected between the positive and negative brushes,

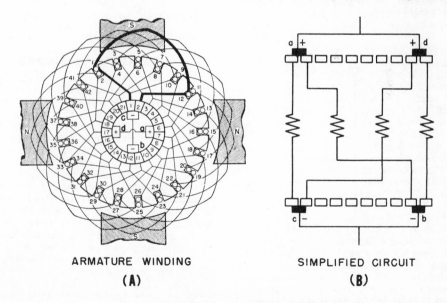

ARMATURE WINDING

(A)

SIMPLIFIED CIRCUIT

(B)

Figure 15-8.—Simplex-lap 4-pole armature winding.

because the voltage of each of the groups is equal and of opposite polarity to the voltages of the other groups.

A simplified schematic of the 4-pole simplex-lap armature winding is shown in figure 15-9. Connecting a load between the positive and negative brushes causes current to flow through the armature in these four paths. The current is distributed equally in the four paths. Thus if the total output current of the armature is 400 amperes, each path through the armature will carry 100 amperes. In this winding there are as many parallel paths for current through the armature as there are poles in the field.

The simplex-lap winding described in this chapter is the simplest type of lap winding. It is identified as a single winding to distinguish it from more complex double and triple lap windings. It is single-reentrant—that is, the winding closes on itself at the end of one complete turn around the armature. This arrangement distinguishes the winding from more complex types that reenter upon themselves after one, two, or three complete turns around the armature. The more complex lap windings are described in the texts that pertain to particular ratings.

The characteristics of the (single) simplex-lap winding may be summarized as follows:

1. There are as many paths for current as there are field poles.

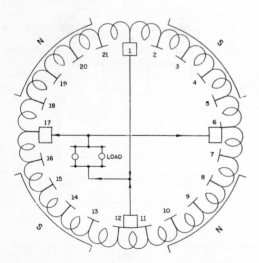

Figure 15-9.—Simplified schematic of simplex-lap 4-pole armature winding.

2. There are as many brush positions on the commutator as there are field poles.

3. The two ends of an armature coil connect to adjacent commutator segments.

4. The armature winding forms a continuous closed circuit.

5. The lap armature winding is used for relatively high-current low-voltage loads.

6. The voltage generated between positive and negative brushes is

$$E = \frac{\Phi ZN}{10^8},$$

where E is the generated e.m.f. in volts, Z the number of armature face conductors, Φ the lines of magnetic flux per pole, and N the armature speed in revolutions per second.

A face conductor lies in a slot and generates a voltage as the armature rotates. An armature coil includes one or more turns, each of which consists of two face conductors and their respective end connections. For example, a 4-pole d-c generator with a simplex-lap armature winding having 10^6 lines of magnetic flux per pole, 440 armature conductors, and a speed of 50 revolutions per second (3,000 r.p.m.) has a generated voltage of

$$E = \frac{10^6 \times 440 \times 50}{10^8} = 220 \text{ volts.}$$

If the load current is 1,000 amperes, each armature coil will carry $\frac{1,000}{4}$, or 250 amperes.

SIMPLEX WAVE WINDING

In the single simplex-wave winding (fig. 15-10) groups of coils under similar pairs of poles at any instant are generating equal voltages and are connected in series. This winding is also called a SERIES WINDING. Each coil has its ends connected to the commutator bars that are two pole spans apart. This distance is measured around the armature circumference from the center of one field pole to the center of the next pole of like sign. In this example, the distance covered by two pole spans is halfway around the commutator; in a 6-pole machine, two pole spans are one-third the way around; and in an 8-pole machine, one-fourth the way around. In the single simplex-wave winding there are as many coils connected in series between adjacent commutator bars as there are pairs of poles in the field. In this example there are two pairs of poles, so there are two coils in series between adjacent commutator bars. This arrangement

276

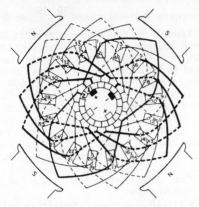

Figure 15-10.—Single simplex-wave winding.

may be seen by starting at segment 1 and tracing through the circuit of the two coils occupying winding spaces 1, 10, 17, and 26, and ending at commutator segment 2.

The single simplex-wave winding is a closed-circuit winding as may be seen by starting with one coil and tracing through the entire armature circuit to complete the trace by ending at the starting position. In the single simplex wave-wound armature there are two paths for current regardless of the number of poles for which it is wound and regardless of the number of brushes. Starting with the upper positive brush, one path includes the armature conductors that occupy winding spaces 1, 10, 17, 26, 33, 8, 15, 24, 31, 6, 13, 22, 29, 4, 11, 20, 27, and 2, returning to the upper negative brush. The other path from the upper positive brush includes the armature conductors that occupy winding spaces 28, 19, 12, 3, 30, 21, 14, 5, 32, 23, 16, 7, 34, 25, 18, and 9, returning to the upper negative brush.

Although four brushes are shown, only two are required. The full voltage of the winding is developed across the upper brushes, and the full voltage is also developed across the lower brushes. The load current divides equally between the two pairs of brushes when they are connected in parallel because the resistance of the two paths through the armature is the same. For example, if the armature has a 20-ampere load at 220 volts the upper brushes alone will carry 20 amperes at 220 volts. Adding the lower brushes will reduce the current to 10 amperes per brush. If the commutator is designed for four brushes, the removal of one pair will overload the remaining brushes unless the load is halved. However, where commutators are inaccessible, wave windings permit the use of two brush positions irrespective of the number of poles, so that servicing the brushes and commutator is facilitated.

The characteristics of the simplex-wave winding may be summarized as follows:

1. There are two parallel paths irrespective of the number of field poles.

2. There is a minimum of two brush positions irrespective of the number of field poles.

3. The two ends of a coil connect to commutator segments that are two pole spans apart (fig. 15-10).

4. The winding has relatively high voltage and low current.

5. The winding forms a continuous closed circuit.

6. There are as many coils in series between adjacent commutator segments as there are pairs of poles in the field.

7. The voltage generated between positive and negative brushes is

$$E = \frac{\Phi ZNP}{10^8},$$

where P is the number of pairs of field poles and the other symbols are the same as those used in the equation for generated voltage in a simplex-lap winding.

For example, a 6-pole d-c generator having a simplex-wave armature winding, 1.05 x 10^6 lines of flux per pole, 3,500 armature conductors, and a speed of 10 revolutions per second (600 r.p.m.) has a generated voltage of

$$E = \frac{\Phi ZNP}{10^8} = \frac{1.05 \times 10^6 \times 3,500 \times 10 \times 3}{10^8} = 1,100 \text{ volts.}$$

If the armature supplies 200 amperes to a load, each armature coil will carry $\frac{200}{2} = 100$ amperes.

Armature Losses

There are three losses in every d-c generator armature. These are (1) the I^2R or copper loss in the winding, (2) the eddy current loss in the core, and (3) the hysteresis loss due to the friction of the revolving magnetic particles in the core.

277

COPPER LOSSES

The copper loss is the power lost in heat in the windings due to the flow of current through the copper coils. This loss varies directly with the armature resistance and as the square of the armature current. The armature resistance varies with the length of the armature conductors and inversely with their cross-sectional area.

Armature conductor size is based on an allowance of from 300 to 1,200 circular mils per ampere. For example, a 2-pole armature that is required to supply 100 amperes may use a wire size based on 800 circular mils per ampere, or $\frac{100}{2}$ x 800 = 40,000 circular mils. This value corresponds to a No. 4 wire. Very small armature windings may use only 300 circular mils per ampere with a resulting high current density. Large generators (5,000 kw.) require an allowance of 1,200 circular mils per ampere with a resulting low current density in the windings. These variations are the result of the variable nature of the heat-radiating ability of the armature conductors.

Very small round conductors have a much higher ratio of surface to volume than do large round conductors. For example, a 0.1-inch diameter round conductor of a given length has a surface-to-volume ratio of

$$\frac{4\pi D}{\pi D^2}, \text{ or } \frac{4}{0.1} = 40.$$

A 1.0-inch diameter conductor of the same length has a surface-to-volume ratio of $\frac{4}{1}$, or 4. Since the heat-radiating ability of a round conductor varies as the ratio of its surface to volume, the 0.1-inch diameter conductor has $\frac{40}{4}$, or 10 times the heat radiating ability of the 1-inch diameter conductor, other factors being equal.

High-speed generators use a lower circular-mil-per-ampere allowance than low-speed generators because of better cooling. The temperature rise is limited by ventilating ducts, and in some cases by the use of forced ventilation, as in aircraft d-c generators.

The hot resistance of an armature winding is higher that its cold resistance. A 2.5° centigrade increase in temperature of a copper conductor corresponds to an increase in resistance of approximately 1 percent. For example, if the no-load temperature of an armature winding is 20° C. and its full-load temperature is 70° C.,

the increase in resistance is $\frac{70 - 20}{2.5}$, or 20 percent. Thus, if the no-load resistance is 0.05 ohm between brushes, the hot resistance will be 1.2 x 0.05, or 0.06 ohm. If the full-load armature current is 100 amperes, the full-load armature copper loss will be $(100)^2$ x 0.06, or 600 watts. The armature copper loss varies more widely with the variation of electrical load on the generator than any other loss occurring in the machine. This is because most generators are constant-potential machines supplying a current output that varies with the electrical load across the brushes. The limiting factor in load on a generator is the allowable current rating of the generator armature.

The armature circuit resistance includes the resistance of the windings between brushes of opposite polarity, the brush contact resistance, and the brush resistance.

EDDY-CURRENT LOSSES

If a d-c generator armature core were made of solid iron (fig. 15-11 (A)) and rotated rapidly in the field, excessive heating would develop even with no-load current in the armature windings. This action would be the result of a generated voltage in the core itself. As the core rotates, it cuts the lines of magnetic field flux at the same time the copper conductors of the armature cut them. Thus, induced currents alternate through the core, first in one direction and then in the other, with accompanying generation of heat.

These induced currents are called EDDY CURRENTS. They are kept to a low value by sectionalizing (laminating) the armature core. For example, if the core is split into two equal parts (fig. 15-11 (B)) and these parts are insulated from each other, the voltage induced in each section of iron is halved and the resistance of the eddy-current paths is doubled (resistance varies inversely with the cross-sectional area). If 10 volts is induced in the core (fig. 15-11 (A)) and the resistance of the path for eddy currents is 1 ohm, the eddy-current loss is $\frac{E^2}{R}$, or $\frac{10^2}{1}$ = 100 watts. The voltage is each section (fig. 15-11 (B)) will be $\frac{10}{2}$, or 5 volts, because the length is halved and the resistance of the eddy-current path for each section is 2 ohms. The loss in each section is $\frac{E^2}{R}$, or $\frac{5^2}{2}$ = 12.5 watts, and the total

278

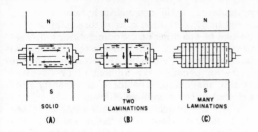

Figure 15-11.—Eddy currents in d-c generator armature cores.

loss in both sections is 12.5 x 2, or 25 watts. This value represents one-fourth of the power loss in figure 15-11 (A).

Reducing the thickness of the core to one-half its original value reduces the loss to one-fourth of the original loss. Thus, eddy-current losses vary as the square of the thickness of the core laminations.

If the armature core is sufficiently subdivided into multiple sections or laminations (fig. 15-11 (C)), the eddy-current loss can be reduced to a negligible value. Reducing the thickness of the laminations reduces the magnitude of the induced e.m.f. in each section and increases the resistance of the eddy-current paths. Laminations in small generator armatures are 1/64 inch thick. The laminations are insulated from each other by a thin coat of lacquer or in some instances simply by the oxidation of the surfaces due to contact with the air while the laminations are being annealed. The insulation need not be high because the voltages induced are very small.

All electrical rotating machines are laminated to reduce eddy-current losses. Transformer cores are laminated for the same reason.

The eddy-current loss is also influenced by speed and flux density. Because the induced voltage, which causes the eddy-currents to flow, varies with the speed and flux density, the power loss, $\dfrac{E2}{R}$, varies as the square of the speed and the square of the flux density.

HYSTERESIS LOSS

When an armature revolves in a stationary magnetic field, the magnetic particles of the armature are held in alinement with the field in varying numbers depending upon the strength of the field. If the field is that of a 2-pole generator, these magnetic particles will rotate, with respect to the particles not held in alinement, one complete turn for each revolution of the armature. The rotation of magnetic particles in the mass of iron produces friction and heat.

Heat produced in this manner is identified as magnetic HYSTERESIS LOSS. The hysteresis loss varies with the speed of the armature and the volume of iron. The flux density varies from approximately 50,000 lines per square inch in the armature core to 130,000 lines per square inch in the iron between the bottom of adjacent armature slots (called the TOOTH ROOT). Heat-treated silicon steel having a low hysteresis loss is used in most d-c generator armatures. After the steel has been formed to the proper shape, the laminations are heated to a dull red heat and allowed to cool. This annealing process reduces the hysteresis loss to a low value.

Armature Reaction

Armature reaction in a generator is the effect on the main field of the armature acting as an electromagnet. With no armature current, the field is undistorted, as shown in figure 15-12 (A). This flux is produced entirely by the ampere-turns of the main field windings. The neutral plane AB is perpendicular to the direction of the main field flux. When an armature conductor moves through this plane its path is parallel to the undistorted lines of force and the conductor does not cut through any flux. Hence no voltage is induced in the conductor. The brushes are placed on the commutator so that they short-circuit coils passing through the neutral plane. With no voltage generated in the coils, no current will flow through the local path formed momentarily between the coils and segments spanned by the brush. Therefore, no sparking at the brushes will result.

When a load is connected across the brushes, armature current flows through the armature conductors, and the armature itself becomes a source of magnetomotive force. The effect of the armature acting as an electromagnet is considered in figure 15-12 (B), with the assumption that the main field coils are deenergized and full-load current is introduced to the armature circuit from an external source. The currents in the conductors on the left of the neutral plane all carry current toward the observer, and those on the right carry current away from the observer. These directions are the same as those in which the current would flow if it were under the influence of the normal e.m.f. generated in the armature with normal field excitation.

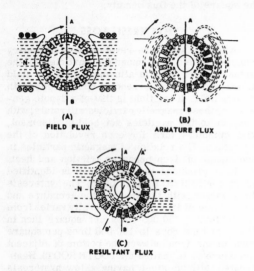

(A) FIELD FLUX

(B) ARMATURE FLUX

(C) RESULTANT FLUX

Figure 15-12.—Flux distribution in a d-c generator.

These armature current-carrying conductors establish a magnetomotive force that is perpendicular to the axis of the main field, and in the figure the force acts downward. This magnetizing action of the armature current is called CROSS MAGNETIZATION and is present only when current flows through the armature circuit. The amount of cross magnetization produced is proportional to the armature current.

When current flows in both the field and armature circuits, the two resulting magnetomotive forces distort each other. They twist in the direction of rotation of the armature. The mechanical (no load) neutral plane, AB (fig. 15-12 (C)), is now advanced to the electrical (load) neutral plane, A'B'. When armature conductors move through plane A'B' their paths are parallel to the distorted field and the conductors cut no flux, hence no voltage is induced in them. The brushes must therefore be moved on the

commutator to the new neutral plane. They are moved in the direction of armature rotation. The absence of sparking at the commutator indicates correct placement. The amount that the neutral plane shifts is proportional to the load on the generator because the amount of cross-magnetizing magnetomotive force is directly proportional to the armature current.

When the brushes are shifted into the electrical neutral plane A'B' the direction of the armature magnetomotive force is downward and to the left, as shown in figure 15-13 (A), instead of vertically downward. The armature magnetomotive force may now be resolved into two components, as shown in figure 15-13 (B).

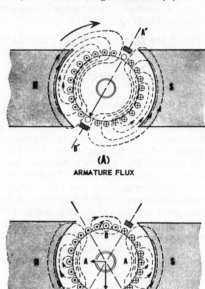

(A) ARMATURE FLUX

(B) DEMAGNETIZING AND CROSS-MAGNETIZING COMPONENTS

Figure 15-13.—Effect of brush shift on armature reaction.

The conductors included at the top and bottom of the armature within sectors BB produce a magnetomotive force that is directly in opposition to the main field and weakens it. This component is called the ARMATURE DEMAGNETIZING M.M.F. The conductors included on the

280

right and left sides of the armature within sector AA produce a cross-magnetizing m.m.f. at right angles to the main field axis. This cross-magnetizing force tends to distort the field in the direction of rotation. As mentioned previously, the distortion of the main field of the generator is the result of ARMATURE REACTION. Armature reaction occurs in the same manner in multipolar machines.

COMPENSATING FOR ARMATURE REACTION

The effects of armature reaction are reduced in d-c machines by the use of (1) high flux density in the pole tips, (2) a compensating winding, and (3) commutation poles.

The cross-sectional area of the pole tips is reduced by building the field poles with laminations having only one tip. These laminations are alternately reversed when the pole core is stacked so that a space is left between alternate laminations at the pole tips. The reduced cross section of iron at the pole tips increases the flux density so that they become saturated and the cross-magnetizing and demagnetizing forces of the armature will not affect the flux distribution in the pole face to as great an extent as they would at reduced flux densities.

The compensating winding consists of conductors imbedded in the pole faces parallel to the armature conductors. The winding is connected in series with the armature and is arranged so that the ampere-turns are equal in magnitude and opposite in direction to those of the armature. The magnetomotive force of the compensating winding therefore neutralizes the armature magnetomotive force, and armature reaction is practically eliminated. Because of the relatively high cost, compensating windings are ordinarily used only on high-speed and high-voltage generators of large capacity.

Commutating poles are discussed after the description of the process of commutation.

Commutation

Commutation is the process of reversing the current in the individual armature coils and conducting the direct current to the external circuit during the brief interval of time required for each commutator segment to pass under a brush. In figure 15-14, commutation occurs simultaneously in the two coils that are undergoing momentary short circuit by the brushes—coil B by the negative brush, and the diametrically opposite coil by the positive brush. As mentioned previously, the brushes are placed on the commutator in a position that short-circuits the coils that are moving through the electrical neutral plane because there is no voltage generated in the coils at the time and no sparking occurs between commutator and brush.

There are two paths for current through the armature winding. If the load current is 100 amperes, each path will contain a current of 50 amperes. Thus each coil on the left side carries 50 amperes in a given direction and each coil on the right side carries a current of 50 amperes in the opposite direction. The reversal of the current in a given coil occurs during the time that particular coil is being short-circuited by a brush. For example, as coil A approaches the negative brush it is carrying the full value of 50 amperes which flows through commutator segment 1 and the left half of the negative brush where it joins 50 amperes from coil C.

At the instant shown, the negative brush spans half of segment 1 and half of segment 2. Coil B is on short circuit and is moving parallel to the field so that its generated voltage is zero, and no current flows through it. As rotation continues in a clockwise direction the negative brush spans more of segment 1 and less of segment 2. Consider, for example, the interval included between the instant shown in the figure and the instant that the negative brush spans only segment 1. During this time the current in segment 1 increases from 50 to 100 amperes and the current in segment 2 decreases from 50 to 0 amperes. When segment 2 leaves the brush, no current flows from segment 2 to the brush and commutation is complete.

As coil A continues into the position of coil B the current in A decreases to zero. Thus, the current in the coils approaching the brush is reducing to zero during the brief interval of time that it takes for coil A to move to the position of coil B. During this time the flux collapses around the coil and induces an e.m.f. of self-induction which opposes the decrease of current. Thus, if the e.m.f. of self-induction is not neutralized, the current will not decrease in coil A

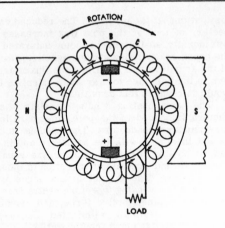

Figure 15-14.—Commutation in a d-c generator.

cut a small amount of flux from the on-coming main pole, sufficient e.m.f. is induced to neutralize the effect of the self-induced e.m.f. This action allows the coil current to decrease to zero and increase to the desired values in the opposite direction without sparking at the brushes.

The flux necessary to generate the e.m.f. that neutralizes the e.m.f. of self-induction is called the COMMUTATING FLUX. This method of reducing sparking at the brushes is satisfactory only under steady-load conditions because the amount of commutating flux required varies with the load and, therefore, the brushes must be shifted with each change in load.

COMMUTATING POLES

Commutating poles, or interpoles, provide the required amount of commutating flux without shifting the brushes from mechanical neutral. They are narrow auxiliary poles located midway between the main poles, as shown in figure 15-2 (F). They establish a flux in the proper direction and of sufficient magnitude to produce satisfactory commutation. They do not contribute to the generated e.m.f. of the armature as a whole because the voltages generated by their fields cancel each other between brushes of opposite polarity.

The interpole magnetomotive force neutralizes that portion of the armature reaction within the zones of commutation and produces the proper flux to generate an e.m.f. in the short-circuited coil that is equal and opposite to the e.m.f. of self-induction. Thus, no sparking occurs at the brushes and "black" commutation indicates the ideal condition. Because both the armature reaction and the self-induced e.m.f. in the commutated coils vary with armature current, the interpole flux varies with the armature current. This condition is obtained by connecting the interpole windings in series with the armature and operating the interpole iron at flux densities well below saturation. The magnetic polarities are such that an interpole always has the same polarity as the adjacent main field pole in the DIRECTION OF ROTATION. This relation always exists for d-c generators.

and the current in the coil lead to segment 1 will not be zero when segment 1 leaves the brush. This delay causes a spark to form between the toe of the brush and the trailing edge of the segment. As the segment breaks contact with the brush, this action burns and pits the commutator.

The reversal of current in the coils takes place very rapidly. For example, in an ordinary 4-pole generator, each coil passes through the process of commutation several thousand times per minute. It is important that commutation be accomplished without sparking to avoid excessive commutator wear.

ADVANCING THE BRUSHES

The e.m.f. of self-induction in the armature coils is caused by the inductance of the coils and the changing current in them and cannot be eliminated. The effects of this e.m.f. can be neutralized however, by introducing into the coil during the process of commutation an e.m.f. that is equal and in opposition to the induced e.m.f. This neutralization can be accomplished by shifting the brushes in the direction of rotation or by using interpoles (commutating poles).

If the brushes are shifted in the direction of rotation until the coils undergoing commutation

Motor Reaction in a Generator

Whenever a generator delivers current to a load, the load current creates an opposition force that opposes the rotation of the generator armature. An armature conductor is represented in figure 15-15. When the conductor is stationary, no voltage is generated and no current flows; hence, no force acts on the conductor. When the conductor is moved downward and the circuit is completed through an external load, current flows through the conductor in the direction indicated, setting up lines of force around it that have a clockwise direction.

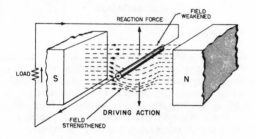

Figure 15-15.—Motor reaction in a generator.

The interaction of the conductor field and the main field of the generator weakens the field above the conductor and strengthens it below the conductor. The field consists of lines that act like stretched rubber bands. Thus, an upward reaction force is produced that acts in opposition to the downward driving force applied to the generator armature. If the current in the conductor increases, the reaction force increases, and more force must be applied to the conductor to keep it from slowing down.

With no armature current, no magnetic reaction exists and the generator input power is low. As the armature current increases, the reaction of each armature conductor against rotation increases and the driving power to maintain the generator armature speed must be increased. If the prime mover driving the generator is a gasoline engine, this effect is accomplished by opening the throttle on the carburetor. If the prime mover is a steam turbine, the main steam-admission valve is opened wider, thus permitting more steam to flow through the turbine.

D-C Generator Characteristics

METHODS OF CONNECTING THE FIELD WINDINGS

Usually d-c generators are classified according to the manner in which the field windings are connected to the armature circuit (fig. 15-16).

A SEPARATELY EXCITED D-C GENERATOR is indicated in the simplified schematic diagram of figure 15-16 (A). In this machine the field windings are energized from a separate d-c source other than its own armature.

A SHUNT GENERATOR has its field windings connected across the armature in shunt with the load, as shown in figure 15-16 (B). The shunt generator is widely used in industry.

A SERIES GENERATOR has its field windings connected in series with the armature and load, as shown in figure 15-16 (B). Series generators are seldom used.

COMPOUND GENERATORS contain both series and shunt field windings, as shown in figure 15-16 (B). Compound generators are widely used in industry.

FIELD SATURATION CURVES

The strength of the field of a d-c generator depends on the number of ampere-turns in the field windings and the reluctance of the magnetic circuit. The number of turns is generally fixed. Hence, the ampere-turns vary directly with the field current. The generated voltage is directly proportional to the product of the field strength and the speed. Thus, if the field strength is zero or the speed is zero, the generated voltage will be zero. As the current through the field windings increases, the field flux and voltage output will increase. The field strength, however, is not directly proportional to the field current because the reluctance of the magnetic circuit

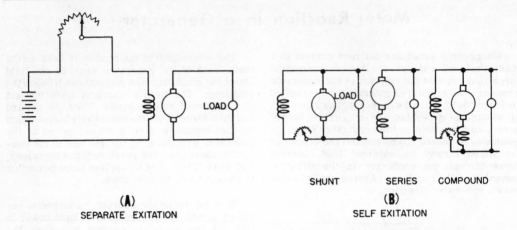

(A)
SEPARATE EXITATION

(B)
SELF EXITATION

SHUNT   SERIES   COMPOUND

Figure 15-16.—Types of d-c generators.

varies with the degree of magnetization. With increasing flux density in the field and armature iron the permeability decreases, thereby increasing the reluctance of the magnetic circuit and it becomes more difficult to increase the voltage.

Certain operating characteristics of the d-c generator are very closely related to the no-load and the full-load field saturation curves of the machine. The no-load saturation curve is determined with no armature current and the full-load saturation is determined with full-load armature current. The speed is held constant for both curves and the field current is increased in equal steps. The terminal voltage corresponding to each value of field current is plotted and forms the field saturation curves as shown in figure 15-17. The no-load saturation curve is preferably taken with the field separately excited. However, for a shunt or a compound generator these curves can be taken with the machine self-excited because the armature voltage drop due to the shunt field current is negligible.

With a certain field current, *OA* (fig. 15-17), a no-load e.m.f. of *AD* volts is generated, but the terminal voltage at full load is *AF*. The difference, *DF*, is caused by the armature *IR* drop and armature reaction. The saturation curves bend to the right at high values of field current and thereby show the tendency of the field iron to saturate. The no-load saturation curve is the magnetization curve of the machine. Because this curve is obtained with no armature current, the observed voltage is the generated e.m.f. of

the machine. At zero field current the e.m.f. is not zero because of the residual flux of the machine. This fact is important because a self-excited generator depends on residual flux to build up its voltage. At low values of field current the voltage varies proportionally, but as the field current increases, the steel portion of the magnetic circuit becomes partly saturated and the voltage increases more slowly.

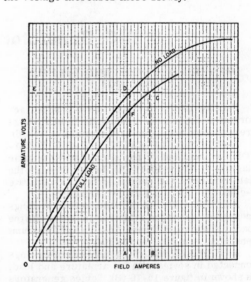

Figure 15-17.—Field saturation curves for d-c generator.

The abrupt bend in the curve is called the KNEE of the curve. Shunt generators are designed to operate at a point slightly above the knee so that a slight change in speed does not cause a great change in voltage. Compound generators operate at a lower point in order to avoid the use of a large series field winding.

SHUNT GENERATOR

The shunt generator (fig. 15-16 (B)) has field coils of many turns of small size wire connected in shunt with the armature and load. The armature current is equal to the sum of the field current and the load current. The field current is small compared with the load current and is approximately constant for normal variations in load. Thus, the armature current varies directly with the load. The field flux produced by the field current is normally constant so that the terminal voltage does not vary widely with load change. Hence, the generator is essentially a constant-potential machine that delivers current to the load in accordance with the load demand.

Build Up of Voltage

After the generator is brought up to normal speed, and before any load is connected across the armature, the generator must "build up" its voltage to the rated value (fig. 15-18). A schematic wiring diagram (fig. 15-18 (A)) is shown without load, and with only a few turns of the field coil around one pole indicated for simplicity in tracing the direction of current flow and the polarity of the voltage generated in the armature winding.

Figure 15-18 (B) indicates the field saturation curve for the generator. Line *OA* represents the relation between voltage and current in the field-coil circuit for one value of field-circuit resistance. Line *OA* is called an *IR*-drop curve for the field circuit and is assumed to be a straight line on the basis of constant temperature operation. The field rheostat permits adjustment of the field current through a relatively wide range and is designed so that its resistance is at least equal to that of the field winding.

At start, the generator is brought up to rated speed. The load is not connected. The armature conductors cut the small residual field and gen-

erate about 10 volts across the brushes (point ① on the saturation curve). The left-hand rule for generator action indicates that the generated voltage is applied to the field winding in a direction to supplement the residual field. Ten volts applied across the field circuit will cause approximately 0.07 ampere to flow through the field coils (point ② on the *IR*-drop curve).

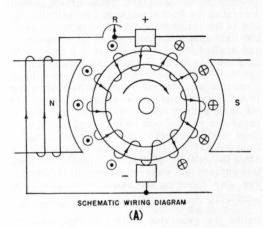

SCHEMATIC WIRING DIAGRAM

(A)

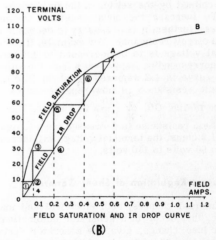

FIELD SATURATION AND IR DROP CURVE

(B)

Figure 15-18.—Buildup of voltage of a shunt generator.

This current strengthens the field, and the armature voltage increases to 30 volts, as shown on the field saturation curve (point ③). During the process of voltage buildup the effect of the armature circuit resistance on the terminal voltage is neglected since the field current is only a small fraction of an ampere. This current flows through the armature and the accompanying *IR* drop is negligible. A generated voltage of 30 volts applied to the field circuit causes a field current of 0.2 ampere to flow, as shown by the *IR*-drop curve (point ④). This current in turn increases the field strength and generated voltage in the armature to 60 volts, as indicated on the field saturation curve (point ⑤). This voltage applied to the field causes 0.4 ampere to flow and this action increases the terminal voltage to 80 volts (point ⑥). The rise in voltage continues until the field current has increased to 0.6 ampere and the terminal voltage levels off at 90 volts (point *A*). No further increase in generated voltage occurs for the given value of field circuit resistance because the amount of field saturation flux produced is enough to generate the voltage required (90 volts) to circulate this current (0.6 ampere) through the field coils. For this condition the resistance of the field circuit is $\frac{90}{0.6}$, or 150 ohms. Field saturation limits the generated voltage to this value as determined by the setting of the field rheostat.

To increase the shunt generator terminal voltage further, it is necessary to decrease the field circuit resistance. For example, if the terminal voltage is to be increased to 110 volts, the corresponding field current from the saturation curve is 1.2 amperes (point *B*). The field circuit resistance is now represented by the slope of line *OB*, or $\frac{110}{1.2}$ = 91.8 ohms. Thus, if the field resistance is decreased from 150 ohms to 91.8 ohms, the terminal voltage will increase from 90 volts to 110 volts.

Inherent Regulation of Shunt Generator

Internal changes, both electrical and magnetic, that occur in a generator automatically with load change, give the generator certain typical characteristics by which it may be identified. These internal changes are referred to as the inherent regulation of a generator. At no load, the armature current is equal to the field current. With low armature resistance and low field current there is little armature *IR* drop, and the generated voltage is equal to the terminal voltage. With load applied, the armature *IR*

drop increases, but is relatively small compared with the generated voltage. Also the armature reaction voltage loss is small. Therefore, the terminal voltage decreases only slightly provided the speed is maintained at the rated value.

Load is added to a shunt generator by increasing the number of parallel paths across the generator terminals. This action reduces the total load circuit resistance with increased load. Since the terminal voltage is approximately constant, armature current increases directly with the load. Since the shunt field is in a separate circuit it receives only a slightly reduced voltage and its current does not change to any great extent.

Thus, with low armature resistance and a relatively strong field there is only a small variation in terminal voltage between no load and full load.

External Voltage Characteristics

A graph of the variation in terminal voltage with load on a shunt generator is shown in curve *A* of figure 15-19. This curve shows that the terminal voltage of a shunt generator falls slightly with increase in load from the no-load condition to the full-load condition. It also shows that with heavy overload the terminal voltage falls more rapidly. The shunt field current is reduced and the magnetization of the field falls to a low value. The dotted portion of curve *A* indicates the way the terminal voltage falls beyond the breakdown point. In large generators the breakdown point occurs at several times rated load current. Generators are not designed to be operated at these large values of load current and will overheat dangerously even at twice the value of full-load current.

Curve *B* represents the external voltage characteristic of a shunt generator with constant field current for variations in load between zero and approximately 25 percent over the rated load condition. Curve *C* represents the external voltage characteristic for the same range of load with simulated conditions of zero armature reaction and constant field current. The divergence of curve *C* from curve *D* represents the voltage variators resulting from the *IR* drop in the armature circuit. As mentioned previously, the terminal voltage of the shunt generator is prevented from varying widely with load change by providing it with a (1) low armature resistance, (2) strong main field with low armature reaction, and (3) separate field circuit in shunt with the armature and load.

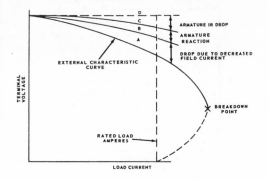

Figure 15-19.—Shunt generator external characteristics.

COMPOUND GENERATOR

Compound generators employ a series field winding in addition to the shunt field winding, as shown in figure 15-16 (B). The series field coils are made of a relatively small number of turns of large copper conductor, either circular or rectangular in cross section, and are connected in series with the armature circuit. These coils are mounted on the same poles on which the shunt field coils are mounted and therefore contribute a magnetomotive force that influences the main field flux of the generator.

Effect of Series Field

If the ampere-turns of the series field act in the same direction as those of the shunt field the combined magnetomotive force is equal to the sum of the series and shunt field components. Load is added to a compound generator in the same manner in which load is added to a shunt generator—by increasing the number of parallel paths across the generator terminals. Thus, the decrease in total load resistance with added load is accompanied by an increase in armature-circuit and series-field circuit current.

The effect of the additive series field is that of increased field flux with increased load. The extent of the increased field flux depends on the degree of saturation of the field iron as determined by the shunt field current. Thus, the terminal voltage of the generator may increase

with load or it may decrease depending upon the influence of the series field coils. This influence is referred to as the degree of compounding.

For example, a FLAT-COMPOUND generator is one in which the no-load and full-load voltages have the same value. An UNDER-COMPOUND generator is one in which the full-load voltage is less than the no-load value. An OVER-COMPOUND generator is one in which the full-load voltage is higher than the no-load value. The way the terminal voltage changes with increasing load depends upon the degree of compounding.

A variable shunt is connected across the series field coils to permit adjustment of the degree of compounding. This shunt is called a DIVERTER. Decreasing the diverter resistance increases the amount of armature circuit current that is bypassed around the series field coils, thereby reducing the degree of compounding.

A field rheostat in the shunt field coil circuit permits adjustment of the no-load voltage of the compound generator. The diverter across the series field coils permits adjustment of the full-load voltage.

External Voltage Characteristics

The variation of terminal voltage with load is indicated in the external characteristic curves of figure 15-20. Curve A is the graph of terminal voltage versus armature current for a flat-compound generator. The no-load and full-load voltages are the same. Neither the diverter nor the field rheostat are altered in this test. The speed is maintained constant at the rated value. The hump in the curve is caused by the increased influence of the series ampere-turns on the field iron at half-load when the degree of saturation is reduced and the armature reaction and armature IR drop are approximately half their normal values.

Curve B is the external characteristic of an over-compound generator. As load is added to this machine its terminal voltage increases so that the field load voltage is higher than the no-load value. Such a characteristic might be desirable where the generator is located some distance from the load and the rise in voltage compensates for the voltage loss in the feeder. This action holds the load voltage approximately

287

constant from no-load to full-load by increasing the generator terminal voltage an amount that is just equal to the voltage drop in the feeder at full load.

Curve C represents the external characteristic for an under-compound generator. The Navy uses a so-called stabilized shunt generator that has a small series field winding of a few turns in the coils to partially compensate for the voltage loss due to armature IR drop and armature reaction. Thus, the external characteristic is almost the same as that of a shunt generator except that the terminal voltage does not fall off quite as rapidly with increased load.

The stabilized shunt generator is the only type of compound generator commonly used in the Navy. This generator is used to supply general lighting and power aboard ship.

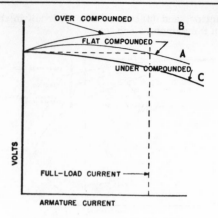

Figure 15-20.—Compound generator external characteristics.

Voltage Regulation

The external characteristic of a generator is sometimes called the VOLTAGE-REGULATION CURVE of the machine. The regulation of a generator refers to the VOLTAGE CHANGE that takes place when the load is changed. It is usually expressed as the change in voltage from no-load to full-load voltage in percent of full-load voltage. Expressed as a formula,

$$\frac{E_{nL} - E_{fL}}{E_{fL}} \times 100 = \text{percent regulation,}$$

where E_{nL} is the no-load terminal voltage and E_{fL} is the full-load terminal voltage of the generator. For example, the percent regulation of a generator having a no-load voltage of 237 volts and a full-load voltage of 230 volts is

$$\frac{237 - 230}{230} \times 100, \text{ or 3 percent.}$$

VOLTAGE CONTROL

Flat-compound generators were formerly used to supply the ship's d-c electric power because they provided a more constant voltage under varying load conditions. Shunt generators are simpler in design and have greater reliability when operating in parallel. The stabilized shunt generator represents a compromise between the two types. As mentioned previously, it has a very light series winding and a slightly

drooping voltage characteristic and is generally used to supply the ship's d-c electric power requirements.

Voltage control is either (1) manual or (2) automatic. In most cases the process involves changing the resistance of the field circuit. By changing field circuit resistance, field current is controlled. Controlling field current permits control of the terminal voltage. Thus, the major difference between various voltage regulator systems is merely the method by which field circuit resistance and current are controlled. When the load changes are infrequent and small, manual control is sufficient to hold the d-c system voltage to the desired value. When the load changes are frequent and large, it may be desirable to employ some form of automatic control.

Inherent voltage regulation should not be confused with voltage control. As described previously, voltage regulation is an internal action occurring within the generator whenever the load changes. Voltage control is a super-imposed action usually by external adjustment. Certain electromechanical devices are used extensively in automatic voltage regulators. These include solenoids, relays, carbon piles, rocking disks, and tilted plates.

Manual Operation

A hand-operated field rheostat (fig. 15-21) connected in series with the shunt field circuit

288

provides the simplest method of controlling the terminal voltage of a d-c generator.

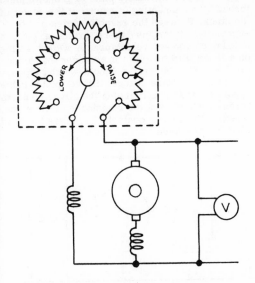

Figure 15-21.—Hand-operated field rheostat.

One form of field rheostat contains tapped resistors with leads to a multiterminal switch. The arm of the switch may be rotated through an arc to make contact with the various resistor taps, thereby varying the amount of resistance in the field circuit. Rotating the arm in the direction of the LOWER arrow increases the resistance and lowers the terminal voltage. Rotating the arm in the direction of the RAISE arrow, decreases the resistance and increases the terminal voltage.

Field rheostats for generators of moderate size employ resistors of alloy wire having a high specific resistance and a low temperature coefficient. These alloys include copper, nickel, manganese, and chromium and are marketed under trade names such as nichrome, advance, manganin, and so forth. Large generator field rheostats use cast-iron grids and a motor-operated switching mechanism.

Automatic Operation

Several types of automatic voltage regulators are used to control the terminal voltage of d-c

generators. One of the earliest types was the vibrating regulator. More recent types include the tilted plate regulator and the rocking disk regulator.

The VIBRATING REGULATOR operates on the principle that an intermittent short circuit applied across the generator field rheostat will cause the terminal voltage of the generator to pulsate within narrow voltage limits and thus it will maintain an average steady value of voltage that is independent of load change. A simplified circuit is shown in figure 15-22.

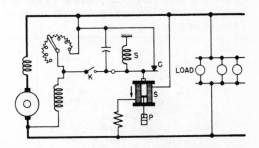

Figure 15-22.—Vibrating type of voltage regulator.

With the generator running at normal speed and switch K open, the field rheostat is adjusted so that the terminal voltage is about 60 percent of normal. Solenoid S is weak and contacts C are held closed by the spring. When K is closed, a short circuit is placed across the field rheostat. This action causes the field current to increase and the terminal voltage to rise.

When the terminal voltage rises above a certain critical value, for example 111 volts, the solenoid downward pull exceeds the spring tension and contact C opens, thus reinserting the field rheostat in the field circuit and reducing the field current and terminal voltage.

When the terminal voltage falls below a certain critical voltage, for example 109 volts, the solenoid armature contact C is closed again by the spring. The field rheostat is now shorted and the terminal voltage starts to rise. The cycle repeats and the action is rapid and continuous. The average voltage of 110 volts is maintained with or without load change.

The dashpot, P, provides smoother operation by acting as a damper to prevent hunting. The capacitor across contacts C eliminates sparking. Added load causes the field rheostat to be shorted

289

for a longer period of time and thus the solenoid armature vibrates more slowly. If the load is reduced and the terminal voltage tends to rise, the armature vibrates more rapidly. Thus the regulator holds the terminal voltage to a steady value for any change in load from no load to full load on the generator.

The TILTED PLATE REGULATOR (fig. 15-23) consists of two or more stacks of graphite plates mounted on metallic supports at the center of each stack. Each plate is balanced on its fulcrum (the metallic support) at the center. On one end of the stack the plates are separated by mica spacers. On the other end they are sepa-rated by silver contacts. Before the silver contacts are closed, the path for field circuit current is from graphite plate to graphite plate through the connecting fulcrums at the center of the stack. Between the graphite plates and their supporting fulcrums there exists a certain amount of contact resistance. A weight acting on a lever tilts the plate in a manner that brings the contacts together. A solenoid, which responds to terminal voltage change, tilts the plates in the opposite direction. Bringing the silver contacts together shorts out the resistance of the stack. Opening the silver contacts increases the field circuit resistance.

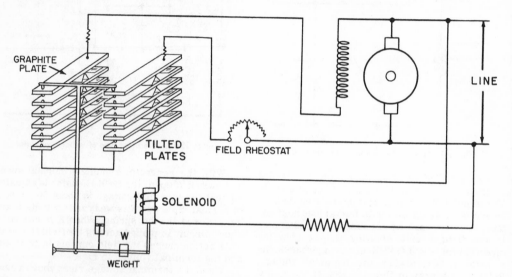

Figure 15-23.—Tilted plate voltage regulator.

The regulator responds to load change and is not designed to overshoot in the manner of the vibrating regulator previously described. For example, at rated voltage the solenoid is in balance with the lever weight and the arm does not move. An increase in load decreases the terminal voltage only slightly because the lever weight immediately overcomes the solenoid and tilts the plates in a direction to lower the resist-ance, thereby strengthening the field and the generated voltage. This action checks the fall of terminal voltage with load.

The ROCKING DISK REGULATOR (fig. 15-24) is another device that is quick acting and sensitive to slight changes in terminal voltage. It may be designed to be in a constant-motion condition of overshooting the voltage a slight amount through each cycle of operation or it may be operated in a static condition in which load change alone causes it to operate.

A spring presses the rocking disk against the flat surface of a silver-plated commutator, the segments of which connect to taps on the field circuit resistors. The disk has a carbon shoe which makes contact with the segments one at a time from top to bottom as the disk is rocked downward. A small range of motion of the spring is converted into a long range of motion of the contact point of the carbon shoe with the various commutator segments. The lever weight tends to rock the disk downward. The solenoid tends to rock the disk upward. For a constant load on the generator, the lever weight and the solenoid are in a state of balance. Thus, the shoe is in contact with one commutator segment, and a portion of the field resistors is short-circuited.

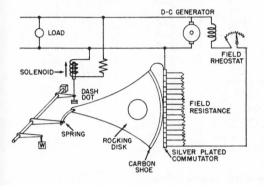

Figure 15-24.—Rocking disk voltage regulator.

When the load on the generator increases, the terminal voltage of the generator starts to fall. The solenoid is weakened and the weight rocks the disk downward, thus short-circuiting more of the field resistors and increasing the generated voltage. The decrease in terminal voltage is almost instantly checked by the increase in field strength and generated voltage, and the weight is now in balance with the solenoid at a new position where the disk contacts a commutator segment nearer the lower end of its travel.

A decrease in load causes the terminal voltage to start to rise and this strengthens the solenoid. Thus the disk rocks in an upward direction and more resistance is inserted in the field circuit, with accompanying decrease in field strength and generated voltage.

The decrease in generated voltage checks the rise in terminal voltage. For example, at one load the generated voltage is 120 volts, the internal voltage loss is 10 volts, and the terminal voltage is 120 - 10, or 110 volts. With decrease in load the internal voltage loss might decrease to 5 volts, and without automatic regulation the terminal voltage would increase to 120 - 5, or 115 volts. However, with automatic regulation the terminal voltage momentarily rises to 111 volts and the regulator causes the generated voltage to fall from 120 volts to 111 + 5, or 116 volts, and to become stable at 115 volts when the terminal voltage is again 115 - 5, or 110 volts.

Regulators for Variable-Speed Generators

VIBRATOR-TYPE REGULATOR

If the speed of a shunt generator varies the output voltage will vary. In cars, trucks, small boats, and some aircraft, the generator is usually driven from the main source of power, which may be a variable-speed internal-combustion engine. If the generator is' of the shunt type, a 3-unit regulator is often employed. One unit consists of a vibrating voltage regulator that places an intermittent short-circuit across a resistor in series with the field. This action is similar to the vibrating-type voltage regulator described earlier in this chapter. The second unit is a current limiter that limits the output current to a value determined by the rating of the generator. The three-unit regulator (fig. 15-25) is designed for use in a power system employing a battery as an auxiliary power supply. The third unit in the regulator is a reverse-current cutout that prevents the battery from motorizing the generator at low speeds by disconnecting the battery from the generator. If the voltage of the generator falls below that of the battery, the battery will discharge through the generator armature; thereby tending to drive the generator as a motor. This action is called "motorizing" the generator, and unless it is prevented, will discharge the battery in a short time.

The action of vibrating contact C1 in the voltage-regulator unit (fig. 15-25) places an intermittent short circuit across R1 and L2. When the generator is not operating, spring S1 holds C1 closed. C2 is also closed by S2, and the shunt field is connected directly across the armature.

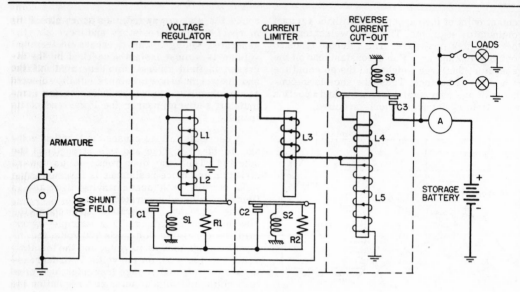

Figure 15-25.—Regulator for variable-speed generator.

When the generator is started, its terminal voltage will rise as the generator comes up to speed, and the armature will apply the field with current through closed contacts $C2$ and $C1$.

As the terminal voltage rises, the current flow through $L1$ increases and the iron becomes more strongly magnetized. At a certain speed and voltage, when the magnetic attraction on the movable arm becomes strong enough to overcome the tension of spring $S1$, contact points $C1$ are separated. The field current now flows through $R1$ and $L2$. Because resistance is added to the field circuit, the field is momentarily weakened and the rise in terminal voltage is checked. Additionally, because the $L2$ winding is opposed to the $L1$ winding, the magnetic pull of $L1$ against $S1$ is partially neutralized, and spring $S1$ closes contact $C1$. $R1$ and $L2$ are again shorted out of the circuit, the field current again increases, the output voltage increases, and $C1$ is opened because of the action of $L1$. The cycle of events occurs very rapidly, many times per second. The terminal voltage of the generator thus varies slightly but rapidly above and below an average value determined by the tension of spring $S1$, which may be adjusted.

The purpose of the vibrator-type current limiter is to limit the output current of the generator automatically to its maximum rated value

in order to protect the generator. As shown in figure 15-25, $L3$ is in series with the main line and load. Thus, the amount of current flowing in the line determines when $C2$ will be opened and $R2$ placed in series with the generator field. By contrast, the voltage regulator is actuated by line voltage, whereas the current limiter is actuated by line current. Spring $S2$ holds contact $C2$ closed until the current through the main line and $L3$ exceeds a certain value, as determined by the tension of spring $S2$, and causes $C2$ to be opened. The increase in current is due to an increase in load. This action inserts R2 into the field circuit of the generator and decreases the field current and the generated voltage. When the generated voltage is decreased, the generator current is reduced. The core of $L3$ is partly demagnetized, and the spring closes the contact points. This causes the generator voltage and current to rise until the current reaches a value sufficient to start the cycle again. A certain minimum value of load current is necessary to cause the current limiter to vibrate.

The purpose of the reverse-current cutout relay (fig. 15-25) is to disconnect the battery automatically from the generator whenever the generator voltage is less than the battery voltage. If this device were not used in the generator

292

circuit, an especially harmful action would occur if the engine were shut off. The battery would discharge through the generator. This would tend to make the generator operate as a motor, but because the generator is coupled to the engine it could not rotate such a heavy load. Under this condition, the generator winding may be severely damaged by excessive current.

There are two windings, $L4$ and $L5$, on the soft-iron core. The current winding, $L4$, consisting of a few turns of heavy wire, is in series with the line and carries the entire line current. The voltage winding, $L5$, consisting of a large number of turns of fine wire, is shunted across the generator terminals.

When the generator is not operating, the contacts, $C3$, are held open by spring $S3$. As the generator voltage builds up, $L5$ magnetizes the iron core. When the current (as a result of the generated voltage) produces sufficient magnetism in the iron core, contact $C3$ is closed, as shown. The battery then receives a charging current. The coil spring, $S3$, is so adjusted that the voltage winding will not close the contact points until the voltage of the generator is in excess of the normal voltage of the battery. The charging current passing through $L4$ aids the current in $L5$ in holding the contacts tightly closed. Unlike $C1$ and $C2$, contacts $C3$ do not vibrate. When the generator slows down, or for any other cause the generator voltage decreases to a certain value below that of the battery, the current reverses through $L4$ and the ampere-turns of $L4$ oppose those of $L5$. Thus, a momentary discharge current from the battery reduces the magnetism of the core and $C3$ is opened, thereby preventing the battery from discharging into the generator and motorizing it. $C3$ will not close again until the generator terminal voltage exceeds that of the battery by a predetermined value.

CARBON-PILE TYPE REGULATOR

The carbon-pile voltage regulator is the type most commonly used in naval aircraft. Its essential parts are shown in figure 15-26. A stack of carbon washers, the "pile," is in series with the shunt field. The resistance of the pile, and thus field current, depends on the mechanical pressure applied to the pile by the wafer spring which acts through the movable iron armature. In a steady-state condition, the magnetic force of the potential coil acts to pull the iron armature away from the pile. This force is balanced by the spring. When a change in line voltage occurs, due to a change in generator speed or load, the potential coil current also changes. Its magnetic strength must also change. As a result, the spring pressure on the carbon pile is INCREASED by a drop in line voltage, and DECREASED by a rise in line voltage. The resultant change in shunt field current will raise or lower the generator output voltage as needed. Variations in voltage characteristics from bench adjustment and aircraft installation may be adjusted by the rheostat, which controls the potential coil current.

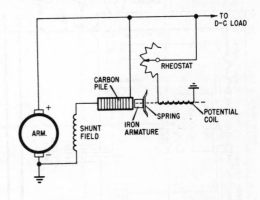

Figure 15-26.—Carbon-pile regulator.

Parallel Operation

Electric power aboard ships may be supplied by more than one generator. When two or more generators are sharing a common load, they are said to be operating in parallel. The generators may be located in different parts of the ship, but are connected to the common load through the ship's power distribution system.

There are a number of reasons for operating generators in parallel. First, the number of generators used may be selected in accordance with the load demand. Thus, by operating each generator as near as possible at its rated capacity, maximum efficiency is achieved. Also, disabled or faulty generators may be taken off the line without interrupting normal operations.

In naval vessels that are provided with d-c electric power systems, the lighting circuits are designed to operate on 115 volts while most motors and other relatively large power-consuming devices are designed to operate on 230 volts. To avoid the use of separate generators for lighting and for power, a 3-wire generator is used that supplies both types of circuits simultaneously. The 3-wire generator is similar to a 2-wire generator except that the armature winding is tapped at points 180 electrical degrees (1-pole span) apart and these are brought out to slip rings on the back of the armature. These rings are connected by means of brushes to a reactance coil. The center tap of the coil connects with the neutral, or third, wire of the 3-wire system.

The reactance coil (or balance coil) provides a method of establishing the potential of the neutral wire, which must be 115 volts positive with respect to one of the outer wires and 115

volts negative with respect to the other. Alternating current is produced in the armature of the d-c generator; and this is taken from the machine through the sliprings to which the balance coil is attached. The action of the alternating current in the balance coil is similar to that occurring in the primary winding of a single-phase transformer. That is, the potential of the center point on the balance coil is at the electrical center of the total voltage generated by the machine. Hence, this point can serve as the neutral, or center, between the positive and negative brushes. The neutral current passes through a portion of the balance coil, which has low resistance to direct current.

The connections for operating stabilized shunt generators in parallel are shown in figure 15-27. Each generator develops 230 volts across the two outside (positive and negative) leads, and 115 volts across either outside leads and neutral. Usually one ammeter and one voltmeter are provided on each generator panel.

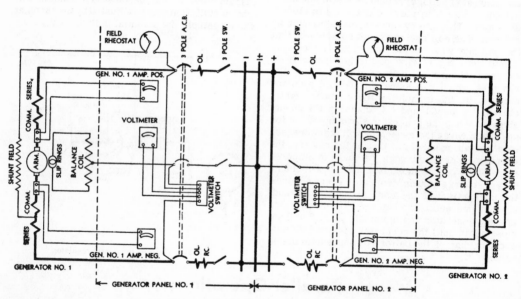

Figure 15-27.—Parallel operation of d-c generators.

Assume that generator No. 1 is supplying the load and it is desired to put generator No. 2 in service. The procedure for paralleling the d-c generators is as follows:

1. The brush rigging and armature of the incoming generator should be inspected for loose gear, and the field rheostat should be adjusted to the lowest voltage position.

2. The prime mover of the incoming generator (No. 2) is brought up to rated speed.

3. The voltage of the incoming machine is adjusted to about 2 volts higher than the bus voltage.

4. Closing the circuit breaker and switch places the generator in parallel with generator No. 1. The ammeter will indicate that generator No. 2 is now carrying a small portion of the load.

5. The field of generator No. 2 is strengthened until the load which it supplies is the proper value. At the same time the field of generator No. 1 should be weakened to maintain the normal voltage.

The procedure for removing a generator from its parallel connection with another is as follows:

1. The field of the generator being secured is weakened at the same time the field of the remaining generator is strengthened until the load on the outgoing machine is about 5 percent of the rated load current.

2. The circuit breaker is tripped and the switch is opened.

TWO-WIRE D-C SYSTEM

The two-wire d-c system is used for d-c power supply on naval aircraft. On multiengine aircraft, the d-c generators are normally operated in parallel. Figure 15-28 is a schematic of the main parts of a typical aircraft d-c power system. Both generators are connected to the main bus, or common load, through their respective reverse-current cutout relays.

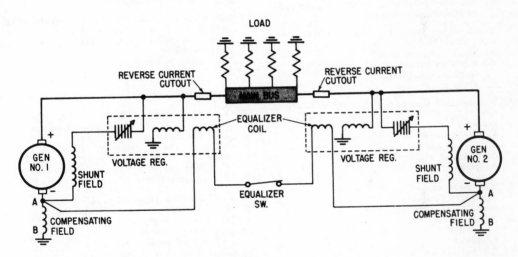

Figure 15-28.—Aircraft d-c power system.

The voltage regulators for aircraft d-c generators are designed and adjusted to permit a slight drooping characteristic. That is, the voltage regulators will permit the terminal voltage of their respective generators to decrease slightly as the bus load is increased. The amount of droop of two or more generators may not be equal, due to internal differences in the generators or adjustment of their regulators. In such cases, one generator will assume more load than the other, as loads are added to the bus.

To assure that the generators will carry equal loads, an automatic load balancing circuit is built into the regulator system. It is referred to as the equalizer. As shown in figure 15-28, the equalizer circuit consists essentially of two equalizer coils and an equalizer switch, all in series, connected between point A in generator No. 1 and point A on generator No. 2. Current through the equalizer circuit flows only when the voltage drops across the compensating fields A-B are unequal. This would be the case when the generators are supplying unequal shares of the total load. The equalizer coils either aid or oppose the regulator potential coils, depending on the DIRECTION of equalizer current. When one generator takes a greater share of the load than the other, the equalizer coil in its regulator will AID the potential coil. This will cause carbon pile decompression, more resistance and less current in the shunt field, less generated voltage, and consequently a decrease in load. The other generator's equalizer coil will OPPOSE its potential coil, increase its shunt field current, raise its generated voltage, and thus cause the generator to assume more of the load.

When only one generator is being operated, the equalizer switch is used to open the equalizer circuit. Otherwise, current would flow from the active generator through the dead generator's compensating field and equalizer coil.

QUIZ

1. A d-c generator is a rotating machine that converts
   a. electrical energy to mechanical energy
   b. mechanical energy to electrical energy
   c. low mechanical energy to a higher level of mechanical energy
   d. low electrical energy to a higher level of electrical energy

2. Commutator segments are insulated from each other by
   a. small strips of wood
   b. a rubber insert
   c. laminated varnish
   d. sheet mica

3. The brushes that carry the current from the commutator to the external circuit are made of
   a. carbon and lead
   b. carbon and graphite
   c. graphite and lead
   d. graphite and zinc

4. The heat-radiating ability of very small armature conductors, as compared to large armature conductors, is
   a. the same
   b. higher
   c. lower
   d. there is no relation

5. The degree that the neutral plane of a generator will shift under load is
   a. inversely proportional to the load
   b. proportional to the load
   c. always less than proportional to the load
   d. independent of the load

6. D-c generators are classified according to the manner in which
   a. they are used
   b. the field windings are connected to the load
   c. the armature circuit is connected to the load
   d. the field windings are connected to the armature circuit

7. The only type of compound generator commonly used in the Navy is the
   a. over compounded
   b. flat compounded
   c. stabilized shunt
   d. cumulative compounded

8. On one end of the tilted plate regulator the graphite plates are separated by mica spacers, while on the other end they are separated by
   a. platinum contacts
   b. silver contacts
   c. zinc contacts
   d. a carbon shoe

9. In the rocking disk regulator, when the terminal voltage of the generator starts to fall, the disk movement
   a. opens the circuit to the solenoid
   b. short-circuits more of the resistors
   c. short-circuits less of the resistors
   d. completes the circuit to the solenoid

10. The 3-wire generator is similar to the 2-wire generator except that the armature winding is tapped at
    a. 30 mechanical degrees
    b. 90 electrical degrees
    c. 180 electrical degrees
    d. 30 electrical degrees

11. The name given to the mechanical power source used to turn the armature of a d-c generator is the
    a. motor driver
    b. machine driver
    c. prime mover
    d. rotor

12. Flashover between the commutator segments in a high-voltage d-c generator is prevented by
    a. reducing the number of segments
    b. increasing the number of segments
    c. reducing the number of field coils
    d. increasing the number of field coils

13. The distance between the two sides of a coil in a d-c generator armature is called
   a. coil pitch
   b. commutator pitch
   c. pole span
   d. pole pitch
14. The effects of armature reaction in a generator are reduced by the use of
   a. commutating windings
   b. interpoles
   c. commutating windings and interpoles
   d. compensating windings and commutating poles
15. The need for shifting the brushes of a d-c generator as its load changes has been eliminated by the use of
   a. interpoles
   b. commutating poles
   c. compensating windings
   d. larger brushes
16. A shunt generator will build up to full terminal voltage with no external load connected to it due to
   a. the large conductors used in the armature
   b. motor action of the generator
   c. interpoles
   d. self-excitation
17. The percent regulation of a generator having a no-load e.m.f. of 220 volts and a full-load e.m.f. of 215 volts is approximately
   a. 3%
   b. 45%
   c. 0.02%
   d. 2%
18. The purpose of the vibrator-type current limiter is to automatically limit the output current of the generator to its
   a. preset value
   b. minimum rated value
   c. maximum rated value
   d. saturation point
19. The main differences between shipboard d-c generators and aircraft d-c generators are
   a. size, rating, and appearance
   b. size, appearance, and function
   c. size and rating only
   d. appearance, rating, and function
20. The part of a d-c generator into which the working voltage is induced is the
   a. yoke
   b. field poles
   c. armature
   d. commutator

21. Power lost in heat in the windings due to the flow of current through the copper is known as
   a. eddy current loss
   b. hysteresis loss
   c. copper loss
   d. none are correct
22. Compensating windings are imbedded in the pole faces parallel to the armature conductors and are electrically connected with the armature windings in
   a. parallel
   b. series-parallel
   c. series
   d. numbers equal to the number of armature conductors
23. As armature current of a generator increases, motor reaction force
   a. decreases
   b. remains the same
   c. increases
   d. has no relation to armature current
24. The small variable shunt connected across the series field coils, to permit adjustment of the degree of compounding, is a
   a. diverter
   b. divider
   c. resistor
   d. rheostat
25. The major difference between various voltage regulator systems is merely the method by which
   a. field circuit resistance and current are controlled
   b. armature circuit resistance is controlled
   c. load circuit resistance is controlled
   d. armature current and load resistance are controlled
26. In the rocking disk regulator (fig. 15-24), when the terminal voltage of the generator starts to fall, the solenoid is weakened and the weight rocks the disk
   a. upward
   b. to the left
   c. to the right
   d. downward
27. In the carbon-pile type regulator, the mechanical pressure on the carbon pile is applied by the
   a. wafer spring
   b. potential coil
   c. iron core of the potential coil
   d. rheostat

CHAPTER 16

DIRECT-CURRENT MOTORS

The construction of a d-c motor is essentially the same as that of a d-c generator. The d-c generator converts mechanical energy into electrical energy, and the d-c motor converts the electrical energy back into mechanical energy. A d-c generator may be made to function as a motor by applying a suitable source of direct voltage across the normal output electrical terminals.

There are various types of d-c motors, depending on the way the field coils are connected. Each has characteristics that are advantageous under given load conditions.

SHUNT MOTORS have the field coils connected in parallel with the armature circuit. This type of motor, with constant potential applied, develops variable torque at an essentially constant speed, even under changing load conditions. Such loads are found in machineshop drives. They include lathes, milling machines, drills, planers, shapers, and so forth.

SERIES MOTORS have the field coils connected in series with the armature circuit. This type of motor, with constant potential applied, develops variable torque but its speed varies widely under changing load conditions. That is, the speed is low under heavy loads, but becomes excessively high under light loads. Series motors are commonly used to drive electric cranes, hoists, winches, and certain types of vehicles (for example, electric trucks). Series motors are used extensively to start internal combustion engines.

COMPOUND MOTORS have one set of field coils in parallel with the armature circuit, and another set of field coils in series with the armature circuit. This type of motor is a compromise between shunt and series motors. It develops an increased starting torque over that of the shunt motor, and has less variation in speed than the series motor. Shunt, series, and compound motors are all d-c motors designed to operate from constant-potential variable-current d-c sources.

STABILIZED SHUNT MOTORS have a light series winding in addition to the shunt field. The action is similar to ordinary shunt motors except that stabilized shunt motors have less field iron and are lighter in weight. Without the stabilizing series field, they have the characteristics of a shunt motor with a strong field and low armature resistance.

Schematic diagrams of the four basic types of d-c motors are shown in figure 16-1.

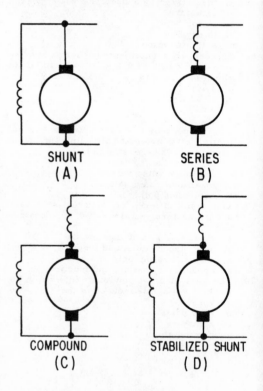

Figure 16-1.—Schematic diagrams of four types of d-c motors.

Direct-current motors may also be classified in other ways. For example, they may be classified according to the degree of enclosure, such as OPEN (fig. 16-2 (A)), DRIP-PROOF (fig. 16-2 (B)), ENCLOSED (fig. 16-2 (C)), and so forth.

The open-type motor shown in figure 16-2 (A) has end bells which offer little or no restriction to ventilation. The drip-proof motor shown in figure 16-2 (B) is protected from falling moisture and dirt from any direction up to a 45° angle with respect to the vertical. A motor of this type has all ventilation openings protected with wire screens or perforated covers, as shown in the figure. An enclosed motor like the one in figure 16-2 (C) is totally enclosed except for openings provided for the admission and discharge of air. These openings are connected to inlet and outlet ducts or pipes.

Other motor types include a spray-tight motor so constructed that a stream of water from a hose may be played upon it from any direction without leakage into the motor.

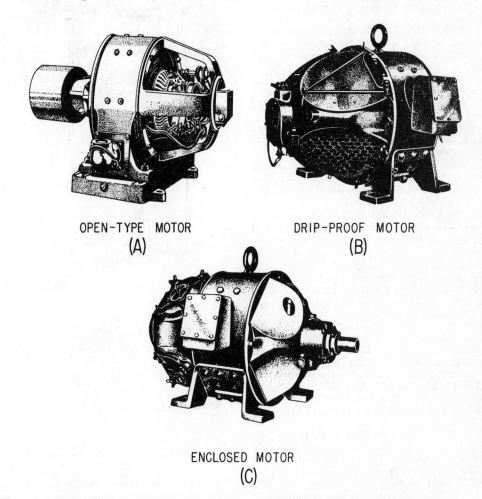

OPEN-TYPE MOTOR

(A)

DRIP-PROOF MOTOR

(B)

ENCLOSED MOTOR

(C)

Figure 16-2.—Types of shipboard d-c motors classified according to enclosure.

A submersible motor is one that will operate while submerged in liquid.

With reference to cooling, the following types of motors are found aboard ship:

1. NATURAL VENTILATED MOTORS, cooled by the natural circulation of the air caused by the rotation of the armature.

2. SELF-VENTILATED MOTORS, cooled by a fan attached to the armature of the motor.

3. SEPARATELY VENTILATED MOTORS, cooled by an independent fan or blower apart from the motor.

With reference to speed, motors are classified as:

1. CONSTANT-SPEED MOTORS in which the speed varies only slightly between no load and full load. A shunt motor is a constant-speed motor.

2. MULTISPEED MOTORS which can be operated at any one of several definite speeds, each speed being nearly constant with load change. Such motors cannot be operated at intermediate speeds. A motor with two windings on the armature is an example of a multispeed motor.

3. ADJUSTABLE-SPEED MOTORS whose speed can be varied gradually over a wide range, but when once adjusted remains at nearly constant speed with load change.

4. VARYING SPEED MOTORS in which the speed varies with the load. Ordinarily the speed decreases as the load increases. The series motor is an example of this type of motor.

5. ADJUSTABLE VARYING SPEED MOTORS in which the speed may be adjusted over a wide range for any given load; but if the speed is adjusted at a given load, the speed will vary with any change in load.

Motors are also classified according to the type of duty they are to perform. For example, a CONTINUOUS-DUTY MOTOR is capable of operating continuously at its rated output without exceeding specified temperature limits. An INTERMITTENT-DUTY MOTOR is capable of being operated at its rated output for a limited period without exceeding its specified temperature limit.

Most d-c motors on Navy vessels are designed to operate on constant-potential 2-wire circuits of either 115 volts or 230 volts. These circuits may be combined in a 3-wire d-c supply with 230 volts between each outside wire, and 115 volts between each outside wire and middle or neutral wire.

D-c motors find extensive use on naval aircraft. The motors used on aircraft operate on the same principles as the larger motors aboard ship. However, the airborne motors differ considerably in size, rating, and appearance, as illustrated in figure 16-3. Also, they are designed to operate from a 24-28 volt d-c source.

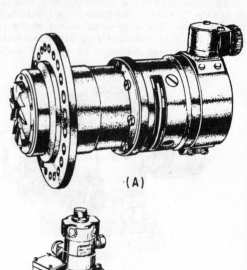

(A)

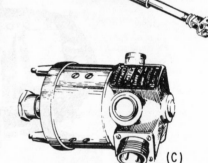

(B)

(C)

Figure 16-3.—Aircraft d-c motors.

Part (A) is an aircraft engine starter motor. Starters are series motors, selected to supply the typically high torque required for engine

300

starting. They are usually the largest motors on the aircraft, with power outputs up to twenty h.p., but are designed only for intermittent use. Part (B) is one of many types of d-c motors used to actuate mechanical loads, in this case cowl flaps. Such loads may include wing flaps, cowl flaps, landing gear, cockpit canopies, and bomb bay doors. Actuator motors are also of the series type, since they must start under full mechanical load. Many airborne actuator motors are of the series split-field type, and are reversible. Most are also designed only for intermittent use. Part (C) is a continuous-duty d-c motor, in this case one that is used to drive windshield wipers. Continuous-duty motors on aircraft are usually of the compound type. The most recent trend in aircraft design is to use d-c motors for intermittent duty, and a-c motors for continuous duty.

Principles of D-C Motors

FORCE ACTING ON A CONDUCTOR

The operation of a d-c motor depends on the principle that a current-carrying conductor placed in, and at right angles to, a magnetic field tends to move at right angles to the direction of the field, as shown in figure 16-4. This action was previously described under the operating principle of the D'Arsonval meter movement.

The magnetic field between a north and a south pole of a magnet is shown in figure 16-4 (A). The lines of force, comprising the field extend from the north pole to the south pole. A cross section of a current-carrying conductor is shown in figure 16-4 (B). The plus sign in the wire indicates that the electron flow is away from the observer. The direction of the flux loops around the wire is counterclockwise, as shown. This follows from the left-hand flux rule which states that if the conductor is grasped in the left hand with the thumb extended in the direction of the current flow, the fingers will curve around the conductor in the direction of the magnetic flux.

If the conductor (carrying the electron flow away from the observer) is placed between the poles of the magnet, as in figure 16-4 (C), both fields will be distorted. Above the wire the field is weakened, and the conductor tends to move upward. The force exerted upward depends on the strength of the field between the poles and on the strength of the current flowing through the wire.

If the current through the conductor is reversed, as in figure 16-4 (D), the direction of the flux around the wire is reversed. The field below the conductor is now weakened, and the conductor tends to move downward.

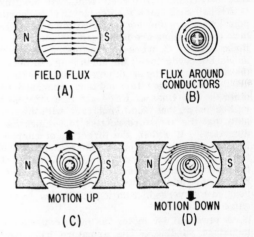

FIELD FLUX
(A)

FLUX AROUND
CONDUCTORS
(B)

MOTION UP
(C)

MOTION DOWN
(D)

Figure 16-4.—Force acting on a current-carrying conductor in a magnetic field.

A convenient method of determining the direction of motion of a current-carrying conductor in a magnetic field is by the use of the right-hand motor rule. Practical d-c motors depend for their operation on the interaction between the field flux and a large number of current-carrying conductors. As in d-c generators, the conductors are wound in slots in the armature; and the armature is mounted in bearings and is free to rotate in the magnetic field. An armature with two slots and two conductors (that is, a single conductor wound in the two slots) is shown in figure 16-5.

Figure 16-5 (A) shows the uniform distribution of the main field flux when the field magnets are energized, and no current flows through the armature. The flux is concentrated in the air gap between the field and armature

301

because of the relatively high permeability of the soft-iron armature core and the low reluctance of the magnetic circuit.

Figure 16-5 (B) shows the magnetic fields surrounding the two active conductors when current flows through the armature coil in the direction indicated, and the field coils are not energized. The direction of the magnetic fields surrounding the two conductors is determined by means of the left-hand flux rule.

Figure 16-5 (C) shows the resultant magnetic field produced by the interaction of the main field magnetomotive force and the armature magnetomotive force. Note that the flux is strengthened below the conductor at the north pole and above the conductor at the south pole because the lines are in the same directions at these points. Conversely, the flux is weakened above the conductor at the north pole and below the conductor at the south pole because the lines are opposite in direction and tend to cancel each other. The lines of force act like stretched rubber bands that tend to contract, with the result that the armature rotates in a clockwise direction. If either the direction of current through the armature coil or the polarity of the field is reversed (but not both), the direction of the force on the armature conductors reverses. If both the field polarity and the armature current are reversed, rotation continues in the same direction.

A practical d-c motor has many coils in the armature winding. The armature has many slots into which are inserted many turns of wire. This increases the number of armature conductors and thus produces a greater, more constant torque. Power output is also increased by increasing the number of poles in the field.

As in the case of the d-c generator, the d-c motor is equipped with a commutator and brushes.

The force, F, acting on a current-carrying conductor in a magnetic field is directly proportional to the field strength, the active length of the conductor (that part of the conductor contained in the armature slot and lying under a pole face), and the current flowing through it. The force, the conductor, and the field are assumed to be mutually perpendicular. This relationship is expressed algebraically as

$$F = \frac{8.85 \times BLI}{10^8},$$

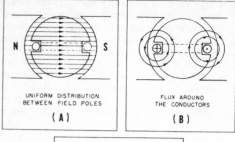

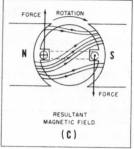

Figure 16-5.—Two-conductor armature.

where F is the force in pounds, B the flux density in lines per square inch, L the active length of the conductor in inches, I the current in amperes flowing through the conductor, and 8.85 is a constant that must be used when the above units are employed.

In a given motor, the length of the conductor is a fixed quantity: therefore, the only variables are the current and the flux. If the field flux is constant, the force acting on the conductor varies directly as the armature current. In other words, F is proportional to I. The following example will illustrate how the force acting on a conductor is calculated.

If a conductor having an active length of 10 inches and a current of 30 amperes is placed in a uniform field of 37,700 lines per square inch, what force will be exerted on the conductor?

$$F = \frac{8.85 \ BLI}{10^8} = \frac{8.85 \times 37,700 \times 10 \times 30}{10^8} = 1 \text{ pound.}$$

If the conductor is wound around an armature (fig. 16-5 (C)) and the armature current flows in the directions shown, there will be an upward force of one pound on the left of the armature and a downward force of one pound on the

302

right of the armature. The net force acting to turn the armature is the sum of these two forces, or two pounds.

TORQUE

The TORQUE (or twist) on the armature is the product of the force acting at the surface of the armature times the perpendicular distance to the center of rotation of the armature. Assume the radius of the armature being considered is 1.5 feet, the torque exerted by each conductor is 1 x 1.5 = 1.5 pound-feet; and the total torque exerted by both conductors is 1.5 + 1.5 = 3 pound-feet.

The armature conductors for a motor are assembled in coils and connected to the commutator riser exactly as in a generator. In the 2-pole motor (fig. 16-6 (A)), the current divides equally in the two paths through the armature. Current flows in one direction in the conductors under the north pole and in the opposite direction in the conductors under the south pole. To develop a continuous motor torque the current in a coil must reverse when the coil passes the dead center position (top and bottom). The function of the commutator is to reverse the current at the proper time to maintain the current flow in the same direction in all conductors under a given pole. The total torque is the sum of the individual torques contributed by all the armature conductors. If there are 200 active conductors each developing a force of 1 pound the total torque will be 200 x 1 x the average moment arm.

The AVERAGE MOMENT ARM is the average of all the perpendicular distances from the armature conductors to the center of rotation. If the field is assumed to consist of uniformly spaced horizontal lines of flux, the average moment arm will be 0.637 of the maximum moment arm, or radius, of the armature.

If the radius of the armature is 1.57 feet, the average moment arm is 0.637 x 1.57 = 1 foot. The total torque exerted by 200 armature conductors developing a force of 1 pound each is 200 x 1 x 1 = 200 pound-feet.

In a 4-pole parallel-wound armature, the current divides into four paths as shown in figure 16-6 (B). The current flows in opposite directions under alternate poles, as in the 2-pole armature, and develops a unidirectional force on all of the armature conductors. The total torque produced by the armature current is equal to the

sum of the individual torques developed by each conductor. This torque, T, is proportional to the product of armature current and field strength.

$$T = K_t \Phi I_a, \tag{16-1}$$

where K_t is a constant that includes the number of armature conductors, number of paths, and other factors which are constant for a particular machine; Φ the flux per pole and I_a the total armature current. When the speed of a motor is constant, the generated torque due to the armature current is just equal to the retarding torque caused by the combined effect of the friction losses in the motor and the mechanical load. The torque developed by the motor armature is a steady one and does not pulsate as in the case of reciprocating steam engines or internal combustion engines.

HORSEPOWER OF A MOTOR

If the number of revolutions that the armature of a motor makes per minute (or per second), the effective armature radius at which the force acts, and the total force acting at and tangent to this effective radius are known, the horsepower may be determined. Briefly, the horsepower may be determined in the following manner.

Work is accomplished when force acts through distance. For example, when a force of one pound acts through a distance of one foot, one foot-pound of work is accomplished. If 33,000 foot-pounds of work is done in one minute, one horsepower of work is accomplished.

Assume that an armature makes 100 revolutions per minute and that the effective radius is 1.59 feet. The circumference (the distance through which the force moves in one revolution of the armature) is

circumference = $2\pi r$

= 2 x 3.14 x 1.59 = 10 feet.

Assuming that a total effective force of 200 pounds acts on the armature tangent to the 10-foot circumference, the work done in one revolution is

work = force x distance = 200 x 10 = 2,000 foot-pounds.

The work done in 100 revolutions (one minute) is

2,000 x 100 = 200,000 foot-pounds.

303

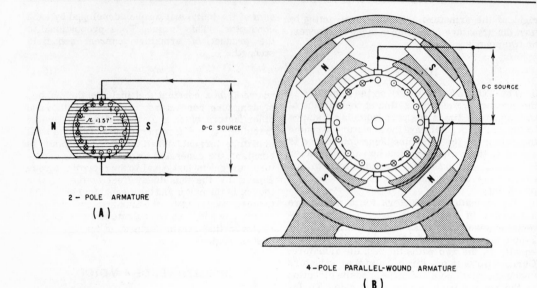

2 – POLE ARMATURE

(A)

4 – POLE PARALLEL-WOUND ARMATURE

(B)

Figure 16-6.—Torque developed in a motor armature.

The horsepower is therefore,

$$\text{h.p.} = \frac{\text{foot-pounds per minute}}{33,000} = \frac{200,000}{33,000} = 6.06 \text{ horsepower.}$$

The horsepower developed by a motor armature may be derived from the general expression.

$$\text{h.p.} = \frac{FV}{33,000}, \qquad (16-2)$$

where F is the total force in pounds tangent to the effective circumference of the armature, and V the velocity of a point on this circumference in feet per minute. Velocity is determined as

$$V = 2\pi r N, \qquad (16-3)$$

where r is the effective radius of the armature in feet, and N is the armature speed in revolutions per minute. The effective circumference is equal to $2\pi r$.

Substituting equation (16-3) in equation (16-2),

$$\text{h.p.} = \frac{2\pi r N F}{33,000} \qquad (16-4)$$

The torque in pound-feet produced by the motor armature is

$$T = rF. \qquad (16-5)$$

Substituting equation (16-5) in equation (16-4) and dividing numerator and denominator by 2π,

$$\text{h.p.} = \frac{NT}{5,252}. \qquad (16-6)$$

Substituting the values $N = 100$ r.p.m. and $T = 1.59 \times 200 = 318$ pound-feet of the preceding example in equation (16-6), the result is

$$\text{h.p.} = \frac{100 \times 318}{5,252} = 6.06.$$

Thus, the horsepower developed by a motor depends on its speed and torque. Large, slow-speed motors develop a large torque; whereas other much smaller motors of the same horsepower rating operate at reduced torque and increased speed.

COUNTER E.M.F.

The MOTOR ACTION of a generator was treated in chapter 15: the GENERATOR ACTION of a motor is now considered. By applying the right-hand motor rule to an armature conductor carrying current in the direction indicated in figure 16-7, it will be found that the conductor is forced upward. As the conductor is moved up through the field, it cuts lines of flux and has a voltage induced in it. Applying the left-hand generator rule, it is found that this generated voltage is in opposition to the impressed e.m.f. This counter voltage is induced in the windings of any rotating motor armature and always opposes the impressed voltage. It is called COUNTER ELECTROMOTIVE FORCE and is directly proportional to the speed of the armature and the field strength. That is, the counter e.m.f. is increased or decreased if the speed is increased or decreased respectively; the same is true if the field strength is increased or decreased.

The EFFECTIVE VOLTAGE (IR drop) in the armature is equal to the impressed voltage minus the counter e.m.f. The armature IR drop varies directly with the current flowing in the armature and the resistance of the armature.

To produce an armature current, I_a, in an armature of resistance, R_a, requires an effective voltage of I_aR_a.

The current flowing through the armature can be found by the equation

$$I_a = \frac{E_a - E_c}{R_a},$$

where I_a is the current flowing through the armature, E_a the impressed (or applied) voltage across the armature, E_c the counter e.m.f., and R_a the armature resistance. This equation can be transposed and written as

$$E_c = E_a - I_aR_a. \qquad (16\text{-}7)$$

In the case of the generator, the generated e.m.f. is equal to the terminal voltage plus the armature resistance drop; and in the case of the motor the generated or counter e.m.f. is equal to the terminal voltage minus the voltage drop in the armature resistance.

Expressing E_a in terms of E_c and I_aR_a,

$$E_a = E_c + I_aR_a.$$

This formula is valid for any d-c motor regardless of speed or load.

The counter e.m.f., E_c, that is induced in a motor armature may be determined by an equation similar to that used to determine the generator voltage in a generator in chapter 15. This equation is

$$E_c = \frac{\Phi ZNP}{10^8p}, \qquad (16\text{-}8)$$

where Φ is the number of lines of flux per pole, Z the number of face conductors, N the armature speed in revolutions per second, P the number of field poles, and p the number of parallel paths through the armature circuit.

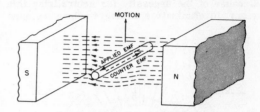

Figure 16-7.—Generator action in a motor.

ARMATURE REACTION

The armature current in a generator flows in the same direction as the generated e.m.f., but the armature current in a motor is forced to flow in the opposite direction to that of the counter e.m.f. Assume that the field of the motor (fig. 16-8 (A)) is of the same polarity as the field of the generator (fig. 15-12 (A)). For the same direction of armature rotation, the armature flux of the motor (fig. 16-8 (B)) is in the opposite direction to that of the generator (fig. 15-12 (B)). In a motor the main field flux is always distorted in the opposite direction to rotation (fig. 16-8 (C)), whereas in a generator the main field flux is distorted (fig. 15-12 (C)) in the same direction as that of rotation. Note that the resultant field in the motor (fig. 16-8 (C)) is strengthened at the leading pole tips and weakened at the trailing pole tips. This action causes the electrical neutral plane to be shifted back to $A'B'$. Thus, to obtain good commutation in a motor without interpoles, it is necessary to shift the brushes from the mechanical neutral, AB, in a direction opposite to that of the armature rotation.

The armature reaction is overcome in a motor by the same methods as for the generator — that is, by the use of laminated pole tips with slotted pole pieces, and compensating windings. In each case the effect produced is the same as that produced in the generator, but it is in the opposite direction.

COMMUTATION

The brush axis, $A'B'$ (fig. 16-8 (C)), could be made to coincide exactly with the neutral plane of the combined field. This would eliminate sparking at the brushes if it were not for the self-induced e.m.f. in the commutated coils. Because of the necessity for neutralizing this e.m.f. to eliminate sparking, the brushes must be set slightly behind the neutral plane in a motor. Thus, in both the generator and the motor, the brushes must be moved from the mechanical neutral slightly beyond the electrical neutral plane to neutralize the effect of self-inductance.

The current flowing in the armature coils of a motor (fig. 16-9) must be periodically reversed when the coils are being short-circuited by the

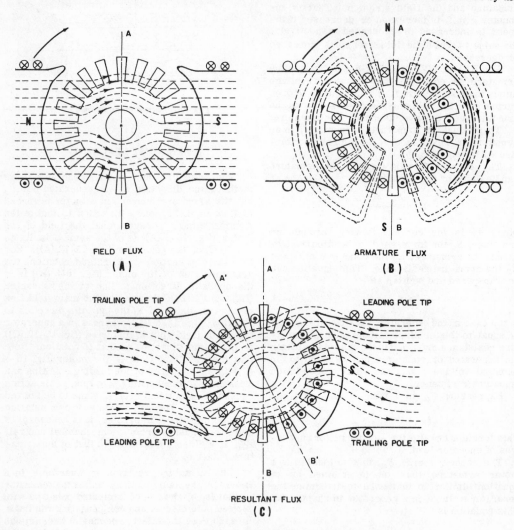

FIELD FLUX

(A)

ARMATURE FLUX

(B)

TRAILING POLE TIP

LEADING POLE TIP

LEADING POLE TIP

TRAILING POLE TIP

RESULTANT FLUX

(C)

Figure 16-8.—Armature reaction in a motor.

306

brushes in order to maintain a unidirectional torque as the coils move under alternate poles. When coil *A* is short circuited by a brush, its current immediately starts to decrease to zero; from zero, the current then builds up to a maximum in the reversed direction by the time the coil moves from position ① to position ②, where the brush no longer short circuits it. As a result of the changing current, a self-induced voltage is set up in the shorted coil, which tends to keep the current from changing. To obtain sparkless commutation it is necessary to overcome this self-induced voltage.

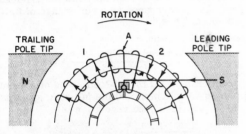

Figure 16-9.—Commutation in a motor.

In any motor the current flows as a result of the applied voltage, and the counter e.m.f. opposes the flow of current. As the current in the commutated coil decreases to zero, the e.m.f. of self-induction tends to keep the current flowing in the same direction, as indicated by the arrow in position ①. Therefore, it aids the applied voltage during this portion of the cycle. As the coil moves into position ② the current increases in the opposite direction, and the self-induced voltage again opposes this current increase. To overcome the self-induced voltage another voltage is introduced into the coil, which opposes the self-induced voltage. The counter e.m.f. is in the proper direction to accomplish this, but the coil being commutated is in the neutral plane and consequently has no counter e.m.f. generated in it.

When the brushes are shifted against the direction of rotation, the coils that are being shorted by the brushes still cut lines of flux from the previous north pole and have a small amount of counter e.m.f. generated in them. Because this counter e.m.f. opposes the applied voltage it also opposes the self-induced voltage, thus resulting in rapid reversal of coil current and in sparkless commutation.

When the load on the motor increases, armature reaction increases and the electrical neutral plane is shifted further in the direction opposite to that of the armature rotation. To maintain sparkless commutation, the plane of the brushes will have to be shifted slightly beyond the electrical neutral plane. When the load is reduced, the brushes are shifted in the opposite direction. Thus, for sparkless commutation, it is necessary to manually shift the brushes when the load varies.

COMMUTATING POLES

Commutating poles are as important in motors as in generators. Nearly all motors of more than one horsepower depend on COMMUTATING POLES, sometimes called INTERPOLES, rather than on the shifting of the brushes to obtain sparkless commutation. Essentially the only difference between the interpole generator and the interpole motor is that in the generator the interpole has the same polarity as the main pole AHEAD of it in the direction of rotation, but in the motor the interpole has the same polarity as the main pole BACK of it.

Without interpoles the e.m.f. of self-induction is overcome by commutating the coil while it is cutting the flux of the main pole it is just leaving. Therefore, if the interpole is to overcome the e.m.f. of self-induction, it must have the same polarity as the main pole it is leaving. This is a north pole in the example of figure 16-9.

The interpole series field coil in a motor is connected to carry the armature current, as in the generator. As the load varies, the interpole flux varies, and commutation is automatic with load change. It is not necessary to shift the brushes when there is an increase or decrease in load. The brushes are located on the no-load neutral and remain in that position for all conditions of load.

The motor may be reversed by reversing the direction of the current in the armature. When the armature current is reversed, the current through the interpole is also reversed, and therefore the interpole still has the proper polarity to provide automatic commutation.

The direction of the counter e.m.f. in the interpole motor with clockwise rotation (fig. 16-10) illustrates that coils under the interpoles do not contribute to the armature counter voltage, but that only those coils under the main

307

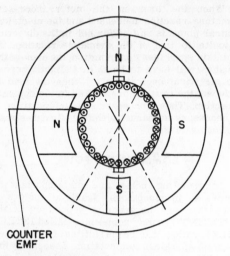

COUNTER
EMF

Figure 16-10.—Effect of interpoles on armature counter e.m.f.

poles contribute to it. The total counter voltage generated in the conductors on each half of the armature is equal to the algebraic sum of the voltages generated in each conductor between the upper and lower brush. Because those under the upper north interpole generate an equal and opposite voltage to those under the lower south interpole, the remaining conductors under the main field poles generate the armature counter e.m.f. that controls the armature load current and the speed-torque characteristics of the motor. It is important that the brushes be set

in the correct neutral plane, otherwise the commutation will be impaired and the motor characteristics will be altered.

SPEED REGULATION

SPEED REGULATION is the ability of a motor to maintain its speed when a load is applied. It is an inherent characteristic of a motor and remains the same as long as the applied voltage does not vary — that is, unless a physical, or mechanical, change is made in the machine. The speed regulation of a motor is a comparison of its no-load speed to its full-load speed and is expressed as a percentage of full-load speed. Thus,

$$\text{percent speed regulation} = \frac{\text{no-load speed} - \text{full-load speed}}{\text{full-load speed}} \times 100 \, .$$

For example, if the no-load speed of a shunt motor is 1,600 r.p.m. and the full-load speed is 1,500 r.p.m. the speed regulation is

$$\frac{1,600 - 1,500}{1,500} \times 100 = 6.6 \text{ percent.}$$

The LOWER the speed-regulation percentage figure of a motor, the more constant the speed will be under varying load conditions and the BETTER will be the speed regulation. The HIGHER the speed-regulation percentage figure, the POORER is the speed regulation.

SPEED CONTROL refers to the external means of varying the speed of a motor under any load.

Shunt Motors

SPEED REGULATION OF A SHUNT MOTORS

The field circuit of a shunt motor is connected across the line and is thus in parallel with the armature the same as it is in the shunt generator (fig. 15-16 (B)). If the supply voltage is constant, the current through the field coils, and consequently the field flux, will be constant.

When there is no load on the shunt motor, the only torque necessary is that required to overcome bearing friction and windage. The rotation of the armature coils through the field flux establishes a counter e.m.f. that limits the armature current to the relatively small value required to establish the necessary torque to run the motor on no load.

When an external load is applied to the shunt motor it tends to slow down slightly. The slight decrease in speed causes a corresponding decrease in counter e.m.f. If the armature resistance is low, the resulting increase in armature current and torque will be relatively large. Therefore, the torque is increased until it matches the resisting torque of the load. The speed of the motor will then remain constant at the new value as long as the load is constant.

Conversely, if the load on the shunt motor is reduced, the motor tends to speed up slightly. The increased speed causes a corresponding increase in counter e.m.f. and a relatively large decrease in armature current and torque.

Thus, it may be seen that the amount of current flowing through the armature of a shunt motor depends on the load on the motor. The larger the load, the larger the current; and conversely, the smaller the load, the smaller the current. The change in speed causes a change in counter e.m.f. and armature current in each case.

Figure 16-11 indicates graphically what happens when the load is applied or removed from a shunt motor. In this figure it is assumed that the field strength remains constant.

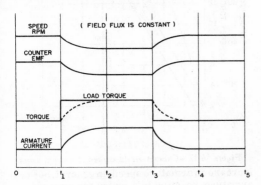

Figure 16-11.—Shunt motor load-speed-torque-e.m.f. relationships with respect to time.

During the interval between 0 and t_1 the motor operates under conditions of equilibrium — that is, the speed, counter e.m.f., torque, and armature current have steady values. At t_1 a load is applied to the motor. Instantly, the load-torque curve rises, but the inertia of the armature prevents the generated torque from rising instantly with it. Because the load torque exceeds

the generated torque in the motor armature, the motor speed is reduced until a balance is again obtained. When the generated torque is again equal to the load torque deceleration ceases and the motor operates at a constant reduced speed.

At time t_2 this state of equilibrium, corresponding to the new load, is reached. At time t_3 the load is suddenly removed. The load torque drops instantly, but the armature inertia prevents the generated torque from falling instantly with it. Likewise, the armature inertia prevents the armature speed from increasing suddenly. Because the generated torque exceeds the load torque, the motor accelerates. As the speed increases, the counter e.m.f. increases proportionately. This opposes the applied e.m.f., and the armature current is reduced until the generated torque and load torque are again in a state of equilibrium. The speed then levels off to a constant value.

The operational features of a shunt motor are indicated in table 16-1. The variation of line current, armature current, counter e.m.f., speed, torque, and efficiency, with varying load conditions are indicated. The values are based on a 1-horsepower 100-volt shunt motor having a field current of 1 ampere and an armature resistance of 1 ohm.

When the armature current is 1 ampere the armature IR drop is 1 volt, and the counter e.m.f. is the difference between the applied voltage and the IR drop, or 100 - 1 = 99 volts. The speed at this load is assumed to be 990 r.p.m. At this load the motor torque is assumed to be 0.7 pound-foot. The output power, P_O, in watts is

$$P_o = \frac{NT}{5,252} \times 746 = 0.142\ NT = 0.142 \times 990 \times 0.7 = 98.4\ \text{watts.}$$

Table 16-1.—Operational features of a shunt motor.

I Line (amperes)	I Armature (amperes)	Counter e.m.f. (volts)	Speed (r.p.m.)	Torque (lb-ft)	Output 0.142NT (watts)	Input (watts)	Efficiency (percent)	Load
[1]2	[1]1	[1]99	[1]990	[1]0.7	98.4	200	49.2	Light.
4	3	97	970	2.1	289	400	72.2	Do.
6	5	95	950	3.5	472	600	78.5	Do.
8	7	93	930	4.9	646	800	80.8	Do.
10	9	91	910	6.3	815	1,000	81.5	Normal.
21	20	80	800	14	1,590	2,100	76	Over.

[1] Assumed.

The constant 746 is used to convert horsepower output into an equivalent number of watts output (1 horsepower = 746 watts).

The total input current to the motor is equal to the sum of the field current and the armature current, or $1 + 1 = 2$ amperes. The input power is the product of the applied voltage and the total input current, or $100 \times 2 = 200$ watts. The efficiency is

$$\frac{\text{output}}{\text{input}} \times 100 = \frac{98.4}{200} = 49.2 \text{ percent at this load.}$$

The torque calculations for other values of load are based on the proportionality between armature current and torque. For example, if the torque is 0.7 pound-foot when the armature current is 1 ampere, the torque for an armature current of 2 amperes will be $2 \times 0.7 = 1.4$ pound-feet.

The speed calculations are based on the proportionality between speed and counter voltage. For example, when the armature current is 2 amperes the armature IR drop is $2 \times 1 = 2$ volts, and the counter e.m.f. is $100 - 2 = 98$ volts. If the speed is 990 r.p.m. when the counter e.m.f. is 99 volts, the speed at 98 volts counter e.m.f. will be 980 r.p.m.

The characteristic curves of a 5-horsepower 230-volt shunt motor are shown in figure 16-12. These curves include speed, torque, efficiency, and input current. The speed curve is almost a horizontal line, and the regulation is good. The torque varies directly with the output load and armature current because the field is approximately constant over the load range.

The speed regulation of a shunt motor is generally better than the voltage regulation of the same machine when operating as a shunt generator. This action is due to the fact that armature reaction in a generator weakens the field and lowers the terminal voltage, whereas armature reaction in a motor weakens the field and tends to increase the motor speed. Armature resistance is low, and a decrease in field strength and counter e.m.f. (for example, of 5 percent) might result in an increase in armature current and accelerating force on the armature conductors of 50 percent with resulting

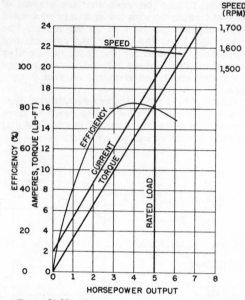

Figure 16-12.—Characteristic curves of a shunt motor.

increase in armature speed. In general, however, armature reaction in a motor weakens the field only slightly and does not cause the speed to increase with load, but to decrease less than it would if the armature reaction were not present.

USES OF SHUNT MOTORS

From the preceding considerations it is evident that a shunt motor is essentially a constant-speed machine. Although the speed may be varied by varying the current through the field winding (for example, by means of a field rheostat), the speed remains nearly constant for a given field current.

The constant-speed characteristic makes the use of shunt motors desirable for driving machine tools or any other device that requires a constant-speed driving source.

Where there is a wide variation in load, or where the motor must start under a heavy load, series motors have desirable features not found in shunt motors.

Series Motors

SPEED REGULATION OF SERIES MOTORS

The field coils of a series motor are connected in series with the armature like those of

the series generator in figure 15-16 (B). With relatively low flux density in the field iron, the series field strength is proportional to armature current I_a. The torque developed by the motor armature is proportional to $I_a \Phi$; and because Φ is also proportional to I_a, the torque is proportional to $I_a{}^2$.

If the supply voltage is constant, the armature current and the field flux will be constant only if the load is constant. If there were no load (this is never done) on the motor, the armature would speed up to such an extent that the windings might be thrown from the slots and the commutator destroyed by the excessive centrifugal forces. The reason why the speed becomes excessive on no load is explained in the following manner.

The speed of a series motor may be expressed mathematically as

$$\text{r.p.m.} = \frac{K[E - I_a(R_a + R_s)]}{\Phi}; \qquad (16\text{-}9)$$

Where K is a constant that depends on such factors as the number of poles, the number of current paths, and the total number of armature conductors; E is the voltage applied across the entire motor; I_a is the armature current; R_a is the armature resistance; R_S is the resistance of the series field; and Φ is the field strength. The factor $E - I_a (R_a + R_S)$ represents mathematically the counter e.m.f., E_c. The applied voltage must then be equal to the counter voltage plus the voltage drop in the armature, or

$$E = E_c + I_a(R_a + R_s). \qquad (16\text{-}10)$$

The armature always tends to rotate at such a speed that the sum of the counter voltage, E_c, and the $I_a R_a$ drop in the armature will equal the applied voltage, E. If the load is removed from the motor, the armature will speed up and a higher counter e.m.f. will be induced in the armature. This reduces the current through the armature and the field. The weakened field causes the armature to turn faster. The counter e.m.f. is thus increased, and the speed is further increased until the machine is destroyed. For this reason, series motors are never belt-connected to their loads. The belt might come off and the motor would then overspeed and destroy itself. Series motors are always connected to their loads directly, or through gears.

As the load increases, the armature slows down and the counter e.m.f. is reduced. The current through the armature is increased and likewise the field strength is increased. This reduces the speed to a very low value. The armature current, however, is not excessive because the torque developed depends on BOTH the field flux and the armature current.

The operational features of a series motor are indicated in table 16-2. The variation of line current, counter e.m.f., speed and torque under varying load conditions are indicated. The values are based on a 0.5-horsepower 100-volt series motor having a field resistance of 1 ohm and an armature resistance of 1 ohm.

When the armature current is 5 amperes, the armature and field IR drop is 10 volts, and the counter e.m.f. is the difference between the applied voltage and the IR drop, or $100 - 10 = 90$ volts. At this load the speed is assumed to be 900 r.p.m. and the motor torque is assumed to be 3 pound-feet. The output power, P_O, in watts is

$$P_o = 0.142NT = 0.142 \times 900 \times 3 = 383.4 \text{ watts.}$$

The input power is the product of the applied voltage and the current through the field and the armature, or $100 \times 5 = 500$ watts. The efficiency

Table 16-2.—Operational features of a series motor.

I Armature (amperes)	Counter e.m.f. (volts)	Speed (r.p.m.)	Torque (lb-ft)	Output 0.142 NT (watts)	Input (watts)	Efficiency (percent)
[1]5	[1]90	[1]900	[1]3	383.4	500	76
10	80	400	12	681.6	1,000	68
15	70	233	27	893.3	1,500	59
20	60	150	48	1,022.4	2,000	51
25	50	100	75	1,065.0	2,500	42

[1] Assumed.

(the output divided by the input) is $\frac{383.4}{500}$, or 76.8 percent.

The speed calculations are based on the following considerations. As has been explained (see equation 16-8), the counter e.m.f., E_c is determined as

$$E_c = \frac{\Phi ZNP}{10^8 p}.$$

It is also determined as

$$E_c = E - I_a (R_a + R_f).$$

These equations may be equated as

$$\frac{\Phi ZNP}{10^8 p} = E - I_a(R_a + R_f).$$

Assume that when 5 amperes flow through the field coil (and the armature) $\Phi = 10^6$ lines of force. Assume also that $Z = 600$ conductors. There are 2 poles ($P = 2$) and 2 paths ($p = 2$) through the armature. If N is divided by 60, the number of revolutions will be determined for an interval of 1 minute. Thus,

$$\frac{10^6 \times 600 \times N \times 2}{10^8 \times 60 \times 2} = 100 - 5(1 + 1),$$

and,

$$N = 900 \text{ r.p.m.}$$

If the current is increased to 10 amperes (doubled), the flux is also assumed to double. Thus,

$$\frac{2 \times 10^6 \times 600 \times N}{10^8 \times 60} = 100 - 10(1 + 1).$$

The number of revolutions per minute becomes

$$N = 400 \text{ r.p.m.}$$

The torque varies as the square of the current. Thus, when the current is doubled, the torque is increased four times.

The characteristic curves of a series motor are shown in figure 16-13. As in the case of the shunt motor, these curves include speed, torque, efficiency, and input current. As stated previously, the torque varies as the square of the armature current (below saturation) and the speed decreases rapidly as the load is increased.

USES OF SERIES MOTORS

As indicated in figure 16-13, the torque increases with load. When the load on a series motor is increased, the speed and the counter e.m.f. decrease and the armature current and field strength increase. There is therefore an increase in torque with decrease in speed with the result that the increased load on the motor is limited by the decrease in speed.

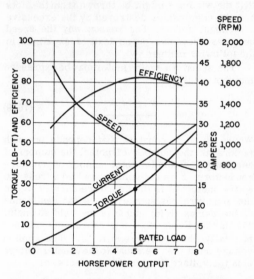

Figure 16-13.—Characteristic curves of a series motor.

When a heavy load is suddenly thrown on a shunt motor, it attempts to take on the load at only slightly reduced speed and counter emf. The flux remains essentially constant and therefore the increased torque is proportional to the increase in armature current. With heavy overload the armature current becomes excessive and the temperature increases to a very high value. The shunt motor cannot slow down appreciably on heavy load, as can the series motor; hence the shunt motor is more susceptible to overload.

For example, assume that a d-c motor is used to move an electric truck up an incline. If it is a shunt motor it will attempt to maintain almost the same speed up the incline as on the level and consequently excessive current may be drawn through the armature, since the field flux remains almost constant. If it is a series motor, the speed must decrease more than the flux increases in order to have a reduction in counter e.m.f. and an increase in armature current $(E_c - \dfrac{\Phi ZNP}{10^8 p})$. The decrease in speed protects the series motor from excessive overload, and the armature current is limited by the counter voltage and the combined resistance of the armature and series field.

The series motor is therefore used where there is a wide variation in both torque and speed such as in traction equipment, blower equipment, hoists, cranes, and so forth.

Compound Motors

Compound motors, like compound generators, have both a shunt and a series field. In most cases the series winding is connected so that its field aids that of the shunt winding, as shown in figure 16-14 (A). Motors of this type are called CUMULATIVE COMPOUND motors. If the series winding is connected so that its field opposes that of the shunt winding, as shown in figure 16-14 (B), the motor is called a DIFFERENTIAL COMPOUND motor. Under full load, the ampere-turns of the shunt coil are greater than the ampere-turns of the series coil.

In the CUMULATIVE COMPOUND motor the speed decreases (when a load is added) more rapidly than it does in a SHUNT motor, but less rapidly than in a series motor. Series field strength increases as in a series motor. Transposing equation (16-10) for armature current,

$$I_a = \frac{E - E_c}{R_a + R_s} .$$

To increase I_a, E_c must decrease. As in the series motor, the decrease in speed is necessary to allow the counter e.m.f. to decrease at the same time the field increases. Because the torque varies directly as the product of the armature current and the field flux (equation 16-1), it is evident that the cumulative compound motor has greater starting torque than does the shunt motor for equal values of armature current and shunt field strength. The performance of this type of motor approaches that of a shunt motor as the ratio of the ampere-turns of the shunt winding to the ampere-turns of the series winding becomes greater. The performance approaches that of a series motor as this ratio becomes smaller.

If the load is removed from this type of motor it tends to speed up, and the counter e.m.f. increases. The current in the series field is reduced, and the greater portion of the field flux is produced by the shunt field coils. The compound motor then has characteristics similar to a shunt motor; and unlike the series motor, there is a definite no-load speed.

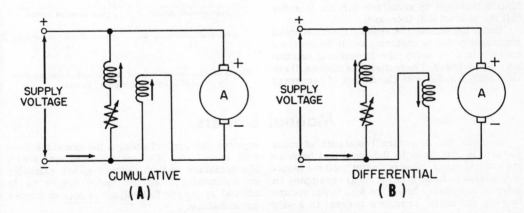

Figure 16-14.—Types of compound motors.

Because the total flux increases when there is an increase in load, there is a greater proportional increase in torque than in armature current. Therefore, for a given torque increase, this type of motor requires less increase in armature current than the shunt motor, but more than the series motor.

In some operations it is desirable to use the cumulative series winding to obtain good starting torque; and when the motor comes up to speed, the series winding is shorted out. The motor then has the improved speed regulation of a shunt motor.

In a differential compound motor, because of the opposition of the series field to the shunt field, the flux decreases as the load and armature current increase. From equation (16-9), it is seen that a decrease in flux causes an increase in speed. However, because the speed is proportional to $\frac{E_c}{\Phi}$, if both factors vary in the same proportion, the speed will remain constant. This action may occur in the differential compound motor. If more turns are added to the series coil, it is possible to cause the motor to run faster as the load is increased.

More armature current is required of the differential compound motor than of the shunt motor for the same increase in torque. This results from the fact that an increase in armature and series-field current reduces the field flux. Since the torque acting on the armature is proportional to the product of armature current and field strength, a decrease in field strength must be accompanied by a disproportionate increase in armature current in order that the product will increase.

Under heavy load the speed of the differential compound motor is unstable; and if the overload current is very heavy, the direction of rotation may be reversed. Thereafter, the motor will run as a series motor with the danger of overspeed

on no load that is the inherent characteristic of all series motors.

The characteristics of the differential compound motor are somewhat similar to those of the shunt motor, only exaggerated in scope. Thus, the starting torque is very low, and the speed regulation is very good if the load is not excessive. However, because of some of the undesirable features, this type of motor does not have wide use.

Figure 16-15 (A) shows the relative speed-load characteristics of shunt motors, cumulative compound motors, and differential compound motors. Although the speed of each of the motors is reduced when the current through the armature is increased (load is increased), the cumulative motor has the greatest decrease in speed. Likewise, in figure 16-15 (B) the cumulative motor has the greatest increase in torque with increase in load.

Cumulative compound motors are used under conditions where large starting torque is necessary, where a relatively large change in speed can be tolerated, and where the load may be removed from the motor with safety. These motors are therefore used for hoists, punches, shears, and so forth.

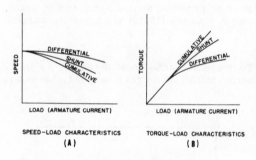

Figure 16-15.—Speed-load and torque-load characteristics of shunt and compound motors.

Manual Starters

Because the armature resistance of many motors is low (0.05 to 0.5 ohm) and because the counter e.m.f. does not exist until the armature begins to turn, it is necessary to employ an external resistance in series with the armature to keep the initial armature current to a safe value. As the armature begins to turn, the counter e.m.f. increases. Because the counter e.m.f.

opposes the applied voltage, the armature current is reduced. The resistance in series with the armature is then reduced either manually or automatically as the motor comes up to normal speed and full voltage is applied across the armature.

The relation between armature current, I_a, applied voltage E_a, counter e.m.f., E_c, armature resistance, R_a, and starting resistance, R_S, for a shunt motor is

$$I_a = \frac{E_a - E_c}{R_a + R_s} .$$

Assume that for the shunt motor shown in figure 16-16, E_a = 100 volts, R_a = 0.1 ohm, R_S = 0.9 ohm, and the normal full-load armature current is 10 amperes. Without the starting resistance, the armature current would be

$$I_a = \frac{E_a}{R_a} = \frac{100}{0.1} = 1,000 \text{ amperes.}$$

This is 100 times the normal current for the motor and would obviously burn up the armature insulation and cause excessive acceleration forces.

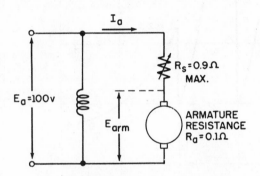

Figure 16-16.—Shunt motor with manual starting resistance.

In order to limit the initial surge of current to a maximum of 100 amperes (arbitrarily, 10 times the full-load current), the starting resistance is

$$R_s = \frac{E_a - I_a R_a}{I_a} = \frac{100 - 100 \times 0.1}{100} = 0.9 \text{ ohm.}$$

The relation of E_a; I_a; the starting resistance, R_S; motor speed, and counter e.m.f. during the accelerating period is shown in the curves of figure 16-17 and in table 16-3.

Initially, the full starting resistance of 0.9 ohm is inserted in series with the armature resistance of 0.1. The speed and counter e.m.f. are zero, and the armature current is limited to 100 amperes by the armature resistance of 0.1 ohm, acting in series with the starting resistance of 0.9 ohm. As the speed and counter e.m.f. increase, the counter e.m.f. subtracts a greater magnitude of voltage from the applied e.m.f., and the armature current is reduced from 100 amperes to some lower value. When the speed is 500 r.p.m. the counter e.m.f. is 50 volts and the current is

$$I_a = \frac{100 - 50}{0.1 + 0.9} = 50 \text{ amperes.}$$

Suppose that at the instant t_1, when the motor speed is 500 r.p.m., the starting switch is moved to the 0.4-ohm tap. The counter e.m.f. of 50 volts subtracts from the 100 volts applied, leaving 50 volts to cause the armature current to again increase to $\frac{100 - 50}{0.4 + 0.1}$ = 100 amperes at time t_1. The armature speed and counter e.m.f. cannot increase suddenly, but rise gradually during the interval from t_1 to t_2. Therefore, the armature current is decreased gradually, and at t_2, when the counter e.m.f. is 75 volts and the speed is 750 r.p.m., the current is

$$I_a = \frac{100 - 75}{0.4 + 0.1} = 50 \text{ amperes.}$$

Moving the starting switch to the 0.15-ohm tap, the 0.025-ohm tap, and the 0-ohm tap at instants t_2, t_3, and t_4 causes the motor to accelerate to a speed of 970 r.p.m. with variations in the armature current as indicated in the figure and in the table.

Automatic Starters

If a motor is at a remote location, or if a large motor is to be started, it is generally desirable to use an automatic starter to bring the motor up to operating speed. Although small motors are started by means of manually operated starters, difficulties are encountered when starting large motors. In the manually-operated starter, the skill with which the operator regulates the magnitude of the starting current is dependent upon his experience. Too much time may be taken by an overcautious operator or the maximum permissible current

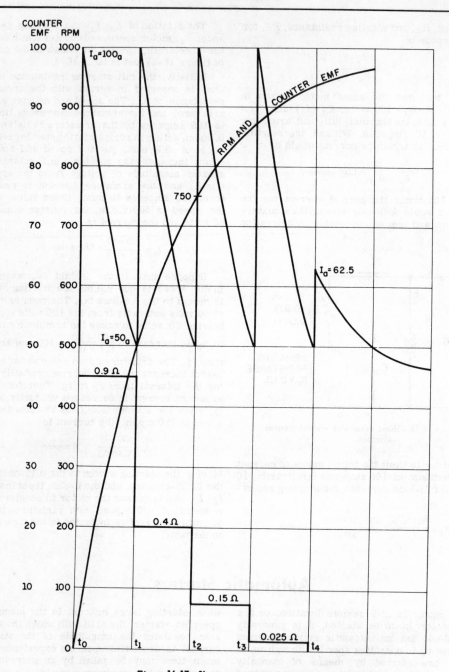

Figure 16-17.—Shunt motor starting curves.

Table 16-3.—Starting characteristics of a shunt motor.

Armature current (amperes)	Starting resistance (ohms)	Armature volts ($E_a - I_a R_s$)	Speed (r.p.m.)	Counter e.m.f. volts $\left[E_a - I_a(R_a + R_s)\right]$
100	0.9	10	0	0
50	0.9	55	500	50
100	0.4	60	500	50
50	0.4	80	750	75
100	0.15	85	750	75
50	0.15	92.5	875	87.5
100	0.025	97.5	875	87.5
50	0.025	98.75	937.5	93.75
62.5	0	100	937.5	93.75
30	0	100	970	97

for the motor may be exceeded by a careless one. In order that time shall not be wasted and the motor receive maximum safe current during the acceleration period, an automatic device should be used that will interpret the conditions of the load and act accordingly.

The following automatic starters will be discussed: (1) The time-element type, (2) the counter e.m.f. type, (3) the shunt current-limit type, and (4) the series current limit type.

TIME-ELEMENT STARTER

A time-element starter is one in which the resistance in series with the armature is reduced a certain amount during each succeeding

unit of time regardless of the load on the motor. One type of time-element starter is shown in figure 16-18. Initially, the full value of the starting resistance is inserted in series with the armature, and its current is therefore limited to a safe value. When the switch is closed, the full-line voltage is impressed across the accelerating solenoid and across the shunt field. The solenoid immediately begins to draw the iron core upwards, and the starting resistance is gradually cut out of the armature circuit. The speed with which the resistance is cut out depends on the size of the orifice (the hole through which the oil flows) in the dashpot. The smaller the orifice, the greater the time delay. The time delay should be such that as

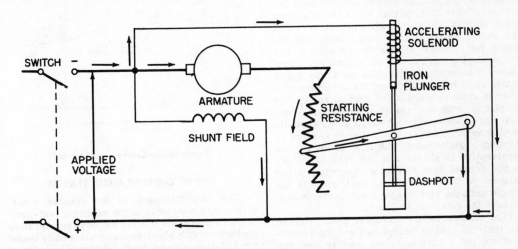

Figure 16-18.—Time-element starter.

317

the speed and the counter e.m.f. builds up, the starting current is maintained at the maximum safe value during the accelerating period. During the time required to reach full speed, the resistance is completely removed from the circuit.

The advantages of the time-element type of automatic starter are that its cost is low, the wiring is simple, and starting is generally sure. The disadvantages are that the amount of load cannot be sensed — that is, the resistance is removed at the same rate whether the load is heavy or light, the motor is not protected on overload, and the dashpot is a source of trouble.

COUNTER E.M.F. STARTER

The counter e.m.f. starter depends for its operation on the counter e.m.f. developed across the armature. As may be seen from figure 16-19 (A), the solenoid that activates the contacts is connected directly across the armature. It therefore responds to armature voltage, which is only slightly higher than the counter e.m.f.

At start (fig. 16-19 (B)), time t_0, the armature current flowing through the starting resistance causes a reduced voltage to be applied to the armature and the accelerating contactor will not immediately close its contacts due to low voltage across its operating coil. As the motor accelerates, the rising counter e.m.f. causes the armature current and voltage drop across the starting resistance to reduce. At the same time, the voltage across the armature increases. When this voltage rises to the proper value, time t_1, the accelerating contactor closes and shorts out the starting resistance, thus applying full voltage across the armature. The accompanying increase in starting current causes continued acceleration until the motor comes up to rated speed, and the armature current is again reduced to the normal value. For simplicity, only one resistor and starting contactor are shown, although large motors usually employ several contactors and several steps of starting resistance. If the load is heavy, the acceleration is slower and the rise in voltage on the accelerating contactor operating coil is delayed so that the starting resistance is not cut out until the rise in speed and counter e.m.f. permits the contactor to close.

The advantages of the counter e.m.f. starter are that the load is interpreted and the resistance cut out accordingly, the cost is low, the wiring is simple, and the dashpot is not used.

The disadvantages of the counter e.m.f. starter are that if the line voltage varies, the acceleration may become erratic. For example, if the line voltage rises, the starting resistance may be removed too soon; and if it falls, the starting contactor may not be activated at all. The starting contactor coils are designed to close the contactor on one value of voltage and to operate continuously on an increased voltage. Thus, they are sensitive to voltage change and will not operate properly if line voltage fluctuations occur.

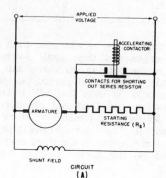

CIRCUIT
(A)

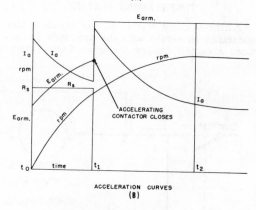

ACCELERATION CURVES
(B)

Figure 16-19.—Counter e.m.f. starter.

SHUNT CURRENT-LIMIT STARTER

The disadvantages of the counter e.m.f. starter are overcome in the shunt current-limit starter. This motor starter employs accelerating contactors with shunt-type operating coils wound for full-line voltage. Each contactor includes an interlocking series relay, the operation of which

318

is limited by the motor starting current. When the series relay closes its contacts, the shunt operating coil of the accelerating contactor is energized and a section of starting resistance is cut out of the armature circuit. This type of motor starter thus derives its name from the fact that the accelerating contactors are shunt operated and the closure of the series relays is limited by the magnitude of the armature current.

Figure 16-20 is a simplified schematic diagram of a shunt current-limit starter operating in connection with a pushbutton starter with no-voltage release holding-contacts. When the ON button is pressed down momentarily, the no-voltage release coil is energized. The holding relay contacts and the line contacts are closed. The series relay is mechanically released, and its contacts would close were it not for the fact that the armature current flows through the series coil and holds its core up, thus keeping its contacts open. Thus, it may be seen that current flows from the negative terminal of the voltage source through the armature, through the starting resistor, through the series relay coil, and back to the positive terminal of the voltage source.

As the motor speeds up, the counter e.m.f. increases, and the armature current is reduced accordingly. The field of the series relay is thereby weakened and the relay contacts are

closed. This action energizes the coil of the accelerating contactor and its contacts close, thus shorting out the starting resistor and the series relay. The full-line voltage is then safely applied across the armature. The series relay and accelerating contactor contacts remain closed until the line contacts are opened.

When the OFF button is pressed, current through the no-voltage release coil is interrupted and the holding relay contacts, the line contacts, and the series relay contacts are opened. Line voltage is thus removed from the motor.

Although for simplicity only one starting resistor is shown in a practical system, two or three are commonly used. Additional accelerating contactors and interlocking series relays are then used to remove the starting resistance in steps as the motor comes up to speed.

The advantage of the shunt current-limit starter is that starting resistance is cut out of the armature circuit only after the speed has built up and the motor current has been reduced to a safe value irrespective of line voltage fluctuations. If the load is too great for the motor to accelerate normally, the counter e.m.f. cannot build up sufficiently to reduce the current through the series relay to cause its contacts to fall closed. Therefore, the starting resistance remains in the circuit and the armature is protected against excessive current.

The disadvantage is that the accelerating units are complicated and expensive.

SERIES CURRENT-LIMIT STARTER

The series current-limit type of motor starter was designed to accelerate motors and to provide the same protection afforded by the shunt current-limit type of starter, but to do the job with less complicated equipment. The interlocking series relays are omitted and the accelerating contactors are designed to lock open on the initial in-rush of starting current. When the current falls to a predetermined value the contactor closes and shorts out the starting resistance.

In the series current-limit starter, the relay coil which operates the accelerating contactor is series wound — that is, it is connected in series with the armature circuit. The simplified circuit, showing only one starting resistor, is shown in figure 16-21 (A).

One type of magnetically operated switch that makes this type of starter possible is shown in figure 16-21 (B). The initial current

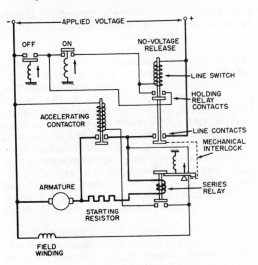

Figure 16-20.—Shunt current-limit starter.

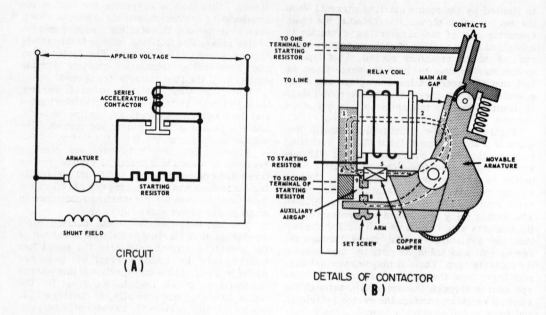

Figure 16-21.—Series current-limit starter.

through the coil causes the accelerating contactor to lock open. When the current falls to a certain predetermined value, the switch will close.

The coil is wound with a few turns of heavy wire. When current flows through the coil, the movable armature is acted upon by two forces, one across the main air gap, the other across the auxiliary air gap. The force across the main air gap tends to close the contactor; that across the auxiliary air gap tends to open it. The flux paths are first 1, 2, 3, 4, 5, 6, 1 ; and second 1, 2, 3, 7, 8, 9, 6, 1. The first path includes only the main air gap. The second includes both gaps. When a small amount of current flows through the coil, the flux path is principally through 1, 2, 3, 4, 5, and 6 and the force exerted across the main air gap tends to close the switch. When a large amount of current flows through the coil, the flux path is through 1, 2, 3, 7, 8, and 9. This path includes both the main and auxiliary air gaps. Because the auxiliary gap is smaller, the force exerted across this gap to

hold the contactor open exceeds the force across the main gap to close it and the contactor locks open.

To prevent the flux from rushing through the shorter path, 4, 5, 6, and closing the contactor before it has time to lock open, a short-circuited coil (damper) is placed around this flux path, as shown in figure 16-21 (B). As the flux links this coil, the induced current in the copper damper sets up a counter magnetomotive force that opposes the original flux and causes it to take the path through 7, 8, and 9 during the time that the current is rising. When the series operating coil current levels off at a high value, the flux path 4, 5, and 6 becomes saturated and sufficient flux is established through 7, 8, and 9 to maintain the contactor in the locked-out condition.

This type of contactor is especially satisfactory when the motor is always under load. The principal disadvantage is that the switch may drop open on light load. However, a shunt holding coil may be used to prevent this.

320

Motor Efficiency

The efficiency of any type of machine is the ratio of the output power to the input power. This ratio is commonly expressed as a percent. Because all machines have some losses, the efficiency will never be 100 percent. Expressed as a percentage, efficiency becomes

$$\text{efficiency} = \frac{\text{output}}{\text{input}} \times 100,$$

or

$$\text{efficiency} = \frac{\text{output}}{\text{output} + \text{losses}} \times 100,$$

$$\text{efficiency} = \frac{\text{input} - \text{losses}}{\text{input}} \times 100.$$

The first equation is general. The second is advantageous when applied to electric generators and transformers. The third is most useful when applied to electric motors. The output must be expressed in the same units as the input. For example, if the output is expressed in horsepower and the input is expressed in watts, they can be changed to common units by means of the relation,

$$746 \text{ watts} = 1 \text{ horsepower}.$$

There are various types of mechanical and electrical losses in d-c motors, some of which are common to other types of motors.

One loss is in BEARING FRICTION. This type of friction is reduced by proper oiling. Roller bearings have less friction loss than sleeve bearings. However, at excessive speed or under excessive load the loss due to bearing friction may be appreciable. A loss is also introduced by BRUSH FRICTION. This may be reduced by the use of a well-polished commutator and properly fitted brushes. WINDAGE LOSS is that due to the resistance of the air to a rapidly revolving armature. IRON LOSSES include eddy-current loss and hysteresis in the armature iron. COPPER LOSSES include the I^2R loss in the armature and field windings.

As an example, assume that the motor shown in figure 16-22 is supplied with 10 amperes at 100 volts.

The COPPER LOSS in the field is

$$I_f^2 \times R_f = 1^2 \times 100 = 100 \text{ watts}.$$

The armature current is 10 - 1, or 9 amperes and the COPPER LOSS in the armature is

$$I_a^2 \times R_a = 9^2 \times 1 = 81 \text{ watts}.$$

Assume that the total MECHANICAL LOSS (friction, windage, and so forth) is 90 watts. The TOTAL LOSS is therefore 271 watts. The input is

$$E_a \times I_L = 100 \times 10 = 1,000 \text{ watts}.$$

The output is

$$\text{input} - \text{losses} = 1,000 - 271 = 729 \text{ watts}.$$

The efficiency is

$$\frac{\text{output}}{\text{input}} \times 100 = \frac{729}{1,000} \times 100 = 72.9 \text{ percent}.$$

If it is determined (by means of a prony brake test) that the power developed by the motor is 0.976 horsepower, the efficiency is also determined as

$$\text{efficiency} = \frac{\text{output}}{\text{input}} \times 100$$

$$= \frac{0.976 \times 746}{1,000} \times 100 = 72.9 \text{ percent}.$$

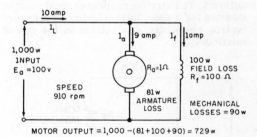

MOTOR OUTPUT = 1,000 − (81+100+90) = 729 w

Figure 16-22.—Distribution of losses in a motor.

Speed Control

The speed, N, of a d-c motor is directly proportional to the armature counter e.m.f., E_c, and inversely proportional to the field strength, Φ.

Transposing equation (16-8) for N, $N = \dfrac{E_c 10^8 p}{\Phi Z P}$.

Such factors as the numbers of poles, P, the number of current paths, p, and the total number of armature conductors, Z, can be lumped into a single constant, K. Simplified, the expression becomes

$$r.p.m. = \frac{KE_c}{\Phi} .$$

In a shunt motor

$$E_c = E_a - I_a R_a .$$

and

$$r.p.m. = \frac{K(E_a - I_a R_a)}{\Phi} , \qquad (16-11)$$

where E_a is the voltage applied across the armature. This is similar to, but not identical with, equation (16-9) for a series motor.

From equation 16-11, it is seen that the speed may be INCREASED by DECREASING the field strength, and vice versa, or the speed may be increased by increasing E_a, and vice versa. Practically, these variations are most simply accomplished by inserting a field rheostat in series with the field circuit, or a variable resistor in series with the armature circuit.

SPEED CONTROL BY ARMATURE SERIES RESISTANCE

Figure 16-23 shows how speed control may be accomplished by means of a variable resistor in series with the armature. The circuit is the same as that used in the motor starter circuit in figure 16-16. However, the wattage rating is different. The starting resistance should only be inserted for a short interval, whereas the speed control resistance can remain in the circuit indefinitely.

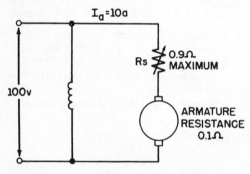

Figure 16-23.—Speed control by means of armature series resistor.

In the example of the motor shown in figure 16-23, assume that $\frac{K}{\Phi}$, as indicated in the previous equation, is replaced by the number 10. The equation for speed in r.p.m. then becomes

$$r.p.m. = 10\left[E_a - I_a(R_s - R_a)\right].$$

When R_S is set at zero, the resistance, R_a, offered by the armature is 0.1 ohm, and I_a is assumed to be 10 amperes. Therefore,

$$r.p.m. = 10\,[\,100 - 10(0 + 0.1)\,] = 990.$$

When R_S is increased to 0.1 ohm, I_a is lowered. The motor speed is reduced, the counter e.m.f. is reduced, and I_a is assumed to come back to the original value of 10 amperes. At the stable condition, the new speed is

$$r.p.m. = 10\,[\,100 - 10(0.1 + 0.1)\,] = 980.$$

The rheostatic losses involved in this method of speed control are appreciable at low speeds and the resultant reduction in efficiency makes this type of control undesirable if the motor is to be operated at greatly reduced speed for prolonged intervals.

SPEED CONTROL BY ADJUSTING THE FIELD STRENGTH

A more economical method of speed control is by rheostatic adjustment of the field current. If the field strength is weakened, the speed of the motor is increased; and if the strength of the field is increased, the speed of the motor is decreased.

Figure 16-24 indicates a method of varying the strength of the field by means of a field rheostat. When the field rheostat is cut out, the field current is 1 ampere. The counter e.m.f. is 90 volts, and the armature current is 10 amperes. The MEASURED speed is 900 r.p.m. When the resistance of the field rheostat is increased to 11.1 ohms, the field current is reduced to 0.9 amperes and the field flux is reduced. This causes a reduction in counter e.m.f. and a sharp increase in armature current, which causes an increase in force on the armature and an increase in armature speed. As the speed builds up, the counter e.m.f. builds up to 90 volts again, and the armature current is again reduced to 10 amperes.

The speed corresponding to a field current of 0.9 ampere may be computed if it is recalled that the speed varies inversely with the flux and that the flux (below saturation) varies directly with the current. Thus, if the speed is 900 r.p.m. when the field current is 1 ampere it will be $900 \times \frac{1}{0.9} = 1,000$ r.p.m. when the field current is 0.9 ampere.

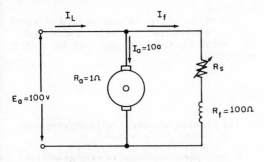

Figure 16-24.—Speed control by varying the strength of the field.

SPEED CONTROL BY WARD-LEONARD SYSTEM

As has been explained in the previous paragraphs, the speed of a d-c motor can be controlled by at least two methods—either the armature voltage can be varied, as in figure 16-23 or the field voltage can be varied as in figure 16-24. The first method gives a range of speeds below the rated full-load speed. The second, gives a range of speed above the rated full-load speed. The first method takes away the constant speed characteristics from the shunt motor when the load varies. The second method permits control with a physically smaller resistor and greatly reduced power and gives essentially constant speed characteristics at any speed setting of the field rheostat provided the field is not weakened excessively. With a very weak field the motor may stall. The inherent difficulties of both methods are removed by the Ward-Leonard method shown in figure 16-25.

The d-c motor armature whose speed is to be controlled, is fed directly from a d-c generator armature which is driven by a constant-speed

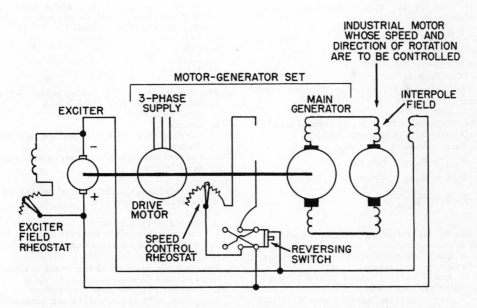

Figure 16-25.—Ward-Leonard speed control system.

prime mover. The d-c field supply to the generator is variable in both magnitude and polarity by means of a rheostat and reversing switch, as shown. Therefore, the motor armature is supplied by a generator having smoothly varying voltage output from zero to full-load value. The motor field is supplied with a constant voltage from the same source as that supplying the generator fields. The generator drive power could be from a single-phase or three-phase a-c motor, from an engine, or other constant-speed source. In the same way, the d-c supply can be supplied from a rectifier, from an exciter on the end of the generator shaft, or from any other suitable d-c source. In the figure

the field exciter is a direct-connected unit on the shaft of the motor-generator set. The drive motor for the M-G (MOTOR-GENERATOR) set is shown as a 3-phase motor. Both the main generator and the speed-control motor have commutating poles, and in some instances, compensating windings.

The advantages of this type of speed control are that it does away with the armature rheostatic losses and instability of speed with variable loads.

The disadvantage of this method of speed control is the initial expense of the added equipment—that is, the M-G set with its control equipment.

QUIZ

1. The most convenient method of determining the direction of induced motion of a current-carrying conductor in a magnetic field is by
   a. applying the right-hand rule for motors
   b. applying the left-hand rule for motors
   c. using a small permament magnet
   d. observation of the location of the conductor

2. The formula for torque developed by a motor is
   a. $T = \dfrac{K_t}{\Phi I_a}$
   b. $T = K_t^2 \, \Phi \, I_a$
   c. $T = K_t \, \Phi \, I_a^2$
   d. $T = K_t \, \Phi \, I_a$

3. The effective voltage (E_{eff}) drop in a motor's armature is determined by
   a. $E_{eff} = E_{app} + c.e.m.f.$
   b. $E_{eff} = E_{app} \times c.e.m.f.$
   c. $E_{eff} = E_{app} - c.e.m.f.$
   d. $E_{eff} = \dfrac{c.e.m.f.}{E_{app}}$

4. Which of the following is true, regarding the speed regulation of a shunt motor?
   a. It has a constant-speed characteristic under varying loads
   b. It has a varying speed characteristic under varying loads
   c. It has a varying speed characteristic under constant loads
   d. None of the above are correct

5. The primary advantage of the differentially compounded motor is that
   a. it is stable under heavy loads
   b. its speed regulation is very good if load is not excessive
   c. it has good speed regulation under varying loads
   d. it will start under a heavy load

6. If the no-load speed of a shunt motor is 1,800 r.p.m. and the full-load speed is 1,475 r.p.m., the speed regulation is
   a. 18%
   b. 22%
   c. 2.2%
   d. 1.8%

7. The input power of a series motor is the product of the applied voltage and
   a. counter e.m.f.
   b. torque
   c. current through the armature and the field
   d. current through the armature and counter e.m.f.

8. The disadvantage of the time-element automatic starter is that the
   a. cost is high
   b. wiring is complicated
   c. construction is too heavy to be practical
   d. motor is not protected on overload

9. The starting resistor of the shunt current-limit starter is connected in
   a. parallel with the motor armature
   b. series with the accelerating contactor
   c. series with the field winding of the motor
   d. series with the armature of the motor

324

10. A motor which has an output of 820 watts and an input of 960 watts has an efficiency of approximately
    a. 90%
    b. 85%
    c. 75%
    d. 70%
11. The horsepower developed by a motor depends mainly upon which of the following two factors?
    a. Speed and voltage
    b. Speed and torque
    c. Torque and voltage
    d. Torque and watts
12. A series motor is more adaptable where a
    a. small variation of torque and speed is needed
    b. wide variation of torque but a small variation of speed is needed
    c. wide variation of torque is required, and wide variations in speed are allowable
    d. constant speed is needed
13. Cumulative compound motors are best suited for use where
    a. small starting torque is required
    b. small changes in speed can be tolerated
    c. the load may be removed from the motor with safety
    d. constant speed under varying load is required
14. What is the output power in watts of a shunt motor of 1 horsepower operating on 100 volts at 910 r.p.m., armature current of 9 amps., and a line current of 10 amps.?
    a. 98.4 watts
    b. 472 watts
    c. 646 watts
    d. 815 watts
15. The counter e.m.f. of a motor is zero when the
    a. motor is at rated speed
    b. armature is not turning
    c. motor is almost up to rated speed
    d. armature has just begun to turn
16. The operation of the c.e.m.f. starter depends upon the
    a. size of the orifice in the dashpot
    b. c.e.m.f. developed across the armature
    c. accelerating contacts
    d. interlocking relays
17. In a shunt current-limit starter the number of starting resistors that are commonly used is
    a. one
    b. two or three
    c. five or six
    d. more than ten

18. The speed of a motor with no load, with an increase of resistance in series with the field winding, will
    a. not be affected
    b. decrease
    c. increase
    d. fluctuate rapidly
19. The generated voltage (c.e.m.f.) of a motor
    a. opposes the impressed (source) voltage
    b. opposes any change in load
    c. aids the impressed (source) voltage
    d. none of the above are correct
20. When a load is applied to a shunt motor, which one of the following will happen?
    a. Speed decreases—c.e.m.f. goes up
    b. Speed increases—c.e.m.f. goes down
    c. Speed increases—c.e.m.f. goes up
    d. Speed decreases—c.e.m.f. goes down
21. On a time-element starter what determines the speed with which the resistance is cut out?
    a. Size of the orifice in the dashpot
    b. Counter e.m.f. of the armature
    c. Interlocking relays
    d. Accelerating contacts
22. The coil of the accelerating contactor of the shunt current-limit starter is caused to become energized by which of the following when the motor speeds up?
    a. Series relay contacts closing
    b. Series relay contacts opening
    c. The no-voltage release
    d. Holding relay contacts
23. In the series current-limit starter the flux is prevented from closing the contactor before it has time to lock open by
    a. an open coil
    b. the spring tension of the contacts
    c. starting resistor
    d. a short-circuited coil
24. The d-c motor armature whose speed is to be controlled by the Ward-Leonard system is fed by a
    a. 3-phase motor
    b. d-c supply in parallel with a rheostat
    c. d-c generator
    d. rectifier

CHAPTER 17

ALTERNATING-CURRENT INSTRUMENTS

In chapter 16, the simpler electrical indicating instruments were discussed. Only a few could measure a.c. Most were used to measure only direct voltage or current. It will be necessary for the technician to become familiar with additional, more advanced a-c indicating instruments. Those that will be discussed in this chapter are (1) rectifier-type a-c meters; (2) wattmeters and watt-hour meters, (3) instrument transformers; (4) bridge meters for measuring resistance, voltage, current, capacitance, and inductance; (5) frequency meters; and (6) the single-phase power-factor meter.

Many of the instruments discussed in this chapter utilize metallic rectifiers. Since these units are common to a number of different instruments, they will be discussed first.

Metallic Rectifiers

A metallic rectifier is a device that offers a high opposition to current flow through it in one direction but not in the other. It is therefore effectively a unidirectional conductor and is used mostly for converting alternating current into a unidirectional current (direct current).

A metallic rectifier element, called a cell, consists of a good conductor and a semiconductor (material of high resistivity) separated by a thin insulating barrier layer. The flow of forward current through a cell consists of a flow of electrons from the good conductor, across the barrier layer, and through the semiconductor.

Metallic rectifier cells are usually made in the form of plates, circular or square in shape, with a hole in the center. A number of cells, with the necessary terminals, spacers, and washers, are assembled on an insulated stud passing through their center holes. This assembly is called a rectifier stack. Some assemblies contain fins, which are used to keep the rectifier from overheating; they afford a large surface area for conducting away the heat. Cells and stacks may be connected in series or parallel, with proper polarities, to obtain the required voltage and current ratings and circuit connections for specific applications.

Two types of metallic rectifiers are used in the Navy—(1) a thin film of copper oxide and copper, and (2) selenium and either iron or aluminum. Metallic rectifier units are represented by the symbol shown in figure 17-1 (A). The arrowhead in the symbol points against the direction of electron flow.

Figure 17-1 (B) shows a simple a-c circuit that utilizes a metallic rectifier. It rectifies the a-c voltage and produces a series of d-c voltage pulses as its output. Although the copper-oxide rectifier is shown, the selenium rectifier may be used instead.

In the copper-oxide rectifier shown in figure 17-2 (A), the oxide is formed on the copper disk before the rectifier unit is assembled. In this type of rectifier the electrons flow more readily from the copper to the oxide than from the oxide to the copper. External electrical connections may be made by connecting terminal lugs between the left pressure plate and the copper and between the right pressure plate and the lead washer.

For the rectifier to function properly, the oxide coating must be very thin. Thus, each individual unit can stand only a low inverse voltage. Rectifiers designed for moderate and high-power applications consist of many of these individual units mounted in series on a single support. The lead washer enables uniform pressure to be applied to the units so that the internal resistance may be reduced. When the units are connected in series, they normally present a

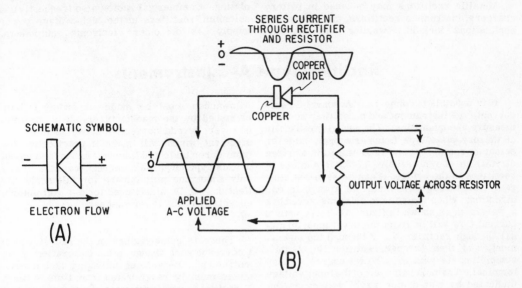

Figure 17-1.–(A) Metallic rectifier symbol; (B) waveforms in simple a-c circuit utilizing a rectifier.

relatively high resistance to the current flow. The resultant heat developed in the resistance must be removed if the rectifier is to operate satisfactorily. Many commercial rectifiers have copper fins between each unit for the purpose of dissipating the excess heat. The useful life of the unit is extended by keeping the temperature low (below 140°F.). The efficiency of this type of rectifier is generally between 60 and 70 percent.

Selenium rectifiers function in much the same manner as copper-oxide rectifiers. A selenium rectifier is shown in figure 17-2 (B). Such a rectifier is made up of an iron disk that is coated with a thin layer of selenium. In this type of rectifier the electrons flow more easily from the selenium to the iron than from the iron to the selenium.

Commercial selenium rectifier units are designed to pass 50 milliamperes per square centimeter of plate area. This type of rectifier may be operated at a somewhat higher temperature than a copper-oxide rectifier of similar rating. The efficiency is between 65 and 85 percent, depending on the circuit and the loading. As in the case of the copper-oxide rectifier, any practical number of units may be bolted together

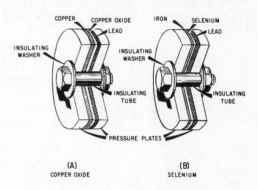

Figure 17-2.–Metallic rectifier construction.

in series to increase the voltage rating. Larger element disks and the necessary cooling fins may be used for higher current ratings. Also, forced-air cooling may be used.

Metallic rectifiers may be used not only as half-wave rectifiers, as shown in figure 17-1, but also in full-wave and bridge circuits. In each of these applications the action of the metallic rectifier is similar to that of a diode.

327

Metallic rectifiers may be used in battery chargers, instrument rectifiers, and many other applications including welding and electro-plating. Commercial radios also frequently use selenium rectifiers in the high-voltage power supply, as do other electronic equipments.

Rectifier-Type A-C Instruments

It is possible to connect a D'Arsonval direct-current type instrument and a rectifier so as to measure a-c quantities. The rectifier is usually of the dry-plate type (such as copper-oxide or selenium rectifiers) and is arranged in a bridge circuit, as shown in figure 17-3. By the use of rectifiers in the bridge, it can be seen that current flow through the meter is always in one direction. When the voltage being measured has a waveform as shown in figure 17-3, the path of current flow will be from the lower input terminal through rectifier No. 3 through the instrument, and then through rectifier No. 2, thus completing its path back to the source's upper terminal. The next half cycle of the input voltage (indicated by dotted sine wave) will cause the current to pass through rectifier No. 1, through the instrument, and through rectifier No. 4, completing its path back to the source.

This type of instrument generally is characterized by errors due to waveform and frequency.

Allowances must be made, according to data furnished by the manufacturer. It is possible, however, to add corrective networks to the instrument which will make it practically free from error up to 100 kilocycles. An instrument of this type requires a current from the line of only about one milliampere for full scale deflection. It is widely used for a-c voltmeters, especially of the lower ranges.

There is some "aging" of the rectifier with a corresponding change in the calibration of the instrument. Because of this aging such instruments must be recalibrated from time to time. A rectifier-type instrument reads the average value of the a-c quantity. However, because the EFFECTIVE, or root-mean-square (r.m.s.), values are more useful, a-c meters are generally calibrated to read r.m.s. values (1.11 times the average of the instantaneous values).

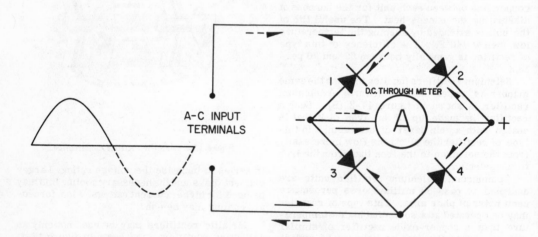

Figure 17-3.—Simple connection of a full-wave, rectifier-type, a-c instrument.

Wattmeter

Electric power is measured by means of a wattmeter. This instrument is of the electrodynamometer type. It consists of a pair of fixed coils, known as current coils, and a movable coil, known as the potential coil. (See fig. 17-4.) The fixed coils are made up of a few turns of comparatively large conductor. The potential coil consists of many turns of fine wire; it is mounted on a shaft, carried in jeweled bearings, so that it may turn inside the stationary coils. The movable coil carries a needle which moves over a suitably graduated scale. Flat coil springs hold the needle to a zero position, as shown in figure 16-10 of chapter 16.

The current coil (stationary coil) of the wattmeter is connected in series with the circuit (load), and the potential coil (movable coil) is connected across the line.

When line current flows through the current coil of a wattmeter, a field is set up around the coil. The strength of this field is proportional to the line current and in phase with it. The potential coil of the wattmeter generally has a high resistance resistor connected in series with it. This is for the purpose of making the

potential-coil circuit of the meter as purely resistive as possible. As a result, current in the potential circuit is practically in phase with line voltage. Therefore, when voltage is impressed on the potential circuit, current is proportional to and in phase with the line voltage.

The actuating force of a wattmeter is derived from the interaction of the field of its current coil and the field of its potential coil. The force acting on the movable coil at any instant (tending to turn it) is proportional to the product of the instantaneous values of line current and voltage.

The wattmeter consists of two circuits, either of which will be damaged if too much current is passed through them. This fact is to be especially emphasized in the case of wattmeters, because the reading of the instrument does not serve to tell the user that the coils are being overheated. If an ammeter or voltmeter is overloaded, the pointer will be indicating beyond the upper limit of its scale. In the wattmeter, both the current and potential circuits may be carrying such an overload that their insulation is burning, and yet the pointer may be only part way up the scale. This is

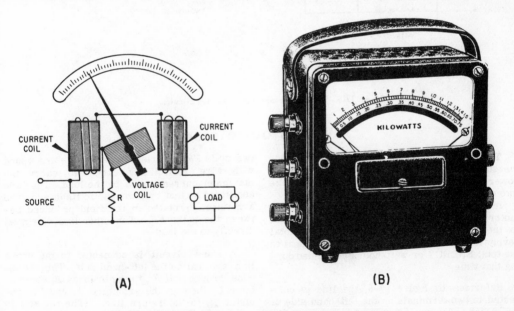

(A)

(B)

Figure 17-4.—Simplified electrodynamomter wattmeter circuit.

because the position of the pointer depends upon the power factor of the circuit as well as upon the voltage and current. Thus, a low power-factor circuit will give a very low reading on the wattmeter even when the current and potential circuits are loaded to the maximum safe limit.

This safe rating is generally given on the face of the instrument.

A wattmeter is always distinctly rated, not in watts but in volts and amperes.

Figure 17-5 shows the proper way to connect a wattmeter in various circuits.

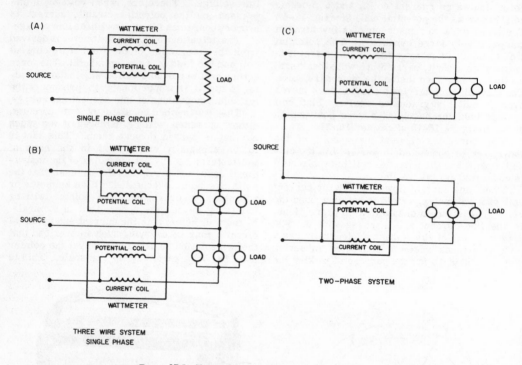

Figure 17-5.—Wattmeter connected in various circuits.

Watt-Hour Meter

The watt-hour meter is an instrument for measuring energy. As energy is the product of power and time; the watt-hour meter must take into consideration both of these factors.

In principle, the watt-hour meter is a small motor whose instantaneous speed is proportional to the POWER passing through it. The total revolutions in a given time are proportional to the total ENERGY or watt-hours consumed during that time.

Referring to figure 17-6, the line is connected to two terminals on the left-hand side of the meter. The upper terminal is connected to

two coils FF in series. These coils are wound with wire sufficiently large to carry the maximum current taken by the load. They are connected so that their magnetic fields add. The armature A rotates in the field produced between the coils FF. The other line wire goes directly to the load.

A shunt circuit is connected to the upper line terminal on the left-hand side. This circuit runs through coil F', to the brushes B, commutator C, through the armature A, and the resistor R, to the return line. (The resistor is omitted in some watt-hour meters.)

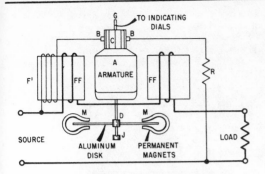

Figure 17-6.–Internal connections of watt-hour meter.

Since the load current is through coils FF and there is no iron in the circuit, the magnetic field produced by these coils is proportional to the LOAD CURRENT. The armature, in series with a resistance, is connected directly across the line. The current in the meter armature is proportional to the LINE VOLTAGE. Neglecting the small voltage drop in FF, the torque acting on the armature must be proportional to the product of the load current and the load voltage. In other words, it must be proportional to the power passing through the meter to the load.

If the meter is to register correctly, there must be a retarding torque acting on the moving element. This force is proportional to the speed of rotation of the moving element. To meet this condition, an aluminum disk D is mounted on the armature shaft. This disk rotates between the poles of two permanent magnets M and M. In cutting the field produced by these magnets, eddy currents are induced in the disk, retarding its motion. The strength of these currents is proportional to the angular velocity of the disk. Since they are acting in conjunction with a magnetic field of constant strength, their retarding effect is proportional to the speed of rotation.

Friction produced by the rotating element cannot be entirely eliminated. Near the rated load of the meter, the effect of the frictional torque is practically negligible. But, at light loads, the friction torque, which is nearly constant at all loads, is a much greater percentage of the load torque. Since the ordinary meter may operate at light loads during a considerable portion of the time, it is desirable that the error due to friction be eliminated. This is accomplished by means of coil F', which is connected in series with the armature. Coil F' is connected so that its field acts in the same direction as that of coils FF. Therefore, it assists armature A to rotate. Since it is connected in the shunt circuit, it acts continuously. The coil is movable and its position can be adjusted so that the friction error is eliminated.

To reduce friction and wear, the rotating element of the meter is made as light as practical. The element rests on a jewel bearing J. This bearing is a sapphire in the smaller types, and a diamond in the larger types of meters. The jewel is supported on a spring. A hardened steel pivot rests in the jewel. In time, the pivot becomes dulled and the jewel roughened, which increases friction and causes the meter to register low unless F' is readjusted. The moving element drives the clockwork of the meter through shaft G.

The following directions should be followed when reading the dials of a watt-hour meter. The meter, in this case, is a four-dial type.

The pointer on the right-hand dial (fig. 17-7) registers 1 kw.-hr. or 1,000 watt-hours for each division on the dial. A complete revolution of the hand on this dial will move the hand of the second dial one division and register 10 kw.-hr. or 10,000 watt-hours. A complete revolution of the hand of the second dial will move the third hand one division and register 100 kw.-hr. or 100,000 watt-hours, and so on.

Accordingly, you must read the hands from left to right, and add three zeros to the reading of the lowest dial to obtain the reading of the meter in watt-hours. The dial hands should always be read as indicating the figure which they have LAST PASSED, and not the one they are approaching.

SINGLE-PHASE INDUCTION WATT-HOUR METER

As in the case of series motors, the Thompson watt-hour meter may be used with alternating or direct current because both the armature and the field flux reverse at the same time, and the armature continues to rotate in the same direction. The induction watt-hour meter, however, has certain advantages over the Thompson watt-hour meter and is more commonly used to measure a-c power.

The SINGLE-PHASE INDUCTION WATT-HOUR METER includes a simple induction-drive

Figure 17-7.—Reading a watt-hour meter.

motor consisting of an aluminum disk, moving magnetic field, drag magnets, current and potential coils, integrating dials, and associated gears. A simplified sketch of an induction watt-hour meter is shown in figure 17-8 (A). The potential coil connected across the load is composed of many turns of relatively small wire. It is wound on one leg of the laminated magnetic circuit. Because of its many turns, the potential coil has high impedance and high inductance, and therefore, the current through it lags the applied voltage by nearly 90°. The two current coils connected in series with the load are

composed of a few turns of heavy wire. They are wound on two legs of the laminated magnetic circuit. Because of the few turns, the current coils have low inductance and low impedance.

The arrangement of the potential coil, the aluminum disk, the current coils, and one of the drag magnets is shown in the phantom view (fig. 17-8 (B)).

The rotating aluminum disk is the moving member that causes the gears to turn and the dials to indicate the amount of energy passed through the meter. This rotation of the aluminum disk is accomplished by eddy currents that are

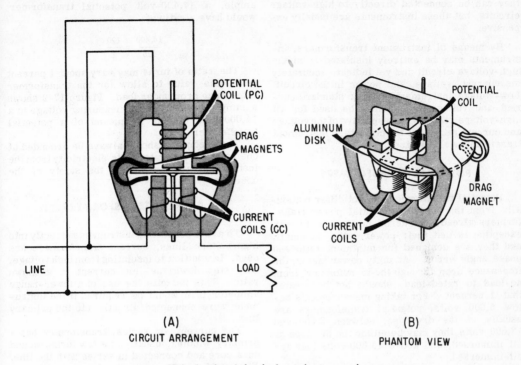

(A)
CIRCUIT ARRANGEMENT

(B)
PHANTOM VIEW

Figure 17-8.—Simplified sketch of an induction watt-hour meter.

established by the current coils and the potential coil. The speed of rotation of the aluminum disk is proportional to the true power supplied through the line to the load. The total energy supplied to the load is proportional to the number of revolutions of the disk during a given period of time.

A small copper shading disk (not shown in the figure) is placed under a portion of the potential pole face. It is in an adjustable mounting and is used to develop a torque in the disk to counteract static friction. The disk has the effect of a shading pole and provides a light-load adjustment for the meter.

The two drag magnets supply the counter torque against which the aluminum disk acts when it turns. The drag is increased (speed of motor is reduced) by moving the magnets toward the edge of the disk. Conversely, the drag is decreased and the speed is increased by moving the magnets toward the center of the disk. Adjustment of the drag magnets will only be made by an authorized instrument and meter technician.

Instrument Transformers

ELECTRICAL MEASUREMENTS AT HIGH VOLTAGES

It is not usually practical to connect instruments and meters directly to high-voltage circuits. Unless the high-voltage circuit is grounded at the instrument, a dangerously high potential-to-ground voltage may exist at the instrument or switchboard. Further, instruments become inaccurate when connected directly to a high voltage, because of the electrostatic forces that act on the indicating element. Specially designed instruments may be constructed so that

333

they can be connected directly to high-voltage circuits, but these instruments are usually expensive.

By means of instrument transformers, instruments may be entirely insulated from the high-voltage circuit and yet indicate accurately the current, voltage, and power in the circuit. Low-voltage instruments having standard current and voltage ranges may be used for all high-voltage circuits, irrespective of the voltage and current ratings of the circuits, if instrument transformers are utilized.

POTENTIAL TRANSFORMERS

Potential transformers do not differ materially from the constant-potential power transformers already discussed in chapter 12. An exception is that their power rating is small, and they are designed for minimum ratio and phase angle error. At unity power factor, the impedance drop through the transformer, from no-load to rated-load, should not be greater than 1 percent. For taking measurements below 5,000 volts, potential transformers are usually of the dry type; between 5,000 and 13,800 volts they may be either the dry type or oil immersed, and above 13,800 volts they are oil-immersed.

Since only instruments, meters, and sometimes indicator lights are ordinarily connected to the secondaries of potential transformers, they have ratings from 40 to 500 watts. For primary voltages of 34,500 volts and higher, the secondaries are rated at 115 volts. For primary voltages less than 34,500 volts, the secondaries are rated at 120 volts. For ex-

ample, a 14,400-volt potential transformer would have a ratio of

$$\frac{14,400}{120} = \frac{120}{1}$$

The ratio of turns may vary about 1 percent from this value to allow for the transformer impedance drop under load. Figure 17-9 shows a simple connection for measuring voltage in a 14,000-volt circuit by means of a potential transformer.

The secondary should always be grounded at one point to eliminate static electricity from the instrument and to insure the safety of the operator.

CURRENT TRANSFORMERS

To avoid connecting instruments directly into high-voltage lines, current transformers are used. In addition to insulating from high voltage, they step down the line current in a known ratio. This permits the use of a lower-range ammeter than would be required if the instrument were connected directly into the primary line.

The current, or series, transformer has a primary winding, usually of a few turns, wound on a core and connected in series with the line. Figure 17-10 shows a simple connection for measuring current in a 14,400-volt circuit by means of a current transformer.

The secondary windings of practically all current transformers are rated at 5 amperes regardless of the primary current rating. For example, a 2,000-ampere current transformer has a ratio of 400 to 1, and 50-ampere transformer has a ratio of 12 to 1.

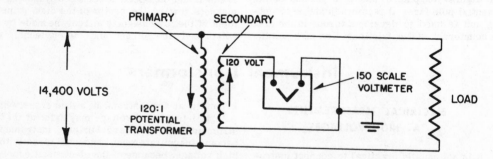

Figure 17-9.—Connections of a potential transformer to a 14,400-volt circuit.

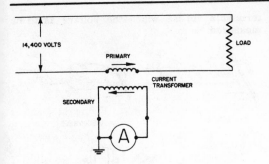

Figure 17-10.—Connections of a current transformer in a 14,400-volt circuit to measure current.

total primary ampere-turns acting alone. This causes a large increase in the flux, producing excessive core loss and heating, as well as a dangerously high voltage across the secondary terminals. THEREFORE, THE SECONDARY OF A CURRENT TRANSFORMER SHOULD NOT BE OPEN-CIRCUITED UNDER ANY CIRCUMSTANCES.

Figure 17-11 shows the method of connecting a complete instrument load, through instrument transformers, to a high-voltage line. The load on the instrument transformers includes an ammeter A, a voltmeter V, a wattmeter, and a watt-hour meter.

The insulation between the primary and the secondary of a current transformer must be sufficient to withstand full circuit voltage. The current transformer differs from the ordinary constant-potential transformer in that its primary current is determined entirely by the load on the system and not by its own secondary load. If its secondary becomes open-circuited, a high voltage will exist across the secondary, because the large ratio of secondary to primary turns causes the transformer to act as a step-up transformer. Also, since the effects of the counter-ampere-turns of the secondary no longer exist, the flux in the core will depend on the

POLARITY MARKING

Instruments, meters, and relays must be connected so that the correct phase relations exist between their potential and current circuits. In instrument transformers it is important that the relation of the instantaneous polarities of the secondary terminals to the primary terminals be known. It has become standard to designate or mark the primary terminals and the secondary terminals that have the same instantaneous polarity.

The primary terminals are marked $H1$, $H2$, etc., and the secondary terminals $X1$, $X2$, etc. In a wiring diagram, primary and secondary

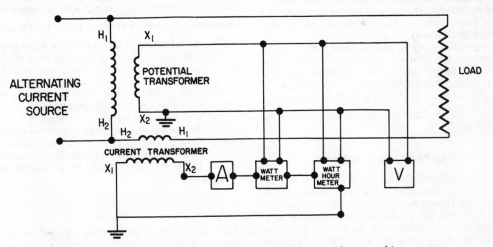

Figure 17-11.—Typical connections of instrument transformers and instruments for single-phase measurements.

terminals having the same instantaneous polarity are marked with a dot. This is shown in figure 17-11.

HOOK-ON TYPE VOLTAMMETER

The hook-on a-c ammeter consists essentially of a current transformer with a split core and a rectifier-type instrument connected to the secondary. The primary of the current transformer is the conductor through which the current to be measured flows. The split core permits the instrument to be "hooked on" the conductor without disconnecting it. Therefore the current flowing through the conductor may be measured safely with a minimum of inconvenience, as shown in figure 17-12.

The instrument is usually constructed so that voltages also may be measured. However, in order to read voltage, the meter switch must be set to VOLTS, and leads must be connected from the voltage terminals on the meter to the terminals across which the voltage is to be measured.

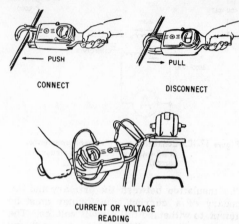

CONNECT — PUSH

DISCONNECT — PULL

CURRENT OR VOLTAGE READING

Figure 17-12.—Hook-on type voltammeter.

A-C Bridges

D-c bridges, called Wheatstone bridges, are covered in chapter 5. Before continuing this section on a-c bridges you should review bridge principles given in chapter 5. Notice particularly the ratio method of determining an unknown value that forms one leg of a bridge. Keep in mind that current varies inversely as resistance—that is, as resistance increases, current decreases.

The same circuit may be used with a fixed-frequency a-c voltage applied, in place of a direct voltage. Figure 17-13 shows bridge circuits using alternating current. Circuit (A) is used to determine an unknown capacitance C_x.

Circuit (B) is used to determine an unknown inductance L_x.

CAPACITANCE BRIDGE

Circuit (A) will be discussed first. You will recall that a capacitor has a certain opposition to current flow. Also, the larger its capacitance the less its opposition becomes. It follows that if an UNKNOWN capacitor is to be measured, there must be a KNOWN capacitor in the bridge with which the unknown capacitor may be compared, as shown in figure 17-13

(A). C_s is the capacitor whose value is known. The resistance of C_s is shown as an equivalent resistance, R_s. This capacitor (with its series resistance) forms one leg of the bridge. The unknown capacitor, C_x, along with its unknown resistance, R_x, forms another leg of the bridge.

The ratio resistors, $R1$ and $R2$, are potentiometers that can be varied to bring the circuit into balance—that is, cause equal currents to flow in the two sides of the bridge. When the circuit is in balance, there will be little or no current flow through the indicator (headphones, or an a-c milliammeter). $R1$ and $R2$ are adjusted by means of accurately calibrated dials. When they are adjusted so that minimum hum is heard in the headphones, the bridge is in balance, and the unknown capacity may be calculated by the formula:

$$\frac{R_1}{R_2} = \frac{C_x}{C_s} \text{ or } C_x = \frac{R_1}{R_2} \times C_s .$$

Notice that this is an inverse proportion because current varies inversely with resistance and directly with capacitance. If the ratio of reactance to resistance is the same in the legs

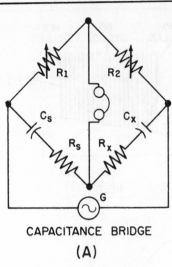

CAPACITANCE BRIDGE

(A)

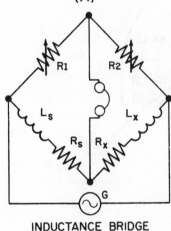

INDUCTANCE BRIDGE

(B)

Figure 17-13.–A-C bridge circuits.

containing capacitance, the following direct proportion exists between the resistive components:

$$\frac{R_1}{R_2} = \frac{R_s}{R_x}$$

$$R_x = \frac{R_2}{R_1} \times R_s$$

Thus, the unknown resistance and capacitance, R_x, and C_x, can be estimated in terms of the known resistances, R_1, R_2, and R_s, and the known capacitance, C_s.

INDUCTANCE BRIDGE

The value of an unknown inductance may be determined in the same manner as an unknown capacitance, as shown in figure 17-13 (B). You will recall that an inductor also has a certain opposition to current flow. Also, the larger the inductance, the greater becomes its opposition. To measure an UNKNOWN inductance (L_x) in a bridge circuit, there must be an inductor of KNOWN VALUE (L_s). This known inductor is compared with the unknown inductor.

The ratio resistors, $R1$ and $R2$, are potentiometers that can be varied to bring the circuit into balance. When there is minimum hum in the headphones, the bridge is said to be in balance, and the unknown inductance may be calculated by the formula:

$$\frac{R_1}{R_2} = \frac{L_s}{L_x},$$

or

$$L_x = \frac{R_2}{R_1} L_s;$$

and

$$\frac{R_1}{R_2} = \frac{R_s}{R_x}$$

or

$$R_x = \frac{R_2}{R_1} R_s.$$

Frequency Meters

VIBRATING-REED FREQUENCY METER

The vibrating-reed type of frequency meter is one of the simplest devices for indicating the frequency of an a-c source. A simplified diagram of one type of vibrating-reed frequency meter is shown in figure 17-14.

The current whose frequency is to be measured flows through the coil and exerts maximum

337

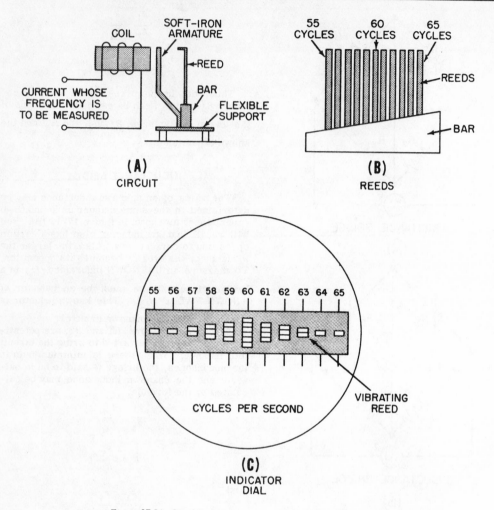

Figure 17-14.—Simplified diagram of a vibrating-reed frequency meter.

attraction on the soft-iron armature TWICE during each cycle (fig. 17-14 (A)). The armature is attached to the bar, which is mounted on a flexible support. Reeds of suitable dimensions to have natural vibration frequencies of 110, 112, 114, and so forth, up to 130 cycles per second are mounted on the bar (fig. 17-14 (B)). The reed having a frequency of 110 cycles is marked "55" cycles, the one having a frequency of 112 cycles is marked "56" cycles, the one having a frequency of 120 cycles is marked "60" cycles, and so forth.

When the coil is energized with a current having a frequency between 55 and 65 cycles, all the reeds are vibrated slightly; but the reed having a natural frequency closest to that of the energizing current (whose frequency is to be measured) vibrates through a larger amplitude. The frequency is read from the scale value opposite the reed having the greatest amplitude of vibration.

338

In some instruments the reeds are the same lengths, but are weighted by different amounts at the top so that they will have different natural rates of vibration.

An end view of the reeds is shown in the indicator dial of figure 17-14 (C). If the energizing current has a frequency of 60 cycles per second, the reed marked "60" cycles will vibrate the greatest amount, as shown.

MOVING-DISK FREQUENCY METER

A moving-disk frequency meter is shown in figure 17-15 (A). Each of the two-pole fields (fig. 17-15 (B)) has a short-circuited turn (shading coil) on one side of the pole face and a magnetizing coil around the associated magnetic circuit. As in a shaded-pole motor, the magnetic field tends to produce rotation toward the shorted turn (A to B). One coil tends to turn the disk clockwise, and the other, counterclockwise. Magnetizing coil A is connected in series with a large value of resistance. Coil B is connected in series with a large inductance and the two circuits are supplied in parallel by the source.

For a given voltage, the current through coil A is practically constant. However, the current through coil B varies inversely with the frequency. At a higher frequency the inductive reactance is greater and the current through coil B is less; the reverse is true at a lower frequency. The disk turns in the direction determined by the stronger coil.

A perfectly circular disk would tend to turn continuously. This is not desirable, and accordingly the disk is constructed so that it will turn only a certain amount clockwise or counterclockwise about the center position, which is commonly marked "60" cycles on commercial equipment. To prevent the disk from turning more than the desired amount, the left half of the disk is mounted so that when motion occurs, the same amount of disk area will always be between the poles of coil A. Therefore, the force produced by coil A to rotate the disk is constant for a constant applied voltage. The right half of the disk is offset, as shown in the figure. When the disk rotates clockwise, an increasing area will come between the poles of coil B; when it rotates counterclockwise, a decreasing area will come between the poles of coil B. The greater

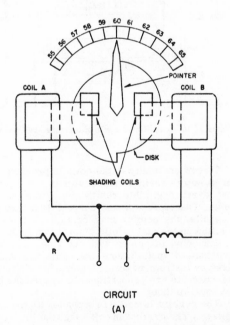

CIRCUIT

(A)

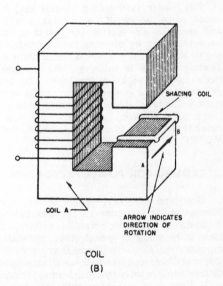

COIL

(B)

Figure 17-15.—Simplified diagram of a moving-disk frequency meter.

339

the area between the poles, the greater will be the disk current and the force tending to turn the disk.

If the frequency applied to the frequency meter should decrease, the reactance offered by L would decrease and the field produced by coil B would increase; the field produced by coil A would remain the same. Thus, the torque produced by coil B would tend to move the disk and the pointer counterclockwise until the area between the poles was reduced sufficiently to make the two torques equal. The scale is calibrated to indicate the correct frequency.

If the frequency should increase, the reactance offered by L would increase and the field produced by coil B would decrease; the field produced by coil A would remain the same. Thus, the decreasing torque produced by coil B would permit a greater disk area to move under the coil, and therefore the disk and the pointer would move clockwise until the two torques were balanced.

If the frequency is constant and the voltage is changed, the currents in the two coils—and therefore the opposing torques—change by the same amount. Therefore, the indication of the instrument is not affected by a change in voltage.

Single-Phase Power-Factor Meter

The power factor of a circuit is the ratio of the true power to apparent power. It is also equal to the cosine of the phase angle between the circuit current and voltage. A pure resistance has a power factor of unity (the current and voltage are in phase and the true power and the apparent power are the same); a pure inductance has a power factor of zero (current lags the voltage by 90°); and a pure capacitance has a power factor of zero (current leads the voltage by 90°).

The power factor of a circuit may be determined by the use of a wattmeter, a voltmeter, and an ammeter—that is, the power factor may be determined by dividing the wattmeter reading by the product of the voltmeter and ammeter readings. This is inconvenient, however, and instruments have been developed that indicate continuously the power factor and at the same time indicate whether the current is leading or lagging the voltage. An instrument that indicates these values is called a POWER-FACTOR METER.

CROSSED-COIL POWER-FACTOR METER

One type of power-factor meter is shown schematically in figure 17-16. The instrument consists of movable potential coils A and B, fixed at right angles to each other, and stationary current coil C. Coils A and B are pivoted, and the assembly, together with the attached pointer, is free to move through an angle of approximately 90°. Coil A is in series with inductor L, and the combination is connected across the line.

Coil B is in series with noninductive resistor R, and the combination is also connected across the line.

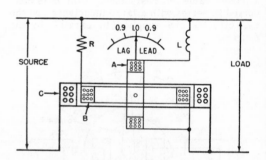

Figure 17-16.—Simplified diagram of a crossed-coil power-factor meter.

Circuit continuity to the coils is provided by three spiral springs (not shown in the figure) that exert negligible restraining force on the coils. Therefore, when no current flows through the coils, the pointer may come to rest at any position on the dial. Coil C (not drawn to scale) is connected in series with the line. In many switchboard installations the coils are energized by instrument transformers, in which case the currents are proportional to line values but not equal to them.

The current in coil B is in phase with the line voltage. The current in coil A lags the line voltage by 90°. When the line current is in phase with the line voltage, the currents in B and C are in phase and a torque is exerted between them that alines their axes so that the pointer indicates unity power factor. The average torque between A and C is zero because these currents are 90° out of phase when the line power factor is unity.

When the current in coil C lags the line voltage—for example, by 45°—the currents in coil A and coil B both will be out of phase with the current in C. The current in A lags the current in C by 45° and the current in B leads the current in C by 45°. The flux around coil C will therefore react with the resultant of the fluxes around coils A and B, which is in phase with the current of C, and the pointer will be moved to an intermediate position (45°) between zero power factor and unity power factor. In most power-factor meters, lagging current causes the pointer to move to the left of the central position (marked "1" on the scale) and a leading current causes the pointer to move to the right of the central position.

MOVING IRON-VANE POWER-FACTOR METER

A diagram of a moving iron-vane type of power-factor meter is shown in figure 17-17.

In part (A) of the figure, potential coil A in series with resistor R comprises a resistive circuit, which is connected across the line. Potential coil B in series with inductor L comprises an inductive circuit, which is also connected across the line. Current coil C, having a few turns of large wire, is connected in series with the line. All coils are fixed in the positions shown, and only the iron vanes are free to move. The current in B lags the line voltage by 90°. The current in A is in phase with the line voltage. Hence, the current in B lags the current in A by 90° and, since the axes of A and B are displaced 90°, a magnetic revolving field is established by these coils when they are energized. The iron vanes are free to rotate about the axis of coil C. These vanes are magnetized alternately north and south by the line current flowing in coil C.

None of the moving parts carry current, and therefore springs are not needed. The movement is free to rotate 360°, but is prevented from rotating with the rotating field by an aluminum disk that rotates in a field produced by drag magnets (disk and magnets not shown).

In figure 17-17 (B), a two-pole rotating field is assumed to revolve at synchronous speed in

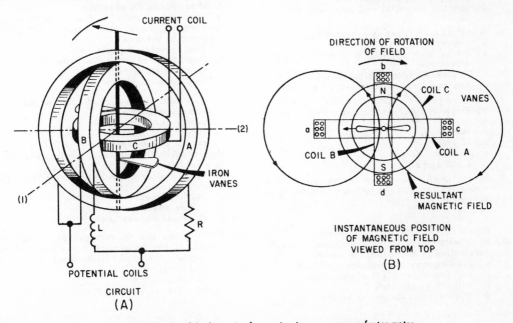

Figure 17-17.—Simplified circuit of a moving iron-vane power-factor meter.

a clockwise direction. The vanes are attracted or repelled by this field depending on the instantaneous direction of the resultant flux produced by A and B and on the instantaneous polarity of the iron vanes as determined by the instantaneous direction of the current through C. The vanes will assume a position out of alinement with the field (position of minimum torque) when the line power factor is unity.

If, at the instant shown in figure 17-17 (B), the current in coil C is maximum and the resultant flux produced by coils A and B passes through the movable element at right angles to the vanes (and has no effect on them), the pointer will indicate unity power factor, as shown. Ninety degrees later, the resultant north-south field will pass through the iron vanes in alinement with them. At this instant the current in magnetizing coil C is zero and the torque on the vanes is again a minimum. If the current through C leads the line voltage by 45° (line power factor 70% leading), the vanes will move 45° to a new position of minimum torque. The current in C will become maximum earlier in the cycle and the revolving field will occupy a new position, again out of alinement with the vanes at this instant.

If the line current lags the line voltage, the pointer will come to rest on the opposite side of the unity power-factor mark.

QUIZ

1. A wattmeter is connected in a circuit with the current coil
   a. and the potential coil in parallel with the load
   b. in parallel and the potential coil in series with the load
   c. in series and the potential coil in parallel with the load
   d. and the potential coil in series with the load

2. A metallic rectifier is a device that
   a. converts d.c. to a.c.
   b. offers high opposition to current in two directions
   c. is classed as a unidirectional conductor
   d. has two good conductors of electricity

3. The amperage rating of the secondary windings of a current transformer is rated at
   a. 400 amps.
   b. 12 amps.
   c. 5 amps.
   d. 2,000 amps.

4. In the iron-vane power factor meter, the vanes are magnetized by current flowing in
   a. coil A
   b. coil B
   c. coil C
   d. all three coils simultaneously

5. In a wattmeter, if the voltage or current safe rating is exceeded, the meter
   a. reading may not indicate overload
   b. will peg to the right of the scale
   c. will not be affected
   d. will not indicate power factor

6. The path for current flow through a rectifier cell is
   a. from the conductor, across the barrier layer, through the semiconductor
   b. from the semiconductor, across the barrier layer, through the conductor
   c. in the direction of the arrow
   d. through the fin assembly

7. In a capacitor bridge, to find the value of an unknown capacitor, what is used to bring the circuit into balance?
   a. Two variable capacitors
   b. Capacitive reactance of capacitors
   c. Two resistors
   d. Two potentiometers

8. A watt-hour meter reads the product of
   a. energy and time
   b. power and current
   c. power and time
   d. power and energy

9. Under normal conditions, the fin assembly in a rectifier is used to
   a. apply uniform pressure to reduce internal resistance
   b. carry current
   c. create resistance
   d. dissipate excess heat

10. When using the vibrating-reed frequency meter, if the frequency of the current is 112 cycles, the reed will be marked
    a. 55 c.p.s.
    b. 56 c.p.s.
    c. 60 c.p.s.
    d. 112 c.p.s.

11. In the iron-vane power factor meter, the spiral springs
    a. are eliminated
    b. return the pointer to zero
    c. oppose torque
    d. carry current to coils A and B
12. Instruments for measuring high voltage circuits become inaccurate when connected directly to high voltage because of
    a. electrostatic forces acting on the transformer
    b. inexpensiveness of instrument indicators
    c. high hysteresis effect on indicating element
    d. electrostatic forces acting on indicating element
13. The normal efficiency of a copper-oxide rectifier is from
    a. 25% to 55%
    b. 55% to 65%
    c. 85% to 100%
    d. 65% to 85%
14. In the moving-disk frequency meter, the magnetic field tends to produce rotation toward
    a. coil A
    b. the magnetizing coil
    c. the shorted coil
    d. coil B
15. When reading a watt-hour meter, the dials are read
    a. from the next highest number that the needle has just passed
    b. left to right
    c. right to left
    d. and subtracted
16. Instruments that are used to measure voltage and current regardless of circuit ratings are
    a. instrument transformers
    b. autotransformers
    c. electrodynamometers
    d. D'Arsonvals
17. A D'Arsonval d-c type instrument can be converted to read a. c. by using
    a. a bridge rectifier unit
    b. four rectifier cells connected in series
    c. a selenium rectifier
    d. a copper-oxide rectifier

18. In the moving-disk frequency meter, the current through coil B (fig. 17-15) varies
    a. inversely with the frequency
    b. directly with the frequency
    c. because it is connected in parallel
    d. because inductive reactance is constant
19. A safety precaution to follow when using a potential transformer is to
    a. ground the secondary
    b. ground the primary
    c. insulate for high current
    d. connect it in series with the line
20. The primary of a current transformer is always connected in
    a. series with the primary
    b. series with the line
    c. parallel with the line
    d. parallel with the power source.
21. The wattmeter is a/ an
    a. D'Arsonval meter
    b. electrodynamometer
    c. potential coil meter
    d. iron-vane meter
22. A power factor meter measures the
    a. phase angle between current and voltage
    b. sine of the phase angle between current and voltage
    c. ratio of apparent power to true power
    d. ratio of true power to apparent power
23. The secondary of a current transformer should not be open-circuited because
    a. of high current in the primary
    b. of high voltage in the secondary
    c. of low current in the primary
    d. it is not grounded
24. In the crossed-coil power factor meter, circuit continuity to the coils is provided by
    a. stationary current coil
    b. the resistor
    c. the inductor
    d. three spiral springs

CHAPTER 18

MAGNETIC AMPLIFIERS

Amplification of voltage and power can be accomplished by means of the magnetic amplifier, which employs as its controllable element an iron-core saturable reactor. The magnitude of the impedance of the saturable reactor depends upon the range of flux change that occurs in its core, and this action, in turn depends upon the magnitude of the control current. If the control current is varied a small amount, the power delivered to a load is varied through a much wider range. Herein lies the action of amplification.

The magnetic amplifier has certain advantages over other types of amplifiers. These include (1) high efficiency (90 percent); (2) reliability (long life, freedom from maintenance, reduction of spare parts inventory); (3) ruggedness (shock and vibration resistance, overload capability, freedom from effects of moisture); and (4) no warmup time. The magnetic amplifier has no moving parts and can be hermetically sealed within a case similar to the conventional dry-type transformer.

Also, the magnetic amplifier has a few disadvantages. For example, it cannot handle low-level signals; it is not useful at high frequencies; it has a time delay associated with magnetic effects; and the output waveform is not an exact reproduction of the input waveform.

The magnetic amplifier is important, however, to many phases of naval engineering because it provides a rugged, trouble-free device that has many applications aboard ship and in aircraft. These applications include throttle controls on the main engines of ships, speed, frequency, voltage, current, and temperature controls on auxiliary equipment; fire control, servomechanisms, and stabilizers for guns, radar, and sonar equipment.

Early Types of Saturable Cores

Early saturable reactors employed ordinary transformer silicon-steel cores. The amplifying qualities of these devices were not very satisfactory because of the relatively low-saturation flux density and high hysteresis losses.

The evolution of a practical magnetic amplifier has resulted from the recent development of high quality steels, gapless construction of the magnetic circuit, special low-leakage rectifiers, and self-saturating magnetic circuits. The improvement in processing magnetic materials and the successful development of dry-disk or metallic rectifiers have contributed principally to the wide use of this device as an amplifier. High-quality steels have increased the power-handling capacity. The dry-disk rectifiers convert either the entire output or part of the output from alternating current to direct current.

Basic Principles of Operation

To introduce the concept of controlling the magnitude of the current through a load by means of the self-induced voltage in a reactor (fig. 18-1), apply a 60-cycle, 117-volt source having a sine-waveform across a series circuit containing a variable inductance (the controlled element) and a fixed resistor (the load). The d-c control voltage is discussed later.

The circuit (fig. 18-1 (A)), although not an accurate analogy of magnetic amplifier action, represents the control of the magnitude of load

344

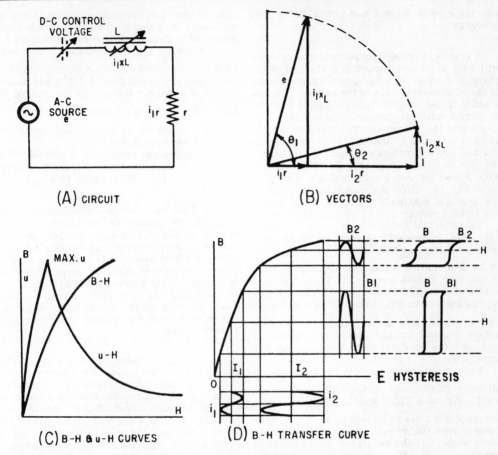

Figure 18-1.—Load current controlled by variable inductance.

current by utilizing the induced voltage inherent in the reactor, L.

Lenz's law states that the induced e.m.f. in any circuit is always in such a direction as to oppose the effect that produces it. Because the current in an a-c circuit is always changing, the opposition of the induced voltage is continuous. Increasing the induced voltage in the series circuit comprising r and L will reduce the magnitude of the circuit current and cause it to lag behind the source voltage by an increasing angle (fig. 18-1 (B)). This action reduces the circuit power factor.

The obvious advantage of controlling the circuit current with adjustable inductance is the absence of appreciable heat loss in the control element. The obvious disadvantage is low circuit power factor.

Magnitude of the inductance may be varied in a number of ways. For example, doubling the number of turns will quadruple the inductance. (Inductance varies as the square of the number of turns.) Also increasing the permeability of the core will increase the inductance. (Inductance varies directly with permeability.)

The latter action may be accomplished in a number of ways. For example, if the reactor core is air, the permeability, μ, will be unity. If a laminated silicon-steel core is gradually inserted into the coil, the permeability will increase (fig. 18-1 (C)) toward the point of maximum μ. The coil impedance will increase

345

and the circuit current and power factor will decrease.

A review of magnetism and magnetic circuits will help in the understanding of the rest of the chapter. Another way to vary the permeability of the silicon-steel core of the reactor is to introduce a d-c control voltage (dotted battery) in series with the circuit of figure 18-1 (A). Increasing the d-c voltage will increase the d-c ampere turns and H (the ampere turns per centimeter are approximately equal to H). Hence, the flux density, B (fig. 18-1 (D)) will increase with H and the d-c control voltage. The permeability ($\mu = B/H$) decreases to the right of the point of maximum, μ (fig. 18-1 (C)) as the d-c control voltage (and H) continue to increase.

The effect of these actions on the load current (a-c component) is represented by projecting the load current curve, i_1 (fig. 18-1 (D)) to the B-H curve and transferring the projection to the flux density curve, $B1$. Thus, with low values of d-c control voltage and direct current I_1, the associated flux variations in the reactor core are relatively large (curve $B1$). The resulting induced voltage across the reactor is high and the load current, curve i_1, has low amplitude.

Voltage $i_1 r$ across the load for the condition of large flux change in the coil is relatively small (fig. 18-1 (B)), and the voltage, $i_1 X_L$, across the coil is relatively large. The circuit current lags the source voltage by a relatively large angle, θ_1, and the circuit power factor is low.

Increasing the d-c control voltage and direct current from I_1 to I_2 will partially saturate the core so that smaller flux variations (curve B2) will occur with a correspondingly reduced magnitude of induced voltage and increased load current (curve i_2). The voltage, $i_2 r$ across the load for the condition of small flux change in the coil is increased (fig. 18-1 (B)), and the voltage, $i_2 X_L$, across the coil is decreased. The angle, θ_2, by which the circuit current lags the source voltage is decreased, and the circuit power factor approaches unity.

With increased values of d-c control voltage and flux density the cycle of magnetization is reduced (fig. 18-1 (E)) from $B1$ to $B2$.

The load current (a-c component) in this example, is relatively insensitive to small changes in d-c control current. Also, the series reactor is never driven very far into saturation so that its impedance never drops to a very low value. For a given value of control current, the full cycle of the corresponding hysteresis loop is completed for each cycle of source voltage. Thus, the gain of the circuit (ratio of a-c load power change to d-c control power change) is relatively low.

To obtain greater circuit gain, certain changes must be made. The reactor core is driven into saturation periodically. This action allows the load current to flow for a controlled portion of each cycle. Before saturation is reached, the flux change prevents current flow through the load for another controlled portion of each cycle. The result of operating the reactor core in the region of saturation for a portion of each cycle will increase the circuit gain materially.

Materials Suitable For Magnetic - Amplifier Cores

Various types of nickel-iron alloys that have more suitable magnetic properties than previous ones for use as core materials for saturable reactors have been developed and are commercially available. These materials are the (1) high permeability alloys and (2) grain-oriented alloys.

High-permeability materials, such as Permalloy A, Mumetal, 1040 alloy and equivalents have low and intermediate values of saturation flux density but relatively narrow and steep hysteresis loops. These materials are used extensively as the cores in low-level input amplifier stages.

Grain-oriented materials, such as Orthonol, Deltamax, Hypernik V, Orthonik, Permeron, and equivalents, have higher values of saturation flux density and more rectangular-shaped hysteresis loops (fig. 18-2 (A)) than the high-permeability materials. Grain-oriented materials are referred to as square-loop materials because of the flat top and bottom of the hysteresis loop. A conventional loop is shown in

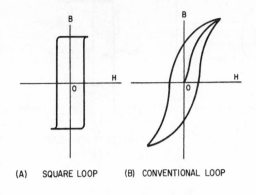

| (A) SQUARE LOOP | (B) CONVENTIONAL LOOP |

Figure 18-2.—Hysteresis loops.

figure 18-2 (B). These materials are used as the cores in high-level output amplifier stages in which maximum permeability occurs close to saturation flux density, resulting in a substantial increase in the power-handling capacity for a given weight of core material.

In the manufacture of saturable cores, the characteristics of the grain structure of the material can be altered considerably by rolling and annealing processes.

A great improvement in the magnetic properties of some materials is obtained by cold-rolling the material before it is annealed. The cold-rolling process develops an orientation of the grain in the direction of rolling. If a magnetizing force is applied to the material so that the flux is in the direction of the grain, a rectangular hysteresis loop is obtained. Thus, in some materials cold rolling produces almost infinite permeability up to the knee and almost complete saturation beyond the knee.

Basic Half-Wave Circuit

A description of a simple half-wave circuit (fig. 18-3 (A)) will be given as an example of the operating principles in general of the magnetic amplifier.

WINDINGS

The magnetic amplifier contains a magnetic core made of a square-loop material upon which two windings are placed. The load, or "gating" winding, L, is connected in series with a rectifier, the load, and an a-c power supply. A second or "control" winding, C, is connected in series with a rectifier, the control signal source, and the same a-c source. The two windings have a 1:1 turns ratio. The magnetic amplifier acts in this circuit like an electrically operated contactor that gates (turns on) the load circuit periodically. A control voltage applied to the closing circuit of the contactor closes the contactor, which completes a circuit to the load. This action can be repeated periodically, for example, by introducing an a-c control voltage in series with a half-wave rectifier and the contactor closing coil.

The action of the control winding of the magnetic amplifier may be compared to that of the closing coil of the contactor. The action of the load winding may be compared to that of the contactor's main contacts. The latter action is that of introducing a high impedance (main contacts open) for a controlled portion of each half cycle and then removing this impedance (main contacts closed) and allowing current to flow through the load during the remaining portion of the half cycle.

POLARITIES

In a previous study it was explained that transformers have polarity markings (fig. 18-4). The solid arrow at the source is marked minus at the head and plus at the tail to represent arbitrarily the positive half cycle of active source voltage. The electron flow is from the negative terminal of the source into the dotted end of the primary and returning to the positive end of the source.

The solid arrow in the secondary of the transformer has the same polarity as that of the source because the secondary is the source for the load.

The dotted (dashed line) arrow in the primary winding represents the induced voltage in the primary for the first half cycle of applied voltage and has the same polarity markings as

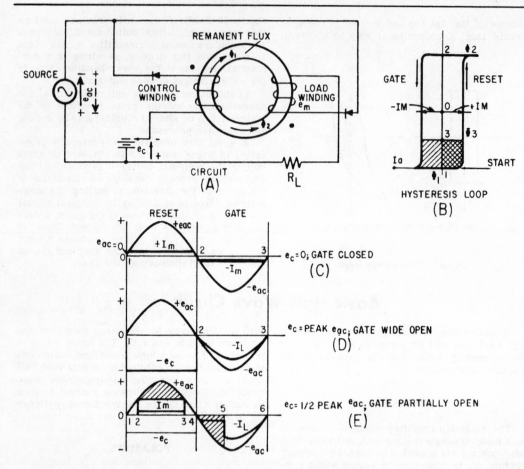

Figure 18-3.—Basic half-wave magnetic amplifier.

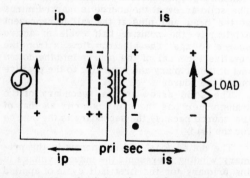

Figure 18-4.—One-half cycle of applied voltage e_{ac}.

the source voltage and the secondary voltage arrows.

The direction of electron flow through the load is represented by a solid arrow, the polarity of which is opposite to that of the other three arrows. This reversal of markings is characteristic of load voltages with respect to source voltages. For voltages across loads, the arrow head is on the positive side and the tail is on the negative side. For voltages originating in generators, transformers, batteries, etc., the arrow head is on the negative side and the tail is on the positive side.

348

In the example of figure 18-3 (A), the solid arrow at the source indicates the direction of electron flow through the circuit during the positive half cycles of applied voltage, e_{ac}. The polarity markings (dots at one end of the windings) are indicative of the way the turns are wound on the core. The dotted ends of the windings of a core are assumed to always have a particular instantaneous polarity with respect to the undotted ends of the windings. Also, the dotted ends of two or more windings on a common core are considered to have the same instantaneous polarity with respect to each other. For example, in figure 18-3 (A), if the voltage applied to the control winding is of a polarity at some instant to cause current to flow INTO the dot-marked end of that winding, the induced voltage of the other winding will be of a polarity (at the same instant) such as to cause current to flow OUT of the dot-marked end of that winding. The control voltage, e_c, is assumed to be a direct voltage. The rectifier arrow-heads are pointed against the direction of electron flow.

FUNCTION OF RECTIFIERS

Rectifiers are placed in the load and control circuits to prohibit current flow in the control circuit during the gating half cycle and in the load, or gating, circuit during the reset half cycle. The magnetic amplifier is not an amplifier in the sense of a step-up transformer. Voltages generated by mutual induction (transformer action) between the control and load windings exist in these windings, but they have only a small effect on the amplifier operation under the established conditions.

During the first half cycle (solid arrow of source) of the applied voltage, the direction of the INDUCED voltages in both windings is INTO, or positive, at the polarity-marked terminals. In the load winding this action is in the forward direction of the rectifier and against e_{ac}. Thus, the rectifier in the load circuit prevents current flow through the load and is subjected to an inverse voltage equal to the difference between e_{ac} and the mutually induced voltage in the load winding. The time interval, corresponding to the first half cycle, is called the "reset" half cycle. The reset action is described later.

ANALYSIS WITH ZERO D-C CONTROL VOLTAGE

As mentioned previously, figure 18-3 is used in the analysis of the action of the basic half-wave magnetic amplifier. Figure 18-3 (A), represents the basic circuit. Figure 18-3 (B) represents the square-type hysteresis loop for the core material used in this circuit. Figure 18-3 (C), (D), and (E), represents the waveforms of current and voltage for three conditions to be considered. The symbol representing a quantity is common to all parts of the figure. For example, the magnetizing current, I_m, is represented in figure 18-3 (B), (C), and (E). The hysteresis loop is enlarged for clarity and is not drawn to the same scale as parts (C), (D), and (E).

Reset Half Cycle

The first condition to be described is with the control voltage, e_c, at zero. At the beginning of the reset half cycle, the core is assumed to possess a residual or negative saturation remanent flux level, Φ_1 (fig. 18-3 (B)). The direction of this flux is indicated by the arrow, Φ_1, in figure 18-3 (A). As e_{ac} increases from 0 in a positive direction (indicated by the solid arrow at the source, fig. 18-3 (A) and by the part of the sine curve, point 1 to point 2 (fig. 18-3 (C)), the current in the control winding establishes an m.m.f. represented by half the width of the hysteresis loop, $+I_m$ (fig. 18-3(B)). The applied voltage establishes an m.m.f. that acts in a direction to oppose the residual core flux, Φ_1, and therefore to demagnetize the core. The amount of change of flux will depend upon the MAGNITUDE of the applied voltage across the control winding and the TIME INTERVAL during which this voltage is applied.

In this example, the first half cycle of applied voltage is assumed to reverse the core magnetism and to establish its flux density at essentially the positive saturation level, Φ_2 (fig. 18-3 (B)). This action is called reset.

As e_{ac} increases from 0 in a positive direction in the vicinity of point 1 (fig. 18-3 (C)), there is no change in core flux until the current increases to the value of $+I_m$, corresponding to

one-half of the width of the hysteresis loop.
Thus, with no flux change, the current rises
abruptly and is limited only by the resistance
of the circuit and the low value of e_{ac}. When
the current reaches the value, $+I_m$, the core
flux starts to change from the Φ_1 level toward
the Φ_2 level (fig. 18-3 (B)). The accompanying
self-induced voltage opposes e_{ac} and limits the
current to a constant small value during the
flux variation from the level Φ_1 to Φ_2.

This flux change continues during the time
interval between point 1 and point 2 (fig.
18-3 (C)). As it continues, the induced voltage
continues to vary in magnitude with e_{ac} and to
oppose e_{ac} in such a manner that I_m remains
constant over the half-cycle interval.

Gating Half Cycle

The next half cycle is called the "gating"
half cycle. It starts at point 2 (fig. 18-3 (C)),
at which time the polarity of the applied voltage
reverses. The direction of e_{ac} for this half cycle
is indicated by the dotted arrow (fig. 18-3 (A)).
During this time interval, the rectifier in the
control circuit blocks the flow of control circuit
current. However, the rectifier in the load circuit permits current from the source to flow in
that circuit. This current will magnetize the
core in a negative direction—that is, in a direction to change the flux from the Φ_2 level to the
Φ_1 level. The applied voltage is assumed to be
of the correct magnitude to cause the core to
be magnetized to the Φ_1 level (fig. 18-3 (B)). A
condition of equilibrium is indicated.

The large flux change from the Φ_2 level to
the Φ_1 level causes a self-induced voltage in the
load winding, L, and a mutually induced voltage
in the control winding, C. The self-induced voltage in the load winding opposes e_{ac}. The mutually induced voltage in the control winding
also opposes e_{ac}. The rectifier in the control
circuit is subject to an inverse voltage equal
to the difference between e_{ac} and the mutually
induced voltage in the control winding. Because

of the maximum flux change in the core, maximum impedance is presented by the load winding
to the circuit containing R_L throughout the gating
half cycle, and therefore e_{ac} will appear across
the load winding and not across R_L. For this
condition, the current through the load is limited
to a very small magnetizing component that is
negligible compared to normal values of load
current. The gate is closed.

**ANALYSIS WITH MAXIMUM D-C CONTROL
VOLTAGE**

The second condition described is for the
condition that e_c is equal to the peak value of
e_{ac}. At point 1 (fig. 18-3 (D)) the remanent
magnetism is again at the Φ_1 level (fig.
18-3 (B)).

First Half Cycle

The applied voltage, e_{ac}, rises from 0 to
maximum during the first 90° of the cycle, but
has no effect on the core flux because the control
voltage, e_c, has a magnitude equal to the maximum value of e_{ac}, and the polarity opposite to
that of e_{ac}. Thus, the rectifier prevents the flow
of battery control current during the time that
e_c is greater than e_{ac}. Because there is no
voltage across the control winding (the rectifier
is essentially an open circuit), no flux change
can occur from point 1 to point 2 (fig. 18-3 (D)).
Figure 18-3 (B), does not apply. Thus, no change
in flux occurs during the reset half cycle for
this assumed condition.

Second Half Cycle

When e_{ac} reverses its polarity (solid to dotted
arrow), the rectifier in the control circuit continues to block the flow of current in that circuit.
In the load circuit the polarity of e_{ac} during the
gating interval, points 2 to 3 (fig. 18-3 (D)), is
such as to tend to drive the core further into
negative saturation (point Ia, fig. 18-3 (B)). Because the core is already saturated, no further

flux change occurs, and e_{ac} appears across R_L because the load winding offers no impedance to I_L.

The full value of load current flows, and its magnitude is e_{ac}/R_L. The gate is wide open. The waveform of this current, $-I_L$, is illustrated in figure 18-3 (D).

ANALYSIS WITH PARTIAL D-C CONTROL VOLTAGE

The third condition assumes that e_C is approximately half peak value of e_{ac}. During the reset half cycle, voltage is applied to the control winding during the time interval from point 2 to point 3 (fig. 18-3 (E)). The magnitude of this voltage is $e_{ac} - e_c$. This voltage will be less than the peak value of e_{ac}, but greater than zero; and a new set of conditions will be established.

First Half Cycle

The reset cycle is just beginning. During the interval 1 to 2 (fig. 18-3 (E)), e_C is greater than e_{ac}, and the rectifier opposes any current flow in the control winding. During the interval 2 to 3, e_{ac} exceeds e_C, and magnetizing current flows in the control winding. As mentioned previously, the extent of the change in core flux will depend on the time interval and magnitude of the voltage applied across the control winding within the half cycle. Because the time interval is very short, and the net voltage applied to the control winding is much less than e_{ac}, the core flux level is assumed to change from Φ_1 to the level along the line through Φ_3 (fig. 18-3 (B)). During the interval 3 to 4 (fig. 18-3 (E)), e_{ac} is again less than e_C, and the rectifier prevents any further flow of control current. As in the previous examples, the rectifier in the load circuit prevents any current flow in that circuit during the reset half cycle.

Second Half Cycle

When e_{ac} reverses, magnetizing current flowing through the load winding changes the core flux from the level through point 3 to the level through point 1 (fig. 18-3 (B)). This change

is assumed to take place during the interval 4 to 5 (fig. 18-3 (E)). The impedance of the load winding is high during this interval, and current flow through the load is restricted to the magnetizing current. However, at point 5 the core becomes saturated, and no further flux change occurs. The impedance of the core drops to zero, and current e_{ac}/R_L flows through the load during the interval 5 to 6. The load voltage is in phase with e_{ac} and has the same waveform as that of e_{ac} for this part of the cycle.

ENERGY CONSIDERATIONS

The area of the portion of the hysteresis loop traversed is a measure of the energy required to complete that particular cycle of magnetization. It may be divided equally by the y axis.

For condition 1 (fig. 18-3 (C)), the entire right-hand area of the loop shown is figure 18-3 (B), is proportional to the area under the $+e_{ac}$ voltage wave (which is proportional to the energy supplied), and the left-hand area is proportional to the area under the $-e_{ac}$ voltage wave.

For condition 2 (fig. 18-3 (D)), the area in both half cycles is zero (no flux change occurs), and the load, R_L, absorbs the entire applied voltage, e_{ac}. No energy is supplied to the control winding.

For condition 3 (fig. 18-3 (E)), the right-hand shaded area of the hysteresis loop (fig. 18-3 (B)) is proportional to the shaded area under $+e_{ac}$ (fig. 18-3 (E)), and the left-hand shaded area of the hysteresis loop is proportional to the shaded area of $-e_{ac}$. In this case the magnitude of $(e_{ac} - e_c)$ applied to the control winding determines how far the core flux is carried from negative saturation toward positive saturation, and consequently, how much of the gating half cycle will be nonconducting.

For condition 3, the energy supplied to the control winding is partially reduced. The corresponding area is reduced from the total area under $+e_{ac}$ for condition 1 to that indicated by the shaded portion under the $+e_{ac}$ curve in figure 18-3 (E). The flux change is not carried to level Φ_2 on the hysteresis loop, but to some point part way up the loop (level Φ_3), as determined by the shaded area under the $+e_{ac}$ curve.

In other words, the time in the gating half cycle at which the core saturates (the firing angle) is determined by the shaded area under the $+e_{ac}$ curve or the amount of energy supplied to the control winding during the reset half cycle. Thus, as e_c is reduced in magnitude, the voltage, $e_{ac} - e_c$, applied to the control winding increases, and the core flux is carried further toward positive saturation during the reset half cycle.

This action increases the firing angle and delays the time in the gating half cycle when the

core saturates and the load winding becomes conducting. Thus, the average load current and voltage are reduced. They both vary with the control voltage.

By way of contrast with the relative low-circuit power factor of the example in figure 18-1, the power factor of the circuit of the example in figure 18-3 is unity for all values of d-c control voltage between zero and maximum.

QUIZ

1. When control current is sufficient to saturate the core, inductance
   a. increases and reactance decreases
   b. decreases and reactance increases
   c. increases and reactance increases
   d. decreases and reactance decreases
2. The power handling capacity of magnetic amplifiers has been improved primarily because of the development of
   a. dry-disk rectifiers
   b. high-quality steels
   c. electron amplifier tubes
   d. high-wattage resistors
3. When the inductive reactance of the load winding is decreased load
   a. current rises and load voltage drops
   b. current drops and load voltage rises
   c. circuit impedance drops and load voltage rises
   d. circuit impedance drops and load voltage drops
4. Doubling the number of turns on a coil will
   a. double the inductance
   b. decrease the inductance by one-half
   c. increase the inductance as the square of the turns
   d. have no effect on inductance
5. Which of the following is a disadvantage of a magnetic amplifier?
   a. High efficiency
   b. Ruggedness
   c. It has no moving parts
   d. It is not useful at high frequencies
6. When a magnetic amplifier is operating at the knee of the magnetization curve, a small increase in control current will
   a. cause a large increase in flux density
   b. desaturate the core
   c. increase permeability of the core
   d. decrease inductance of the load winding

7. Transformer action between the a-c load windings and d-c control winding is
   a. necessary to increase amplification
   b. desired in order to reduce the required control current
   c. desired to increase response time
   d. not desired
8. Which of the following is considered an advantage of a magnetic-amplifier circuit over a vacuum-tube circuit?
   a. Little distortion
   b. Frequency response time
   c. Shock resistance
   d. Impedance matching
9. Current flow in the load circuit can be increased by
   a. increasing the impedance of the circuit
   b. decreasing the permeability of the core
   c. increasing the permeability of the core
   d. decreasing the control current
10. The basic control action of a magnetic amplifier depends upon
    a. variations in the load impedance
    b. changes in inductance
    c. type of core material
    d. construction of the core
11. Permeability of a substance is defined as the
    a. ease with which it conducts magnetic lines of flux
    b. opposition it offers to a-c current flow
    c. opposition if offers to d-c current flow
    d. ease with which it retains magnetic properties
12. Which of the following is an advantage of a magnetic amplifier?
    a. It has a time delay associated with magnetic effects
    b. The output waveform is not an exact reproduction of the input waveform
    c. No warmup time
    d. It cannot handle low-level signals

13. Rectifiers are placed in the control circuits to prohibit current flow in the control winding during the
    a. warmup time
    b. gating half cycle
    c. reset half cycle
    d. complete cycle

14. Silicon steel cores were not satisfactory for saturable reactors because of
    a. low saturation flux density and high hysteresis losses
    b. high saturation flux density and high hysteresis losses
    c. low saturation flux density and low hysteresis losses
    d. high saturation flux density and low hysteresis losses

15. An important advantage of controlling circuit current by an adjustable inductor is
    a. low circuit power factor
    b. high circuit power factor
    c. absence of heat loss in the control element
    d. high heat loss in the control element

16. Operating the reactor core in the region of saturation for a portion of each cycle will cause the circuit gain to
    a. hold steady
    b. fluctuate rapidly
    c. decrease
    d. increase

CHAPTER 19

SYNCHROS AND SERVOMECHANISMS

Synchros

Synchros, as identified by the Armed Forces, are electromagnetic devices which are used primarily for the transfer of angular-position data. Synchros are, in effect, single-phase transformers whose primary-to-secondary coupling may be varied by physically changing the relative orientation of these two windings.

Synchro systems are used throughout the Navy to provide a means of transmitting the position of a remotely located device to one or more indicators located away from the transmitting area.

Figure 19-1 (A) shows a simple synchro system. The synchro transmitter sends an electrical signal to the synchro receivers, via interconnecting leads. The synchro transmitter signal is generated when the handwheel turns the transmitter's shaft, and the indicator's shaft will rotate to aline with the transmitter's shaft.

Figure 19-1 (B) shows a simple mechanical system that uses gears and shafts for transmitting position data. Mechanical systems are usually impractical because of associated belts, pulleys, and flexible rotating shafts.

In appearance, synchros resemble small electric motors. They consist of a rotor (R) and a stator (S). The letters R and S are used to identify rotor and stator connections in wiring diagrams and blueprints. Synchros are represented schematically by the symbols shown in figure 19-2. The symbols shown in (A) and (B) are used when it is necessary to show only the external connections to a synchro, while those shown in (C), (D), and (E) are used when it is important to see the positional relationship between the rotor and stator. The small arrow on the rotor indicates the angular displacement of the rotor; in these illustrations the displacement is zero degrees.

SYNCHRO CONSTRUCTION

Knowledge of a synchro's construction and its characteristics will enable you to better understand synchro operation. As stated previously, synchros are, in effect, transformers whose primary-to-secondary coupling may be varied by physically changing the relative orientation of the two windings. This is accomplished by mounting one of the windings so that it is free to rotate inside the other. The inner, usually movable, winding is called the rotor, and the outer, usually stationary, winding is called the stator. The rotor consists of either one or three coils wound on sheet-steel laminations. The stator normally consists of three coils wound in internally slotted laminations. In some units the rotor is the primary and the stator is the secondary, in other units the reverse is true.

Rotor Construction

The laminations of the rotor core are stacked together and rigidly mounted on a shaft. Sliprings are mounted on, but insulated from, the shaft. The ends of the coil or coils are connected to these sliprings. Brushes riding on the sliprings provide continuous electrical contact during rotation, and low-friction ball bearings permit the shaft to turn easily. In standard synchros, the bearings must permit rotation from very low speeds to speeds as high as 1,200 r.p.m.

There are two common types of synchro rotors now in use, (1) the salient-pole rotor, and (2) the drum or wound rotor.

The salient-pole rotor, which frequently is called a "dumb-bell" or "H" rotor because of the shape of its core laminations, is shown in figure 19-3.

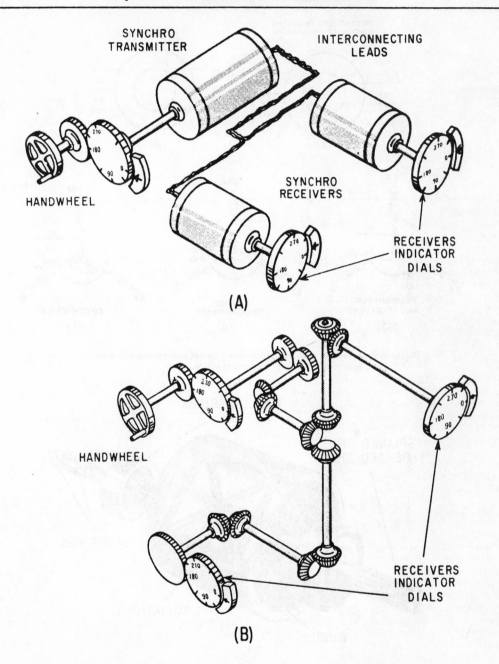

Figure 19-1.–(A) Data transfer with synchros; (B) data transfer with gears.

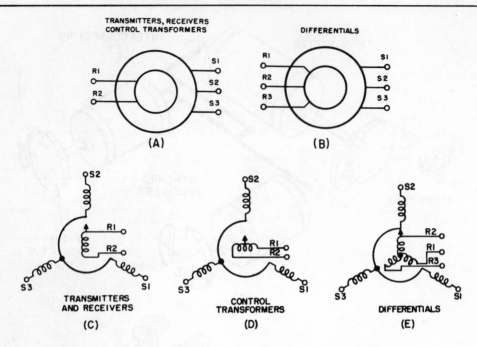

Figure 19-2.—Schematic symbols used to show external connections and relative positions of windings for Navy synchros.

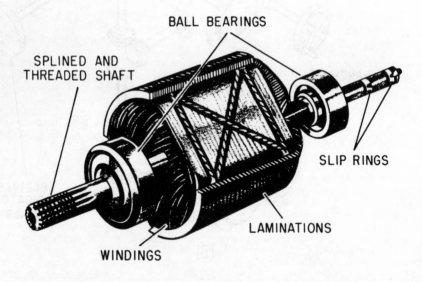

Figure 19-3.—Salient-pole rotor.

The winding consists of a single machine-wound coil whose turns lie in planes perpendicular to a line through the center called the axis of the coil and along which the m.m.f. of the coil is developed. The coil axis coincides with that of the salient poles. When used in transmitters and receivers, the rotor functions as the excitation or primary winding of the synchro. When energized, it becomes an a-c electromagnet with the poles assuming opposite magnetic polarities. During one complete excitation cycle, the magnetic polarity changes from zero to maximum in one direction, to zero and reversing to maximum in the opposite direction, returning to zero.

The drum or wound rotor is shown in figure 19-4. This type of rotor is used in most synchro control transformers. The winding of the wound rotor may consist of three coils, so wound that their axes are displaced from each other by 120 degrees. One end of each coil terminates at one of three sliprings on the shaft, while the other ends are connected together. Synchro windings of this type are called Y-connected. In other wound rotors, a single coil of wire or group of coils is connected in series to produce either a concentrated winding effect, or the same distributed winding effect as that of the salient-pole rotor.

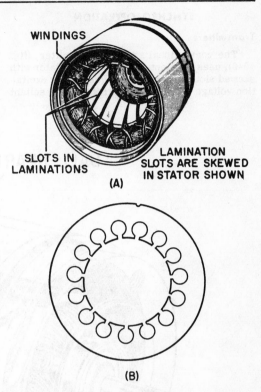

WINDINGS

SLOTS IN LAMINATIONS

LAMINATION SLOTS ARE SKEWED IN STATOR SHOWN

(A)

(B)

Figure 19-5.—(A) Typical stator; (B) stator lamination.

WINDINGS

SLIP RINGS

LAMINATIONS

Figure 19-4.—Drum or wound rotor.

Stator Construction

The stator of a synchro is a cylindrical structure of slotted laminations on which three Y-connected coils are wound with their axes 120 degrees apart. Figure 19-5 (A) shows a typical stator assembly and figure 19-5 (B) shows a stator lamination.

Stator windings function as the secondary windings in synchro transmitters and receivers. Normally, stators are not connected directly to an a-c source. Their excitation is supplied by the a-c magnetic field of the rotor.

Some synchros are constructed so that both the stator and rotor may be turned. Connections to the stator of this type are made via sliprings and brushes. In some units, the sliprings are secured to the housing and the brushes turn with the stator. In other units, the brushes are fixed and the sliprings are mounted on a flat insulated plate secured to the stator.

Unit Assembly

The rotor is mounted so that it may turn within the stator. A cylindrical frame houses the assembled synchro. Standard synchros have an insulated terminal block secured to one end of the housing at which the internal connections to the rotor and stator terminate, and to which external connections are made. Special type synchros often have pigtail leads brought out from inside the unit, rather than terminals.

SYNCHRO OPERATION

Transmitters

The conventional synchro transmitter, (fig. 19-6), uses a salient-pole rotor and a stator with skewed slots (fig. 19-5 (A)). When an a-c excitation voltage is applied to the rotor, the resultant current produces an a-c magnetic field. The lines of force, or flux, vary continually in amplitude and direction, and, by transformer action, induce voltages into the stator coils. The effective voltage induced in any stator coil depends upon the angular position of that coil's axis with respect to the rotor axis.

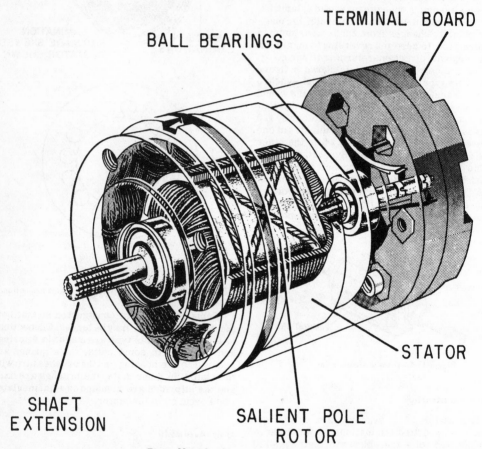

Figure 19-6.—Synchro transmitter or receiver.

When the maximum coil effective (r.m.s.) voltage is known, the effective voltage induced at any angular displacement can be determined. Figure 19-7 is a cross section of a synchro transmitter and shows the effective voltages induced in one stator coil as the rotor is turned to different positions.

The turns ratio between the rotor and stator is such that when single-phase 115-volt power is applied to the rotor, the highest value of effective voltage that will be induced in any one stator coil will be 52 volts. For example, the highest effective voltage that can be induced in stator coil A will occur when the rotor is turned

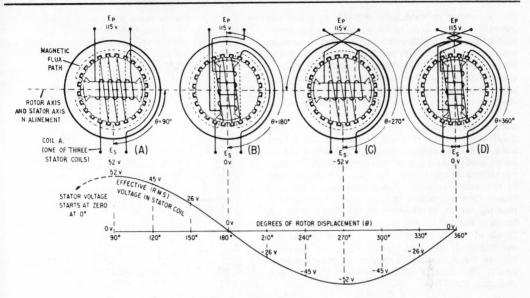

Figure 19-7.—Simple synchro transmitter stator voltages.

to angle θ (fig. 19-7 (A)). In this position the rotor axis is in alinement with the axis of winding A and the magnetic coupling between the primary and secondary coil A is maximum.

The effective voltage, E_s, induced in any one of the secondary windings A, B, or C is approximately equal to the product of the effective voltage, E_p, on the primary; the secondary-to-primary turns ratio, N; and the magnetic coupling between primary and secondary which depends upon the cosine of the angle, θ, between the rotor axis and the axis of the corresponding secondary winding. Expressed mathematically,

$$E_s = E_p \times N \times \cos \theta.$$

Therefore, because the effective primary voltage and the turns ratio are constant, the effective secondary voltage varies with angle θ.

Terminal-to-Terminal Stator Voltages

Because the common connection between the stator coils is not accessible, it is possible to measure only the terminal-to-terminal voltages. When the maximum terminal-to-terminal effective voltage is known, the terminal-to-terminal effective voltage for any rotor displacement can be determined. Figure 19-8 shows how these voltages vary as the rotor is turned. Values are above the line when the terminal-to-terminal voltage is in phase with the $R1$ to $R2$ voltage and below the line when the voltage is 180 degrees out of phase with the $R1$ to $R2$ voltage thus negative values indicate a phase reversal. As an example, when the rotor is turned 50 degrees from the reference (zero degree) position, the $S3$ to $S1$ voltage will be about 70 volts and in phase with the $R1$ to $R2$ voltage, the $S2$ to $S3$ voltage will be about 16 volts and also in phase with the $R1$ to $R2$ voltage, and the $S1$ to $S3$ voltage will be about 85 volts, 180 degrees out of phase with the $R1$ to $R2$ voltage. Although the curves of figure 19-8 resemble timegraphs of a-c voltages, they show only the variations in effective voltage amplitude and phase as a function of the mechanical rotor position.

Receivers

Receivers are electrically identical to transmitters of the same size. In some sizes of the 400-cycle standard synchros, the units may be used as transmitters or receivers.

Normally the receiver rotor is unrestrained in movement except for brush and bearing friction. When power is first applied to a system, the transmitter position quickly changes, or if the receiver is switched into the system, the receiver rotor turns to correspond to the position of the transmitter rotor. This sudden motion can cause the rotor to oscillate (swing back and forth) around the synchronous position; should the movement of the rotor be great enough it may even spin. Some method of preventing excessive oscillations or spinning must be used.

In small synchro units, a retarding action may be produced by a shorted winding on the quadrature axis, at right angles to the direct axis. In larger units, a mechanical device known as an inertia damper is more effective. Several variations of the inertia damper are in use. One of the more common types consists of a heavy brass flywheel which is free to rotate around a bushing which is attached to the rotor shaft. A tension spring on the bushing rubs against the flywheel so that they both turn during normal operation. If the rotor shaft turns or tends to change its speed or direction of rotation suddenly, the inertia of the damper opposes the changing condition.

SIMPLE SYNCHRO SYSTEM

A simple synchro transmission system consists of a transmitter connected to a receiver, as shown in figure 19-9. The $R1$ transmitter and $R1$ receiver leads are connected to one side of the a-c supply line and the $R2$ transmitter and $R2$ receiver leads are connected to the other side of the supply line. The stators of both the transmitter and the receiver are connected $S1$ to $S1$, $S2$ to $S2$, and $S3$ to $S3$ so that the voltage in each of the transmitter stator coils opposes the voltage in the corresponding coils of the receiver stator. The voltage directions are indicated by arrows for the instant of time shown by the dot on the sine wave of the rotor supply voltage. The a-c generator symbol inserted in series with each of the synchro windings indicates the presence of a transformer-induced voltage.

The field of the transmitter is alined with the axis of $S2$ (fig. 19-9 (A)) because the transmitter rotor axis is alined with $S2$. Assume for the moment that the receiver rotor is not connected to the single-phase supply. Under this condition the voltage induced in the transmitter stator windings will be impressed on the receiver stator windings through the three leads connecting the $S1$, $S2$, and $S3$ terminals. Exciting currents that are proportional to the transmitter stator voltages will flow in the receiver stator windings, and the magnetomotive forces

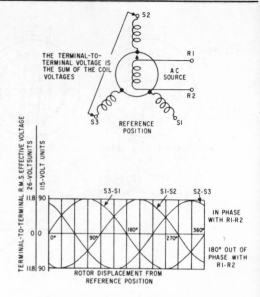

Figure 19-8.—Terminal-to-terminal voltages.

produced by these currents will establish a 2-pole field that orients itself in the receiver stator in exactly the same manner that the transmitter field is oriented in its own stator. Thus, if the transmitter field is turned by turning the transmitter rotor, the receiver field will also turn in exact synchronism with the transmitter rotor.

A soft-iron bar placed in a magnetic field will always tend to aline itself so that its longest axis is parallel to the axis of the field. Thus, the salient pole receiver rotor will also aline itself with the receiver field even though the receiver rotor winding is open-circuited. Operation with an open-circuited rotor is not desirable, however, because for a given position of the transmitter rotor and field there are two positions, 180° apart, in which the salient pole receiver rotor may come into alinement with the receiver field. This difficulty is eliminated by energizing the receiver rotor with alternating current of the same frequency and phase as that supplied to the transmitter rotor. Now the receiver rotor electromagnet comes into alinement with the receiver field in such a position as to always aid the magnetomotive forces of the three windings of the receiver stator. A rotor position in which the magnetomotive force of the rotor opposes the magnetomotive forces of the stator would not be stable. For example, a compass

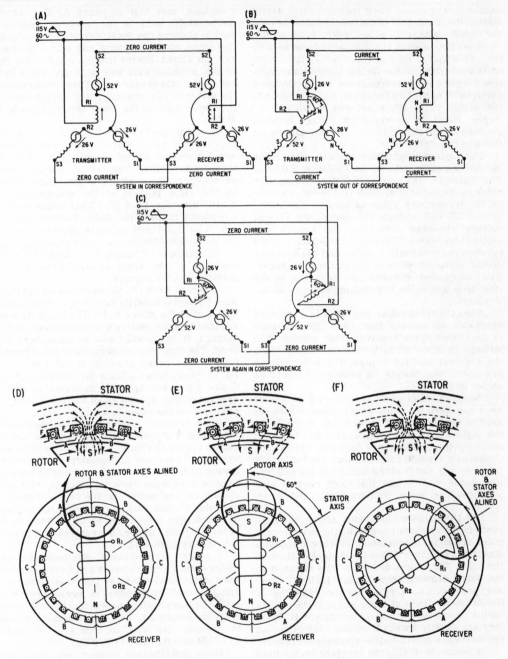

Figure 19-9.—Development of torque in a synchro.

needle always alines itself with the earth's field so that the north pole of the needle points toward the south magnetic pole (north geographic).

When both rotors are displaced from zero by the same angle, they are properly alined with their respective stator fields. Under this condition they are in correspondence and the induced voltages in each of the three pairs of corresponding stator coils are equal and in opposition. Hence, there is no resultant voltage between corresponding stator terminals and no current flows in the stator coils.

The angle through which a transmitter rotor is mechanically rotated is called a SIGNAL. For example, the angle that the transmitter rotor is displaced (fig. 19-9 (B)) is 60°. As soon as the transmitter rotor is turned, the transmitter S2 coil voltage decreases, the S1 coil voltage reverses direction, and the S3 coil voltage increases. Current immediately flows between the transmitter stator and the receiver stator in the direction of the stronger voltages. The unbalanced voltages are absorbed in the line drop and in the internal impedances of the windings.

When the transmitter (fig. 19-9 (A)) is turned clockwise 60 degrees (fig. 19-9 (B)), a torque is developed in the receiver rotor causing it to attempt to follow through the same angle. When the receiver and the transmitter are again in alinement, the torque is reduced to zero, as shown in 19-9 (C).

Receiver alinement is pictured in figure 19-9 (D). Here the rotor axis coincides with the axis of the stator field. Notice that currents on the right side of the vertical axis are back and those on the left side are forward. This action produces a magnetic field as shown by the letters S at the top and N at the bottom of the salient-pole rotor. Notice that the rotor current also produces the same polarity (left-hand rule).

For the balanced condition shown, the currents in the conductors opposite the salient rotor poles are equal in magnitude and flow in opposite directions on either side of the centerline through the poles. The forces developed are pictured in the detail drawing above figure 19-9 (D). They are developed as a result of the crowding of the magnetic lines of force at the right of conductor A and at the left of conductor B. Since they are equally spaced from the centerline, no net unbalance exists and the rotor torque is zero.

In figure 19-9 (E), the receiver stator field is rotated clockwise 60 degrees so that its axis

coincides with that of phase A. The rotor is deliberately held in the vertical position to enable showing the development of the torque on the rotor when the rotor and stator field axes are not alined. Notice that currents to the right of the A-phase axis are back and those to the left of the axis are forward. This action produces the stator field across the rotor and extends from the upper right to the lower left portions of the stator.

Now the currents in the stator conductors opposite the rotor salient poles are all in the same direction on both sides of the centerline through the poles. The forces are unbalanced as shown by the crowding of the magnetic lines on the right portion of the conductors. (See detail above fig. 19-9 (E).) This action indicates a tendency to force the stator conductors to the left. The equal and opposite reaction force on the rotor tends to turn it in a clockwise direction.

The amount of torque developed varies with the sine of the angle of displacement and is maximum at 90 degrees.

In figure 19-9 (F), the rotor has turned clockwise 60 degrees and its axis is again in alinement with that of the stator field. The torque is again reduced to zero. Notice that the current in conductors B is forward and in conductors C is back. The flux lines crowd to the right of conductors B (see detail drawing at right) and to the left of conductors C. Since the currents in B and C are equal and opposite in direction and are symmetrically spaced about the rotor axis, the net force on the rotor is zero.

As a receiver approaches correspondence, the stator voltages of the transmitter and receiver approach equality. This action decreases the stator currents and produces a decreasing torque on the receiver that reduces as the position of correspondence is reached. At correspondence, the torque on the receiver rotor is only the amount that is caused by the tendency of the salient-pole rotor to aline itself in the receiver field. Hence, a receiver can position only a very light load.

Synchro transmission systems are used where torque requirements are small. However, when drive power heavier than that required to drive a dial or pointer is necessary, some method of amplifying the synchro's weak torque must be employed. Two common methods used to provide this amplification are the SERVO SYSTEM and the AMPLIDYNE .

Many installations connect one transmitter to several receivers in parallel. This procedure requires a transmitter large enough to carry the total load current of all the receivers. All the $R1$ rotor leads are connected to one side of the a-c power supply, and all the $R2$ rotor leads are connected to the other side of the supply. The receiver stator leads are connected lead for lead to the transmitter stator leads.

The sizes of Navy synchro transmitters are designated by numbers. Synchro transmitters in general use are sizes 1, 5, 6, and 7. Synchro receivers in general use are sizes 1 and 5. A size-1 transmitter can control one or two size-1 receivers; a size-5 transmitter can control two size-5 receivers; a size-6 transmitter can control as many as nine size-5 receivers; and a size-7 transmitter can control as many as eighteen size-5 receivers.

Synchros employed in airborne equipments are usually designed for 400-cycle operation, and as a result, are considerably lighter in weight and smaller in size than those that operate with 60-cycle line voltages.

Reversing Direction of Receiver Rotation

When the teeth of two mechanical gears are meshed and a turning force is applied, the gears turn in opposite directions. If a third gear is added, it turns in the same direction as the first. This is important here because synchro receivers are often connected through a train of mechanical gears to the device which they operate, and whether or not force is applied to

the device in the same direction as that in which the receiver rotor turns depends on whether the number of gears in the train is odd or even.

The important thing, of course, is to move the dial or other device in the proper direction, and even when there are no gears involved, this may be opposite to the direction in which the receiver rotor of a normally connected system would turn.

Either of these two factors, and sometimes a combination of both, may make it necessary to have the transmitter turn the receiver rotor in a direction opposite to that of its own rotor. This is accomplished by reversing the $S1$ and $S3$ connections of the transmitter-receiver system, so that $S1$ of the transmitter is connected to $S3$ of the receiver and vice versa. This is shown in figure 19-10.

With both rotors at zero degrees, conditions within the system remain the same as during normal stator connections, since the rotor coupling to $S1$ and $S3$ is equal. But suppose that the transmitter rotor is turned counterclockwise to 60 degrees, as shown in figure 19-10. In the transmitter, maximum rotor coupling induces maximum voltage across $S1$, which causes maximum current to flow through $S3$ in the receiver. The magnetic forces produced turn the receiver rotor clockwise into line with $S3$, the rotor's 300-degree position, at which point the rotor again induces voltages in its stator coils which equal those of the transmitter coils to which

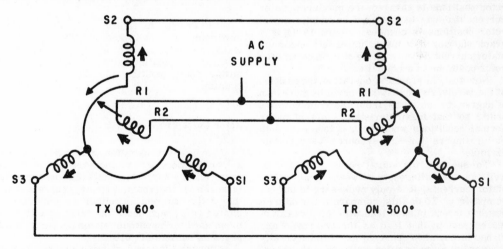

Figure 19-10.—Effect of reversing S1 and S3 connections between the transmitter and receiver.

they are connected. Notice that only the direction of rotation changes, not the amount; the 300-degree position is the same as the minus 60-degree position.

It is important to emphasize that the *S1* and *S3* connections are the only ones ever interchanged in a standard synchro system. Since *S2* represents electrical zero, changing the *S2* lead would introduce 120-degree errors in indication, and also reverse the direction of rotation.

Stator Currents

Whenever the rotors of two interconnected synchros are in different positions, current flows in the stator windings. The amount of current flowing in each stator lead depends on the difference between the voltages induced in the two coils to which that lead connects. This voltage unbalance, in turn, depends on two things -- (1) the actual positions of the rotors, and (2) the difference between the two positions.

To observe the effect of the latter, suppose that an ammeter is inserted in any one of the stator leads, the *S2* lead for example. Also, suppose that the two rotors are held so that there is a constant difference between their positions while they are rotated together until a point is found at which the ammeter indicates maximum stator current. If the difference between rotor positions is then increased and the rotation repeated, a different maximum reading is obtained. Each time the difference between rotor positions is changed, the maximum stator current that can be obtained by varying actual rotor positions is changed. Figure 19-11 is a graph showing how the value of this maximum stator current depends on the difference between rotor positions in a typical case.

Note that, in practical operation, the position of the receiver's shaft would never be more than a degree or so away from the transmitter's shaft, so that maximum stator current under normal conditions would be less than one-tenth of an ampere for the synchros used in this example.

To see how the actual rotor positions, as well as the difference between them, affect stator currents, it is only necessary to make a comparison. To do this, compare the maximum stator current in each lead with the strength of the current in that lead as the two rotors are turned through 360 degrees, maintaining the difference in rotor position with which the maximum stator current was established.

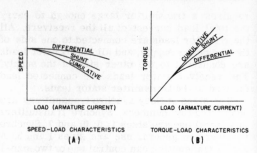

SPEED-LOAD CHARACTERISTICS
(A)

TORQUE-LOAD CHARACTERISTICS
(B)

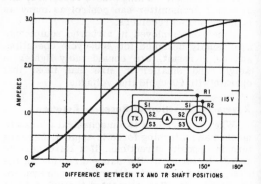

Figure 19-11.—Effect of rotor position difference on maximum stator current.

The graphs in figure 19-12 show how the maximum current in each of the three stator leads depends on the mean (average) shaft position; the position halfway between the transmitter rotor position and the receiver rotor position.

Rotor Currents

A synchro transmitter or receiver acts like a transformer, and an increase in the stator, or secondary current, results in a corresponding increase in the rotor, primary, current. When the rotor current of either of the units is plotted on a graph under the same conditions as those used for maximum stator currents, it appears as shown in figure 19-13.

Although all three stator currents are zero when the shafts are in the same positions, the

ALL CURRENTS ARE RMS VALUE.
CURRENTS SHOWN ABOVE THE O LINE ARE IN PHASE
  WITH S1 CURRENT AT 0°
CURRENTS SHOWN BELOW THE O LINE ARE 180° OUT
  OF PHASE WITH S1 CURRENT AT 0°

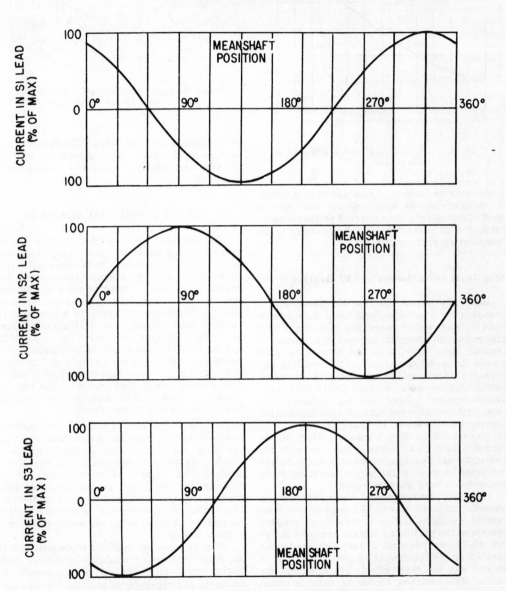

Figure 19-12.—Effect of actual rotor position on individual stator current.

365

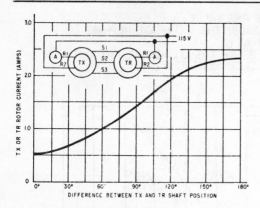

Figure 19-13.—Effect of rotor position difference on rotor current.

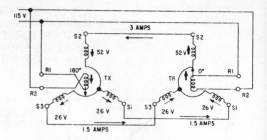

Figure 19-14.—Internal conditions in TX-TR system when TX and TR rotors are 180° apart.

rotor current is not. As in any transformer, the primary draws some current with no load on the secondary. This current produces magnetization of the rotor and is equivalent to the transformer exciting current.

Why There Is No Torque at 180 Degrees

Since the stator current increases with a change in rotor position, and since the magnetic field of each stator increases in strength with the stator current, it appears the torque or turning force exerted by the receiver's shaft should be greatest when the transmitter and receiver rotors are 180 degrees apart. However, exactly the opposite is true. Under these circumstances the torque is zero. To understand this, first consider the current conditions in the synchro system shown in figure 19-14.

Since all the voltages aid each other, strong currents flow in all three stator leads. If the two units are the same size, the currents are the same as those which would flow if the three stator leads were shorted together.

Obviously, these strong currents produce powerful magnetic forces. To see why no torque results, consider the polarities existing in the system at the particular instant assumed in figure 19-15. As powerful as they are, the forces exerted on the rotor work against each other in such a way that their effects are equal and opposite. The resulting torque is zero. In actual situations, the two shafts do not stay in these

positions unless held there. The slightest displacement of either one destroys the balance, and they are rapidly brought into corresponding positions.

TORQUE DIFFERENTIAL SYNCHROS

The demands on a synchro system are not always as simple as the positioning of an indicating device in response to the information received from a single source (transmitter). For example, an error detector used in checking fire-control equipment employs a synchro system to determine the error in a gun turret's position with respect to the training order supplied by a dummy director. To do this, the synchro system must accept two signals, one containing the training order and the other corresponding to the turret's actual position. The system must then compare the two and position an indicator to show the difference between them, which is the error.

Obviously, the simple synchro transmitter-receiver system considered up to now could not handle a job of this sort. A different type of synchro is needed, one which can accept two position-data signals simultaneously, add or subtract the data, and furnish an output proportional to the sum or difference of the two. This is where the synchro differential enters the picture. A differential can perform all three of these functions.

In a differential synchro transmitter, both the rotor and stator windings consist of three Y-connected coils. The stator is normally the primary, and receives its excitation from a synchro transmitter. The voltages appearing across

366

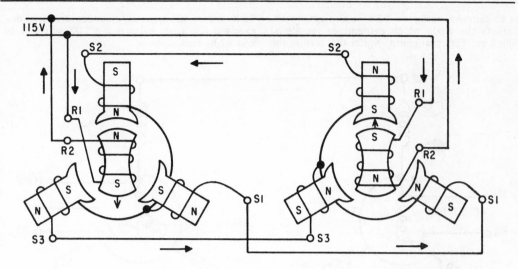

Figure 19-15.—Magnetic polarities at a particular instant when TX and TR rotors are 180° apart.

the differential's rotor terminals are determined by the magnetic field produced by the stator currents AND the physical position of the rotor. The magnetic field created by the stator currents assumes an angle corresponding to that of the magnetic field in the transmitter supplying the excitation. If the rotor position changes, the voltages induced into its windings also change, so that the voltages present at the rotor terminals change.

Differential Receivers

As torque receivers were previously compared to torque transmitters, so may torque differential receivers be compared to torque differential transmitters. Both rotor and stator receive energizing currents from torque transmitters. The two resultant magnetic fields interact and the rotor turns.

In a torque differential synchro system, the system will consist either of a torque transmitter (TX), a torque differential transmitter (TDX), and a torque receiver (TR); or the system may consist of two torque transmitters (TX) and one torque differential receiver (TDR).

TX-TDX-TR Synchro System

Assume that the stator leads of a torque transmitter are connected to the corresponding stator leads of a torque differential transmitter, as shown in figure 19-16. The resultant stator m.m.f., shown by the open arrow, produced in the TX directly opposes the TX rotor m.m.f., shown by the solid arrow. Corresponding stator coils of the two units are in series; for example, S2 of TX is in series with S2 of the TDX, and the current flow produces a resultant stator m.m.f. of equal strength in the TDX. However, currents in corresponding stator coils of the TDX are opposite in direction. The direction of the stator m.m.f. in the TDX is therefore opposite to the direction of the TX stator m.m.f., but identical to the direction of its rotor m.m.f.

The TDX rotor coils are angularly spaced 120 degrees apart, in the same manner as the TX stator coils. The TDX stator m.m.f. is identical to the TX rotor m.m.f., neglecting small circuit losses.

Before considering such an arrangement, however, it must be made clear that the controlling relationship in the TDX is the position of the TDX stator field with respect to the rotor, not with respect to the TDX stator. Suppose that the TX rotor in the previous example is turned to 75 degrees, and the TDX rotor to 30 degrees, as shown in figure 19-17. The TDX stator field is now positioned at 75 degrees with respect to S2, but the angle at which it cuts the TDX rotor is 45 degrees, using the *R2* axis as a reference. This is the angle which determines the signal which the TDX transmits. Notice that turning the TDX rotor 30 degrees counterclockwise decreased the angle between the TDX stator field and *R2* by that amount.

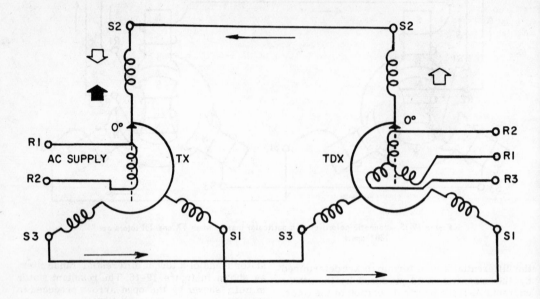

Figure 19-16.—Position of TDX stator m.m.f. when TX rotor is at zero degree.

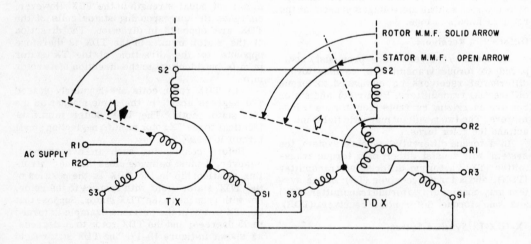

Figure 19-17.—Rotating TDX stator field by turning the TX rotor.

How the Differential Transmitter Subtracts

The manner in which the torque system containing a TDX subtracts or adds two inputs can be figuratively described as the positioning of magnetomotive forces. Figure 19-18 shows such a system connected for subtraction. A mechanical input of 75 degrees is applied to the TX and converted to an electrical signal which the TX transmits to the TDX stator. The TDX subtracts its own mechanical input from this signal, and transmits the result to the TR, which indicates the torque system's mechanical output by the position of its rotor.

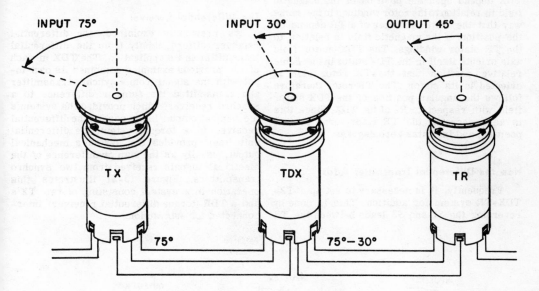

Figure 19-18.—Subtraction with TDX.

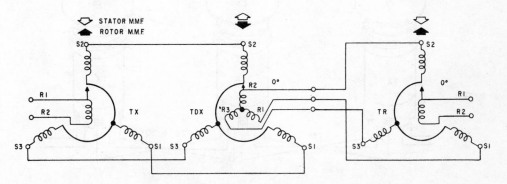

Figure 19-19.—Magnetomotive force positions in TX-TDX-TR system with all rotors at zero degree.

To understand how this result is accomplished, first consider the conditions in a TX-TDX-TR system when the TX and TDX rotors are turned to zero degrees, as in figure 19-19.

It has been shown how torque is developed in a synchro receiver to bring its rotor into a position which corresponds to that of an associated transmitter. The rotor voltages of the TDX depend upon the position of the magnetic field in relation to the rotor windings in the same way that the stator voltages of a TR depend on the position of the magnetic field in relation to the TR stator windings. The TDX stator field axis orients itself in the TDX stator in the same relative position that the TX rotor axis is oriented in its stator. The TR rotor therefore follows the angular position of the TDX stator field with respect to $R2$ of the TDX. Since this is zero degrees, the TR rotor turns to that position, and indicates zero degrees.

How the Differential Transmitter Adds

Frequently, it is necessary to set up a TX-TDX-TR system for addition. This is done by reversing the $S1$ and $S3$ leads between the TX and TDX stators, and the $R1$ and $R3$ leads between the TDX rotor and the TR. With these connections the system behaves as illustrated in figure 19-20. The 75-and 30-degree mechanical inputs, applied respectively to the rotor of the TX and the rotor of the TDX, are added and transmitted to the TR, whose rotor provides an output equal to their sum by turning to 105 degrees.

The Differential Receiver

As previously explained, the differential receiver differs chiefly from the differential transmitter in its application. The TDX in each of the previous examples combined its own input with the signal from a synchro transmitter and transmitted the sum or difference to a synchro receiver, which provided the system's mechanical output. In the case of the differential receiver in a torque system, the differential unit itself provides the system's mechanical output, usually as the sum or difference of the electrical signals received from two synchro transmitters. Figure 19-21 illustrates this operation in a system consisting of two TX's and a TDR (torque differential receiver) interconnected for subtraction.

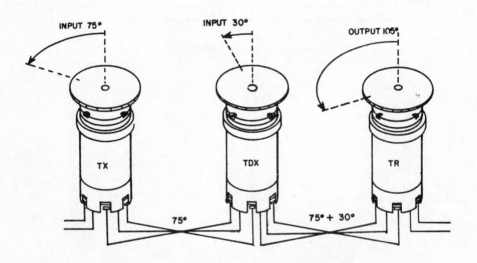

Figure 19-20.—Addition with TDX.

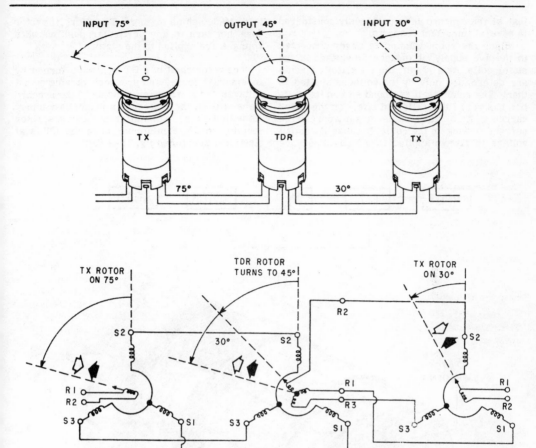

Figure 19-21.—Subtraction with TDR.

CONTROL SYNCHRO SYSTEMS

There is wide usage of synchros as followup links in automatic control systems. Synchros alone do not possess sufficient torque (turning power), to rotate such loads as radar antennas or gun turrets; however, they can control power amplifying devices, which in turn can move these heavy loads. For such applications, servo motors are used. They are placed in a closed-loop servo mechanism employing a special type of synchro called a synchro control transformer (CT) to detect the difference (error) signal between the input and output of the loop. A block diagram of

such a transformer is shown in figure 19-22 (A). Figure 19-22 (B) is a phantom view of a typical transformer, CT, with a drum rotor.

The Control Transformer

The distinguishing unit of any synchro control system is the control transformer, CT. The CT is a synchro designed to supply, from its rotor terminals, an a-c voltage whose magnitude and phase is dependent on the rotor position, and on the signal applied to the three stator windings. The behavior of the CT in a system differs from

371

that of the synchro units previously considered in several important respects.

Since the rotor winding is never connected to the a-c supply, it induces no voltage in the stator coils. As a result, the CT stator currents are determined only by the voltages applied to them. The rotor itself is wound so that its position has very little reflected effect on the stator currents. Also, there is never any appreciable current flowing in the rotor, because its output voltage is always applied to a high-impedance

load, 10,000 ohms or more. Therefore, the rotor does not turn to any particular position when voltages are applied to the stators.

The rotor shaft of a CT is always turned by an external force, and produces varying output voltages from its rotor winding. Like synchro transmitters, the CT requires no inertia damper, but unlike either transmitter or receivers, rotor coupling to S2 is minimum when the CT is at electrical zero. (See fig. 19-2 (D)).

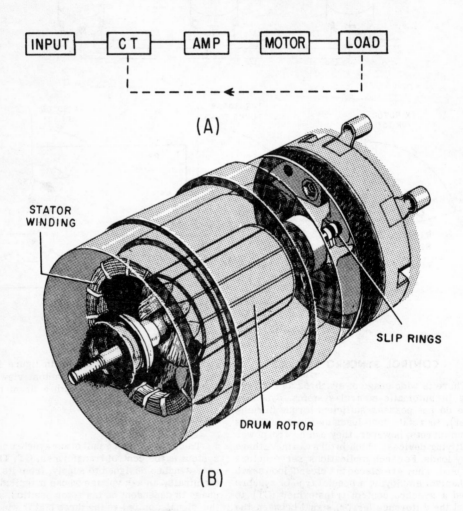

(A)

STATOR WINDING

SLIP RINGS

DRUM ROTOR

(B)

Figure 19-22.—(A) Block diagram with control transforming; (B) typical control transformer.

Relationship of the Stator Voltages in a CT to the Resultant Magnetic Field

When current flows in the stator circuits of a CT, a resultant magnetic field is produced. This resultant field can be rotated by the signal from a synchro transmitter, or synchro differential transmitter, in the same manner as the resultant stator field of the TDX previously considered. When the field of the CT stator is at right angles to the axis of the rotor winding, the voltage induced in the rotor winding is zero. When the stator field and the rotor's magnetic axis are alined, the induced rotor voltage is maximum. Since the CT's output is expressed in volts, it is convenient to consider its operation in terms of stator voltages as well as in terms of the position of the resultant magnetic field, but it should be remembered that it is the ANGULAR POSITION, with respect to the rotor axis, that determines the output of the CT.

Operation of the Control Transformer With a Synchro Transmitter

Consider the conditions existing in the system shown in figure 19-23, where a CT is connected for operation with a CX (control transmitter) and the rotors of both units are positioned at zero degrees. The relative phases of the individual stator voltages with respect to the R1 to R2 voltage of the transmitter are indicated by the small arrows. The resultant stator field of the CT is shown in the same manner as for the TDX. With both rotors in the same position, the CT stator field is at right angles to the axis of the rotor coil. Since no voltage is induced in a coil by an alternating magnetic field perpendicular to its axis, the output voltage appearing across the rotor terminals of the CT is zero.

Now assume that the CT rotor is turned to 90 degrees, as in figure 19-24, while the CX rotor remains at zero degrees. Since the CT's rotor position does not affect stator voltages or currents, the resultant stator field of the CT remains alined with S2. The axis of the rotor coil is now in alinement with the stator field. Maximum voltage, approximately 55 volts, is induced in the coil and appears across the rotor terminals as the output of the CT.

Next, assume the CX rotor is turned to 180 degrees, as in figure 19-25. The electrical positions of the CX and CT are 90 degrees apart, the CT stator field and rotor axis are alined, and the CT's output is maximum again, but the direction of the rotor's winding is now reversed with respect to the direction of the stator field. The phase of the output voltage is therefore opposite to that of the CT in the preceding example. This means that the phase of the CT's output voltage indicates the direction in which the CT

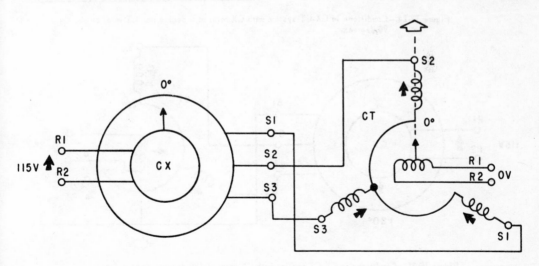

Figure 19-23.—Conditions in CX-CT system with rotors in correspondence.

rotor is displaced with respect to the position-data signal applied to its stators.

It is evident that the CT's output can be varied by rotating either its rotor or the position-data signal applied to its stators. It can also be seen that the magnitude and phase of the output depend on the relationship between signal and rotor rather than on the actual position of either.

Servomechanisms

In the operation of electrical and electronic equipment, it is often necessary to operate a mechanical load that is remotely located from its source of control. Examples of this are the movement of heavy radar antennas or small indicator motors. The mechanical load may require either high or low torque movement.

It can be stated that a servomechanism is an electromechanical device that positions an

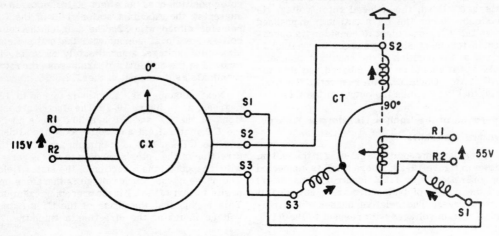

Figure 19-24.—Conditions in CX-CT system with CX rotor at 0 degree and CT rotor at 90 degrees.

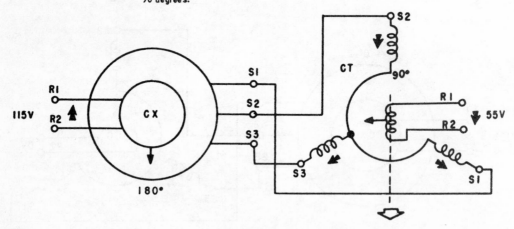

Figure 19-25.—Conditions in CX-CT system with CX rotor at 180 degrees and CT rotor at 90 degrees.

object in accordance with a variable signal. The signal source may be capable of supplying only a small amount of power. A servomechanism operates to reduce difference (error) between two quantities. These quantities are usually the CONTROL DEVICE position and the LOAD position.

The essential components of a servomechanism system are the INPUT CONTROLLER and OUTPUT CONTROLLER.

INPUT CONTROLLER

The input controller provides the means whereby the human operator may actuate or operate the remotely located load. This may be achieved either mechanically or electrically. Electrical means are most commonly used. Synchro systems and bridge circuits are most widely used for input control of servomechanism systems.

OUTPUT CONTROLLER

The output controller of a servomechanism system is the component or components in which power amplification and conversion occur. This power is usually amplified by vacuum-tube amplifiers or magnetic amplifiers. In many applications a combination of these are used. The power from the amplifier is then converted by the servomotor into mechanical motion of the direction required to produce the desired function. This sequence of functions is shown in figure 19-26. The figure shows a simplified block diagram of a simple servomechanism system.

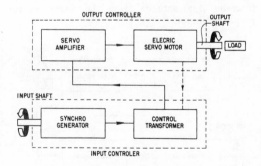

Figure 19-26.—Simplified block diagram of a servomechanism.

OPERATION OF BASIC SERVOMECHANISM

The block diagram of figure 19-26, is shown schematically in figure 19-27. Its basic principles of operation are as follows:

The INPUT CONTROLLER, which consists of a synchro control transmitter (CX) and a synchro controller transformer (CT), originates, or commands, the system movement. The CX's rotor is attached to a shaft, which is turned by hand or by a controlling mechanical device. Movement of the CX rotor from its electrical zero will cause an unbalance of voltages in the stator windings S2, S1, and S3. (This was explained under the heading, Control Synchro Systems.) A voltage is induced in the rotor of the control transformer. Its MAGNITUDE depends on the AMOUNT of displacement of the CX rotor; its PHASE RELATIONSHIP depends on the DIRECTION of displacement from electrical zero. This voltage represents the ERROR voltage. Since a control transformer is not designed to furnish enough power to drive a load of any significant size, the error voltage must be amplified before it is powerful enough to drive the servomotor, and thus move the load.

The servoamplifier, as stated before, may be a vacuum-tube type or magnetic type. In many cases, it is a combination of both. In the combination type, the vacuum-tube section amplifies the ERROR VOLTAGE, and the error voltage in turn controls a magnetic amplifier. The POWER amplification occurs in the magnetic amplifier. The various ways that a magnetic amplifier does this are explained in chapter 18, Magnetic Amplifiers.

Regardless of the type of amplifier used, the output of the power amplifier is connected to the control field of the servomotor. In this illustration, a single-phase induction motor is used. The fixed field is energized at all times but cannot turn the motor shaft unaided. The control field is energized only when an error voltage appears at the control transformer When the control field is energized, the motor operates.

The direction of rotation of the motor is determined by the phase relationship of the voltage applied to the fixed field to that of the control field. Varying phase relationships occur in the

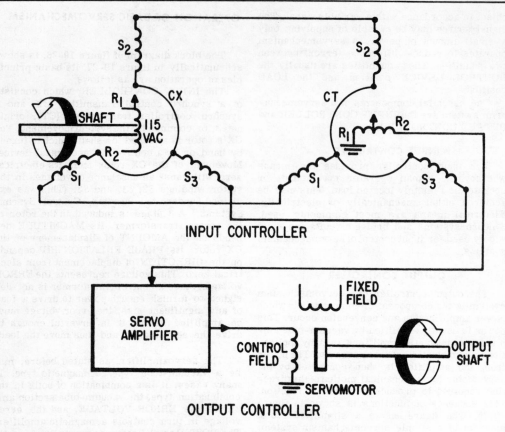

Figure 19-27.—Schematic diagram of figure 19-26.

control field only, because its voltage (magnitude and phase relationship) is determined by the direction of displacement of the control transmitter rotor.

Once the input controller in the system just discussed produces an error voltage, the servomotor continues to turn until the rotor of the control transmitter is again in its electrical zero (null) position. This is called an OPEN LOOP control system, because the servo output has no means of changing the input during operation.

Figure 19-28 shows the simplified block diagram of a servomechanism system that is much more widely used. It is the CLOSED-LOOP control system. Note that it is similar to the open-loop system, except that an additional

function line extends from the servo to the amplifier input.

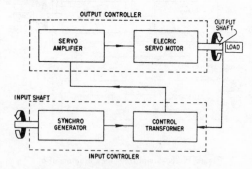

Figure 19-28.—Closed-loop servomechanism.

376

In the closed-loop control system, the servomotor can be made to stop at any position, without returning the rotor of the control transmitter to its electrical zero position. To accomplish this, an error voltage controlled by the servo is necessary. This error voltage is called a FOLLOWUP voltage.

To provide this followup voltage, there is usually a bridge element or a control transformer driven by the servo's output shaft. The electrical connection is such that the bridge or control transformer will generate a voltage opposing the error voltage of the input controller. Figure 19-29 shows a schematic diagram of the closed-loop control system.

The followup control transformer is basically the same in construction as those discussed earlier. Note that the stator is excited by the same a-c voltage as the rotor of the control transmitter. This voltage is connected only across two of the stator windings. The third stator winding is not used. With a voltage applied across the two windings 120 degrees apart, a resultant magnetic field appears midway (60°) between the two windings. If the rotor of the followup control transmitter is placed so that its axis is 90 degrees from the field axis, the voltage induced in the rotor from the two stator windings is zero. It can be seen that if the rotor is moved from this zero-voltage position, a

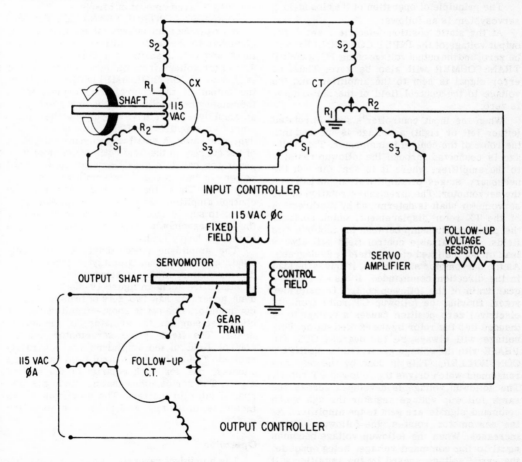

Figure 19-29.—Closed-loop control system.

377

voltage will be induced into the rotor. The magnitude and phase-relationship of this voltage is dependent upon the amount of displacement, and the direction of rotation of the rotor from its zero position.

When a followup control transformer is used in a servomechanism system, as illustrated in figure 19-29, the rotor is usually driven through a gear train by the servomotor's output shaft. The gear ratio will be such that the output shaft will turn many times before the rotor is turned any appreciable amount. Ratios of 1,500 to 1 are common. The servomotor output shaft may either be connected directly to its load, or geared up or down.

The principle of operation of the closed-loop servosystem is as follows:

At the static position (electrical zero) the output voltage of the INPUT CONTROLLER will be zero, and the output voltage of the FOLLOWUP TRANSFORMER will also be zero. Thus, no error signal is sent to the amplifier, and the voltage to the control field of the servomotor is zero.

When the input controller's shaft is rotated (either left or right) a voltage is induced into the rotor of the control transformer. This voltage is connected through the followup resistor to the amplifier, where it is sent through the necessary stages of amplification, and drives the servomotor. The direction of rotation of the servomotor shaft is determined by the direction of the TX rotor displacement, which controls the phase relationship between the motor's two fields. The variable control field will always lead or lag the fixed control field by 90 degrees. As the servomotor shaft turns, it drives the load in the direction commanded. It also drives the gear train of the followup control transformer rotor. Driving the followup CT rotor from its electrical zero position causes a voltage to be induced into the rotor by the excited stator. This voltage will always be 180 degrees OUT OF PHASE with the voltage generated by the INPUT CONTROLLER. (This is done by the gear arrangement which drives the followup CT rotor). The followup voltage is developed across the same followup voltage resistor through which command signals are sent to the amplifier. As the servomotor rotates, the followup voltage increases. When the followup voltage becomes equal to the command voltage, being opposite, the error voltage sensed by the amplifier will be zero. The servomotor stops rotating. Note

that it is unnecessary to reposition the control transmitter's rotor (input controller) to electrical zero in order to stop rotation of the servomotor. The servomotor will rotate to move the load to whatever position is commanded by the control transmitter.

AMPLIDYNES

As has been stated earlier in this chapter, SYNCHROS are used for the transmission of angular motion without developing a large amount of torque.

DIFFERENTIAL SYNCHROS are used for combining, in the desired manner angular motion from two different sources, again without developing a large amount of torque.

SYNCHRO CONTROL TRANSFORMERS are used to produce an output voltage that is proportional to the angular difference between the input and output shafts of a servomechanism. The error voltage from the control transformer is fed to a CONTROL AMPLIFIER (amplifies the output of the control transformer) which increases the amplitude of the error signal. In an amplidyne power drive the output of the control amplifier supplies the field coils of an amplidyne generator. A small variation in the strength of the current in the field coils of the amplidyne generator causes a great variation in its output power. In this respect the amplidyne is a d-c amplifier. Thus, the signal developed in the control amplifier can cause the amplidyne generator to supply enough output power to operate the d-c servomotor which has sufficient torque to move a heavy load.

The amplidyne power drive, as commonly used, consists of an amplidyne generator, a driving motor, and a d-c servomotor, as shown in simplified form in figure 19-30. The amplidyne generator has two sets of brushes on the commutator. One set is short-circuited and the other set supplies the armature of the servomotor. The field of the servomotor and the control field of the amplidyne are separately excited. The amplidyne control field has a split winding, one for each polarity of the applied signal. The series compensating winding is discussed later in the text. The amplidyne drive motor is ordinarily a 3-phase a-c induction motor.

Operation

The amplidyne generator is a small separately excited direct-current generator having a

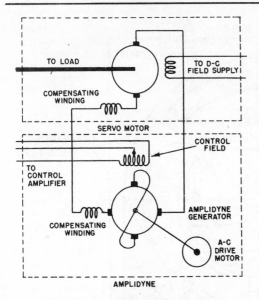

Figure 19-30.—Basic amplidyne drive.

The armature acting as an electromagnet establishes a quadrature, or cross, magnetomotive force having an axis that coincides with that of the brushes. The relative strength and position of this armature cross magnetizing force is indicated by vector OB in figure 19-31 (B). It has about the same length as the control field vector, OA, and is perpendicular to it.

If the strength of the control field in figure 19-31 (A) is reduced to 1 percent of normal, the armature generated voltage will fall to 1 percent of normal, or to about 1 volt in this example. The output current from the armature will fall to 1 ampere through the 1-ohm load.

Normal armature current may be restored by short-circuiting the brushes, as shown in figure 19-32 (A). One volt acting through an internal armature resistance of 0.01 ohm will circulate 100 amperes between the brushes. The control field strength is still 1 percent of its normal value (vector OA, fig. 19-32 (B)), but the armature crossfield m.m.f. has been restored to its normal value, as indicated by vector OB.

The armature crossfield is cut by the armature conductors and may be regarded as being responsible for normal load voltage, which is obtained across an additional pair of brushes, as shown in figure 19-33 (A). The axis of these brushes is perpendicular to that of the shorted brushes. The load is connected in series with these new brushes and a compensating winding, shown schematically around the south field pole, S.

Armature load current is toward the observer around the upper half of the armature windings and away from the observer around the lower half. The armature acts like an electromagnet, which creates an m.m.f. directly opposed (in this case) to the control field m.m.f. and in the same axis as that of the control field.

The purpose of the compensating winding is to create an opposing m.m.f. along this same axis to counterbalance the armature load current m.m.f. This counterbalance is made automatic for any degree of load by connecting the compensating winding in series with the load brushes and the load. Vector OC (fig. 19-33 (B)) represents the relative magnitude and direction of the compensating winding m.m.f. with respect to the control field m.m.f. OA; the armature load current m.m.f. OD; and the armature crossfield m.m.f. OB.

control field that requires a low power input. The armature output voltage may be 100 volts and the output load current 100 amperes, giving an output power of 10 kilowatts (kw.). The amplidyne is essentially a control device that is extremely sensitive. For example, an increase in control field power from zero to 1 watt can cause the generator output power to increase from zero to 10 kw. It is thus a power amplifier that increases the power by an amplification factor of 10,000. The following analysis shows how this high amplification is accomplished.

In an ordinary 2-pole generator (fig. 19-31) the separately excited control field may take an input power of 100 watts in order to establish normal magnetism in the field poles and a normal armature voltage of 100 volts. When this voltage is impressed on a 1-ohm load the armature will deliver 100 amperes, or an output power of 10 kw. The circles with dots represent armature conductors carrying current toward the observer; those with crosses represent electron flow away from the observer. The control field winding develops a north pole (N) on the left-hand field pole and a south pole (S) on the right-hand field pole.

The relative strength of the control field is represented by vector OA in figure 19-31 (B).

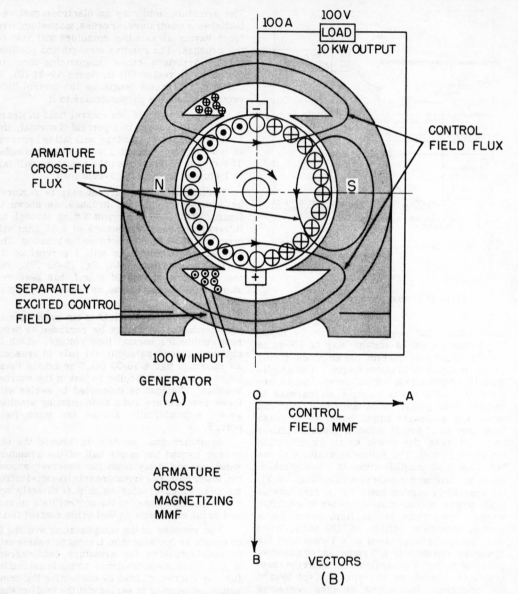

Figure 19-31.—Ordinary d-c generator.

The main field poles are shown slotted along the load-brush (horizontal) axis to indicate a method of achieving satisfactory commutation in the coils being shorted by these brushes. A restriction in the size of the amplidyne is the self-induced voltage in the coils being commutated and the resultant sparking at the commutator.

380

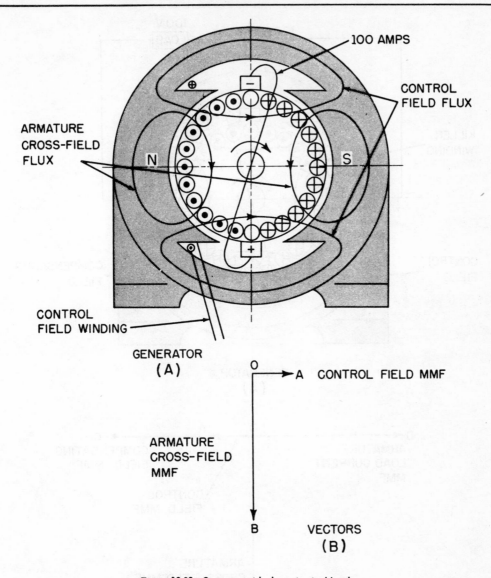

100 AMPS

CONTROL
FIELD FLUX

ARMATURE
CROSS-FIELD
FLUX

N   S

CONTROL
FIELD WINDING

GENERATOR
(A)

O ————► A   CONTROL FIELD MMF

ARMATURE
CROSS-FIELD
MMF

B   VECTORS
(B)

Figure 19-32.—Generator with short-circuited brushes.

Because any residual magnetism along the **axis** of the control field would have an appreciable effect on the amplidyne output, it is necessary to demagnetize the core material when the control field winding is deenergized. This demagnetization is accomplished by means of a small a-c magneto generator (mounted on the amplidyne frame) which supplies a suitably placed demagnetizing winding, known as a KILLER WINDING (fig. 19-33 (A)).

381

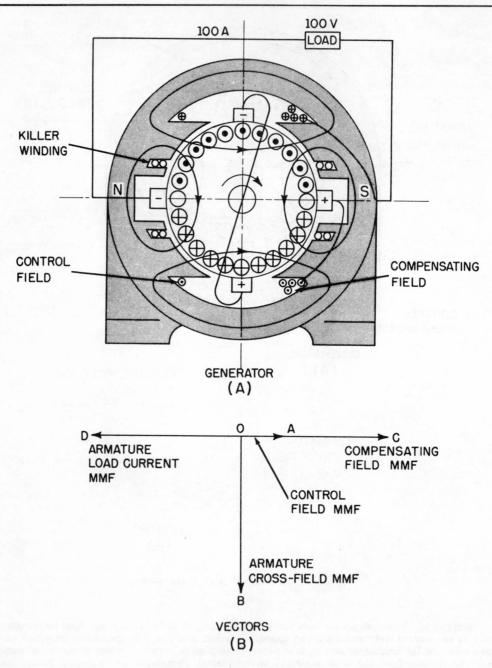

Figure 19-33.—Amplidyne generator.

The action of the amplidyne is summarized as follows:

1. A very low power (1 watt) input to the control field creates an armature short-circuit current of 100 amperes, thus producing a relatively strong armature crossfield. This is responsible, in turn, for the generation of a normal output voltage of 100 volts across the output load brushes. The output load of 1 ohm is supplied with a current of 100 amperes and an output power of 10,000 watts.

2. In larger size amplidyne generators, a control field input power of 4 watts will develop an output voltage of 200 volts and an armature load current of 200 amperes, or 40,000 watts output.

3. Because of the high power amplification, any residual magnetism in the poles would greatly interfere with the proportion between the input and output. Residual magnetism is removed by means of a small a-c magneto generator which supplies a demagnetizing winding having the same axis as the control field winding.

4. The laminated armature and stator cores are worked at a low flux density in order to maintain a straight-line proportion between input and output.

5. Amplidyne generators are driven at relatively high speeds (1,800 r.p.m. to 4,000 r.p.m.) in order that they may be of small size and light weight.

6. The amplidyne generator has a quick response to changes in control field current. The lapse in time between a change in the magnitude of the control field current and the load output response is about 0.1 second.

ANTIHUNT CONSIDERATIONS

One problem in the application of the servo-system is that of hunting. Hunting refers to the tendency of a mechanical system to oscillate about a normal position. Thus, in figure 19-34 the steel ball, if depressed from its normal position and suddenly released, oscillates vertically because of its inertia and the forces exerted by the springs. In time, the oscillation is damped out by the frictional losses in the oscillating system.

Although other factors are involved, a somewhat similar effect is observed in radar fire

control, and other equipments employing servo drive. Because the connection between the handwheel or other device controlling the position

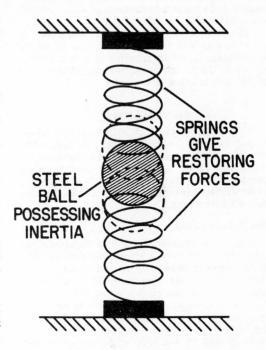

Figure 19-34.—Mechanical demonstration of hunting.

of the equipment (antenna, gun, etc., to be moved) and the equipment itself is somewhat elastic (because of the action of the electrical and magnetic circuits involved), the inertia of the equipment causes it to overtravel its required position. An error voltage is developed in the servosystem in the opposite direction and the equipment reverses. Successive overtravels by the equipment would be less and less, and the mechanical oscillation would die out except for one factor: there may be a time lag in the servosystem, which causes reinforced oscillations. In such a case, the equipment would continue to oscillate or HUNT about its normal position. This action would cause harmful mechanical vibration of the entire rotating system.

In order to eliminate hunting, an ANTIHUNT device or circuit is used. This device commonly consists of arrangements to slow up the drive motor as the equipment to be moved approaches its final position. If the drive power is reduced soon enough, the inertia of the moving part causes it to coast into its final position without any overtravel.

The antihunt circuit commonly connects the servo or followup motor to the control amplifier. A feedback signal is supplied by means of this circuit to the control amplifier where the hunting problem is handled electrically.

SERVOMOTORS

The output drive motor in a servosystem should have the required power, be easily reversible, and be capable of speed control over a fairly wide range. The d-c motor has characteristics that make its use advantageous. However, under certain circumstances the a-c motor has distinct advantages.

The D-C Servomotor

The d-c servomotor used with the amplidyne generator must have a constant magnetic field if its output is to be proportional to the voltage applied across its armature. This voltage is supplied by the controlled output of the amplidyne generator. A constant field can be produced by a field winding supplied by a constant-voltage d-c source, or supplied by means of a suitable rectifier and an a-c source. A simpler method is to use permanent magnets that are capable of establishing the necessary flux. These are restricted to small-size, low-horsepower motors.

A disadvantage in using permanent magnets is that they may become demagnetized by armature reaction. However, this condition may be counteracted by the use of a compensating winding. This winding is connected in series with the armature and so placed around the pole faces that the armature reaction effect is completely eliminated.

The A-C Servomotor

As has been stated, the output drive motor in a servosystem should be easily reversible and should be capable of speed control over a fairly wide range. Ordinarily, an a-c motor cannot fulfill the requirements of a servo drive motor as completely as a d-c motor because the range of speed control is less. However, the use of an a-c motor may provide a much simpler drive system, especially where a-c power is the only source available and where some sacrifice in range of speed control can be made.

An a-c motor that can be adapted for servosystem use is the single-phase induction motor. This motor contains two stator windings. They are the starting and running windings and are displaced 90 degrees. Their currents are displaced in time phase to produce a revolving magnetic field. The rotor may be either a WOUND rotor or a CAGE rotor. The latter type is the most common. It consists of heavy conducting bars embedded in the armature slots and connected at the ends by conducting rings. The revolving magnetic field originating in the stator cuts the rotor windings when power is applied at start and induces voltages in them. The resulting rotor currents react with the field to start the motor in the direction of the revolving field.

The starting winding is frequently designed to operate continuously with a capacitor to increase the phase displacement between the currents at start and to improve the motor power factor when the motor comes up to speed. When this arrangement is used it is called a CAPACITOR MOTOR. In order to reduce the size of the phase-splitting capacitor required for induction motor applications (and to produce essentially the same result), a high voltage capacitor of smaller capacitance and a small autotransformer are used. The operation of the capacitor motor and the method of employing the capacitor are explained in chapter 13.

In order to give the necessary range of speed control and higher starting torque for certain applications, it is possible to modify the two-phase motor in other ways. These include increasing the resistance of the rotor bars and end rings and the use of a tapped autotransformer, one arrangement of which is shown in figure 19-35. In this circuit the phase-splitting capacitor and autotransformer are placed in parallel with one coil, and the combination is placed in series with the second coil. The current through coil 1 is the vector sum of the lagging current through coil 2 and the leading current through the primary of the autotransformer. Because the current through the capacitor is leading the current through coil 2, the total current through coil 1 leads that through coil 2. The capacitor is chosen to give approximately a 90-degree phase shift between the currents in coils 1 and 2. Thus, the desired rotating magnetic field is produced. However, the efficiency of this type of motor is relatively poor because of the high resistance rotor.

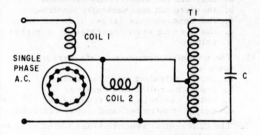

Figure 19-35.—Single-phase capacitor motor with series stator coil connections.

The DIRECTION of rotation of the capacitor motor is reversed either by reversing the connections to one stator coil or by shifting the capacitor from one coil to the other. The SPEED of the motor is varied over a limited range by changing the voltage applied to the motor. The voltage may be changed by placing a variable impedance in series with one or both phases. The effect of such an impedance is to lower the voltage, and hence the current, input to the windings. This action weakens the field and lowers the induced voltage in the rotor bars, hence reduces the motor torque and speed. The basic requirements of this system are: (1) a means of using an error signal to vary the impedance in series with the motor in order to control the speed, and (2) a means of comparing the phase of the error signal with a reference voltage in order to control the direction of rotation of the motor.

The block diagram of a servosystem in which a capacitor motor is used to provide the output power is shown in figure 19-36. A synchro control transformer is used to provide an error signal that is proportional to the difference between the actual antenna position and the desired

position, represented by the position of the handwheel. The rotor of the control transformer is geared to the load so that rotation of the load turns the rotor toward the position in which the error voltage is zero. The antenna is rotated by turning the handwheel connected to the rotor of the synchro transmitter. The turning of the rotor shifts the position of the stator field of the control transformer and thus causes an error voltage to be induced in its rotor. The error voltage is fed to the control amplifier where it is amplified and used to lower the impedance in series with the a-c motor in order to start the motor, and to control (within limits) the speed of rotation. The error voltage is simultaneously fed to another section of the amplifier where its phase is compared with the phase of a reference voltage in order to control the direction of rotation. The output of this section of the amplifier is fed to a relay which selects the stator winding with which the phase-splitting capacitor is to be connected in series.

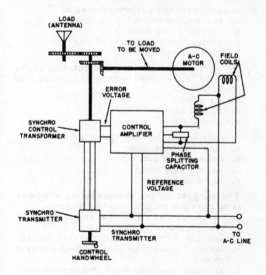

Figure 19-36.—Servosystem using capacitor motor.

QUIZ

1. The direction of rotation of a capacitor motor can be reversed by
   a. reversing connections to the noncapacitor phase
   b. reversing connection to the capacitor phase
   c. reversing source power connections
   d. shifting the capacitor from one phase to the other

2. A synchro transmitter is connected to a synchro motor
   a. mechanically
   b. magnetically
   c. directly
   d. electrically

3. If S2 and either S1 or S3 are reversed at the receiver, the rotor will
   a. reverse direction with no error
   b. be 180° in error
   c. be 120° in error
   d. not be affected

4. A basic synchro system is used to
   a. transmit position information
   b. control drive motors
   c. control large amounts of current
   d. transfer energy

5. To reverse the direction of rotation of the rotor of the receiver (with no error) reverse
   a. S1 and S2
   b. R1 and R2
   c. S2 and S3
   d. S1 and S3

6. A control transformer synchro uses a
   a. squirrel cage rotor
   b. drum wound rotor
   c. salient pole rotor
   d. lap wound rotor

7. The purpose of the compensating windings is to create a magnetomotive force to
   a. counterbalance the armature load current m.m.f.
   b. aid the armature load current m.m.f.
   c. counterbalance the control field current m.m.f.
   d. aid the control field current m.m.f.

8. The a-c servomotor is a
   a. 3Φ induction motor
   b. 1Φ repulsion induction motor
   c. 1Φ induction motor
   d. 1Φ series motor

9. A synchro is comparable to a
   a. single-phase transformer
   b. generator
   c. synchronous motor
   d. three-phase transformer

10. Synchro generators and motors are usually not interchangeable because
    a. they are not electrically identical
    b. they are not mechanically identical
    c. the generator is larger than the motor
    d. the generator operates at a higher voltage

11. The essential components of a servomechanism are
    a. input controller and transmitter
    b. input controller and receiver
    c. output controller and transmitter
    d. output controller and input controller

12. The differential synchro transmitter uses a rotor having
    a. a single coil
    b. three separately connected coils
    c. three wye-connected coils
    d. three delta-connected coils

13. With both rotors in the same position and maximum voltage induced in winding S2, there is
    a. minimum current flow in the system
    b. maximum current flow in the system
    c. minimum current flow in stator windings
    d. maximum current flow in stator windings

14. Driving the followup center tap rotor from the electrical zero position causes a voltage to be induced into the rotor by the excited stator. This voltage will be
    a. in phase with the voltage generated by the input controller
    b. out of phase with the voltage generated by the output controller
    c. in phase with the voltage generated by the output controller
    d. out of phase with the voltage generated by the input controller

15. The generator and motor rotors are connected
    a. in parallel
    b. in series
    c. to separate sources
    d. by mutual inductance

16. The stator voltages are
    a. in phase and subtractive
    b. out of phase and subtractive
    c. in phase and additive
    d. out of phase and additive

17. The motor rotor will follow the generator rotor because of
    a. magnetic coupling
    b. induced e.m.f.
    c. c.e.m.f.
    d. generator movement

18. The windings of the synchro stators are displaced from each other by
    a. 45°
    b. 90°
    c. 120°
    d. 240°
19. An amplidyne is a/an
    a. a-c amplifier
    b. d-c amplifier
    c. ac-dc amplifier
    d. d-c servomotor
20. The rotor of a synchro must continuously draw current to
    a. produce heat
    b. maintain a magnetized rotor
    c. set up a reference voltage
    d. produce an induced voltage in the stator

21. Synchro systems will be at a null when induced e.m.f.'s are
    a. in phase and equal
    b. out of phase and equal
    c. in phase and not equal
    d. out of phase and not equal

22. The amplidyne drive motor is usually a
    a. d-c compound motor
    b. d-c series motor
    c. one-phase a-c induction motor
    d. three-phase a-c induction motor

19. The windings of the synchro stator are displaced from each other by

a. 90°

b. 120°

CHAPTER 20

ELECTRICAL DRAWINGS AND TECHNICAL MANUALS

This course has presented the basic principles of electricity. These principles are widely applicable. For instance, the laws of voltage distribution around a closed circuit apply equally to a-c and d-c circuits irrespective of the number of voltage sources or the nature of the components of the circuit. When analyzing the operation of even the most complex circuit or equipment, the principles of its functions may be explained by one or more of the widely applicable electrical laws. Thus, the first step in your technical training is learning these laws, most of which are set forth in the preceding parts of this text. The second step, gained largely through experience, is learning the methods and practices by which these principles are put to work, in the form of actual hardware, in hundreds of different types of equipment.

One of the best ways to learn these methods and common practices is to become familiar with the language of practical electricity. This language is found in the technical manual (instruction book) written for each equipment and in the diagrams for each system. You cannot hope to memorize every detail of every circuit in the

complex systems and equipments you must maintain. A good technician does not even attempt it. Instead, you should be able to obtain this information as you need it from the manuals and drawings provided for that purpose. To do this, you must be able to read electrical drawings and diagrams. The ability to read a particular drawing, coupled with the basic principles of electricity, will make it much easier for you to understand, adjust, operate, and repair any particular equipment or circuit.

In the construction of a wiring or schematic diagram of a circuit or system, it would not be practical, and rarely even useful, to draw pictures of each part as they actually appear. Instead, each part in a wiring or schematic diagram is represented by a symbol. Electrical symbols are to the technician as shorthand is to the stenographer. All parts, such as resistors, capacitors, switches, relays, and so forth, have symbols that are standard Navy-wide. The most important ability in reading electrical drawings is the ability of the technician to form a mental correlation between the symbol for a part as it appears in a diagram, and the actual appearance and function of that part.

Electrical Symbols

Table 20-1 is a listing of some of the most common standard electrical parts. The name and standard symbol for each part are given, along with a picture. By studying this list, and others similar to it, you will be able to mentally correlate parts and their symbols, which is necessary in developing the ability to read electrical diagrams.

A brief discussion of some of the most common parts that are used in electrical circuits follows the list of symbols.

RESISTOR COLOR CODING

As you probably know, a resistor is a device used to limit current flow. Resistors are of two types: fixed and variable. Fixed resistors may be made of wire wound on a core and coated with ceramic or they may be made of carbon. The majority of fixed resistors have axial leads. Resistance value is indicated by 3 colored bands. A fourth band is sometimes used to indicate tolerance as follows: gold = ±5 percent, silver = ±10 percent. When no fourth band is present,

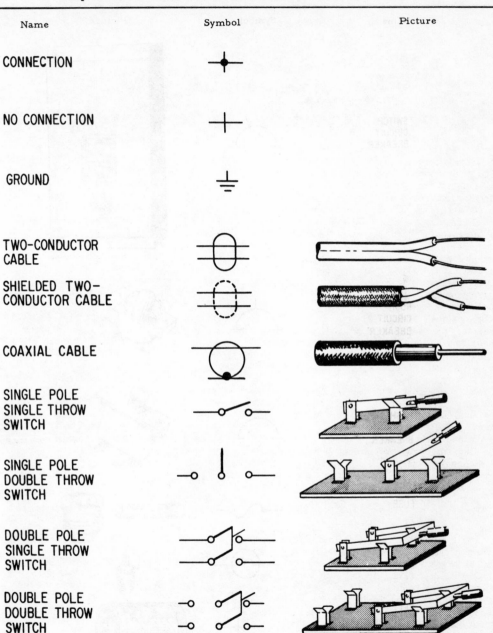

Name	Symbol	Picture
CONNECTION		
NO CONNECTION		
GROUND		
TWO-CONDUCTOR CABLE		
SHIELDED TWO-CONDUCTOR CABLE		
COAXIAL CABLE		
SINGLE POLE SINGLE THROW SWITCH		
SINGLE POLE DOUBLE THROW SWITCH		
DOUBLE POLE SINGLE THROW SWITCH		
DOUBLE POLE DOUBLE THROW SWITCH		

Table 20-1. — Electrical symbols.

389

Name	Symbol	Picture
SWITCH CIRCUIT BREAKER		
PUSH CIRCUIT BREAKER		
PUSH-PULL CIRCUIT BREAKER		
FUSE		
LAMP		
CELL (LONG VERTICAL LINE IS ALWAYS POSITIVE)		

Table 20-1. — Electrical symbols — Continued

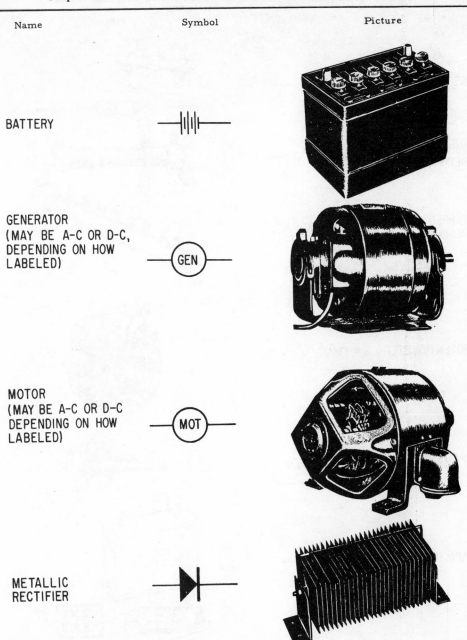

Name	Symbol	Picture
BATTERY		
GENERATOR (MAY BE A-C OR D-C, DEPENDING ON HOW LABELED)	GEN	
MOTOR (MAY BE A-C OR D-C DEPENDING ON HOW LABELED)	MOT	
METALLIC RECTIFIER		

Table 20-1. — Electrical symbols — Continued

391

Name	Symbol	Picture

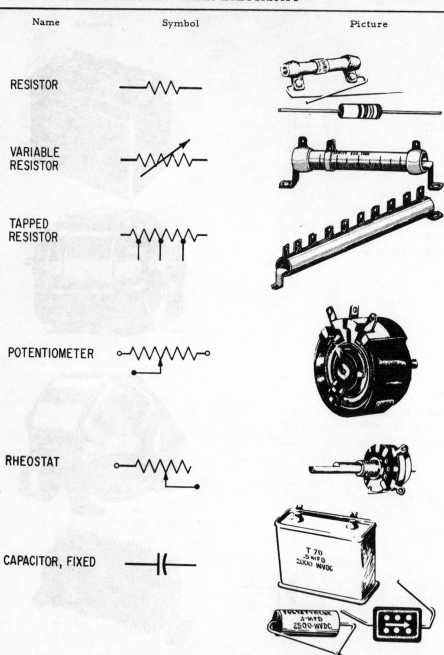

RESISTOR

VARIABLE RESISTOR

TAPPED RESISTOR

POTENTIOMETER

RHEOSTAT

CAPACITOR, FIXED

Table 20-1. – Electrical symbols – Continued

Name	Symbol	Picture
CAPACITOR, VARIABLE		
CAPACITOR, GANGED		
INDUCTOR, AIR CORE		
INDUCTOR, IRON CORE		

Table 20-1. — Electrical symbols — Continued

Name	Symbol	Picture
TRANSFORMER, AIR CORE		
TRANSFORMER, IRON CORE		
RELAY COIL WITH CONTACTS	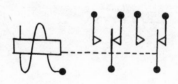	
PIEZOELECTRIC CRYSTAL UNIT		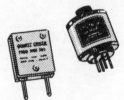

Table 20-1. — Electrical symbols — Continued

Name	Symbol	Picture

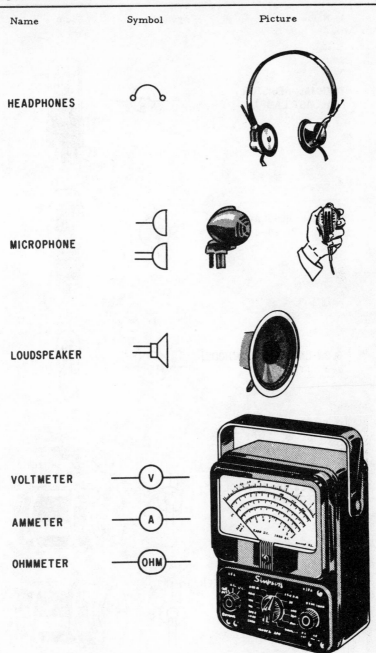

HEADPHONES

MICROPHONE

LOUDSPEAKER

VOLTMETER

AMMETER

OHMMETER

Table 20-1. — Electrical symbols — Continued

Name	Symbol	Picture
THERMAL RESISTOR (BALLAST LAMP)		
VOLTAGE REGULATOR OR GLOW TUBE (d-c TYPE)		
GLOW LAMP (COLD CATHODE) a-c TYPE		
SYNCHRO TRANSMITTER RECEIVER OR CONTROL TRANSFORMER		MECHANICAL INPUT TO TRANSMITTER ROTOR 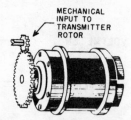
DIFFERENTIAL TRANSMITTER OR RECEIVER		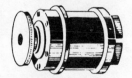

Table 20-1. — Electrical symbols — Continued

396

the resistor has a ±20 percent tolerance. For example, colored bands of red, orange, blue, and gold would indicate that the value of the resistor was 23 megohms (23,000,000 ohms) with a resistance tolerance of ±5 percent. (See fig. 20-1 and table 20-2.)

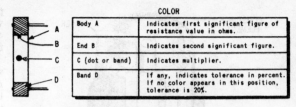

		COLOR
Body A		Indicates first significant figure of resistance value in ohms.
End B		Indicates second significant figure.
C (dot or band)		Indicates multiplier.
Band D		If any, indicates tolerance in percent. If no color appears in this position, tolerance is 20%.

Figure 20-2.—Color coding for radial-lead resistors.

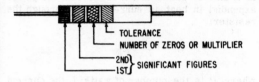

Figure 20-1.—Standard resistor coding.

Some fixed resistors are constructed with radial leads as shown in figure 20-2. The method of interpreting the color code to determine the value of these resistors is somewhat different from the method used with axial-lead resistors. (See fig. 20-2.) For example, if the body of the resistor is brown, end B is green, and dot C is yellow, the resistor will have a resistance of 150,000 ohms with a tolerance of 20% (no band D indicated).

Variable resistors are of two general types: rheostats and potentiometers.

A rheostat is a variable resistor which is normally used to adjust the current in a circuit without opening the circuit; however, some rheostats are constructed so that the circuit may also be opened. Generally, a rheostat has two terminals; one terminal is connected to one end of the resistance element, and the other terminal to the sliding contact. (See fig. 20-3.) As shown in this figure, the resistance element is circular in shape and is made of resistance wire wound around an insulating form usually made of a ceramic material. The resistance is decreased by rotating the wiper toward the end contact.

The potentiometer (often called a "pot") is a control device used to vary the amount of voltage applied to an electrical device. The term

Color	Significant figure or number of zeros	Decimal multiplier	Resistance tolerance
			Percent ±
BLACK	0	- - -	- - -
BROWN	1	- - -	- - -
RED	2	- - -	- - -
ORANGE	3	- - -	- - -
YELLOW	4	- - -	- - -
GREEN	5	- - -	- - -
BLUE	6	- - -	- - -
VIOLET	7	- - -	- - -
GRAY	8	- - -	- - -
WHITE	9	- - -	- - -
GOLD	- - -	0.1	5(J)*
SILVER	- - -	0.01	10(K)*
NO COLOR	- - -	- - -	20(M)*

* SYMBOL DESIGNATION ALTERNATE FOR COLOR

Table 20-2. — Standard color code for resistors.

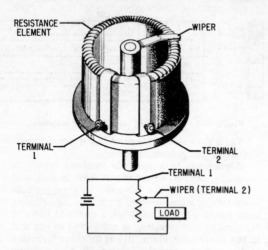

Figure 20-3.—Rheostat.

potentiometer is usually used to refer to any adjustable resistor having three terminals, two of which are connected to the ends of the resistance element and the third to the wiper contact. (See fig. 20-4.) By positioning the sliding contact, any desired voltage within the range of the

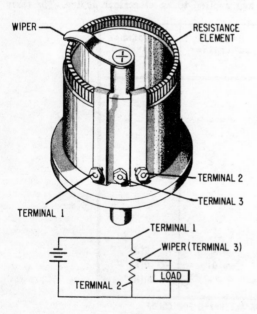

Figure 20-4.—Potentiometer.

potentiometer may be "picked off" and used where needed. As a rule, potentiometers are constructed to carry smaller currents than rheostats.

Resistors are rated according to the heat they will safely dissipate. Heat is produced by current flow through a resistance; and as current increases, the temperature will rise. The watt is a unit of power and it represents the power expended in heat as current flows through the resistor:

$$P = I^2R$$

where P is the number of watts; I, the current flow through the resistor; and R, the resistance of the resistor.

The wattage rating of resistors is dependent on both the composition of the resistor and the physical size; as resistor size increases, wattage rating increases. Resistors used in Navy equipment usually have a wattage rating of at least 50 percent above the wattage that can be expected to be developed across them. For example, 5 watts would be developed across a 5-megohm resistor if 1 milliampere of current flowed through it.

$$P = I^2R$$
$$P = (1 \times 10^{-3})^2 \times 5 \times 10^6$$
$$P = 1 \times 10^{-6} \times 5 \times 10^6 \ = 5 \text{ watts}$$

Thus, this resistor should have a wattage rating of at least 7.5 watts.

Carbon resistors generally have a wattage rating of one-half to two watts. For wattage ratings of more than two watts, wire-wound resistors are generally used.

CAPACITOR COLOR CODING

The various types of capacitors were described in chapter 9 of this training course. Many capacitors are stamped with their working voltage and their value of capacitance. The capacitance is given in microfarads. (See fig. 20-5.) When the value of capacitance is not stamped on capacitors, it is indicated by the use of a color code as shown in table 20-3. On molded capacitors, colors are applied in the form of dots, four different marking systems being

Figure 20.5.—Capacitors stamped with value of capacitance.

Capacitance			
Color	Significant figure	Multiplier	Tolerance
BLACK	0	1	20%
BROWN	1	10	1%
RED	2	100	2%
ORANGE	3	1,000	3%
YELLOW	4	10,000	4%
GREEN	5	100,000	5%
BLUE	6	1,000,000	6%
VIOLET	7	10,000,000	7%
GRAY	8	100,000,000	8%
WHITE	9	1,000,000,000	9%
GOLD	- - -	0.1	5%
SILVER	- - -	0.01	10%

Table 20-3. — Color code for molded capacitors.

used to indicate the value of capacitance in micromicrofarads.

To read the three-dot system correctly, the capacitor must be held so that the arrows point to the right. The first and second dots indicate the first and second significant figures, respectively, and the third dot indicates the multiplier. (See fig. 20-6 (A).) For example, if the three colors were red, green, and orange, the value of the capacitor would be 25,000 micromicrofarads or 0.025 microfarads.

The five-dot system is interpreted by holding the capacitor so that three dots are in the top row and two dots in the bottom row. The three dots in the top row indicate the first three significant figures. The lower left dot in the bottom row is the multiplier, and the lower right dot is the tolerance. (See fig. 20-6 (B).)

The value of a capacitor coded with the six-dot system can be found by holding the capacitor so that the dot arrows point to the right. As shown in figure 20-6 (C), the three dots indicate the first, second, and third significant figures. The lower right dot specifies the multiplier; the

lower middle dot, the tolerance; and the lower left dot, the voltage rating in hundreds of volts. This is the most frequently used color coding system. Assuming the top row of dots, reading from left to right, to be brown, red, and orange, and the bottom row, again reading from left to right, to be blue, green, and red, the capacitance would be 12,300 micromicrofarads; the voltage rating, 600 volts; and the tolerance, 5 percent.

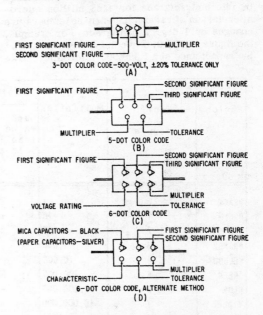

Figure 20-6.—Capacitor color coding. (A) Three-dot color code; (B) five-dot color code; (C) six-dot color code; (D) six-dot color code, alternate method.

The fourth color coding system also uses six dots, arranged in two rows, and again the capacitor must be held so that the arrows point to the right. However, in this system, the top left dot is either black, signifying a mica capacitor; or silver, signifying a paper capacitor. The second and third dots in the top row indicate the first two significant figures; the lower right dot, the multiplier, the lower center dot, the tolerance; and the lower left, the characteristics. "Characteristics" refer to such factors as the type case, dielectric, and temperature coefficient. (Temperature coefficient is the change in capacitance which occurs when a change in temperature takes place.) (See fig. 20-6 (D).)

399

Ceramic capacitors are color-coded as shown in figure 20-7.

The color code is the same as for molded capacitors except for certain values of multipliers and temperature coefficients. Table 20-4 shows the color code for ceramic capacitors. In the temperature coefficient column, the heading "parts per million per degree centigrade" means the amount the capacitance may change in micromicrofarads for each million micromicrofarads of rated value when the temperature changes by 1 degree centigrade. For example, the figure "-30" in this column would mean that the capacitance of a 1,000,000-micromicrofarad

capacitor would decrease to 999,970 micromicrofarads if the temperature increased 1 degree centigrade.

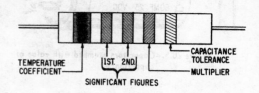

Figure 20-7.—Color code for ceramic capacitors.

Color	Significant figure	Multiplier	Tolerance of capacitance		Temperature coefficient parts per million per degree, centigrade
			Capacitors of value greater than 10 mmfd. in percent	Capacitors of 10 mmfd. or less in mmfd.	
BLACK	0	1	20(M)	2.0(G)	0
BROWN	1	10	1(F)	- - -	-30
RED	2	100	2(G)	- - -	-80
ORANGE	3	1,000	- - -	- - -	-150
YELLOW	4	10,000	- - -	- - -	-220
GREEN	5	100,000	5(J)	0.5(D)	-330
BLUE	6	1,000,000	- - -	- - -	-470
VIOLET	7	10,000,000	- - -	- - -	-750
GRAY	8	0.01	- - -	0.25(C)	+ 30
WHITE	9	0.1	10(K)	1.0(F)	+550

Table 20-4. – Color code for ceramic capacitors.

Transformers

Chapter 13 of this training course describes several different types of transformers. Since it is essential that all windings be correctly connected, the technician should understand the coding used in marking transformer leads.

Small power transformers, of the size used in electronic equipment, are generally color coded as shown in figure 20-8. In an untapped primary, both leads are black. If the primary is tapped, one lead is common and is colored black, the tap lead is black and yellow, and the

other lead is black and red.

On the transformer secondary, the high-voltage winding has two red leads if untapped, or two red leads and a yellow tap lead if tapped. On the rectifier filament windings, yellow leads are used across the whole winding, and the tap lead is yellow and blue. If there are other filament windings, they will be either green, brown, or slate. The tapped wire will be yellow in combination with one of the colors just named, that is green and yellow, brown and yellow, or slate and yellow.

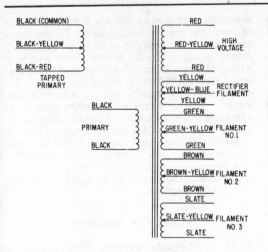

Figure 20-8.—Color coding of small power transformer leads.

this connection will equal the difference in the voltages of the two windings. The voltage of the low-voltage winding opposes that of the high-voltage winding and subtracts from it, hence the term "subtractive polarity."

When the $H1$ and $X1$ leads are brought out on opposite corners of the transformer (fig. 20-9 (B)), the polarity is ADDITIVE. Navy shipboard transformers have additive polarity. If the $H1$ and $X2$ leads are connected and a reduced voltage is applied across the $H1$ and $H2$ leads, the resultant voltage across the $H2$ and $X1$ leads in the series circuit formed by this connection will equal the sum of the voltages of the two windings. The voltage of the low-voltage winding aids the voltage of the high-voltage winding and adds to it, hence the term "additive polarity."

Polarity markings do not indicate the internal voltage stress in the windings but are useful only in making external connections between transformers, as previously mentioned.

The leads of large power transformers, such as those used for shipboard lighting and public utilities, are marked with numbers, letters, or a combination of both. This type of marking is shown in figure 20-9. Terminals for the high-voltage windings are marked $H1$, $H2$, $H3$, and so forth. The increasing numerical subscript designates an increasing voltage. Thus, the voltage between $H1$ and $H3$ is higher than the voltage between $H1$ and $H2$.

The secondary terminals are marked $X1$, $X2$, $X3$, and so forth. There are two types of markings that may be employed on the secondaries. These are shown in figure 20-9. When the $H1$ and $X1$ leads are brought out on the same side of the transformer (fig. 20-9 (A)), the polarity is called SUBTRACTIVE. The reason this arrangement is called subtractive is as follows: If the $H1$ and $X1$ leads are connected and a reduced voltage is applied across the $H1$ and $H2$ leads, the resultant voltage which appears across the $H2$ and $X2$ leads in the series circuit formed by

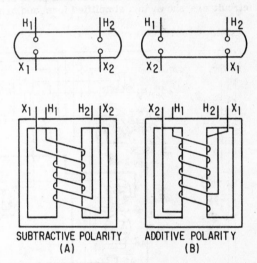

SUBTRACTIVE POLARITY (A)

ADDITIVE POLARITY (B)

Figure 20-9.—Polarity markings for large transformers.

Drawings

There are many different types of drawings, but it would be impractical to attempt to discuss all of them. Therefore, only those drawings that you, the technician, are apt to use frequently will be explained.

For each ship or aircraft there is a master electrical drawing. This drawing shows the entire electrical system and includes such information as power generation, distribution, and utilization. You can easily realize that because of size it would be impractical for the entire electrical drawing to be made available each time information concerning a particular circuit was needed. Therefore, needed sections of this drawing are made available to the technician who maintains that particular part of the system. These sections are usually placed in maintenance manuals.

Many different names are used to describe the various drawings that are constructed to aid in the understanding of electrical systems and equipments. Most all of these drawings are adaptations of some section of the master drawing. Some of the names used to identify particular types of drawings are isometric, expanded, master, wiring, schematic, pictorial, orthographic, and elementary.

The drawings that will be used most often in connection with maintenance work are the wiring diagram and the schematic diagram.

WIRING DIAGRAM

In a wiring diagram the structural parts of a circuit are shown in a simplified form and are generally arranged so that the physical location of parts is similar to the layout in the actual equipment. An example of this type drawing is shown in figure 20-10, which shows a typical wiring diagram of an automobile electrical system. Through the use of such a diagram, the location and interconnection of parts can be determined. Wiring diagrams are often used in the assembly and maintenance of electrical and electronic circuits in which the placement of parts is critical. For example, the lengths of the leads and the position of a capacitor, coil, or resistor may have a noticeable effect on the performance of a circuit, and this could be clearly specified on a wiring diagram.

SCHEMATIC DIAGRAM

In a schematic diagram (generally called simply a "schematic"), parts are represented by symbols, and may be arranged quite differently from their actual physical arrangement.

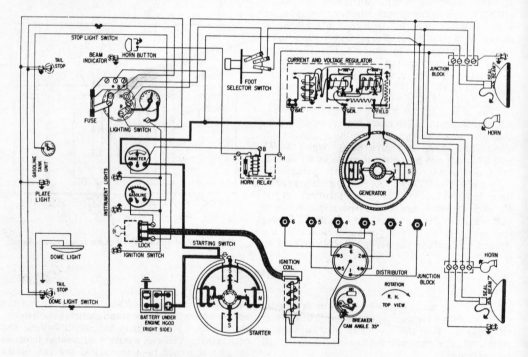

Figure 20-10.—Wiring diagram of automobile electrical system.

Figure 20-11 is a schematic of the same electrical system shown in figure 20-10. Since this type of diagram is much easier to draw and more compact than a wiring diagram, it is frequently used in connection with troubleshooting and maintenance, particularly in complicated electrical and electronic equipment.

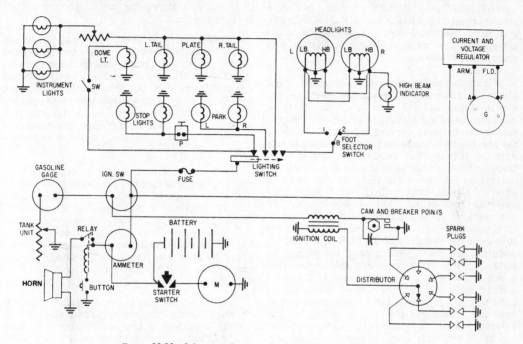

Figure 20-11.—Schematic diagram of automobile electrical system.

Circuit Analysis

You cannot hope to work effectively on a circuit or system you do not understand. Before attempting to make adjustments or correct faults in a circuit, you must first know at least the following:

1. What the circuit is supposed to do in normal operation, and how to operate it.

2. What each part or piece of equipment in the circuit contributes, and how each functions.

3. The location of every part, and routing of conductors.

4. The most likely cause of any given malfunction.

5. The best places to "get into" the circuit for making tests.

If you need any or all of this information, refer to the maintenance manual or master diagram for a particular circuit or system. These publications are prepared by the builder of the ship or aircraft, and contain the most complete descriptions and explanations available.

Also included in these manuals are wiring and schematic diagrams. After the purpose and operation of a circuit is understood, these diagrams are extremely useful in analyzing the details of its installation and operation. They show actual electrical connections between various parts and points in the circuit. When using these diagrams, you can start at the source of power for a particular circuit, trace along the conductors through control devices such as resistors, coils, capacitors, switches, connecting plugs, terminal points, the load, and finally back to the source. Thus, you gain a mental picture of the whole circuit before attempting to work on it. (See figs. 20-10 and 20-11.) By thoroughly analyzing the schematic or wiring diagram for a circuit and then operating it to observe the fault, you should have a pretty good idea of WHAT and WHERE a trouble is before you ever pick up a tool. For instance, suppose you have been told that the headlights on an automobile are not operating properly and you must make repairs.

First, before going to the automobile, you study the schematic diagram (for example, the one in figure 20-11). You determine that the complete headlight circuit is as follows: Starting at the battery, current flows to one side of the starter switch, through the ammeter, to one side of the ignition switch, through a fuse, through the lighting switch when it is down and contacting all four terminals, through the foot selector switch, out terminal 1 or 2, through the selected high-beam (HB) or low-beam (LB) filaments, to ground, and thence back to the battery, one side of which is grounded. When the foot selector switch is in the high-beam (No. 2) position, the beam indicator lamp should be lighted. With the circuit in mind, or carrying a schematic with you, you proceed to the automobile to make an operational check. Upon actuating the lighting switch, you observe that both low beams are lighted. Stepping the foot selector switch to position 2, you observe that the beam indicator lamp is operating, but only the left high-beam headlight is operating. With a glance at the schematic, this indicates that the wiring is sound between terminal 2 and the beam indicator lamp, and between terminal 2 and the left high-beam filament. It also shows that power is being delivered to the right high-beam filament, even though it is not lighting. This indicates that the trouble is in the right headlight. You now know WHERE the trouble is, simply by studying the schematic and operating the circuit. You should also have an idea of WHAT the trouble is (burned-out high-beam filament). It is now time to TURN OFF THE POWER, take up your tools, and go to work on the inoperative headlight.

After exposing the rear terminals of the headlight, you disconnect the wiring and make a continuity check through the high-beam filament with an ohmmeter. To your surprise, the filament checks good. You know that power has been reaching the right high-beam terminal, because it also supplies power to the left high-beam which works properly. Since power is reaching the filament terminal, and the filament is good, this can only mean that the connection is poor. Cleaning and tightening the connection should correct the fault.

The foregoing procedure is usually referred to as "troubleshooting". Troubleshooting and repair consists in locating the fault and correcting it. Repairing the trouble usually involves the replacement of defective parts, but locating trouble is often a more tedious job, requiring knowledge of the system or equipment plus mechanical know-how. Efficient troubleshooting requires an orderly and systematic procedure.

As a technician, much of your time will be spent troubleshooting the equipment you are required to maintain. This is reason enough for you to become a proficient troubleshooter. Much of the equipment you are required to maintain is quite complex, and you may feel that it is beyond your ability to keep it operative. However, the most complex job will usually become much easier if it is first broken up into successive steps.

Figure 20-12 shows, in chart form, a general troubleshooting procedure. The steps given in blocks 1 through 5 are to be used in locating trouble, and the steps given in blocks 6 and 7 are used in making repairs. Steps 2, 3, 4, and 5 may sometimes be eliminated, but never steps 6 and 7.

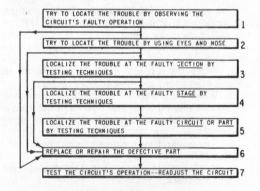

Figure 20-12.—Troubleshooting procedure.

Maintenance Publications

Many different maintenance publications are written to aid naval technicians in installing, adjusting, maintaining, and testing electrical and electronic equipment. Most of the publications that you will use will be written by the manufacturer of the equipment or by the Navy. These publications usually follow a prescribed pattern and are written so that they present the information in such style that it is easily understood and covers the operation and maintenance procedures thoroughly. In order for you to perform the duties of your job efficiently, it will be necessary for you to refer to these publications. The primary objective of this section of this chapter is to let you know that written material is available and that you should formulate the habit of referring to it.

A brief description of some of the more common publications will be given.

BUREAU OF SHIPS MAINTENANCE PUBLICATIONS

Publications that pertain to the operation and maintenance of electrical equipment and systems are kept in the log room, which is an office of the engineering department. It is important to refer to the applicable publications before working on any equipment or circuits with which you are not thoroughly familiar.

Publications of primary interest to the technician are (1) manufacturers' instruction books, (2) *Bureau of Ships Technical Manual*, (3) *Ship Information Book*, Volume 3, and (4) ship's plans.

Manufacturers Instruction Books

Manufacturers' instruction books contain technical information and instructions for the operation and maintenance of specific apparatus. This information usually includes a general description of the equipment, principles of operation, installation instructions, operating data, maintenance procedures, and safety precautions.

On most ships, instruction books are issued to responsible personnel who must sign custody receipts.

Bureau Of Ships Technical Manual

The Bureau of Ships Technical Manual is the most important Bureau of Ships publication. This manual contains the administrative and engineering instructions for the use of the engineering department. It describes methods of conducting tests, procedures for making repairs, and many helpful maintenance suggestions. It is the official authority on operating procedures.

Ship Information Book, Volume 3

The General Specifications for Ships of the United States Navy require that the contractor furnish copies of the *Ship Information Book*, which consists of several volumes, to each ship built in accordance with these specifications. Power and Lighting, Volume 3 of the *Ship Information Book* serves a particular ship, and replaces the *Record of Electrical Installations and Electrically Operated Auxiliaries*, previously required. Volume 3 consists of two parts. Part 1 contains a general description, and design information of each electrical auxiliary and equipment including the interior communications systems. Part 2 contains the manufacturers' and shipbuilders' test data. This part is particularly valuable as a basis for comparison of test results obtained after the equipment has operated over a period of time.

Ship's Plans

A complete file of standard plans and blueprints is available in the log room for reference and study. At the time a vessel is delivered, the shipbuilder furnishes a set of blueprints to the commanding officer via the supervisor of shipbuilding. These blueprints are in accordance with a list of working plans corrected to show the equipment as installed. Two copies of the *Ship's Plan Index* are also furnished to the ship. This index lists all plans under the cognizance of the Bureau of Ships which apply to the vessel concerned.

The plans furnished to the ship include wiring diagrams of all circuits, lists of telephones, loudspeakers, microphone control stations, voice tubes, calls, message-passing facilities, assembly plans, and wiring diagrams of interior communication and action cutout switchboards and panels; arrangement of electrical equipment in the ship control, command, and plotting stations; and a summary of interior communication and fire control equipment.

BUREAU OF NAVAL WEAPONS MAINTENANCE PUBLICATIONS

(NOTE: A relatively recent Department of the Navy change affects the designation of many aeronautical publications. As of 1 December, 1959 all responsibilities of the Bureau of Aeronautics were transferred to the Bureau of Naval Weapons. Publications that were already printed carry a BUAER designation. As new publications are printed they carry a BUWEP designation.)

The *Naval Aeronautic Publications Index*, NavWeps 00-500, contains a listing of all available naval aeronautic publications. These publications relate to the various naval aircraft and the equipment that is installed in them, as well as associated test equipment. The index is kept current through semiannual revisions. By referring to this index, the technician should be able to determine the identifying number and title of any publication that relates to the equipment he must maintain.

Handbooks

For each model of airborne electronic equipment, four handbooks are prepared. These are (1) the *Handbook of Operating Instructions* (HOI), (2) the *Handbook of Service Instructions* (HSI), (3) the *Handbook of Overhaul Instructions* (O/H), and (4) the *Illustrated Parts Breakdown* (IPB). These handbooks, which are authorized for publication by the Chief of the Bureau of Naval Weapons, contain information based on the results of countless tests and checks. This information will assist the technician and operator in obtaining the best possible performance from the equipment.

The *Handbook of Operating Instructions* contains information pertaining to the operation of the specific equipment and the necessary checks and adjustments required for obtaining optimum operation. This handbook is divided into the following sections—(1) a general description of the equipment, (2) the operating procedures, (3) the

operating checks and adjustments, and (4) provisions for emergency operation of the system.

The *Handbook of Service Instructions* presents information on preparing the specific equipment for use. It also tells how to maintain this equipment in an operational squadron, or supporting activity. The handbook is divided into sections which include such information as general principles of operation, special test equipment and tools needed for testing and adjusting the equipment, preparation for use and reshipment, theory of operation, maintenance instructions, and complete schematic, wiring, voltage, and resistance diagrams along with cabling charts for connection of the equipment units.

The *Handbook of Operating Instructions*, the *Handbook of Service Instructions*, and the *Illustrated Parts Breakdown* can be of most help to the technician at the operating level. The *Handbook of Overhaul Instructions* finds greater use at higher levels of maintenance.

THE TECHNICAL LIBRARY

In order that all necessary maintenance publications may be procured, properly filed, kept current, and made available to persons who need them, technical libraries are established.

The technical library contains all letter publications and technical manuals that pertain to the equipment to be maintained. In addition, material of a generally informative nature and also publications useful for training purposes may be available. The technical library should be kept in an orderly manner and its facilities made available to all personnel needing them. When many people use the library, it is essential that a checkout system be set up so that publications may be easily located when needed, and will not be misplaced.

If the technical library contains classified publications, a system is set up that will insure adequate security for its stowage and issuance. Proper procedures for the stowage and handling of classified matter are given in the *Security Manual for Classified Information*, OpNav Instruction 5510.1 series.

QUIZ

1. A molded capacitor on which the top row of dots (left to right) is silver, brown, and gray and the bottom row (left to right) is yellow, gold, and orange will have a value of
   a. 0.018 mfd.
   b. 18 mfd.
   c. 0.183 mfd.
   d. 183 mfd.

2. The publication that is the official authority on operating procedures is the
   a. Bureau of Ships Technical Manual
   b. Handbook of Operating Instructions
   c. Handbook of Service Instructions
   d. Ship Information Book, Vol. III

3. The electrical symbol used to indicate a potentiometer is
   a. ───/\/\/\/───

   b. ───/\/\/\/───

   c. ○──/\/\/\/──○

   d. ○──/\/\/\/──○

4. The lower left dot in a five-dot capacitor indicates the
   a. multiplier
   b. tolerance
   c. working voltage
   d. characteristic

5. Small power transformer primary leads are color coded
   a. red
   b. black
   c. green
   d. yellow

6. The temperature coefficient of a ceramic capacitor is indicated by the
   a. first dot
   b. last dot
   c. first band
   d. last band

7. A carbon resistor color coded red, blue, green, and gold would indicate a tolerance of
   a. 2%
   b. 5%
   c. 10%
   d. 20%

8. A carbon resistor color coded brown, black, and silver has a resistance value of
   a. 0.01Ω
   b. 0.1Ω
   c. 1Ω
   d. 10Ω

9. The secondary high voltage windings of a small power transformer are color coded
   a. black
   b. green
   c. white
   d. red

10. Before making any adjustments on a faulty circuit, the maintenance man should
    a. check all resistors and capacitors in the circuit
    b. make sure he understands what the circuit is supposed to do in normal operation
    c. check the circuit power supply
    d. observe the circuit's faulty operation

11. The value of a radial carbon resistor with a red end, blue body, and an orange dot would be
    a. 26,000 Ω ±20%
    b. 6,300 Ω ±20%
    c. 3,600 Ω ±20%
    d. 62,000 Ω ±20%

12. The drawings most often used in maintenance work are
    a. master electrical drawings and schematics
    b. schematics and wiring diagrams
    c. wiring diagrams and isometric drawings
    d. isometric drawings and schematics

13. In a standard Navy circuit drawing 1 milliampere, the power rating of a 4-megohm resistor should be
    a. 3 watts
    b. 4 watts
    c. 5 watts
    d. 6 watts

14. A molded capacitor on which the top row of dots (left to right) is red, violet, and yellow and the bottom row of dots (left to right) is green, silver, and orange will have a voltage rating of
    a. 200 volts
    b. 300 volts
    c. 400 volts
    d. 500 volts

15. The type of diagram that is consulted to find location and interconnection of parts is called a
    a. schematic diagram
    b. master diagram
    c. wiring diagram
    d. pictorial diagram

16. The Naval Aeronautics Publications Index, NavWeps 00-500,
    a. contains a list of parts available for issue in supply
    b. contains a list of equipment and material necessary to place an activity in readiness condition
    c. lists publications currently in effect
    d. is revised annually

CHAPTER 21

SAFETY

In the performance of your duties as a technician you will install, maintain, and repair electrical and electronic equipment in which dangerously high voltages are frequently present. This work is often done in very limited spaces. Among the hazards of this work are electric shock, electrical fires, harmful gases which are sometimes generated by faulty electrical and electronic devices, and injuries which may be caused by the improper use of tools.

Because of these dangers, you should be aware that the formation of safe and intelligent work habits is fully as important as your knowledge of electrical equipment. One of your primary objectives should be to train yourself to recognize and correct dangerous conditions and to avoid unsafe acts. You must also know the authorized methods for dealing with fires of electric origin, for treating burns, and for giving artificial respiration to persons suffering from electric shock.

Under the heading "Basic Precepts," the *United States Navy Safety Precautions* (OpNav 34P1) makes the following statement:

"Most accidents which occur in noncombat operations can be prevented if the full cooperation of personnel is gained and vigilance is exercised to eliminate unsafe acts."

This publication then gives the following general safety rules which apply to personnel in all types of activities:

"Each individual concerned shall strictly observe all safety precautions applicable to his work or duty."

"a. REPORTING UNSAFE CONDITIONS. Each individual concerned shall report any unsafe condition, or any equipment or material which he considers to be unsafe.

"b. WARNING OTHERS. Each individual concerned shall warn others whom he believes to be endangered by known hazards or by failure to observe safety precautions.

"c. PERSONAL PROTECTIVE EQUIPMENT. Each individual concerned shall wear or use protective clothing or equipment of the type approved for the safe performance of his work or duty.

"d. REPORT OF INJURY OR ILL HEALTH. All personnel shall report to their supervisors any injury or evidence of impaired health occurring in the course of work or duty.

"e. EMERGENCY CONDITIONS. In the event of an unforeseen hazardous occurrence, each individual concerned is expected to exercise such reasonable caution as is appropriate to the situation."

Electrical Safety Precautions

EFFECTS OF ELECTRIC SHOCK

Electric shock may cause instant death or may cause unconsciousness, cessation of breathing, and burns of all degrees. If a 60-cycle alternating current is passed through a person from hand to hand or from hand to foot, the effects when current is gradually increased from zero are as follows:

1. At about 1 milliampere (0.001 ampere) the shock can be felt.

2. At about 10 milliamperes (0.010 ampere) the shock is severe enough to paralyze muscles so that a person is unable to release the conductor.

3. At about 100 milliamperes (0.100 ampere) the shock is fatal if it lasts for one second or more.

IT IS IMPORTANT TO REMEMBER THAT CURRENT IS THE SHOCK FACTOR RATHER THAN THE AMOUNT OF VOLTAGE. You should clearly understand that the resistance of the human body is not great enough to prevent fatal shock from a voltage of as low as 115 volts. In many cases, voltages less than 115 volts are fatal. When the skin is dry, it has a high resistance. The resistance may be high enough to protect a person from a fatal shock even if one hand touches a high voltage while another part of the body touches the chassis or another ground.

Contact resistance decreases when the skin is moist and body resistance may drop to as low as 300 ohms. With this low body resistance, it can be seen that a very low voltage could supply enough current to cause death.

GENERAL SAFETY PRECAUTIONS IN
ELECTRICAL MAINTENANCE

Because of the possibility of injury to personnel, the danger of fire, and possible damage to material, all repair and maintenance work on electrical equipment should be performed only by duly authorized and assigned persons.

When any electrical equipment is to be overhauled or repaired, the main supply switches or cutout switches in each circuit from which power could possibly be fed should be secured in the open position and tagged. The tag should read, "This circuit was ordered open for repairs and shall not be closed except by direct order of...." (usually the person directly in charge of the repairs). After the work has been completed, the tag (or tags) should be removed by the same person.

The covers of fuse boxes and junction boxes should be kept securely closed except when work is being done. Safety devices such as interlocks, overload relays, and fuses should never be altered or disconnected except for replacements. Safety or protective devices should never be changed or modified in any way without specific authorization.

The interlock switch is ordinarily wired in series with the power-line leads to the electronic power supply unit, and is installed on the lid or door of the enclosure so as to break the circuit when the lid or door is opened. A true interlock switch is entirely automatic in action; it does not have to be manipulated by the operator. Multiple interlock switches, connected in series, may be used for increased safety. One switch may be installed on the access door of a device, and another on the cover or the power-supply section. Complex interlock systems are provided when several separate circuits must be opened for safety.

Because electrical and electronic equipment may have to be serviced without deenergizing the circuits, interlock switches are constructed so that they can be disabled by the technician. However, to minimize the danger of disabling them accidentally, they are generally located in such a manner that a certain amount of manipulation is necessary in order to operate them.

Fuses should be removed and replaced only after the circuit has been deenergized. When a fuse blows, it should be replaced only with a fuse of the same current and voltage ratings. When possible, the circuit should be carefully checked before making the replacement, since the burned-out fuse is often the result of circuit fault.

HIGH-VOLTAGE PRECAUTIONS

Personnel should never work alone near high-voltage equipment. Tools and equipment containing metal parts, such as brushes and brooms, should not be used in any area within four feet of high-voltage circuits or any electric wiring having exposed surfaces. The handles of all metal tools, such as pliers and cutters, should be covered with rubber insulating tape. (The use of plastic or cambric sleeving or of friction tape alone for this purpose is prohibited.) It is also necessary to insulate the shanks of certain screwdrivers (particularly those used inside electronic equipment) with insulating sheaths. Only 3/16 of an inch of the blade need be exposed. Where it is not practicable to tape or otherwise insulate a surface, electricians' insulating varnish may be used.

Before a worker touches a capacitor which is connected to a deenergized circuit, or which is disconnected entirely, he should short-circuit the terminals to make sure that the capacitor is completely discharged. Grounded shorting prods should be permanently attached to workbenches where electronic devices are regularly serviced.

Do not work on any type of electrical apparatus with wet hands or while wearing wet clothing, and do not wear loose or flapping clothing. The use of thin-soled shoes with metal plates or hobnails is prohibited. Safety shoes with nonconducting soles should be worn if available. Flammable articles, such as celluloid cap visors, should not be worn.

Before working on electronic or electrical apparatus, all rings, wristwatches, bracelets, and similar metal items should be removed. Care should be taken that the clothing does not contain exposed zippers, metal buttons, or any type of metal fasteners.

Warning signs and suitable guards should be provided to prevent personnel from coming into accidental contact with high voltages.

WORK ON ENERGIZED CIRCUITS

Insofar as is practicable, repair work on energized circuits should NOT be undertaken. When repairs on operating equipment must be made in order to make proper adjustments, every known safety precaution should be carefully observed. Ample light for good illumination should be provided; and the worker should be insulated from ground with some suitable nonconducting material such as several layers of dry canvas, dry wood, or a rubber mat of approved construction. The worker should, if possible, use only one hand in accomplishing the necessary repairs, keeping the other hand well away from the energized circuit. Helpers should be stationed near the main switch or the circuit breaker so that the equipment can be deenergized immediately in case of emergency. A man qualified in first aid for electric shock should stand by during the entire period of the repair.

GROUNDING OF PORTABLE ELECTRICAL EQUIPMENT

Navy specifications for portable tools require that the electric cord for such tools be provided with a distinctively marked ground wire in addition to the conductors for supplying power to the tool. The end of the ground wire within the tool must be connected to the tool's metal housing. The other end must be connected to ground. For this ground connection, specially designed grounded-type plugs and receptacles, which automatically make this connection when the plug is inserted in the receptacle, must be used.

Portable tools not provided with the grounded-type plug, and miscellaneous portable electric equipment, which do not have a cord with a grounded conductor and grounded plug, must be provided with a 3-conductor cord and with a standard Navy grounded-type plug. The ground wire must be connected to a positive ground, and the total resistance from the tool enclosure to the ground to which it is connected must not exceed a small fraction of an ohm. Extreme care must be exercised to see that the ground connection is made correctly. If the grounding conductor, which is connected to the metallic equipment casing, is connected by mistake to a line contact of the plug, a dangerous potential will be placed on the equipment casing. This might easily result in a fatal shock to the operator.

BATTERY SAFETY PRECAUTIONS

The principal hazard in connection with batteries is the danger of acid burns when refilling or handling batteries. These burns can be prevented by the proper use of eyeshields, rubber gloves, rubber aprons, and rubber boots with nonslip soles. The rubber boots and apron need be worn only when batteries are being refilled. It is a good practice, however, to wear the eyeshields whenever working around batteries to prevent the possibility of acid burns of the eyes. Wood slat floorboards, if kept in good condition, are helpful in preventing slips and falls as well as electric shock from the high-voltage side of charging equipment.

Another hazard is the danger of explosion due to the ignition of hydrogen gas given off during the battery charging operation. This is especially true where the accelerated charging method is used. Open flames or smoking should not be permitted in the battery charging room, and the charging rate should be held at a point that will prevent the rapid liberation of hydrogen gas. Manufacturers' recommendations as to the charging rates for various size batteries should be closely followed, and a shop exhaust system should be used.

Particular care should be taken by battery men to prevent short circuits while batteries are being charged, tested, or handled, because of the danger of serious burns and explosion of any accumulated hydrogen gas as a result of the spark generated.

PRECAUTIONS WITH CHEMICALS

Volatile liquids such as insulating varnish, lacquer, turpentine, and kerosene are dangerous when used near energized electronic or electrical equipment because of the danger of igniting the fumes by sparks. When these liquids are used in spaces containing nonoperating equipment, be sure that there is sufficient ventilation to avoid an accumulation of fumes and that all fumes are cleared before the equipment is energized.

Alcohol should never be used for cleaning electrical equipment since it not only constitutes a fire hazard but it also results in damage to many kinds of insulation. Neither should carbon tetrachloride be employed as a cleaning agent. Unlike alcohol, the use of carbon tetrachloride does not create a fire hazard; but it is dangerous because of the injurious effects of breathing its vapor. Also, it forms an insulating film on the material to which it is applied. The careless use of carbon tetrachloride may result in headache, dizziness, and nausea. If the fumes are breathed in poorly ventilated spaces, the effect may be loss of consciousness or even death. For these reasons, the use of carbon tetrachloride as a solvent or cleaner has been specifically prohibited in Navy maintenance operations. When cleaning electrical or electronic equipments or parts, always use an approved cleaning agent such as Dry Cleaning Solvent, Federal Specification P-S-661.

Safety From Fire

PREVENTING FIRES

General cleanliness of the work area and of electronic apparatus is essential for the prevention of electrical fires. Oil, grease, and carbon dust can be ignited by electrical arcing. Therefore, electrical and electronic equipment should be kept absolutely clean and free of all such deposits.

Wiping rags and other flammable waste material must always be placed in tightly closed metal containers, which must be emptied at the end of the day's work.

Containers holding paints, varnishes, cleaners, or any volatile solvents should be kept tightly closed when not in actual use. They must be stored in a separate building or in a fire-resisting room which is well-ventilated and where they will not be exposed to excessive heat or to the direct rays of the sun.

FIREFIGHTING

In case of electrical fires, the following steps should be taken:

1. Deenergize the circuit.
2. Call the Fire Department.
3. Control or extinguish the fire, using the correct type of fire extinguisher.
4. Report the fire to the appropriate authority.

For combating electrical fires, use a CO_2 (carbon dioxide) fire extinguisher and direct it toward the base of the flame. Carbon tetrachloride should never be used for firefighting since it changes to phosgene (a poisonous gas) upon contact with hot metal, and even in open air this creates a hazardous condition. The application of water to electrical fires is dangerous; the foam-type fire extinguishers should not be used since the foam is electrically conductive.

In cases of cable fires in which the inner layers of insulation or insulation covered by armor are burning, the only positive method of preventing the fire from running the length of the cable is to cut the cable and separate the two ends.

When selenium rectifiers burn out, fumes of selenium dioxide are liberated which cause an overpowering stench. The fumes are poisonous and should not be breathed. If a rectifier burns out, deenergize the equipment immediately and ventilate the room. Allow the damaged rectifier to cool before attempting any repairs. If possible, move the equipment containing it out of doors. Do not touch or handle the defective rectifier while it is hot since a skin burn might result, through which some of the selenium compound could be absorbed.

Fires involving wood, paper, cloth, or explosives should be fought with water. Water works well on them. Therefore, advantage is taken of its inexpensiveness, availability, and safety in handling.

A steady stream of water does not work in extinguishing fires involving substances like oil, gasoline, kerosene, or paint, because these substances will float on top of the water and keep right on burning. Also, a stream of water will scatter the burning liquid and spread the fire. For this reason, foam or fog must be used in fighting such fires.

Safety Precautions When Using Tools

As a general precaution, be sure that all tools used conform to Navy standards as to quality and type. Use each tool only for the purpose for which it is intended. All tools in active use should be maintained in good repair and all damaged or nonworking tools should be returned to the toolkeeper.

HANDTOOLS

Care must be taken when selecting pliers, side cutters, or diagonal cutters. Pliers or cutters should never be used on nuts or pipefittings. Always hold the pliers or cutters so that the fingers are not wrapped around the handle in such a way that they can be pinched or jammed if the tool slips. When cutting short pieces, take care that parts of the work do not fly and cause injury. Never put extensions on tool handles to increase leverage.

When selecting a screwdriver for electrical work, be sure that it has a nonconducting handle. The screwdriver selected should be of the proper size to fit the screw and should never be used as a substitute for a punch or a chisel. The points of screwdrivers can be kept in proper shape with a file or a grinding wheel.

Use wrenches only if they are right for the job and only if they are in good condition. An adjustable wrench should be faced so that the movable jaw is located forward in the direction in which the handle is to be turned.

PORTABLE POWER TOOLS

All portable power tools should be inspected before use to see that they are clean, well oiled, and in the proper state or repair. The switches should operate normally, and the cords should be clean and free of defects. The case of any electrically driven power tool should be well grounded; and sparking electric tools should never be used in places where flammable gases or liquids or exposed explosives are present.

Drills must be straight, undamaged, and properly sharpened. Tighten the drill securely in the chuck using the key provided; never secure it with pliers or with a wrench. It is important that the drill be set straight and true in the chuck. The work should be firmly clamped and, if of metal, a center punch should be used to score the material before drilling is started.

Be sure that power cords do not come in contact with sharp objects. The cords should not be allowed to kink, nor should they be allowed to come in contact with oil, grease, hot surfaces, or chemicals. When cords are damaged, they should be replaced instead of being patched with tape.

SHOP MACHINERY

In your work as a technician, you may be required to use a few pieces of shop machinery such as a power grinder or a drill press. In addition to the general precautions on the use of tools, there are several other precautions which should be observed when you work with machinery. The more important ones are:

1. Never remove a guard or cover from a running machine.

2. Never operate mechanical or powered equipment unless you are thoroughly familiar with its controls. When in doubt, consult the appropriate instruction or ask someone who knows.

3. Always make sure that everyone is clear before starting or operating mechanical equipment.

4. Never try to clear jammed machinery without first cutting off the source of power.

5. When hoisting heavy machinery (or equipment) by a chain fall, always keep everyone clear, and guide the hoist with lines attached to the equipment.

6. Never plug in portable electric machinery without insuring that the source is the kind of electricity (a.c. or d.c.) called for on the nameplate of the machine.

First Aid

TREATMENT FOR ELECTRICAL SHOCK

Electric shock is a jarring, shaking sensation resulting from contact with electric circuits or from the effects of lightning. The victim usually feels that he has received a sudden blow; and if the voltage is sufficiently high, he may become unconscious. Severe burns may appear on the skin at the place of contact; muscular spasm can occur, causing him to clasp the apparatus or wire which caused the shock and be unable to turn it loose. Electric shock can kill its victim by stopping the heart or by stopping breathing, or both. It may sometimes damage nerve tissue and result in a slow wasting away of muscles that may not become apparent until several weeks or months after the shock was received.

The following procedure is recommended for rescue and care of shock victims:

1. Remove the victim from electrical contact at once, but DO NOT ENDANGER YOURSELF. This can be done by: (1) Throwing the switch if it is nearby; (2) cutting the cable or wires to the apparatus, using an ax with a wooden handle while taking care to protect your eyes from the flash when the wires are severed; (3) use of a dry stick, rope, leather belt, coat, blanket, or any other nonconductor of electricity.

2. Determine whether the victim is breathing. If he is, keep him lying down in a comfortable position. Loosen the clothing about his neck, chest, and abdomen so that he can breathe freely. Protect him from exposure to cold, and watch him carefully.

3. Keep him from moving about. In this condition, the heart is very weak, and any sudden muscular effort or activity on the part of the patient may result in heart failure.

4. Do not give stimulants or opiates. Send for a medical officer at once and do not leave the patient until he has adequate medical care.

5. If the victim is not breathing, it will be necessary to apply artificial respiration without delay, even though he may appear to be lifeless.

RESUSCITATION FROM THE EFFECTS OF ELECTRIC SHOCK

Artificial respiration is the process of promoting breathing by mechanical means. It is used to resuscitate persons whose breathing has stopped, not only as a result of electric shock, but also from causes such as drowning, asphyxiation, strangling, or the presence of a foreign body in the throat.

When a shock victim must be revived, begin artificial respiration as soon as possible. If there is any serious bleeding, stop it first, but do not waste time on anything else. Seconds count; and the longer you wait to begin, the less are the chances of saving the victim. (See fig. 21-1.)

Personnel in all rates and ratings, E-2 and above, are required to be able to administer artificial respiration by the back-pressure arm-lift method and the back-pressure hip-lift method. Detailed coverage on the Navy's standardized procedures on these methods of artificial respiration are given in the *Standard First Aid Training Course*, NavPers 10081. Additional material such as that on pole-top resuscitation, mechanical aids for resuscitation, and treatment during recovery are also contained in this first aid course. Future revisions of Nav-Pers 10081 will contain information on new standardized first aid procedures adopted by the Navy such as the mouth-to-mouth method of resuscitation.

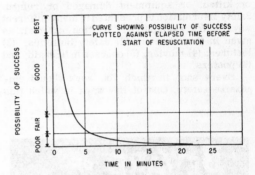

Figure 21-1.—Importance of speed in commencing artificial respiration.

TREATMENT OF BURNS AND WOUNDS

In administering first aid for burns, the objectives are to relieve the pain, to make the patient as comfortable as possible, to prevent infection, and to guard against shock which often accompanies burns of a serious nature. Detailed information on the proper method for treating various types of burns is contained in the *Standard First Aid Training Course*, NavPers 10081.

Any break in the skin is dangerous because it allows germs to enter the wound. Although infection may occur in any wound, it is of particular danger in wounds which do not bleed freely, wounds in which torn tissue or skin falls back into place and so prevents the entrance of air, and wounds which involve crushing of tissues.

Minor wounds should be washed immediately with soap and clean water, dried, and painted with a mild, nonirritating antiseptic. Benzalkonium chloride tincture, which is now found in most Navy first aid kits, is a good antiseptic; it does not irritate the skin but it effectively destroys many of the micro-organisms which cause infection. (Benzalkonium chloride is commonly sold under the name of Zephiran or Zepherin chloride.) Apply a dressing if necessary.

Larger wounds should be treated only by medical personnel. Merely cover the wound with a dry sterile compress and fasten the compress in place with a bandage.

Since the saving of a person's life often depends on prompt and correct first aid treatment, all Navy personnel should become thoroughly familiar with the material in the *Standard First Aid Training Course*, NavPers 10081.

Safety Education

Safety is an all-hand responsibility. It is the job of every person in the Navy to exercise precaution to insure that people will not be injured or killed, or equipment damaged or ruined. Safety information is presented in many different ways — for example: (1) Written material, as given in this chapter; (2) safety bulletins; (3) lectures; (4) movies; (5) courses in first aid; and (6) posters.

Every shop in which you work should emphasize safety. One of the ways in which this can be done is through the use of posters. The Navy makes available numerous safety posters. Some of these are general in nature and some relate to specific types of work. These posters should be placed in a conspicuous area and as new ones are printed they should replace the older ones.

Four of the current posters that relate to shop and electrical safety follow.

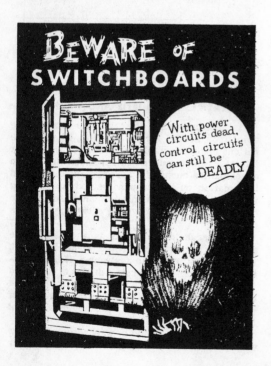

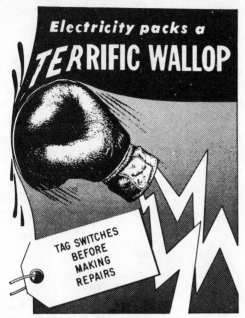

NATIONAL SAFETY COUNCIL

QUIZ

1. It is dangerous to touch a burned-out selenium rectifier when it is hot because
   a. some of the selenium compound could
      be absorbed through a skin burn
   b. direct current could cause shock
   c. fumes of selenium dioxide could be
      liberated
   d. all of the above are correct
2. When using an adjustable wrench, it should
   be so faced that the movable jaw is located
   a. forward in the direction in which the
      handle is turned
   b. aft of the direction in which the handle
      is turned
   c. free of all obstructions
   d. between the worker and the work to be
      performed
3. If electrical or electronic equipment is to
   be repaired, what must be done before the
   actual work is begun?
   a. The fuse for the associated circuit must
      be removed
   b. The main supply switches must be
      shorted out
   c. A man must be stationed nearby with a
      fire extinguisher
   d. The main supply switches must be se-
      cured open and tagged

4. The handles of all metal tools used for
   working on electrical circuits should be
   covered with
   a. friction tape
   b. plastic sleeving
   c. rubber insulating tape
   d. cambric sleeving
5. To check whether a capacitor is completely
   discharged, a worker should
   a. short-circuit the terminals
   b. take a resistance reading
   c. lightly tap the leads with his finger
   d. none of the above are correct
6. The principal hazard(s) when handling and
   charging batteries is/are due to the danger
   of
   a. electrical shock
   b. asphyxiation
   c. acid burns and explosion
   d. acid burns and asphyxiation
7. When fighting an electrical fire, you should
   use
   a. foam
   b. soda and acid
   c. carbon dioxide
   d. carbon tetrachloride

8. If you desire to drill a hole in metal, always be sure to
   a. apply extra pressure to prevent bucking
   b. use a dull drill and oil
   c. secure the drill in the chuck with a wrench
   d. score the material with a center punch

9. Carbon tetrachloride is specifically prohibited as a cleaning agent because it may
   a. create a fire hazard
   b. cause dizziness and nausea
   c. explode if exposed to an electrical spark
   d. cause blood poisoning

10. Paints and varnishes should be stored in a
    a. tightly closed metal locker
    b. sealed fire-resisting room or separate building
    c. separate building or fire-resisting room which is well-ventilated
    d. warm and sunlit location

11. Damaged cords for power tools should be
    a. coated with flux and covered with rubber tape
    b. repaired with insulating tape
    c. replaced
    d. shortened to remove the damaged section

12. Electrical shock is fatal when_____of current is passed through a person from hand to hand for one second or more.
    a. 0.10 ampere
    b. 0.01 ampere
    c. 1 milliampere
    d. 10 milliamperes

13. Water is a good firefighting agent on wood, paper,
    a. cloth, or kerosene
    b. cloth, or explosives
    c. oil, or paint
    d. oil, or gasoline

14. The shock factor of electricity is dependent on the amount of
    a. resistance
    b. voltage
    c. current
    d. all of the above

15. In case of an electrical fire, the first step is to
    a. deenergize the circuit
    b. call the fire department
    c. extinguish the fire
    d. notify the proper authority

16. What cleaning agent should be used for cleaning electrical or electronic equipment or parts?
    a. Alcohol
    b. Drycleaning solvent
    c. Carbon tetrachloride
    d. Turpentine

17. The proper treatment for a person who has received a severe electric shock but is still breathing is to
    a. give him an opiate to relieve his anxiety
    b. keep him walking or moving about so that he will not lose consciousness
    c. apply artificial respiration to assist him in breathing
    d. keep him lying down

APPENDIX I
ANSWERS TO QUIZZES

Chapter 1
FUNDAMENTAL CONCEPTS OF ELECTRICITY

1. c.	8. d.	14. b.	20. d.
2. d.	9. c.	15. d.	21. d.
3. d.	10. a.	16. d.	22. d.
4. c.	11. c.	17. c.	23. c.
5. c.	12. b.	18. a.	24. d.
6. b.	13. a.	19. b.	25. b.
7. a.			

Chapter 2
BATTERIES

1. c.	6. a.	11. c.	16. c.
2. c.	7. d.	12. b.	17. d.
3. d.	8. b.	13. b.	18. c.
4. c.	9. c.	14. c.	19. a.
5. b.	10. c.	15. c.	20. a.

Chapter 3
THE SIMPLE ELECTRIC CIRCUIT

1. a.	6. c.	11. b.	16. b.
2. b.	7. b.	12. d.	17. a.
3. d.	8. c.	13. b.	18. d.
4. a.	9. b.	14. b.	19. b.
5. b.	10. c.	15. a.	20. b.

Chapter 4
DIRECT-CURRENT SERIES AND PARALLEL CIRCUITS

1. c.	7. b.	13. d.	19. b.
2. a.	8. b.	14. b.	20. d.
3. c.	9. b.	15. c.	21. c.
4. b.	10. a.	16. a.	22. d.
5. c.	11. a.	17. a.	23. a.
6. a.	12. a.	18. d.	24. b.

Chapter 5

DIRECT-CURRENT COMPOUND AND BRIDGE CIRCUITS

1. b.	6. c.	11. a.	16. c.
2. c.	7. d.	12. c.	17. b.
3. d.	8. a.	13. a.	18. a.
4. b.	9. d.	14. b.	19. c.
5. a.	10. d.	15. d.	20. b.

Chapter 6

ELECTRICAL CONDUCTORS AND WIRING TECHNIQUES

1. c.	6. b.	11. c.	16. d.
2. d.	7. a.	12. c.	17. a.
3. d.	8. c.	13. b.	18. b.
4. c.	9. a.	14. d.	19. b.
5. a.	10. b.	15. c.	20. a.

Chapter 7

ELECTROMAGETISM AND MAGNETIC CIRCUITS

1. b.	7. b.	12. c.	17. c.
2. d.	8. b.	13. d.	18. c.
3. b.	9. a.	14. a.	19. b.
4. b.	10. b.	15. a.	20. c.
5. d.	11. a.	16. d.	21. c.
6. c.			

Chapter 8

INTRODUCTION TO ALTERNATING-CURRENT ELECTRICITY

1. c.	8. c.	15. b.	22. d.
2. a.	9. b.	16. b.	23. d.
3. d.	10. c.	17. d.	24. a.
4. c.	11. b.	18. a.	25. d.
5. b.	12. b.	19. b.	26. b.
6. d.	13. c.	20. c.	27. c.
7. c.	14. d.	21. c.	

Chapter 9

INDUCTANCE AND CAPACITANCE

1. b.	8. d.	14. a.	20. d.
2. c.	9. c.	15. d.	21. b.
3. c.	10. b.	16. b.	22. b.
4. b.	11. c.	17. a.	23. a.
5. a.	12. a.	18. d.	24. d.
6. b.	13. b.	19. b.	25. a.
7. d.			

Chapter 10

INDUCTIVE AND CAPACITIVE REACTANCE

1. c.	7. a.	13. b.	19. d.
2. c.	8. a.	14. d.	20. a.
3. c.	9. d.	15. a.	21. a.
4. a.	10. d.	16. c.	22. b.
5. a.	11. a.	17. b.	23. a.
6. b.	12. d.	18. b.	

Chapter 11

FUNDAMENTAL ALTERNATING-CURRENT CIRCUIT THEORY

1. b.	7. d.	13. a.	19. c.
2. b.	8. d.	14. c.	20. d.
3. c.	9. a.	15. d.	21. b.
4. a.	10. c.	16. d.	22. a.
5. c.	11. c.	17. c.	23. b.
6. b.	12. a.	18. b.	24. c.

Chapter 12

BASIC ELECTRICAL INDICATING INSTRUMENTS

1. b.	7. b.	13. b.	19. b.
2. c.	8. c.	14. c.	20. d.
3. c.	9. b.	15. c.	21. b.
4. c.	10. b.	16. d.	22. a.
5. b.	11. a.	17. a.	23. c.
6. d.	12. b.	18. d.	

Chapter 13

ALTERNATING-CURRENT GENERATORS AND TRANSFORMERS

1. c.	7. d.	13. c.	18. b.
2. c.	8. a.	14. c.	19. c.
3. c.	9. a.	15. c.	20. a.
4. d.	10. b.	16. b.	21. c.
5. d.	11. d.	17. a.	22. c.
6. b.	12. b.		

Chapter 14

ALTERNATING-CURRENT MOTORS

1. d.	8. b.	14. c.	20. c.
2. b.	9. d.	15. d.	21. d.
3. d.	10. d.	16. c.	22. b.
4. b.	11. b.	17. a.	23. d.
5. a.	12. b.	18. d.	24. b.
6. a.	13. c.	19. b.	25. c.
7. a.			

419

Chapter 15

DIRECT-CURRENT GENERATORS

1. b.	8. b.	15. a.	22. c.
2. d.	9. b.	16. d.	23. c.
3. b.	10. c.	17. d.	24. a.
4. b.	11. c.	18. c.	25. a.
5. b.	12. b.	19. a.	26. d.
6. d.	13. a.	20. c.	27. a.
7. c.	14. d.	21. c.	

Chapter 16

DIRECT-CURRENT MOTORS

1. a.	7. c.	13. c.	19. a.
2. d.	8. d.	14. d.	20. d.
3. c.	9. d.	15. b.	21. a.
4. a.	10. b.	16. b.	22. a.
5. b.	11. b.	17. b.	23. d.
6. b.	12. c.	18. c.	24. c.

Chapter 17

ALTERNATING-CURRENT INSTRUMENTS

1. c.	7. d.	13. d.	19. a.
2. c.	8. c.	14. c.	20. b.
3. c.	9. d.	15. c.	21. b.
4. c.	10. b.	16. a.	22. d.
5. a.	11. a.	17. a.	23. b.
6. a.	12. d.	18. a.	24. d.

Chapter 18

MAGNETIC AMPLIFIERS

1. d.	5. d.	9. b.	13. b.
2. b.	6. d.	10. b.	14. a.
3. c.	7. d.	11. a.	15. c.
4. c.	8. c.	12. c.	16. d.

Chapter 19

SYNCHROS AND SERVOMECHANISMS

1. d.	7. a.	13. a.	18. c.
2. d.	8. d.	14. b.	19. b.
3. c.	9. a.	15. a.	20. b.
4. a.	10. b.	16. a.	21. a.
5. d.	11. d.	17. a.	22. d.
6. b.	12. c.		

Chapter 20

ELECTRICAL DRAWINGS AND TECHNICAL MANUALS

1. a.	5. b.	9. d.	13. d.
2. a.	6. c.	10. b.	14. d.
3. c.	7. b.	11. d.	15. c.
4. a.	8. b.	12. b.	16. c.

Chapter 21

SAFETY

1. a.	6. c.	10. c.	14. c.
2. a.	7. c.	11. c.	15. a.
3. d.	8. d.	12. a.	16. b.
4. c.	9. b.	13. b.	17. d.
5. a.			

APPENDIX II

NAVY CABLE TYPE AND SIZE DESIGNATIONS

All cables described herein are identified by NAVY CABLE TYPE AND SIZE DESIGNATIONS, which consists of a letter followed by numerals.

I. The TYPE DESIGNATION indicates the type or construction of the cable and and consists of the first letters of the words used in describing the cable:

Example: Type SHFA-Single, Heat and Flame-resistance, Armored.

II. The SIZE DESIGNATION relates to the copper conductors. No set rule has been established for application of SIZE DESIGNATIONS since the numerals used may indicate one or more of the following:

(1) Size of copper conductor.
(2) Stranding of conductors.
(3) Number of copper conductors.
(4) Number of twisted pairs.

Examples of the most common uses of SIZE DESIGNATIONS are given below:

(1) To indicate approximate cross-sectional area of the conductor expressed in thousands of circular mils (abbreviated C.M.).

Example: The conductor area of SHFA-3 is approximately 3000 C.M. (exactly 2828 C.M.)

(2) To indicate approximate cross-sectional area with stranding shown in parentheses.

Example: The conductor area of SRI-2-1/2 (26) is approximately 2500 C.M. (exactly 2613 C.M.), and consists of 26 individual wire strands.

(3) To indicate number of conductors.

Example: MCOP-7 is a cable comprised of seven conductors.

(4) To indicate number of twisted pairs.

Example: TTOP-10 is a 20-conductor cable comprised of 10 twisted pairs.

The following are typical examples of type designations and constructions:

FLA—Four conductor, Lighting, Armored. Varnished cambric or rubber insulation, rubber hose jacket, armored.

MCMB—Multiple Conductor, Marker-Buoy. Rubber insulated identifying colors, steel supporting cable, tape over assembly, tough rubber sheath.

SHFA—Single conductor, Heat and Flame-resistant, Armored. Asbestos-varnished cambric-asbestos insulation, impervious sheath, armored.

THFR—Triple conductor, Heat and Flame-resistant, Radio. Synthetic resin-varnished cambric and felted asbestos insulation, asbestos belt, impervious sheath, armored.

TTHFA—Twisted pairs, Telephone, Heat and Flame-resistant, Armored. Solid conductor, textile wrap or synthetic resin insulation, twisted pair, felted asbestos belt, impervious sheath, armored.

APPENDIX III
GREEK ALPHABET

Name	Capital	Lower Case	Designates
Alpha	A	α	Angles.
Beta	B	β	Angles, flux density.
Gamma . . .	Γ	γ	Conductivity.
Delta	Δ	δ	Variation of a quantity, increment.
Epsilon . . .	E	ϵ	Base of natural logarithms (2.71828).
Zeta	Z	ζ	Impedance, coefficients, coordinates.
Eta	H	η	Hysteresis coefficient, efficiency, magnetizing force.
Theta	Θ	θ	Phase angle.
Iota	I	ι	
Kappa	K	κ	Dielectric constant, coupling coefficient, susceptibility.
Lambda . . .	Λ	λ	Wavelength.
Mu	M	μ	Permeability, micro, amplification factor.
Nu	N	ν	Reluctivity.
Xi	Ξ	ξ	
Omicron . . .	O	o	
Pi	Π	π	3.1416
Rho	P	ρ	Resistivity.
Sigma	Σ	σ	
Tau	T	τ	Time constant, time-phase displacement.
Upsilon . . .	Υ	υ	
Phi	Φ	φ	Angles, magnetic flux.
Chi	X	χ	
Psi	Ψ	ψ	Dielectric flux, phase difference.
Omega	Ω	ω	Ohms (capital), angular velocity ($2\pi f$).

COMMON ABBREVIATIONS AND LETTER SYMBOLS

Term	Abbreviation or Symbol
alternating current (noun)	a.c.
alternating-current (adj.)	a-c
ampere	a.
area	A
audiofrequency (noun)	AF
audiofrequency (adj.)	A-F
capacitance	C
capacitive reactance	X_C
centimeter	cm.
conductance	G
coulomb	Q
counterelectromotive force	c.e.m.f.
current (d-c or r.m.s. value)	I
current (instantaneous value)	i
cycles per second	c.p.s.
dielectric constant	K,k
difference in potential (d-c or r.m.s. value)	E
difference in potential (instantaneous value)	e
direct current (noun)	d.c.
direct-current (adj.)	d-c
electromotive force	e.m.f.
frequency	f
henry	h.
horsepower	hp.
impedance	Z
inductance	L
inductive reactance	X_L
kilovolt	kv.
kilovolt-ampere	kv.-a.
kilowatt	kw.
kilowatt-hour	kw.-hr.
magnetic field intensity	H
magnetomotive force	m.m.f.
megohm	M
microampere	μ a.
microfarad	μ f.
microhenry	μ h.
micromicrofarad	$\mu\mu$ f.
microvolt	μ v.
milliampere	ma.
millihenry	mh.
milliwatt	mw.
mutual inductance	M
power	P
resistance	R
revolutions per minute	r.p.m.
root mean square	r.m.s.
time	t
torque	T
volt	v.
watt	w.

ELECTRICAL TERMS AND FORMULAS

Terms

AGONIC.--An imaginary line of the earth's surface passing through points where the magnetic declination is 0°; that is, points where the compass points to true north.

AMMETER.--An instrument for measuring the amount of electron flow in amperes.

AMPERE.-- The basic unit of electrical current.

AMPERE-TURN.--The magnetizing force produced by a current of one ampere flowing through a coil of one turn.

AMPLIDYNE.--A rotary magnetic or dynamo-electric amplifier used in servomechanism and control applications.

AMPLIFICATION.--The process of increasing the strength (current, power, or voltage) of a signal.

AMPLIFIER.--A device used to increase the signal voltage, current, or power, generally composed of a vacuum tube and associated circuit called a stage. It may contain several stages in order to obtain a desired gain.

AMPLITUDE.--The maximum instantaneous value of an alternating voltage or current, measured in either the positive or negative direction.

ARC.-A flash caused by an electric current ionizing a gas or vapor.

ARMATURE.--The rotating part of an electric motor or generator. The moving part of a relay or vibrator.

ATTENUATOR.-A network of resistors used to reduce voltage, current, or power delivered to a load.

AUTOTRANSFORMER.--A transformer in which the primary and secondary are connected together in one winding.

BATTERY.-- Two or more primary or secondary cells connected together electrically. The term does not apply to a single cell.

BREAKER POINTS.--Metal contacts that open and close a circuit at timed intervals.

BRIDGE CIRCUIT.--The electrical bridge circuit is a term referring to any one of a variety of electric circuit networks, one branch of which, the "bridge" proper, connects two points of equal potential and hence carries no current when the circuit is properly adjusted or balanced.

BRUSH.--The conducting material, usually a block of carbon, bearing against the commutator or sliprings through which the current flows in or out.

BUS BAR.--A primary power distribution point connected to the main power source.

CAPACITOR.--Two electrodes or sets of electrodes in the form of plates, separated from each other by an insulating material called the dielectric.

CHOKE COIL.--A coil of low ohmic resistance and high impedance to alternating current.

CIRCUIT.--The complete path of an electric current.

CIRCUIT BREAKER.--An electromagnetic or thermal device that opens a circuit when the current in the circuit exceeds a predetermined amount. Circuit breakers can be reset.

CIRCULAR MIL.--An area equal to that of a circle with a diameter of 0.001 inch. It is used for measuring the cross section of wires.

COAXIAL CABLE.--A transmission line consisting of two conductors concentric with and insulated from each other.

COMMUTATOR.-- The copper segments on the armature of a motor or generator. It is cylindrical in shape and is used to pass power into or from the brushes. It is a switching device.

CONDUCTANCE.-- The ability of a material to conduct or carry an electric current. It is the reciprocal of the resistance of the material, and is expressed in mhos.

CONDUCTIVITY.-- The ease with which a substance transmits electricity.

CONDUCTOR.--Any material suitable for carrying electric current.

CORE.--A magnetic material that affords an easy path for magnetic flux lines in a coil.

COUNTER E.M.F.--Counter electromotive force; an e.m.f. induced in a coil or armature that opposes the applied voltage.

CURRENT LIMITER.--A protective device similar to a fuse, usually used in high amperage circuits.

CYCLE.--One complete positive and one complete negative alternation of a current or voltage.

DIELECTRIC.--An insulator; a term that refers to the insulating material between the plates of a capacitor.

DIODE.—Vacuum tube—a two element tube that contains a cathode and plate; semiconductor —a material of either germanium or silicon that is manufactured to allow current to flow in only one direction. Diodes are used as rectifiers and detectors.

DIRECT CURRENT.—An electric current that flows in one direction only.

EDDY CURRENT.—Induced circulating currents in a conducting material that are caused by a varying magnetic field.

EFFICIENCY.—The ratio of output power to input power, generally expressed as a percentage.

ELECTROLYTE.—A solution of a substance which is capable of conducting electricity. An electrolyte may be in the form of either a liquid or a paste.

ELECTROMAGNET.—A magnet made by passing current through a coil of wire wound on a soft iron core.

ELECTROMOTIVE FORCE (e.m.f.).—The force that produces an electric current in a circuit.

ELECTRON.—A negatively charged particle of matter.

ENERGY.—The ability or capacity to do work.

FARAD.—The unit of capacitance.

FEEDBACK.—A transfer of energy from the output circuit of a device back to its input.

FIELD.—The space containing electric or magnetic lines of force.

FIELD WINDING.—The coil used to provide the magnetizing force in motors and generators.

FLUX FIELD.—All electric or magnetic lines of force in a given region.

FREE ELECTRONS.—Electrons which are loosely held and consequently tend to move at random among the atoms of the material.

FREQUENCY.—The number of complete cycles per second existing in any form of wave motion; such as the number of cycles per second of an alternating current.

FULL-WAVE RECTIFIER CIRCUIT.—A circuit which utilizes both the positive and the negative alternations of an alternating current to produce a direct current.

FUSE.—A protective device inserted in series with a circuit. It contains a metal that will melt or break when current is increased beyond a specific value for a definite period of time.

GAIN.—The ratio of the output power, voltage, or current to the input power, voltage, or current, respectively.

GALVANOMETER.—An instrument used to measure small d-c currents.

GENERATOR.—A machine that converts mechanical energy into electrical energy.

GROUND.—A metallic connection with the earth to establish ground potential. Also, a common return to a point of zero potential. The chassis of a receiver or a transmitter is sometimes the common return, and therefore the ground of the unit.

HENRY.—The basic unit of inductance.

HORSEPOWER.—The English unit of power, equal to work done at the rate of 550 foot-pounds per second. Equal to 746 watts of electrical power.

HYSTERESIS.—A lagging of the magnetic flux in a magnetic material behind the magnetizing force which is producing it.

IMPEDANCE.—The total opposition offered to the flow of an alternating current. It may consist of any combination of resistance, inductive reactance, and capacitive reactance.

INDUCTANCE.—The property of a circuit which tends to oppose a change in the existing current.

INDUCTION.—The act or process of producing voltage by the relative motion of a magnetic field across a conductor.

INDUCTIVE REACTANCE.—The opposition to the flow of alternating or pulsating current caused by the inductance of a circuit. It is measured in ohms.

INPHASE.—Applied to the condition that exists when two waves of the same frequency pass through their maximum and minimum values of like polarity at the same instant.

INVERSELY.—Inverted or reversed in position or relationship.

ISOGONIC LINE.—An imaginary line drawn through points on the earth's surface where the magnetic deviation is equal.

JOULE.—A unit of energy or work. A joule of energy is liberated by one ampere flowing for one second through a resistance of one ohm.

KILO.—A prefix meaning 1,000.

LAG.—The amount one wave is behind another in time; expressed in electrical degrees.

LAMINATED CORE.—A core built up from thin sheets of metal and used in transformers and relays.

LEAD.—The opposite of LAG. Also, a wire or connection.

LINE OF FORCE.–A line in an electric or magnetic field that shows the direction of the force.

LOAD.–The power that is being delivered by any power producing device. The equipment that uses the power from the power producing device.

MAGNETIC AMPLIFIER.–A saturable reactor type device that is used in a circuit to amplify or control.

MAGNETIC CIRCUIT.–The complete path of magnetic lines of force.

MAGNETIC FIELD.–The space in which a magnetic force exists.

MAGNETIC FLUX.–The total number of lines of force issuing from a pole of a magnet.

MAGNETIZE.–To convert a material into a magnet by causing the molecules to rearrange.

MAGNETO.–A generator which produces alternating current and has a permanent magnet as its field.

MEGGER.–A test instrument used to measure insulation resistance and other high resistances. It is a portable hand operated d-c generator used as an ohmmeter.

MEGOHM.–A million ohms.

MICRO.–A prefix meaning one-millionth.

MILLI.–A prefix meaning one-thousandth.

MILLIAMMETER.–An ammeter that measures current in thousandths of an ampere.

MOTOR-GENERATOR.–A motor and a generator with a common shaft used to convert line voltages to other voltages or frequencies.

MUTUAL INDUCTANCE.–A circuit property existing when the relative position of two inductors causes the magnetic lines of force from one to link with the turns of the other.

NEGATIVE CHARGE.–The electrical charge carried by a body which has an excess of electrons.

NEUTRON.–A particle having the weight of a proton but carrying no electric charge. It is located in the nucleus of an atom.

NUCLEUS.–The central part of an atom that is mainly comprised of protons and neutrons. It is the part of the atom that has the most mass.

NULL.–Zero.

OHM.–The unit of electrical resistance.

OHMMETER.–An instrument for directly measuring resistance in ohms.

OVERLOAD.–A load greater than the rated load of an electrical device.

PERMALLOY.–An alloy of nickel and iron having an abnormally high magnetic permeability.

PERMEABILITY.–A measure of the ease with which magnetic lines of force can flow through a material as compared to air.

PHASE DIFFERENCE.–The time in electrical degrees by which one wave leads or lags another.

POLARITY.–The character of having magnetic poles, or electric charges.

POLE.–The section of a magnet where the flux lines are concentrated; also where they enter and leave the magnet. An electrode of a battery.

POLYPHASE.–A circuit that utilizes more than one phase of alternating current.

POSITIVE CHARGE.–The electrical charge carried by a body which has become deficient in electrons.

POTENTIAL.–The amount of charge held by a body as compared to another point or body. Usually measured in volts.

POTENTIOMETER.–A variable voltage divider; a resistor which has a variable contact arm so that any portion of the potential applied between its ends may be selected.

POWER.–The rate of doing work or the rate of expending energy. The unit of electrical power is the watt.

POWER FACTOR.–The ratio of the actual power of an alternating or pulsating current, as measured by a wattmeter, to the apparent power, as indicated by ammeter and voltmeter readings. The power factor of an inductor, capacitor, or insulator is an expression of their losses.

PRIME MOVER.–The source of mechanical power used to drive the rotor of a generator.

PROTON.–A positively charged particle in the nucleus of an atom.

RATIO.–The value obtained by dividing one number by another, indicating their relative proportions.

REACTANCE.–The opposition offered to the flow of an alternating current by the inductance, capacitance, or both, in any circuit.

RECTIFIERS.–Devices used to change alternating current to unidirectional current. These may be vacuum tubes, semiconductors such as germanium and silicon, and dry-disk rectifiers such as selenium and copper-oxide.

RELAY.–An electromechanical switching device that can be used as a remote control.

RELUCTANCE.–A measure of the opposition that a material offers to magnetic lines of force.

RESISTANCE.–The opposition to the flow of current caused by the nature and physical dimensions of a conductor.

RESISTOR.–A circuit element whose chief characteristic is resistance; used to oppose the flow of current.

RETENTIVITY.—The measure of the ability of a material to hold its magnetism.

RHEOSTAT.—A variable resistor.

SATURABLE REACTOR.—A control device that uses a small d-c current to control a large a-c current by controlling core flux density.

SATURATION.—The condition existing in any circuit when an increase in the driving signal produces no further change in the resultant effect.

SELF-INDUCTION.—The process by which a circuit induces an e.m.f. into itself by its own magnetic field.

SERIES-WOUND.—A motor or generator in which the armature is wired in series with the field winding.

SERVO.—A device used to convert a small movement into one of greater movement or force.

SERVOMECHANISM.—A closed-loop system that produces a force to position an object in accordance with the information that originates at the input.

SOLENOID.—An electromagnetic coil that contains a movable plunger.

SPACE CHARGE.—The cloud of electrons existing in the space between the cathode and plate in a vacuum tube, formed by the electrons emitted from the cathode in excess of those immediately attracted to the plate.

SPECIFIC GRAVITY—The ratio between the density of a substance and that of pure water, at a given temperature.

SYNCHROSCOPE—An instrument used to indicate a difference in frequency between two a-c sources.

SYNCHRO SYSTEM.—An electrical system that gives remote indications or control by means of self-synchronizing motors.

TACHOMETER.—An instrument for indicating revolutions per minute.

TERTIARY WINDING.—A third winding on a transformer or magnetic amplifier that is used as a second control winding.

THERMISTOR.—A resistor that is used to compensate for temperature variations in a circuit.

THERMOCOUPLE.—A junction of two dissimilar metals that produces a voltage when heated.

TORQUE.—The turning effort or twist which a shaft sustains when transmitting power.

TRANSFORMER.—A device composed of two or more coils, linked by magnetic lines of force, used to transfer energy from one circuit to another.

TRANSMISSION LINES.—Any conductor or system of conductors used to carry electrical energy from its source to a load.

VARS.—Abbreviation for volt-ampere, reactive.

VECTOR.—A line used to represent both direction and magnitude.

VOLT.—The unit of electrical potential.

VOLTMETER.—An instrument designed to measure a difference in electrical potential, in volts.

WATT.—The unit of electrical power.

WATTMETER.—An instrument for measuring electrical power in watts.

Formulas

Ohm's Law for d-c Circuits

$$I = \frac{E}{R} = \frac{P}{E} = \sqrt{\frac{P}{R}}$$

$$R = \frac{E}{I} = \frac{P}{I^2} = \frac{E^2}{P}$$

$$E = IR = \frac{P}{I} = \sqrt{PR}$$

$$P = EI = \frac{E^2}{R} = I^2 R$$

Resistors in Series

$$R_T = R_1 + R_2 \ldots$$

Resistors in Parallel
Two resistors

$$R_T = \frac{R_1 R_2}{R_1 + R_2}$$

More than two

$$\frac{1}{R_T} = \frac{1}{R_1} + \frac{1}{R_2} + \frac{1}{R_3}$$

R-L Circuit Time Constant equals

$$\frac{L \text{ (in henrys)}}{R \text{ (in ohms)}} = t \text{ (in seconds), or}$$

$$\frac{L \text{ (in microhenrys)}}{R \text{ (in ohms)}} = t \text{ (in microseconds)}$$

R-C Circuit Time Constants equals

R (ohms) X C (farads) = t (seconds)

R (megohms) x C (microfarads) = t (seconds)

R (ohms) x C (microfarads) = t (microseconds)

R (megohms) x C (micromicrofrads = t (microseconds)

Comparison of Units in Electric and Magnetic Circuits.

	Electric circuit	Magnetic circuit
Force	Volt, E or e.m.f.	Gilberts, F, or m.m.f.
Flow	Ampere, I	Flux, Φ, in maxwells
Opposition	Ohms, R	Reluctance, R
Law	Ohm's law, $I = \frac{E}{R}$	Rowland's law $\Phi = \frac{F}{R}$
Intensity of force	Volts per cm. of length	$H = \frac{1.257IN}{L}$, gilberts per centimeter of length
Density	Current density— for example, amperes per cm^2.	Flux density—for example, lines per cm^2., or gausses

Capacitors in Series

Two capacitors

$$C_T = \frac{C_1 C_2}{C_1 + C_2}$$

More than two

$$\frac{1}{C_T} = \frac{1}{C_1} + \frac{1}{C_2} + \frac{1}{C_3} \cdots$$

Capacitors in Parallel

$$C_T = C_1 + C_2 \cdots$$

Capacitive Reactance

$$X_c = \frac{1}{2\pi fC}$$

Impedance in an R-C Circuit (Series)

$$Z = \sqrt{R^2 + X_c^2}$$

Inductors in Series

$$L_T = L_1 + L_2 \ldots \text{ (No coupling between coils)}$$

Inductors in Parallel

Two inductors

$$L_T = \frac{L_1 L_2}{L_1 + L_2} \text{ (No coupling between coils)}$$

More than two

$$\frac{1}{L_T} = \frac{1}{L_1} + \frac{1}{L_2} + \frac{1}{L_3} \ldots \text{ (No coupling between coils)}$$

Inductive Reactance

$$X_L = 2\pi fL$$

Q of a Coil

$$Q = \frac{X_L}{R}$$

Impedance of an R-L Circuit (series)

$$Z = \sqrt{R^2 + X_L^2}$$

Impedance with R, C, and L in Series

$$Z = \sqrt{R^2 + (X_L - X_C)^2}$$

Parallel Circuit Impedance

$$Z = \frac{Z_1 Z_2}{Z_1 + Z_2}$$

Sine-Wave Voltage Relationships

Average value

$$E_{ave} = \frac{2}{\pi} \times E_{max} = 0.637 E_{max}$$

Effective or r.m.s. value

$$E_{eff} = \frac{E_{max}}{\sqrt{2}} = \frac{E_{max}}{1.414} = 0.707 E_{max} = 1.11 E_{ave}$$

Maximum value

$$E_{max} = \sqrt{2} E_{eff} = 1.414 E_{eff} = 1.57 E_{ave}$$

Voltage in an a-c circuit

$$E = IZ = \frac{P}{I \times P.F.}$$

Current in an a-c circuit

$$I = \frac{E}{Z} = \frac{P}{E \times P.F.}$$

Power in A-C Circuit
Apparent power = EI
True power

$$P = EI \cos \theta = EI \times P.F.$$

Power factor

$$P.F. = \frac{P}{EI} = \cos \theta$$

$$\cos \theta = \frac{\text{true power}}{\text{apparent power}}$$

Transformers
Voltage relationship

$$\frac{E}{E} = \frac{N}{N} \text{ or } E = E \times \frac{N}{N}$$

Current relationship

$$\frac{I_p}{I_s} = \frac{N_s}{N_p}$$

Induced voltage

$$E_{eff} = 4.44 \, BA f N 10^{-8}$$

Turns ratio equals

$$\frac{N_p}{N_s} = \sqrt{\frac{Z_p}{Z_s}}$$

Secondary current

$$I_s = I_p \frac{N_p}{N_s}$$

Secondary voltage

$$E_s = E_p \frac{N_s}{N_p}$$

Three Phase Voltage and Current Relationships
With wye connected windings

$$E_{line} = 1.732 E_{coil} = \sqrt{3} E_{coil}$$

$$I_{line} = I_{coil}$$

With delta connected windings

$$E_{line} = E_{coil}$$

$$I_{line} = 1.732 I_{coil}$$

With wye or delta connected winding

$$P_{coil} = E_{coil} I_{coil}$$

$$P_t = 3 P_{coil}$$

$$P_t = 1.732 E_{line} I_{line}$$

(To convert to true power multiply by $\cos \theta$)

Synchronous Speed of Motor

$$\text{r.p.m.} = \frac{120 \times \text{frequency}}{\text{number of poles}}$$

APPENDIX VI
TRIGONOMETRIC FUNCTIONS

In a right triangle, there are several relationships which always hold true. These relationships pertain to the length of the sides of a right triangle, and the way the lengths are affected by the angles between them. An understanding of these relationships, called trigonometric functions, is essential for solving many problems in a-c circuits such as power factor, impedance, voltage drops, and so forth.

To be a RIGHT triangle, a triangle must have a "square" corner; one in which there is exactly 90° between two of the sides. Trigonometric functions do not apply to any other type of triangle. This type of triangle is shown in figure VI-1.

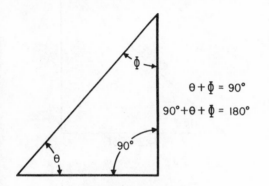

$$\theta + \Phi = 90°$$
$$90° + \theta + \Phi = 180°$$

Figure VI-1.—A right triangle.

By use of the trigonometric functions, it is possible to determine the UNKNOWN length of one or more sides of a triangle, or the number of degrees in UNKNOWN angles, depending on what is presently known about the triangle. For instance, if the lengths of any two sides are known, the third side and both angles θ (theta) and Φ (phi) may be determined. The triangle may also be solved if the length of any one side and one of the angles (θ or Φ in fig. VI-I) are known.

The first basic fact to accept, regarding triangles, is that IN ANY TRIANGLE, THE SUM OF THE THREE ANGLES FORMED INSIDE THE TRIANGLE MUST ALWAYS EQUAL 180°. If one angle is always 90° (a right angle) then the sum of the other two angles must always be 90°.

$$\theta + \Phi = 90°$$
and
$$90° + \theta + \Phi = 180°$$
or
$$90° + 90° = 180°$$

thus, if angle θ is known, Φ may be quickly determined.

For instance, if θ is 30°, what is Φ ?

$$90° + 30° + \Phi = 180°$$
Transposing $\quad \Phi = 180° - 90° - 30°$
$$\Phi = 60°$$

Also, if Φ is known, θ may be determined in the same manner.

The second basic fact you must understand is that FOR EVERY DIFFERENT COMBINATION OF ANGLES IN A TRIANGLE, THERE IS A DEFINITE RATIO BETWEEN THE LENGTHS OF THE THREE SIDES. Consider the triangle in figure VI-2, consisting of the base, side B; the altitude, side A; and the hypotenuse, side C. (The hypotenuse is always the longest side, and is always opposite the 90° angle.) If angle θ is 30°, Φ must be 60°. With θ equal to 30°, the ratio of the length of side B to side C is 0.866 to 1. That is, if the hypotenuse is 1 inch long, the side adjacent to θ, side B, is 0.866 inch long. Also, with θ equal to 30°, the ratio of side A to side C is 0.5 to 1. That is, with the hypotenuse 1 inch long, the side opposite to θ (side A) is 0.5 inch long. With θ still at 30°, side A is 0.5774 of the length of B. With the combination of angles given (30° - 60° - 90°) these are the ONLY ratios of lengths that will "fit" to form a right triangle.

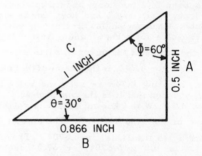

Figure VI-2.—A 30° - 60° - 90° triangle.

Note that three ratios are shown to exist for the given value of θ : the ratio $\frac{B}{C}$, which is always referred to as the COSINE (ratio of θ, the ratio $\frac{A}{C}$, which is always the SINE ratio of θ, and the ratio $\frac{A}{B}$, which is always the TANGENT ratio of θ. If θ changes, all three ratios change, because the lengths of the sides (base and altitude) change. There is a set of ratios for every increment between 0° and 90°. These angular ratios, or sine, cosine, and tangent functions, are listed for each degree and tenth of degree in a table at the end of this appendix. In this table, the length of the hypotenuse of a triangle is considered fixed. Thus, the ratios of length given refer to the manner in which sides A and B vary with relation to each other and in relation to side C, as angle θ is varied from 0° to 90°.

The solution of problems in trigonometry (solution of triangles) is much simpler when the table of trigonometric functions is used properly. The most common ways in which it is used will be shown by solving a series of exemplary

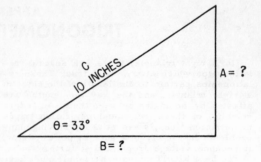

Problem 1: If the hypotenuse of the triangle (side C) in figure VI-3(A) is 10 inches long, and angle θ is 33°, how long are sides B and A?

Solution: The ratio $\frac{B}{C}$ is the cosine function. By checking the table of functions, you will find that the cosine of 33° is 0.8387. This means that the length of B is 0.8387 the length of side C. If side C is 10 inches long, then side B must be 10 x 0.8387, or 8.387 inches in length. To determine the length of side A, use the sine function, the ratio $\frac{A}{C}$. Again consulting the table of functions, you will find that the sine of 33° is 0.5446. Thus, side A must be 10 x 0.5446, or 5.446 inches in length.

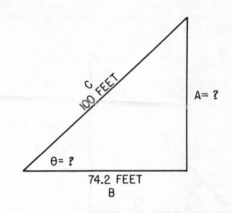

Problem 2: The triangle in figure VI-3 (B) has a base 74.2 feet long, and a hypotenuse 100 feet long. What is θ , and how long is side A? Solution: When no angles are given, you must always solve for a known angle first. The ratio $\frac{B}{C}$ is the cosine of the unknown angle θ ; therefore $\frac{74.2}{100}$, or 0.742, is the cosine of the unknown angle. Locating 0.742 as a cosine value in the table, you find that it is the cosine of 42.1°. That is, θ= 42.1°. With θ known, side A is solved for by use of the sine ratio $\frac{A}{C}$. The sine of 42.1°, according to the table, is 0.6704. Therefore, side A is 100 x 0.6704, or 67.04 feet long.

Problem 3: In the triangle in figure VI-3 (C), the base is 3 units long, and the altitude is 4 units. What is θ , and how long is the hypotenuse? Solution: With the information given, the tangent of θ may be determined. Tan θ = $\frac{A}{B}$ = $\frac{4}{3}$ = 1.33

Locating the value 1.33 as a tangent value in the table of functions, you find it to be the tangent of 53.2° . Therefore, θ = 53.2°. Once θ is known, either the sine or cosine ratio may be used to determine the length of the hypotenuse. The cosine of 53.2° is 0.6004. This indicates that the

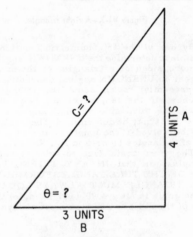

Figure VI-3.—Trigonometric problems.

base of 3 units is 0.6004, the length of the hypotenuse. Therefore, the hypotenuse is $\dfrac{3}{0.6004}$, or 5 units in length. Using the sine ratio, the hypot- is $\dfrac{4}{0.7997}$, or 5 units in length.

In the foregoing explanations and problems, the sides of triangles were given in inches, feet, and units. In applying trigonometry to a-c circuit problems, these units of measure will be replaced by such measurements as ohms, amperes, volts, and watts. Angle θ will often be referred to as the phase angle. However, the solution of these a-c problems is accomplished in exactly the same manner as the foregoing problems. Only the units and some terminology are changed.

NATURAL SINES, COSINES, AND TANGENTS

0° - 14.9°

Degs.	Function	0.0°	0.1°	0.2°	0.3°	0.4°	0.5°	0.6°	0.7°	0.8°	0.9°
0	sin	0.0000	0.0017	0.0035	0.0052	0.0070	0.0087	0.0105	0.0122	0.0140	0.0157
	cos	1.0000	1.0000	1.0000	1.0000	1.0000	1.0000	0.9999	0.9999	0.9999	0.9999
	tan	0.0000	0.0017	0.0035	0.0052	0.0070	0.0087	0.0105	0.0122	0.0140	0.0157
1	sin	0.0175	0.0192	0.0209	0.0227	0.0244	0.0262	0.0279	0.0297	0.0314	0.0332
	cos	0.9998	0.9998	0.9998	0.9997	0.9997	0.9997	0.9996	0.9996	0.9995	0.9995
	tan	0.0175	0.0192	0.0209	0.0227	0.0244	0.0262	0.0279	0.0297	0.0314	0.0332
2	sin	0.0349	0.0366	0.0384	0.0401	0.0419	0.0436	0.0454	0.0471	0.0488	0.0506
	cos	0.9994	0.9993	0.9993	0.9992	0.9991	0.9990	0.9990	0.9989	0.9988	0.9987
	tan	0.0349	0.0367	0.0384	0.0402	0.0419	0.0437	0.0454	0.0472	0.0489	0.0507
3	sin	0.0523	0.0541	0.0558	0.0576	0.0593	0.0610	0.0628	0.0645	0.0663	0.0680
	cos	0.9986	0.9985	0.9984	0.9983	0.9982	0.9981	0.9980	0.9979	0.9978	0.9977
	tan	0.0524	0.0542	0.0559	0.0577	0.0594	0.0612	0.0629	0.0647	0.0664	0.0682
4	sin	0.0698	0.0715	0.0732	0.0750	0.0767	0.0785	0.0802	0.0819	0.0837	0.0854
	cos	0.9976	0.9974	0.9973	0.9972	0.9971	0.9969	0.9968	0.9966	0.9965	0.9963
	tan	0.0699	0.0717	0.0734	0.0752	0.0769	0.0787	0.0805	0.0822	0.0840	0.0857
5	sin	0.0872	0.0889	0.0906	0.0924	0.0941	0.0958	0.0976	0.0993	0.1011	0.1028
	cos	0.9962	0.9960	0.9959	0.9957	0.9956	0.9954	0.9952	0.9951	0.9949	0.9947
	tan	0.0875	0.0802	0.0910	0.0928	0.0945	0.0963	0.0981	0.0998	0.1016	0.1033
6	sin	0.1045	0.1063	0.1080	0.1097	0.1115	0.1132	0.1149	0.1167	0.1184	0.1201
	cos	0.9945	0.9943	0.9942	0.9940	0.9938	0.9936	0.9934	0.9932	0.9930	0.9928
	tan	0.1051	0.1069	0.1086	0.1104	0.1122	0.1139	0.1157	0.1175	0.1192	0.1210
7	sin	0.1219	0.1236	0.1253	0.1271	0.1288	0.1305	0.1323	0.1340	0.1357	0.1374
	cos	0.9925	0.9923	0.9921	0.9919	0.9917	0.9914	0.9912	0.9910	0.9907	0.9905
	tan	0.1228	0.1246	0.1263	0.1281	0.1299	0.1317	0.1334	0.1352	0.1370	0.1388
8	sin	0.1392	0.1409	0.1426	0.1444	0.1461	0.1478	0.1495	0.1513	0.1530	0.1547
	cos	0.9903	0.9900	0.9898	0.9895	0.9893	0.9890	0.9888	0.9885	0.9882	0.9880
	tan	0.1405	0.1423	0.1441	0.1459	0.1477	0.1495	0.1512	0.1530	0.1548	0.1566
9	sin	0.1564	0.1582	0.1599	0.1616	0.1633	0.1650	0.1668	0.1685	0.1702	0.1719
	cos	0.9877	0.9874	0.9871	0.9869	0.9866	0.9863	0.9860	0.9857	0.9854	0.9851
	tan	0.1584	0.1602	0.1620	0.1638	0.1655	0.1673	0.1691	0.1709	0.1727	0.1745
10	sin	0.1736	0.1754	0.1771	0.1788	0.1805	0.1822	0.1840	0.1857	0.1874	0.1891
	cos	0.9848	0.9845	0.9842	0.9839	0.9836	0.9833	0.9829	0.9826	0.9823	0.9820
	tan	0.1763	0.1781	0.1799	0.1817	0.1835	0.1853	0.1871	0.1890	0.1908	0.1926
11	sin	0.1908	0.1925	0.1942	0.1959	0.1977	0.1994	0.2011	0.2028	0.2045	0.2062
	cos	0.9816	0.9813	0.9810	0.9806	0.9803	0.9799	0.9796	0.9792	0.9789	0.9785
	tan	0.1944	0.1962	0.1980	0.1998	0.2016	0.2035	0.2053	0.2071	0.2089	0.2107
12	sin	0.2079	0.2096	0.2113	0.2130	0.2147	0.2164	0.2181	0.2198	0.2215	0.2232
	cos	0.9781	0.9778	0.9774	0.9770	0.9767	0.9763	0.9759	0.9755	0.9751	0.9748
	tan	0.2126	0.2144	0.2162	0.2180	0.2199	0.2217	0.2235	0.2254	0.2272	0.2290
13	sin	0.2250	0.2267	0.2284	0.2300	0.2318	0.2334	0.2351	0.2368	0.2385	0.2402
	cos	0.9744	0.9740	0.9736	0.9732	0.9728	0.9724	0.9720	0.9715	0.9711	0.9707
	tan	0.2309	0.2327	0.2345	0.2364	0.2382	0.2401	0.2419	0.2438	0.2456	0.2475
14	sin	0.2419	0.2436	0.2453	0.2470	0.2487	0.2504	0.2521	0.2538	0.2554	0.2571
	cos	0.9703	0.9699	0.9694	0.9690	0.9686	0.9681	0.9677	0.9673	0.9668	0.9664
	tan	0.2493	0.2512	0.2530	0.2549	0.2568	0.2586	0.2605	0.2623	0.2642	0.2661
Degs.	Function	0′	6′	12′	18′	24′	30′	36′	42′	48′	54′

NATURAL SINES, COSINES, AND TANGENTS

15° - 29.9°

Degs.	Function	0.0°	0.1°	0.2°	0.3°	0.4°	0.5°	0.6°	0.7°	0.8°	0.9°
15	sin	0.2588	0.2605	0.2622	0.2639	0.2656	0.2672	0.2689	0.2706	0.2723	0.2740
	cos	0.9659	0.9655	0.9650	0.9646	0.9641	0.9636	0.9632	0.9627	0.9622	0.9617
	tan	0.2679	0.2698	0.2717	0.2736	0.2754	0.2773	0.2792	0.2811	0.2830	0.2849
16	sin	0.2756	0.2773	0.2790	0.2807	0.2823	0.2840	0.2857	0.2874	0.2890	0.2907
	cos	0.9613	0.9608	0.9603	0.9598	0.9593	0.9588	0.9583	0.9578	0.9573	0.9568
	tan	0.2867	0.2886	0.2905	0.2924	0.2943	0.2962	0.2981	0.3000	0.3019	0.3038
17	sin	0.2924	0.2940	0.2957	0.2974	0.2990	0.3007	0.3024	0.3040	0.3057	0.3074
	cos	0.9563	0.9558	0.9553	0.9548	0.9542	0.9537	0.9532	0.9527	0.9521	0.9516
	tan	0.3057	0.3076	0.3096	0.3115	0.3134	0.3153	0.3172	0.3191	0.3211	0.3230
18	sin	0.3090	0.3107	0.3123	0.3140	0.3156	0.3173	0.3190	0.3206	0.3223	0.3239
	cos	0.9511	0.9505	0.9500	0.9494	0.9489	0.9483	0.9478	0.9472	0.9466	0.9461
	tan	0.3249	0.3269	0.3288	0.3307	0.3327	0.3346	0.3365	0.3385	0.3404	0.3424
19	sin	0.3256	0.3272	0.3289	0.3305	0.3322	0.3338	0.3355	0.3371	0.3387	0.3404
	cos	0.9455	0.9449	0.9444	0.9438	0.9432	0.9426	0.9421	0.9415	0.9409	0.9403
	tan	0.3443	0.3463	0.3482	0.3502	0.3522	0.3541	0.3561	0.3581	0.3600	0.3620
20	sin	0.3420	0.3437	0.3453	0.3469	0.3486	0.3502	0.3518	0.3535	0.3551	0.3567
	cos	0.9397	0.9391	0.9385	0.9379	0.9373	0.9367	0.9361	0.9354	0.9348	0.9342
	tan	0.3640	0.3659	0.3679	0.3699	0.3719	0.3739	0.3750	0.3779	0.3799	0.3819
21	sin	0.3584	0.3600	0.3616	0.3633	0.3649	0.3665	0.3681	0.3697	0.3714	0.3730
	cos	0.9336	0.9330	0.9323	0.9317	0.9311	0.9304	0.9298	0.9291	0.9285	0.9278
	tan	0.3839	0.3859	0.3879	0.3899	0.3919	0.3939	0.3959	0.3979	0.4000	0.4020
22	sin	0.3746	0.3762	0.3778	0.3795	0.3811	0.3827	0.3843	0.3859	0.3875	0.3891
	cos	0.9272	0.9265	0.9259	0.9252	0.9245	0.9239	0.9232	0.9225	0.9219	0.9212
	tan	0.4040	0.4061	0.4081	0.4101	0.4122	0.4142	0.4163	0.4183	0.4204	0.4224
23	sin	0.3907	0.3923	0.3939	0.3955	0.3971	0.3987	0.4003	0.4019	0.4035	0.4051
	cos	0.9205	0.9198	0.9191	0.9184	0.9178	0.9171	0.9164	0.9157	0.9150	0.9143
	tan	0.4245	0.4265	0.4286	0.4307	0.4327	0.4348	0.4369	0.4390	0.4411	0.4431
24	sin	0.4067	0.4083	0.4099	0.4115	0.4131	0.4147	0.4163	0.4179	0.4195	0.4210
	cos	0.9135	0.9128	0.9121	0.9114	0.9107	0.9100	0.9092	0.9085	0.9078	0.9070
	tan	0.4452	0.4473	0.4494	0.4515	0.4536	0.4557	0.4578	0.4599	0.4621	0.4642
25	sin	0.4226	0.4242	0.4258	0.4274	0.4289	0.4305	0.4321	0.4337	0.4352	0.4368
	cos	0.9063	0.9056	0.9048	0.9041	0.9033	0.9026	0.9018	0.9011	0.9003	0.8996
	tan	0.4663	0.4684	0.4706	0.4727	0.4748	0.4770	0.4791	0.4813	0.4834	0.4856
26	sin	0.4384	0.4399	0.4415	0.4431	0.4446	0.4462	0.4478	0.4493	0.4509	0.4524
	cos	0.8988	0.8980	0.8973	0.8965	0.8957	0.8949	0.8942	0.8934	0.8926	0.8918
	tan	0.4877	0.4899	0.4921	0.4942	0.4964	0.4986	0.5008	0.5029	0.5051	0.5073
27	sin	0.4540	0.4555	0.4571	0.4586	0.4602	0.4617	0.4633	0.4648	0.4664	0.4679
	cos	0.8910	0.8902	0.8894	0.8886	0.8878	0.8870	0.8862	0.8854	0.8846	0.8838
	tan	0.5095	0.5117	0.5139	0.5161	0.5184	0.5206	0.5228	0.5250	0.5272	0.5295
28	sin	0.4695	0.4710	0.4726	0.4741	0.4756	0.4772	0.4787	0.4802	0.4818	0.4833
	cos	0.8829	0.8821	0.8813	0.8805	0.8796	0.8788	0.8780	0.8771	0.8763	0.8755
	tan	0.5317	0.5340	0.5362	0.5384	0.5407	0.5430	0.5452	0.5475	0.5498	0.5520
29	sin	0.4848	0.4863	0.4879	0.4894	0.4909	0.4924	0.4939	0.4955	0.4970	0.4983
	cos	0.8746	0.8738	0.8729	0.8721	0.8712	0.8704	0.8695	0.8686	0.8678	0.8669
	tan	0.5543	0.5566	0.5589	0.5612	0.5635	0.5658	0.5681	0.5704	0.5727	0.5750
Degs.	Function	0′	6′	12′	18′	24′	30′	36′	42′	48′	54′

NATURAL SINES, COSINES, AND TANGENTS

30° - 44.9°

Degs.	Function	0.0°	0.1°	0.2°	0.3°	0.4°	0.5°	0.6°	0.7°	0.8°	0.9°
30	sin	0.5000	0.5015	0.5030	0.5045	0.5060	0.5075	0.5090	0.5105	0.5120	0.5135
	cos	0.8660	0.8652	0.8643	0.8634	0.8625	0.8616	0.8607	0.8599	0.8590	0.8581
	tan	0.5774	0.5797	0.5820	0.5844	0.5867	0.5890	0.5914	0.5938	0.5961	0.5985
31	sin	0.5150	0.5165	0.5180	0.5195	0.5210	0.5225	0.5240	0.5255	0.5270	0.5284
	cos	0.8572	0.8563	0.8554	0.8545	0.8536	0.8526	0.8517	0.8508	0.8499	0.8490
	tan	0.6009	0.6032	0.6056	0.6080	0.6104	0.6128	0.6152	0.6176	0.6200	0.6224
32	sin	0.5299	0.5314	0.5329	0.5344	0.5358	0.5373	0.5388	0.5402	0.5417	0.5432
	cos	0.8480	0.8471	0.8462	0.8453	0.8443	0.8434	0.8425	0.8415	0.8406	0.8396
	tan	0.6249	0.6273	0.6297	0.6322	0.6346	0.6371	0.6395	0.6420	0.6445	0.6469
33	sin	0.5446	0.5461	0.5476	0.5490	0.5505	0.5519	0.5534	0.5548	0.5563	0.5577
	cos	0.8387	0.8377	0.8368	0.8358	0.8348	0.8339	0.8329	0.8320	0.8310	0.8300
	tan	0.6494	0.6519	0.6544	0.6569	0.6594	0.6619	0.6644	0.6669	0.6694	0.6720
34	sin	0.5592	0.5606	0.5621	0.5635	0.5650	0.5664	0.5678	0.5693	0.5707	0.5721
	cos	0.8290	0.8281	0.8271	0.8261	0.8251	0.8241	0.8231	0.8221	0.8211	0.8202
	tan	0.6745	0.6771	0.6796	0.6822	0.6847	0.6873	0.6899	0.6924	0.6950	0.6976
35	sin	0.5736	0.5750	0.5764	0.5779	0.5793	0.5807	0.5821	0.5835	0.5850	0.5864
	cos	0.8192	0.8181	0.8171	0.8161	0.8151	0.8141	0.8131	0.8121	0.8111	0.8100
	tan	0.7002	0.7028	0.7054	0.7080	0.7107	0.7133	0.7159	0.7186	0.7212	0.7239
36	sin	0.5878	0.5892	0.5906	0.5920	0.5934	0.5948	0.5962	0.5976	0.5990	0.6004
	cos	0.8090	0.8080	0.8070	0.8059	0.8049	0.8039	0.8028	0.8018	0.8007	0.7997
	tan	0.7265	0.7292	0.7319	0.7346	0.7373	0.7400	0.7427	0.7454	0.7481	0.7508
37	sin	0.6018	0.6032	0.6046	0.6060	0.6074	0.6088	0.6101	0.6115	0.6129	0.6143
	cos	0.7986	0.7976	0.7965	0.7955	0.7944	0.7934	0.7923	0.7912	0.7902	0.7891
	tan	0.7536	0.7563	0.7590	0.7618	0.7646	0.7673	0.7701	0.7729	0.7757	0.7785
38	sin	0.6157	0.6170	0.6184	0.6198	0.6211	0.6225	0.6239	0.6252	0.6266	0.6280
	cos	0.7880	0.7869	0.7859	0.7848	0.7837	0.7826	0.7815	0.7804	0.7793	0.7782
	tan	0.7813	0.7841	0.7869	0.7898	0.7926	0.7954	0.7983	0.8012	0.8040	0.8069
39	sin	0.6293	0.6307	0.6320	0.6334	0.6347	0.6361	0.6374	0.6388	0.6401	0.6414
	cos	0.7771	0.7760	0.7749	0.7738	0.7727	0.7716	0.7705	0.7694	0.7683	0.7672
	tan	0.8098	0.8127	0.8156	0.8185	0.8214	0.8243	0.8273	0.8302	0.8332	0.8361
40	sin	0.6428	0.6441	0.6455	0.6468	0.6481	0.6494	0.6508	0.6521	0.6534	0.6547
	cos	0.7660	0.7649	0.7638	0.7627	0.7615	0.7604	0.7593	0.7581	0.7570	0.7559
	tan	0.8391	0.8421	0.8451	0.8481	0.8511	0.8541	0.8571	0.8601	0.8632	0.8662
41	sin	0.6561	0.6574	0.6587	0.6600	0.6613	0.6626	0.6639	0.6652	0.6665	0.6678
	cos	0.7547	0.7536	0.7524	0.7513	0.7501	0.7490	0.7478	0.7466	0.7455	0.7443
	tan	0.8693	0.8724	0.8754	0.8785	0.8816	0.8847	0.8878	0.8910	0.8941	0.8972
42	sin	0.6691	0.6704	0.6717	0.6730	0.6743	0.6756	0.6769	0.6782	0.6794	0.6807
	cos	0.7431	0.7420	0.7408	0.7396	0.7385	0.7373	0.7361	0.7349	0.7337	0.7325
	tan	0.9004	0.9036	0.9067	0.9099	0.9131	0.9163	0.9195	0.9228	0.9260	0.9293
43	sin	0.6820	0.6833	0.6845	0.6858	0.6871	0.6884	0.6896	0.6909	0.6921	0.6934
	cos	0.7314	0.7302	0.7290	0.7278	0.7266	0.7254	0.7242	0.7230	0.7218	0.7206
	tan	0.9325	0.9358	0.9391	0.9424	0.9457	0.9490	0.9523	0.9556	0.9590	0.9623
44	sin	0.6947	0.6959	0.6972	0.6984	0.6997	0.7009	0.7022	0.7034	0.7046	0.7059
	cos	0.7193	0.7181	0.7169	0.7157	0.7145	0.7133	0.7120	0.7108	0.7096	0.7083
	tan	0.9657	0.9691	0.9725	0.9759	0.9793	0.9827	0.9861	0.9896	0.9930	0.9965
Degs.	Function	0′	6′	12′	18′	24′	30′	36′	42′	48′	54′

NATURAL SINES, COSINES, AND TANGENTS

45° - 59.9°

Degs.	Function	0.0°	0.1°	0.2°	0.3°	0.4°	0.5°	0.6°	0.7°	0.8°	0.9°
45	sin	0.7071	0.7083	0.7096	0.7108	0.7120	0.7133	0.7145	0.7157	0.7169	0.7181
	cos	0.7071	0.7059	0.7046	0.7034	0.7022	0.7009	0.6997	0.6984	0.6972	0.6959
	tan	1.0000	1.0035	1.0070	1.0105	1.0141	1.0176	1.0212	1.0247	1.0283	1.0319
46	sin	0.7193	0.7206	0.7218	0.7230	0.7242	0.7254	0.7266	0.7278	0.7290	0.7302
	cos	0.6947	0.6934	0.6921	0.6909	0.6896	0.6884	0.6871	0.6858	0.6845	0.6833
	tan	1.0355	1.0392	1.0428	1.0464	1.0501	1.0538	1.0575	1.0612	1.0649	1.0686
47	sin	0.7314	0.7325	0.7337	0.7349	0.7361	0.7373	0.7385	0.7396	0.7408	0.7420
	cos	0.6820	0.6807	0.6794	0.6782	0.6769	0.6756	0.6743	0.6730	0.6717	0.6704
	tan	1.0724	1.0761	1.0799	1.0837	1.0875	1.0913	1.0951	1.0990	1.1028	1.1067
48	sin	0.7431	0.7443	0.7455	0.7466	0.7478	0.7490	0.7501	0.7513	0.7524	0.7536
	cos	0.6691	0.6678	0.6665	0.6652	0.6639	0.6626	0.6613	0.6600	0.6587	0.6574
	tan	1.1106	1.1145	1.1184	1.1224	1.1263	1.1303	1.1343	1.1383	1.1423	1.1463
49	sin	0.7547	0.7559	0.7570	0.7581	0.7593	0.7604	0.7615	0.7627	0.7638	0.7649
	cos	0.6561	0.6547	0.6534	0.6521	0.6508	0.6494	0.6481	0.6468	0.6455	0.6441
	tan	1.1504	1.1544	1.1585	1.1626	1.1667	1.1708	1.1750	1.1792	1.1833	1.1875
50	sin	0.7660	0.7672	0.7683	0.7694	0.7705	0.7716	0.7727	0.7738	0.7749	0.7760
	cos	0.6428	0.6414	0.6401	0.6388	0.6374	0.6361	0.6347	0.6334	0.6320	0.6307
	tan	1.1918	1.1960	1.2002	1.2045	1.2088	1.2131	1.2174	1.2218	1.2261	1.2305
51	sin	0.7771	0.7782	0.7793	0.7804	0.7815	0.7826	0.7837	0.7848	0.7859	0.7869
	cos	0.6293	0.6280	0.6266	0.6252	0.6239	0.6225	0.6211	0.6198	0.6184	0.6170
	tan	1.2349	1.2393	1.2437	1.2482	1.2527	1.2572	1.2617	1.2662	1.2708	1.2753
52	sin	0.7880	0.7891	0.7902	0.7912	0.7923	0.7934	0.7944	0.7955	0.7965	0.7976
	cos	0.6157	0.6143	0.6129	0.6115	0.6101	0.6088	0.6074	0.6060	0.6046	0.6032
	tan	1.2799	1.2846	1.2892	1.2938	1.2985	1.3032	1.3079	1.3127	1.3175	1.3222
53	sin	0.7986	0.7997	0.8007	0.8018	0.8028	0.8039	0.8049	0.8059	0.8070	0.8080
	cos	0.6018	0.6004	0.5990	0.5976	0.5962	0.5948	0.5934	0.5920	0.5906	0.5892
	tan	1.3270	1.3319	1.3367	1.3416	1.3465	1.3514	1.3564	1.3613	1.3663	1.3713
54	sin	0.8090	0.8100	0.8111	0.8121	0.8131	0.8141	0.8151	0.8161	0.8171	0.8181
	cos	0.5878	0.5864	0.5850	0.5835	0.5821	0.5807	0.5793	0.5779	0.5764	0.5750
	tan	1.3764	1.3814	1.3865	1.3916	1.3968	1.4019	1.4071	1.4124	1.4176	1.4229
55	sin	0.8192	0.8202	0.8211	0.8221	0.8231	0.8241	0.8251	0.8261	0.8271	0.8281
	cos	0.5736	0.5721	0.5707	0.5693	0.5678	0.5664	0.5650	0.5635	0.5621	0.5606
	tan	1.4281	1.4335	1.4388	1.4442	1.4496	1.4550	1.4605	1.4659	1.4715	1.4770
56	sin	0.8290	0.8300	0.8310	0.8320	0.8329	0.8339	0.8348	0.8358	0.8368	0.8377
	cos	0.5592	0.5577	0.5563	0.5548	0.5534	0.5519	0.5505	0.5490	0.5476	0.5461
	tan	1.4826	1.4882	1.4938	1.4994	1.5051	1.5108	1.5166	1.5224	1.5282	1.5340
57	sin	0.8387	0.8396	0.8406	0.8415	0.8425	0.8434	0.8443	0.8453	0.8462	0.8471
	cos	0.5446	0.5432	0.5417	0.5402	0.5388	0.5373	0.5358	0.5344	0.5329	0.5314
	tan	1.5399	1.5458	1.5517	1.5577	1.5637	1.5697	1.5757	1.5818	1.5880	1.5941
58	sin	0.8480	0.8490	0.8499	0.8508	0.8517	0.8526	0.8536	0.8545	0.8551	0.8563
	cos	0.5299	0.5284	0.5270	0.5255	0.5240	0.5225	0.5210	0.5195	0.5180	0.5165
	tan	1.6003	1.6066	1.6128	1.6191	1.6255	1.6319	1.6383	1.6447	1.6512	1.6577
59	sin	0.8572	0.8581	0.8590	0.8599	0.8607	0.8616	0.8625	0.8634	0.8643	0.8652
	cos	0.5150	0.5135	0.5120	0.5105	0.5090	0.5075	0.5060	0.5045	0.5030	0.5015
	tan	1.6643	1.6709	1.6775	1.6842	1.6909	1.6977	1.7045	1.7113	1.7182	1.7251
Degs.	Function	0′	6′	12′	18′	24′	30′	36′	42′	48′	54′

NATURAL SINES, COSINES, AND TANGENTS

60° - 74.9°

Degs.	Function	0.0°	0.1°	0.2°	0.3°	0.4°	0.5°	0.6°	0.7°	0.8°	0.9°
60	sin	0.8660	0.8669	0.8678	0.8686	0.8695	0.8704	0.8712	0.8721	0.8729	0.8738
	cos	0.5000	0.4985	0.4970	0.4955	0.4939	0.4924	0.4909	0.4894	0.4879	0.4863
	tan	1.7321	1.7391	1.7461	1.7532	1.7603	1.7675	1.7747	1.7820	1.7893	1.7966
61	sin	0.8746	0.8755	0.8763	0.8771	0.8780	0.8788	0.8796	0.8805	0.8813	0.8821
	cos	0.4848	0.4833	0.4818	0.4802	0.4787	0.4772	0.4756	0.4741	0.4726	0.4710
	tan	1.8040	1.8115	1.8190	1.8265	1.8341	1.8418	1.8495	1.8572	1.8650	1.8728
62	sin	0.8829	0.8838	0.8846	0.8854	0.8862	0.8870	0.8878	0.8886	0.8894	0.8902
	cos	0.4695	0.4679	0.4664	0.4648	0.4633	0.4617	0.4602	0.4586	0.4571	0.4555
	tan	1.8807	1.8887	1.8967	1.9047	1.9128	1.9210	1.9292	1.9375	1.9458	1.9542
63	sin	0.8910	0.8918	0.8926	0.8934	0.8942	0.8949	0.8957	0.8965	0.8973	0.8980
	cos	0.4540	0.4524	0.4509	0.4493	0.4478	0.4462	0.4446	0.4431	0.4415	0.4399
	tan	1.9626	1.9711	1.9797	1.9883	1.9970	2.0057	2.0145	2.0233	2.0323	2.0413
64	sin	0.8988	0.8996	0.9003	0.9011	0.9018	0.9026	0.9033	0.9041	0.9048	0.9056
	cos	0.4384	0.4368	0.4352	0.4337	0.4321	0.4305	0.4289	0.4274	0.4258	0.4242
	tan	2.0503	2.0594	2.0686	2.0778	2.0872	2.0965	2.1060	2.1155	2.1251	2.1348
65	sin	0.9063	0.9070	0.9078	0.9085	0.9092	0.9100	0.9107	0.9114	0.9121	0.9128
	cos	0.4226	0.4210	0.4195	0.4179	0.4163	0.4147	0.4131	0.4115	0.4099	0.4083
	tan	2.1445	2.1543	2.1642	2.1742	2.1842	2.1943	2.2045	2.2148	2.2251	2.2355
66	sin	0.9135	0.9143	0.9150	0.9157	0.9164	0.9171	0.9178	0.9184	0.9191	0.9198
	cos	0.4067	0.4051	0.4035	0.4019	0.4003	0.3987	0.3971	0.3955	0.3939	0.3923
	tan	2.2460	2.2566	2.2673	2.2781	2.2889	2.2998	2.3109	2.3220	2.3332	2.3445
67	sin	0.9205	0.9212	0.9219	0.9225	0.9232	0.9239	0.9245	0.9252	0.9259	0.9265
	cos	0.3907	0.3891	0.3875	0.3859	0.3843	0.3827	0.3811	0.3795	0.3778	0.3762
	tan	2.3559	2.3673	2.3789	2.3906	2.4023	2.4142	2.4262	2.4383	2.4504	2.4627
68	sin	0.9272	0.9278	0.9285	0.9291	0.9298	0.9304	0.9311	0.9317	0.9323	0.9330
	cos	0.3746	0.3730	0.3714	0.3697	0.3681	0.3665	0.3649	0.3633	0.3616	0.3600
	tan	2.4751	2.4876	2.5002	2.5129	2.5257	2.5386	2.5517	2.5649	2.5782	2.5916
69	sin	0.9336	0.9342	0.9348	0.9354	0.9361	0.9367	0.9373	0.9379	0.9385	0.9391
	cos	0.3584	0.3567	0.3551	0.3535	0.3518	0.3502	0.3486	0.3469	0.3453	0.3437
	tan	2.6051	2.6187	2.6325	2.6464	2.6605	2.6746	2.6889	2.7034	2.7179	2.7326
70	sin	0.9397	0.9403	0.9409	0.9415	0.9421	0.9426	0.9432	0.9438	0.9444	0.9449
	cos	0.3420	0.3404	0.3387	0.3371	0.3355	0.3338	0.3322	0.3305	0.3289	0.3272
	tan	2.7475	2.7625	2.7776	2.7929	2.8083	2.8239	2.8397	2.8556	2.8716	2.8878
71	sin	0.9455	0.9461	0.9466	0.9472	0.9478	0.9483	0.9489	0.9494	0.9500	0.9505
	cos	0.3256	0.3239	0.3223	0.3206	0.3190	0.3173	0.3156	0.3140	0.3123	0.3107
	tan	2.9042	2.9208	2.9375	2.9544	2.9714	2.9887	3.0061	3.0237	3.0415	3.0595
72	sin	0.9511	0.9516	0.9521	0.9527	0.9532	0.9537	0.9542	0.9548	0.9553	0.9558
	cos	0.3090	0.3074	0.3057	0.3040	0.3024	0.3007	0.2990	0.2974	0.2957	0.2940
	tan	3.0777	3.0961	3.1146	3.1334	3.1524	3.1716	3.1910	3.2106	3.2305	3.2506
73	sin	0.9562	0.9568	0.9573	0.9578	0.9583	0.9588	0.9593	0.9598	0.9603	0.9608
	cos	0.2924	0.2907	0.2890	0.2874	0.2857	0.2840	0.2823	0.2807	0.2790	0.2773
	tan	3.2709	3.2914	3.3122	3.3332	3.3544	3.3759	3.3977	3.4197	3.4420	3.4646
74	sin	0.9613	0.9617	0.9622	0.9627	0.9632	0.9636	0.9641	0.9646	0.9650	0.9655
	cos	0.2756	0.2740	0.2723	0.2706	0.2689	0.2672	0.2656	0.2639	0.2622	0.2605
	tan	3.4874	3.5105	3.5339	3.5576	3.5816	3.6059	3.6305	3.6554	3.6806	3.7062
Degs.	Function	0′	6′	12′	18′	24′	30′	36′	42′	48′	54′

NATURAL SINES, COSINES, AND TANGENTS

75° – 89.9°

Degs.	Function	0.0°	0.1°	0.2°	0.3°	0.4°	0.5°	0.6°	0.7°	0.8°	0.9°
75	sin	0.9659	0.9664	0.9668	0.9673	0.9677	0.9681	0.9686	0.9690	0.9694	0.9699
	cos	0.2588	0.2571	0.2554	0.2538	0.2521	0.2504	0.2487	0.2470	0.2453	0.2436
	tan	3.7321	3.7583	3.7848	3.8118	3.8391	3.8667	3.8947	3.9232	3.9520	3.9812
76	sin	0.9703	0.9707	0.9711	0.9715	0.9720	0.9724	0.9728	0.9732	0.9736	0.9740
	cos	0.2419	0.2402	0.2385	0.2368	0.2351	0.2334	0.2317	0.2300	0.2284	0.2267
	tan	4.0108	4.0408	4.0713	4.1022	4.1335	4.1653	4.1976	4.2303	4.2635	4.2972
77	sin	0.9744	0.9748	0.9751	0.9755	0.9759	0.9763	0.9767	0.9770	0.9774	0.9778
	cos	0.2250	0.2232	0.2215	0.2198	0.2181	0.2164	0.2147	0.2130	0.2113	0.2096
	tan	4.3315	4.3662	4.4015	4.4374	4.4737	4.5107	4.5483	4.5864	4.6252	4.6646
78	sin	0.9781	0.9785	0.9789	0.9792	0.9796	0.9799	0.9803	0.9806	0.9810	0.9813
	cos	0.2079	0.2062	0.2045	0.2028	0.2011	0.1994	0.1977	0.1959	0.1942	0.1925
	tan	4.7046	4.7453	4.7867	4.8288	4.8716	4.9152	4.9594	5.0045	5.0504	5.0970
79	sin	0.9816	0.9820	0.9823	0.9826	0.9829	0.9833	0.9836	0.9839	0.9842	0.9845
	cos	0.1908	0.1891	0.1874	0.1857	0.1840	0.1822	0.1805	0.1788	0.1771	0.1754
	tan	5.1446	5.1929	5.2422	5.2924	5.3435	5.3955	5.4486	5.5026	5.5578	5.6140
80	sin	0.9848	0.9851	0.9854	0.9857	0.9860	0.9863	0.9866	0.9869	0.9871	0.9874
	cos	0.1736	0.1719	0.1702	0.1685	0.1668	0.1650	0.1633	0.1616	0.1599	0.1582
	tan	5.6713	5.7297	5.7894	5.8502	5.9124	5.9758	6.0405	6.1066	6.1742	6.2432
81	sin	0.9877	0.9880	0.9882	0.9885	0.9888	0.9890	0.9893	0.9895	0.9898	0.9900
	cos	0.1564	0.1547	0.1530	0.1513	0.1495	0.1478	0.1461	0.1444	0.1426	0.1409
	tan	6.3138	6.3859	6.4596	6.5350	6.6122	6.6912	6.7720	6.8548	6.9395	7.0264
82	sin	0.9903	0.9905	0.9907	0.9910	0.9912	0.9914	0.9917	0.9919	0.9921	0.9923
	cos	0.1392	0.1374	0.1357	0.1340	0.1323	0.1305	0.1288	0.1271	0.1253	0.1236
	tan	7.1154	7.2066	7.3002	7.3962	7.4947	7.5958	7.6996	7.8062	7.9158	8.0285
83	sin	0.9925	0.9928	0.9930	0.9932	0.9934	0.9936	0.9938	0.9940	0.9942	0.9943
	cos	0.1219	0.1201	0.1184	0.1167	0.1149	0.1132	0.1115	0.1097	0.1080	0.1063
	tan	8.1443	8.2636	8.3863	8.5126	8.6427	8.7769	8.9152	9.0579	9.2052	9.3572
84	sin	0.9945	0.9947	0.9949	0.9951	0.9952	0.9954	0.9956	0.9957	0.9959	0.9960
	cos	0.1045	0.1028	0.1011	0.0993	0.0976	0.0958	0.0941	0.0924	0.0906	0.0889
	tan	9.5144	9.6768	9.8448	10.02	10.20	10.39	10.58	10.78	10.99.	11.20
85	sin	0.9962	0.9963	0.9965	0.9966	0.9968	0.9969	0.9971	0.9972	0.9973	0.9974
	cos	0.0872	0.0854	0.0837	0.0819	0.0802	0.0785	0.0767	0.0750	0.0732	0.0715
	tan	11.43	11.66	11.91	12.16	12.43	12.71	13.00	13.30	13.62	13.95
86	sin	0.9976	0.9977	0.9978	0.9979	0.9980	0.9981	0.9982	0.9983	0.9984	0.9985
	cos	0.0698	0.0680	0.0663	0.0645	0.0628	0.0610	0.0593	0.0576	0.0558	0.0541
	tan	14.30	14.67	15.06	15.46	15.89	16.35	16.83	17.34	17.89	18.46
87	sin	0.9986	0.9987	0.9988	0.9989	0.9990	0.9990	0.9991	0.9992	0.9993	0.9993
	cos	0.0523	0.0506	0.0488	0.0471	0.0454	0.0436	0.0419	0.0401	0.0384	0.0366
	tan	19.08	19.74	20.45	21.20	22.02	22.90	23.86	24.90	26.03	27.27
88	sin	0.9994	0.9995	0.9995	0.9996	0.9996	0.9997	0.9997	0.9997	0.9998	0.9998
	cos	0.0349	0.0332	0.0314	0.0297	0.0279	0.0262	0.0244	0.0227	0.0209	0.0192
	tan	28.64	30.14	31.82	33.69	35.80	38.19	40.92	44.07	47.74	52.08
89	sin	0.9998	0.9999	0.9999	0.9999	0.9999	1.000	1.000	1.000	1.000	1.000
	cos	0.0175	0.0157	0.0140	0.0122	0.0105	0.0087	0.0070	0.0052	0.0035	0.0017
	tan	57.29	63.66	71.62	81.85	95.49	114.6	143.2	191.0	286.5	573.0
Degs.	Function	0′	6′	12′	18′	24′	30′	36′	42′	48′	54′

INDEX

441

CATALOGUE OF DOVER BOOKS

Books Explaining Science and Mathematics

WHAT IS SCIENCE?, N. Campbell. The role of experiment and measurement, the function of mathematics, the nature of scientific laws, the difference between laws and theories, the limitations of science, and many similarly provocative topics are treated clearly and without technicalities by an eminent scientist. "Still an excellent introduction to scientific philosophy," H. Margenau in PHYSICS TODAY. "A first-rate primer . . . deserves a wide audience," SCIENTIFIC AMERICAN. 192pp. 5⅜ x 8.   S43 Paperbound **$1.25**

THE NATURE OF PHYSICAL THEORY, P. W. Bridgman. A Nobel Laureate's clear, non-technical lectures on difficulties and paradoxes connected with frontier research on the physical sciences. Concerned with such central concepts as thought, logic, mathematics, relativity, probability, wave mechanics, etc. he analyzes the contributions of such men as Newton, Einstein, Bohr, Heisenberg, and many others. "Lucid and entertaining . . . recommended to anyone who wants to get some insight into current philosophies of science," THE NEW PHILOSOPHY. Index. xi + 138pp. 5⅜ x 8.   S33 Paperbound **$1.25**

EXPERIMENT AND THEORY IN PHYSICS, Max Born. A Nobel Laureate examines the nature of experiment and theory in theoretical physics and analyzes the advances made by the great physicists of our day: Heisenberg, Einstein, Bohr, Planck, Dirac, and others. The actual process of creation is detailed step-by-step by one who participated. A fine examination of the scientific method at work. 44pp. 5⅜ x 8.   S308 Paperbound **75¢**

THE PSYCHOLOGY OF INVENTION IN THE MATHEMATICAL FIELD, J. Hadamard. The reports of such men as Descartes, Pascal, Einstein, Poincaré, and others are considered in this investigation of the method of idea-creation in mathematics and other sciences and the thinking process in general. How do ideas originate? What is the role of the unconscious? What is Poincaré's forgetting hypothesis? are some of the fascinating questions treated. A penetrating analysis of Einstein's thought processes concludes the book. xiii + 145pp. 5⅜ x 8.   T107 Paperbound **$1.25**

THE NATURE OF LIGHT AND COLOUR IN THE OPEN AIR, M. Minnaert. Why are shadows sometimes blue, sometimes green, or other colors depending on the light and surroundings? What causes mirages? Why do multiple suns and moons appear in the sky? Professor Minnaert explains these unusual phenomena and hundreds of others in simple, easy-to-understand terms based on optical laws and the properties of light and color. No mathematics is required but artists, scientists, students, and everyone fascinated by these "tricks" of nature will find thousands of useful and amazing pieces of information. Hundreds of observational experiments are suggested which require no special equipment. 200 illustrations; 42 photos. xvi + 362pp. 5⅜ x 8.   T196 Paperbound **$1.95**

THE UNIVERSE OF LIGHT, W. Bragg. Sir William Bragg, Nobel Laureate and great modern physicist, is also well known for his powers of clear exposition. Here he analyzes all aspects of light for the layman: lenses, reflection, refraction, the optics of vision, x-rays, the photoelectric effect, etc. He tells you what causes the color of spectra, rainbows, and soap bubbles, how magic mirrors work, and much more. Dozens of simple experiments are described. Preface. Index. 199 line drawings and photographs, including 2 full-page color plates. x + 283pp. 5⅜ x 8.   T538 Paperbound **$1.85**

SOAP-BUBBLES: THEIR COLOURS AND THE FORCES THAT MOULD THEM, C. V. Boys. For continuing popularity and validity as scientific primer, few books can match this volume of easily-followed experiments, explanations. Lucid exposition of complexities of liquid films, surface tension and related phenomena, bubbles' reaction to heat, motion, music, magnetic fields. Experiments with capillary attraction, soap bubbles on frames, composite bubbles, liquid cylinders and jets, bubbles other than soap, etc. Wonderful introduction to scientific method; natural laws that have many ramifications in areas of modern physics. Only complete edition in print. New Introduction by S. Z. Lewin, New York University. 83 illustrations; 1 full-page color plate. xii + 190pp. 5⅜ x 8½.   T542 Paperbound **95¢**

CATALOGUE OF DOVER BOOKS

THE STORY OF X-RAYS FROM RONTGEN TO ISOTOPES, A. R. Bleich, M.D. This book, by a member of the American College of Radiology, gives the scientific explanation of x-rays, their applications in medicine, industry and art, and their danger (and that of atmospheric radiation) to the individual and the species. You learn how radiation therapy is applied against cancer, how x-rays diagnose heart disease and other ailments, how they are used to examine mummies for information on diseases of early societies, and industrial materials for hidden weaknesses. 54 illustrations show x-rays of flowers, bones, stomach, gears with flaws, etc. 1st publication. Index. xix + 186pp. 5⅜ x 8. **T622 Paperbound $1.35**

SPINNING TOPS AND GYROSCOPIC MOTION, John Perry. A classic elementary text of the dynamics of rotation — the behavior and use of rotating bodies such as gyroscopes and tops. In simple, everyday English you are shown how quasi-rigidity is induced in discs of paper, smoke rings, chains, etc., by rapid motions; why a gyrostat falls and why a top rises; precession; how the earth's motion affects climate; and many other phenomena. Appendix on practical use of gyroscopes. 62 figures. 128pp. 5⅜ x 8. **T416 Paperbound $1.00**

SNOW CRYSTALS, W. A. Bentley, M. J. Humphreys. For almost 50 years W. A. Bentley photographed snow flakes in his laboratory in Jericho, Vermont; in 1931 the American Meteorological Society gathered together the best of his work, some 2400 photographs of snow flakes, plus a few ice flowers, windowpane frosts, dew, frozen rain, and other ice formations. Pictures were selected for beauty and scientific value. A very valuable work to anyone in meteorology, cryology; most interesting to layman; extremely useful for artist who wants beautiful, crystalline designs. All copyright free. Unabridged reprint of 1931 edition. 2453 illustrations. 227pp. 8 x 10½. **T287 Paperbound $3.00**

A DOVER SCIENCE SAMPLER, edited by George Barkin. A collection of brief, non-technical passages from 44 Dover Books Explaining Science for the enjoyment of the science-minded browser. Includes work of Bertrand Russell, Poincaré, Laplace, Max Born, Galileo, Newton; material on physics, mathematics, metallurgy, anatomy, astronomy, chemistry, etc. You will be fascinated by Martin Gardner's analysis of the sincere pseudo-scientist, Moritz's account of Newton's absentmindedness, Bernard's examples of human vivisection, etc. Illustrations from the Diderot Pictorial Encyclopedia and De Re Metallica. 64 pages. **FREE**

THE STORY OF ATOMIC THEORY AND ATOMIC ENERGY, J. G. Feinberg. A broader approach to subject of nuclear energy and its cultural implications than any other similar source. Very readable, informal, completely non-technical text. Begins with first atomic theory, 600 B.C. and carries you through the work of Mendelejeff, Röntgen, Madame Curie, to Einstein's equation and the A-bomb. New chapter goes through thermonuclear fission, binding energy, other events up to 1959. Radioactive decay and radiation hazards, future benefits, work of Bohr, moderns, hundreds more topics. "Deserves special mention . . . not only authoritative but thoroughly popular in the best sense of the word," Saturday Review. Formerly, "The Atom Story." Expanded with new chapter. Three appendixes. Index. 34 illustrations. vii + 243pp. 5⅜ x 8. **T625 Paperbound $1.45**

THE STRANGE STORY OF THE QUANTUM, AN ACCOUNT FOR THE GENERAL READER OF THE GROWTH OF IDEAS UNDERLYING OUR PRESENT ATOMIC KNOWLEDGE, B. Hoffmann. Presents lucidly and expertly, with barest amount of mathematics, the problems and theories which led to modern quantum physics. Dr. Hoffmann begins with the closing years of the 19th century, when certain trifling discrepancies were noticed, and with illuminating analogies and examples takes you through the brilliant concepts of Planck, Einstein, Pauli, Broglie, Bohr, Schroedinger, Heisenberg, Dirac, Sommerfeld, Feynman, etc. This edition includes a new, long postscript carrying the story through 1958. "Of the books attempting an account of the history and contents of our modern atomic physics which have come to my attention, this is the best," H. Margenau, Yale University, in "American Journal of Physics." 32 tables and line illustrations. Index. 275pp. 5⅜ x 8. **T518 Paperbound $1.50**

SPACE AND TIME, E. Borel. Written by a versatile mathematician of world renown with his customary lucidity and precision, this introduction to relativity for the layman presents scores of examples, analogies, and illustrations that open up new ways of thinking about space and time. It covers abstract geometry and geographical maps, continuity and topology, the propagation of light, the special theory of relativity, the general theory of relativity, theoretical researches, and much more. Mathematical notes. 2 Indexes. 4 Appendices. 15 figures. xvi + 243pp. 5⅜ x 8. **T592 Paperbound $1.45**

FROM EUCLID TO EDDINGTON: A STUDY OF THE CONCEPTIONS OF THE EXTERNAL WORLD, Sir Edmund Whittaker. A foremost British scientist traces the development of theories of natural philosophy from the western rediscovery of Euclid to Eddington, Einstein, Dirac, etc. The inadequacy of classical physics is contrasted with present day attempts to understand the physical world through relativity, non-Euclidean geometry, space curvature, wave mechanics, etc. 5 major divisions of examination: Space; Time and Movement; the Concepts of Classical Physics; the Concepts of Quantum Mechanics; the Eddington Universe. 212pp. 5⅜ x 8. **T491 Paperbound $1.35**

CATALOGUE OF DOVER BOOKS

*THE EVOLUTION OF SCIENTIFIC THOUGHT FROM NEWTON TO EINSTEIN, A. d'Abro. A detailed account of the evolution of classical physics into modern relativistic theory and the concommitant changes in scientific methodology. The breakdown of classical physics in the face of non-Euclidean geometry and the electromagnetic equations is carefully discussed and then an exhaustive analysis of Einstein's special and general theories of relativity and their implications is given. Newton, Riemann, Weyl, Lorentz, Planck, Maxwell, and many others are considered. A non-technical explanation of space, time, electromagnetic waves, etc. as understood today. "Model of semi-popular exposition," NEW REPUBLIC. 21 diagrams. 482pp. 5⅜ x 8.
T2 Paperbound **$2.00**

EINSTEIN'S THEORY OF RELATIVITY, Max Born. Nobel Laureate explains Einstein's special and general theories of relativity, beginning with a thorough review of classical physics in simple, non-technical language. Exposition of Einstein's work discusses concept of simultaneity, kinematics, relativity of arbitrary motions, the space-time continuum, geometry of curved surfaces, etc., steering middle course between vague popularizations and complex scientific presentations. 1962 edition revised by author takes into account latest findings, predictions of theory and implications for cosmology, indicates what is being sought in unified field theory. Mathematics very elementary, illustrative diagrams and experiments informative but simple. Revised 1962 edition. Revised by Max Born, assisted by Gunther Leibfried and Walter Biem. Index. 143 illustrations. vii + 376pp. 5⅜ x 8.
S769 Paperbound **$2.00**

PHILOSOPHY AND THE PHYSICISTS, L. Susan Stebbing. A philosopher examines the philosophical aspects of modern science, in terms of a lively critical attack on the ideas of Jeans and Eddington. Such basic questions are treated as the task of science, causality, determinism, probability, consciousness, the relation of the world of physics to the world of everyday experience. The author probes the concepts of man's smallness before an inscrutable universe, the tendency to idealize mathematical construction, unpredictability theorems and human freedom, the supposed opposition between 19th century determinism and modern science, and many others. Introduces many thought-stimulating ideas about the implications of modern physical concepts. xvi + 295pp. 5⅜ x 8.
T480 Paperbound **$1.65**

THE RESTLESS UNIVERSE, Max Born. A remarkably lucid account by a Nobel Laureate of recent theories of wave mechanics, behavior of gases, electrons and ions, waves and particles, electronic structure of the atom, nuclear physics, and similar topics. "Much more thorough and deeper than most attempts . . . easy and delightful," CHEMICAL AND ENGINEERING NEWS. Special feature: 7 animated sequences of 60 figures each showing such phenomena as gas molecules in motion, the scattering of alpha particles, etc. 11 full-page plates of photographs. Total of nearly 600 illustrations. 351pp. 6⅛ x 9¼.
T412 Paperbound **$2.00**

THE COMMON SENSE OF THE EXACT SCIENCES, W. K. Clifford. For 70 years a guide to the basic concepts of scientific and mathematical thought. Acclaimed by scientists and laymen alike, it offers a wonderful insight into concepts such as the extension of meaning of symbols, characteristics of surface boundaries, properties of plane figures, measurement of quantities, vectors, the nature of position, bending of space, motion, mass and force, and many others. Prefaces by Bertrand Russell and Karl Pearson. Critical introduction by James Newman. 130 figures. 249pp. 5⅜ x 8.
T61 Paperbound **$1.60**

MATTER AND LIGHT, THE NEW PHYSICS, Louis de Broglie. Non-technical explanations by a Nobel Laureate of electro-magnetic theory, relativity, matter, light and radiation, wave mechanics, quantum physics, philosophy of science, and similar topics. This is one of the simplest yet most accurate introductions to the work of men like Planck, Einstein, Bohr, and others. Only 2 of the 21 chapters require a knowledge of mathematics. 300pp. 5⅜ x 8.
T35 Paperbound **$1.75**

SCIENCE, THEORY AND MAN, Erwin Schrödinger. This is a complete and unabridged reissue of SCIENCE AND THE HUMAN TEMPERAMENT plus an additional essay: "What Is an Elementary Particle?" Nobel Laureate Schrödinger discusses such topics as nature of scientific method, tne nature of science, chance and determinism, science and society, conceptual models for physical entities, elementary particles and wave mechanics. Presentation is popular and may be followed by most people with little or no scientific training. "Fine practical preparation for a time when laws of nature, human institutions . . . are undergoing a critical examination without parallel," Waldemar Kaempffert, N. Y. TIMES. 192pp. 5⅜ x 8.
T428 Paperbound **$1.35**

CONCERNING THE NATURE OF THINGS, Sir William Bragg. The Nobel Laureate physicist in his Royal Institute Christmas Lectures explains such diverse phenomena as the formation of crystals, how uranium is transmuted to lead, the way X-rays work, why a spinning ball travels in a curved path, the reason why bubbles bounce from each other, and many other scientific topics that are seldom explained in simple terms. No scientific background needed—book is easy enough that any intelligent adult or youngster can understand it. Unabridged. 32pp. of photos; 57 figures. xii + 232pp. 5⅜ x 8.
T31 Paperbound **$1.35**

*THE RISE OF THE NEW PHYSICS (formerly THE DECLINE OF MECHANISM), A. d'Abro. This authoritative and comprehensive 2 volume exposition is unique in scientific publishing. Written for intelligent readers not familiar with higher mathematics, it is the only thorough explanation in non-technical language of modern mathematical-physical theory. Combining both history and exposition, it ranges from classical Newtonian concepts up through the electronic theories of Dirac and Heisenberg, the statistical mechanics of Fermi, and Einstein's relativity theories. "A must for anyone doing serious study in the physical sciences," J. OF FRANKLIN INST. 97 illustrations. 991pp. 2 volumes.
T3 Vol. 1, Paperbound **$2.00**
T4 Vol. 2, Paperbound **$2.00**

CATALOGUE OF DOVER BOOKS

SCIENCE AND HYPOTHESIS, Henri Poincaré. Creative psychology in science. How such concepts as number, magnitude, space, force, classical mechanics were developed and how the modern scientist uses them in his thought. Hypothesis in physics, theories of modern physics. Introduction by Sir James Larmor. "Few mathematicians have had the breadth of vision of Poincaré, and none is his superior in the gift of clear exposition," E. T. Bell. Index. 272pp. 5⅜ x 8.
S221 Paperbound **$1.35**

THE VALUE OF SCIENCE, Henri Poincaré. Many of the most mature ideas of the "last scientific universalist" conveyed with charm and vigor for both the beginning student and the advanced worker. Discusses the nature of scientific truth, whether order is innate in the universe or imposed upon it by man, logical thought versus intuition (relating to mathematics through the works of Weierstrass, Lie, Klein, Riemann), time and space (relativity, psychological time, simultaneity), Hertz's concept of force, interrelationship of mathematical physics to pure math, values within disciplines of Maxwell, Carnot, Mayer, Newton, Lorentz, etc. Index. iii + 147pp. 5⅜ x 8.
S469 Paperbound **$1.35**

THE SKY AND ITS MYSTERIES, E. A. Beet. One of the most lucid books on the mysteries of the universe; covers history of astronomy from earliest observations to modern theories of expanding universe, source of stellar energy, birth of planets, origin of moon craters, possibilities of life on other planets. Discusses effects of sunspots on weather; distance, age of stars; methods and tools of astronomers; much more. Expert and fascinating. "Eminently readable book," London Times. Bibliography. Over 50 diagrams, 12 full-page plates. Fold-out star map. Introduction. Index. 238pp. 5¼ x 7½.
T627 Clothbound **$3.50**

OUT OF THE SKY: AN INTRODUCTION TO METEORITICS, H. H. Nininger. A non-technical yet comprehensive introduction to the young science of meteoritics: all aspects of the arrival of cosmic matter on our planet from outer space and the reaction and alteration of this matter in the terrestrial environment. Essential facts and major theories presented by one of the world's leading experts. Covers ancient reports of meteors; modern systematic investigations; fireball clusters; meteorite showers; tektites; planetoidal encounters; etc. 52 full-page plates with over 175 photographs. 22 figures. Bibliography and references. Index. viii + 336pp. 5⅜ x 8.
T519 Paperbound **$1.85**

THE REALM OF THE NEBULAE, E. Hubble. One of great astronomers of our day records his formulation of concept of "island universes." Covers velocity-distance relationship; classification, nature, distances, general types of nebulae; cosmological theories. A fine introduction to modern theories for layman. No math needed. New introduction by A. Sandage. 55 illustrations, photos. Index. iv + 201pp. 5⅜ x 8.
S455 Paperbound **$1.50**

AN ELEMENTARY SURVEY OF CELESTIAL MECHANICS, Y. Ryabov. Elementary exposition of gravitational theory and celestial mechanics. Historical introduction and coverage of basic principles, including: the ecliptic, the orbital plane, the 2- and 3-body problems, the discovery of Neptune, planetary rotation, the length of the day, the shapes of galaxies, satellites (detailed treatment of Sputnik I), etc. First American reprinting of successful Russian exposition. Follow actual methods of astrophysicists with only high school math! Appendix. 58 figures. 165pp. 5⅜ x 8.
T756 Paperbound **$1.25**

GREAT IDEAS AND THEORIES OF MODERN COSMOLOGY, Jagjit Singh. Companion volume to author's popular "Great Ideas of Modern Mathematics" (Dover, $1.55). The best non-technical survey of post-Einstein attempts to answer perhaps unanswerable questions of origin, age of Universe, possibility of life on other worlds, etc. Fundamental theories of cosmology and cosmogony recounted, explained, evaluated in light of most recent data: Einstein's concepts of relativity, space-time; Milne's a priori world-system; astrophysical theories of Jeans, Eddington; Hoyle's "continuous creation"; contributions of dozens more scientists. A faithful, comprehensive critical summary of complex material presented in an extremely well-written text intended for laymen. Original publication. Index. xii + 276pp. 5⅜ x 8½.
T925 Paperbound **$1.85**

BASIC ELECTRICITY, Bureau of Naval Personnel. Very thorough, easily followed course in basic electricity for beginner, layman, or intermediate student. Begins with simplest definitions, presents coordinated, systematic coverage of basic theory and application: conductors, insulators, static electricity, magnetism, production of voltage, Ohm's law, direct current series and parallel circuits, wiring techniques, electromagnetism, alternating current, capacitance and inductance, measuring instruments, etc.; application to electrical machines such as alternating and direct current generators, motors, transformers, magnetic magnifiers, etc. Each chapter contains problems to test progress; answers at rear. No math needed beyond algebra. Appendices on signs, formulas, etc. 345 illustrations. 448pp. 7½ x 10.
S973 Paperbound **$2.95**

ELEMENTARY METALLURGY AND METALLOGRAPHY, A. M. Shrager. An introduction to common metals and alloys; stress is upon steel and iron, but other metals and alloys also covered. All aspects of production, processing, working of metals. Designed for student who wishes to enter metallurgy, for bright high school or college beginner, layman who wants background on extremely important industry. Questions, at ends of chapters, many microphotographs, glossary. Greatly revised 1961 edition. 195 illustrations, tables. ix + 389pp. 5⅜ x 8.
S138 Paperbound **$2.25**

BRIDGES AND THEIR BUILDERS, D. B. Steinman & S. R. Watson. Engineers, historians, and every person who has ever been fascinated by great spans will find this book an endless source of information and interest. Greek and Roman structures, Medieval bridges, modern classics such as the Brooklyn Bridge, and the latest developments in the science are retold by one of the world's leading authorities on bridge design and construction. BRIDGES AND THEIR BUILDERS is the only comprehensive and accurate semi-popular history of these important measures of progress in print. New, greatly revised, enlarged edition. 23 photos; 26 line-drawings. Index. xvii + 401pp. 5⅜ x 8. **T431 Paperbound $2.00**

FAMOUS BRIDGES OF THE WORLD, D. B. Steinman. An up-to-the-minute new edition of a book that explains the fascinating drama of how the world's great bridges came to be built. The author, designer of the famed Mackinac bridge, discusses bridges from all periods and all parts of the world, explaining their various types of construction, and describing the problems their builders faced. Although primarily for youngsters, this cannot fail to interest readers of all ages. 48 illustrations in the text. 23 photographs. 99pp. 6⅛ x 9¼. **T161 Paperbound $1.00**

HOW DO YOU USE A SLIDE RULE? by A. A. Merrill. A step-by-step explanation of the slide rule that presents the fundamental rules clearly enough for the non-mathematician to understand. Unlike most instruction manuals, this work concentrates on the two most important operations: multiplication and division. 10 easy lessons, each with a clear drawing, for the reader who has difficulty following other expositions. 1st publication. Index. 2 Appendices. 10 illustrations. 78 problems, all with answers. vi + 36 pp. 6⅛ x 9¼. **T62 Paperbound 60¢**

HOW TO CALCULATE QUICKLY, H. Sticker. A tried and true method for increasing your "number sense" — the ability to see relationships between numbers and groups of numbers. Addition, subtraction, multiplication, division, fractions, and other topics are treated through techniques not generally taught in schools: left to right multiplication, division by inspection, etc. This is not a collection of tricks which work only on special numbers, but a detailed well-planned course, consisting of over 9,000 problems that you can work in spare moments. It is excellent for anyone who is inconvenienced by slow computational skills. 5 or 10 minutes of this book daily will double or triple your calculation speed. 9,000 problems, answers. 256pp. 5⅜ x 8. **T295 Paperbound $1.00**

MATHEMATICAL FUN, GAMES AND PUZZLES, Jack Frohlichstein. A valuable service for parents of children who have trouble with math, for teachers in need of a supplement to regular upper elementary and junior high math texts (each section is graded—easy, average, difficult —for ready adaptation to different levels of ability), and for just anyone who would like to develop basic skills in an informal and entertaining manner. The author combines ten years of experience as a junior high school math teacher with a method that uses puzzles and games to introduce the basic ideas and operations of arithmetic. Stress on everyday uses of math: banking, stock market, personal budgets, insurance, taxes. Intellectually stimulating and practical, too. 418 problems and diversions with answers. Bibliography. 120 illustrations. xix + 306pp. 5⅝ x 8½. **T789 Paperbound $1.75**

GREAT IDEAS OF MODERN MATHEMATICS: THEIR NATURE AND USE, Jagjit Singh. Reader with only high school math will understand main mathematical ideas of modern physics, astronomy, genetics, psychology, evolution, etc. better than many who use them as tools, but comprehend little of their basic structure. Author uses his wide knowledge of non-mathematical fields in brilliant exposition of differential equations, matrices, group theory, logic, statistics, problems of mathematical foundations, imaginary numbers, vectors, etc. Original publication. 2 appendixes. 2 indexes. 65 illustr. 322pp. 5⅜ x 8. **S587 Paperbound $1.75**

*MATHEMATICS IN ACTION, O. G. Sutton. Everyone with a command of high school algebra will find this book one of the finest possible introductions to the application of mathematics to physical theory. Ballistics, numerical analysis, waves and wavelike phenomena, Fourier series, group concepts, fluid flow and aerodynamics, statistical measures, and meteorology are discussed with unusual clarity. Some calculus and differential equations theory is developed by the author for the reader's help in the more difficult sections. 88 figures. Index. viii + 236pp. 5⅜ x 8. **T440 Clothbound $3.50**

*INTRODUCTION TO SYMBOLIC LOGIC AND ITS APPLICATIONS, Rudolph Carnap. One of the clearest, most comprehensive, and rigorous introductions to modern symbolic logic, by perhaps its greatest living master. Not merely elementary theory, but demonstrated applications in mathematics, physics, and biology. Symbolic languages of various degrees of complexity are analyzed, and one constructed. "A creation of the rank of a masterpiece," Zentralblatt für Mathematik und Ihre Grenzgebiete. Over 300 exercises. 5 figures. Bibliography. Index. xvi + 241pp. 5⅜ x 8. **S453 Paperbound $1.85**

*HIGHER MATHEMATICS FOR STUDENTS OF CHEMISTRY AND PHYSICS, J. W. Mellor. Not abstract, but practical, drawing its problems from familiar laboratory material, this book covers theory and application of differential calculus, analytic geometry, functions with singularities, integral calculus, infinite series, solution of numerical equations, differential equations, Fourier's theorem and extensions, probability and the theory of errors, calculus of variations, determinants, etc. "If the reader is not familiar with this book, it will repay him to examine it," CHEM. & ENGINEERING NEWS. 800 problems. 189 figures. 2 appendices; 30 tables of integrals, probability functions, etc. Bibliography. xxi + 641pp. 5⅜ x 8. **S193 Paperbound $2.25**

CATALOGUE OF DOVER BOOKS

THE FOURTH DIMENSION SIMPLY EXPLAINED, edited by Henry P. Manning. Originally written as entries in contest sponsored by "Scientific American," then published in book form, these 22 essays present easily understood explanations of how the fourth dimension may be studied, the relationship of non-Euclidean geometry to the fourth dimension, analogies to three-dimensional space, some fourth-dimensional absurdities and curiosities, possible measurements and forms in the fourth dimension. In general, a thorough coverage of many of the simpler properties of fourth-dimensional space. Multi-points of view on many of the most important aspects are valuable aid to comprehension. Introduction by Dr. Henry P. Manning gives proper emphasis to points in essays, more advanced account of fourth-dimensional geometry. 82 figures. 251pp. 5⅜ x 8. **T711 Paperbound $1.35**

TRIGONOMETRY REFRESHER FOR TECHNICAL MEN, A. A. Klaf. A modern question and answer text on plane and spherical trigonometry. Part I covers plane trigonometry: angles, quadrants, trigonometrical functions, graphical representation, interpolation, equations, logarithms, solution of triangles, slide rules, etc. Part II discusses applications to navigation, surveying, elasticity, architecture, and engineering. Small angles, periodic functions, vectors, polar coordinates, De Moivre's theorem, fully covered. Part III is devoted to spherical trigonometry and the solution of spherical triangles, with applications to terrestrial and astronomical problems. Special time-savers for numerical calculation. 913 questions answered for you! 1738 problems; answers to odd numbers. 494 figures. 14 pages of functions, formulae. Index. x + 629pp. 5⅜ x 8. **T371 Paperbound $2.00**

CALCULUS REFRESHER FOR TECHNICAL MEN. A. A. Klaf. Not an ordinary textbook but a unique refresher for engineers, technicians, and students. An examination of the most important aspects of differential and integral calculus by means of 756 key questions. Part I covers simple differential calculus: constants, variables, functions, increments, derivatives, logarithms, curvature, etc. Part II treats fundamental concepts of integration: inspection, substitution, transformation, reduction, areas and volumes, mean value, successive and partial integration, double and triple integration. Stresses practical aspects! A 50 page section gives applications to civil and nautical engineering, electricity, stress and strain, elasticity, industrial engineering, and similar fields. 756 questions answered. 556 problems; solutions to odd numbers. 36 pages of constants, formulae. Index. v + 431pp. 5⅜ x 8.
T370 Paperbound $2.00

PROBABILITIES AND LIFE, Emile Borel. One of the leading French mathematicians of the last 100 years makes use of certain results of mathematics of probabilities and explains a number of problems that for the most part, are related to everyday living or to illness and death: computation of life expectancy tables, chances of recovery from various diseases, probabilities of job accidents, weather predictions, games of chance, and so on. Emphasis on results not processes, though some indication is made of mathematical proofs. Simple in style, free of technical terminology, limited in scope to everyday situations, it is comprehensible to laymen, fine reading for beginning students of probability. New English translation. Index. Appendix. vi + 87pp. 5⅜ x 8½. **T121 Paperbound $1.00**

POPULAR SCIENTIFIC LECTURES, Hermann von Helmholtz. 7 lucid expositions by a pre-eminent scientific mind: "The Physiological Causes of Harmony in Music," "On the Relation of Optics to Painting," "On the Conservation of Force," "On the Interaction of Natural Forces," "On Goethe's Scientific Researches" into theory of color, "On the Origin and Significance of Geometric Axioms," "On Recent Progress in the Theory of Vision." Written with simplicity of expression, stripped of technicalities, these are easy to understand and delightful reading for anyone interested in science or looking for an introduction to serious study of acoustics or optics. Introduction by Professor Morris Kline, Director, Division of Electromagnetic Research, New York University, contains astute, impartial evaluations. Selected from "Popular Lectures on Scientific Subjects," 1st and 2nd series. xii + 286pp. 5⅜ x 8½. **T799 Paperbound $1.45**

SCIENCE AND METHOD, Henri Poincaré. Procedure of scientific discovery, methodology, experiment, idea-germination—the intellectual processes by which discoveries come into being. Most significant and most interesting aspects of development, application of ideas. Chapters cover selection of facts, chance, mathematical reasoning, mathematics, and logic; Whitehead, Russell, Cantor; the new mechanics, etc. 288pp. 5⅜ x 8. **S222 Paperbound $1.35**

HEAT AND ITS WORKINGS, Morton Mott-Smith, Ph.D. An unusual book; to our knowledge the only middle-level survey of this important area of science. Explains clearly such important concepts as physiological sensation of heat and Weber's law, measurement of heat, evolution of thermometer, nature of heat, expansion and contraction of solids, Boyle's law, specific heat. BTU's and calories, evaporation, Andrews's isothermals, radiation, the relation of heat to light, many more topics inseparable from other aspects of physics. A wide, non-mathematical yet thorough explanation of basic ideas, theories, phenomena for laymen and beginning scientists illustrated by experiences of daily life. Bibliography. 50 illustrations. x + 165pp. 5⅜ x 8½. **T978 Paperbound $1.00**

History of Science and Mathematics

THE STUDY OF THE HISTORY OF MATHEMATICS, THE STUDY OF THE HISTORY OF SCIENCE, G. Sarton. Two books bound as one. Each volume contains a long introduction to the methods and philosophy of each of these historical fields, covering the skills and sympathies of the historian, concepts of history of science, psychology of idea-creation, and the purpose of history of science. Prof. Sarton also provides more than 80 pages of classified bibliography. Complete and unabridged. Indexed. 10 illustrations. 188pp. 5⅜ x 8.   T240 Paperbound **$1.25**

A HISTORY OF PHYSICS, Florian Cajori, Ph.D. First written in 1899, thoroughly revised in 1929, this is still best entry into antecedents of modern theories. Precise non-mathematical discussion of ideas, theories, techniques, apparatus of each period from Greeks to 1920's, analyzing within each period basic topics of matter, mechanics, light, electricity and magnetism, sound, atomic theory, etc. Stress on modern developments, from early 19th century to present. Written with critical eye on historical development, significance. Provides most of needed historical background for student of physics. Reprint of second (1929) edition. Index. Bibliography in footnotes. 16 figures. xv + 424pp. 5⅜ x 8.   T970 Paperbound **$2.00**

A HISTORY OF ASTRONOMY FROM THALES TO KEPLER, J. L. E. Dreyer. Formerly titled A HISTORY OF PLANETARY SYSTEMS FROM THALES TO KEPLER. This is the only work in English which provides a detailed history of man's cosmological views from prehistoric times up through the Renaissance. It covers Egypt, Babylonia, early Greece, Alexandria, the Middle Ages, Copernicus, Tycho Brahe, Kepler, and many others. Epicycles and other complex theories of positional astronomy are explained in terms nearly everyone will find clear and easy to understand. "Standard reference on Greek astronomy and the Copernican revolution," SKY AND TELESCOPE. Bibliography. 21 diagrams. Index. xvii + 430pp. 5⅜ x 8.   S79 Paperbound **$1.98**

A SHORT HISTORY OF ASTRONOMY, A. Berry. A popular standard work for over 50 years, this thorough and accurate volume covers the science from primitive times to the end of the 19th century. After the Greeks and Middle Ages, individual chapters analyze Copernicus, Brahe, Galileo, Kepler, and Newton, and the mixed reception of their startling discoveries. Post-Newtonian achievements are then discussed in unusual detail: Halley, Bradley, Lagrange, Laplace, Herschel, Bessel, etc. 2 indexes. 104 illustrations, 9 portraits. xxxi + 440pp. 5⅜ x 8.   T210 Paperbound **$2.00**

PIONEERS OF SCIENCE, Sir Oliver Lodge. An authoritative, yet elementary history of science by a leading scientist and expositor. Concentrating on individuals—Copernicus, Brahe, Kepler, Galileo, Descartes, Newton, Laplace, Herschel, Lord Kelvin, and other scientists—the author presents their discoveries in historical order, adding biographical material on each man and full, specific explanations of their achievements. The full, clear discussions of the accomplishments of post-Newtonian astronomers are features seldom found in other books on the subject. Index. 120 illustrations. xv + 404pp. 5⅜ x 8.   T716 Paperbound **$1.65**

THE BIRTH AND DEVELOPMENT OF THE GEOLOGICAL SCIENCES, F. D. Adams. The most complete and thorough history of the earth sciences in print. Geological thought from earliest recorded times to the end of the 19th century—covers over 300 early thinkers and systems: fossils and hypothetical explanations of them, vulcanists vs. neptunists, figured stones and paleontology, generation of stones, and similar topics. 91 illustrations, including medieval, renaissance woodcuts, etc. 632 footnotes and bibliographic notes. Index. 511pp. 5⅜ x 8.   T5 Paperbound **$2.25**

THE STORY OF ALCHEMY AND EARLY CHEMISTRY, J. M. Stillman. "Add the blood of a red-haired man"—a recipe typical of the many quoted in this authoritative and readable history of the strange beliefs and practices of the alchemists. Concise studies of every leading figure in alchemy and early chemistry through Lavoisier, in this curious epic of superstition and true science, constructed from scores of rare and difficult Greek, Latin, German, and French texts. Foreword by S. W. Young. 246-item bibliography. Index. xiii + 566pp. 5⅜ x 8.   S628 Paperbound **$2.45**

HISTORY OF MATHEMATICS, D. E. Smith. Most comprehensive non-technical history of math in English. Discusses the lives and works of over a thousand major and minor figures, from Euclid to Descartes, Gauss, and Riemann. Vol. I: A chronological examination, from primitive concepts through Egypt, Babylonia, Greece, the Orient, Rome, the Middle Ages, the Renaissance, and up to 1900. Vol. 2: The development of ideas in specific fields and problems, up through elementary calculus. Two volumes, total of 510 illustrations, 1355pp. 5⅜ x 8. Set boxed in attractive container.   T429,430 Paperbound the set **$5.00**

Classics of Science

THE DIDEROT PICTORIAL ENCYCLOPEDIA OF TRADES AND INDUSTRY, MANUFACTURING AND THE TECHNICAL ARTS IN PLATES SELECTED FROM "L'ENCYCLOPEDIE OU DICTIONNAIRE RAISONNE DES SCIENCES, DES ARTS, ET DES METIERS" OF DENIS DIDEROT, edited with text by C. Gillispie. The first modern selection of plates from the high point of 18th century French engraving, Diderot's famous Encyclopedia. Over 2000 illustrations on 485 full page plates, most of them original size, illustrating the trades and industries of one of the most fascinating periods of modern history, 18th century France. These magnificent engravings provide an invaluable glimpse into the past for the student of early technology, a lively and accurate social document to students of cultures, an outstanding find to the lover of fine engravings. The plates teem with life, with men, women, and children performing all of the thousands of operations necessary to the trades before and during the early stages of the industrial revolution. Plates are in sequence, and show general operations, closeups of difficult operations, and details of complex machinery. Such important and interesting trades and industries are illustrated as sowing, harvesting, beekeeping, cheesemaking, operating windmills, milling flour, charcoal burning, tobacco processing, indigo, fishing, arts of war, salt extraction, mining, smelting iron, casting iron, steel, extracting mercury, zinc, sulphur, copper, etc., slating, tinning, silverplating, gilding, making gunpowder, cannons, bells, shoeing horses, tanning, papermaking, printing, dying, and more than 40 other categories. 920pp. 9 x 12. Heavy library cloth.   T421 Two volume set **$18.50**

THE PRINCIPLES OF SCIENCE, A TREATISE ON LOGIC AND THE SCIENTIFIC METHOD, W. Stanley Jevons. Treating such topics as Inductive and Deductive Logic, the Theory of Number, Probability, and the Limits of Scientific Method, this milestone in the development of symbolic logic remains a stimulating contribution to the investigation of inferential validity in the natural and social sciences. It significantly advances Boole's logic, and describes a machine which is a foundation of modern electronic calculators. In his introduction, Ernest Nagel of Columbia University says, "(Jevons) . . . continues to be of interest as an attempt to articulate the logic of scientific inquiry." Index. liii + 786pp. 5⅜ x 8.
S446 Paperbound **$2.98**

*DIALOGUES CONCERNING TWO NEW SCIENCES, Galileo Galilei. A classic of experimental science which has had a profound and enduring influence on the entire history of mechanics and engineering. Galileo based this, his finest work, on 30 years of experimentation. It offers a fascinating and vivid exposition of dynamics, elasticity, sound, ballistics, strength of materials, and the scientific method. Translated by H. Crew and A. de Salvio. 126 diagrams. Index. xxi + 288pp. 5⅜ x 8.   S99 Paperbound **$1.75**

DE MAGNETE, William Gilbert. This classic work on magnetism founded a new science. Gilbert was the first to use the word "electricity," to recognize mass as distinct from weight, to discover the effect of heat on magnetic bodies; invented an electroscope, differentiated between static electricity and magnetism, conceived of the earth as a magnet. Written by the first great experimental scientist, this lively work is valuable not only as an historical landmark, but as the delightfully easy-to-follow record of a perpetually searching, ingenious mind. Translated by P. F. Mottelay. 25 page biographical memoir. 90 fix. lix + 368pp. 5⅜ x 8.   S470 Paperbound **$2.00**

*OPTICKS, Sir Isaac Newton. An enormous storehouse of insights and discoveries on light, reflection, color, refraction, theories of wave and corpuscular propagation of light, optical apparatus, and mathematical devices which have recently been reevaluated in terms of modern physics and placed in the top-most ranks of Newton's work! Foreword by Albert Einstein. Preface by I. B. Cohen of Harvard U. 7 pages of portraits, facsimile pages, letters, etc. cxvi + 412pp. 5⅜ x 8.   S205 Paperbound **$2.25**

A SURVEY OF PHYSICAL THEORY, M. Planck. Lucid essays on modern physics for the general reader by the Nobel Laureate and creator of the quantum revolution. Planck explains how the new concepts came into being; explores the clash between theories of mechanics, electrodynamics, and thermodynamics; and traces the evolution of the concept of light through Newton, Huygens, Maxwell, and his own quantum theory, providing unparalleled insights into his development of this momentous modern concept. Bibliography. Index. vii + 121pp. 5⅜ x 8.
S650 Paperbound **$1.15**

A SOURCE BOOK IN MATHEMATICS, D. E. Smith. English translations of the original papers that announced the great discoveries in mathematics from the Renaissance to the end of the 19th century: succinct selections from 125 different treatises and articles, most of them unavailable elsewhere in English—Newton, Leibniz, Pascal, Riemann, Bernoulli, etc. 24 articles trace developments in the field of number, 18 cover algebra, 36 are on geometry, and 13 on calculus. Biographical-historical introductions to each article. Two volume set. Index in each. Total of 115 illustrations. Total of xxviii + 742pp. 5⅜ x 8.   S552 Vol I Paperbound **$1.85**
S553 Vol II Paperbound **$1.85**
The set, boxed **$3.50**

CATALOGUE OF DOVER BOOKS

*THE THIRTEEN BOOKS OF EUCLID'S ELEMENTS, edited by T. L. Heath. This is the complete EUCLID — the definitive edition of one of the greatest classics of the western world. Complete English translation of the Heiberg text with spurious Book XIV. Detailed 150-page introduction discusses aspects of Greek and medieval mathematics: Euclid, texts, commentators, etc. Paralleling the text is an elaborate critical exposition analyzing each definition, proposition, postulate, etc., and covering textual matters, mathematical analyses, refutations, extensions, etc. Unabridged reproduction of the Cambridge 2nd edition. 3 volumes. Total of 995 figures, 1426pp. 5⅜ x 8.   S88, 89, 90 — 3 vol. set, Paperbound **$6.75**

*THE GEOMETRY OF RENE DESCARTES. The great work which founded analytic geometry. The renowned Smith-Latham translation faced with the original French text containing all of Descartes' own diagrams! Contains: Problems the Construction of Which Requires Only Straight Lines and Circles; On the Nature of Curved Lines; On the Construction of Solid or Supersolid Problems. Notes. Diagrams. 258pp.   S68 Paperbound **$1.60**

*A PHILOSOPHICAL ESSAY ON PROBABILITIES, P. Laplace. Without recourse to any mathematics above grammar school, Laplace develops a philosophically, mathematically and historically classical exposition of the nature of probability: its functions and limitations, operations in practical affairs, calculations in games of chance, insurance, government, astronomy, and countless other fields. New introduction by E. T. Bell. viii + 196pp. S166 Paperbound **$1.35**

DE RE METALLICA, Georgius Agricola. Written over 400 years ago, for 200 years the most authoritative first-hand account of the production of metals, translated in 1912 by former President Herbert Hoover and his wife, and today still one of the most beautiful and fascinating volumes ever produced in the history of science! 12 books, exhaustively annotated, give a wonderfully lucid and vivid picture of the history of mining, selection of sites, types of deposits, excavating pits, sinking shafts, ventilating, pumps, crushing machinery, assaying, smelting, refining metals, making salt, alum, nitre, glass, and many other topics. This definitive edition contains all 289 of the 16th century woodcuts which made the original an artistic masterpiece. It makes a superb gift for geologists, engineers, libraries, artists, historians, and everyone interested in science and early illustrative art. Biographical, historical introductions. Bibliography, survey of ancient authors. Indices. 289 illustrations. 672pp. 6¾ x 10¾. Deluxe library edition.   S6 Clothbound **$10.00**

GEOGRAPHICAL ESSAYS, W. M. Davis. Modern geography and geomorphology rest on the fundamental work of this scientist. His new concepts of earth-processes revolutionized science and his broad interpretation of the scope of geography created a deeper understanding of the interrelation of the landscape and the forces that mold it. This first inexpensive unabridged edition covers theory of geography, methods of advanced geographic teaching, descriptions of geographic areas, analyses of land-shaping processes, and much besides. Not only a factual and historical classic, it is still widely read for its reflections of modern scientific thought. Introduction. 130 figures. Index. vi + 777pp. 5⅜ x 8.
                              S383 Paperbound **$2.95**

CHARLES BABBAGE AND HIS CALCULATING ENGINES, edited by P. Morrison and E. Morrison. Friend of Darwin, Humboldt, and Laplace, Babbage was a leading pioneer in large-scale mathematical machines and a prophetic herald of modern operational research—true father of Harvard's relay computer Mark I. His Difference Engine and Analytical Engine were the first successful machines in the field. This volume contains a valuable introduction on his life and work; major excerpts from his fascinating autobiography, revealing his eccentric and unusual personality; and extensive selections from "Babbage's Calculating Engines," a compilation of hard-to-find journal articles, both by Babbage and by such eminent contributors as the Countess of Lovelace, L. F. Menabrea, and Dionysius Lardner. 11 illustrations. Appendix of miscellaneous papers. Index. Bibliography. xxxviii + 400pp. 5⅜ x 8.   T12 Paperbound **$2.00**

*THE WORKS OF ARCHIMEDES WITH THE METHOD OF ARCHIMEDES, edited by T. L. Heath. All the known works of the greatest mathematician of antiquity including the recently discovered METHOD OF ARCHIMEDES. This last is the only work we have which shows exactly how early mathematicians discovered their proofs before setting them down in their final perfection. A 186 page study by the eminent scholar Heath discusses Archimedes and the history of Greek mathematics. Bibliography. 563pp. 5⅜ x 8.   S9 Paperbound **$2.25**

Teach Yourself

These British books are the most effective series of home study books on the market! With no outside help they will teach you as much as is necessary to have a good background in each subject, in many cases offering as much material as a similar high school or college course. They are carefully planned, written by foremost British educators, and amply provided with test questions and problems for you to check your progress; the mathematics books are especially rich in examples and problems. Do not confuse them with skimpy outlines or ordinary school texts or vague generalized popularizations; each book is complete in itself, full without being overdetailed, and designed to give you an easily-acquired branch of knowledge.

TEACH YOURSELF ALGEBRA, P. Abbott. The equivalent of a thorough high school course, up through logarithms. 52 illus. 307pp. 4¼ x 7.　　　　　　　　　**T680 Clothbound $2.00**

TEACH YOURSELF GEOMETRY, P. Abbott. Plane and solid geometry, covering about a year of plane and six months of solid. 268 illus. 344pp. 4½ x 7.　　　　　　**T681 Clothbound $2.00**

TEACH YOURSELF TRIGONOMETRY, P. Abbott. Background of algebra and geometry will enable you to get equivalent of elementary college course. Tables. 102 illus. 204pp. 4½ x 7.
　　　　　　　　　　　　　　　　　　　　　　　　　　　T682 Clothbound $2.00

TEACH YOURSELF THE CALCULUS, P. Abbott. With algebra and trigonometry you will be able to acquire a good working knowledge of elementary integral calculus and differential calculus. Excellent supplement to any course textbook. 380pp. 4¼ x 7.　　　　**T683 Clothbound $2.00**

TEACH YOURSELF THE SLIDE RULE, B. Snodgrass. Basic principles clearly explained, with many applications in engineering, business, general figuring, will enable you to pick up very useful skill. 10 illus. 207pp. 4¼ x 7.　　　　　　　　　　　　　**T684 Clothbound $2.00**

TEACH YOURSELF MECHANICS, P. Abbott. Equivalent of part course on elementary college level, with lever, parallelogram of force, friction, laws of motion, gases, etc. Fine introduction before more advanced course. 163 illus. 271pp. 4½ x 7.　　　　**T685 Clothbound $2.00**

TEACH YOURSELF ELECTRICITY, C. W. Wilman. Current, resistance, voltage, Ohm's law, circuits, generators, motors, transformers, etc. Non-mathematical as much as possible. 115 illus. 184pp. 4¼ x 7.　　　　　　　　　　　　　　　　　　**T230 Clothbound $2.00**

TEACH YOURSELF HEAT ENGINES E. DeVille. Steam and internal combustion engines; non-mathematical introduction for student, for layman wishing background, refresher for advanced student. 76 illus. 217pp. 4¼ x 7.　　　　　　　　　　**T237 Clothbound $2.00**

TEACH YOURSELF TO PLAY THE PIANO, King Palmer. Companion and supplement to lessons or self study. Handy reference, too. Nature of instrument, elementary musical theory, technique of playing, interpretation, etc. 60 illus. 144pp. 4¼ x 7.　　　　**T959 Clothbound $2.00**

TEACH YOURSELF HERALDRY AND GENEALOGY, L. G. Pine. Modern work, avoiding romantic and overpopular misconceptions. Editor of new Burke presents detailed information and commentary down to present. Best general survey. 50 illus. glossary; 129pp. 4¼ x 7.
　　　　　　　　　　　　　　　　　　　　　　　　　　　T962 Clothbound $2.00

TEACH YOURSELF HANDWRITING, John L. Dumpleton. Basic Chancery cursive style is popular and easy to learn. Many diagrams. 114 illus. 192pp. 4¼ x 7.　　　**T960 Clothbound $2.00**

TEACH YOURSELF CARD GAMES FOR TWO, Kenneth Konstam. Many first-rate games, including old favorites like cribbage and gin and canasta as well as new lesser-known games. Extremely interesting for cards enthusiast. 60 illus. 150pp. 4¼ x 7.　　　　**T963 Clothbound $2.00**

TEACH YOURSELF GUIDEBOOK TO THE DRAMA, Luis Vargas. Clear, rapid survey of changing fashions and forms from Aeschylus to Tennessee Williams, in all major European traditions. Plot summaries, critical comments, etc. Equivalent of a college drama course; fine cultural background 224pp. 4¼ x 7.　　　　　　　　　　　　　　　　**T961 Clothbound $2.00**

TEACH YOURSELF THE ORGAN, Francis Routh. Excellent compendium of background material for everyone interested in organ music, whether as listener or player. 27 musical illus. 158pp. 4¼ x 7.　　　　　　　　　　　　　　　　　　**T977 Clothbound $2.00**

TEACH YOURSELF TO STUDY SCULPTURE, William Gaunt. Noted British cultural historian surveys culture from Greeks, primitive world, to moderns. Equivalent of college survey course. 23 figures, 40 photos. 158pp. 4¼ x 7.　　　　　　　　　**T976 Clothbound $2.00**

Miscellaneous

THE COMPLETE KANO JIU-JITSU (JUDO), H. I. Hancock and K. Higashi. Most comprehensive guide to judo, referred to as outstanding work by Encyclopaedia Britannica. Complete authentic Japanese system of 160 holds and throws, including the most spectacular, fully illustrated with 487 photos. Full text explains leverage, weight centers, pressure points, special tricks, etc.; shows how to protect yourself from almost any manner of attack though your attacker may have the initial advantage of strength and surprise. This authentic Kano system should not be confused with the many American imitations. xii + 500pp. 5⅜ x 8.
T639 Paperbound **$2.00**

THE MEMOIRS OF JACQUES CASANOVA. Splendid self-revelation by history's most engaging scoundrel—utterly dishonest with women and money, yet highly intelligent and observant. Here are all the famous duels, scandals, amours, banishments, thefts, treacheries, and imprisonments all over Europe: a life lived to the fullest and recounted with gusto in one of the greatest autobiographies of all time. What is more, these Memoirs are also one of the most trustworthy and valuable documents we have on the society and culture of the extravagant 18th century. Here are Voltaire, Louis XV, Catherine the Great, cardinals, castrati, pimps, and pawnbrokers—an entire glittering civilization unfolding before you with an unparalleled sense of actuality. Translated by Arthur Machen. Edited by F. A. Blossom. Introduction by Arthur Symons. Illustrated by Rockwell Kent. Total of xlviii + 2216pp. 5⅜ x 8.
T338 Vol I Paperbound **$2.00**
T339 Vol II Paperbound **$2.00**
T340 Vol III Paperbound **$2.00**
The set **$6.00**

BARNUM'S OWN STORY, P. T. Barnum. The astonishingly frank and gratifyingly well-written autobiography of the master showman and pioneer publicity man reveals the truth about his early career, his famous hoaxes (such as the Fejee Mermaid and the Woolly Horse), his amazing commercial ventures, his fling in politics, his feuds and friendships, his failures and surprising comebacks. A vast panorama of 19th century America's mores, amusements, and vitality. 66 new illustrations in this edition. xii + 500pp. 5⅜ x 8.
T764 Paperbound **$1.65**

THE STORY OF THE TITANIC AS TOLD BY ITS SURVIVORS, ed. by Jack Winocour. Most significant accounts of most overpowering naval disaster of modern times: all 4 authors were survivors. Includes 2 full-length, unabridged books: "The Loss of the S.S. Titanic," by Laurence Beesley, "The Truth about the Titanic," by Col. Archibald Gracie; 6 pertinent chapters from "Titanic and Other Ships," autobiography of only officer to survive, Second Officer Charles Lightoller; and a short, dramatic account by the Titanic's wireless operator, Harold Bride. 26 illus. 368pp. 5⅜ x 8.
T610 Paperbound **$1.50**

THE PHYSIOLOGY OF TASTE, Jean Anthelme Brillat-Savarin. Humorous, satirical, witty, and personal classic on joys of food and drink by 18th century French politician, litterateur. Treats the science of gastronomy, erotic value of truffles, Parisian restaurants, drinking contests; gives recipes for tunny omelette, pheasant, Swiss fondue, etc. Only modern translation of original French edition. Introduction. 41 illus. 346pp. 5⅝ x 8⅜.
T591 Paperbound **$1.50**

THE ART OF THE STORY-TELLER, M. L. Shedlock. This classic in the field of effective story-telling is regarded by librarians, story-tellers, and educators as the finest and most lucid book on the subject. The author considers the nature of the story, the difficulties of communicating stories to children, the artifices used in story-telling, how to obtain and maintain the effect of the story, and, of extreme importance, the elements to seek and those to avoid in selecting material. A 99-page selection of Miss Shedlock's most effective stories and an extensive bibliography of further material by Eulalie Steinmetz enhance the book's usefulness. xxi + 320pp. 5⅜ x 8.
T635 Paperbound **$1.50**

CREATIVE POWER: THE EDUCATION OF YOUTH IN THE CREATIVE ARTS, Hughes Mearns. In first printing considered revolutionary in its dynamic, progressive approach to teaching the creative arts; now accepted as one of the most effective and valuable approaches yet formulated. Based on the belief that every child has something to contribute, it provides in a stimulating manner invaluable and inspired teaching insights, to stimulate children's latent powers of creative expression in drama, poetry, music, writing, etc. Mearns's methods were developed in his famous experimental classes in creative education at the Lincoln School of Teachers College, Columbia Univ. Named one of the 20 foremost books on education in recent times by National Education Association. New enlarged revised 2nd edition. Introduction. 272pp. 5⅜ x 8.
T490 Paperbound **$1.75**

FREE AND INEXPENSIVE EDUCATIONAL AIDS, T. J. Pepe, Superintendent of Schools, Southbury, Connecticut. An up-to-date listing of over 1500 booklets, films, charts, etc. 5% costs less than 25¢; 1% costs more; 94% is yours for the asking. Use this material privately, or in schools from elementary to college, for discussion, vocational guidance, projects. 59 categories include health, trucking, textiles, language, weather, the blood, office practice, wild life, atomic energy, other important topics. Each item described according to contents, number of pages or running time, level. All material is educationally sound, and without political or company bias. 1st publication. Second, revised edition. Index. 244pp. 5⅜ x 8.
T663 Paperbound **$1.50**

CATALOGUE OF DOVER BOOKS

GEOMETRY OF FOUR DIMENSIONS, H. P. Manning. Unique in English as a clear, concise introduction to this fascinating subject. Treatment is primarily synthetic and Euclidean, although hyperplanes and hyperspheres at infinity are considered by non-Euclidean forms. Historical introduction and foundations of 4-dimensional geometry; perpendicularity; simple angles; angles of planes; higher order; symmetry; order, motion; hyperpyramids, hypercones, hyperspheres; figures with parallel elements; volume, hypervolume in space; regular polyhedroids. Glossary of terms. 74 illustrations. ix + 348pp. 5⅜ x 8. S182 Paperbound **$2.00**

PAPER FOLDING FOR BEGINNERS, W. D. Murray and F. J. Rigney. A delightful introduction to the varied and entertaining Japanese art of origami (paper folding), with a full, crystal-clear text that anticipates every difficulty; over 275 clearly labeled diagrams of all important stages in creation. You get results at each stage, since complex figures are logically developed from simpler ones. 43 different pieces are explained: sailboats, frogs, roosters, etc. 6 photographic plates. 279 diagrams. 95pp. 5⅝ x 8⅜. T713 Paperbound **$1.00**

SATELLITES AND SCIENTIFIC RESEARCH, D. King-Hele. An up-to-the-minute non-technical account of the man-made satellites and the discoveries they have yielded up to September of 1961. Brings together information hitherto published only in hard-to-get scientific journals. Includes the life history of a typical satellite, methods of tracking, new information on the shape of the earth, zones of radiation, etc. Over 60 diagrams and 6 photographs. Mathematical appendix. Bibliography of over 100 items. Index. xii + 180pp. 5⅜ x 8½. T703 Paperbound **$2.00**

LOUIS PASTEUR, S. J. Holmes. A brief, very clear, and warmly understanding biography of the great French scientist by a former Professor of Zoology in the University of California. Traces his home life, the fortunate effects of his education, his early researches and first theses, and his constant struggle with superstition and institutionalism in his work on microorganisms, fermentation, anthrax, rabies, etc. New preface by the author. 159pp. 5⅜ x 8. T197 Paperbound **$1.00**

THE ENJOYMENT OF CHESS PROBLEMS, K. S. Howard. A classic treatise on this minor art by an internationally recognized authority that gives a basic knowledge of terms and themes for the everyday chess player as well as the problem fan: 7 chapters on the two-mover; 7 more on 3- and 4-move problems; a chapter on selfmates; and much more. "The most important one-volume contribution originating solely in the U.S.A.," Alain White. 200 diagrams. Solutions, viii + 212pp. 5⅜ x 8. T742 Paperbound **$1.25**

SAM LOYD AND HIS CHESS PROBLEMS, Alain C. White. Loyd was (for all practical purposes) the father of the American chess problem and his protégé and successor presents here the diamonds of his production, chess problems embodying a whimsy and bizarre fancy entirely unique. More than 725 in all, ranging from two-move to extremely elaborate five-movers, including Loyd's contributions to chess oddities—problems in which pieces are arranged to form initials, figures, other by-paths of chess problem found nowhere else. Classified according to major concept, with full text analyzing problems, containing selections from Loyd's own writings. A classic to challenge your ingenuity, increase your skill. Corrected republication of 1913 edition. Over 750 diagrams and illustrations. 744 problems with solutions. 471pp. 5⅜ x 8½. T928 Paperbound **$2.25**

FABLES IN SLANG & MORE FABLES IN SLANG, George Ade. 2 complete books of major American humorist in pungent colloquial tradition of Twain, Billings. 1st reprinting in over 30 years includes "The Two Mandolin Players and the Willing Performer," "The Base Ball Fan Who Took the Only Known Cure," "The Slim Girl Who Tried to Keep a Date that was Never Made," 42 other tales of eccentric, perverse, but always funny characters. "Touch of genius," H. L. Mencken. New introduction by E. F. Bleiler. 86 illus. 208pp. 5⅜ x 8. T533 Paperbound **$1.00**

Prices subject to change without notice.

Dover publishes books on art, music, philosophy, literature, languages, history, social sciences, psychology, handcrafts, orientalia, puzzles and entertainments, chess, pets and gardens, books explaining science, intermediate and higher mathematics, mathematical physics, engineering, biological sciences, earth sciences; classics of science, etc. Write to:

Dept. catrr.
Dover Publications, Inc.
180 Varick Street, N. Y. 14, N. Y.